MEDICAL ASSISTANT

Integumentary, Sensory, and Nervous Systems/
Patient Care and Communication

Module A

MEDICAL ASSIS

Integumentary, Sensory, and Nervo
Patient Care and Communic
Module A

Material Selected from:

Mastering Healthcare Terminology
Second Edition
by
Betsy J. Shiland, MS, RHIA, CPHQ, CTR

Saunders Textbook of Medical Assist
(textbook and workbook)
by
Diane M. Klieger, RN, MBA, CMA

Medical Transcription: Techniques and Pro
Sixth Edition
by
Marcy O. Diehl, BVE, CMA-A, CMT, FAAMT

SAUND
ELSEVI

11830 West
St. Louis, M

INTEGUME
PATIENT C

Copyright

Chapters 1,
Copyright (

Chapters 2,
assisting, St
Copyright (

Chapter 14
Copyright (

Appendixes
medical assi
Copyright (

Portions of

All rights
form or by
information
Permissions
3804 (US) (
elsevier.com
http://www

Knowledg
experienc
become n
informati
product t
duration
relying or
determine
appropria
the Autho
arising ou

ISBN: 978-

SAUNDERS

ELSEVIER

Printed in t

Last digit is

ERS
ER

ine Industrial Drive
issouri 63146

NTARY, SENSORY, AND NERVOUS SYSTEMS/
RE AND COMMUNICATION—MODULE A   ISBN: 978-1-4377-0340-5

5, and 12 from Shiland BJ: *Mastering healthcare terminology*, ed 2, St Louis.
2006, Mosby.

3, 4, 6, 7, 8, 9, 10, 11, and 13 from Klieger DM: *Saunders textbook of medical*
Louis.
2005, Elsevier.

from Diehl MO: *Medical transcription: techniques and procedures*, ed 6, St Louis.
2007, Saunders.

A and B from Klieger DM: *Workbook to accompany Saunders textbook of*
ting, St Louis.
2005, Elsevier.

Appendixes A and B copyright © 2010 by Corinthian Colleges, Inc.

Notice

and best practice in this field are constantly changing. As new research and
broaden our knowledge, changes in practice, treatment and drug therapy may
cessary or appropriate. Readers are advised to check the most current
n provided (i) on procedures featured or (ii) by the manufacturer of each
be administered, to verify the recommended dose or formula, the method and
f administration, and contraindications. It is the responsibility of practitioners,
their own experience and knowledge of the patient, to make diagnoses, to
dosages and the best treatment for each individual patient, and to take all
e safety precautions. To the fullest extent of the law, neither the Publisher nor
rs assumes any liability for any injury and/or damage to persons or property
of or related to any use of the material contained in this book.

The Publisher

4-4377-0340-5

ie United States of America

the print number: 9   8   7   6   5   4   3

ACKNOWLEDGMENTS

Thank you to our advisory board members and the CCi Medical Assisting Program community for your dedication, teamwork, and support over the years.

This textbook has been designed for your success. Each feature has been chosen to help you learn medical assisting quickly and effectively. Colorful boxes, tables, and illustrations will visually spark your interest, add to your knowledge, and aid in your retention of the material. Most chapters end with a review that asks you to apply the terms and concepts you have learned.

USE ALL THE FEATURES IN THE CHAPTER

Key Terms

The key terms list provides you with a quick overview of the terms you will encounter as you work your way through the chapter. You can also use this page to help you review for tests.

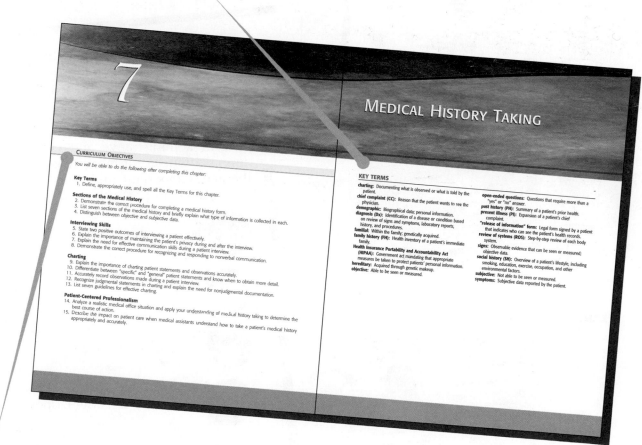

Objectives

Each objective is a goal for you. You should refer to these objectives before you study the chapter to see what your goals are and then again at the end of the chapter to see if you have accomplished them.

Exercises

Some chapters have exercises located after passages of information. Make sure you do these exercises to help you retain your new knowledge. Your instructor can check your work.

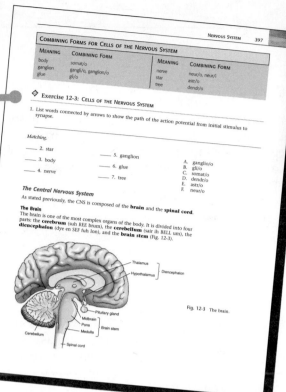

Procedures

Many chapters will contain illustrated step-by-step procedures showing you how to perform administrative and clinical procedures. Rationales for most steps explain why the step is important, and icons let you know which standard precautions to follow:

 Handwashing

 Gloving

 Personal Protective Equipment

 Biohazardous Waste Disposal

 Sharps Disposal

Plus, sample documentation shows you how to chart clinical procedures.

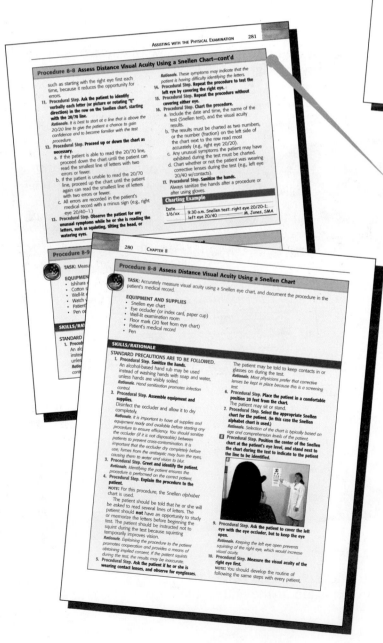

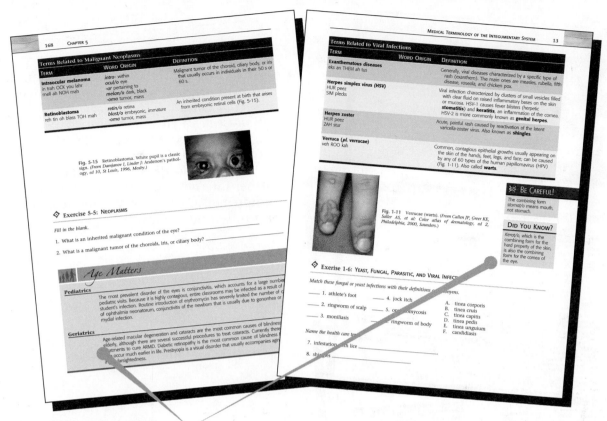

Special Information Boxes

Special information boxes that offer interesting facts or cautions are scattered throughout each chapter.

- *Did You Know?* boxes highlight the fascinating, sometimes strange history that underlies the origins of health care terms.
- *Be Careful!* boxes point out common pitfalls that you might experience when health care terms and word parts are spelled similarly but have different meanings.
- *Age Matters* boxes highlight important concepts and terminology for both pediatric and geriatric patients.

- *Careers* boxes are intended to give you more information about the job outlook, tasks, and educational requirements for the other members of the health care team.

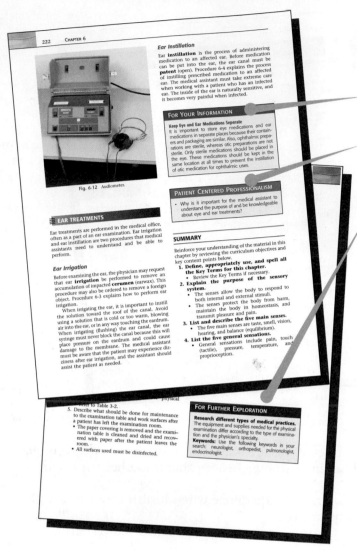

• *For Your Information* boxes provide interesting informational "tid-bits" on topics related to the subject at hand.
• *Patient-Centered Professionalism* boxes prompt you to think about the patient's perspective and encourage empathy.
• *For Further Exploration* boxes suggest topics for further Internet research to expand your comprehension of concepts and inspire you to "learn beyond the text."

Chapter Review

A variety of exercises, including reviews of chapter terminology, theory, and critical-thinking, are included at the end of each chapter to help you test your knowledge. Most chapter reviews also include case studies to give you the opportunity to apply your recently gained knowledge to real-life situations. Your instructor can check your work on the chapter review section.

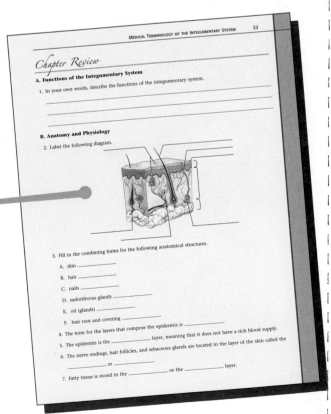

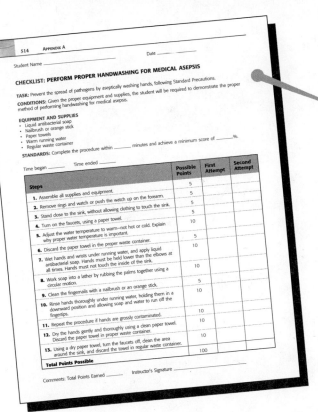

514   APPENDIX A

Student Name _____   Date _____

CHECKLIST: PERFORM PROPER HANDWASHING FOR MEDICAL ASEPSIS

TASK: Prevent the spread of pathogens by aseptically washing hands, following Standard Precautions.

CONDITIONS: Given the proper equipment and supplies, the student will be required to demonstrate the proper method of performing handwashing for medical asepsis.

EQUIPMENT AND SUPPLIES
- Liquid antibacterial soap
- Nailbrush or orange stick
- Paper towels
- Warm running water
- Regular waste container

STANDARDS: Complete the procedure within _____ minutes and achieve a minimum score of _____%.

Time began _____   Time ended _____

Steps	Possible Points	First Attempt	Second Attempt
1. Assemble all supplies and equipment.	5		
2. Remove rings and watch or push the watch up on the forearm.	5		
3. Stand close to the sink, without allowing clothing to touch the sink.	5		
4. Turn on the faucets, using a paper towel.	5		
5. Adjust the water temperature to warm—not hot or cold. Explain why proper water temperature is important.	10		
6. Discard the paper towel in the proper waste container.	5		
7. Wet hands and wrists under running water, and apply liquid antibacterial soap. Hands must be held lower than the elbows at all times. Hands must not touch the inside of the sink.	10		
8. Work soap into a lather by rubbing the palms together using a circular motion.	10		
9. Clean the fingernails with a nailbrush or an orange stick.	5		
10. Rinse hands thoroughly under running water, holding them in a downward position and allowing soap and water to run off the fingertips.	10		
11. Repeat the procedure if hands are grossly contaminated.	10		
12. Dry the hands gently and thoroughly using a clean paper towel. Discard the paper towel in proper waste container.	10		
13. Using a dry paper towel, turn the faucets off, clean the area around the sink, and discard the towel in regular waste container.	10		
Total Points Possible	100		

Comments: Total Points Earned _____   Instructor's Signature _____

Appendixes

Appendixes include competency checklists. They are organized into two groups. There are Core Competency Checklists for core skills, such as taking vital signs, giving injections, and assigning insurance codes, that you will be practicing in every module. The Core Competency Checklists are followed by the Procedure Competency Checklists, which are unique to the topics you are learning in this module. Each group of checklists has a Grade Sheet to summarize your performance scores when demonstrating your competencies to your instructor.

CONTENTS

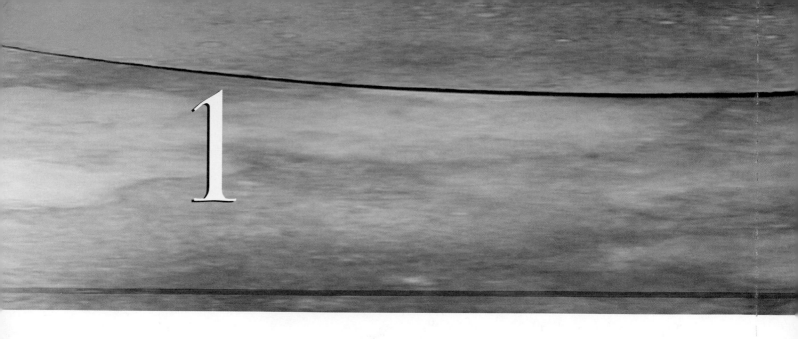

"Genius is one percent inspiration and ninety-nine percent perspiration."
—Thomas Edison

OBJECTIVES

1. Recognize and use terms related to the anatomy and physiology of the integumentary system.
2. Recognize and use terms related to the pathology of the integumentary system.
3. Recognize and use terms related to the diagnostic procedures for the integumentary system.
4. Recognize and use terms related to the therapeutic interventions for the integumentary system.

MEDICAL TERMINOLOGY OF THE INTEGUMENTARY SYSTEM

CHAPTER AT A GLANCE

ANATOMY AND PHYSIOLOGY

dermis	nail bed	subcutaneous tissue
epidermis	nail body	sudoriferous glands
eponychium	nail root	
hair follicle	sebaceous glands	

KEY WORD PARTS

PREFIXES	SUFFIXES	COMBINING FORMS
anti-	-ectomy	cutane/o
epi-	-itis	dermat/o, derm/o
hyper-	-oma	follicul/o
intra-	-osis	hidr/o
sub-	-plasty	kerat/o
trans-	-tomy	myc/o
	-ule	onych/o
		seb/o
		trich/o
		ungu/o

KEY TERMS

acne	ecchymosis	impetigo	pediculosis
alopecia	eczema	incision and drainage (I&D)	psoriasis
biopsy (Bx)	escharotomy	intradermal (ID)	tinea pedis
curettage	folliculitis	keloid	tuberculosis (TB) skin tests
cyst	hematoma	nevus	verruca
debridement	herpes simplex virus (HSV)	onychomycosis	vesicle
decubitus ulcer (decub)	herpes zoster	paronychia	wheal

≋ FUNCTIONS OF THE INTEGUMENTARY SYSTEM

The most important function of the skin (integument) is that it acts as the first line of defense in protecting the body from disease by providing an external barrier. It also helps regulate the temperature of the body, provides information about the environment through the sense of touch, assists in the synthesis of vitamin D (essential for the normal formation of bones and teeth), and helps eliminate waste products from the body. It is the largest organ of the body and accomplishes its diverse functions with assistance from its accessory structures, which include the hair, nails, and two types of glands: sebaceous (oil) and sudoriferous (sweat). Any impairment of the skin has the potential to lessen its ability to carry out these functions, the result of which can lead to disease.

COMBINING FORMS FOR THE INTEGUMENTARY SYSTEM

MEANING	COMBINING FORM	MEANING	COMBINING FORM
gland	aden/o	skin	derm/o, dermat/o and cutane/o
hair	trich/o, pil/o	sudoriferous gland	hidraden/o
nails	onych/o, ungu/o	sweat	hidr/o
sebum, oil	seb/o		

◈ Exercise 1-1: FUNCTIONS OF THE INTEGUMENTARY SYSTEM

Fill in the blanks.

1. The functions of the integumentary system are as follows:

   A. To help eliminate _Disease_ from the body.

   B. To protect the body from disease by providing an external _Barrier_

   C. To provide information about the external environment through the sense of _touch_

   D. To regulate _Vitamin D_

   E. To synthesize vitamin D, which is essential for the normal formation of _Bones_ and _Teeth_.

Match the combining forms for the integumentary system with their meanings.

_F_ 2. cutane/o, dermat/o   _A_ 5. trich/o, pil/o   A. hair
                                                                   B. sweat
_D_ 3. ungu/o, onych/o   _B_ 6. hidr/o   C. oil
                                                                   D. nail
_E_ 4. hidraden/o   _C_ 7. seb/o   E. sweat gland
                                                                   F. skin

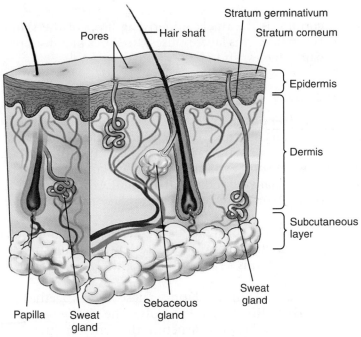

Fig. 1-1 Diagram of the skin.

ANATOMY AND PHYSIOLOGY

Skin

The skin is composed of two layers: the **epidermis** (eh pih DUR mis), which forms the outermost layer, and the **dermis** or **corium** (KORE ee um), the inner layer (Fig. 1-1). The dermis is attached to a layer of connective tissue called the **hypodermis** or the **subcutaneous** (sub kyoo TAY nee us) layer, which is mainly composed of adipose (fatty) tissue.

Epidermis

The top layer, the epidermis, is composed of several different layers, or strata, (*sing.* stratum) of epithelial (eh pih THEE lee ul) tissue. Epithelial tissue covers many of the external and internal surfaces of the body. Because the type of epithelial tissue that covers the body has a microscopic scaly appearance, it is referred to as **stratified squamous epithelium** (SKWAY muss eh pih THEE lee um).

Although there is a limited blood supply to the epidermis (it is **avascular** [a VAS kyoo lur]—i.e., it contains no blood vessels), constant activity is taking place. New skin cells are formed in the **basal** (BAY sul) (bottom) layer of the epidermis: the **stratum germinativum** (STRA tum jur mih nuh TIH vum). These cells then move outward toward the **stratum corneum** (top layer). During the transition from the lowest layer to the outer layer, the cells become filled with **keratin** (KAIR ah tin), which is a hard protein material. The nature of the keratin adds to the protective nature of the skin, giving it a waterproof property that helps retain moisture within the body.

The epidermis also protects the body by producing **melanocytes** (MEL an oh sites), the cells that produce pigment. When the skin is exposed to ultraviolet light, the melanocytes secrete more **melanin** (MELL ah nin) (pigment) to protect the layers underneath from radiation. People have different skin colors because of the varying amounts of melanin.

⊗ BE CAREFUL!

Don't confuse *strata*, meaning layers, with *striae*, meaning stretch marks.

⊗ BE CAREFUL!

Don't confuse *papill/o*, meaning papilla, and *papul/o*, which means pimple.

DID YOU KNOW?

As the ability to see smaller and smaller body structures became possible, early anatomists named them according to what they resembled that was already named. For example, the nipple was the first structure called a papilla. Later, the term *papilla* was also used to name the projecting capillaries at the bottom of a hair shaft, the conical-shaped entrance to the optic nerve, and the taste buds on the tongue.

Dermis

The dermis, or corium, is the thick, underlying layer of the skin composed of vascular connective tissue. This layer houses the skin's blood supply, lymphatics, nervous tissue, hair follicles, and glands.

Accessory Structures

GLANDS.   The **sudoriferous** (soo dur IF uh rus), or sweat, glands are located in the dermis and provide one means of thermoregulation for the body. They secrete sweat through tiny openings in the surface of the skin called **pores.** The secretion of sweat is called **perspiration.** These glands are present throughout the body but are especially abundant in the following areas: the soles of the feet, the palms of the hands, the armpits or axillae (*sing.* axilla), the upper lip, and the forehead.

The **sebaceous** (seh BAY shus) glands secrete an oily, acidic substance called **sebum** (SEE bum), which helps to lubricate hair and the surface of the skin. The acidic nature of sebum is key in inhibiting the growth of bacteria.

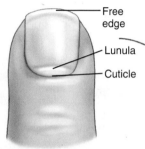

HAIR.   The hair has its roots in the dermis; these roots, together with their coverings, are called **hair follicles** (FALL ih kuls). The visible part is called the hair **shaft.** Underneath the follicle is a structure that encloses the capillaries called the **papilla** (pah PILL ah) (*pl.* papillae). The epithelial cells on top of the papilla are responsible for the formation of the hair shaft. When these cells die, the hair can no longer regenerate, and hair loss occurs. The main function of hair is to assist in thermoregulation by holding heat near the body. When cold, the hair stands on end, holding a layer of air as insulation near the body.

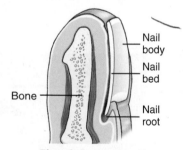

Fig. 1-2   The nail.

NAILS.   Nails cover and thus protect the dorsal surfaces of the distal bones of the fingers and toes (Fig. 1-2). The part that is visible is the **nail body,** whereas the **nail root** is in a groove under a small fold of skin at the base of the nail. The **nail bed** is the highly vascular tissue under the nail that appears pink when the blood is oxygenated or blue/purple when it is oxygen deficient. The moonlike white area at the base of the nail is called the **lunula** (LOON yoo lah), beyond which new growth occurs. The small fold of skin surrounding the lower part of the nail is called the **cuticle** (KYOO tih kul) or **eponychium** (eh puh NEE kee um).

COMBINING FORMS FOR ANATOMY AND PHYSIOLOGY

MEANING	COMBINING FORM	MEANING	COMBINING FORM
base	bas/o	horny	corne/o
black	melan/o	papilla	papill/o
fat	adip/o	scaly	squam/o
follicle	follicul/o	sebum	seb/o
hard, horny	kerat/o	vessel	vascul/o

❖ Exercise 1-2: ANATOMY AND PHYSIOLOGY

Match the combining forms with their meanings. More than one answer may be correct.

D 1. vessel   E 4. scaly   A. bas/o   E. squam/o
                                          B. melan/o   F. adip/o
F 2. fat   A 5. base   C. corne/o   G. kerat/o
                                          D. vascul/o
B 3. black   G+C 6. horny

Circle the correct term in parentheses.

7. The health care term for the sweat glands is the (sebaceous, **sudoriferous**) glands.
8. Perspiration is excreted through (**pores**, papillae).
9. The acidic nature of the skin helps to inhibit (perspiration, **bacteria**).
10. The hair root and its covering is called the (**follicle**, adipose tissue).
11. When hair stands on end, it is performing one of the functions of the skin called (**thermoregulation**, elimination).
12. The small fold of skin surrounding the base of the nail is called the (lunula, **cuticle**).
13. The pigment produced by cells in the epidermis that gives skin its color is (melanocytes, **melanin**).
14. A hard protein material that adds to the protective nature of the skin is (**keratin**, eponychium).
15. The highly vascular tissue under the nail is the nail (**bed**, body).

Selvidge Memorial Hospital
17201 Northridge Dr.
St. Paul, MN 55407

OPERATIVE REPORT

Surgeon:	Scott Dover, MD
Anesthetist:	Gabriela Dixon, MD
Anesthesia:	General
Date:	08/15/XX
Preoperative Diagnosis:	Chronic nail bed deformity and nail plate deformity, right middle finger
Postoperative Diagnosis:	Same
Operation:	Nail bed and nail plate ablation and shortening of distal phalanx and primary flap coverage, tip, right middle finger

Patient was brought into the operating suite and middle carpal block was induced into the right middle finger. The right upper extremity was then prepped with Betadine and draped in a sterile fashion. Digital tourniquet was applied and with 4× magnification loupes, we ablated the nail plate with rongeurs. We then excised the nail bed, elliptically excising this and excising it directly off the distal phalanx. The underlying distal phalanx was extremely rough and pitted. After complete ablation of the nail bed, we removed the tuft of the distal phalanx with the rongeurs. This freed up enough volar skin so that we could close this flap up primarily. We sutured this with 5-0 nylon and then excised dog ears and both radial and ulna sides and closed with 5-0 nylon suture. Appearance was excellent. Xeroform was applied, the digital tourniquet was removed, and good circulation returned to the finger. Tube gauze dressing was then applied.

Patient will be dismissed as an outpatient and arrangements made for follow-up in 2 weeks for suture removal.

Scott Dover, MD

◈ **Exercise 1-3: OPERATIVE REPORT**

Using the above operative report, answer the following questions:

1. What are the two structures, nail bed and nail plate, that are being removed (ablated)?

   _____

2. What is the name of the finger bone that is being operated on? _____

3. What is a "digital tourniquet," and why do you think it was used? _____

4. From your knowledge of the anatomy of a nail, what if any parts of the nail do you think remain?

   _____

≋ PATHOLOGY

Skin Lesions

A skin **lesion** (LEE zhun) is any visible, localized abnormality of skin tissue. It can be described as either primary or secondary. **Primary lesions** (Fig. 1-3) are early skin changes that have not yet undergone natural evolution or change caused by manipulation. **Secondary lesions** (Fig. 1-4) are the result of a natural evolution or manipulation of a primary lesion.

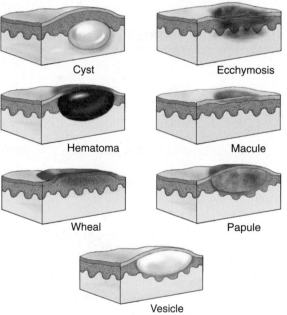

Cyst

Ecchymosis

Hematoma

Macule

Wheal

Papule

Fig. 1-3   Primary lesions.

Vesicle

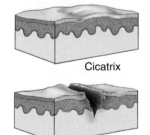

Cicatrix

Fissure

Fig. 1-4   Secondary lesions.

Terms Related to Primary Skin Lesions

TERM	WORD ORIGIN	DEFINITION
Bulla (*pl.* bullae) BULL ah		Vesicle larger than $\frac{1}{2}$ cm; seen with second-degree burns.
Cyst sist		Nodule filled with a semisolid material, such as a keratinous cyst (see Fig. 1-3).
Ecchymosis (*pl.* ecchymoses) eck ih MOH sis	*ec-* out *chym/o-* juice *-osis* abnormal condition	Hemorrhage or extravasation of blood into the subcutaneous tissue as a result of trauma to the underlying blood vessels or fragility of the vessel walls. The resultant darkening is commonly described as a **bruise** (see Fig. 1-3).
Hematoma hee mah TOH mah	*hemat/o* blood *-oma* mass, swelling	Collection of extravasated blood trapped in the tissues and palpable to the examiner (see Fig. 1-3).
Macule MACK yool	*macul/o* spot	Flat blemish or discoloration less than 1 cm, such as a freckle (see Fig. 1-3).
Nodule NOD yool	*nod/o* knot *-ule* diminutive	Palpable, solid lesion that may or may not be elevated less than 2 cm, such as a small lipoma.
Papule PAP yool	*Papul/o* pimple	Solid skin lesion raised less than 1 cm, such as a pimple (see Fig. 1-3).
Patch		Large, flat, nonpalpable macule, larger than 1 cm.
Petechiae (*sing.* petechia) peh TEEK ee ee		Tiny ecchymoses within the dermal layer.
Plaque plack		Raised plateau-like papule greater than 1 cm, such as a psoriatic lesion or seborrheic keratosis.
Purpura PUR pur ah	*purpur/o* purple	Massive hemorrhage into the tissues under the skin.
Pustule PUS tyool	*pustul/o* pustule	Superficial, elevated lesion containing pus that may be the result of an infection, such as acne.
Telangiectasia tell an jee eck TAY zsa	*tel/e-* distant *angi/o* vessel *-ectasia* dilation	Permanent dilation of groups of superficial capillaries and venules.
Tumor TOO mur		Nodule more than 2 cm; any mass or swelling, including neoplasms.
Vesicle VESS ih kul	*vesicul/o* blister or small sac	Circumscribed, elevated lesion containing fluid and smaller than $\frac{1}{2}$ cm, such as an insect bite (see Fig. 1-3).
Wheal wheel		Circumscribed, elevated papule caused by localized edema, commonly resulting from an allergic reaction, called **urticaria**. Also called **hives** (see Fig. 1-3).

Terms Related to Secondary Skin Lesions

TERM	WORD ORIGIN	DEFINITION
Atrophy AT troh fee	*a-* no, not, without ***troph/o*** development *-y* process	Paper-thin, wasted skin often occurring in the aged or as stretch marks (**striae**, *sing.* stria) (STRY ay) from rapid weight gain.
Cicatrix (*pl.* cicatrices) SICK ah tricks		A scar—an area of fibrous tissue that replaces normal skin after destruction of some of the dermis (see Fig. 1-4).
Crust		Dried serum, blood, and/or pus. May occur in inflammatory and infectious diseases, such as impetigo. Also called a **scab.**
Erosion eh ROH zhun		Destruction of the surface layer of the skin by physical or inflammatory processes, such as that seen with herpes virus.
Excoriation ecks kore ee A shun		Hollowed-out or linear crusted area caused by traumatic scratching, abrasion, or burning. The sensation of itching is called **pruritus** (pyoor RYE tus).
Fissure FISH ur		Cracklike lesion of the skin, such as an anal fissure (see Fig. 1-4).
Keloid KEE loyd		Type of scar that is an overgrowth of tissue at the site of injury in excess of the amount of tissue necessary to repair the wound. The extra tissue is partially due to an accumulation of collagen at the site (Fig. 1-5).
Lichenification lye ken ih fih KAY shun		Thickening and hardening of the skin, often resulting from the irritation caused by repeated scratching of a pruritic lesion.
Scales		Small, thin flakes of keratinized epithelium frequently seen in rashes, such as psoriasis.
Ulcer UL sur		Circumscribed crater-like lesion of the skin or mucous membrane resulting from **necrosis** (neck KROH sis), or tissue death, that can accompany an inflammatory, infectious, or malignant process. An example is the **decubitus ulcer** (deh KYOO bih tus) seen sometimes in bedridden patients.

DID YOU KNOW?

The term *extravasation* means the process of a substance (blood or lymph) leaking outside of a vessel into surrounding tissues. Petechia, ecchymosis, hematoma, and purpura are examples of extravasation. The term is easy to analyze. *Extra-* means outside, *vas/o* is a combining form for a vessel, and *-tion* means the process of.

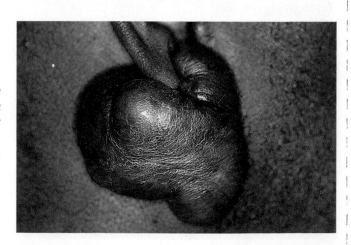

Fig. 1-5 Keloid caused by ear piercing. *(From Callen JP, Greer KE, Saller AS, et al: Callen atlas of dermatology, ed 2, Philadelphia, 2000, Saunders.)*

Exercise 1-4: Skin Lesions

1. What is the term that means *an itching sensation?* (And be careful to spell it correctly!)

PRURITUS

2. What is the difference between primary and secondary lesions?

Primary are early stages that have not gone under evolution.
Secondary = result in natural evolution or manipulation.

Match the primary lesions with their definitions.

_E_ 3. vesicle   _B_ 7. macule   A. extravasated blood into subcutaneous tissue caused by trauma
_F_ 4. papule   _D_ 8. pustule   B. flat blemish or discoloration
_C_ 5. wheals   C. circumscribed, raised papule
                                                D. superficial, elevated lesion containing pus
_A_ 6. ecchymosis   E. circumscribed, raised lesion containing fluid
                                                F. solid, raised skin lesion

Match the smaller version of a primary skin lesion with the larger version.

_C_ 9. petechia   _E_ 12. macule   A. plaque
_D_ 10. vesicle   _B_ 13. nodule   B. tumor
                                                C. ecchymosis
_A_ 11. papule   D. bulla
                                                E. patch

Match the following secondary lesions with their definitions.

_F_ 14. ulcer   _H_ 18. lichenification   A. paper-thin, wasted skin
_G_ 15. cicatrix   _B_ 19. crust   B. scab
_D_ 16. fissure   _A_ 20. atrophy   C. destruction of the surface layer
_E_ 17. excoriation   _C_ 21. erosion   D. cracklike lesion
                                                  E. hollowed-out crusted area
                                                  F. circumscribed, crater-like lesion
                                                  G. scar
                                                  H. thickening and hardening of the skin

Terms Related to Dermatitis and Bacterial Infections

TERM	WORD ORIGIN	DEFINITION
Atopic dermatitis a TOP ick dur mah TYE tis	*a-* without *top/o* place *-ic* pertaining to *dermat/o* skin *-itis* inflammation	Chronic, pruritic superficial inflammation of the skin usually associated with a family history of allergic disorders.
Carbuncle KAR bun kul		Furuncle with interconnecting subcutaneous pockets; commonly located on the back of the neck and the buttocks.
Cellulitis sell yoo LYE tis	*cellul/o* cell *-itis* inflammation	Diffuse, spreading, acute inflammation within solid tissues. The most common cause is a *Streptococcus pyogenes* infection (Fig. 1-6).

Continued

Terms Related to Dermatitis and Bacterial Infections—cont'd

TERM	WORD ORIGIN	DEFINITION
Contact dermatitis	*dermat/o* skin *-itis* inflammation	Irritated or allergic response of the skin that can lead to an acute or chronic inflammation (Fig. 1-7).
Eczema ECK suh muh		Superficial inflammation of the skin, characterized by vesicles, weeping, and pruritus. Also called **dermatitis**.
Folliculitis foh lick yoo LYE tis	*Follicul/o* follicle *-itis* inflammation	Inflammation of the hair follicles, which may be superficial or deep, acute or chronic.
Furuncle FYOOR ung kul		Localized, suppurative staphylococcal skin infections originating in a gland or hair follicle and characterized by pain, redness, and swelling.
Impetigo Im peh TYE goh		Superficial vesiculopustular skin infection, normally seen in children but possible in adults.
Paronychia pair ah NICK ee ah	*par-* near, beside *onych/o* nail *-ia* condition	Infection of the fold of the skin at the margin of the nail.
Seborrheic dermatitis seh boh REE ick	*seb/o* sebum *-rrheic* Pertaining to discharge *-dermat/o* skin *-itis* inflammation	Inflammatory scaling disease of the scalp and face. In newborns, this is known as **cradle cap**.

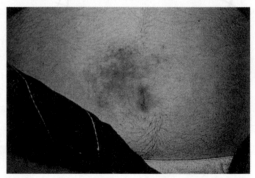

⊗ BE CAREFUL!

Paronychium is the structure that surrounds the nail. *Paronychia* is an infection of the nail.

Fig. 1-6   Cellulitis of the lower leg. *(From Wilson SF, Giddens JF: Health assessment for nursing practice, ed 3, St Louis, 2005, Mosby.)*

Fig. 1-7   Contact dermatitis caused by allergy to metal snap. *(From Epstein E: Common skin disorders, ed 5, Philadelphia, 2001, Saunders.)*

◆   **Exercise 1-5: DERMATITIS AND BACTERIAL INFECTIONS**

Circle the correct term.

1. Another term for dermatitis is (eczema, carbuncle).
2. A chronic, pruritic superficial inflammation of the skin associated with a family history of allergic disorders is called (atopic dermatitis, seborrheic dermatitis).

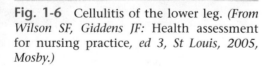

3. An irritated or allergic response of the skin that can lead to an acute or chronic inflammation is called (cellulitis, contact dermatitis).
4. An inflammatory scaling disease of the scalp and face is termed (impetigo, seborrheic dermatitis).
5. An infection of the fold of the skin at the margin of the nail is called (onychomycosis, paronychia).
6. A diffuse, spreading, acute inflammation within solid tissues as a result of a streptococcal infection describes (cellulitis, dermatitis).
7. A superficial vesiculopustular skin infection normally seen in children is called (contact dermatitis, impetigo).
8. A localized, suppurative staphylococcal skin infection in a gland or hair follicle is called a (carbuncle, furuncle).
9. Inflammation of the hair follicles is called (trichomycosis, folliculitis).
10. A group of furuncles interconnected by subcutaneous pockets is called (carbuncles, cellulitis).

Terms Related to Yeast and Fungal Infections

TERM	WORD ORIGIN	DEFINITION
Candidiasis kan dih DYE ah sis		Yeast infection in moist, occluded areas of the skin (armpits, inner thighs, underneath pendulous breasts) and mucous membranes. Also called **moniliasis** (mah nih LYE ah sis).
Dermatomycosis dur muh toh mye KOH sis	*dermat/o* skin *myc/o* fungus *-osis* abnormal condition	Fungal infection of the skin.
Onychomycosis on ih koh mye KOH sis	*onych/o* nail *myc/o* fungus *-osis* abnormal condition	Fungal infection of the nails (Fig. 1-8).
Tinea capitis TIN ee ah KAP ih tis	*capit/o* head *-is* noun ending	Fungal infection of the scalp; also known as **ringworm**.
Tinea corporis TIN ee ah KOR poor is	*corpor/o* body *-is* noun ending	Ringworm of the body, manifested by pink to red papulosquamous annular (ringlike) plaques with raised borders; also known as **ringworm** (Fig. 1-9).
Tinea cruris TIN ee ah KROO ris	*crur/o* leg *-is* noun ending	A fungal infection that occurs mainly on external genitalia and upper legs in males, particularly in warm weather; also known as **jock itch.**
Tinea pedis TIN ee ah PEH dis	*ped/o* foot *-is* noun ending	Fungal infection of the foot; also known as **athlete's foot.**
Tinea unguium TIN ee ah UN gwee um	*ungu/o* nail *-ium* noun ending	Fungal infection of the nails; also known as **onychomycosis**.

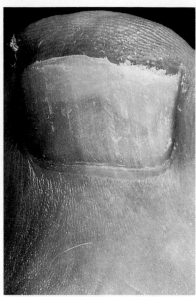

Fig. 1-8 Subungual onychomycosis. Early changes show subungual debris at the distal end of the nail plate. *(From Habif TP: Clinical dermatology, ed 4, St Louis, 2004, Mosby.)*

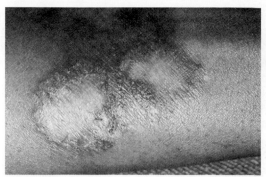

Fig. 1-9 Tinea corporis. *(From Hill MJ: Skin disorders, St Louis, 1994, Mosby.)*

Terms Related to Parasitic Infestations

TERM	WORD ORIGIN	DEFINITION
Pediculosis peh dick yoo LOH sis	*pedicul/o* louse *-osis* abnormal condition	Parasitic infestation with lice, involving the head, body, or genital area (Fig. 1-10).
Scabies SKAY bees		Parasitic infestation caused by mites; characterized by pruritic papular rash.

Fig. 1-10 Lice in hair. *(From Frazier MS, Drzymkowski JW: Essentials of human diseases and conditions, ed 3, Philadelphia, 2004, Saunders.)*

Terms Related to Viral Infections

TERM	WORD ORIGIN	DEFINITION
Exanthematous diseases eks an THEM ah tus		Generally, viral diseases characterized by a specific type of rash (exanthem). The main ones are measles, rubella, fifth disease, roseola, and chicken pox.
Herpes simplex virus (HSV) HUR peez SIM plecks		Viral infection characterized by clusters of small vesicles filled with clear fluid on raised inflammatory bases on the skin or mucosa. HSV-1 causes fever blisters (herpetic **stomatitis**) and **keratitis**, an inflammation of the cornea. HSV-2 is more commonly known as **genital herpes**.
Herpes zoster HUR peez ZAH stur		Acute, painful rash caused by reactivation of the latent varicella-zoster virus. Also known as **shingles**.
Verruca (*pl.* verrucae) veh ROO kah *warts*		Common, contagious epithelial growths usually appearing on the skin of the hands, feet, legs, and face; can be caused by any of 60 types of the human papillomavirus (HPV) (Fig. 1-11). Also called **warts**.

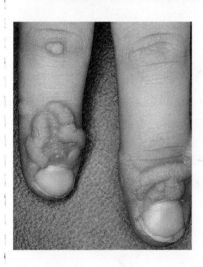

Fig. 1-11 Verrucae (warts). *(From Callen JP, Greer KE, Saller AS, et al: Color atlas of dermatology, ed 2, Philadelphia, 2000, Saunders.)*

⊠ BE CAREFUL!

The combining form *stomat/o* means mouth, not stomach.

DID YOU KNOW?

Kerat/o, which is the combining form for the hard property of the skin, is also the combining form for the cornea of the eye.

◆ **Exercise 1-6: YEAST, FUNGAL, PARASITIC, AND VIRAL INFECTIONS**

Match these fungal or yeast infections with their definitions or synonyms.

D 1. athlete's foot   B 4. jock itch   A. tinea corporis
C 2. ringworm of scalp   E 5. onychomycosis   B. tinea cruis
F 3. moniliasis   A 6. ringworm of body   C. tinea capitis
                                                        D. tinea pedis
                                                        E. tinea unguium
                                                        F. candidiasis

Name the health care term.

7. infestation with lice *Pediculosis*

8. shingles *Herpes zoster*

9. warts (be sure to use plural spelling) _____.

10. virus causing stomatitis _____.

11. infestation with mites _____.

12. fungal infection of the skin _____.

13. term for a "rash" _____.

Terms Related to Disorders of Hair Follicles and Sebaceous Glands

TERM	WORD ORIGIN	DEFINITION
Acne ACK nee		Inflammatory disease of the sebaceous glands characterized by papules, pustules, inflamed nodules, and **comedones** (kah mih DOH neez) (*sing.* comedo), which are plugs of sebum that partially or completely block a pore. Blackheads are open comedones, and whiteheads are closed comedones.
Alopecia al oh PEE shee ah		Baldness, or hair loss, resulting from genetic factors, aging, or disease (Fig. 1-12).
Hypertrichosis hye pur trih KOH sis	*hyper-* excessive *trich/o* hair *-osis* abnormal condition	Abnormal excess of hair; also known as **hirsutism** (HER soo tih zum).
Keratinous cyst kur AT tin us	*kerat/o* hard, horny	Benign cavity lined by keratinizing epithelium and filled with sebum and epithelial debris.
Milia MILL ee ah		Tiny superficial keratinous cysts caused by clogged oil ducts.
Rosacea roh ZAY shah		Chronic inflammatory disorder that occurs in fair-skinned individuals and is characterized by telangiectasia, erythema, papules, and pustules on the face.
Trichotillomania trick oh till oh MAY nee ah	*trich/o* hair *till/o* to pull *mania* excessive preoccupation	Disorder characterized by an impulsive tendency to pull one's hair out.

DID YOU KNOW?

Alopecia comes from the Greek term *alopekia*, meaning fox mange. Mange is an animal disease in which the hair comes out in clumps.

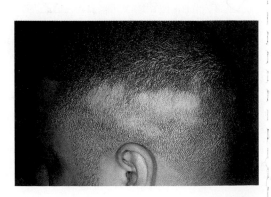

Fig. 1-12 Alopecia. *(From Bork K, Brauninger W: Skin diseases in clinical practice, ed 2, Philadelphia, 1999, Saunders.)*

Term Related to Scaling Papular Diseases

TERM	WORD ORIGIN	DEFINITION
Psoriasis sur EYE ah sis		Common chronic skin disorder characterized by circumscribed, salmon-red patches covered by thick, dry, silvery scales that are the result of excessive development of epithelial cells (Fig. 1-13).

Terms Related to Cornification and Pressure Injuries

TERM	WORD ORIGIN	DEFINITION
Callus KAL us		Common painless thickening of the stratum corneum at locations of external pressure or friction.
Corn		Horny mass of condensed epithelial cells overlying a bony prominence resulting from pressure or friction; also referred to as a **clavus** (KLA vus).
Decubitus ulcer deh KYOO bih tus		Inflammation, ulcer, or sore in the skin over a bony prominence. Most often seen in aged, debilitated, cachectic (wasted), or immobilized patients; pressure sores or ulcers are graded by stages of severity. The highest stage, stage 6, involves muscle, fat, and bone. Also known as a **bedsore**, **pressure ulcer**, or **pressure sore** (Fig. 1-14).
Ichthyosis ick thee OH sis	*ichthy/o* fish, scalelike *-osis* abnormal condition	Category of dry skin that has the scaly appearance of a fish. It ranges from mild to severe. The mild form is known as **xeroderma** (zir oh DUR mah). Xer/o means "dry."

Fig. 1-13 Psoriasis. *(From Hill MJ: Skin disorders, St Louis, 1994, Mosby.)*

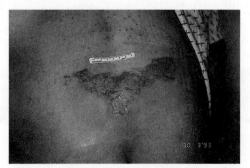

Fig. 1-14 Stage 2 decubitus ulcer. *(From Surrentino SA: Assisting with patient care, ed 2, St Louis, 2004, Mosby.)*

DID YOU KNOW?

The term *decubitus* comes from a Latin noun meaning a lying down and the adjective, related to the elbow. Romans rested on their elbows when reclining. One assumes they eventually suffered pressure sores on their elbows from this constant position.

◆ Exercise 1-7: DISORDERS OF HAIR FOLLICLES AND SEBACEOUS GLANDS, SCALING PAPULAR DISEASES, AND PRESSURE INJURIES

Fill in the blanks with the correct terms from the list below.

acne, alopecia, clavus, decubitus ulcer, hypertrichosis, keratinous cyst, milia, pressure sore, psoriasis, rosacea, trichotillomania, xeroderma

1. What is a chronic inflammatory disorder characterized by telangiectasia, erythema, papules, and pustules on the face? _____

2. What is a disorder of circumscribed salmon-red patches covered with thick, silvery scales?

    _____

3. What is another name for hirsutism? _____

4. What is the term for the tendency to pull one's hair out? _____

5. What is the term for baldness? _____

6. What is the term for a benign cavity filled with sebum and epithelial debris and lined with keratinized epithelium? _____

7. What is the common inflammatory disease of the sebaceous glands characterized by comedones, papules, pustules, and inflamed nodules? _____

8. What is another term for a corn? _____

9. What are two alternative terms for bedsores? _____

10. What are tiny, superficial keratinous cysts? _____

11. What is the term for mildly dry skin? _____

Terms Related to Pigmentation Disorders

TERM	WORD ORIGIN	DEFINITION
Albinism AL bih niz um	*albin/o* white *-ism* condition	Complete lack of melanin production by existing melanocytes, resulting in pale skin, white hair, and pink irides (*sing.* iris).
Hyperpigmentation	*hyper-* excessive *pigment/o* paint *-ation* condition	Abnormally increased pigmentation.
Hypopigmentation	*hypo-* deficient *pigment/o* paint *-ation* condition	Congenital or acquired decrease in melanin production.

Terms Related to Pigmentation Disorders—cont'd

TERM	WORD ORIGIN	DEFINITION
Melasma mah LAZ mah		Hyperpigmentation of the forehead, cheeks, and/or nose as a result of the effect of pregnancy or oral contraceptives. The pigmentation recedes gradually, although sometimes incompletely, when the pregnancy concludes or the oral contraceptives are discontinued. Also called **chloasma** (kloh AZ muh).
Vitiligo vih tih LYE goh		Benign acquired disease of unknown origin, consisting of irregular patches of various sizes lacking in pigment (Fig. 1-15).

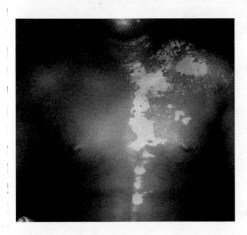

Fig. 1-15 Vitiligo. *(From Callen JP, Greer KE, Saller AS, et al: Color atlas of dermatology, ed 2, Philadelphia, 2000, Saunders.)*

⊠ BE CAREFUL!

Hidr/o- with an *i* means sweat; *hydr/o-* with a *y* means water. Both are pronounced HYE droh.

⊠ BE CAREFUL!

Don't confuse *milia*, a condition resulting from oil-filled ducts, with *miliaria*, a condition resulting from sweat-filled ducts.

Terms Related to Disorders of Sweating

TERM	WORD ORIGIN	DEFINITION
Hyperhidrosis hye pur hye DROH sis	*hyper-* excessive *hidr/o* sweat *-osis* abnormal condition	Excessive perspiration caused by heat, strong emotion, menopause, hyperthyroidism, or infection.
Miliaria mill ee AIR ee uh		Minute vesicles and papules, often with surrounding **erythema** (redness), caused by occlusion of sweat ducts during times of exposure to heat and high humidity.

◈ Exercise 1-8: PIGMENTATION DISORDERS AND DISORDERS OF SWEATING

Build the term.

1. an abnormal condition of excessive perspiration _____

2. an abnormal condition of deficient pigmentation _____

Fill in the blank.

3. An acquired disorder of irregular patches of various sizes lacking in pigment is _____.

4. A patient whose body produces no melanin has a diagnosis of _____.

5. Minute vesicles and papules caused by occlusion of sweat ducts are called

_____.

6. Hyperpigmentation of the face during pregnancy or while taking oral contraceptives is called

_____ or _____.

Terms Related to Benign (Noncancerous) Skin Growths

TERM	WORD ORIGIN	DEFINITION
Angioma an jee OH mah	*angi/o* vessel *-oma* swelling, mass	Localized vascular lesion that includes hemangiomas, vascular nevi, and lymphangiomas (Fig. 1-16).
Dermatofibroma dur mat toh fye BROH mah	*dermat/o* skin *fibr/o* fiber *-oma* swelling, mass	Skin nodule that is painless, round, firm, red or gray, elevated, and usually found on the extremities.
Dysplastic nevus (*pl.* nevi) dis PLAS tick NEE vus	*dys-* abnormal *plast/o* formation *-ic* pertaining to	Various abnormal changes of a pigmented congenital skin blemish that give rise to a concern for progression to malignancy. Changes of concern are categorized as ABCD: **a**symmetry **b**orders, irregular **c**olors, changes in or uneven pigmentation **d**iameter, increasing size or >6 mm
Lipoma lih POH mah	*lip/o* fat *-oma* mass, swelling	Fatty tumor that is a soft, movable, subcutaneous nodule.
Nevus		Pigmented lesion often present at birth. Also called a **mole**.
Seborrheic keratosis seh boh REE ick kair ah TOH sis	*seb/o* sebum *-rrheic* pertaining to discharge *kerat/o* hard, horny *-osis* abnormal condition	Benign, circumscribed, pigmented, superficial warty skin lesion that may be accompanied by pruritus.
Skin tags		Small, soft, pedunculated lesions that are harmless outgrowths of epidermal and dermal tissue, usually occurring on the neck, eyelids, armpits, and groin; usually occur in multiples. Also known as **acrochordons** (ack roh KORE dons).

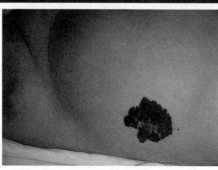

Fig. 1-16 Hemangioma. *(From Callen JP, Greer KE, Saller AS, et al: Color atlas of dermatology, ed 2, Philadelphia, 2000, Saunders.)*

◈ Exercise 1-9: BENIGN SKIN GROWTHS

Matching.

_____ 1. pigmented lesion

_____ 2. acrochordon

_____ 3. fatty tumor

_____ 4. painless skin lesion

_____ 5. benign warty skin lesion

_____ 6. vascular nevus

A. skin tag
B. lipoma
C. seborrheic keratosis
D. mole
E. dermatofibroma
F. angioma

Terms Related to Malignant Neoplasms

TERM	WORD ORIGIN	DEFINITION
Basal cell carcinoma (BCC) BAY suhl	*bas/o* base *-al* pertaining to *carcin/o* cancer of epithelial origin *-oma* tumor, mass *Flesh colored*	The most common form of skin cancer, it originates in the basal layer of the epidermis. It usually occurs on the face as a result of sun exposure and rarely metastasizes (spreads to distant sites). (Appear as formed flesh-colored, waxy papules with ulcerations)
Kaposi sarcoma (KS) Keh POH see	*sarc/o* connective tissue cancer *-oma* tumor, mass	A rare form of skin cancer that takes the form of red/blue/brown/purple nodules, usually on the extremities. One form appears most often in patients with deficient immune systems.
Malignant melanoma	*melan/o* black, dark *-oma* tumor, mass	This cancerous tumor arises from mutated melanocytes. This particular cancer is the leading cause of death for all skin diseases (Fig. 1-17).
Squamous cell carcinoma (SCC) SKWAY muss	*squam/o* scaly *-ous* pertaining to *carcin/o* cancer of epithelial origin *-oma* tumor, mass *Flat reddish patches*	The second most common type of skin cancer, also caused by sun exposure, but grows slower than the other types of skin cancer. (Appears as a papule with a rough, scaly surface and flat reddish patches)

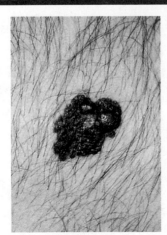

Fig. 1-17 Malignant melanoma on arm.

◈ Exercise 1-10: Malignant Neoplasms

Fill in the blank.

1. What is a common skin cancer that grows slower than BCC? _____

2. What is a rare form of skin cancer that often occurs in patients with a deficient immune system?

   _____

3. What is a malignant skin tumor that arises from mutated melanocytes?

   _____

4. What is the most common type of skin cancer (originating in the basal layer of the epidermis)?

   _____

Burns

Burns are injuries to tissues that result from exposure to thermal, chemical, electrical, or radioactive agents. They may be classified into four different degrees of severity, depending on the layers of the skin that are damaged. Coders must categorize burns higher than second degree according to the "rule of nines" (Fig. 1-18) that divides the body into percentages that are, for the most part, multiples of nine: the head and neck equaling 9%, each upper limb 9%, each lower limb 9%, the front and back of the torso 36%, and the genital area 1%. Fig. 1-19 is an illustration of the different degrees of burns.

- **First degree:** Burn in which only the first layer of the skin, the epidermis, is damaged; also known as a *superficial burn.* Characterized by redness (erythema), tenderness, and hyperesthesia, with no scar development.
- **Second degree:** Burn in which the first and second layers of the skin (epidermis and part of the dermis) are affected; sometimes called a *partial-thickness burn.* Characterized by redness, blisters, and pain, with possible scar development.
- **Third degree:** Burn that damages the epidermis, dermis, and subcutaneous tissue; also known as a *full-thickness burn.* Pain is not present because the nerve endings in the skin have been destroyed. Skin appearance may be deep red, pale gray, brown, or black. Scar formation is likely.
- **Fourth degree:** Although not a universally accepted category, some burn specialists use this category to describe a rare burn that extends beyond the subcutaneous tissue into the muscle and bone.
- **Eschar** (ESS kar): Scab or dry crust that results from a burn, trauma, or infection.

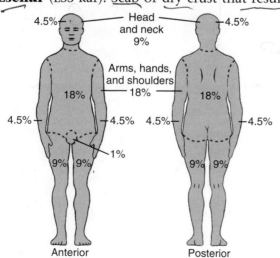

Fig. 1-18 Rule of nines for estimating extent of burns. *(From Habif TP:* Clinical dermatology, *ed 4, St Louis, 2004, Mosby.)*

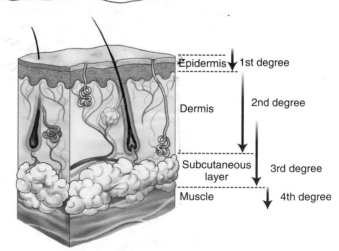

Fig. 1-19 Degree of burns and depth of tissue involvement. *(From Damjanov I, Linder J:* Anderson's pathology, *ed 10, St Louis, 1996, Mosby.)*

❖ Exercise 1-11: BURNS

Match the characteristics of the burns listed with their degree.

_____ 1. first degree

_____ 2. second degree

_____ 3. third degree

_____ 4. fourth degree

A. Ironing a blouse for work, Rhonda burned her hand, resulting in blisters and erythema.

B. John suffered burns over two thirds of his body with many areas of tissue burned to the bone.

C. Because Kristin forgot to reapply her sunblock, she sustained a sunburn that resulted in painful reddened skin.

D. Smoking in bed resulting in burns that destroyed the epidermis, dermis, and extended through the hypodermis on the victim's chest and shoulders.

Fill in the blank.

5. The health care term for a crust or scab especially related to burns is _____.

6. The rule of nines is used to categorize the _____ of a burn, depending on the body surfaces affected.

 Age Matters

Pediatrics

Children routinely appear at physician offices with skin disorders. Some of the most common are impetigo, acne, seborrheic dermatitis, cellulitis, and pediculosis. Although none of these are serious disorders, impetigo and pediculosis are highly contagious. Also seen are the different degrees of burns, usually accidental but potentially life threatening.

Geriatrics

Elderly patients have a completely different set of diagnoses. The disorders categorized as those relating to cornification, especially corns and calluses, are seen routinely in medical offices. These masses or thickenings of the skin are formed as a defensive response to constant friction, usually in shoes. Pressure sores (also called bedsores or decubitus ulcers) are most often seen in bedridden patients whose skin may already be atrophied and thin. Eczema, actinic keratoses, cellulitis, and fungal infections are also common complaints. The last category of skin disorders often seen in the elderly is the area of neoplasms. Although younger patients are routinely seen with skin cancers, the older patient, by definition, has had a longer time period to be exposed to the sun.

DIAGNOSTIC PROCEDURES

Terms Related to Biopsies

TERM	WORD ORIGIN	DEFINITION
Excisional biopsy		Biopsy in which the entire tumor may be removed with borders as a means of diagnosis and treatment.
Exfoliation ecks foh lee A shun		Scraping or shaving off samples of friable (easily crushed) lesions for a laboratory examination called **exfoliative cytology.**
Incisional biopsy		Biopsy in which larger tissue samples may be obtained by excising a wedge of tissue and suturing the incision.
Needle aspiration		Aspiration of fluid from lesions to obtain samples for culture and examination.
Punch biopsy		Biopsy in which a tubular punch is inserted through to the subcutaneous tissue, and the tissue is cut off at the base (Fig. 1-20).

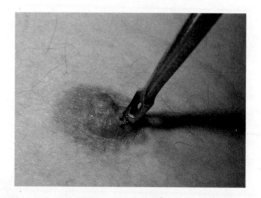

Fig. 1-20   Punch biopsy.

Terms Related to Laboratory Tests

TERM	WORD ORIGIN	DEFINITION
Bacterial analyses		Culture and serology of lesions to help diagnose such disorders as impetigo.
Fungal tests		Cultures of scrapings of lesions used to identify fungal infections, such as tinea pedis, tinea capitis, and tinea cruris.
Sweat tests		Laboratory test for abnormally high levels of sodium and chloride present in the perspiration of persons with cystic fibrosis.
Tuberculosis (TB) skin tests		Intradermal test (e.g., Mantoux test) using purified protein derivative (PPD) to test for either dormant or active tuberculosis; much more accurate test than the multiple puncture tine test, which has been used for screening purposes.
Tzanck test tzahnk		Microscopic examination of lesions for the purpose of diagnosing herpes zoster and herpes simplex.
Viral culture		Sampling of vesicular fluid for the purpose of identifying viruses.

Terms Related to Laboratory Tests—cont'd

TERM	WORD ORIGIN	DEFINITION
Wood's light examination		Method to identify a variety of skin infections through the use of a Wood's lamp, which produces ultraviolet light; tinea capitis and pseudomonas infections in burns are two of the disorders it can reveal (Fig. 1-21).
Wound and abscess cultures		Lab samplings that can identify pathogens in wounds, such as diabetic or decubitus ulcers, postoperative wounds, or abscesses.

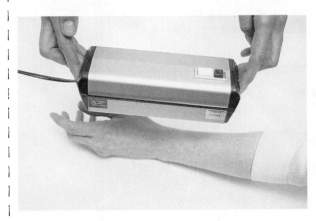

Fig. 1-21   Wood's lamp. The purple color on the skin indicates that no fungal infection is present. *(From Seidel HM, Ball JW, Dains JI, et al: Mosby's guide to physical examination, ed 5, St Louis, 2003, Mosby.)*

◈ Exercise 1-12: DIAGNOSTIC PROCEDURES

Fill in the blanks with the correct terms from the list below.

excisional, exfoliation, incisional, needle aspiration, punch

1. An entire tumor is removed in a(n) _____ biopsy.

2. Fluid from a lesion is aspirated to obtain samples for culture in a(n) _____ biopsy.

3. A wedge of tissue is removed and the incision is sutured in a(n) _____ biopsy.

4. Samples of friable lesions are scraped or shaved off in _____.

5. A cylindrical punch is inserted into the subcutaneous tissue layer, and the tissue is cut off at the base

   in _____ biopsy.

Match the following disorders with the tests that may be used to diagnose them.

_____ 6. ringworm

_____ 7. impetigo

_____ 8. cystic fibrosis

_____ 9. tuberculosis

_____ 10. herpes zoster, herpes simplex

_____ 11. tinea capitis, pseudomonas

_____ 12. bedsore, infection

A. Wood's light examination
B. Mantoux test
C. bacterial analysis
D. wound abscess culture
E. sweat test
F. fungal test
G. Tzanck test

Selvidge Memorial Outpatient Clinic
17201 Northridge Dr.
St. Paul, MN 55407

PROGRESS NOTE

Patient presents for her initial evaluation complaining of severe pruritic rash on her left and right antecubital fossa × 4 days. She reports the rash began on her arms but has also erupted on her forearms and lower extremities. Also has multiple lesions across her chest. Denies any new lotions, soaps, detergents, clothes, pets. No different foods or exposure to poison ivy. Has no previous history of dermatitis.

Denies fevers, chills; other than rash all other systems are unremarkable.

PHYSICAL EXAMINATION: Diffuse vesicular lesions across the upper torso, forearms, and thighs. She has erythematous area of vesicular lesions in her right and left popliteal fossa.
Vesicular diffuse lesions, cause unclear.

Patient referred to dermatology for further examination and treatment. Most likely this represents a viral exanthem. She was given topical hydrocortisone cream and advised to use Benadryl for itching.

Maurice Doate, MD

 Exercise 1-13: PROGRESS NOTE

Review the progress note above and answer the following questions:

1. How do we know that her rash is itchy?

_____

2. What phrase tells us that she has had no skin inflammations diagnosed in the past?

_____

3. What characteristic would "vesicular" lesions have?

_____

4. "Exanthem" is a medical term for what?

_____

☰ THERAPEUTIC INTERVENTIONS

Terms Related to Grafting Techniques and Other Therapies

Term	Word Origin	Definition
Allograft AL oh graft	*all/o* other	Harvest of skin from another human donor for temporary transplant until an autograft is available.
Autograft AH toh graft	*auto-* self	Harvest of the patient's own skin for transplant (Fig. 1-22).
Dermatome DUR mah tohm	*dermat/o* skin *-tome* instrument to cut	Instrument used to remove split-skin grafts.
Flap		Section of skin transferred from one location to an immediately adjacent one.
Full-thickness graft		Free skin graft using full portions of both the epidermis and dermis.
Laser therapy		Procedure to repair or destroy tissue, particularly in the removal of tattoos, warts, port wine stains, and psoriatic lesions.
Occlusive therapy	*occlus/o* to close *-ive* pertaining to	Use of a nonporous occlusive dressing to cover a treated area to increase the absorption and effectiveness of a medication; used to treat psoriasis, lupus erythematosus, and chronic hand dermatitis.
Psoralen plus ultraviolet A (PUVA) therapy SORE ah lin		Directing a type of ultraviolet light on psoriatic lesions.
Skin grafting (SG)		Skin transplant performed when normal skin cover has been lost as a result of burns, ulcers, or operations to remove cancerous tissue.
Split-thickness skin graft (STSG)		Skin graft using the epidermis and parts of the dermis.
Xenograft ZEE noh graft	*xen/o* foreign	Temporary skin graft from another species, often a pig, used until an autograft is available.

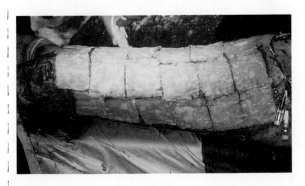

Fig. 1-22 Epithelial autografts. Thin sheets of skin are attached to gauze backing. *(From McCance KL, Huether SE: Pathophysiology: the biologic basis for disease in adults and children, ed 4, St Louis, 2002, Mosby.)*

DID YOU KNOW?

The term *dermatome* also describes an area on the surface of the body that receives innervation from afferent fibers of a spinal root.

Terms Related to Tissue Removal

TERM	WORD ORIGIN	DEFINITION
Cauterization kah tur rye ZAY shun	*cauter/o* burn *-zation* process of	Destruction of tissue by burning with heat.
Cryosurgery KRY oh sur juh ree	*cryo-* extreme cold	Destruction of tissue through the use of extreme cold, usually liquid nitrogen.
Curettage KYOOR uh tahz	*scrab*	Scraping material from the wall of a cavity or other surface to obtain tissue for microscopic examination; this is done with an instrument called a **curette**.
Debridement dah breed MON		First step in wound treatment, involving removal of dirt, foreign bodies (FB), damaged tissue, and cellular debris from the wound or burn to prevent infection and to promote healing.
Escharotomy ess kar AH tuh mee	*eschar/o* scab *-tomy* incision	Surgical incision into necrotic tissue resulting from a severe burn. This may be necessary to prevent edema leading to ischemia (loss of blood flow) in underlying tissue.
Incision and drainage (I&D)		To cut open and remove the contents of a wound, cyst, or other lesion.
Shaving (paring)		Slicing of thin sheets of tissue to remove lesions.

Terms Related to Cosmetic Procedures

TERM	WORD ORIGIN	DEFINITION
Blepharoplasty BLEF ar oh plas tee	*blephar/o* eyelid *-plasty* surgical repair	Surgical restructuring of the eyelid.
Chemical peel		Use of a mild acid to produce a mild, superficial burn; normally done to remove wrinkles.
Dermabrasion dur mah BRAY zhun	*derm/o* skin *-abrasion* scraping	Surgical procedure to resurface the skin; used to remove acne scars, nevi, wrinkles, and tattoos.
Dermatoplasty dur mat toh PLAS tee	*dermat/o* skin *-plasty* surgical repair	Transplant of living skin to correct effects of injury, operation, or disease.

Terms Related to Cosmetic Procedures—cont'd

TERM	WORD ORIGIN	DEFINITION
Lipectomy lih PECK toh mee	*lip/o* fat *-ectomy* removal	Resection of fatty tissue.
Liposuction LYE poh suck shun	*lip/o* fat	Technique for removing adipose tissue with a suction pump device.
Rhytidectomy rye tih DECK tuh mee	*rhytid/o* wrinkle *-ectomy* removal	Surgical operation to remove wrinkles. Commonly known as a "face-lift."

◈ **Exercise 1-14: THERAPEUTIC INTERVENTIONS**

1. Explain the differences among the following.

   A. autograft _____

   B. allograft _____

   C. xenograft _____

2. Which type of graft includes the epidermis and the dermis? _____

3. What instrument is used to cut skin for grafting? _____

Fill in the blanks with the correct terms from the list below.

cauterization, cryosurgery, curettage, debridement, incision and drainage, laser therapy, occlusive therapy, shaving

4. _____ is used to destroy tattoos.

5. Removing dirt, foreign bodies, damaged tissue, and cellular debris from a wound is called

   _____.

6. The destruction of tissue by burning with heat is called _____.

7. The destruction of tissue through the use of extreme cold is called _____.

8. Scraping of material from the wall of a cavity is called _____.

9. I&D is _____.

10. Another term for paring is _____.

11. A covered treatment area is called _____.

Matching.

_____ 12. resection of fatty tissue

_____ 13. excision of wrinkles

_____ 14. resurfacing the skin

_____ 15. restructuring of eyelids

_____ 16. therapeutic superficial burn

_____ 17. suction of adipose tissue

_____ 18. transplant of skin

A. chemical peel
B. liposuction
C. blepharoplasty
D. rhytidectomy
E. lipectomy
F. dermabrasion
G. dermatoplasty

⚶ PHARMACOLOGY

Routes of Administration

Several medications are administered on, within, or through the skin. The most common of these routes of administration include the following:

Hypodermic (H): General term that refers to any injection under the skin.
Intradermal (ID): Route of injection within the dermis (Fig. 1-23, *A*). Also called **intracutaneous.**
Subcutaneous (Sub Q, Sub-Q): Route for injection into the fat layer beneath the skin (Fig. 1-23, *B*).
Topical: Type of drug applied directly on the skin as a cream, gel, lotion, or ointment.
Transdermal therapeutic system (TTS): Use of a transdermal patch; involves placing medication in a gel-like material that is applied to the skin, allowing for a specified timed release of the medicine. Examples are nitroglycerin for angina pectoris and Nicoderm for smoking cessation.

> ⊠ BE CAREFUL!
>
> *ID* means intradermal; *I&D* means incision and drainage.

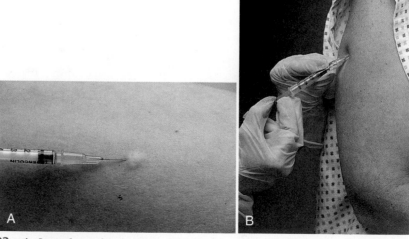

Fig. 1-23   A, Intradermal injection. **B,** Subcutaneous injection. *(From Brody HJ: Chemical peeling, ed 2, St Louis, 1997, Mosby.)*

Dermatological Drugs

Traditional Pharmacology

Anesthetic agents: Drugs to reduce pain and discomfort; can be given topically on an affected area. Examples include lidocaine and Solarcaine.

Antibacterials: Drugs that prevent and treat bacterial growth. Topical agents such as erythromycin (Ery 2% Pads) and clindamycin (Benzaclin) are used to treat acne, while Triple Antibiotic Ointment (bacitracin, polymixin B, and neomycin), silver sulfadiazine (Silvadene), and mupirocin (Bactroban) are used to prevent and treat skin or wound infections. Oral agents for the treatment of acne include erythromycin (Ery-Tab), tetracycline (Sumycin), and minocycline (Minocin).

Antifungals: Drugs that attack fungi. Agents that target topical fungal infections include nystatin (Nystat), butenafine (Lotrimin), ciclopirox (Loprox), and econazole (Spectazole).

Antihistamines: Drugs that lessen itching by reducing an allergic response. Diphenhydramine (Benadryl) is available in oral or topical formulations. Other oral agents include loratadine (Claritin), chlorpheniramine (Chlor-Trimeton), and cetirizine (Zyrtec).

Anti-inflammatories: Used to reduce inflammation and pain. Oral agents include prednisone and aspirin, while topical agents include hydrocortisone (Cortizone), fluocinonide (Lidex), and triamcinolone (Kenalog).

Antipsoriatics: Agents that specifically treat psoriasis. Examples include anthralin (Drithocreme) and calcipotriene (Dovonex).

Antiseptics: Topical agents used to prevent infection by destroying microbials. Examples include iodine and chlorhexidine (Peridex).

Antivirals: Drugs designed to lessen the effect of viruses. Examples include valacyclovir (Valtrex) and acyclovir (Zovirax) for the treatment of herpes simplex virus (cold sores or genital herpes) and herpes zoster (shingles).

Emollients (ih MOLL yents): Topical substances that soften the skin. Examples include mineral oil, lanolin, cetyl alcohol, and stearyl alcohol. A well-known product containing emollients is Lubriderm.

Immunomodulators or **immunosuppressants:** Agents that suppress the body's immune system. Topical agents such as pimecrolimus (Elidel) and tacrolimus (Protopic) are used to treat atopic dermatitis and eczema.

Keratolytics (kair ah toh LIT icks): Topical substances used to break down hardened skin and shed the top layer of dead skin to treat warts, calluses, corns, acne, rosacea, and psoriasis. Examples include salicylic acid, cantharidin, benzoyl peroxide (Benzac, Oxy10), and podofilox (Condylox).

Pediculicides: Destroy lice. Examples include malathion (Ovide), lindane, and permethrin (Nix).

Protectives: Topicals with sun protection factors (SPFs) to protect the skin against ultraviolet A and B in sunlight. A wide variety of these are available over the counter.

Retinoids: Derived from vitamin A; alters the growth of the top layer of skin and may be used to treat acne, reduce wrinkles, and treat psoriasis. Examples include tretinoin (Retin-A), isotretinoin (Accutane), and tazarotene (Tazorac).

Scabicides: Destroy mites and scabies. Examples include lindane, permethrin (Elimite), and crotamiton (Eurax).

Alternative and Complementary Methods of Treatment

Herbal medicine: Drugs from minimally altered plant sources, such as aloe vera (to treat sunburn and stomach ulcers) or tea tree oil (used for its antibacterial, antiviral, and antifungal properties to treat boils, wound infections, and acne). Also, therapeutic use of essential oils is useful in treating dry flaky skin, decubitus ulcers, diabetic ulcers, herpes zoster, and herpes simplex type 1.

DID YOU KNOW?

Many dermatological drugs share the prefixes *anti-*, meaning that they are against whatever is named, *-lytics*, meaning that they destroy or break down something, or *-cides*, meaning that they are intended to kill something.

◆ Exercise 1-15: PHARMACOLOGY

Build terms to describe the following.

1. Medication injected "within the dermis" is given by the _Intradermal_ route.

2. Medications applied directly to the skin are given by the _Topical_ route.

3. A general term meaning *under the skin* is _Hypodermic_

4. Medications delivered via a patch through the skin are given by _Transdermal Therapeutic Route_.

5. Medication applied to an affected area to reduce pain and discomfort is called a(n) _Anesthetic_.

6. Salicylic acid, benzoyl peroxide, and podofilox are examples of _Keratolytics Agent_

7. Oral erythromycin, tetracycline, and minocycline are all used to treat _~~Antibacterials~~ Acne_

8. Medications that target bacteria are called _Antibacterials_.

9. Butenafine, nystatin, and econazole are all _Antifungal_ medications.

10. Give three examples of anti-inflammatory medications: _Prednisone, Aspirin, Flocinonide_

Match the following pharmaceutical agents with their actions.

_D_ 11. softens the skin

_C_ 12. breaks down hardened skin

_A_ 13. lessens itching

_B_ 14. prevents infection

_E_ 15. treats herpes simplex virus

_G_ 16. treats lice

_F_ 17. treats mites

A. antihistamine
B. antiseptic
C. keratolytic
D. emollient
E. antiviral
F. scabicide
G. pediculicide

Abbreviations

Abbreviation	Meaning	Abbreviation	Meaning
Bx	Biopsy	PPD	Purified protein derivative
Decub	Pressure ulcer	PUVA	Psoralen plus ultraviolet A
ED	Emergency department	SG	Skin graft
FB	Foreign body	SPF	Sun protection factor
H	Hypodermic	STSG	Split-thickness skin graft
HPV	Human papillomavirus	Sub Q, Sub-Q	Subcutaneous
HSV-1	Herpes simplex virus 1	TB	Tuberculosis
HSV-2	Herpes simplex virus 2	TTS	Transdermal therapeutic system
I&D	Incision and drainage	ung	Ointment
ID	Intradermal	UV	Ultraviolet (light)

◇ Exercise 1-16: ABBREVIATIONS

Write the abbreviation for each of the following.

1. a route of administration within the dermis: _____ID_____

2. radiation from sunlight: _____

3. skin graft: _____

4. pressure ulcer: _____

5. example of material removed from a wound during debridement: _____

6. biopsy: _____

7. patch to deliver medicine: _____

8. ointment: _____

Careers

Health Information

Are you fascinated by medicine but do not want to have direct patient contact? You might want to consider a career in health information. Projected to be one of the careers that is expected to grow much faster than average for all professions, the field offers careers as clinical coders, department directors, privacy officers, information security officers, insurance claims analysts, and physician practice managers. Although most job settings are in hospitals, insurance companies and physician practices also hire health information professionals.

Registered Health Information Administrators (RHIAs) are graduates of approved baccalaureate-level programs who have successfully passed the registration exam for health information administrators given by the American Health Information Management Association (AHIMA). Their duties include the collection, interpretation, and analysis of health care data. Coursework and practice in management qualify these individuals to be administrators of health information management departments.

Registered Health Information Technicians (RHITs) are graduates of approved associate degree programs who have passed their AHIMA registration exam. They analyze patient records for completeness, oversee the appropriate release of patient information, and supervise other employees in health information management departments.

Clinical coders are certified by two associations: the AHIMA and the American Academy of Professional Coders (AAPC). The AHIMA certifications are the Certified Coding Associate (CCA), the Certified Coding Specialist (CCS), and the Certified Coding Specialist for Physician offices (CCS-P). The AAPC credentials are the Certified Professional Coder (CPC) and the Certified Professional Coder-Hospital (CPC-H). The CCA credential is an entry-level coding credential. The CCS is normally for those individuals who will code inpatient hospital records, including ambulatory surgery and emergency room care, and the CCS-P is for those who code in physician-based settings. The CPC is a coding specialist in the area of physician practice coding. The CPC-H is the credential offered by the AAPC for outpatient facilities.

For more information about the RHIA, RHIT, CCA, CCS, or CCS-P credentials, visit: The American Health Information Management Association at: http://www.ahima.org.

For information about the CPC or CPC-H credentials, visit: The American Academy of Professional Coders at: http://www.aapc.com.

Medical Transcription

Most medical transcriptionists listen to physician dictation and transcribe the recordings into health care reports, correspondence, or other types of reports. They must have a good command of English grammar and punctuation, medical terminology, anatomy and physiology, pharmacology, and diagnostic procedures. Current job settings are hospitals, physician offices, transcription services, or at home. Training may be a 1-year certificate or a 2-year associate degree program. For further information, visit: The American Association for Medical Transcription at http://www.aamt.org.

Careers Related to the Integumentary System

Dermatologist

For those of you who wish to explore the career of a dermatologist, you might want to go back to the first chapter to consult the AMA site. Be aware that after 4 years of college with specific prerequisites and 4 years of medical school, a dermatologist must spend 3 years in a dermatology residency. Most dermatologists work in hospitals or in private practice. Duties include treating patients, performing skin surgeries, and interpreting slides of skin biopsies. For more information, visit: American Academy of Dermatology at http://www.aad.org/default.htm.

Medical Esthetician

Students who consider a career in cosmetology but want to work in a medical setting now have a career option: medical esthetician. These individuals usually work in dermatology practices but may also work in oncology departments. Duties may include the following: postoperative skin care treatment for patients who have undergone plastic surgery, assisting with microdermabrasion, teaching burn patients to apply makeup to conceal injuries, or helping chemotherapy patients learn to measure their natural brow line to draw eyebrows lost to treatment. Interested students will need to check with their own state boards of cosmetology for certification requirements.

Chapter Review

A. Functions of the Integumentary System

1. In your own words, describe the functions of the integumentary system.

   _____

   _____

   _____

B. Anatomy and Physiology

2. Label the following diagram.

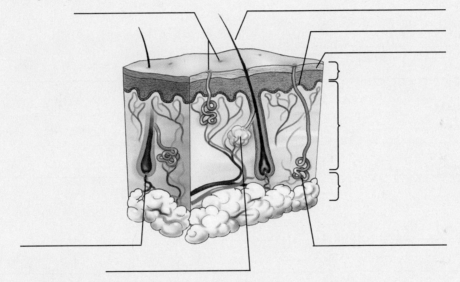

3. Fill in the combining forms for the following anatomical structures.

   A. skin _____

   B. hair _____

   C. nails _____

   D. sudoriferous glands _____

   E. oil (glands) _____

   F. hair root and covering _____

4. The term for the layers that compose the epidermis is _____.

5. The epidermis is the _____ layer, meaning that it does not have a rich blood supply.

6. The nerve endings, hair follicles, and sebaceous glands are located in the layer of the skin called the

   _____ or _____.

7. Fatty tissue is stored in the _____ or the _____ layer.

C. Pathology

Decode the medical term by writing the meaning of the word part in the space provided, then using the parts to form a definition.

Example: *dermatology*

      (dermat/o- *skin* + -logy *the study of*)

      the study of the skin

8. **dermatitis**

    (dermat/o _____ + -itis _____)

    _____

9. **folliculitis**

    (follicul/o _____ + -itis _____)

    _____

10. **onychomycosis**

    (onych/o _____ + myc/o _____ + -osis _____)

    _____

11. **angioma**

    (angi/o _____ + -oma _____)

    _____

12. **hyperhidrosis**

    (hyper- _____ + hidr/o _____ + -osis _____)

    _____

13. **hypertrichosis**

    (hyper- _____ + trich/o _____ + -osis _____)

    _____

14. **seborrheic dermatitis**

    (seb/o _____ + -rrheic _____ dermat/o _____

    + -itis _____)

    _____

15. **lipoma**

   (lip/o _____ + -oma _____)

   _____

16. **dysplastic (nevus)**

   (dys- _____ + plast/o _____ + -ic _____)

   _____

17. **xeroderma**

   (xer/o _____ + -derma _____)

   _____

18. Define "lesion."

   _____

   _____

19. What is the difference between a primary lesion and a secondary lesion?

   _____

   _____

   _____

20. Define the following.

   A. petechia _____

   B. ecchymosis _____

   C. purpura _____

   D. hematoma _____

   E. telangiectasia _____

21. What do the terms in Question 20 have in common?

   _____

22. Given the following examples, name the type of lesion:

    A. 0.4-cm blister _____

    B. scab _____

    C. freckle _____

    D. scar _____

    E. bruise _____

    F. bedsore _____

    G. stria _____

23. Jeremy had a localized suppurative staph infection in hair follicles on his neck. What type of infection did he have? _____

24. Manuel developed athlete's foot after showering in his local gym without shower shoes. The health care term for athlete's foot is _____.

25. Irene developed a yeast infection after she had been on a course of antibiotics. The health care term for one type of yeast infection is _____.

26. Shri had to send home notices about a child who had lice in his classroom. The term for a louse infestation is _____.

27. A parasitic infection caused by mites is _____.

28. Roseanne had verrucae on the plantar surface of her feet. Verrucae are _____.

29. Shingles is the common name for _____.

30. Roberta went to see her dermatologist because of thinning hair. She was diagnosed with _____.

31. Extremely dry skin, named for its scaly appearance, is called _____.

32. What is the difference between a corn and a callus?

    _____

33. Give an example of hypopigmentation: _____

34. Give an example of hyperpigmentation: _____

35. What is eschar? _____

36. List the depth of skin or body tissue affected and the observable changes for each of the four degrees of burns listed.

   A. first degree _____

   B. second degree _____

   C. third degree _____

   D. fourth degree _____

D. Diagnostic Procedures

37. The entire tumor is removed in a(n) _____ biopsy.

38. Fluid from a lesion is aspirated to obtain samples for culture in a(n)

   _____ biopsy.

39. A wedge of tissue is removed, and the incision is sutured in a(n) _____ biopsy.

40. Samples of friable lesions are scraped or shaved off in _____.

41. A tubular punch is inserted into the subcutaneous tissue layer, and the tissue is cut off at the base in

   a(n) _____ biopsy.

42. A test to diagnose herpes zoster or herpes simplex is _____.

43. Tinea capitis and *Pseudomonas* infections are two disorders tested by

   _____.

44. The Mantoux test is used to diagnose _____.

45. A test for cystic fibrosis is the _____ test.

46. Postoperative wound drainage would indicate the need for _____ and _____ cultures.

47. Vesicular fluid can be tested through a(n) _____ culture.

48. Impetigo is tested by a(n) _____ analysis.

49. Tinea pedis is tested by a(n) _____ test.

E. Therapeutic Interventions

50. Decode the medical term by writing the meaning of the word part in the space provided, then using the parts to form a definition.

   A. **dermatome**

      (dermat/o _____ + -tome _____)

      _____

B. **dermatoplasty**

(dermat/o _____ + -plasty _____)

_____

C. **escharotomy**

(eschar/o _____ + -tomy _____)

_____

D. **cryosurgery**

(cry/o_____) + surgery

_____

E. **lipectomy**

(lip/o _____ + -ectomy _____)

_____

F. **rhytidectomy**

(rhytid/o _____ + -ectomy _____)

_____

G. **dermabrasion**

(derm/o _____ + -abrasion _____)

_____

51. Explain the differences among the following.

A. autograft _____

B. allograft _____

C. xenograft _____

52. The difference between cryosurgery and cauterization is that the first uses extreme _____

to destroy tissue, whereas the latter uses _____ to destroy tissue.

53. Differentiate among the following.

A. shaving _____

B. debridement _____

C. curettage _____

54. Covering a treated area with a nonporous dressing to increase absorption and effectiveness is

_____ therapy.

F. Pharmacology

55. Medications injected within the dermis are given by the _____ route.

56. Medications applied directly on the skin are given by the _____ route.

57. Essential oils used to treat disease are part of a discipline called _____.

58. Aloe is a type of _____ medicine.

59. Samantha applied a medication to reduce the pain and discomfort of her sunburn. It is classified as

a/an _____.

60. Keratolytics are designed to _____.

61. Dr. Wong prescribed a(n) _____ to treat a louse infestation.

62. Monica was prescribed a type of medication to lessen itching classified as a/an

_____.

63. Topical substances that soften skin are _____.

G. Abbreviations

Write out the abbreviations for the following questions.

64. If Paula had a Bx, she had a(n) _____.

65. An STSG means that someone has had a(n) _____.

66. A fever blister is caused by _____.

67. I&D performed on a cyst is _____ and _____.

68. Darius had the abbreviation "Decub" recorded on his chart. What does that mean?

_____

69. A patient's treatment includes TTS, which means _____.

70. A type of light treatment for psoriasis is called _____.

H. Singulars and Plurals

Change the following singular terms to plural.

71. stria _____

72. bulla _____

73. onychomycosis _____

74. decubitus _____

75. ecchymosis _____

76. petechia _____

77. comedo _____

78. verruca _____

79. stratum _____

I. Translations

Rewrite the following to explain the underlined terms.

80. The patient had a <u>verruca</u> on the <u>plantar</u> surface of his foot removed with <u>cryosurgery</u>.

_____

81. The elderly patient developed a <u>decubitus ulcer</u> from lack of proper care during an extended hospital stay.

_____

_____

82. The patient bought a wig to cover her <u>alopecia</u> caused by <u>trichotillomania</u>.

_____

_____

83. Mr. Hassan complained of intense <u>pruritus</u> from <u>urticaria</u>.

_____

_____

84. The burn patient was in for an <u>escharotomy</u> and a consultation for a possible <u>allograft</u>.

_____

_____

85. Write the synonyms for the following terms.

A. acrochordon _____

B. clavus_____

C. nevus _____

D. hirsutism _____

    E. verruca _____

    F. cicatrix _____

    G. pressure sore _____

J. Be Careful

Explain the difference between these paired terms.

86. hidr/o and hydr/o _____

87. milia and miliaria _____

88. stria and strata _____

89. ID and I&D _____

90. papill/o and papul/o _____

Case Study With Accompanying Medical Report

Eleven-month-old Ben Warner was enjoying himself as he practiced walking in his family's living room. His training circuit consisted of pulling up on the coffee table, edging around to the side near the couch, and then launching himself for a wobbly step before collapsing on the carpet. Unfortunately, Ben's dad left his newspaper and a fresh cup of hot coffee on the table when he went to answer the phone. It only took seconds for Ben to pull the newspaper and coffee onto himself, and his resulting howls brought his father running back to find his little boy with a nasty burn on his arm. Ben was taken to the emergency department (ED) of their local hospital.

In the Health Information Management department the following day, Olivia Crawford, Registered Health Information Technician (RHIT), Certified Coding Specialist (CCS) assigned codes to Ben's ED record.

The coffee that scalded Ben caused a mottled, sensitive, and painful area on his arm that soon developed a large blister. He was diagnosed as having a second-degree burn. His dad was told that he would need to try to keep Ben from picking at the blister because patients with this type of burn are at risk for developing scar tissue.

If Ben's burn had been more serious, he might have needed a grafting procedure, possibly harvesting of some of his own tissue from his buttocks. Fortunately, the burn did not appear to be severe enough to warrant the need for grafting. If the wound does not heal properly and a disfiguring scar develops, he may be a candidate for revision of the scar at a later date.

(From Barkauskas VH: Health and physical assessment, *ed 3, St Louis, 2002, Mosby.)*

(From Lewis SM: Medical-surgical nursing: assessment and management of clinical problems, *ed 6, St Louis, 2005, Mosby.)*

Before leaving the ED, Ben's forearm was treated with Silvadene cream, an antibiotic, and covered with a loose dressing. His dad was advised to keep the burn covered with sterile bandages and to return in a week to have it checked.

Selvidge Memorial Hospital
17201 Northridge Drive
St. Paul, MN 55407

ED RECORD

Patient Name: Benjamin Warner

Allergies: NKDA

Physician Name: Dr. James

Med Report: #59776

Patient Complaint: Second-degree burns on forearm of African-American male, 11 months. Father states that child pulled hot coffee off table onto arm. Denies other injuries. + erythema, 3-cm bulla

Impression: 2-degree burn to right arm, 1%

Rx: Silvadene dressing, Children's Advil prn
Condition on Discharge: Stable

ICD-9-CM Codes Assigned:
943.21—Burn of forearm: blisters, epidermal loss (second degree)
948.00—Burns classified according to extent of body surface involved: less than 10% or unspecified
E924.0—Accident caused by hot substance or object, caustic or corrosive material, and steam; hot liquids and vapors, including steam

K. Health Care Report

91. What type of burn is described?
    A. superficial
    B. partial thickness
    C. full thickness

92. What are the characteristics present that make this a second-degree burn?

    _____

93. E codes categorize the external cause of the injury. What did the E code describe in this case?

    _____

94. How big was the blister on the child's arm?

    _____

References

Edison TA: Life. In Bartlett J, Kaplan J, editors: *Bartlett's familiar quotations: a collection of passages, phrases, and proverbs traced to their sources in ancient and modern literature,* ed 16, New York, 1992, Little, Brown.

Micozzi MS: *Fundamentals of complementary and alternative medicine,* ed 2, New York, 2001, Churchill Livingstone.

Novey DW: *Clinician's complete reference to complementary and alternative medicine,* St Louis, 2000, Mosby.

2

OBJECTIVES

You will be able to do the following after completing this chapter:

Key Terms
1. Define, appropriately use, and spell all the Key Terms for this chapter.

Function and Structure of the Integumentary System
2. List the three main functions of the skin.
3. Explain how the body is able to maintain a constant temperature.
4. Identify the three layers of the skin and describe the structure and function of each.
5. Identify the three types of substructures of the skin and explain the function of each.

Damage to the Skin
6. List and briefly describe nine common skin lesions.
7. Define actinic keratosis, basal cell carcinoma, malignant melanoma, and squamous cell carcinoma, and determine how to identify each.
8. List four treatment options for malignant skin lesions.
9. Explain the difference between *open* and *closed* wounds.
10. List and describe the three phases of wound healing.
11. Distinguish between a partial-thickness and a full-thickness burn as a means to assessing the depth of a burn.
12. Explain the purpose and use of the "rule of nines."

Diseases and Disorders of the Integumentary System
13. List and describe seven signs and symptoms of skin disease.
14. List five types of diagnostic tests and procedures for the skin and describe the use of each.
15. List 10 diseases and disorders of the integumentary system and briefly describe the etiology, signs and symptoms, diagnosis, therapy, and interventions for each.

Patient-Centered Professionalism
16. Analyze a realistic medical office situation and apply your understanding of the integumentary system to determine the best course of action.
17. Describe the impact on patient care when medical assistants have a solid understanding of the structure and function of the integumentary system.

ANATOMY AND PHYSIOLOGY OF THE INTEGUMENTARY SYSTEM

KEY TERMS

The Key Terms for this chapter have been organized into sections so that you can easily see the terminology associated with each aspect of the integumentary system.

dermatologist Physician who specializes in the treatment of diseases and conditions of the skin.

dermatology Study of the skin.

integumentary system Body system made up of the skin, hair, nails, and sweat glands.

turgor (turgidity) Normal tension in the skin.

Structure of the Skin

albinism Genetic condition with a total or partial loss of pigment caused by the inability to use melanin.

dermis Layer of the skin that lies beneath the epidermis.

epidermis Thin upper layer of the skin.

keratin Waterproof protein that toughens the skin.

melanin Dark pigment that provides color to the skin and protects against the sun's ultraviolet rays.

subcutaneous layer Skin layer that lies beneath the dermis and consists mainly of adipose tissue and loose connective tissue.

whorls Ridges that fit snugly over the papillae on top of the dermis; coils or spirals that form fingerprints.

Substructures of the Skin

Hair

follicle Sac or tube that anchors and contains an individual hair.

root Part of the hair that lies beneath the surface of the skin or scalp.

shaft Part of the hair that is seen extending above the skin or scalp.

Glands

acne Disease of the sebaceous gland associated with excessive sebum.

comedo Blackhead; pore that is blocked, usually with sebum and bacteria; may be pustular (whitehead) in closed form.

pore Opening on the surface of the skin that provides a pathway for fluid to leave the body.

sebaceous glands Oil glands; release oil that lubricates the skin and hair.

sebum Oil that lubricates the skin and hair.

sudoriferous glands Sweat glands; maintain body temperature.

Nails

cuticle Narrow band of epidermis at the base and sides of the nail.

free edge Edge of the nail extending beyond the nail body.

lunula White, moon-shaped base of the nail.

nail body Fingernail that covers the nail bed.

nail root Part of the nail that lies under the cuticle.

nails Growths of hard keratin that protect the ends of the fingers and toes.

Damage to the Skin

Lesions

cyst Thick-walled sac that contains fluid or semisolid material.

fissure Split or crack in the skin.

lesion Area of tissue that has pathologically changed.

macule Flat, discolored area of the skin.

papule Small, solid, raised area of the skin.

polyp Flat or stalklike growth extending out from the mucous membrane.

pustule Small, raised, red area of the skin containing pus; pimple.

ulcer Erosion of the skin.

vesicle Blister; collection of clear fluid under the skin.

wheal Slightly elevated area on the skin; bump resembling a hive (e.g., insect bite) or seen after a properly placed intradermal injection.

KEY TERMS—*cont'd*

Skin Lesions

actinic keratosis Precancerous skin growth caused by excessive exposure to the sun.

basal cell carcinoma Malignant skin lesion that is raised, with blood vessels around the edges.

benign Not malignant.

malignant Invasive and destructive growth; having the potential to metastasize; frequently fatal, cancerous.

malignant melanoma Black, asymmetrical lesion with uneven borders that grows faster than normal moles.

nevus A mole or birthmark.

squamous cell carcinoma Skin cancer that appears as a firm papule with ulcerations.

Wounds

abrasion Epidermis is scraped off in an injury or through mechanical means.

closed wound Damage to the tissues beneath the skin without a visible break in the skin.

contusion Blood vessels rupture and blood seeps into the tissue; bruise.

granulation phase Phase 2 of the healing process; flesh begins to form to later support scar tissue.

incision Smooth cut into the skin.

inflammatory phase Phase 1 of the healing process; blood clot forms and stops blood from flowing.

laceration Jagged cuts; wound tissue edges are irregular.

maturation phase Phase 3 of the healing process; scar tissue forms.

open wound Contusion where the skin is broken and the tissue below is exposed.

puncture Sharp object pierces the skin.

wound Break in the skin.

Burns

first-degree burn Reddened area of the epidermis that has slight pain and is hot to the touch; no blisters. Also called a superficial burn.

full-thickness burn Third-degree burn.

partial-thickness burn First-degree and second-degree burns.

"rule of nines" System for evaluating the burns on a patient's total body surface area.

second-degree burn Reddened, blistered tissue involving the epidermis and dermis.

third-degree burn Deep burn that destroys the epidermis and dermis and results in nerve and tissue destruction.

Diseases and Disorders of the Integumentary System

Signs and Symptoms

abscess Localized collection of pus that occurs on the skin or in body tissue.

alopecia Baldness; loss of hair.

carbuncles Large abscesses that involve connecting furuncles.

cicatrix Scar formation after a wound heals.

crust Scab; dried serum, blood, and pus.

decubitus ulcer Pressure sore (bedsore).

diaphoresis Excessive sweating.

ecchymosis Collection of blood under the skin causing the skin to turn blue-black in color.

eczema Itchy, red rash with pustules, scales, crusts, or scabs caused by sensitivity to a substance.

erosion Destruction of the surface layer of skin.

excoriation Removal of the surface epidermis by scratching, burn, abrasion, or chemicals.

furuncle Abscess that occurs around a hair follicle.

ichthyosis Dry, scaly skin condition resembling fish scales.

keloid Overgrowth of fibrous tissue at the site of scar tissue.

petechiae Flat, pinpoint red spots.

pruritus Severe itching.

purpura Small hemorrhages into the skin and tissues.

ulcer Area of open skin caused by a loss of superficial tissue, usually accompanied by the sloughing of inflamed and dead tissue.

urticaria Hives; raised areas that are smooth and cause itching.

vitiligo Loss of pigment in the skin; milk-white patches.

Diseases and Disorders

cellulitis Infection of the skin and subcutaneous or connective tissue.

erythema Redness of the skin.

herpes simplex Viral infection of the skin at the site where skin and mucous membranes meet; "cold sores" or "fever blisters."

impetigo Bacterial infection that forms pustules that rupture and form crusts; usually caused by streptococcal or staphylococcal infection.

Lyme disease Bacterial skin disease that also affects the joints and connective tissue; carried by the tick as a vector.

onychomycosis Fungal infection of the nail.

pediculosis Parasitic skin disorder caused by lice.

psoriasis Idiopathic, hereditary dermatitis with dry, scaly, silver patches with definite borders, usually on both arms, legs, and the scalp.

scabies Parasitic skin disorder caused by an itch mite.

scleroderma Idiopathic, progressive chronic systemic disease of the skin.

tinea Fungal infection of the skin.

warts (verrucae) Contagious raised epithelial growths caused by the papillomavirus.

What Would You Do?

Read the following scenario and keep it in mind as you learn about the integumentary system in this chapter.

Marilyn was taking a shower 2 weeks ago and found a large black mole on her shoulder. At first she ignored it, but after talking with her friend, she decided that she should see her family practice physician. This physician sent her to Dr. Nelson, a dermatologist, who diagnosed her lesion as a possible malignant melanoma. Dr. Nelson asked Marilyn if she had any pruritus, a fissure, or crusting of the lesion. As Dr. Nelson examined Marilyn's shoulder, he noticed petechiae, ecchymosis, and purpura. When asked about these findings, Marilyn told the physician that the mole had itched and she had scratched the area in her sleep. On her leg was a furuncle that was inflamed, hot, and appeared to have a pus formation. On completing the physical examination, Dr. Nelson noticed that Marilyn had the tendency to keloid formation based on the appearance of her appendectomy scar.

Marilyn had quite a few questions for the medical assistant about the meaning of some of the terms used by Dr. Nelson. Marilyn left the dermatologist's office with surgery scheduled for removal of the melanoma in 2 days.

Would you be able to answer Marilyn's questions?

The skin, along with the hair, nails, and sweat glands, makes up the **integumentary system.** The skin is the largest organ of the body systems and provides protection against the environment. The skin is also involved with body temperature regulation, sensory perception, and elimination of toxins. The condition of people's skin reflects their general health, and skin changes throughout a person's life (Table 2-1). The physician evaluates the patient's skin **turgor** (normal tension in the skin) as part of the patient's physical assessment. The integumentary system is very important in working with the other body systems to maintain homeostasis. **Dermatology** is the study of the skin.

FUNCTION AND STRUCTURE OF THE INTEGUMENTARY SYSTEM

Functions of the Skin

The skin serves three main functions to maintain homeostasis in the body: protection, temperature regulation, and sensation.

TABLE 2-1	Life Cycle of the Skin		
Texture	**Flexibility**	**Glands**	**Healing**
Children Smooth Unwrinkled	Very elastic and flexible	Few sweat glands (rely on increased blood flow to cool the body)	Rapid
Adults Skin reacts to the environment; can toughen if too much sun exposure	Flexibility and elasticity continue unless exposed to harmful external environment	Well-developed sebaceous and sweat glands Increased sweat production, thus body odor Increased sebum production leads to acne formation	Heals readily unless an underlying disease process is present
Older Adults Toughened Wrinkled	Less elastic	Decreased sebaceous and sweat glands activity Body loses ability to cool itself effectively	Slow

Protection

The skin protects the body and is the first line of defense against bacterial invasion. The skin is constantly exposed to heat, cold, and toxic substances. It can be scraped, bruised, or cut, but when the body is in a healthy state, skin can heal itself. The skin prevents excessive loss of electrolytes and fluids so the body and skin do not totally dry out. Melanin provides protection from the harmful effects of ultraviolet (UV) rays by providing pigment to the skin. When exposed to the sun's UV rays, the skin manufactures vitamin D, which is needed for the absorption of calcium.

Temperature Regulation

The ability of the body to maintain a constant body temperature is important to the functioning of other processes in the body. For example, many chemical reactions take place in the body. These reactions depend on the action of certain enzymes. Without a constant body temperature, enzymes do not function properly. To maintain a constant body temperature, the body must balance the amount of heat it produces with the amount it loses. To prevent heat loss, the blood vessels within the skin constrict, causing "goose bumps." This "goose flesh" (cutis anserina) prevents heat loss by not allowing body heat to escape through blood vessels near the skin. When the body temperature rises above the normal range, the skin's capillaries dilate, and the sweat glands increase their secretions. This allows the body to maintain a constant body temperature because the sweat that is generated will cool hot skin (Fig. 2-1).

Sensation

Within the skin are sensory receptors that detect pain, heat, cold, and pressure. When stimulated, these receptors make it possible for the body to respond to changes in both the external and the internal environment.

PATIENT-CENTERED PROFESSIONALISM

- Why is it important for the medical assistant to understand the function of the skin?

Structure of the Skin

The skin is composed of the epidermis, dermis, and subcutaneous layer (Fig. 2-2).

Epidermis

The **epidermis** is the thin upper layer of the skin. The outer cells of the epidermis are filled with **keratin,** a waterproof protein that toughens the skin. As new cells are produced, they move to the top. The top layer of the epidermis is composed of flat (scalelike) dead cells. The top layer is shed and replaced constantly.

The epidermis is full of ridges that fit snugly over the papillae on top of the dermis. These ridges form the **whorls** (coils or spirals) or patterns that are known as fingerprints.

Some cells within the epidermis produce **melanin,** which provides color to the skin and protects against the sun's UV rays. The more melanin a person has, the darker his or her skin. A person unable to form melanin will have very white skin with no pigmentation, a condition called **albinism.** Fig. 2-3 illustrates the many factors that contribute to a person's skin color.

Dermis

The **dermis** is thicker than the epidermis and lies beneath it. The dermis is composed of connective tissue and contains blood vessels, nerve endings, hair follicles, lymph vessels, and sweat glands. The connective tissue is mostly collagen fibers; these fibers provide for the elasticity and strength of the skin. The dermis adds support and nourishment to the skin.

Subcutaneous Layer

The **subcutaneous layer** lies below the dermis and consists mainly of adipose tissue and loose connective tissue. It attaches the skin to muscles and other tissue. This layer acts as a shock absorber for organs and conserves the body's heat.

Substructures of the Skin

Several important substructures are located within the skin. The hair, specific glands, and nails are all part of the integumentary system.

HAIR

Hair is distributed over the body except on the palms of the hands and soles of the feet. Hair develops within a **follicle** and grows from within the deep layers of the skin. Hair protects the skin. It is composed of nonliving material, mostly keratin. The **shaft** of the hair is the part you can see extending from the skin, and it does not contain nerves. The **root** lies below the surface.

GLANDS

There are several types of glands in the skin, including sweat glands and oil glands (Fig. 2-4).

The **sudoriferous glands,** or sweat glands, are small, coiled glands. Sweat glands maintain body temperature by releasing sweat, a watery fluid with dissolved body salts. Sweat evaporates to cool the

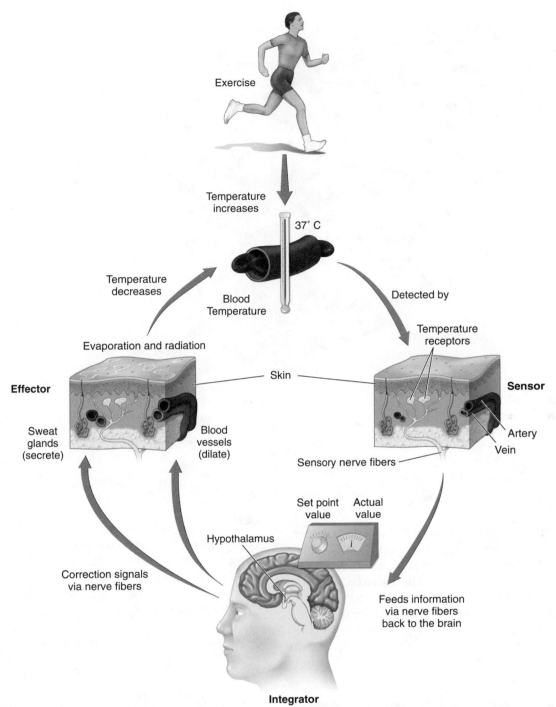

Exercise

Temperature increases

37° C

Blood Temperature

Temperature decreases

Detected by

Temperature receptors

Evaporation and radiation

Effector

Skin

Sensor

Sweat glands (secrete)

Blood vessels (dilate)

Artery

Vein

Sensory nerve fibers

Set point value   Actual value

Hypothalamus

Feeds information via nerve fibers back to the brain

Correction signals via nerve fibers

Integrator

Fig. 2-1 Role of the skin in homeostasis of body temperature. *(Modified from Thibodeau GA, Patton KT:* Anatomy and physiology, *ed 5, St Louis, 2003, Mosby.)*

body. Sweat glands are numerous in the hands, feet, and underarms (axilla). Sweat is released through pores. A **pore** is the duct opening that provides a pathway for fluid to leave the body.

The **sebaceous glands,** or oil glands, are located around hair follicles. Oil glands release **sebum** (oil) that lubricates the skin and hair. This prevents drying by minimizing water loss. Sebum also functions to inhibit the growth of certain bacteria. The

activity of these glands increases at puberty because of increased hormone production in the body. This overstimulation can lead to **acne,** which is when the ducts of the glands become blocked. Once blocked, the sebum combines with dead cells and a blackhead, or **comedo,** forms or the comedo may be pustular (whitehead). The blackened area is actually a collection of melanin, not dirt. When the duct ruptures, a pimple forms.

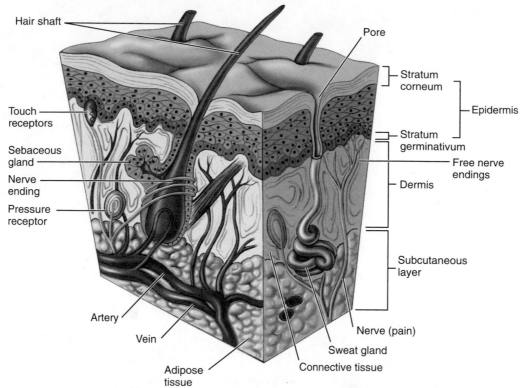

Fig. 2-2   The skin. (*From Herlihy B, Maebius NK:* The human body in health and illness, *ed 2, Philadelphia, 2003, Saunders.*)

NAILS

Nails protect the ends of the fingers and toes. They develop from epidermal cells and consist mainly of hard keratin. The nails appear pink because of the rich blood supply to the area. The **lunula,** or half-moon shape, is at the base of the nail and is white. The **cuticle** is a narrow band of epidermis at the base and sides of the nail. Under the cuticle lies the **nail root.** The **nail body** is the fingernail that covers the nail bed, and the part that extends out is referred to as the **free edge** (Fig. 2-5).

PATIENT-CENTERED PROFESSIONALISM

- Why is it important for the medical assistant to understand basic skin structure and substructure?

〰 DAMAGE TO THE SKIN

The skin provides protection for our bodies, but it can be damaged in the process. Lesions, wounds, and burns are ways in which the skin can be damaged.

Lesions

Lesions are changes in the skin caused by an underlying disease or trauma that alters the basic structure of the skin. A skin lesion is any visible abnormality of the tissues. Common lesions include the following (Fig. 2-6):

- **Cyst:** Thick-walled sac that contains fluid or semisolid material (e.g., sebaceous cyst)
- **Fissure:** Split or crack in the skin (e.g., anal fissure is a split in the anus)
- **Macule:** Flat, discolored area (e.g., freckle, age spot)
- **Papule:** Small, solid, raised area of the skin, less than 1 cm (e.g., pimple)
- **Polyp:** Flat or stalklike growth from a mucous membrane (e.g., nasal polyps, intestinal polyps) that is often precancerous
- **Pustule:** Small, raised area of the skin containing pus (e.g., acne)
- **Ulcer:** Erosion of the skin (bedsore)
- **Vesicle:** Blister; a collection of clear fluid under the skin (e.g., herpes or burn)
- **Wheal:** Slightly elevated central area on the skin; bump resembling a hive (e.g., insect bite)

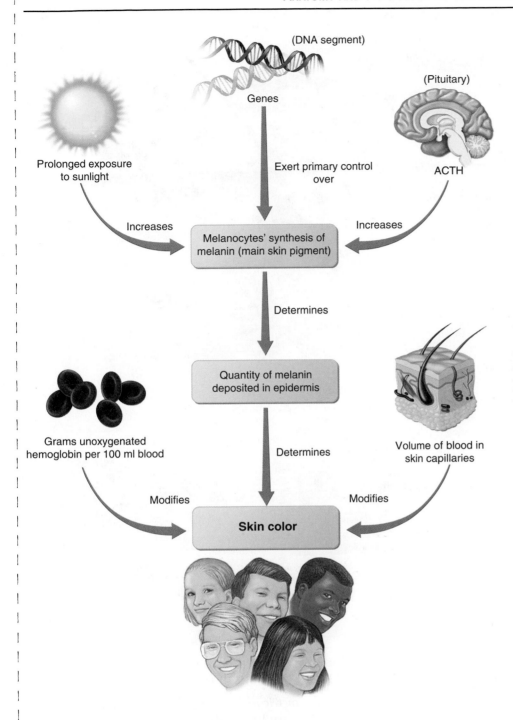

Fig. 2-3 How genes affect skin color. *(Modified from Thibodeau GA, Patton KT:* Anatomy and physiology, *ed 5, St Louis, 2003, Mosby.)*

or seen after a properly placed intradermal injection

Precancerous Skin Lesions

Actinic keratoses are precancerous skin growths. This type of lesion is caused by prior sun exposure. Actinic keratoses are slightly scaly papules that appear pinkish to reddish. If left untreated, these lesions spread into the dermis to become squamous cell carcinomas (Fig. 2-7).

Malignant Skin Lesions

Some types of skin lesions are **malignant,** or cancerous. Examples include basal cell carcinoma, malignant melanoma, and squamous cell carcinoma.

Basal Cell Carcinoma

Basal cell carcinomas are malignant skin lesions that appear as raised, flesh-colored papules with

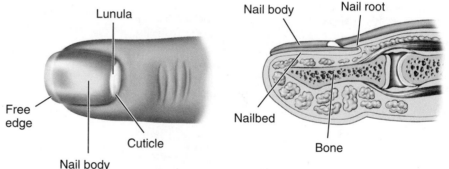

Fig. 2-4 Glands of the skin. *(Modified from Herlihy B, Maebius NK: The human body in health and illness, ed 2, Philadelphia, 2003, Saunders.)*

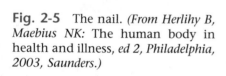

Fig. 2-5 The nail. *(From Herlihy B, Maebius NK: The human body in health and illness, ed 2, Philadelphia, 2003, Saunders.)*

blood vessels around the edges. These lesions are slow growing, with local destruction and usually without metastasis (spreading). These lesions can appear anywhere in sun-exposed areas but usually appear on the face, nose, and neck (Fig. 2-8).

Malignant Melanoma

Malignant melanomas are the most dangerous of all skin cancers. They can appear anywhere on the body. This type of cancer often develops from a **nevus,** or mole or birthmark. The danger of this form of cancer is that it can *metastasize* (spread) to any organ.

Fig. 2-9 shows a typical malignant melanoma. Fig. 2-10 shows a typical **benign** mole. Table 2-2 compares the appearance of a benign nevus to a malignant melanoma. The characteristics of a mela-

noma are easy to remember with the following "ABCDE rule" of self-examination:

- **A**symmetrical (uneven) in appearance. If an imaginary line is drawn through the middle of a melanoma, it will not produce matching halves.
- **B**orders are uneven. The edges of a melanoma appear irregular or scalloped.
- **C**olor changes appear. The area changes from shades of brown to black.
- **D**iameter of a melanoma tends to grow faster than normal moles.
- **E**levation or thickness increases in a melanoma.

Pathophysiologists recognize that genetic predisposition is a factor in forming melanomas. They also cite that exposure to UV radiation is a contributing factor for common skin cancers. UV rays

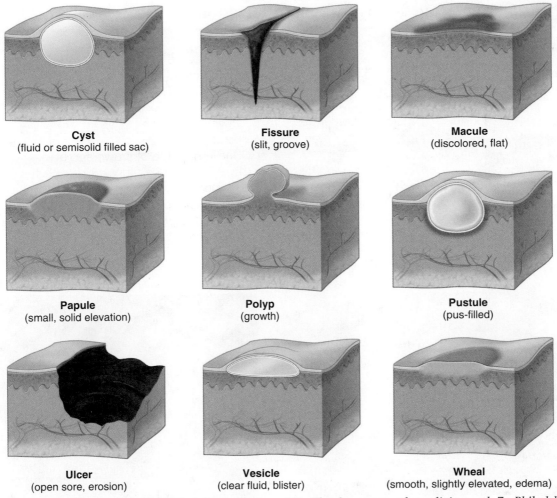

Cyst
(fluid or semisolid filled sac)

Fissure
(slit, groove)

Macule
(discolored, flat)

Papule
(small, solid elevation)

Polyp
(growth)

Pustule
(pus-filled)

Ulcer
(open sore, erosion)

Vesicle
(clear fluid, blister)

Wheal
(smooth, slightly elevated, edema)

Fig. 2-6 Common skin lesions. *(Modified from Chabner DE:* The language of medicine, *ed 7, Philadelphia, 2004, Saunders.)*

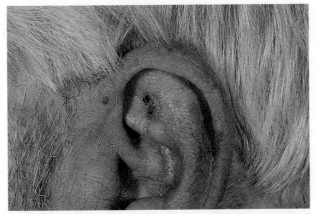

Fig. 2-7 Actinic keratosis. *(From Callen JP et al:* Color atlas of dermatology, *ed 2, Philadelphia, 2000, Saunders.)*

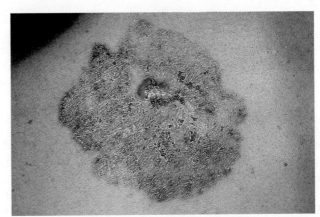

Fig. 2-8 Superficial basal cell epithelioma. *(From Callen JP et al:* Color atlas of dermatology, *ed 2, Philadelphia, 2000, Saunders.)*

TABLE 2-2	Benign Mole versus Malignant Melanoma ("ABCDE Rule")	
Characteristic	**Benign Mole**	**Malignant Melanoma**
Asymmetry	Symmetrical; each half is mirror image of other half	Asymmetrical
Border	Outlined by a defined border	Lopsided in appearance Outline irregular
Color	Shades of brown color are even	Black Uneven mixture of brown and black In extreme cases, white
Diameter	<6 mm (¼ inch)	>6 mm
Elevation	Flat or raised mole that does not change	Flat mole becomes raised above the skin or rough in surface; change in thickness, cracks in surface, bleeding

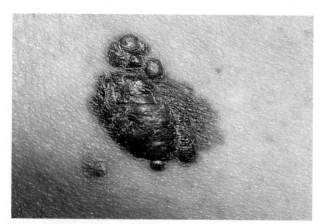

Fig. 2-9 Malignant melanoma. *(From Callen JP et al: Color atlas of dermatology, ed 2, Philadelphia, 2000, Saunders.)*

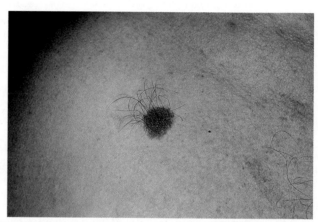

Fig. 2-10 Congenital melanocytic nevus (benign mole). *(From Callen JP et al: Color atlas of dermatology, ed 2, Philadelphia, 2000, Saunders.)*

damage the deoxyribonucleic acid (DNA) in skin cells, causing a change during mitosis that produces cancer cells.

Squamous Cell Carcinoma

Squamous cell carcinomas are skin cancers that appear as firm papules with ulcerations (Fig. 2-11). This type of cancer can appear anywhere on the body, but most notably on the lower lip, scalp, forehead, face, top of the ears, and back of the hands.

Therapy

Treatment options for malignant skin lesions vary but include the following:

- *Cryosurgery:* Use of liquid nitrogen to burn off tissue by freezing.

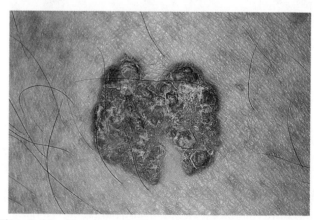

Fig. 2-11 Squamous cell carcinomas (Bowen's type or in situ). *(From Callen JP et al: Color atlas of dermatology, ed 2, Philadelphia, 2000, Saunders.)*

- *Topical chemotherapy:* Use of chemicals to destroy tissue.
- *Excision:* Surgical removal of tissue.
- *Radiation:* Use of radiation to destroy tissue.

Wounds

A **wound** is some form of a break in the skin. Wounds may be intentional (e.g., surgical incision) or accidental (e.g., stepping on a nail protruding from a board). Wounds are considered to be either open or closed, based on whether the skin has been broken.

Closed Wound

A **closed wound** occurs when damage is done to the tissues beneath the skin without a visible break in the skin. An example of a closed wound is a **contusion,** which occurs when blood vessels rupture and blood seeps into the tissue, giving the area under the skin a mottled, dark appearance, as with a bruise. Injuries to the musculoskeletal system often produce a contusion (e.g., sprains, strains, fractures).

Open Wound

Open wounds occur when the skin is damaged and the tissue below is exposed. The four basic types of open wounds are as follows (Fig. 2-12).

- An **incision** is a smooth cut into the skin (e.g., surgical incision).
- A **laceration** is a wound where the tissue edges are irregular (e.g., knife wound).
- A **puncture** is a wound made by a sharp object that pierces the skin (e.g., stepping on a nail).

- An **abrasion** is a wound in which the epidermis is scraped off (e.g., scraping a knee on the sidewalk when roller-blading).

Healing Process

Wound healing can be separated into three phases:

- *Phase 1* is the **inflammatory phase** and begins when the skin is damaged. A blood clot forms and stops blood from flowing. The blood supply to the damaged area increases, allowing white blood cells and nutrients to aid in the healing process.
- *Phase 2* is the **granulation phase** or **proliferation phase.** This phase allows flesh to begin forming collagen, a protein that adds strength to the repairing tissue. A capillary supply forms to create a blood supply to the newly formed tissue.
- *Phase 3* is the **maturation phase.** Tissue continues to form and eventually hardens to form scar tissue. Scar tissue does not have nerve tissue or a blood supply and may have a raised or "puckered" appearance when healed.

Burns

A burn is damage to the skin caused by heat or severe cold, chemicals, electricity, or radiation. Burns are classified according to their depth and their surface area. Depth classifications include the following (Fig. 2-13, *A*):

- **Partial-thickness** burns can be divided into first-degree and second-degree burns.

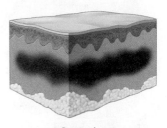
Contusion

Incision

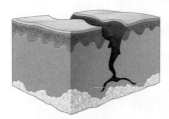
Laceration

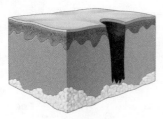
Puncture

Abrasion

Fig. 2-12 Types of wounds. *(Modified from Bonewit-West K:* Clinical procedures for medical assistants, *ed 6, Philadelphia, 2004, Saunders.)*

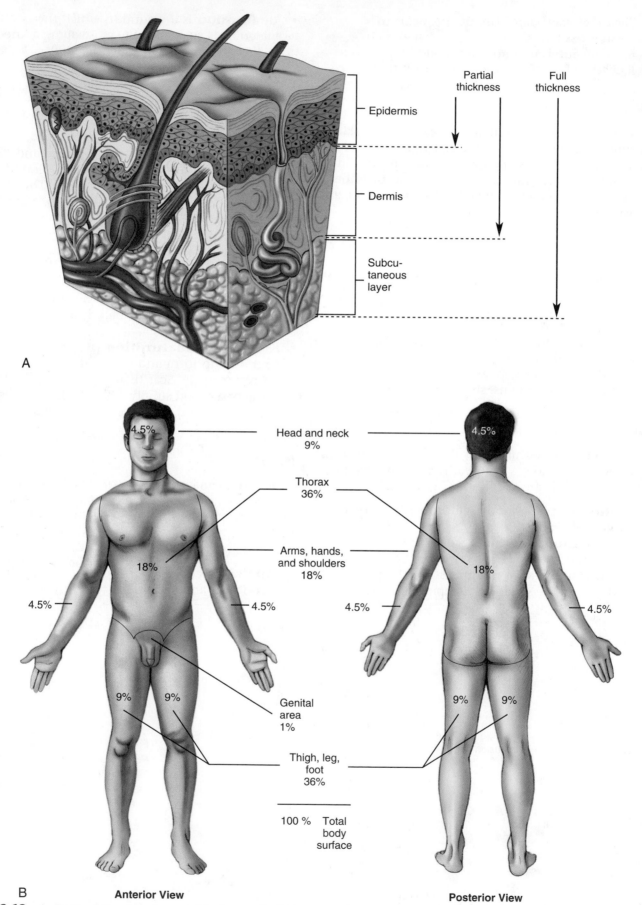

Fig. 2-13 **A,** Parts of the skin damaged by burns. **B,** Estimating the extent of burns using the "rule of nines." *(Modified from Herlihy B, Maebius NK: The human body in health and illness, ed 2, Philadelphia, 2003, Saunders.)*

First-degree burns involve only the epidermis, which appears reddened, with slight pain. A mild sunburn and brief contact with a hot object (e.g., iron, stove) are examples of first-degree burns.

Second-degree burns involve both the epidermis and the dermis. Damage to tissue is greater and the area is blistered and severely swollen. Examples include severe sunburn and burns caused by hot liquids (e.g., coffee) or chemicals.

- **Full-thickness** burns are referred to as third-degree burns.

Third-degree burns destroy the epidermis and the dermis. There is deep tissue destruction and less pain because of nerve destruction. The appearance of the skin is charred or white. Examples include burns from electric shocks, flames, or chemicals.

A burn patient's total body surface (TBS) or body surface area (BSA) is evaluated according to the **"rule of nines"** (Fig. 2-13, *B*). By dividing the body into regions and assigning a number related to 9, a burn area can be assessed. Thus, when an accident victim is described as being "burned over 90% of his body," this is the percentage of the TBS involved in the burn. When determining treatment, the physician assesses the depth of the burn, the BSA of the burn, and the particular body parts involved. Burns on the face, neck, and genital areas are especially painful to treat. First-degree burns over 50% of the body's extremities may not be as difficult to treat as third-degree burns over 25% of the body, including the facial and neck area.

PATIENT-CENTERED PROFESSIONALISM

- Tissue damage can occur in several ways. Why must the medical assistant be aware of methods to prevent skin damage?
- How does this awareness translate to better patient care?

DISEASES AND DISORDERS OF THE INTEGUMENTARY SYSTEM

Diseases and disorders of the integumentary system are often exhibited as alterations of surface skin tissue. Conditions of the skin may be caused by bacteria, parasites, fungi, or viruses, or may have no apparent known cause. A **dermatologist** can treat diseases and conditions of the integumentary system, and drugs may be prescribed to treat these disorders (Table 2-3).

As a medical assistant you need to be able to recognize the common signs and symptoms of and the diagnostic tests for the different types of skin disorders and diseases.

- Study Box 2-1 to familiarize yourself with the common signs and symptoms.
- Study Box 2-2 to learn about common diagnostic tests and procedures.
- Study Table 2-4 to understand the diseases and disorders that affect the integumentary system.

BOX 2-1 Common Signs and Symptoms of Skin Disease

Abscess	Localized collection of pus that occurs on the skin or any body tissue
Alopecia	Loss of hair; baldness
Carbuncles	Large abscesses that involve connecting furuncles
Cicatrix	Scar formation
Crust	Dried serum, blood, and pus; scab
Decubitus ulcer	Pressure sore; caused by decreased circulation to tissue, which leads to death of tissue and bacterial infection
Diaphoresis	Excessive sweating
Ecchymosis	Collection of blood under the skin; skin has blue-black appearance
Eczema	Most common inflammation of the skin; accompanied by papules, vesicles, and crusts; usually an underlying condition of another disorder
Erosion	Destruction of the surface layer of skin
Excoriation	Removal of surface epidermis by scratching, burn, or abrasion
Fissure	Split or crack in the skin
Furuncle	Abscess that occurs around a hair follicle
Ichthyosis	Dry, scaly skin condition; skin has appearance of fish scales
Keloid	Overgrowth of fibrous tissue at site of scar tissue
Petechiae	Flat, pinpoint red spots
Pruritus	Severe itching
Purpura	Small hemorrhages into the skin and tissues
Ulcer	Erosion of the epidermis and dermis
Urticaria	Hives; raised areas that are smooth and cause itching
Vitiligo	Loss of pigment in the skin in patches; milk-white patches

TABLE 2-3 Integumentary (Skin) Drug Classifications

Drug Classification	Common Generic (Brand) Drugs
Anesthetics (local) Block pain at site where administered	lidocaine (Xylocaine)
Anti-acne drugs Treat acne vulgaris	procaine (Novocain)
Antifungals Inhibit the growth of fungi	tetracycline (Achromycin)
Anti-infectives Inhibit growth of microorganisms on skin	tretinoin (Avita)
Antipsoriatics Treat the effects of psoriasis	ciclopirox (Loprox)
Antivirals Inhibit the effects of herpes simplex	clotrimazole (Lotrimin)
Burn preparations Treat burned tissue	mupirocin (Bactroban)
Corticosteroids Act against inflammation	neomycin (Neosporin)
Keratolytics Remove warts, corns, and calluses	anthralin (Anthra-Derm)
Scabicides, pediculicides Kill parasites and destroy eggs	methotrexate (Methotrexate)
Antipruritics Temporarily relieve itching	acyclovir (Zovirax)
	penciclovir (Denavir)
	nitrofurazone (Furacin)
	mafenide (Sulfamylon)
	amcinonide (Cyclocort)
	hydrocortisone (Cort-Dome)
	salicylic acid (Compound W)
	cantharidin (Verr-Canth)
	lindane 1% (Scabene)
	5% permethrin (Elimite)
	diphenhydramine (Benadryl)
	hydroxyzine pamoate (Vistaril)

PATIENT-CENTERED PROFESSIONALISM

- Why should the medical assistant be aware of the causes of skin disorders?

CONCLUSION

The skin is the body's protective covering, and along with the hair, nails, and glands, the skin makes up the integumentary system. The skin provides support and protection and plays an important role in maintaining homeostasis. The appearance of the skin (color, texture, and temperature) is an indicator of a person's physical condition. Diseases and disorders of the skin can be diagnosed and treated using several different methods.

Understanding the structure and function of the integumentary system is important in understanding how it works with the other body systems to maintain homeostasis. This understanding will help you provide better care to the patients who come to the physician's office with skin diseases or disorders.

BOX 2-2 Diagnostic Tests and Procedures for the Skin

Tissue scraping	Identifies bacterial or fungal disease
Skin biopsy	Removes section of lesion for pathological examination
Wood's light examination	Detects skin infections (usually fungal) by using an ultraviolet light filtered through a special type of glass
Blood antibody titer	Blood test that indicates whether a person has or has had an infection
Tzanck test	Microscopic examination of skin lesions to screen for herpes virus
Skin test	Determines the reaction of the body to an allergen

- *Intradermal:* Subcutaneously injecting the patient with an allergy extract.
- *Patch:* Small patch of paper impregnated with suspected allergen is placed on the skin.
- *Scratch:* Minute amount of solution containing the suspected allergen is placed on a scratched area of the skin.

TABLE 2-4	Diseases and Disorders of the Integumentary System				
Disease and Description	**Etiology**	**Signs and Symptoms**	**Diagnosis**	**Therapy**	**Interventions**
Bacterial Infections					
Cellulitis Infection of skin and subcutaneous tissue caused by microorganisms	Usually *Streptococcus* or *Staphylococcus* bacteria that enter skin through a cut or lesion	Redness of skin **(erythema)** with edema; area is hot and tender to the touch	Clinical symptoms of affected limb; blood culture	Antibiotic therapy; affected area is elevated and kept immobile; warm compresses applied to affected area to increase blood circulation; analgesic usually prescribed for discomfort	Encourage patient to pay attention to skin care after scratches and other seemingly minor injuries
Impetigo Infection causes pustules that rupture and form crusts (Fig. 2-14)	Causative bacteria are either *Streptococcus* or *Staphylococcus aureus*	Small pustular lesions that appear on face, legs, and arms; spreads easily, especially after scratching an infected area	Clinical appearance and Gram stain of exudates	Use of antibiotics on affected areas	Encourage good hygiene, especially handwashing

Continued

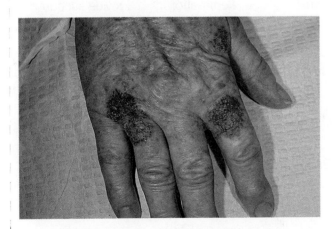

Fig. 2-14   Impetigo. *(From Callen JP et al: Color atlas of dermatology, ed 2, Philadelphia, 2000, Saunders.)*

| TABLE 2-4 | Diseases and Disorders of the Integumentary System—cont'd |

Disease and Description	Etiology	Signs and Symptoms	Diagnosis	Therapy	Interventions
Idiopathic Disorders					
Psoriasis					
Hereditary dermatitis with dry, scaly, silvery patches, usually on both arms, legs, and scalp	Unknown; possibly an autoimmune response, stress, allergies, and pregnancy	Thick, flaky, red patches with white, silvery scales	Clinical presentation reveals obvious symptoms	Ultraviolet light therapy, steroid creams, and antihistamines	Provide emotional support for patient
Scleroderma					
Chronic progressive systemic disease of skin and body systems	Unknown; possibly from an autoimmune condition	Skin hardens (becomes leathery); some organs are affected by decreasing in size; joints swell and are painful	Physical examination, patient history, skin biopsy, and x-ray studies	Palliative Physical therapy to maintain strength of muscle tone	Provide emotional support for patient
Parasitic Diseases					
Lyme disease					
Skin disease that also affects joints and connective tissues	Caused by a spirochete that is transmitted by a bite from a deer tick	Red, itchy rash with bull's-eye appearance; joint pain and malaise	Physical examination, patient history, lesions; blood sample drawn for titer level	Removal of tick; antibiotics and medications for joint pain and fever	Provide emotional support for patient
Scabies					
Skin disorder caused by itch mite (*Sarcoptes scabiei*)	Mite spreads from person to person by close physical contact	Pruritus and rash in affected area	Visual examination of affected area	Removal of mites by shampoos, application of creams, and topical steroid preparations for itching	Provide support to family and encouragement to treat patient's environment (e.g., bedding, comb, brush)
Pediculosis					
Skin disorder caused by lice (*Pediculus humanus*)*	Caused by lice and spread by human contact or sharing of personal items	Rash; presence of nits (eggs) on hair shaft, skin, or clothing	Visual examination	Prescription shampoo with repeat application in 7 to 10 days	Provide emotional support

*P. humanus capitis, head lice; P. humanus corporis, body lice; Phthirus pubis, pubic lice.

TABLE 2-4 **Diseases and Disorders of the Integumentary System—cont'd**

Disease and Description	Etiology	Signs and Symptoms	Diagnosis	Therapy	Interventions
Fungal Infections					
Tinea					
Skin infection caused by fungus; classified according to body region affected	Direct contact with fungus or spores	Clinical presentation of patient; usually, scaly lesions and itching	Appearance and location of lesions; culture of lesions	Topical and oral antifungal medications as indicated	Encourage good hygiene

Tinea corporis: affects body; also called "ringworm"
Tinea pedis: affects feet; also called "athlete's foot" (Fig. 2-15)
Tinea unguium: affects nails; also called **onychomycosis**
Tinea cruris: affects genital region; also called "jock itch" (Fig. 2-16)
Tinea faciei: affects face (Fig. 2-17)
Tinea capitis: affects scalp (Fig. 2-18)

Disease and Description	Etiology	Signs and Symptoms	Diagnosis	Therapy	Interventions
Viral Infections					
Herpes Simplex					
Skin infection caused by virus; "cold sores," "fever blisters" (Fig. 2-19)	Caused by herpes simplex virus type 1 (HSV-1)	Blisters appear on lips, inside of mouth, and occasionally in nose; lesions usually at the junction of mucous membranes and skin	Physical examination	Antiviral medications; topical antivirals to heal and relieve pain	Encourage good handwashing because virus can be spread by contact
Warts (Verrucae)					
Contagious epithelial growths	Caused by human papillomavirus (HPV); spread by contact with skin shed from a wart	Elevated growths of epidermis	Visual examination	Surgical excision; cryosurgery	Provide emotional support

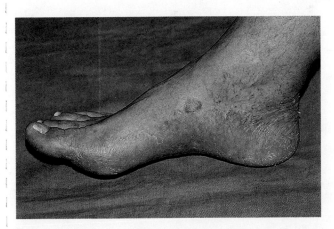

Fig. 2-15 Tinea pedis resulting from *Trichophyton rubrum* infection. *(From Callen JP et al: Color atlas of dermatology, ed 2, Philadelphia, 2000, Saunders.)*

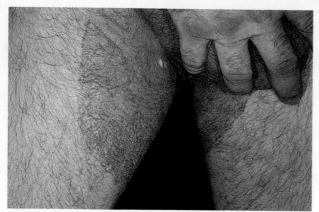

Fig. 2-16   Tinea cruris. *(From Callen JP et al: Color atlas of dermatology, ed 2, Philadelphia, 2000, Saunders.)*

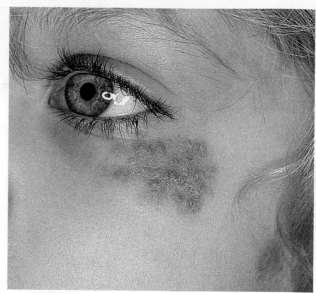

Fig. 2-17   Tinea faciei. *(From Callen JP et al: Color atlas of dermatology, ed 2, Philadelphia, 2000, Saunders.)*

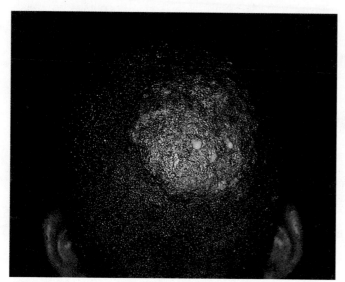

Fig. 2-18   Kerion (nodular swelling with pustules) form of tinea capitis. *(From Callen JP et al: Color atlas of dermatology, ed 2, Philadelphia, 2000, Saunders.)*

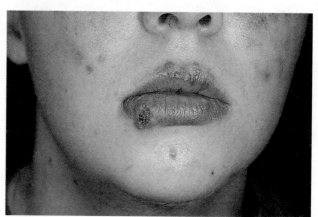

Fig. 2-19   Herpes simplex infection. *(From Callen JP et al: Color atlas of dermatology, ed 2, Philadelphia, 2000, Saunders.)*

SUMMARY

Reinforce your understanding of the material in this chapter by reviewing the curriculum objectives and key content points below.

1. Define, appropriately use, and spell all the Key Terms for this chapter.
   - Review the Key Terms if necessary.
2. List the three main functions of the skin.
   - The skin serves to protect the body, regulate temperature, and detect sensations.
3. Explain how the body is able to maintain a constant temperature.
   - Enzymes do not function properly without a constant body temperature.
   - When the body becomes too cold, heat loss can be prevented by "goose bumps."
   - When the body becomes too hot, sweating cools the body.
4. Identify the three layers of the skin and describe the structure and function of each.
   - The epidermis and the dermis are the two upper layers of the skin.
   - The epidermis is the thin upper layer of flat, dead cells. This layer protects the skin against the sun's ultraviolet rays.
   - The dermis is thicker than the epidermis and contains the blood vessels, nerve endings, hair follicles, lymph vessels, and sweat glands.
   - The subcutaneous layer is mainly fatty adipose tissue and loose connective tissue and is located beneath the dermis. It provides shock absorption for organs and conserves heat.
5. Identify the three types of substructures of the skin and explain the function of each.
   - Hair protects the skin.
   - Sweat glands help maintain body temperature; oil glands prevent drying by reducing water loss.
   - Nails protect the ends of fingers and toes.
6. List and briefly describe nine common skin lesions.
   - Cysts are sacs filled with fluid or semisolid material.
   - Fissures are splits or cracks in the skin.
   - Macules are flat, discolored areas.
   - Papules are small, solid, raised areas of the skin.
   - Polyps are flat or stalklike growths from a mucous membrane.
   - Pustules are small, raised areas of the skin that contain pus.
   - Ulcers are erosions of the skin.
   - Vesicles are blisters, collections of clear fluid under the skin.
   - Wheals are slightly elevated areas on the skin; bumps resembling hives.
7. Define actinic keratosis, basal cell carcinoma, malignant melanoma, and squamous cell carcinoma and determine how to identify each.
   - Actinic keratoses are precancerous growths that are scaly papules.
   - Basal cell carcinomas are slow-growing malignant skin lesions that can appear anywhere on sun-exposed skin.
   - Malignant melanomas are a type of skin cancer with black coloring that can appear anywhere on the body and will metastasize.
   - Squamous cell carcinomas appear as firm papules with ulcerations.
   - Use the "ABCDE rule" to check for skin cancer.
8. List four treatment options for malignant skin lesions.
   - Cryosurgery, topical chemotherapy, excision, and radiation are some of the treatments for malignant skin lesions.
9. Explain the difference between *open* and *closed* wounds.
   - In an open wound the skin is damaged, and the tissue below is exposed.
   - In a closed wound the tissues beneath the skin are damaged, but there is no visible break in the skin.
10. List and describe the three phases of wound healing.
    - Blood clotting occurs in the inflammatory phase.
    - Collagen is added and a capillary supply is formed during the granulation phase.
    - Scar tissue forms during the maturation phase.
11. Distinguish between a partial-thickness and a full-thickness burn as a means of assessing the depth of a burn.
    - First-degree and second-degree burns are considered partial-thickness burns.
    - Third-degree burns are considered full-thickness burns.
    - Emergency medical assistance is needed for second- and third-degree burns.
12. Explain the purpose and use of the "rule of nines."
    - The "rule of nines" is a method of assessing the surface area involved in burns.
    - Treatment is based on the severity of the burn and total body surface involved.
13. List and describe seven signs and symptoms of skin disease.
    - Refer to Box 2-1.
14. List five types of diagnostic tests and procedures for the skin and describe the use of each.
    - Refer to Box 2-2.

15. List 10 diseases and disorders of the integumentary system and briefly describe the etiology, signs and symptoms, diagnosis, therapy, and interventions for each.
    • Refer to Table 2-4.
16. Analyze a realistic medical office situation and apply your understanding of the integumentary system to determine the best course of action.
    • Medical assistants must understand the terminology and processes associated with the integumentary system so that they can provide better care to patients.
17. Describe the impact on patient care when medical assistants have a solid understanding of the structure and function of the integumentary system.
    • Medical assistants who understand the physiology of the integumentary system are better able to work with patients who come to the office for diseases and disorders of the skin.

FOR FURTHER EXPLORATION

Research skin cancers to learn more about origins and the predisposition of the skin to cancer. Discover how skin type, sun exposure, family history, age, and immunological factors play a role in the development of skin cancers.

Keywords: Use the following keywords in your search: skin cancer, basal cell carcinoma, squamous cell carcinoma, malignant melanoma, melanoma.

WORD PARTS: INTEGUMENTARY SYSTEM

Combining Forms

albin/o	white
cutane/o	skin
derm/o, dermat/o	skin
hidr/o	sweat
histi/o, hist/o	tissue
ichthy/o	fish; scalelike
kerat/o	horny, hard
melan/o	black; dark
myc/o	fungus
onych/o	nail (finger or toe)
seb/o	oil; sebum
trich/o	hair
xanth/o	yellow
xer/o	dry

Abbreviations: Integumentary System

BSA	body surface area
Bx	biopsy (removal of tissue for examination)
Decub	decubitus ulcer (bedsore)
Derm	dermatology
I&D	incision and drainage
TBS	total body surface
Ung	ointment
UV	ultraviolet (light)

Chapter Review

Vocabulary Review

Matching

Match each term with the correct definition.

A. dermatologist

B. turgor

C. dermis

D. keratin

E. melanin

F. whorls

G. sebaceous glands

H. sudoriferous glands

I. nails

J. cyst

K. polyp

L. benign

M. malignant melanoma

N. abrasion

O. contusion

P. laceration

Q. rule of nines

_____ 1. Black, asymmetrical lesion with uneven borders that grows faster than normal moles

_____ 2. Sweat glands; maintain body temperature

_____ 3. Contagious epithelial growths caused by a virus

_____ 4. Localized collection of pus that occurs on the skin or any body tissue

_____ 5. Specialist in the treatment of diseases and conditions of the skin

_____ 6. Abscess that occurs around a hair follicle

_____ 7. Not malignant

_____ 8. Ridges that fit snugly over the papillae on top of the dermis; coils or spirals that form fingerprints

_____ 9. Parasitic skin disorder caused by lice

_____ 10. Scar formation

_____ 11. Stalklike growth extending out from the mucous membrane

_____ 12. Pressure sore; bedsore

_____ 13. Waterproof protein that toughens the skin

_____ 14. Growths of hard keratin that protect the ends of the fingers and toes

R. abscess

S. cicatrix

T. decubitus ulcer

U. furuncle

V. pruritus

W. vitiligo

X. herpes simplex

Y. pediculosis

Z. verrucae

—— 15. Blood vessels rupture and blood seeps into the tissue

—— 16. Viral infection of the skin characterized by "cold sores" and "fever blisters"

—— 17. Oil glands; release oil that lubricates the skin and hair

—— 18. Severe itching

—— 19. Jagged cuts; tissue edges are irregular

—— 20. Thick-walled sac that contains fluid or semisolid material

—— 21. Normal tension in the skin

—— 22. Loss of pigment in the skin; milk-white patches

—— 23. Epidermis is scraped off

—— 24. Layer of skin that lies beneath the epidermis

—— 25. System for evaluating the burns on a patient's total body surface area

—— 26. Dark pigment that provides color to the skin and protects against the sun's ultraviolet rays

Theory Recall

True/False

Indicate whether the sentence or statement is true or false.

—— 1. The skin is composed of the dermis, epidermis, and subcutaneous layer.

—— 2. The epidermis is the deepest layer of the skin.

—— 3. The dermis is thicker than the epidermis and lies beneath it.

—— 4. A macule is a split or crack in the skin.

—— 5. An incision is a smooth cut into the skin.

Multiple Choice

Identify the letter of the choice that best completes the statement or answers the question.

1. _____ is the most common inflammation of the skin; accompanied by papules, vesicles, and crusts.
   A. Furuncle
   B. Keloid
   C. Eczema
   D. Urticaria

2. Xylocaine is an example of a(n) _____ that blocks pain at the site where it is administered.
   A. anti-inflammatory
   B. analgesic
   C. antiviral
   D. none of the above

3. Salicylic acid is a(n) _____ medication used to remove warts.
   A. keratolytic
   B. antiviral
   C. corticosteroid
   D. anti-infective

4. _____ is a microscopic examination of skin lesions to screen for herpes virus.
   A. Wood's light examination
   B. Blood antibody titer
   C. Tzanck test
   D. Skin biopsy

5. Signs and symptoms of _____ include red, itchy rash with bull's eye appearance; joint pain and malaise.
   A. impetigo
   B. Lyme disease
   C. scleroderma
   D. scabies

6. _____ is a skin infection caused by fungus; classified according to body region.
   A. Lyme disease
   B. Scabies
   C. Tinea
   D. Pediculosis

7. A narrow band of epidermis at the base and sides of the nail is called the _____.
   A. nail bed
   B. lunula
   C. nail root
   D. cuticle

8. The medical term for "baldness" is _____.
   A. alopecia
   B. cicatrix
   C. onychomycosis
   D. none of the above

9. _____ is a parasitic skin disorder caused by lice.
   A. Onychomycosis
   B. Pediculosis
   C. Scabies
   D. Tinea

10. _____ are large abscesses that involve connecting furuncles.
   A. Cicatrix
   B. Melanoma
   C. Polyps
   D. Carbuncles

11. A sac or tube that anchors and contains an individual hair is called the _____.
   A. shaft
   B. follicle
   C. root
   D. none of the above

12. The medical term for a "precancerous growth of the skin" is _____.
   A. polyp
   B. vesicle
   C. actinic keratosis
   D. comedo

13. The skin layer that is mainly composed of adipose tissue and loose connective tissue is the _____.
   A. subcutaneous
   B. dermis
   C. epidermis
   D. both B and C

14. The medical term for a "flat discolored area of the skin" is _____.
   A. papule
   B. lesion
   C. wheal
   D. macule

15. Which degree of burn is reddened blistering of the dermis and epidermis layers of the skin?
   A. First
   B. Second
   C. Third
   D. Fourth

16. The medical term for "removal of surface epidermis by scratching, burning, or abrasion" is _____.
   A. erosion
   B. ichthyosis
   C. excoriation
   D. none of the above

17. An idiopathic hereditary dermatitis with dry, scaly, silver patches, usually on both arms, legs, and the scalp, is called _____.
   A. psoriasis
   B. eczema
   C. urticaria
   D. scleroderma

18. The medical term for an "erosion of the skin" (bedsore) is _____.
    A. lesion
    B. pustule
    C. polyp
    D. decubitus ulcer

19. Phase 1 of the healing process is known as the _____ phase.
    A. inflammation
    B. granulation
    C. maturation
    D. none of the above

20. A(n) _____ is an overgrowth of fibrous tissue at the site of scar tissue.
    A. ulcer
    B. polyp
    C. keloid
    D. furuncle

21. Benadryl is an example of a(n) _____ medication.
    A. antipruritic
    B. antiviral
    C. antifungal
    D. anesthetic

22. _____ is an infection of the skin and subcutaneous tissue caused by bacteria.
    A. Psoriasis
    B. Cellulitis
    C. Pediculosis
    D. Impetigo

23. In the condition of _____, the skin hardens and becomes leathery. Organs may also be affected by decreasing in size, and joints may swell and be painful.
    A. Lyme disease
    B. psoriasis
    C. scleroderma
    D. scabies

24. The combining form for "skin" is _____.
    A. albino/o
    B. diaphor/o
    C. histi/o
    D. dermat/o

25. The maturation phase of healing is phase _____.
    A. 1
    B. 2
    C. 3
    D. 4

Sentence Completion

Complete each sentence or statement.

1. A person unable to form melanin will have very white skin with no pigmentation and is referred to as a(n) _____.

2. A(n) _____ is the duct opening that provides a pathway for fluid to leave the body.

3. The _____ is a white half-moon shape at the base of the nail.

4. Oil glands release _____.

5. A clear blister is called a(n) _____.

6. A(n) _____ is a thick-walled sac that contains fluid or semisolid material.

7. _____ are skin cancers that appear as firm papules with ulcerations.

8. The abbreviation for "ointment" is _____.

9. The abbreviation for "biopsy" is _____.

10. The term for "scalelike" is _____.

Short Answers

1. List the three main functions of the skin.

   _____

   _____

   _____

2. Identify the three layers of the skin and describe the structure and function of each.

   _____

   _____

   _____

   _____

   _____

   _____

3. List and briefly describe nine common skin lesions.

_____

_____

_____

_____

_____

_____

_____

_____

4. What is the rule of nines?

_____

_____

_____

_____

5. Describe how the skin changes through the life cycle.

_____

_____

_____

_____

Critical Thinking

1. Mrs. Kimerfield called the office this afternoon because her 8-year-old daughter Melanie brought a note home from school informing Mrs. Kimerfield that several of Melanie's classmates have head lice and that there is the potential that Melanie may also have it. Explain to Mrs. Kimerfield what to look for and how to treat it.

2. Identify the following types of fungal infections, by stating their location and a typical treatment of each.

- Tinea corporis _____

- Tinea pedis _____

- Tinea unguium _____

- Tinea cruris _____

- Tinea faciei _____

- Tinea capitis _____

Use your text, your institution's resource reference library, and/or the Internet to address the above as needed.

Internet Research

Keyword: (Use the name of the condition or disease you select to write about)

Select one condition or disease from Table 2-4 or another related condition or disease. Write a two-paragraph report regarding the condition or disease you selected, listing the etiology, signs and symptoms, diagnosis, therapy, and interventions. Cite your source. (You may not use the information on the tables exclusively for your report.) Be prepared to give a 2-minute oral presentation should your instructor assign you to do so.

What Would You Do?

If you have accomplished the objectives in this chapter, you will be able to make better choices as a medical assistant. Take another look at this situation and decide what you would do.

Marilyn was taking a shower 2 weeks ago and found a large black mole on her shoulder. At first she wanted to ignore it, but after talking with her friend, she decided that she should see her family practice physician. This physician sent her to Dr. Nelson, a dermatologist, who diagnosed her lesion as a possible malignant melanoma. Dr. Nelson asked if she had any pruritus, a fissure, or crusting of the lesion. As Dr. Nelson examined Marilyn's shoulder, he noticed petechiae, ecchymosis, and purpura. When asked about these findings, Marilyn told the physician that the mole had itched and she had scratched the area in her sleep. On her leg was a furuncle that was inflamed and hot and appeared to have a pus formation. Upon completing the physical examination, Dr. Nelson noticed that Marilyn had the tendency to keloid formation based on the appearance of her old appendectomy scar. Marilyn had quite a few questions for the medical assistant about the meaning of some of the terms used by Dr. Nelson. Marilyn left the dermatologist's office with surgery scheduled for removal of the melanoma 2 days later.

1. What is the etiology of a malignant melanoma?

_____

_____

2. How do the signs of a malignant melanoma differ from those of a benign lesion?

_____

_____

_____

3. What is pruritus? Fissure? Crusting?

_____

_____

_____

_____

4. What are petechiae? What is ecchymosis? Purpura?

_____

_____

_____

_____

5. What is the difference between a furuncle and a carbuncle?

_____

_____

_____

_____

6. Why would the physician be concerned that Marilyn had a history of keloids?

_____

_____

_____

_____

7. What are the stages of the healing process that you could expect Marilyn to have following surgery?

_____

_____

_____

_____

8. What is a closed wound? Give two examples.

_____

_____

_____

_____

9. What is an open wound? Give two examples.

_____

_____

_____

_____

Application of Skills

Label the diagrams.

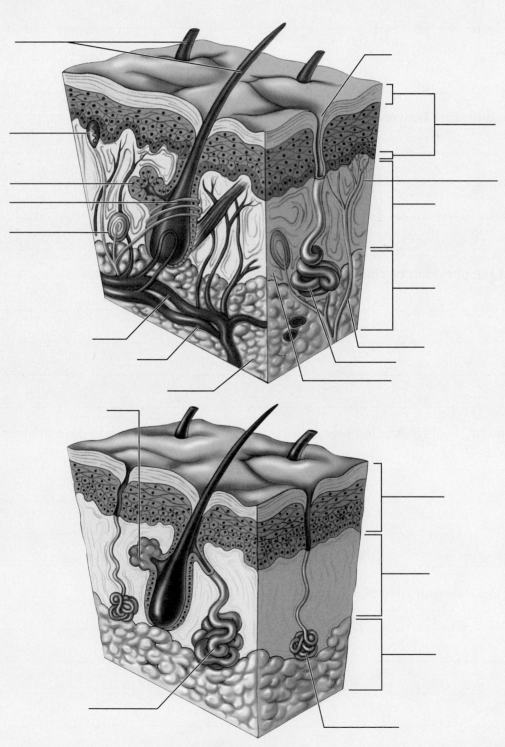

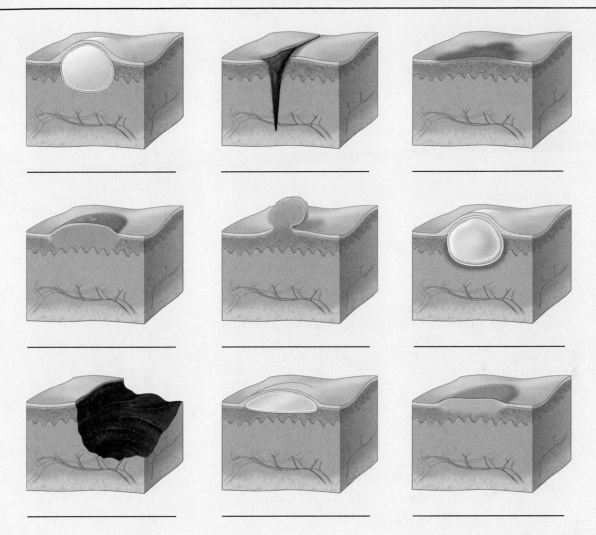

Chapter Quiz

Multiple Choice

Identify the letter of the choice that best completes the statement or answers the question.

1. A(n) _____ has jagged cuts and tissue edges that are irregular.
   A. laceration
   B. incision
   C. abrasion
   D. contusion

2. _____ is an idiopathic, chronic systemic disease of the skin in which the skin hardens and become leathery.
   A. Impetigo
   B. Scleroderma
   C. Cellulitis
   D. Psoriasis

3. A(n) _____ is a split or crack in the skin.
   A. purpura
   B. contusion
   C. fissure
   D. onychomycosis

4. _____ are flat, pinpoint red spots.
   A. Ichthyosis
   B. Purpura
   C. Urticaria
   D. Petechiae

5. The deepest layer of skin is the _____.
   A. subcutaneous tissue
   B. epidermis
   C. dermis
   D. none of the above

6. A(n) _____ is an abscess that occurs around a hair follicle.
   A. carbuncle
   B. ulcer
   C. furuncle
   D. excoriation

7. _____ are oil glands that release oil that lubricates the skin and hair.
   A. Sudoriferous glands
   B. Sebaceous glands
   C. Lymph glands
   D. Adenoids

8. The _____ is phase 2 of the healing process; collagen forms.
   A. inflammatory phase
   B. maturation phase
   C. granulation phase
   D. none of the above

9. _____ is the normal tension of skin.
   A. Turgor
   B. Rigor
   C. Flaccidity
   D. Cicatrix

10. A(n) _____ is a malignant skin lesion that is raised, with blood vessels around the edges.
    A. squamous cell carcinoma
    B. basal cell carcinoma
    C. malignant melanoma
    D. actinic keratosis

11. _____ is a skin disorder caused by itch mites.
    A. Lyme disease
    B. Pediculosis
    C. Scabies
    D. Tinea cruris

12. A patient with _____ exhibits blisters on the lips, inside of the mouth, and occasionally the nose.
    A. pediculosis
    B. verrucae
    C. tinea corporis
    D. herpes simplex

13. A combining form for "tissue" is _____.
    A. kerat/o
    B. histi/o
    C. hidr/o
    D. onych/o

14. Ung is the abbreviation for _____.
    A. "ointment"
    B. "nail border"
    C. "urgent"
    D. none of the above

15. Tetracycline is an example of a medication used for treating _____.
    A. fungi
    B. acne
    C. lice
    D. psoriasis

16. Zovirax is an example of a medication used for treating _____.
    A. scabies
    B. herpes simplex
    C. athletes foot
    D. burns

17. A Wood's light examination is used to detect _____.
    A. fungal skin infections
    B. reaction of the body to allergens
    C. viral infections
    D. bacterial infections

18. A burn patient's total body surface area is evaluated according to the _____ to determine the extent and/or severity of the burn.
    A. core body temperature
    B. full-thickness measurement
    C. rule of nines
    D. total body weight

19. The medical term for "ringworm" is _____.
    A. tinea capitis
    B. tinea cruris
    C. tinea faciei
    D. tinea pedis

20. The medical term for a "pore that is blocked, usually with sebum and dead cells" is _____.
    A. polyp
    B. furuncle
    C. comedo
    D. fissure

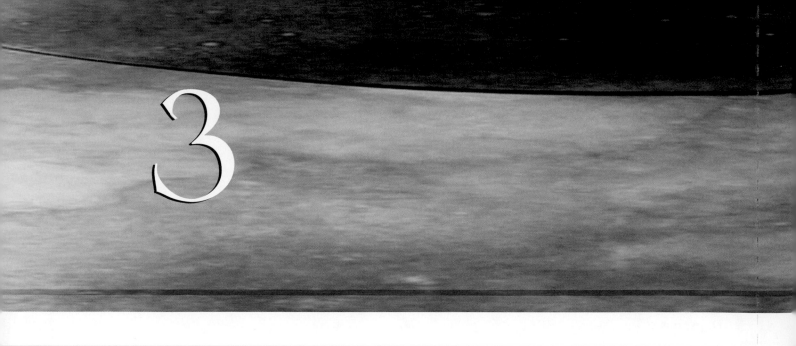

OBJECTIVES

You will be able to do the following after completing this chapter:

Key Terms
1. Define, appropriately use, and spell all the Key Terms for this chapter.

Room Preparation
2. List four general considerations for examination room arrangement and preparation.
3. List and briefly describe the purpose of seven instruments typically stocked in an examination room.
4. List and briefly describe the purpose of six general supplies kept in an examination room.

Room Maintenance
5. Describe what should be done for maintenance to the examination table and work surfaces after a patient has left the examination room.
6. Describe what should be done to the instruments used during the examination after a patient has left the examination room.

Patient Preparation
7. Explain the medical assistant's role in preparing the patient to comply with the plan of care.

Patient-Centered Professionalism
8. Analyze a realistic medical office situation and apply your understanding of examination room preparation to determine the best course of action.
9. Describe the impact on patient care when medical assistants understand how to prepare the examination room for patients.

PREPARING THE EXAMINATION ROOM

KEY TERMS

audiometer Electronic instrument used to test hearing.

lubricant Agent used to reduce friction by making a surface moist; used to facilitate anal and vaginal examinations.

ophthalmoscope Instrument used to examine the internal structure of the eye.

otoscope Instrument used to examine the ear canal and eardrum.

penlight Instrument used to enhance examination in a cavity and to check for pupillary response to light.

percussion hammer Instrument used to measure tendon reflexes.

specimen Sample of a larger part, such as body tissue or cells.

speculum Instrument for viewing a cavity (e.g., ear, nose).

tape measure Device used to measure body parts and wound length.

tongue depressor Instrument used to hold the tongue down or move it from side to side when examining the mouth.

tuning fork Instrument used to test hearing acuity by air or bone conduction.

What Would You Do?

Read the following scenario and keep it in mind as you learn about preparing the examination room for patients.

Julie, a medical assistant who was not educated in a medical assisting program, has been hired by a local family physician to assist with physical examinations. Today is her second day on the job. Her mentor has called in sick, so Julie is responsible for the clinical area by herself. Another physician, Dr. Johnson, will be performing the invasive procedures, and Julie is expected to have the room and patient ready for Dr. Johnson's examinations.

Julie finds the room too warm for her comfort, and she knows that it will be too warm for the physician in a lab coat, so she lowers the thermostat to 67° F. As Mrs. Sito is undressing, Julie barges into the room and leaves the door open. A male patient walks by and sees Mrs. Sito undressed.

During the examination Dr. Johnson asks for the ophthalmoscope and otoscope. When he tries to use these, the necessary light will not work, so he asks for a penlight. Julie leaves the room to find the penlight and a tape measure. Dr. Johnson reaches for a cotton-tipped applicator and tongue depressors. Noticing that the supply is low, he asks Julie, "Would you please fill these containers?" Julie immediately departs to fill the jars, leaving Dr. Johnson alone with the patient, who needs a pelvic examination.

After Mrs. Sito leaves the room, Julie decides that the table paper does not look used. Thinking she will save the physician some money in supplies, she does not change the paper covering and brings in 5-year-old Joey Novelle, placing him on the table Mrs. Sito has just left. The sink still contains the dirty instruments used for the other patients. Joey's mother tells Dr. Johnson that she has never seen someone placed on dirty table paper, and she does not want her child to see dirty instruments in the sink.

At the end of Joey's physical examination, Dr. Johnson takes Julie to his office and explains that if she cannot properly prepare and clean the examination room in the future, he will have to find someone to replace her.

If you worked with Julie, what are some suggestions you would make to help her perform her duties more effectively?

The medical assistant is responsible for preparing the examination room and the patient for the procedure that the physician will perform. How an examination room is stocked depends on the type of medical practice and the purpose for which the room will be used. Certain items are kept in all examination rooms because of the frequency of their use, such as nonsterile disposable gloves and alcohol pads.

All examination rooms in the medical office should be stocked in the same manner with supplies stored in the same location in each room. This assists the physician and other health care team members and helps prevent delays in caring for the patient. When a specialty examination is planned, the medical assistant will set up the examination room to accommodate the needs and preferences of the practitioner (e.g., physician, nurse practitioner, physician's assistant).

Preparing for a patient examination or procedure involves readying the examination room, maintaining the room, and preparing the patient.

ROOM PREPARATION

It is important for the examination room to be prepared before the patient arrives and the health care provider begins the examination or procedure. As shown in the scenario above, an improperly prepared room, without the necessary equipment or supplies readily available, causes delays in caring for the patient. This is a failure to provide good service to the patient.

A helpful organizational tool for the medical assistant is to list all equipment and supplies needed for a particular procedure on an index card. Also, labeling the contents of the drawers helps when restocking items. Prescription pads should not be left on the counter in the examination room; pads should be safely stored away to prevent theft or misuse.

General Considerations

The examination room should provide privacy for patient interviews and examinations, should be appealing to the eye and comfortable, and should accommodate those with disabilities.

Privacy

Privacy is a key issue for patients. The patient may reveal sensitive information during the interview, so it is important that the door is closed and the medical assistant speaks in a voice that will not be overheard by others. This protects the patient's right to privacy and confidentiality as mandated by the Health Insurance Portability and Accountability Act (HIPAA).

If a patient is required to disrobe for the examination, the medical assistant should provide a gown and show the patient where to place removed clothing. Instructions should be given and even demonstrated to the patient on whether the gown should open in the front or back, which is usually based on the physician's preference. The assistant then should leave the room unless the patient requires assistance. Before re-entering, the assistant should always knock to alert the patient that the door is opening.

Decor and Temperature
Room decor should be functional but should also promote a sense of warmth, friendliness, and tranquility. Lighting should not be overstimulating or too harsh. The room should not appear cluttered. Artwork may be placed on the walls and reading materials or pamphlets provided.

Room temperature should not be too warm or too cold. The elderly patient may be more sensitive to a cool room because of loss of body fat and diminished circulation, and a blanket may need to be provided for comfort.

Accessibility and Safety
Appropriate accommodations need to be made in examination rooms to ensure that the room is accessible to all patients, including those in wheelchairs, as required by the Americans with Disabilities Act (ADA).

Safety measures should be taken to ensure patients do not injure themselves in the office. Such measures include slip-resistant flooring and a reception area free of obstacles that could cause a patient to trip (e.g., cords, throw rugs).

Equipment and Supplies

Equipment and supplies typically stocked in an examination room are those used during a general physical examination by the physician to evaluate the patient's health status. Medical assistants need to know some of the common instruments, equipment, and supplies needed and how each is used.

Equipment
In addition to blood pressure equipment (*sphygmomanometer* and *stethoscope*), other equipment typically kept in the examination room for physical examinations includes the following (Table 3-1 and Fig. 3-1):

- **Ophthalmoscope:** Used to examine the internal structure of the eye. The head has a light, magnifying lenses, and an opening to look into the eye (Fig. 3-2). Occasionally, the ophthalmoscope and the otoscope share a battery handle, and the heads of each are interchangeable.
- **Otoscope:** Used to examine the ear canal and eardrum (Fig. 3-3). The head has a light and magnifying lens and is attached to a battery handle. Most ear speculums are disposable and are long and narrow. Replacing this type of

TABLE 3-1 Equipment in the Examination Room

Device or Item	Use
Ophthalmoscope	Inspect internal eye structure
Otoscope (with disposable speculum)	Inspect inner ear
Sphygmomanometer	Measure blood pressure
Stethoscope	Listen to heart, lung, and bowel sounds
Percussion hammer	Test reflex reactions
Tuning fork	Test for hearing loss
Thermometer	Measure body temperature
Sharps container	Hold used needles and other sharps for disposal
Tape measure	Measure length and diameter of surfaces
Gooseneck lamp	Allow for better inspection and viewing of body parts
Examination table (with footrest)	Allow for positioning of patient for examination
Penlight	Illuminate eyes to allow testing for dilation and constriction of pupils
Biohazard container	Hold biohazardous wastes (other than sharps)
Waste container with liner	Hold nonbiohazardous waste materials
Nasal speculum	View internal surfaces of nostrils

Fig. 3-1 Instruments and supplies typically used for the physical examination. **A,** Specimen cup. **B,** Tape measure. **C,** Stethoscope. **D,** Reflex hammer. **E,** Tongue depressor. **F,** Tuning fork. **G,** Nasal speculum. **H,** Guaiac card and developer.

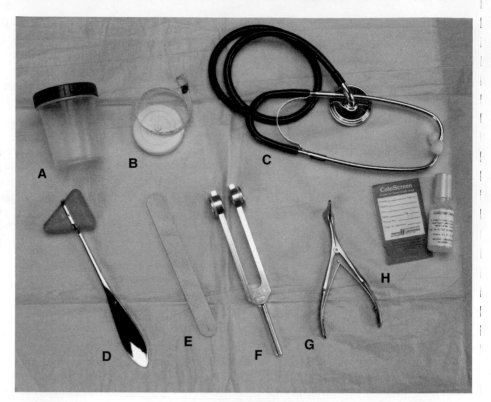

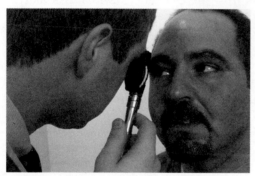

Fig. 3-2 Physician using ophthalmoscope to view internal structure of the eye.

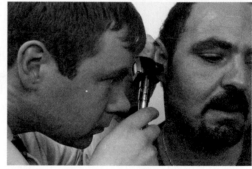

Fig. 3-3 Physician using otoscope to examine the ear canal.

speculum with a short and wide speculum allows the physician to examine the nasal area.
- **Penlight:** A small flashlight used to allow the physician to better examine the nose and the mouth; also used to check response of the pupils to light.
- **Tape measure:** Used to measure various body parts (e.g., head circumference of infant, body length) and the length of wounds.
- **Percussion hammer:** Instrument with a rubber triangle-shaped head used for tapping the tendon in the elbow, wrist, ankle, and knee to test for reflex action. The end of the stainless steel handle can be used on the sole of the foot to test for sensory perception. Fig. 3-4 illustrates

how the practitioner uses the hammer to test for various reflex actions.
- **Tuning fork:** Aluminum instrument with a handle (stem) and two prongs used to test hearing acuity (Fig. 3-5). The physician strikes the prongs against the hand or knee, causing a vibration. The vibrating tuning fork stem is first placed behind the ear on the mastoid process to test hearing by bone conduction, then removed. The vibrating end is held near the ear canal to test hearing by air conduction. This is called the *Rinne test* and compares air conduction to bone conduction. The *Weber test* is used when the patient states hearing is better in one ear than the other. The vibrating tuning fork stem is placed in the center of the skull or

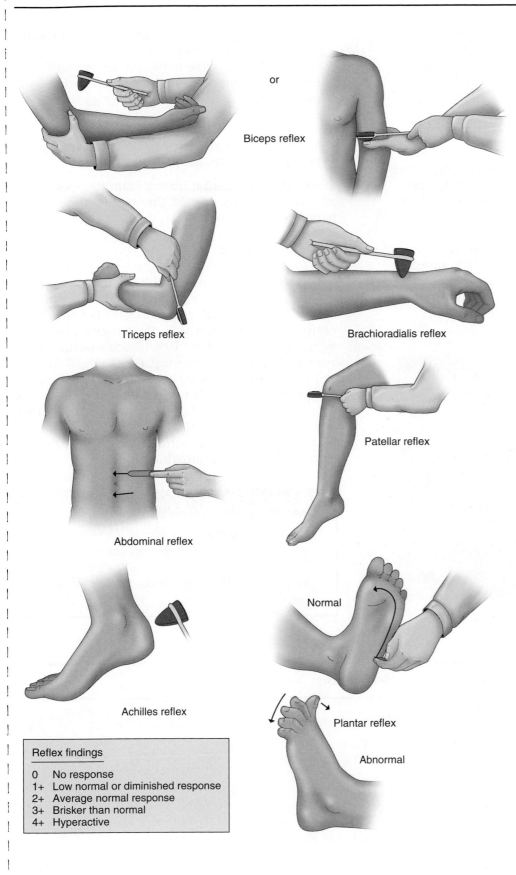

or

Biceps reflex

Triceps reflex

Brachioradialis reflex

Abdominal reflex

Patellar reflex

Achilles reflex

Normal

Plantar reflex

Abnormal

Reflex findings

0   No response
1+   Low normal or diminished response
2+   Average normal response
3+   Brisker than normal
4+   Hyperactive

Fig. 3-4 Testing reflexes with percussion hammer. *Inset,* Rating scale: 0 to 4+. *(Modified from Leahy J, Kizilay P:* Foundations of nursing practice, *Philadelphia, 1998, Saunders.)*

on top of the head to see if the patient hears equally in both ears.

- **Audiometer:** Electronic device used to test hearing.

Supplies

General supplies kept in the examination room include the following (Table 3-2):

- *Disposable gloves.* **Gloves are always worn when coming in contact with body secretions.** A gloved hand can be used to examine the mucous membranes of the mouth and other body parts.
- **Lubricant.** Water-soluble lubricant is used in conjunction with gloves to provide moisture when examining the rectal and vaginal areas.
- **Tongue depressor.** This disposable wooden device is used to hold the tongue down,

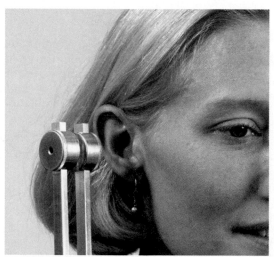

Fig. 3-5 Tuning fork is used to test hearing acuity.

allowing the physician to better see the mouth and throat (the oral cavity).

- *Tissues:* Used to wipe body secretions and excess lubricant (e.g., anal area after rectal examination).
- *Cotton-tipped applicators:* Used to collect specimens.
- *Specimen containers:* Used to hold and transport **specimens** to the laboratory.

The medical assistant must maintain the room with adequate supplies needed throughout the day for patient examinations.

Examination Table

The examination room will have an examination table. Most examination tables can be raised or lowered by pushing or pulling a lever on the side of the table. The tables are usually covered with nonpermeable vinyl, which allows for easy cleaning with a disinfectant (e.g., 10% bleach solution, EPA-approved product) between patients (Fig. 3-6).

To cover the table's surface, paper is often pulled from a roll underneath the head of the table and is secured at the bottom (Fig. 3-7). A footrest or pullout platform at the end of the table should be available in the room for patients who may require assistance getting onto the examination table.

PATIENT-CENTERED PROFESSIONALISM

- Why must the examination room promote privacy and offer appropriate accommodations for patient accessibility?
- What is the medical assistant's role in room preparation?

TABLE 3-2 Supplies in the Examination Room

Item	Use
Alcohol wipes	Disinfect skin and equipment surfaces
Tongue depressors	Hold tongue during full-mouth or throat examination
Tissues	Wipe body secretions
Cotton-tipped applicators	Collect specimens; remove debris
Disposable gloves (nonsterile)	Provide protection against contact with body fluids
Lubricant (water soluble)	Assist in examination of rectal and vaginal areas by moistening area
Patient gowns and capes	Cover body and allow easy access for examination
Drapes	Provide privacy and warmth
Hypoallergenic tape of various sizes	Secure dressings in place
Gauze squares (2 × 2, 4 × 4)	Wipe or cover an area
Sterile dressings	Cover wounds
Guaiac card and developer	Test for occult blood (usually fecal)

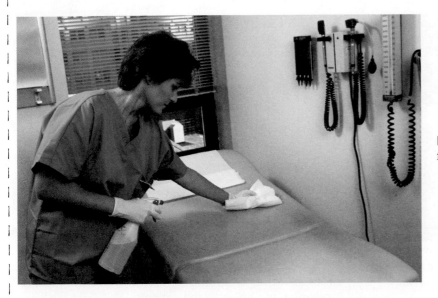

Fig. 3-6 Examination table must be disinfected between patients.

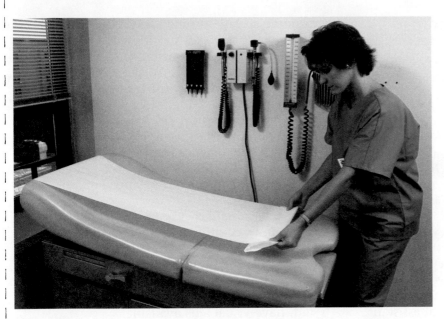

Fig. 3-7 The medical assistant pulls clean paper covering down over the examination table.

ROOM MAINTENANCE

After a patient has left the room and has been escorted to the front of the office, the paper covering the examination table is removed, and the table is cleaned, dried, and recovered with clean paper. Never bring a patient into a dirty examination room. Ensure that the room is clean and odor free before bringing in the next patient.

Occupational Safety and Health Administration (OSHA) regulations state that all contaminated work surfaces must be decontaminated using an appropriate disinfectant as soon as possible after a procedure, or immediately if potentially infectious contamination has occurred (e.g., contaminated body fluids). Medical assistants need to be especially careful to hold the dirty paper covering away from their clothing when removing it (Fig. 3-8). Besides the table, all equipment and surfaces used must be sanitized and disinfected.

All instruments used during the examination need to be removed, cleaned, and sterilized if necessary. Instruments and equipment are then assembled and arranged to be neat and orderly. All supplies and equipment will be added to the room as required for the next patient. Any equipment for specialty examinations should be added to the examination tray as necessary (e.g., vaginal speculum, Pap smear supplies).

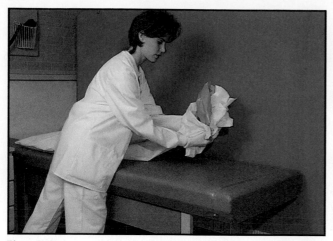

Fig. 3-8 The medical assistant keeps the soiled paper table covering away from her clothing. *(From Chester GA: Modern medical assisting, Philadelphia, 1998, Saunders.)*

Fig. 3-9 Patient teaching is made easier when written instructions are provided and the patient is allowed to ask questions. Keep in mind that some patients may not be able to read; therefore any teaching materials must be explained, not given to the patient.

PATIENT-CENTERED PROFESSIONALISM

- What key element in infection control is the medical assistant providing by performing room sanitization?

PATIENT PREPARATION

The medical assistant has an important role in helping the patient comply with the physician-designed treatment plan. This involves preparing patients for procedures as well as preparing them to comply with the plan of care after they leave the medical office. Once the physician has made the diagnosis, implementation of the plan of care requires patient cooperation. The medical assistant must be aware of barriers that would prevent the patient from following the plan.

To prepare the patient for carrying out the treatment plan, the medical assistant can address four major areas with the following questions:

1. *Does the patient understand the instructions?* Shaking the head "yes" does not mean the patient fully understands what is expected. Ask the patient to explain or demonstrate to you what is expected. Any additional teaching or clarification can take place during this "show and tell" time. Provide written instructions when available, and allow the patient to ask questions (Fig. 3-9).
2. *Do the patient and family understand the time demands needed to follow the procedure preparation or treatment plan successfully?* For

example, a patient scheduled for a sigmoidoscopy needs to follow a bowel evacuation procedure before the examination. The patient who needs to take medication with food in the morning must take enough time to eat breakfast.
3. *Will the patient's living environment allow the treatment plan to be followed?* For example, a patient newly diagnosed with diabetes has food concerns. Is the family supportive to help make certain the patient has a balanced diet or special foods?
4. *Is the patient hard of hearing or does the patient have other medical problems that could hinder understanding?* The medical assistant should always face the patient when speaking. Speak naturally and use nonverbal communication to send the message. To reinforce what is being said, have visual aids available.

PATIENT-CENTERED PROFESSIONALISM

- In what ways can the medical assistant help the patient prepare for a procedure and comply with the treatment plan?

CONCLUSION

An important part of the medical assistant's duties involves preparation for patient treatment. Before the patient arrives, the examination room must be prepared for the type of examination or procedure to be performed. In addition, the necessary supplies and equipment must be ready for the physician or other provider to use during the examination or procedure. Finally, medical assistants need to prepare patients for the procedure by educating them about anything they need to do before the procedure, as well as how they can comply with the treatment plan. Effective preparation saves time for the health care provider and the patient, ultimately providing for more effective patient care.

SUMMARY

Reinforce your understanding of the material in this chapter by reviewing the curriculum objectives and key content points below.

1. Define, appropriately use, and spell all the Key Terms for this chapter.
   - Review the Key Terms if necessary.
2. List four general considerations for examination room arrangement and preparation.
   - Privacy, room decor, room temperature, and accessibility are four important considerations for examination rooms.
3. List and briefly describe the purpose of seven instruments typically stocked in an examination room.
   - An ophthalmoscope, otoscope, penlight, tape measure, reflex hammer, and tuning fork are kept in the examination room and used for physical examinations.
   - An audiometer is an electronic device used to test hearing.
   - Refer to Table 3-1.
4. List and briefly describe the purpose of six general supplies kept in an examination room.
   - Gloves, water-soluble lubricant, tongue depressors, tissues, cotton-tipped applicators, and specimen containers are usually kept in the examination room and used for physical examinations.
   - Refer to Table 3-2.
5. Describe what should be done for maintenance to the examination table and work surfaces after a patient has left the examination room.
   - The paper covering is removed and the examination table is cleaned and dried and recovered with paper after the patient leaves the room.
   - All surfaces used must be disinfected.

6. Describe what should be done to the instruments used during the examination after a patient has left the examination room.
   - All instruments used during the examination must be removed, sanitized, and if necessary, sterilized.
7. Explain the medical assistant's role in preparing the patient to comply with the plan of care.
   - Medical assistants focus on the patient's understanding of instructions, time demands, living environment, and possible disabilities that may hinder understanding in helping patients comply with their treatment plans.
8. Analyze a realistic medical office situation and apply your understanding of examination room preparation to determine the best course of action.
   - The effective preparation of the examination room affects not only the functioning of the medical office but also the care that patients receive.
   - Proper examination room preparation breaks the chain of infection.
9. Describe the impact on patient care when medical assistants understand how to prepare the examination room for patients.
   - The patient tends to have more confidence in the ability of the health care team (and the team's decision-making capability) when the equipment and supplies are readily available.
   - Infections may be prevented when proper room decontamination procedures are followed.

FOR FURTHER EXPLORATION

Research different types of medical practices. The equipment and supplies needed for the physical examination differ according to the type of examination and the physician's specialty.
Keywords: Use the following keywords in your search: neurologist, orthopedist, pulmonologist, endocrinologist.

Chapter Review

Vocabulary Review

Matching

Match each term with the correct definition.

A. audiometer

B. tuning fork

C. otoscope

D. specimen

E. percussion hammer

F. tape measure

G. ophthalmoscope

H. tongue depressor

I. lubricant

J. penlight

_____ 1. Instrument used to hold the tongue down or move it from side to side when examining the mouth

_____ 2. Agent used to reduce friction by making a surface moist; used to facilitate anal and vaginal examinations

_____ 3. Instrument used to test hearing acuity by air or bone conduction

_____ 4. Instrument used to measure tendon reflexes

_____ 5. Instrument used to examine internal structure of the eye

_____ 6. Electronic instrument used to test hearing

_____ 7. Sample of a larger part, such as body tissue or cells

_____ 8. Instrument used to examine the ear canal and eardrum

_____ 9. Device used to measure body parts and wound length

_____ 10. Instrument used to enhance examination in a cavity and to check for papillary response to light

Theory Recall

True/False

Indicate whether the sentence or statement is true or false.

_____ 1. Confidentiality is a key issue for patients.

_____ 2. It is acceptable to leave prescription pads on the counter in examination rooms, because even if a patient took the pad he or she could not use it.

_____ 3. A medical assistant should be present while a patient changes into a gown.

_____ 4. Otoscope may have a short and wide speculum attached and can be used by the physician to examine the nasal area.

_____ 5. Examination tables must be covered with nonpermeable latex as directed by OSHA.

Multiple Choice

Identify the letter of the choice that best completes the statement or answers the question.

1. An instrument used to measure tendon reflexes is a(n) _____.
   A. audiometer
   B. percussion hammer
   C. tape measure
   D. tuning fork

2. The _____ test is used when a patient states hearing is better in one ear than in the other.
   A. audiometer
   B. Rinne
   C. verbal
   D. Weber

3. Appropriate accommodations need to be made in examination rooms to ensure that the room is accessible to all patients, including those in wheelchairs, as directed by _____.
   A. CDC
   B. OSHA
   C. ADA
   D. none of the above

4. Which one of the following is the correct spelling for the medical term for a blood pressure cuff?
   A. Syphgmomanometer
   B. Sphygmomanometer
   C. Syfigmomanometer
   D. None of the above

5. A _____ holds used needles and other sharps for disposal.
   A. biohazardous waste container
   B. puncture-resistant container
   C. sealable stainless steel canister
   D. none of the above

6. _____ requires that all contaminated work surfaces be decontaminated using appropriate disinfectant as soon as possible after a procedure or immediately if potential infectious contamination has occurred.
   A. CDC
   B. Office procedure manual
   C. State law
   D. Exposure control plan

7. _____ is(are) used to collect specimens and remove debris.
   A. Cotton-tipped applicator
   B. Lubricant
   C. Sterile saline
   D. Sharp/sharp operating scissors

8. _____ is an instrument used to test hearing acuity through vibration.
   A. Audiometer
   B. Otoscope
   C. Percussion hammer
   D. Tuning fork

9. _____ is an instrument used for viewing a cavity.
   A. Penlight
   B. Tongue depressor
   C. Speculum
   D. None of the above

10. The _____ test compares air conduction with bone conduction.
    A. audiometer
    B. percussion hammer
    C. Rinne
    D. Weber

11. _____ disinfects skin and equipment surfaces.
    A. Sterile saline
    B. Isopropyl alcohol 70%
    C. Johnson & Johnson "Wet Wipes"
    D. None of the above

12. Lubricants used in a medical office should be _____.
    A. water soluble
    B. oil based
    C. consistent with the ingredients of household detergent
    D. none of the above

13. Examination tables and counter surfaces must be cleaned in between patients with _____.
    A. sterile saline
    B. 70% isopropyl alcohol wipe
    C. 10% bleach solution
    D. all of the above

14. All instruments used during an examination must be removed, cleaned, and _____.
    A. sanitized
    B. disinfected
    C. sterilized
    D. all of the above

15. Which one of the following is a specialty item that would be added to an examination tray for a Pap smear?
    A. Sigmoidoscope
    B. Ophthalmoscope
    C. Tuning fork
    D. Vaginal speculum

Sentence Completion

Complete each sentence or statement.

1. _____ measures should be taken to ensure patients do not injure themselves in the office.

2. _____ mandates the privacy and confidentiality of patients.

3. Gloves are always worn when coming in contact with _____.

4. _____ is used for taping the tendon in the elbow, wrist, ankle, and knee to test for reflex action.

5. _____ is used to examine the internal structures of the eye.

Short Answers

1. Describe what safety measures need to be taken in the medical office so that patients do not injure themselves.

   _____

   _____

   _____

   _____

2. List equipment for a physical examination typically found in an examination room.

   _____

   _____

   _____

   _____

3. List the four major areas of treatment plan preparation that the medical assistant can address.

   _____

   _____

   _____

   _____

4. List four general considerations taken when preparing an examination room for a patient.

   _____

   _____

   _____

   _____

Critical Thinking

Today is your first day of externship, and the medical assistant that you will be training with has asked you to set up Room 3 for a routine physical examination. List the items you will need to have available for the physician, and describe the preparation of the examination room.

Internet Research

Keywords: Health Insurance Portability and Accountability Act (HIPAA) regulations on patient privacy, Americans with Disabilities Act (ADA) accessibility requirements for medical offices and clinics

Choose one of the following topics to research: Health Insurance Portability and Accountability Act (HIPAA) regulations on patient privacy or Americans with Disabilities Act (ADA) accessibility requirements for medical offices and clinics. Prepare a one-page report, and cite your source. Be prepared to give a 2-minute oral presentation should your instructor assign you to do so.

What Would You Do?

If you have accomplished the objectives in this chapter, you will be able to make better choices as a medical assistant. Take another look at this situation and decide what you would do.

Julie, a medical assistant who was not educated in a medical assisting program, has been hired by a local family physician to assist with physical examinations. Today is her second day on the job. Her mentor has called in sick, so Julie is responsible for the clinical area by herself. Another physician, Dr. Johnson, will be performing the invasive procedures, and Julie is expected to have the room and patient ready for Dr. Johnson's examinations. Julie finds the room too warm for her comfort, and she knows that it will be too warm for the physician in a lab coat, so she lowers the thermostat to 67° F. As Mrs. Sito is undressing, Julie barges into the room and leaves the door open. A male patient walks by and sees Mrs. Sito undressed. During the examination Dr. Johnson asks for the ophthalmoscope and otoscope. When he tries to use these, the necessary light will not work, so he asks for a penlight. Julie leaves the room to find the penlight and a tape measure. Dr. Johnson reaches for a cotton-tipped applicator and tongue depressors. Noticing that the supply is low, he asks Julie, "Would you please fill these containers?" Julie immediately departs to fill the jars, leaving Dr. Johnson alone with the patient, who needs a pelvic examination. After Mrs. Sito leaves the room, Julie decides that the table paper does not look used. Thinking she will save the physician some money in supplies, she does not change the paper covering and brings in 5-year-old Joey Novelle, placing him on the table Mrs. Sito has just left. The sink still contains the dirty instruments used for the other patients. Joey's mother tells Dr. Johnson that she has never seen someone placed on dirty table paper, and she does not want her child to see dirty instruments in the sink. At the end of Joey's physical examination, Dr. Johnson takes Julie to his office and explains that if she cannot properly prepare and clean the examination room in the future, he will have to find someone to replace her.

If you worked with Julie, what are some suggestions you would make to help her perform her duties more effectively?

1. What part did the lack of education in the medical assisting field play in Julie making mistakes?

_____

_____

_____

2. What temperature is appropriate for the patient examination room?

_____

3. Why should Julie have been very careful to keep the door closed to the examination room where a patient was placed?

_____

_____

_____

4. What is the use of the ophthalmoscope and otoscope?

_____

_____

_____

5. Should Julie have left the room to fill the containers of cotton-tipped applicators and tongue depressors? Explain your answer.

_____

_____

_____

6. Why is changing the examination table's paper covering such an important task?

_____

_____

_____

7. Do you think that Joey's mother and Dr. Johnson had a right to be upset?

_____

_____

_____

8. What effect did the room's lack of preparation have on the appointments for that day?

_____

_____

_____

Application of Skills

Discuss with a partner why room maintenance and room preparation are important for maintaining the efficiency of the office's workflow.

Chapter Quiz

Multiple Choice

Identify the letter of the choice that best completes the statement or answers the question.

1. _____ is used when a patient states that the hearing is better on one side than the other.
   A. Audiometer test
   B. Tuning fork
   C. Rinne test
   D. Weber test

2. _____ are always worn when coming in contact with patient body secretions.
   A. Latex gloves
   B. Powdered gloves
   C. Disposable gloves
   D. Sterile gloves

3. A _____ should be available in the exam room for a patient to access an exam table.
   A. stepstool
   B. footrest
   C. pullout platform
   D. any of the above

4. Prescription pads should not be left on the counter in examination rooms.
   A. True
   B. False

5. The medical assistant should prepare the examination room _____ the patient arrives.
   A. after
   B. before
   C. when
   D. none of the above

6. The Americans with Disabilities Act requires that appropriate accommodations be made in examination rooms so that all patients, including those in wheelchairs, have access.
   A. True
   B. False

7. _____ is a piece of equipment typically kept in examination rooms for physical examination.
   A. Cotton-tipped applicators
   B. Disposable gloves
   C. Tongue depressors
   D. Otoscope

8. Confidentiality is not an issue for most patients.
   A. True
   B. False

9. _____ regulates that all contaminated work surfaces must be decontaminated using an appropriate disinfectant as soon as the patient leaves.
   A. Office policy manual
   B. CDC
   C. Exposure control plan
   D. State law

10. _____ protects the patient's right to privacy.
    A. CDC
    B. OSHA
    C. HIPAA
    D. Office policy

11. Examination table paper needs to be changed _____.
    A. every morning
    B. twice a day
    C. end of the day
    D. after each patient

12. When the medical assistant is preparing the patient for carrying out the treatment plan, the medical assistant should _____.
    A. make sure the patient understands the instructions
    B. make sure the patient's living environment will allow for compliance
    C. make sure the patient is not hearing impaired
    D. all of the above

13. A(n) _____ is an instrument for viewing a cavity.
    A. penlight
    B. otoscope
    C. speculum
    D. tongue depressor

14. _____ is an instrument to view the internal structure of the eye.
    A. Audiometer
    B. Otoscope
    C. Ophthalmoscope
    D. Penlight

15. The medical assistant should stay in the examination room while a patient changes into a gown.
    A. True
    B. False

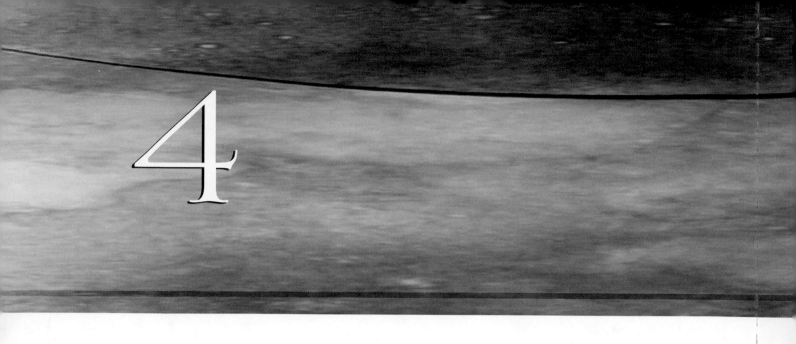

OBJECTIVES

You will be able to do the following after completing this chapter:

Key Terms
1. Define, appropriately use, and spell all the Key Terms for this chapter.

Greeting Patients
2. Describe how a warm, professional greeting affects patients.
3. Demonstrate the correct procedure for giving patients verbal instructions on how to locate the medical office.
4. Explain the purpose of the medical practice information booklet.
5. Demonstrate the correct procedure for constructing a patient information brochure.

Managing the Telephone
6. Describe how a medical assistant's tone of voice affects telephone conversations.
7. List 12 guidelines for telephone etiquette and explain the importance of each.
8. Demonstrate the correct procedure for answering a multiline telephone system.
9. Explain the considerations for screening incoming calls.
10. Explain the importance of a triage (protocol guidelines) manual.
11. Describe the process of placing a caller on hold when needed.
12. List the seven types of information documented when taking a phone message.
13. List three types of outgoing calls that administrative medical assistants may make.

Scheduling Appointments
14. Explain the importance for patients, medical assistants, and physicians of managing office appointments efficiently and consistently.
15. Demonstrate the correct procedure for preparing and maintaining the office appointment book.
16. List one method of blocking off, or reserving, time *not* to be used for patient scheduling.
17. Explain the considerations for canceling a patient appointment.
18. List 10 abbreviations commonly used in scheduling appointments.
19. Demonstrate the correct procedure for scheduling a new patient for an office visit.
20. List six appointment-scheduling techniques and explain the advantages and disadvantages of each.
21. List two special problems that can occur in scheduling appointments and explain what can be done to prevent each.
22. Explain the purpose of an appointment reminder.
23. Demonstrate the correct procedure for scheduling a patient for outpatient diagnostic testing.

MEDICAL OFFICE COMMUNICATION

Handling Mail
24. Explain why it is important to sort incoming mail.
25. List four classifications of U.S. mail.
26. List eight special services offered by the post office that can help medical offices track, insure, and receive delivery confirmation for the mail they send.
27. Demonstrate the correct preparation of an envelope.

Managing Written Correspondence
28. Explain the proper use of a letter and a memo in medical office communication.
29. List nine guidelines for preparing effective written communication in the medical office.
30. Identify proofreader's marks used to edit written correspondence.
31. Demonstrate the correct procedure for composing, keying, and proofreading a business letter and preparing the envelope.
32. Demonstrate the correct procedure for composing a memo.
33. Describe the format used to prepare a manuscript based on clinical research performed in the office.
34. List seven types of medical office reports and describe the purpose of each.
35. Demonstrate the correct procedure for transcribing a machine-dictated document.

Patient-Centered Professionalism
36. Analyze a realistic medical office situation and apply your understanding of medical office communication to determine the best course of action.
37. Describe the impact on patient care when medical assistants have a solid understanding of communication in the medical office.

KEY TERMS

abstract Brief summary of the contents of a manuscript or publication.

autopsy report Medical report that provides details about the cause of a person's illness and death through both internal and external examination findings.

certified mail Special mail-handling method used to prove an item was mailed and received.

cluster scheduling Appointment scheduling technique that groups several appointments for similar types of examination; also called *categorization scheduling*.

consultation report Medical report written by a specialist after seeing a patient for a primary physician.

discharge summary Medical report that provides a comprehensive review of a patient's hospital stay.

double booking Appointment scheduling technique that schedules more than one patient during the same appointment time period.

emergency Situation in which a delay in treatment could be life threatening.

established patient Patient who has received professional services from the physician or the medical office in the past 3 years.

full-block format Letter format that has all lines flush with the left margin.

KEY TERMS—*cont'd*

history and physical (H&P) report Medical report that consists of a patient's subjective (medical history) and objective (physical examination) data.

manuscript Document used for publication.

matrix Format used to mark off or reserve time in a schedule.

medical practice information booklet Booklet or brochure that provides nonmedical information for patients about standard office policies (e.g., billing, inclement weather) of a medical practice.

memo Informed written form of communication for interoffice use.

modified-block format Letter format that has all lines flush with left margin, except for first line of new paragraph (which is indented five spaces) and date, closing, and signature (which are centered).

modified-wave scheduling Appointment scheduling technique based on the theory that each patient visit will not require the allotted time.

necropsy Autopsy.

new patient Patient who has not received professional services from the physician or the medical office in the past 3 years.

open-hour scheduling Appointment scheduling technique that allows patients to be seen without an appointment.

operative report Medical report that lists a surgical procedure done, any pathological specimens, the findings, and the medical personnel involved.

patient information brochure See *medical practice information booklet.*

progress notes Written findings of a patient's condition.

proofreading Reviewing a written work for errors.

radiology report Medical report that describes the findings and interpretations of a radiologist.

registered mail Special mail-handling method used when the contents have a declared monetary value.

time-specified scheduling Appointment scheduling technique that provides a definite time period for the patient to be seen.

transcriptionist Person who listens to recorded dictation and converts it to a written document.

wave scheduling Appointment scheduling technique that divides an hour block into average-appointment time slots.

What Would You Do?

Read the following scenario and keep it in mind as you learn about the importance of communicating effectively in the medical office in this chapter.

Tara is a new medical assistant at a physician's office. Dr. Vickers has hired her to answer the phone and to greet patients as they arrive, as well as to assist with making appointments as needed. On a particularly busy day, the phone is ringing with two lines already on hold, and a new patient arrives at the reception desk. Steve, the physician's assistant, asks Tara to make an appointment for another patient to see Dr. Vickers as soon as possible. Because the office makes appointments in a modified wave, Steve tells the patient to wait to be seen

because Tara has found an opening in about a half-hour. In all the confusion, Tara does not return to the patients who are on hold for several minutes, and one of the calls is an emergency. Furthermore, Tara is short-tempered with the new patient who has arrived at the office. Tara's frustration about the busy schedule she is expected to keep shows, and the new patient states that she is not sure that she has chosen the best physician's office for her medical care.

What effect will Tara's frustration have on this medical office? How would you have handled this situation differently?

The daily functioning of a medical practice relies on good communication skills. As you have learned in previous chapters, effective communication involves excellent skills not only in speaking and listening, but also in conveying nonverbal and written messages. Medical assistants and other health professionals must use effective communication skills in such daily activities as the following:

- Greeting patients
- Speaking with patients and other professionals on the telephone
- Scheduling appointments
- Corresponding with patients and other health professionals in writing

When applying effective communication skills in these areas, health professionals must meet patient expectations for professionalism, as well as HIPAA regulations on how patient information can be communicated or disclosed (Box 4-1).

≋ GREETING PATIENTS

As a medical assistant, you may serve as a receptionist. The receptionist is the first person a patient sees in the medical office. Make sure the patient's first impression of you and the medical practice is positive. If a patient is calling for the first time to schedule an appointment, make sure the patient knows how to find the office. Procedure 4-1 shows how to use verbal instructions to give patients directions for locating the medical office.

The reception desk should be accessible to patients when they enter the office. In addition, the counter height needs to be high enough to maintain the confidentiality of patient information. You must keep several considerations in mind when greeting **new patients** and **established patients**, as well as other visitors to the medical office.

New Patients

Patients new to the medical office (first visit or first visit to the office in 3 years) need to feel welcome. Some practices will mail a "new patient packet" before the patient's first office visit. If forms have not been sent previously, give the new patient a pen and the forms that must be completed. Explain the policies of the medical office, or give the patient a **medical practice information booklet**, or **patient information brochure**, that provides this information (Box 4-2). An information booklet or brochure should provide answers to nonmedical questions. Procedure 4-2 explains information necessary to construct an information brochure.

Let patients know that when they finish reviewing the brochure, you will be glad to answer any questions about the medical practice. In addition, inform patients that you are available to help them complete the forms, if necessary. Sometimes patients have trouble reading or seeing, and just handing them a form to be completed may be seen as uncaring. People unable to read are embarrassed to say so, and therefore they may not fill out the forms correctly. Some may not understand the questions being asked because of medical terminology used in the forms. Patients may not want to admit they need help or may be confused.

Helping patients with forms also saves time. Some offices have a private area set aside to answer

BOX 4-1   HIPAA: The Privacy Rule

The Health Insurance Portability and Accountability Act (HIPAA) of 1996 mandates that the privacy and security of patient information be maintained in a confidential manner. This process begins when the individual arrives for their first appointment. Patients must be given detailed *written* information concerning their privacy rights. This includes the steps the practice will take to protect their privacy and how the medical practice will use patients' *protected health information* (PHI).

To document that the medical practice made an effort to comply with this regulation, the practice must obtain a written acknowledgment from the patient that he or she has reviewed these rights. Acknowledgment may be in the form of a signature or the patient's initials on the notice signifying that he or she has received the required information. If the patient declines to acknowledge receiving a *Notice of Privacy Practices,* this must be documented in the patient's chart. This documentation shows a good faith effort was made by the practice to inform the patient and details the reason for failure to accomplish this act and comply with the regulation.

Medical practices must also post a *Notice of Privacy Practices* in the office, usually in the reception area. Additional copies of the notice should be made available if a patient requests a copy. The regulation also requires medical practices to have a written policy and procedure in place for determining who has access to patient medical information. For example, the policy may state that the receptionist may view the names of the patients coming into the office but may *not* view patients' records.

To accommodate computerized information, two types of access codes (passwords) should be used. The first set would allow the receptionist to view the physician's schedule but would not allow the receptionist to view patient records. The second set would allow the physician, nurse, and medical assistant to view the patient records for the purpose of patient care. A tracking system that keeps detailed information of all staff members viewing a patient's medical record should be in place.

The HIPAA regulation also addresses the issues of sign-in sheets and calling the names of patients who are sitting in the waiting area.

Can a medical practice use patient sign-in sheets and call out the names of patients in the waiting room?

Yes; the practice can do both, as long as the information disclosed is appropriately limited. The Privacy Rule allows for *incidental disclosure* as long as appropriate safeguards are in place. For example, the sign-in sheet cannot contain confidential patient information (e.g., reason for the visit, medical problem). It is best to change used sheets with clean ones periodically during the day. Calling patients by name is still the most acceptable, courteous, and respectful way to "invite" patients into the examination area.

BOX 4-2   Patient Information Booklet

The patient information booklet (or brochure) communicates policies of the practice (e.g., payment must be made at the time of service). It clarifies appointment policies, office hours, prescription refill policies, and so on. It should avoid technical terminology and should be written as if the staff is speaking to the patient (e.g., "We want to make your medical care our number-one priority").

A patient brochure, or medical practice information booklet, should answer frequently asked questions, thus saving staff time by limiting the need to repeat information. This reduces telephone calls about office policies (e.g., office hours). The booklet invites the patient to be an active participant in his or her care.

questions and to fill out forms. This allows for minimal distractions and patient privacy.

Established Patients

Personalize the greeting when returning patients come into the office (e.g., "The doctor will be with you shortly, Ms. Jones; please make yourself comfortable in the reception area"). Remember to not address a patient by first name unless the patient has given you permission to do so. If other patients approach the desk while you are speaking with a patient, stop long enough to acknowledge their presence and tell them you will be available shortly. This lets them know that they are important as well and will receive your full attention. Every patient should be made to feel that he or she has the full attention of the office staff and that his or her needs have priority, no matter how busy the office is that day.

Procedure 4-1 Give Verbal Instructions on How to Locate the Medical Office

TASK: Provide verbal instructions to a caller on how to locate the medical office.

EQUIPMENT AND SUPPLIES
- Telephone
- City map
- Pen or pencil

SKILLS/RATIONALE

1. **Procedural Step. Address the patient or caller in a polite and professional manner.**
   Rationale. Tone and pitch of voice promote a positive first impression.

2. **Procedural Step. Ask the person, "Where will you be coming from?"**
   Rationale. This provides the medical assistant with a location on which to base directions. Find the location on a city map if needed. An Internet mapping service (e.g., MapQuest) may also be helpful in providing door-to-door directions.

3. **Procedural Step. Determine the most direct route to the medical office, with alternate routes if possible. Provide the person with major cross streets and landmarks.**
   Rationale. Providing the most direct route will save the patient or caller time and will lessen the likelihood of not finding the office. Having alternate routes, cross streets, and landmarks available will be helpful for people unfamiliar with the area. For example, "turn left on McCleary, take the next right onto Dearborne. Our parking lot is across the street from the bank." Keep in mind that the person may be driving, walking, or taking public transportation.

4. **Procedural Step. Allow the patient or caller sufficient time to write down the directions.**
   a. Repeat the directions back to the person, as needed, with a cheerful and pleasant tone.
   b. Ask the person to repeat the directions back to you if the location is somewhat difficult to find.
   Rationale. This provides for excellent customer service and a favorable impression of the medical office.

5. **Procedural Step. Provide the caller with the office's phone number in case the person needs to call for further clarification of directions en route. If time permits, the medical assistant may mail written directions and a map to the patient before the appointment.**
   Rationale. Again, this provides for excellent customer service and a favorable impression of the medical office. Written directions and a map may be included in the office's informational brochure, which is often mailed to new patients.

Procedure 4-2 Create a Medical Practice Information Brochure

TASK: Create a "mock" patient information booklet for the medical practice.

EQUIPMENT AND SUPPLIES
- Computer
- Software program that allows for brochure layouts
- Examples of local medical practice brochures and local medical office policies
- Pen or pencil

SKILLS/RATIONALE

1. **Procedural Step. Determine the content information to include in the informational brochure to be provided to patients.**
   Rationale: Provides an effective means to communicate with patients about office policies.
   Items for consideration may include the following:
   - Practice's philosophy statement
   - Goals of the practice
   - Description of the practice
   - Physical location of the office (address), including a map
   - Parking options, public transportation routes

Continued

Procedure 4-2 Create a Medical Practice Information Brochure—cont'd

- Telephone numbers, e-mail address, Web page
- Office hours, day and time
- Names and credentials of staff members*
- Types of services
- Appointment scheduling and cancellation policies
- Payment options
- Prescription refill policy
- Types of insurance accepted
- Policy regarding no-shows and canceled appointments
- Referral policy
- Release of records policy
- Emergency protocols
- Who to contact if the physician is unavailable
- Frequently asked questions
- Any special considerations

2. **Procedural Step. Write and key a short paragraph describing each of the topics to be included in the brochure. Proofread the keyed information.**
   Rationale. The medical assistant can read the content and make corrections as needed. A brochure should

never be sent out with incorrect information or "typos." Remember, this may be the first interaction a patient has with your office and an impression will be formed.

3. **Procedural Step. Determine the layout of the brochure.**
   a. The layout should be visually pleasing.
   b. Consider the placement of the office logo.
   c. Ensure that the name of the practice, address, and phone number are prominent.
   d. Some software programs have a brochure template that may work for creating this booklet. If a separate program is not available, any word-processing program can be used.

4. **Procedural Step. Have the office manager or physician approve the final draft.**
   a. Make corrections as requested.
   b. The physician has final approval.

5. **Procedural Step. Print the brochure.**
   This may be done at the office if the office photocopier can provide quality copies. Otherwise, submit the brochure electronically to a printing company for professional-looking brochures.

*Some offices choose *not* to include this information.

Other Visitors

Occasionally, people other than patients request to see the physician, such as family members, sales representatives, and other physicians. If possible, answer questions concerning when the physician can see them, or assist them with making an appointment. The office should have a procedure to let the receptionist know which visitors the physician will see without an appointment. All visitors should be treated courteously.

PATIENT-CENTERED PROFESSIONALISM

- Why must the medical assistant greet patients and all visitors to the medical office in a professional manner?
- Why is it important that the medical practice information brochure be structured to anticipate patients' most common nonmedical questions?

MANAGING THE TELEPHONE

Every caller who phones the medical office forms an impression of the physician and all health care

workers in the office. In fact, people often form a mental picture of the person they are speaking with according to the way his or her voice sounds on the telephone. When people talk face to face, an impression is formed based on many factors. When talking on the telephone, a speaker projects his or her personality by the voice alone. The receptionist's voice should be businesslike, courteous, pleasant, and friendly.

Telephone Voice

The quality of your voice is important because it is a major way to express your ideas to others. A person's voice tends to project that person's personality to listeners. The voice is a valuable tool to promote a professional image. You have probably heard this before, but it is true: If you smile while talking on the phone, callers can tell.

Tone

Your *tone*, or the sound of your voice, should be expressive and pleasant, not monotone. The *pitch* (highs and lows) should be low because this projects and carries the voice better and tends to be calming. In emphasizing a word or important point the pitch should be raised. Raising the inflection of the voice at the end of a sentence is useful because people tend to remember what they heard last.

Volume

The volume used when delivering a message must be appropriate for what is being said and for the physical condition of the patient. Speaking loudly is irritating to most patients. They may feel they are being spoken to rudely (e.g., "yelled at") or disrespectfully.

Clarity

You need to speak distinctly so that it will be easy for patients to understand your message. Patients also need to understand the terms used. Speak in lay terms (nontechnical terms); the message is lost if the patient does not understand the terminology. Pronounce words correctly, and ask patients to pronounce or spell their last name if you are unsure how to say it correctly.

Rate of Speed

If you speak too rapidly you will not be well understood, and time is wasted repeating yourself. Speaking too slowly causes your words to sound disconnected, which can also irritate the listener. Speaking too quickly or too slowly can make it difficult for the listener to follow the conversation, and the person may lose interest. Speaking clearly requires that you adjust your rate of speed according to the listener's needs.

Telephone Etiquette

The word *etiquette* essentially means "manners." Using good etiquette on the medical office telephone helps make a good impression on those who call. Good telephone manners reflect the qualities of pleasantness, promptness, politeness, and helpfulness. Guidelines for proper telephone etiquette follow.

Before the Call

1. Prepare yourself by checking your body posture.
2. Make sure you have the supplies to take messages (pens, paper, message pad, appointment book, watch to record time).

When Speaking with the Caller

1. Always identify yourself and the office so that callers know they have reached the correct number (e.g., "Good morning, Westside Medical Office, this is Lisa. How can I help you?").
2. Be as courteous over the telephone as you would be with someone face to face.

3. Avoid slang terms and technical terms.
4. Listen attentively. Do not interrupt callers until they finish saying everything they want to say. If you speak too quickly, an important fact may be missed. Do provide feedback to let people know you are listening. Sound alert and helpful.
5. Think about how the caller feels. Be empathetic and show concern for what a patient is saying. The patient's needs are critical to the medical practice. Concentrate on what is being said, keeping in mind that the patient needs to feel important.
6. Ask questions if you do not understand something.
7. Listen for overtones; much can be learned from a person's tone of voice and rate of speech.
8. Take notes to help you remember the important points and to gain clarification, especially date and time.
9. Give clear explanations.
10. Try to avoid placing callers on hold. When it is necessary, ask the caller first, and thank the caller for holding when returning to the line. Be sure their time on hold is minimal.

When the Call Is over

Leave the caller with a pleasant feeling when the conversation is finished (e.g., "Thank you for calling, Ms. Jones").

Incoming Calls

When the medical assistant uses proper telephone techniques, screening incoming calls becomes easier. Procedure 4-3 explains the proper techniques for answering a multiline telephone in a medical office. When a caller requests to speak to "the doctor," the medical assistant can use these techniques to process the requests in a professional manner. Calls from other physicians should be put through to the physician promptly, if he or she is available.

Tact must be used when a caller requests to speak to the physician. The callers must never feel that the physician is trying to avoid them. It is best to acknowledge that the physician is not available, or is with a patient, before asking for the caller's identity. If the caller wants to hold for the physician, keep the caller informed about what is happening (e.g., "The doctor is still unavailable. Would you like to continue to hold?"). Always offer to take a message.

Office policy should list the types of situations for which the medical assistant can interrupt the physician. Table 4-1 provides protocol to be used as

Procedure 4-3 Answer a Multiline Telephone System

TASK: Answer a multiline telephone system in a physician's office or clinic in a professional manner. Respond to a request for action, place a call on hold, transfer a call to another party, and accurately record a message.

EQUIPMENT AND SUPPLIES
- Telephone
- Appointment book
- Message pad
- Telephone emergency triage reference guide
- Physician referral sheet
- Pen or pencil
- Headset (optional)

SKILLS/RATIONALE

1. **Procedural Step. Answer the phone.**
   a. Smile before answering the phone.
      Rationale. The caller may not be able to see the smile but will hear it in your voice. Often, a telephone call to make an appointment is the first interaction the patient has with the office or clinic. Make the first impression a pleasant one.
   b. Answer the telephone by the third ring; speak directly into the transmitter, with the mouthpiece positioned 1 inch from the mouth.
      Rationale. Answering promptly conveys interest in the caller. The voice carries better when the mouthpiece is properly positioned.
   c. Speaking distinctly with a pleasant tone and expression, at a moderate rate, and with sufficient volume, identify the office and yourself. The greeting should start with the time of day (such as "Good morning" or "Good afternoon"), and a request to help should be included.
      Rationale. When you speak distinctly with a pleasant tone, at a moderate rate, and with sufficient volume, the caller will be able to understand what is being said. By identifying the facility and yourself, the caller will know that the correct number has been reached and to whom he or she is speaking.
         Example: "Good morning, Dr. Smith's office, this is Stacey speaking. How may I help you?"
   d. Verify the identity of the caller and request the caller's phone number.
      Rationale. This confirms the origin of the call and provides a phone number to return the call should it be disconnected or if the intended receiver of the call is unavailable.
   e. Provide the caller with the requested information or service, whenever possible.
         Medical assistants handle four types of calls on a routine basis:

   (1) **Appointments.** Because these are typically the most common phone calls made to the medical office, it is important to have the appointment book or electronic scheduling program easily accessible and near the telephone.
   (2) **Payment or account balance information.** If the medical facility does not have a separate department that handles these calls, it is best to have patient records close to the phone so that the medical assistant answering the phone has access.
   (3) **Physician referrals.** Most medical facilities have a physician referral list typed and located near the phone. The list should contain physicians, laboratories, hospitals, and other medical services frequently used by the physician in patient referral.
   (4) **Emergencies.** Emergency calls may or may not be made to the medical facility. If this is a common occurrence for the practice, an emergency triage reference guide should be located near the phone. Along with the screening reference guide, emergency phone numbers for fire, police, poison control, and ambulance services should be readily accessible if 911 does not connect with these services in your area.
   Rationale. The medical assistant can handle many calls and conserve the time and energy of the physician or other staff members.
   f. If you are unable to assist the caller, transfer the caller to the person who can assist. First, ask if you may put the caller on hold. Wait for a response, and place the call on hold. Then transfer the call to the appropriate staff member. (Note: Some telephone systems allow you to

Procedure 4-3 Answer a Multiline Telephone System—cont'd

immediately transfer the caller without placing him or her on hold.)

Example: "I would like to transfer you to the accounting department. May I put you on hold? Thank you. Please hold."

NOTE: *Never* leave a caller on hold for more than 90 seconds. If the line is not answered within this time, return to the caller and ask to take a message. If the caller does not want to be put back on hold, ask the caller for a phone number at which the call can be returned.

2. **Procedural Step. If more than one line is ringing at once put a caller on hold:**
   a. Answer the first line, and ask if you can put the caller on hold (remember to wait for a response).
   b. Answer the second line, and ask the caller to please hold (again, waiting for a response first).
   c. Return to the first call, and either help the caller or direct the call to the correct person, using the appropriate hold request, or ask for a phone number at which the call can be returned as soon as possible.
   d. Return to the second call, and repeat the process for subsequent incoming calls.
   Rationale. This ensures that all callers are treated with courtesy and respect.

3 Procedural Step. Take a message.
   a. Collect complete and accurate information that you can pass on to the party with whom the caller wishes to speak.

Rationale. Complete, accurate information helps the person quickly and efficiently return the call and addresses the needs or concerns of the caller.

   b. Record the following information:
   (1) Recipient of the message.
      Rationale. When taking a telephone message, it is important to know to whom the message needs to be directed so that the message is received promptly.
   (2) Name of the caller. If you are unsure of the spelling of the caller's name or did not understand the caller, ask the caller to spell it for you.
      Rationale. When taking a telephone message, it is important to determine the relationship of the caller to the patient if the caller is someone other than the patient, to ensure that the caller has a legal right to ask questions or be given information about the patient.
   (3) Date and time the message is taken.
   (4) Urgency of the message.
      Rationale. It is important for the physician or other health professional to know if this situation must be handled immediately, as in an emergency.
   (5) Allergies. If no allergies exist, write "none" or "0" in the box. Allergy information is available in the patient's medical record but any changes need to be noted. (This information may be unnecessary if no drug therapy is needed for the patient.)

3

MESSAGE FROM								
For Dr. Hughes	Name of Caller	Ref. to pt.	Patient Roland Aiken	Pt. Age 40+	Pt. Temp.	Message Date 10/13/xx	Message Time 3:00 PM	Urgent ☐ Yes ☒ No
Message: needs more Aldactazide (25mg tabs) — takes I daily							Allergies 0	

Respond to Phone # 814-555-2010	Best Time to Call AM PM	Pharmacy Name / # West Side 814-555-9817	Patient's Chart Attached ☒ Yes ☐ No	Patient's chart #	Initials KJ

DOCTOR - STAFF RESPONSE

Doctor's / Staff Orders / Follow-up Action

OK – call to pharmacy JH
#30
12 refills
Sig: T po qam

	Call Back ☐ Yes ☐ No	Chart. Mes. ☐ Yes ☐ No	Follow-up Date / /	Follow-up Completed-Date/Time / /	AM PM	Response By:

Product # 78-9156-Pkg, #78-9157-Pads, Bibbero Systems, Inc., Petaluma, CA.

Continued

Procedure 4-3 Answer a Multiline Telephone System—cont'd

Rationale. The condition reported may require a prescription.

(6) Message content. Record what the patient tells you.

Rationale. The "heart" of the message includes the reason why the call was made and the caller's question for the physician or other allied health professional (or action the caller wants the physician to take).

(7) Return phone number.

Rationale. The person for whom the call was placed must have the phone number of the caller to return the call.

(8) Pharmacy name and phone number. This information may be found in the patient's medical record.

Rationale. Including the name and number of the patient's pharmacy in the message provides the physician with a ready means of contacting the pharmacy should the need arise and ensures the correct pharmacy is called.

(9) Initials of message taker.

Rationale. For purposes of accountability and in case a question arises, the identification of the person taking the message needs to be indicated and should be recorded during the course of the phone call.

(10) Physician and staff response. This section of the form is completed by the individual to whom the message was directed. It is used whenever a telephone encounter with a patient results in, for example, the reporting of symptoms or a change in treatment. The provider writes in the action taken or to be taken (e.g., physician writes prescription that medical assistant will call in to pharmacy), call back (yes or no), chart message (yes or no), and follow-up date.

NOTE: If the medical assistant is assigned to make the follow-up call, the provider usually writes his or her initials immediately following the narrative. Sometimes both the provider and the medical assistant place their initials in the response box.

Rationale. Completing this portion of the form and placing it in the medical record is necessary after such calls, as this action must be documented in the medical record as part of the continuous record of care given.

4. **Procedural Step. Terminate the call in a pleasant manner, and replace the receiver gently.**

a. Be sure to thank the caller, and ask if there is anything further you can do to assist the caller, before hanging up.

b. It is best if the caller ends the call first. The proper language to end a call is to say, "Good-bye, Ms. Jones, and thank you for calling." It is never appropriate to say "bye-bye" or to use any other form of familiarization when ending a call.

Rationale. Proper telephone technique is often the first impression a new patient has of the medical practice.

---

a guide when certain situations arise. The medical assistant is not permitted to exercise independent judgment, but must limit their activities to preset protocols established by the physician. When this information is firmly and competently relayed, callers gain confidence in the office's ability to assist them. Often a new patient will call and request directions to the facility; it is important that this information be provided accurately and with clarity (see Procedure 4-1).

Placing the Caller on Hold

The telephone in a medical practice is in constant use. Most offices have more than one telephone line, and more than one call can come into the office at the same time. See Procedure 4-3 for a more detailed explanation of the process for putting a caller on hold.

Telephone Messages

When you take a message, certain information should be obtained (see Procedure 4-3 for details). Remember always record what the patient tells you. Write the message in a duplicate telephone logbook. Give the original to the appropriate person for follow-up.

Outgoing Calls

You must also be prepared to place outgoing calls. Have all needed information available before making the call. Before dialing the number, always listen for a dial tone. Many times a call may be coming in to the office at the same time you are trying to dial out. In this case, a loud noise on the phone line will be heard. Outgoing calls that medical assistants may need to make include the following:

TABLE 4-1	Protocols for Screening Telephone Calls	
Type of Call	**Action Taken by Medical Administrative Assistant**	**Call Handled by Whom**
Patient requests appointment	If not a potential emergency, schedule appointment	Medical administrative assistant
Patient requests prescription refill	Take a message with medication name and patient's pharmacy name and number. Send message with patient's medical record to physician.	Physician will call pharmacy if approved; clinical medical professional will phone patient to inform patient as to action taken by the physician (refilled or not refilled).
Patient asks to talk with physician or clinical medical professional because patient is ill or needs some medical information	Take a message, send message with patient's medical record to physician or clinical medical professional. (Depending on the severity of the patient's illness, the call may need to be transferred immediately to the physician or clinical medical professional.)	Physician or clinical medical professional
Patient is returning a call to the physician or clinical medical professional	Transfer call directly to physician or clinical medical professional as requested	Physician or clinical medical professional
Another physician calls for the physician	Transfer call directly to physician as requested; no need to ask the reason for the call	Physician
Outside laboratory calls with test results	Transfer call directly to individual requested by the laboratory	Identified staff member
Patient is uncomfortable identifying the reason for calling	Ask the patient if the call is an emergency. If not, ask the patient if you can have the clinical medical professional return a call to the patient.	Clinical medical professional
Patient calls for test results	Take a message; send message with patient's medical record to physician or clinical medical professional.	Physician or clinical medical professional
Patient calls with insurance or billing question	After confirming the identity of the patient and if the patient is entitled to the information, answer the patient's question. Some information may not be able to be released over the phone and may need to be mailed directly to the patient's home.	Medical administrative assistant
Insurance company calls requesting information on a patient	Identify requested information and identity of caller. Usually, only limited information may be given over the phone, and the caller should send a written request for information that has been authorized by the patient.	Medical administrative assistant

Continued

TABLE 4-1	Protocols for Screening Telephone Calls—cont'd	
Type of Call	**Action Taken by Medical Administrative Assistant**	**Call Handled by Whom**
Personal calls for a member of the office staff	Transfer directly to the staff member. If the call is for the physician and the physician is with a patient, notify the caller of that fact, and ask if you should interrupt (i.e., "The doctor is with a patient right now; would you like me to interrupt?") Note: Follow office protocol regarding physician interruptions.	Identified staff member
Administration calls for a member of the office staff	Transfer directly to the staff member. If the call is for the physician and the physician is with a patient, notify the caller of that fact, and ask if you should interrupt (i.e., "The doctor is with a patient right now; would you like me to interrupt?") Note: Follow office protocol regarding physician interruptions.	Identified staff member
Patient has a complaint	Attempt to handle the situation if at all possible; otherwise, take a message or transfer the call to the appropriate individual. If necessary, notify physician of complaint.	Medical administrative assistant or identified staff member
Patient has been poisoned	Immediately give caller telephone number of poison control center and obtain identification of patient. Poison control centers are properly equipped to handle poisonings in a rapid manner; assist with emergency help as appropriate.	Notify physician, and document call in patient's medical chart
Pharmaceutical sales representative wants appointment to give sales talk to physician and clinical medical professional	Make appointment under the guidelines established for the office	Medical administrative assistant
Office supply sales representative	Take message and give to staff member chiefly responsible for buying office supplies	Identified staff member

Modified from Potter BA: *Medical office administration: a worktext,* Philadelphia, 2003, Saunders.

- Changing or confirming a patient's appointment.
- Making outpatient appointments or patient referrals.
- Ordering supplies or laboratory forms.

Long-Distance Calls

When you need to call a person or company in a different state, it is important to know in which *time zone* the person or company is located. Fig. 4-1 shows the time zones of the United States and Canada. For example, if you were in an office in Massachusetts and needed to make a call to Nevada,

you would need to remember that Nevada is 3 hours *behind* Massachusetts in time. Therefore 9 a.m. in Massachusetts is 6 a.m. in Nevada. Some medical offices require that all long-distance phone calls be recorded in a long-distance phone log (caller, time, reason for calling). Check your office policy manual for any special considerations for long-distance calling.

Telephone Directory

At times you may need to look up a phone number and use a telephone directory. The telephone directory's "white pages" list residential phone numbers

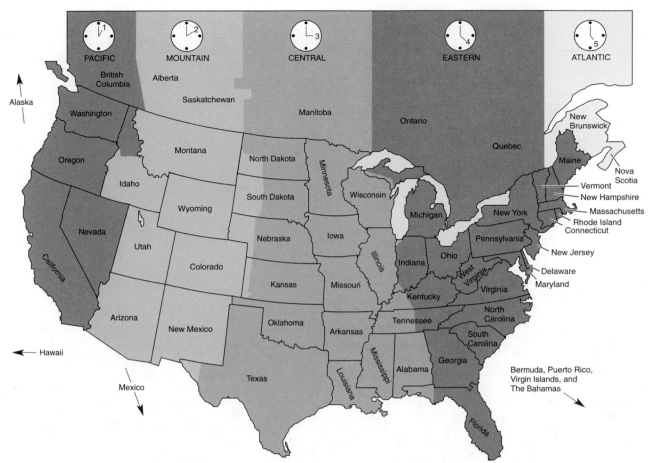

Fig. 4-1 Time zones in the United States and Canada. *(From Hunt SA: Fundamentals of medical assisting, Philadelphia, 2002, Saunders.)*

and addresses in alphabetical order by residents' last names. The "yellow pages" list area businesses' contact information in alphabetical order by the business (or business owner's) name and type of business. Some telephone directories contain a special section that lists local government or municipal contact information (city hall, public works, governmental offices, schools). Many medical offices keep a listing of frequently called phone numbers (laboratories, local hospitals and pharmacies, supply companies). This may be a printed list or a file stored on the office computer system.

PATIENT-CENTERED PROFESSIONALISM

- What telephone techniques would you use if you were responsible for answering the telephone at the medical office? What impact will this have on patients who call?
- Why must the medical assistant be aware of telephone etiquette? What are some general guidelines to follow?

SCHEDULING APPOINTMENTS

An administrative medical assistant is often the person who schedules appointments in the medical office. For consistency, it is best if only one person schedules the appointments, but this is not always possible, especially in a large practice. Although offices should have their own set of policies and procedures, some general principles apply when scheduling appointments effectively. Medical assistants need to understand the importance of effective scheduling, how to use the office appointment book, and the techniques available for scheduling appointments or the computerized scheduling feature of their practice management software.

Effective Scheduling

Good scheduling management allows for efficient office functioning. The scheduling system chosen must be flexible enough to handle emergency situations as well as the routine daily schedule. Patients do not find it acceptable to wait for long periods.

Monday - January 2

Dr. Jones		Dr. Smith		Dr. Doe	
8		8		8	
:10		:10		:10	
:20		:20		:20	
:30		:30		:30	
:40		:40		:40	
:50		:50		:50	
9		9		9	

	Dr. Link Monday February 2			Dr. Link Tuesday February 3	
8^{00}			8^{00}		
:15			:15		
:30			:30		
:45			:45		
9^{00}			9^{00}		
:15			:15		
:30			:30		

Fig. 4-2 The appointment book allows for appointments of differing lengths of time to be recorded (e.g., 10 minutes to 60 minutes).

Few patients are willing to wait longer than 20 minutes. Having an appointment schedule that accommodates the physician's preferences and commitments allows for a smoothly operating practice. Each office should have a standard for the time needed for each type of procedure so that the medical assistant can gauge the time needed for the appointment and assign appointments accordingly.

Making the schedule flow smoothly can be a challenge for the medical office. It takes the cooperation of all staff members to make it happen. But effective scheduling is the backbone of an efficient medical practice.

Appointment Book

Many types of appointment books are used in medical offices today. Often, appointment books are spiral-bound, and each page is dated and contains a day of the week. The time allotted for appointments varies from every 10 minutes to every 60 minutes (Fig. 4-2). The appointment book must be accurate because the daily workflow depends on its contents.

Before appointments can be made, it must be determined when the physician is available. Most offices establish a **matrix** (reserved time) or develop some other format to block off time that is *not* to be used in patient scheduling. Using a slanted line or an "x" to mark off the nonpatient appointment periods informs staff about when the physician is not able to see patients. A brief statement explaining this notation is used (e.g., "hospital rounds"; Fig. 4-3). Open appointment times are indicated by the blank boxes in the grid.

Procedure 4-4 explains the process of establishing the matrix of an appointment book page and scheduling a patient appointment in detail. When appointments are entered, the patient's name and phone number are entered. If a patient is a "no-show" or cancels the day of the appointment, a notation next to the patient's name must be placed in ink. This documentation protects the

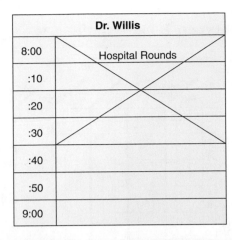

Dr. Willis	
8:00	Hospital Rounds
:10	
:20	
:30	
:40	
:50	
9:00	

Fig. 4-3 Time is blocked off of the appointment book when Dr. Willis will be out of the office doing hospital rounds.

Procedure 4-4 Prepare and Maintain an Appointment Book

TASK: Establish the matrix of an appointment book page and schedule a new and established patient appointment.

EQUIPMENT AND SUPPLIES
• Appointment book
• Office policy for office hours and list of physician's availability
• Pencil
• Calendar

SKILLS/RATIONALE

1 Procedural Step. "Matrix" the appointment book.
a. Identify and mark with an "X" in an appointment book those times when the office is not open for patient care.
b. Determine the hours that each physician will not be available for appointments.
C Block out time for emergency visits, and reserve time for unexpected needs.
NOTE: This can be accomplished manually in an appointment book or electronically in a computer software program. (For the purposes of this procedure, this task is performed manually in an appointment book.)
Rationale. Predetermined time(s) must be blocked out on the appointment book so that patients are not inadvertently scheduled to be seen during these times. "Matrixing" the appointment book shows the available time slots that can be used for patient appointments.

2. Procedural Step. Schedule an appointment.
a. When a patient requests an appointment time, identify the patient's chief complaint to determine the amount of time needed for the appointment.
Rationale. The patient's chief complaint determines the amount of time required for the visit. Office policies should be established to provide standard procedure times for patient scheduling.

b. Identify whether the patient is a new or an established patient.
Rationale. New patients often require a longer office visit than established patients.
c. Enter the patient's full name, reason for the visit, and patient's day phone number (home, work, or cell number) in the appointment book.
Rationale. Writing in a reason for the visit allows the clinical assistant to prepare equipment and supplies needed for the visit. Writing in a telephone number allows for quick reference if the patient must be rescheduled for any reason. If the patient is new to the facility, write "NP" (new patient) after his or her name.
NOTE: An appointment book is a legal document and can be subpoenaed as evidence in court. Because of this, appointments should be entered in ink. However, if a manual appointment book is kept, standard practice is to enter the appointments in pencil to allow for changes such as rescheduling. A record of no-show appointments should be kept and documented in patient records. A photocopy of the appointment page is accepted as a permanent record.

Continued

Procedure 4-4 Prepare and Maintain an Appointment Book—cont'd

1-c

APPOINTMENT SCHEDULE

	Dr. Lawler	Dr. Hughes	Dr. Lopez	DAY	Mon. 10/13	Tue. 10/14	Wed. 10/15	Thu. 10/16	Fri. 10/17	Sat. 10/18

Dr. Lawler — hospital rounds

Dr. Lopez — satellite office

lunch

catch-up

meeting at hospital

medical practice in case of a lawsuit. The appointment book is a legal document; this is why most offices require that only dark-blue or black ink can be used to write in it. Other important aspects of scheduling appointments include the use of computerized appointment systems and abbreviations in scheduling.

Computerized Appointments

Computerized systems for appointment scheduling offer medical assistants great flexibility. The system will search a physician's schedule to locate an available appointment time. The schedule can be printed daily (Fig. 4-4). As with any computerized data, a backup system should be in place if the system fails.

Abbreviations

When an appointment is made, a reason should be recorded. Using an abbreviation allows the medical assistant to indicate the reason for the appointment without writing out the reason using complete words and sentences (e.g., "complete physical exam" is "CPE"). This is much quicker and also helps prevent spelling errors and hard-to-read explanations. Box 4-3 shows common abbreviations used for appointment setting.

New Patient Appointments

When a new patient calls the medical office for an appointment, you should obtain the following information:

Schedule for 10/13/XX for Dr. Howard Lawler

Time	Patient	Phone	Comments
8:00a	HOSPITAL ROUNDS		
8:20a	↓		
8:40a	↓		
9:00a	Wayne Harris	452-8117	New Patient; Complete Physical
9:20a	*****************		
9:40a	~~Ella Jones~~	~~932-8174~~	~~recheck~~ _cancel 8am 10/13_
10:00a	Fred Linstatt	452-0667	recheck
10:20a	Mary Higgens	731-8241	recheck; URI 2 weeks ago
10:40a	Tina Leggett	931-0451	PE
11:00a			
11:20a	Tracey Jones	462-0157	2-yr PE; father Robert
11:40a	Keth Jones		3-yr PE
12:00p	LUNCH		
12:20p	↓		
12:40p	↓		
1:00p	↓		
1:20p			
1:40p			
2:00p	Winston Hill	648-0791	PE
2:20p			
2:40p			
3:00p			
3:20p			
3:40p			
4:00p	Meeting at hospital		
4:20p	↓		
4:40p	↓		
5:00p			
5:20p			
5:40p			

Fig. 4-4 Computer-generated appointment schedule. *(From Hunt SA: Fundamentals of medical assisting, Philadelphia, 2002, Saunders.)*

BOX 4-3	Common Abbreviations Used in Appointment Setting

BP	Blood pressure check
Bx	Biopsy
Can	Cancelled
Cons	Consultation
CPE, CPX	Complete physical examination
ECG, EKG	Electrocardiography
FB	Foreign body
FU	Follow up (follow-up)
I&D	Incision and drainage
Lab	Laboratory
N&V	Nausea and vomiting
NP	New patient
NS	No-show
OV	Office visit
PAP	Pap (Papanicolaou) smear (test)
Pgt	Pregnancy test
PX	Physical
ReC, RECK	Recheck
Ref	Referral
RS	Reschedule
Surg	Surgery
S/R	Suture removal
UTI	Urinary tract infection
URI	Upper respiratory infection

Fig. 4-5 Medical assistant scheduling an appointment.

1. *Name.* Obtain the patient's last name, first name, and middle initial. Ask the patient to spell the last name to prevent an error.
2. *Address.* Obtain the home address and the billing address, if different from the home address.
3. *Telephone number.* Obtain the telephone numbers for home, cellular phone, and work so that an appointment time can be confirmed, canceled, or changed.
4. *Purpose of the visit.* This information is necessary to schedule the correct length of time for the appointment.
5. *Referral.* If another physician is referring the patient, try to schedule the patient as soon as possible. The patient needs to bring any applicable documents to the appointment.
6. *Insurance coverage.* Insurance information can be verified to save time when the patient comes into the office.

Procedure 4-5 explains the process of scheduling new patients in detail, both manually and using the computer.

Established-Patient Appointments

An established patient is any patient who has been seen in the past 3 years by the physician or another physician in the practice, no matter what the locale (patients who have not been to the office in 3 years should be considered "new" patients). The following information is needed when established patients call:

1. *Telephone.* Obtain the telephone numbers for both home and work for the same reason as a new patient.
2. *Purpose of the visit.* This is obtained, as with the new patient, for scheduling purposes.
3. *Insurance information.* Ask if the patient's insurance information has changed.

Appointment Techniques

Medical assistants are often responsible for scheduling appointments. An office policy listing time periods for the various types of medical services allows the medical assistant to assign appointment times accordingly. Routine office visits require an average of 15 to 20 minutes when only basic equipment and staff are needed (Fig. 4-5).

Each office must choose a method of scheduling appointments that fits the activities of the physician and needs of the office. Various techniques are used for scheduling patients.

Time-Specified or Streaming

Time-specified scheduling gives each patient an appointment for a definite period (e.g., 10-10:15

Procedure 4-5 Schedule a New Patient

TASK: Schedule a new patient for an office visit.

EQUIPMENT AND SUPPLIES
- Appointment book
- Telephone
- Pencil and paper

SKILLS/RATIONALE

1 Procedural Step. Obtain preliminary information.
  a Name of the physician for whom to book the appointment.
  b. Purpose of the appointment.
  c. Scheduling preferences of the patient.
  Rationale. It is important to have this information so you can then locate and schedule an appropriate appointment time slot in the appointment book.

2. Procedural Step. Obtain the patient's demographic information and chief complaint.
  a. Patient's name (verify the spelling of the name).
  b. Patient's address.
  c. Patient's daytime phone number, including cell or work number.
  d. Patient's date of birth.
  Rationale. Not all the information, such as the address and date of birth, will be recorded in the appointment book. This information will be used to start the patient's medical record. However, it is important that this information be gathered at the time the first appointment is scheduled.
  e. Determine the new patient's chief complaint, and ask when the first symptoms occurred.
  Rationale. This information is needed to help determine the length of time needed for the appointment and the degree of urgency.

3. Procedural Step. Determine whether the patient was referred by another physician.
  Reference the patient history form for this information or ask the patient directly. You may need to request additional information from the referring physician, and your physician will want to send a consultation report and a thank-you letter.

4. Procedural Step. Enter the appointment in the appointment book.
  a. Search the appointment book for the first available appointment time and an alternate time. Offer the patient a choice of these dates and times. It is best to give the patient two appointment options: a morning appointment on one date and an afternoon appointment on another date.
  Rationale. Patients are better satisfied if they are given a choice.
  b. Enter the time agreed on in the appointment book, followed by the patient's daytime telephone number, reason for visit, and the abbreviation "NP."
  Rationale. Writing in a reason for the visit allows the clinical assistant to prepare equipment and supplies needed for the visit. Writing in a telephone number allows for quick reference if the patient must be rescheduled for any reason. "NP" establishes the new patient status.

5. Procedural Step. Obtain additional information at the time the appointment is made.
  a. Request insurance information and explain any financial policies at the time the appointment is made.
  Rationale. This ensures that the patient will be aware of the payment policy and that the office can verify insurance benefits before the appointment.
  b. Provide directions to the office, as well as any special parking instructions.
  Rationale. This provides for excellent customer service and relieves any patient anxiety about being able to find the medical facility. (See Procedure 4-1.)
  c. Repeat the day, date, and time of the appointment, and ask if the patient has any questions before ending the conversation.
  Rationale. This helps to verify that the patient understands when the appointment is scheduled and allows the patient one more opportunity to ask questions or clarify the office payment policy.

Continued

Procedure 4-5 Schedule a New Patient—cont'd

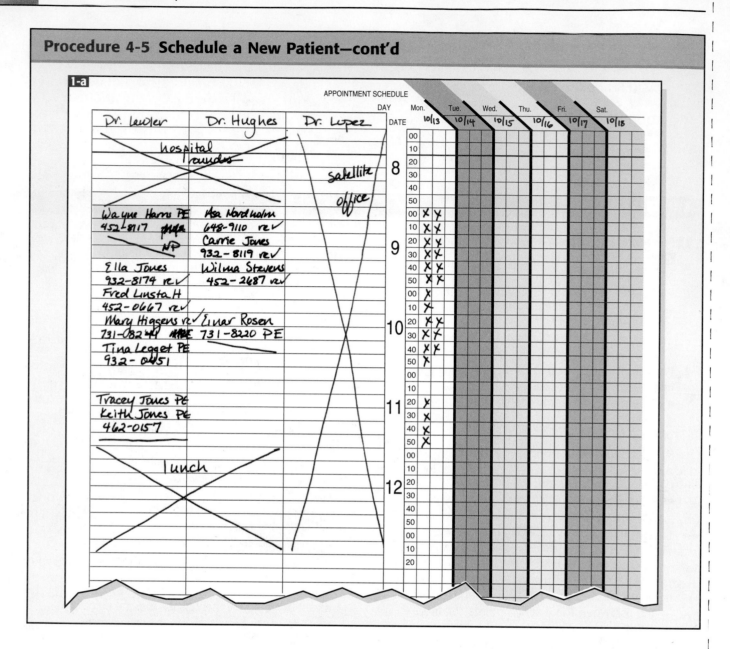

a.m.). The medical assistant scheduling the appointment needs to know exactly why the patient is being scheduled. A 15-minute appointment is adequate for a blood pressure check, but more time is needed for a well-patient visit. Streaming gives each patient a different length of time for his or her appointment based on the patient's chief complaint.

Wave

Wave scheduling is not as structured as the time-specified system and allows for more flexibility. Wave scheduling is designed to self-adjust and avoid backups. This type of scheduling takes into account no-shows and late arrivals. Each hour block is divided into the average-appointment time. For

example, if the average amount of time used for each appointment is 15 minutes, four patients could be scheduled between 9 and 10 a.m.. In this case the four patients would be given an appointment time at the beginning of the hour (9 a.m.). Patients are seen in the order of their arrival. The idea of this flexible appointment system is that each patient will not arrive at exactly the same time, or require the entire time, and by the end of the hour, all patients will be seen and the schedule will be on track.

Modified Wave

As with the wave method, **modified-wave scheduling** is also based on the idea that each visit will not take the required time. However, instead of scheduling the entire group of patients at the beginning of the hour, the group is split in half. One half of the group is scheduled for the beginning of the hour and the remaining on the half hour. Thus, using the example given in the wave method, two patients would be given a 9 a.m. appointment, and the other two would be given a 9:30 a.m. appointment. This allows time for catching up before the next hour begins.

Double Booking

Double booking is similar to wave scheduling, but instead of more than one patient being scheduled at the beginning of the hour, two patients are scheduled to see the physician at the same time. This is similar to an airline selling more seats than available. The assumption is there will be cancellations and no-shows. This form of scheduling is helpful if a patient needs to be seen that day and has no appointment, but it often causes the office schedule to fall behind. This type of scheduling should not be done on a regular basis, and patients should be informed that they are being double-booked, and that they will probably have to wait after arrival.

Cluster (Group) or Categorization

In **cluster scheduling**, several appointments for similar types of examinations are grouped. For instance, some medical offices will do complete physical examinations only on the last Friday of the month or only on Fridays. Grouping specialty examinations allows the practice to meet patient demands and is a better use of resources. Often, specialty personnel must see these patients (e.g., nutritionist), and the time they can be scheduled is limited.

Open Hours

Open-hour scheduling allows patients to be seen any time within a specified time frame on a first-come, first-served basis. This type of scheduling is typically used in walk-in clinics because of their steady flow of patients. An appointment book is often needed to establish a matrix and to mark which patient has arrived first. A disadvantage of this scheduling method is that patients may have to wait for a considerably long time, depending on the number of patients already there when they arrive.

Acute Needs

From time to time, patients call and request to see the physician the same day. The medical assistant will have to screen the patient to determine the urgency of the call and the need for an immediate office appointment. Office criteria should be developed to determine what constitutes an **emergency.** The physician or other supervisory medical staff must be available to help with the decision process. Some patients will be advised to go directly to the emergency room because of their condition. If a patient is scheduled to come in on an emergency basis, it usually means the patient is told to arrive at the end of the day, or to come in right away, but the patient may have to wait.

Some offices build a "buffer period" into their schedule to accommodate emergencies or walk-in patients. This buffer period is a designated flexible hour in the schedule that is used to meet the needs of patients while not disrupting the rest of the schedule. After all, patients cannot predict when they will become sick or injured.

Special Circumstances

Problems that disrupt the scheduling process include "no-shows," cancellations, late arrival of patients, late arrival of the physician, and unexpected times when the physician is called away from the office. Inclement weather can make travel dangerous, resulting in cancelled appointments. An electrical power loss can cause a medical practice to close, resulting in the cancelling or rescheduling of appointments.

NO-SHOWS AND CANCELLATIONS

Patients sometimes fail to keep an appointment or cancel an appointment without rescheduling. A follow-up call should be made to the patient when this occurs to find out the reason and to reschedule if necessary. "No-show" information needs to be noted in the appointment book and on the patient's health record for legal purposes. Patients who do this chronically are "noncompliant with treatment."

LATE ARRIVAL OF PATIENTS

If a patient is repeatedly late for a scheduled appointment, scheduling the person at the end of the day helps to alleviate the resulting delay.

LATE ARRIVAL OR UNEXPECTED ABSENCE OF PHYSICIAN

Patients understand occasionally waiting for the physician, usually 20 minutes, but repeated lengthy waits result in agitation and stress. Patients should be notified if they will be required to wait more than 20 minutes. This shows respect for their time and allows them an opportunity to reschedule. Always notify patients if the physician will be delayed, and give an approximate time of the physician's arrival. Patients may take this opportunity to run an errand or make some phone calls. This reduces their stress and the resulting stress placed on the office staff.

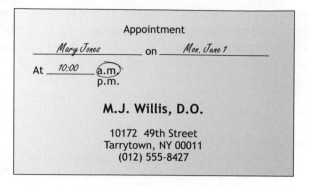

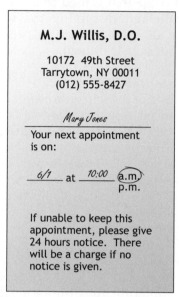

Fig. 4-6 Appointment reminder card.

Appointment Reminder

An appointment reminder card helps patients remember their next appointment. Many patients will carry the card in their wallet or purse for easy reference. It should be given to patients before they leave the office. If a new patient schedules an appointment, an appointment card can be sent with the patient information packet.

The appointment card takes many forms, but the information it contains is standard. The following information is imprinted on the card (Fig. 4-6):

- Line to record patient's name
- Line(s) to record date and time of appointment
- Physician's name, address, and telephone number
- Sometimes, office policy concerning cancellations

Another way to remind patients about upcoming appointments is with a phone call. The medical assistant may call each patient scheduled for an appointment the day before as a reminder.

Scheduling Ancillary Appointments for Patients

Sometimes medical assistants schedule patients for surgery, x-ray consultations, referrals, and outpatient diagnostic testing (Procedure 4-6). To make certain these things are done in a timely manner, the medical assistant will often call and schedule the appointment as a convenience for the patient.

Each health care plan has its own requirements before providing an authorization number. For an example of information often required before admitting or scheduling a procedure for a patient, review Table 4-2.

PATIENT-CENTERED PROFESSIONALISM

- Why is it important to follow established guidelines when scheduling patients? What are the established guidelines?
- How would you handle the situation of a physician being delayed for his afternoon appointments? How are patients affected by this situation?

HANDLING MAIL

Handling correspondence is an important administrative medical office duty. Incoming and outgoing medical office mail needs to be handled properly to make sure patients and office staff alike receive their correspondence. Setting protocol for the efficient handling of incoming and outgoing mail is key in an organized daily routine, which will include other duties for the medical assistant. Medical assistants responsible for handling the mail should familiarize themselves with postal laws, regulations, and procedures. The United States Postal Service (USPS) Website, www.usps.com, is a great resource for this information.

Interoffice mail, the mail coming from within the office, or from other offices of the same practice, can be handled in a variety of ways, according to office protocol. This type of correspondence does not go through the USPS.

Incoming Mail

When mail arrives, it needs to be sorted into categories before being opened. Many different types of mail will be sent to the medical office: payments, insurance correspondence, journals, personal mail, magazines, brochures, and advertisements. The sorting of mail saves valuable time for the physician and office staff. Letters marked "Personal" are separated from other mail and delivered unopened to

Procedure 4-6 Schedule Outpatient and Inpatient Appointments

TASK: Schedule a patient for a physician-ordered diagnostic test or procedure, either in an outpatient or inpatient setting, or inpatient admission within the time frame requested by the physician, confirm the appointment with the patient, and issue all required instructions.

EQUIPMENT AND SUPPLIES
- Physician's order for either an outpatient or inpatient diagnostic test, procedure, or inpatient admission
- Name, address, and telephone number of diagnostic facility performing the test, or the admitting facility
- Patient medical record
- Test preparation or pre-admission instructions
- Telephone
- Pencil

SKILLS/RATIONALE

1. **Procedural Step. Schedule appointment using an order for an outpatient or inpatient diagnostic test, procedure, or admission and the expected time frame for results.**
   Rationale. A physician's order is required before scheduling diagnostic tests, procedures, or inpatient admissions. The urgency of receiving the test results, having procedures done, or patient care affects the timing of the appointment.

2. **Procedural Step. Precertify the procedure with the patient's insurance company.**
   Rationale. In some cases it is important to confirm that a patient's insurance benefits are valid and the needed procedure will be covered by the patient's insurance policy. This is accomplished by contacting the insurance company directly.

3. **Procedural Step. Determine patient availability.**
   a. Call the patient to determine the availability of dates and times before scheduling the appointment.
   Rationale. This ensures that the patient will be able to comply with all arrangements. The best practice is to obtain an alternate date and time as well.
   b. Pull the patient's record before calling to schedule the test or admission.
   Rationale. All of the patient's information such as address, phone number, and insurance information will be requested by the facility. Having the patient's record accessible before calling ensures that information is readily available.

4. **Procedural Step. Contact the facility and schedule the procedure, test, or admission.**
   a. Provide the facility with the information needed for arrangements.
   - Order the specific test or procedure needed, or inform the facility of the admitting order.
   - Provide the patient's diagnosis.
   - Give the patient's name, address, daytime telephone number, and date of birth.
   - Provide the patient's insurance information, including policy numbers and addresses.
   - Establish the date and time of the procedure, or time of admission.
   - Determine any special instructions or requirements for the patient.
   - Notify the facility of any urgency for test or procedure results.

5. **Procedural Step. Notify the patient of arrangements, including the following:**
   a. Name, address, and telephone number of the facility.
   b. Date and time to report for the test, procedure, or admission.
   c. Instructions concerning preparation for the test or procedure (such as eating restrictions, fluids, medications, etc.).
   d. Tell what, if any, preparation is necessary.
   e. Directions to the facility and parking instructions.
   f. Ask the patient to repeat the instructions.
   g. Send written instructions to the patient, if applicable.
   Rationale. These details are provided to ensure that the patient understands the preparation necessary for the test and the importance of keeping the appointment.

6. **Procedural Step. Document.**

7. **Procedural Step. Conduct follow-up.**
   a. Place a reminder of the test, procedure, or admission on the physician's desk calendar or appropriate tickler file.
   b. Record the scheduled test, procedure, or admission on an office tracking log for follow-up with the facility if the results are not received in a timely manner.
   c. Place the notification for the test or procedure in the patient's record and make it available to the physician.
   Rationale. This allows for timely follow-up of the results, which will affect patient care.

TABLE 4-2 Scheduling Criteria for Inpatient and Outpatient Admissions and Procedures

Inpatient Elective Admission	Inpatient Direct Admission (Emergency from Medical Office)	Inpatient Procedure	Outpatient Admission	Outpatient Procedure
Patient demographics	Patient demographics	Patient demographics	Patient demographics	Patient demographics
Patient diagnosis	Patient diagnosis	Patient diagnosis	Patient diagnosis	Patient diagnosis
Physician admitting	Physician admitting	Physician admitting	Physician admitting	Physician admitting
Type of bed or floor	Type of bed or floor	Procedure room schedule	Type of bed or floor	Procedure room schedule
Insurance authorization	Insurance authorization	Insurance authorization	Insurance authorization	Insurance authorization
Patient preparation (fax admit orders to hospital on admission date)	Patient preparation (fax admit orders directly to designated floor)	Patient preparation (provide patient with instructions)	Patient preparation (fax admit orders to hospital on admission date)	Patient preparation (provide patient with instructions)
Preadmission testing		Preadmission testing	Preadmission testing	Preadmission testing
		Length of procedure		Length of procedure
		Anesthesia required		Anesthesia required
Notify patient of dates and other information	Notify physician	Notify patient of dates and other information	Notify patient of dates and other information	Notify patient of dates and other information

the person to whom they are addressed. If a "Personal" letter is accidentally opened, "Opened in error" should be noted on the envelope with the opener's initials.

The USPS classifies U.S. mail into several types, or classes (Box 4-4). Considerations for handling incoming mail include the following:

- First-class mail should be opened with a letter opener (to avoid damaging the contents), date stamped, and inspected for signatures, enclosures, and complete addresses.
- Envelopes should be attached to the correspondence to which they belong, if the date of mailing might become an issue (e.g., legal notices, delinquent bill payments).
- Correspondence received from patients or other physicians regarding a patient's illness, laboratory reports, pathology reports, and operative reports should be attached to the patient's medical record and placed on the physician's desk.
- When payments are received, the payment is entered in the daily journal and posted on the

BOX 4-4 U.S. Postal Service (USPS) Mail Classifications

- *First-class* mail includes all sealed or unsealed letters up to and including 11 ounces (e.g., correspondence, statements).
- *Second-class* mail includes newspapers, journals, and magazines.
- *Third-class* mail includes circulars and advertising materials that weigh less than 16 ounces.
- *Fourth-class* mail includes library material, packages, and manuscripts weighing 1 to 70 pounds with a combined girth of 108 inches.

patient's ledger card or account by the appropriate person.
- Mail should be arranged according to importance and placed on the physician's desk (i.e., first-class mail on top).
- The physician will need to initial all papers that require proof that he or she has read them (e.g.,

laboratory reports, pathology reports). Initials signify that the physician has reviewed the material personally.

Outgoing Mail

Correspondence that leaves the medical office should be prepared properly. This helps ensure it will arrive at its destination quickly and will create a professional impression. General guidelines for properly preparing outgoing mail are as follows:

- Copies of all correspondence should be made, providing a record of what was sent, and filed in the patient's record. The original letter and a typed envelope should be clipped together and placed on the physician's desk for signature.
- Use the appropriate handling method to send the mail (Box 4-5).
- Fold the letter or correspondence correctly before placing inside the envelope.
- Prepare the envelope properly.

These guidelines are discussed in detail in the following sections. The volume of mail leaving the office will increase when patient statements are sent out. A postage meter reduces the time spent in stamping the envelopes and saves frequent trips to the post office to purchase stamps. The postage meter can be set for the proper class of mail and the correct amount and date.

Folding Letters

The folding and inserting of a letter will depend on the letterhead used and the envelopes provided. The letter should be faceup and folded into thirds to fit into a #10 envelope (Fig. 4-7). If a #6¾ envelope is being used, the letter should be folded in half, and then into thirds (Fig. 4-8).

Envelope Preparation

When addressing an envelope, following simple guidelines helps the post office speed the mail to its destination.

1. A business letter envelope is $4\frac{1}{8} \times 9\frac{1}{2}$ inches (#10). The address should begin 14 lines from the top and 4 inches from the left edge of the envelope. This is the most common envelope used for correspondence.
2. A standard size envelope is $3\frac{5}{8} \times 6\frac{1}{2}$ inches (#6¾). The address should begin 12 lines down from the top and 2 inches from the left edge.
3. Use only capital letters to start words throughout the address.
4. Do not use punctuation.
5. Use single spacing and block format.
6. Use two-letter abbreviation for state, district, or territory. State abbreviations of two

---

BOX 4-5 Special Handling Methods for Mail

Most medical office mail is sent first class, but certain items require special handling.

- **Registered mail** is used when items have a declared monetary value and are being sent via first-class mail. Registered mail can be insured for a maximum amount of $25,000.
- *Insured mail* is also used when items have a monetary value, but it is used for items valued at $400 or less and being mailed via third- or fourth-class or priority mail.
- *Return receipt* is used when the medical office needs proof that an item mailed was received by the intended person. The recipient must sign the return receipt, which is returned to the sender, and this provides proof that the sender's mail was received.
- *Restricted delivery* is used when the item needs to be delivered only to a specific recipient. It can be used to help maintain patient privacy (e.g., delivery is restricted to only the patient, and no one else is authorized to receive the mail).
- **Certified mail** is used when it is necessary to prove that a letter was delivered. The recipient signs a return receipt to verify that the delivery was made. Certified mail is used for items that are considered urgent. It also provides proof that that an item was mailed. A letter sent to discharge a patient from the practice must be sent by certified mail. The receipt is kept with the patient's record.
- *Express mail* guarantees overnight delivery within the United States.
- *Priority mail* is first-class mail weighing more than 11 ounces and up to 70 pounds. It is the fastest method to have heavier mail delivered within 2 or 3 days.
- *Mailgrams* are special services offered by both the U.S. Postal Service (USPS) and Western Union.

---

letters without periods or spaces were developed to use with the *optical character reader* (OCR), which reads numbers, capitals, and small letters typed by machine or word processor. OCR has all post office locations and zip code numbers and can recognize the state abbreviation faster than the whole word. Box 4-6 provides a list of acceptable state abbreviations.

7. The last line in the address must have the city, state, and zip code. Using zip codes speeds mail to its destination. A zip code directory can be

Fig. 4-7 Method of folding a letter to place inside a #10 envelope. *(From Young AP, Kennedy DB: Kinn's the medical assistant, ed 9, Philadelphia, 2003, Saunders.)*

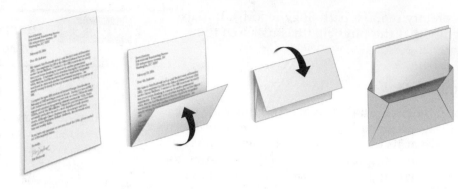

Fig. 4-8 Method of folding a letter to place inside a #6¾ envelope. *(From Young AP, Kennedy DB: Kinn's the medical assistant, ed 9, Philadelphia, 2003, Saunders.)*

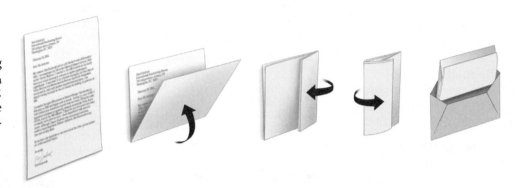

BOX 4-6	State Abbreviations for Mailing Addresses							
AK	Alaska	GU	Guam*	ME	Maine	NJ	New Jersey	SD	South Dakota
AL	Alabama	HI	Hawaii	MI	Michigan	NM	New Mexico	TN	Tennessee
AR	Arkansas	IA	Iowa	MN	Minnesota	NV	Nevada	TX	Texas
AZ	Arizona	ID	Idaho	MO	Missouri	NY	New York	UT	Utah
CA	California	IL	Illinois	MS	Mississippi	OH	Ohio	VA	Virginia
CO	Colorado	IN	Indiana	MT	Montana	OK	Oklahoma	VI	Virgin Islands*
CT	Connecticut	KS	Kansas	NC	North Carolina	OR	Oregon	VT	Vermont
DC	District of	KY	Kentucky	ND	North Dakota	PA	Pennsylvania	WA	Washington
	Columbia*	LA	Louisiana	NE	Nebraska	PR	Puerto Rico*	WI	Wisconsin
DE	Delaware	MA	Massachusetts	NH	New	RI	Rhode Island	WV	West Virginia
FL	Florida	MD	Maryland		Hampshire	SC	South Carolina	WY	Wyoming
GA	Georgia							

*Not a state, but this abbreviation is used.

purchased at the post office or can be found on-line. It is important to recognize that only 27 characters are to be used in the last line, including spaces.

8. If mail is to be sent via special handling (e.g., registered mail), this needs to be identified in all-capital letters and placed below the stamp.

Fig. 4-9 shows properly addressed envelopes.

PATIENT-CENTERED PROFESSIONALISM

- Why is it important to sort the mail in a planned sequence?
- How important is it to follow USPS guidelines when addressing an envelope?
- How might patients be affected if mail is not handled efficiently?

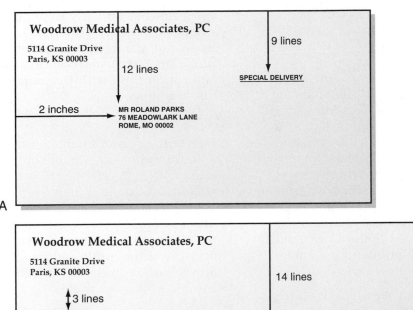

Fig. 4-9 Correct format for addressing **(A)** #6¾ envelope and **(B)** #10 envelope.

MANAGING WRITTEN CORRESPONDENCE

All written correspondence from the medical office must create a good impression. It should be neat, in the correct format, professional and courteous in tone, and error-free. You need to understand the basic guidelines for effective written correspondence as well as the writing formats used for business letters, memos, and manuscripts.

Guidelines for Effective Written Correspondence

All written correspondence, whether sent within the office or out to patients or other organizations, needs to be written in a clear, concise, professional way. Basic guidelines for effective written correspondence are as follows:

1. Before writing, plan the message so that it meets the needs of the reader. The message should contain all the information the receiver needs to have, written in good grammatical style.

2. Present ideas positively (e.g., "Please feel free to call if I can be of assistance" instead of "If I can be of further help, please do not hesitate to let me know").

3. Include all essential information. Confusion or errors can result when a letter does not include all essential information. Often, time is wasted because a second letter needs to be written to add to or clarify the first communication.

4. Ensure clarity. Written communications need to be written clearly so that they cannot be misunderstood.

5. Write in an action-oriented style (e.g., "We will mail you the lab report" instead of "The lab report will be mailed to you"). Clear, direct writing is effective and efficient.

6. Use concrete, or specific, language (e.g., "a fever of 106.4° F" instead of "a high fever"). Confusion exists when general statements are used because the reader may have difficulty understanding the meaning.

7. Use proper sentence structure.

8. Use proper paragraph structure.

9. Edit and proofread messages carefully. Reviewing basic grammar, punctuation,

capitalization, and word usage rules will assist in the editing process.

Proofreading

As you know, any communication a patient receives from the medical office creates an impression. Clear, well-organized, accurate communication creates a good impression; communication that is not clear, organized, or accurate creates a negative impression. Before sending anything you write or type, you need to proofread it to be certain the document is free of errors. Some medical assistants proofread directly from the computer screen, scrolling line by line. Others prefer to print out the document and proofread the hard copy. Key points to remember when **proofreading** are as follows:

1. When reviewing a letter, pay close attention to the date, enclosure notation, and recipient's name.
2. Concentrate as you read, and check for keying errors. Even though most word processors have a spelling checker, it will not detect a miskeyed word if it is another word spelled correctly (e.g., mistakenly keying "spat" instead of "stat," or "two" instead of "too").
3. Use the correct word (e.g., affect/effect, advice/advise)
4. Check punctuation after proofreading for spelling and word usage.

Table 4-3 lists frequently used proofreading symbols and proofreader's marks. Always be sure to read over the printed copy of a document before sending it.

Letter and Memo Preparation

Medical office correspondence is often in the form of letters, memos, and electronic mail (e-mail, discussed in Chapter 9). Medical assistants need to use the correct form when using these types of correspondence.

Business Letters

A business letter includes the following elements:

1. *Date line.* The position of the date line on the page depends on the style of the letter used.
   - Typed three lines below the letterhead.
   - Written as month, day, and year (e.g., October 1, 2009, not 10/1/09).
   - Date the letter using the day it was dictated or written, not the day typed.
2. *Inside address.* When using letterhead, the inside address contains the name and address (with zip code and any suite numbers) to whom the letter is written. If not using letterhead, the name and address of the physician and medical office are also included and appear flush with the margin before the inside address.
   - Typed three to eight lines below the date line.
   - Place the person's name on the first line and the company's name on the second line.
   - Contains no more than five lines.
   - Single-space the address.
3. *Attention line.* May be used if a person's name is not known or is not stated on the first line of the inside address. The attention line is flush with the left margin of the letter.

EXAMPLE:

QRS Insurance Company

41 Main Street

Buxton, OR 11000

(skip 2 lines)

ATTENTION: Medical Director

4. *Salutation.* This is the opening greeting of the letter.
   - Typed two to four lines below the inside address.
   - If an "attention" line is used, type the salutation two spaces below the attention line.
   - Capitalize the first word, the title, and the surname. "Mrs." is used for married females; "Miss" or "Ms." may be a matter of personal preference.
   - Use a colon following the salutation (e.g., Dear Dr. Smith:).
   - Use "To Whom It May Concern" as a salutation in letters not addressed to any particular person.
5. *Subject or regarding line.*
   - Typed two lines below the salutation.
   - Should be short and to the point (e.g., Subject: Disability Evaluation).
6. *Body.* This is all the material between the salutation and the closing (the message).
   - Begins two lines below the salutation.
   - If the message is short, double-space; otherwise, single spacing is recommended.
   - Double-space between paragraphs.
   - If entire body is double-spaced, use indentation with new paragraphs.

TABLE 4-3 Proofreading Marks

Symbol or Margin Notation	Meaning	Example
ℒ or ɤ or ⟋	Delete	take it out
⌒	Close up	print as o ne word
ℰ	Delete and close up	cloʂse up
∧ or ⟩ or ⋏	Insert	insert here (something
#	Insert a space	put onehere
ℰ#	Space evenly	space evenly where indicated
stet	Let stand	let marked text stand as set
tr	Transpose	change order the
[	Set farther to left	too far to the right
]	Set farther to right	too far to the left
¶	Begin a new paragraph	the same is true. ¶In conclusion
ⓈⓅ	Spell out	set 5 lbs as five pounds
cap	Set in CAPITALS	set nato as NATO
lc	Set in lowercase	set South as south
ital	Set in italic	set oeuvre as oeuvre
bf	Set in boldface	set important as **important**
∨	Superscript or superior	3 as in πr^2
∧	Subscript or inferior	2 as in H_2O
⁀	Comma	red blue, and yellow
⌄	Apostrophe	Calvin's lizard was green.
⊙	Period	The end is near ⊙
; or ;/	Semicolon	1, this; 2, that
: or ⊙	Colon	is the following :
ℐℐ or ↶↷	Quotation marks	He said, I did it.
( )	Parentheses	Run fast now.

BOX 4-7 Examples of Complimentary Closing in Business Letters

Great Respect
Respectfully yours
Yours respectfully
Very respectfully yours

Formal
Yours very truly
Very truly yours

Less Formal
Sincerely yours
Yours truly
Yours sincerely

Friendly
Cordially yours
Yours cordially
Very cordially yours

7. *Closing.* This is the "goodbye" of the letter.
   - Typed two lines below the last line of the message (e.g., "Sincerely yours,").
   - Box 4-7 shows examples of acceptable closings.
8. *Signature line.* This is the name and title of the person who signs the letter.
   - Typed four lines below the complimentary close.
9. *Reference notation.* This is used when a person does not type his or her own letter. If the writer's initials are included, they are in all-capital letters, followed by a slash mark or colon, and then followed by the typist's initials in lowercase letters (e.g., TLM/rgn or TLM:rgn).
   - Typed two lines below the signature line, flush with the left margin.
10. *Enclosure notation.* Informs reader of any enclosures, or additional items, included in the mailing (e.g., Enclosure: Résumé).
    - Indicate the number of enclosures (e.g., Enc: 5).
    - Typed two lines below the last entry, flush with the left margin.
11. *Copy notation.* The courtesy "carbon" copy (CC) notation lists all the people receiving the letter in addition to the addressee.
    - Typed two lines below the last entry, flush with the left margin.

EXAMPLE:

CC: Audit ctm

Finance ctm

When letters are two or more pages long, the additional pages are printed on plain paper of the same quality and color as the letterhead used for the first page.

Procedure 4-7 explains the process of composing and proofreading business correspondence and preparing envelopes.

The letter in Fig. 4-10 illustrates the basic elements of a typical business letter in block-style format.

- Full-block format has all lines flush with the left margin, and punctuation at the end of the salutation and complimentary close is omitted. This type of formatting does not include indented paragraphs, which tend to slow a typist. This type of letter also appears more formal and business-like.
- Modified-block format has all letter parts flush with the left margin. The date, closing, and signature lines are centered on the page. This type of format is more traditional and appears more balanced.

There are other business letter styles, but currently, most correspondence is written in one of these two formats.

Memos

A **memo,** or memorandum, is written for employees within the medical office setting. Memos might provide details about an upcoming meeting or relay office policy decisions. The elements of a memo are simple and include the following:

1. *Heading.* The heading should include the name of the person receiving the memo, the sender's name, the subject, and the date. Fig. 4-11 shows two different formats.
2. *Body.* The body of the memo should be typed, single-spaced, with double spacing between paragraphs.

Memo writing should be concise. Copies of all memos circulated to office staff should be filed alphabetically by subject or by date in a binder. Many offices require staff initials as proof that everyone concerned has read the memo. See Procedure 4-8 for more details about composing a memo.

Manuscript and Report Preparation

A **manuscript** is an article for a journal or other publication. You may be asked by the physician to type a manuscript describing clinical research performed in the office. In addition, you may be asked to type various kinds of procedure reports and records.

Manuscripts

A manuscript begins with an **abstract,** which provides a brief summary of each section of the manuscript. The margin settings depend on if the document will be bound or unbound. An unbound

Procedure 4-7 Compose Business Correspondence

TASK: Compose, key, and proofread a business letter using the guidelines of a common style.

EQUIPMENT AND SUPPLIES
- Word processor, computer with printer, or typewriter
- Paper
- Letterhead stationery
- Pen or pencil
- Envelope

SKILLS/RATIONALE

1. **Procedural Step. Assemble all needed equipment and supplies.**
   a. Determine the letter style.
   b. Obtain the name and address of the recipient.
   Rationale. This allows for efficient use of time and ensures the letter will be sent to the correct recipient.

2. **Procedural Step. Prepare a rough draft of the letter.**
   a. Use established business correspondence guidelines. (Refer to Fig. 4-10.)
   Rationale. This ensures that all topics are covered, that the appearance of the letter is professional, and that the correct format has been used. Working from a draft allows for quick corrections and ease of additions or rearrangement of information.
   b. Edit and proofread the draft carefully for grammatical, spelling, and punctuation errors. If the document was keyed, proofread for miskeyed information. (Refer to Table 4-3 for correct use of proofreading marks.)
   Rationale. All business correspondence represents the image of the practice. No correspondence should be sent from the office with errors, as it will reflect poorly on the medical practice. Spelling errors, and often grammatical and punctuation errors, can be corrected through the "spell check" function of the word processor. Remember, however, that if a miskeyed term is an actual word, it will not be identified as an error. The spell check function of a word processor must never replace careful and thorough proofreading of a draft.
   c. Correct errors on the rough draft.
   If the rough draft was handwritten, the correspondence should now be keyed. If the rough draft was originally keyed, make corrections and save.

3. **Procedural Step. Prepare the final draft of the letter.**
   a. Set the correct line spacing and margins for attractive placement of the letter.
   b. Print a copy on plain paper and review for errors and overall appearance of the final draft.
   Rationale. This avoids wasting letterhead if you decide changes need to be made once you have reviewed the hard copy.
   c. Insert letterhead into the printer. Print a hard copy of the final draft.
   This is the copy of the correspondence that will be sent.
   d. Remove the completed document and sign it, or present it to the physician for his or her signature.
   If the document is written under the medical assistant's name, the medical assistant will sign it. Remember that the medical assistant can send out correspondence requesting information for the office. The physician should sign all other correspondence.

4. **Procedural Step. Print copy of letter.**

5. **Procedural Step. Prepare the correspondence for mailing or electronic transmission.**
   a. Select the envelope size.
   b. Address the envelope according to postal OCR guidelines. (Refer to Fig. 4-9 for the correct method.)
   c. Trifold the letter with neat creases. (Refer to Figs. 4-7 and 4-8 for the correct method.)
   d. Insert the letter into the envelope. (Refer to Figs. 4-7 and 4-8 for the correct method.)
   e. Add postage.
   f. Mail the letter.
   Rationale. The appearance of the envelope is as important as the content. The envelope should be free of errors.
   NOTE: If the document is prepared for electronic transmission, the letter is sent as an e-mail attachment.

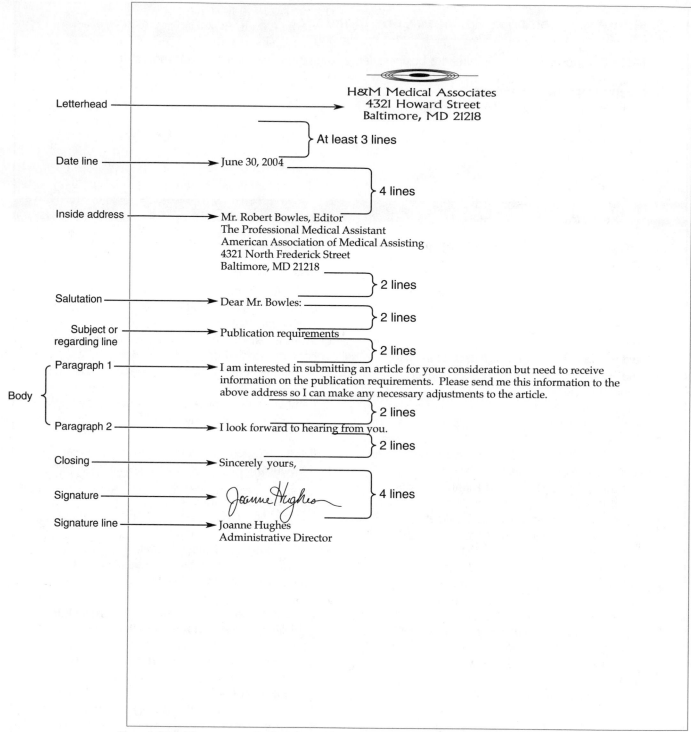

Fig. 4-10 Elements of a business letter (block style in full block format).

manuscript will have a 1-inch margin all around. A bound edition will have a 1½-inch left margin to allow for binding. Each publisher or journal will have set guidelines for submission of papers to be published. Manuscripts often include, but are not limited to, the following sections: title, abstract, introduction, main discussion, materials and methods, results or findings and discussion, conclu-sion, acknowledgments, references, and appendices. Manuscripts accepted for publication must follow the strict style format set by the individual publisher.

Medical Reports

A detailed record of the patient's care is necessary every time a patient is seen in a hospital, outpatient

Jones Medical Clinic

To: Office Staff

From: Sandy Wilton, Office Manager

Date: May 2, 2009

Subject: Staff Meeting

On Monday, May 9, 2009 Justin Collman, a representative from the Alliance Corporation will be here to discuss the new pension and profit sharing plan.

The meeting will be held from 12 to 2 in the office library. The doctors will permit the office to be closed 2 hours, with the answering service on for patient calls. No office appointments or lab services are to be scheduled for this time.

The booklets describing the plan were mailed to each employee's home a week ago. Please read through the booklet and come prepared for any questions you might have concerning the plan.

If you are unable to attend this meeting for any reason, please notify me in advance. Thank you.

Jones Medical Clinic

To: Office Staff   Date: May 2, 2009

From: Sandy Wilton, Office Manager   Subject: Staff Meeting

On Monday, May 9, 2009 Justin Collman, a representative from the Alliance Corporation will be here to discuss the new pension and profit sharing plan.

The meeting will be held from 12 to 2 in the office library. The doctors will permit the office to be closed 2 hours, with the answering service on for patient calls. No office appointments or lab services are to be scheduled for this time.

The booklets describing the plan were mailed to each employee's home a week ago. Please read through the booklet and come prepared for any questions you might have concerning the plan.

If you are unable to attend this meeting for any reason, please notify me in advance. Thank you.

Fig. 4-11 Memo formats.

clinic, or physician's office. This record is created when the health care provider dictates the results of tests, examinations, and procedures. Each facility will establish a format for the reports to satisfy auditing procedures and accrediting standards.

A medical office initiates the H&P, progress notes, and sometimes x-ray reports, whereas other report forms may be done by the hospital. Even so, it is important to be aware of the content of all types of reports because they are often copied to the medical office. Following are several types of basic medical reports used by facilities.

HISTORY AND PHYSICAL REPORT

The **history and physical (H&P) report** is the primary document because it must be in the patient's medical record before treatment is initiated. In a hospital setting the H&P must be transcribed within 24 hours of the patient's admission. Fig. 4-12 provides an example of a history in full-block format. The H&P details the patient's past medical history, surgery, allergies, and social and family histories. A review of the patient's body systems is done as well. The history consists of subjective findings as related by the patient (e.g., chief complaint, symptoms), and the physical examination provides objective data as determined by the physician (e.g., vital signs, height, weight).

CONSULTATION REPORT

A physician specializing in a specific field of medicine provides **consultation reports.** The primary physician requests a consultation from another physician when his or her expertise in that disease process is needed. The consulting physician examines the patient and then dictates a report of the examination, opinions about a course of treatment, and prognosis. This report is sent to the referring physician.

OPERATIVE REPORT

Immediately following a surgical procedure an **operative report** is dictated by the surgeon about the procedure (Fig. 4-13). Preoperative and postoperative diagnoses are included. The procedure done, any pathological specimens, the findings as a result of the procedure, and people involved in the surgical procedure are included.

RADIOLOGY REPORT

A **radiology report** describes the findings and the interpretation of all radiographs by a radiologist (Fig. 4-14). Some x-ray images require a dye (contrast media), use of ultrasound, or sensitive x-ray film. Each radiology format will include the date, type of study done, ordering physician's name, age of the patient, and the findings. The report will be signed by the radiologist who interpreted the film and made a clinical judgment.

DISCHARGE SUMMARY

The **discharge summary** is a final progress note about a patient who is leaving the hospital. It is a comprehensive review of the patient's hospital stay. It also includes the patient's condition at discharge, postdischarge medications prescribed for the patient, discharge diagnosis, and instructions for follow-up care and office visits.

Procedure 4-8 Compose a Memo

TASK: Compose, key, and proofread a memo.

EQUIPMENT AND SUPPLIES
- Word processor, computer with printer, or typewriter
- Paper
- Pen or pencil

SKILLS/RATIONALE

1. **Procedural Step. Assemble all needed equipment and supplies.**
   Rationale. This allows for efficient use of time and ensures the memo will be sent to the correct recipient(s).

2. **Procedural Step. Create a memo form, or access a template file.**
   Access a memo template from the word-processing template file. If a template is not available for use, key a Memo Form using the guidelines below. Save the blank document for future use.

   NOTE: If using Microsoft Word, a memo template may be accessed and created by performing the following steps:
   - On the **File** menu, click **New**.
   - In the **New Document** task pane, under **New Form Template,** click **General Templates**.
   - Click the **Memos** tab.
     If you do not see the Wizard in the **Templates** dialog box, you might need to install it.
   - Follow the steps in the Wizard.
     NOTE: You can use the Memo Wizard to create a memo for printing, e-mail distribution, or faxing.

3. **Procedural Step. Fill in the required data. (Refer to Fig. 4–11.)**
   a. *Date:* When keying the date, use the same rules as if writing a business letter.
   b. *To:* List the names of all recipients. Names can be listed by hierarchy or alphabetically.

   If sending the memo to a group or department, the department or group name can be listed (e.g., All Employees, Department Managers).
   c. *From:* List the name and title of the person sending the memo.
   d. *Subject:* Key a brief description of the purpose of the memo.
   e. *Body:* Key the memo message.
      NOTE: Salutations and closings are not used when sending memos.

4. **Procedural Step. Ensure the format is correct.**
   a. All lines of a memo are justified flush left.
   b. One-inch margins are used.
   c. The words *Date, To, From,* and *Subject* are double-spaced.
   d. The body is single-spaced, with double spacing between paragraphs.

5. **Procedural Step. Distribute the memo.**
   a. Proofread and edit the memo carefully using proofreader's marks (see Table 4-2).
   b. Make corrections as necessary.
   c. Print the memo from the computer and photocopy the required number of copies. Place a memo on each recipient's desk or in the person's "in-house" mailbox. Some facilities require the recipient to initial the memo and return it to the sender as an acknowledgment of receipt.
      NOTE: Memos can also be sent electronically in the form of e-mail or an e-mail attachment.

ST. VINCENT'S HOSPITAL
153 West 11th Street
New York, NY 10011-0000

HISTORY AND PHYSICAL

PATIENT: Gregory Williams   DATE: July 9, 20XX

MEDICAL RECORD NO: 86-90-14

PHYSICIAN: M. J. Willis, DO

CHIEF COMPLAINT: Gregory Williams, a 17-year-old white male, presented himself to the emergency room at 7:45 a.m. complaining that he had a pain in his abdomen, which started last evening and has persisted and worsened throughout the night.

DETAILS OF PRESENT ILLNESS: The pain was originally in the mid portion of his abdomen, but it gradually shifted and is mainly in his right lower quadrant. He had no nausea or vomiting. He ate a normal dinner, but he has had nothing by mouth since he awakened at 6:00 a.m. He did not sleep well during the night because of his discomfort. He has never had an attack like this before. His bowels have not moved. He has urinated twice without discomfort and with no effect on the abdominal pain.

PAST HISTORY: His only previous illnesses were tonsillitis, measles, and chickenpox with no complications or sequelae.

PHYSICAL EXAMINATION: Physical examination reveals a tall, thin, well-developed white male in obvious discomfort who is more uncomfortable when he moves. He is alert and answers all questions intelligently. His temperature was 99.4° F, pulse 100, blood pressure 110/78. Examination of his nose and throat were normal. Physical examination of his chest failed to show any abnormalities. Abnormal findings were primarily in the abdomen, without contact. His abdominal musculature seemed tense and he was holding himself tense. He was not breathing deeply. Excursions were flat. On abdominal palpation, his abdominal muscles were tense in the epigastrium and in the right lower quadrant. On palpation, he had severe tenderness and board-like rigidity in the lower right quadrant. Rebound tenderness was most pronounced in the right lower quadrant. Bowel sounds were not remarkable. On rectal examination, his rectum was clear and there was marked tenderness in his rectum, high on the right side. There were no hernias.

LABORATORY RESULTS: A blood count revealed a WBC of 16,000 with an increase in his differential. Urinalysis was normal.

IMPRESSION: On the basis of the blood count, history, and physical examination, a diagnosis of acute appendicitis was made and immediate operation was recommended. He agreed. Prior to operation, he had a physical examination by the surgical resident who found no contraindications to spinal anesthesia or an appendectomy.

PLAN: Gregory was admitted to the hospital and immediate appendectomy was performed.

_____

M. J. Willis, D.O.

MJW: bp
D: 9/9/20XX
T: 9/10/20XX

Fig. 4-12 Example of history and physical (H&P) report for patient with acute appendicitis admitted to hospital through emergency department. *(Modified from Sloane S, Fordney MT:* Saunders manual of medical transcription, *Philadelphia, 1994, Saunders.)*

ST. VINCENT'S HOSPITAL
153 West 11th Street
New York, NY 10011-0000

OPERATIVE REPORT

PATIENT: Sharon Crawford   DATE: May 18, 20XX

MEDICAL RECORD NO: 74-34-65   ASSISTANT: Isaac Jones, M.D.

SURGEON: M. J. Willis, D.O.

ANESTHESIOLOGIST: Steven Holt, M.D.

PREOPERATIVE DIAGNOSIS: Carcinoma of the transverse colon.

POSTOPERATIVE DIAGNOSIS: Same

OPERATION: Colectomy. Colocolostomy.

PROCEDURE: Two weeks ago the patient was operated on at this hospital for an intestinal obstruction, which was due to a carcinoma of the transverse colon. A bar colostomy was performed. In the interim period, the colon was cleaned out proximally and distally. No other lesions were found.

The patient was placed on the operating table in a supine position. Anesthesia was begun with intravenous sodium Pentothal. An endotracheal tube was inserted and inhalation endotracheal anesthesia was continued throughout the operation. There was a functioning transverse colostomy in the right upper quadrant. The abdomen was doubly prepped and draped. Using sharp dissection the colostomy was freed from the skin of the abdomen. This merely freed the colostomy from the adhered abdominal skin. The abdomen was not entered. The colostomy wall was closed with interrupted silk sutures. Drapes were removed and a full new abdominal prep carried out.

The colon was freed with sharp dissection from the abdominal wall opening in the peritoneal cavity. This allowed the closed colostomy to drop into the peritoneal cavity.

The entire peritoneal cavity was examined. The liver was free of any tumor. The entire large and small bowel was examined. There was a 4 cm irregular tumor in the mid-portion of the transverse colon encircling the colon. There was no evidence of any more tumor in the abdomen. The mesenteries were all clear of tumor. It was decided to resect en masse the tumor, the hepatic and splenic flexures, the transverse mesocolon and the omentum.

The omentum was freed, the midcolic artery was divided within 1 cm of the superior mesenteric artery. The arcade of the hepatic flexure was divided where it came off the right colic artery. On the left side the arcade was divided at the left colic artery. Hemostasis was established. It was possible to bring the remaining right colon and left colon together in an end-to-end anastomosis. A very adequate anastomosis was made.

The rents in the mesentery were closed. Hemostasis was established. The wound was closed with interrupted silk sutures. The specimen was examined. There was adequate margin. No lymph nodes were noted.

The patient tolerated the procedure well and left the operating room in good condition. Patient discharged from the hospital with wound well healed and bowels moving satisfactorily.

_____   MJW: ssb
M. J. Willis, D.O.   D: 5/18/20XX
                                               T: 5/19/20XX

Fig. 4-13 Example of operative report. *(Modified from Sloane S, Fordney MT:* Saunders manual of medical transcription, *Philadelphia, 1994, Saunders.)*

University Radiological Group, Inc.
1234 Main Street
Los Angeles, CA 90012-0000

NAME: Jane Doe DOB: 03/17/50 RM/BD: 513301 EDP# 75033 ORD# 00034
REFERRING PHYSICIAN: John Smith, M.D. PERFORMED BY CMK
DATE: 04/16/XXXX TIME: 1735
MJ DATE: 04/17/XXXX TIME: 1012
RADIOLOGIST: James Jones, M.D.
DATE AND TIME OF FINAL REPORT: 04/18/XX 1036
X-RAY# 000097959

EXAMINATION: CHEST PA & LATERAL

The heart size and contour are normal. There is streaky infiltration in the
left infraclavicular region extending back down toward the left hilar area.
There is somewhat similar interstitial infiltration in the projection of the 2nd
right anterior interspace. There are several smooth, rounded areas of
radiolucency within the infiltrate.

There are also interstitial infiltrations in the right, mid, and left paracardiac
regions.

The costophrenic angles are clear.

Impression: BILATERAL UPPER LOBE INFILTRATIONS WITH PROBABLE CAVITY
FORMATION WITH BRONCHOGENIC SPREAD TO THE RIGHT, MID, AND LEFT
LOWER LUNG FIELDS.

THE FINDINGS ARE MOST LIKELY ON THE BASIS OF TUBERCULOSIS, BUT THE
EXACT ETIOLOGY AND ACTIVITY MUST BE ESTABLISHED CLINICALLY.

James Jones, M.D.

JJ/alb
D: 4/18/XX
T: 4/18/XX

Fig. 4-14 Example of radiology report. *(Modified from Sloane S, Fordney MT: Saunders manual of medical transcription, Philadelphia, 1994, Saunders.)*

AUTOPSY REPORT

An **autopsy report** includes the preliminary diagnosis for a patient's cause of death, patient's medical history (if known), both internal and external examination impressions, and the results of microscopic examination of tissues. When a **necropsy** (autopsy) is done, the report should be part of the final medical record within 60 days.

PROGRESS NOTES

Progress notes are added to a patient's medical record each time the patient is treated. The physician records the patient's chief complaint, noting any significant aspect of the patient's condition, and the course of treatment, prescribed medications, and diagnosis. Progress notes are always recorded in chronological order, as are prescrip-

ROLAND, SARA   **MEDICAL RECORD NO: 678-99-08-02**

SUBJECTIVE:
Mrs. Roland returns today for a followup of her incontinence. A review of the history with the patient today indicates that she has had stress-related incontinence for 1 or 2 years requiring the use of pads. Interestingly, the patient has had marked urinary frequency of one or two times every hour for the past 15 or possibly 20 to 25 years. She has also had nocturia two or three times a night for a long period of time. This may be somewhat worsened by the diuretics she is currently using, but I suspect that she may have had this even prior to diuretic therapy.

OBJECTIVE:
ABDOMEN: The physical examination today demonstrates a massively obese abdomen. There is a well-healed midline infraumbilical incision from prior hysterectomy.

PELVIC: The pelvic examination demonstrates a mild cystocele and a moderate to severe rectocele. The speculum examination demonstrates no abnormalities, and the bimanual examination is not remarkable for tenderness or mass.

A renal sonogram has been performed and demonstrates normal renal units bilaterally. The remainder of the abdominal sonogram is likewise unremarkable. Cystoscopy demonstrates slight descensus of the bladder neck. There is diffuse erythema throughout the bladder. Upon distention of the bladder, punctate glomerulations or hemorrhages developed. The remainder of the examination is unremarkable. No tumors or stones are appreciated. The trigone is normal. The cystometrogram demonstrates an increased residual urine of approximately 100 mL. The first sensation, however, is at 75 mL and by 200 to 250 mL, the patient has moderately severe urgency with a maximum volume threshold of only 250 mL, which is about half of the normal capacity. A Marshall test was then performed and does demonstrate definite stress-related urinary incontinence. The Bonnie, or O-Tip, test suggests urethral hypermobility with a resting angulation of 45°. With Valsalva, there is some worsening of this. The patient has definite correction of the stress-related incontinence with elevation of the bladder neck during examination.

ASSESSMENT:
Mrs. Roland does definitely have urethral hypermobility with stress-related urinary incontinence and a rectocele that is currently asymptomatic. Unfortunately, the patient also has severe detrusor instability, a decreased volume threshold, and changes in the bladder, which may indicate a mild form of interstitial cystitis. This would certainly explain her chronic history of frequency and her diminished bladder capacity.

PLAN:
I discussed the various treatment alternatives with the patient. Although a bladder neck suspension may correct the incontinence, she would still be left with urgency, frequency, and possibly an inability to void successfully and would, therefore, require intermittent catheterizations. For these reasons, I do not feel this patient is an ideal candidate for a bladder neck suspension. I will, therefore, try to treat her medically. First, I will concentrate on the urgency and the frequency. The patient was given a prescription of Ditropan, 5 mg p.o.t.i.d., p.r.n. for 1 month with refills. I will see her in 2 months. If she has had some response to this, I could consider adding Ornade to improve her bladder neck tone.

D: 01–02–XX   T: 01–03–XX   Hal Griswold, M.D./mtf

Fig. 4-15 Sample chart entry using SOAP format (subjective, objective, assessment, plan). *(Modified from Sloane S, Fordney MT: Saunders manual of medical transcription, Philadelphia, 1994, Saunders.)*

tions, laboratory reports, and consultations (Fig. 4-15).

Medical Transcription

Occasionally, a medical assistant may be asked to perform the duties of a medical transcriptionist. A **transcriptionist** is a person who listens to recorded dictation and converts it to a written docu-ment. The process begins when the physician speaks into a machine (dictaphone) and the information is recorded. The transcriptionist listens to the recorded information through a headset and keys it into a word processor (or types it using a typewriter) (Fig. 4-16). This action produces a printed document, which is proofread and edited. Procedure 4-9 explains how to transcribe a machine-dictated document.

Procedure 4-9 Transcribe a Machine-Dictated Document

TASK: Transcribe a machine-dictated document, error free, in the correct format.

EQUIPMENT AND SUPPLIES
- Transcription machine with foot pedal and headset
- Computer with word-processing software and spelling checker, or typewriter
- Reference materials (English dictionary, medical dictionary)
- Paper
- Cassette tape with dictated materials

SKILLS/RATIONALE

1 **Procedural Step. Assemble supplies and equipment.**
Rationale. This allows for efficient use of time.

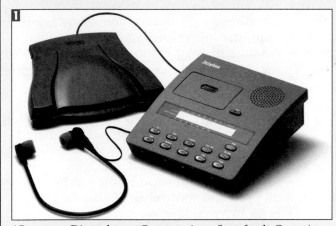

(Courtesy Dictaphone Corporation, Stratford, Conn.)

2. **Procedural Step. Turn on the computer and transcription equipment.**

3. **Procedural Step. Adjust the volume and speed control to comfortable levels.**
Rationale. The transcription machine allows for slowing down or speeding up the rate at which you can listen to the tape. This accommodates your typing speed.

4. **Procedural Step. Listen to the dictated report and key the document using the appropriate format.**

5. **Procedural Step. Proofread and edit the document using proofreading marks and reference material.**
Rationale. The completed document must be error free because it becomes part of the patient's permanent record and is considered a legal document.

6. **Procedural Step. Make corrections.**
   a. Once you have edited and proofread the document, carefully make the corrections.
   b. Proofread the document one more time.

7. **Procedural Step. Print the document.**
Rationale. The printed document is provided to the physician for his or her signature, and a copy is then placed in the patient's file.

8. **Procedural Step. Erase the tape, then rewind the tape back to the beginning.**
Rationale. This ensures that the tape is ready to use for the next dictation.

9. **Procedural Step. Turn off the transcriber.**

10. **Procedural Step. Remove the cassette from the transcriber, and store.**

PATIENT-CENTERED PROFESSIONALISM

- Why is it important for the medical assistant to develop good writing skills?
- Give an example of how a medical assistant's poor writing can negatively affect a patient.

〰 CONCLUSION

A medical practice must make a good impression on patients and other people involved in its services. A good reputation is important for keeping current patients and attracting new patients. Effective communication in the medical office makes new patients feel welcome, helps established patients continue to feel important, and ultimately ensures good patient care by preventing misunderstandings and errors. In the same way, written correspondence should reflect the medical practice's high standards for patient care and effective communication. Communicating effectively with patients instills confidence and can even help ensure that patients will follow their treatment plans.

Good communication is not just something medical office professionals should "try" to do. It is

Fig. 4-16 The medical assistant performing transcription.

something they *must* do to provide effective patient care.

SUMMARY

Reinforce your understanding of the material in this chapter by reviewing the curriculum objectives and key content points below.

1. Define, appropriately use, and spell all the Key Terms for this chapter.
   - Review the Key Terms if necessary.
2. Describe how a warm, professional greeting affects patients.
   - A cheerful, sincere personal greeting will make patients feel welcome and put them at ease.
3. Demonstrate the correct procedure for giving patients verbal instructions on how to locate the medical office.
   - Review Procedure 4-1.
4. Explain the purpose of the medical practice information booklet.
   - All new patients should be given information about the practice's policies and services.
   - The booklet will answer questions that patients might not think to ask.
5. Demonstrate the correct procedure for constructing a patient information brochure.
   - Review Procedure 4-2.

6. Describe how a medical assistant's tone of voice affects telephone conversations.
   - A person's telephone voice projects the professional attitude of the medical office.
7. List 12 guidelines for telephone etiquette and explain the importance of each.
   - Using good telephone etiquette is important when promoting a positive image of the medical practice.
   - Review the lists under "Telephone Etiquette."
8. Demonstrate the correct procedure for answering a multiline telephone system.
   - Review Procedure 4-3.
9. Explain the considerations for screening incoming calls.
   - Incoming calls should be handled promptly and messages taken accurately to promote an efficient and effective medical office.
   - Emergency calls receive immediate priority.
10. Explain the importance of a triage manual.
    - A triage manual (protocol guidelines) helps the receptionist screen incoming calls and determine the level of urgency.
    - Refer to Table 4-1.
11. Describe the process of placing a caller on hold when needed.
    - Avoid placing callers on hold whenever possible.
    - Always ask permission before placing a caller on hold and wait for their answer.
    - Refer to Procedure 4-3.
12. List the seven types of information documented when taking a phone message.
    - It is very important to obtain the necessary information in a phone message so that the call can be returned.
    - Review Procedure 4-3.
13. List three types of outgoing calls that administrative medical assistants may make.
    - Confirming appointments, referrals to other physician offices, and ordering office supplies are examples of outgoing calls an administrative medical assistant may make.
    - Outgoing calls are necessary to confirm appointments and to assist in making outpatient appointments.
14. Explain the importance for patients, medical assistants, and physicians of managing office appointments efficiently and consistently.
    - Daily workflow depends on the accuracy of the appointment book.
    - Everyone's stress levels in the medical office are reduced when appointments are scheduled and managed effectively.
    - Patients appreciate an office that runs on time.

15. Demonstrate the correct procedure for preparing and maintaining the office appointment book.
    - Review Procedure 4-4.
    - Appointment books may be on paper or on the computer.
    - Appointment slots should be assigned according to the type of procedure to be done.
16. List one method of blocking off, or reserving, time *not* to be used for patient scheduling.
    - Establishing a matrix is an effective way to block off time in the medical office schedule.
    - Time may be blocked out for physician vacations, meetings, court appearances, and so on.
17. Explain the considerations for canceling a patient appointment.
    The office may need to cancel patient appointments when:
    - An emergency dictates the physician is needed elsewhere.
    - Inclement weather makes traveling dangerous for patients and staff.
    - Facility problems occur, such as loss of electricity.

    If a patient cancels an appointment:
    - Make the rescheduling as convenient as possible for the patient.
    - If this is a noncompliant patient pattern, it needs to be documented in the patient's record.
18. List 10 abbreviations commonly used in scheduling appointments.
    - Using the correct abbreviation is vital.
    - Abbreviations save time and space when keeping the schedule.
    - Review Box 4-3.
19. Demonstrate the correct procedure for scheduling a new patient for an office visit.
    - Review Procedure 4-5.
    - Always follow the medical office's procedures for scheduling new and established patients.
    - Complete name, address, telephone numbers, purpose of visit, name of referring physician, and type of insurance coverage are essential pieces of information.
    - Inaccurate information gathered at the first new patient visit can generate multiple billing problems later.
20. List six appointment-scheduling techniques and explain the advantages and disadvantages of each.
    There are many techniques used for scheduling, and the one chosen for the office setting should complement the available resources.

Time specified. Every patient has an appointment for a definite time, so the office knows exactly how many patients to expect. The schedule runs smoothly as long as everyone shows up on time. Cancellations and no-shows leave time gaps in the schedule, resulting in underutilization of resources.

Wave. Four patients are given appointments for 15-minute time slots (e.g., for 9 a.m., and all seen by 10 a.m.). Schedule is flexible and self-adjusts (eventually all four patients will be seen within the hour). If all four patients show up at exactly the same time, however, some will have to wait.

Modified wave. Instead of the wave scenario above, two patients are given appointments at the hour (e.g., 9 a.m.) and two patients at the half-hour (e.g., 9:30 a.m.). All are seen within the hour (e.g., by 10 a.m.), but you are accommodating only two patients each half-hour, so the patient load is better distributed than with wave. Again, late arrivals, cancellations, and no-shows will affect the schedule.

Double booking. The time slot has two patients scheduled at the same appointment time, first come, first served. The method least favored by patients, double booking often involves more waiting, and patients feel rushed when they are with the physician. The advantage to the office is a "backup patient" in that time slot if the other patient scheduled cancels or is a no-show.

Cluster. Several appointments for similar visits are grouped (e.g., all physicals on Fridays). This scheduling allows for better utilization of staff resources but is often inconvenient for the patient.

Open hour. This method works best for walk-in clinics. No appointment is necessary; first come, first served. Advantages are patient convenience and often, evening and weekend hours. Disadvantage is not being able to predict the number of patients.

21. List two special problems that can occur in scheduling appointments and explain what can be done to prevent each.
    - Cancellations and "no-shows" mean office resources are not being used optimally because the physician is waiting for the patients. No-shows should be documented in the patient medical record. Chronic late offenders should be scheduled at the end of the day, and confirming reminder calls should be made a day before the appointment.
    - Emergency visits must fit into the schedule. Some offices will double-book in this case or

will have an allotted time in the schedule used only for emergencies.

22. Explain the purpose of an appointment reminder.
    - Patients can be reminded of appointments with cards or phone calls.
    - Appointment reminders minimize the number of missed appointments.

23. Demonstrate the correct procedure for scheduling a patient for outpatient diagnostic testing.
    - Review Procedure 4-6.

24. Explain why it is important to sort incoming mail.
    - Mail should be categorized when received according to order of importance to the recipient.
    - Sorting mail in order of importance saves time for the physician.

25. List four classifications of U.S. mail.
    - Understanding the classifications of mail will make it easier to process incoming mail and outgoing mail in the medical office.
    - Review Box 4-4.

26. List eight special services offered by the post office that can help medical offices track, insure, and receive delivery confirmation for the mail they send.
    - Special mailing services may be used depending on the type of item or correspondence being sent.
    - Certified mail and return receipts must be filed in the patient chart for legal purposes.
    - Review Box 4-5.

27. Demonstrate the correct preparation of an envelope.
    - Envelope preparation should follow the post office guidelines to promote efficiency of delivery.
    - Refer to Fig. 4-7 to 4-9.

28. Explain the proper use of a letter and a memo in medical office communication.
    - Memos are used for interoffice communication.
    - Letters are used to communicate with those outside the medical office (patients, vendors, other physicians).

29. List nine guidelines for preparing effective written communication in the medical office.
    - Plan the message.
    - Present the message positively.
    - Include all essential information.
    - Ensure clarity.
    - Use active, not passive voice ("action oriented style").
    - Use specific language the reader will understand.
    - Use proper sentence structure.

- Use proper paragraph structure.
- Edit and proofread the message carefully before sending.

30. Identify proofreader's marks used to edit written correspondence.
    - Proofreader's marks help the proofreader see what needs to be corrected before the correspondence is sent.
    - All correspondence must be proofread before being sent out of the office.
    - Refer to Table 4-3.

31. Demonstrate the correct procedure for composing, keying, and proofreading a business letter and preparing the envelope.
    - Review Procedure 4-7.
    - Correct formatting of a business letter creates a good impression of the medical practice and its staff.

32. Demonstrate the correct procedure for composing a memo.
    - Review Procedure 4-8.
    - Memos should be clear and concise.
    - Memos are used for interoffice correspondence.

33. Describe the format used to prepare a manuscript based on clinical research performed in the office.
    - Manuscript preparation follows defined guidelines and styles set by individual publishers.

34. List seven types of medical office reports and describe the purpose of each.
    - *History and physical* (H&P) reports are initiated by the medical office before treatment begins.
    - *Progress notes* provide documentation of every patient encounter and are a record of the patient's current status, including chief complaint, course of treatment, and diagnosis.
    - *Consultation* reports contain information about the examination, opinions of treatment, and the patient's prognosis as rendered by a specialist or another physician asked for a second opinion.
    - *Operative* reports describe the surgical procedure and include pathological specimens, results, and personnel involved.
    - *Radiology* reports describe the findings and the interpretation of all radiographs.
    - *Discharge summary* is the final progress note of the patient's stay in the hospital.
    - *Autopsy* report includes both internal and external examination of tissues and probable cause of death.

35. Demonstrate the correct procedure for transcribing a machine-dictated document.
    - Review Procedure 4-9.

- Transcription requires someone to listen to recorded information and produce the information in a written document.
- Transcription must be accurate; it becomes a part of the patient's record.

36. Analyze a realistic medical office situation and apply your understanding of medical office communication to determine the best course of action.
    - How does the medical assistant's attitude and treatment of callers and patients affect the functioning of the practice?

37. Describe the impact on patient care when medical assistants have a solid understanding of communication in the medical office.
    - Patient perception of the medical practice is formed in part through the communication they receive.
    - Greeting patients, answering the telephone, scheduling appointments, and writing effectively will create a positive impression of the medical practice.

FOR FURTHER EXPLANATION

Communication in the medical office is handled in several ways. The telephone is an important tool when doing business. Creating good first impressions by using telephone techniques that will make phone conversations more effective is vital.

1. **Research additional theories on telephone techniques.** How a caller is treated provides the person with an impression about the capabilities of the medical practice.

   Keywords: Use the following keywords in your search: telephone etiquette, phone etiquette.

2. **Research appointment scheduling.** For the medical office to operate smoothly, appointment scheduling must be done efficiently.

   Keywords: Use the following keywords in your search: appointments, appointment quest, medical appointments.

Chapter Review

Vocabulary Review

Matching

Match each term with the correct definition.

A. autopsy report

B. certified mail

C. cluster scheduling

D. consultation report

E. discharge summary

F. double booking

G. established patient

H. full-block format

I. history and physical (H&P) report

J. matrix

K. medical practice information booklet

L. modified-block format

M. modified-wave scheduling

N. new patient

O. open-hour scheduling

P. operative report

Q. progress notes

R. registered mail

S. time-specified scheduling

T. wave scheduling

___F___ 1. Appointment scheduling technique that schedules more than one patient during the same appointment time period

___M___ 2. Appointment scheduling technique based on the theory that each patient visit will not require the allotted time

_____ 3. Special mail-handling method used when the contents have a declared monetary value

___C___ 4. Appointment scheduling technique that groups several appointments for similar types of examination; also called *categorization scheduling*

___T___ 5. Appointment scheduling technique that divides an hour block into average-appointment time slots

_____ 6. Booklet or brochure that provides nonmedical information for patients about standard office policies

_____ 7. Letter format in which all lines are flush with the left margin, except the first line of new paragraph, date, closing, and signature (which are centered)

_____ 8. Medical report that lists a surgical procedure performed, any pathological specimens, the findings, and the medical personnel involved

___S___ 9. Appointment scheduling technique that provides a definite time period for the patient to be seen

_____ 10. Letter format that has all lines flush with the left margin

_____ 11. Medical report written by a specialist who sees a patient for a primary physician and then returns care to the primary physician

_____ 12. Appointment scheduling technique that allows patients to be seen without an appointment

_____ 13. Medical report that provides details about the cause of a person's illness and death through both internal and external examination findings

_____ 14. Written findings of a patient's condition

_____ 15. Patient who has not received professional services from the physician or the medical office in the past 3 years

_____ 16. Medical report that provides a comprehensive review of a patient's hospital stay

_____ 17. Patient who has received professional services from the physician or the medical office in the past 3 years

_____ 18. Format used to mark off or reserve time in a schedule

_____ 19. Special mail-handling method used to prove an item was mailed and received

_____ 20. Medical report that consists of a patient's subjective and objective data

Theory Recall

True/False

Indicate whether the sentence or statement is true or false.

_____ 1. The HIPAA privacy rule allows for incidental disclosure of patient information as long as appropriate safeguards and rules are in place and followed.

_____ 2. Cluster scheduling is similar to wave scheduling, but instead of more than one patient being scheduled at the beginning of the hour, two patients are scheduled to see the physician at the same time.

_____ 3. A patient should be notified if he or she will be required to wait more than 20 minutes for the physician.

_____ 4. Mail should be arranged in order of importance and placed on the physician's desk.

_____ 5. The subject line of a business letter should be typed four lines below the salutation.

Multiple Choice

Identify the letter of the choice that best completes the statement or answers the question.

1. What is the purpose of the medical information booklet/brochure?
   A. Provides answers to nonmedical questions
   B. Outlines a treatment plan
   C. Provides the patient with a wound care instruction sheet
   D. None of the above

2. A medical assistant's/receptionist's voice should be _____ when answering the telephone.
   A. high pitched and loud
   B. expressive but pleasant
   C. low pitched and monotone
   D. none of the above

3. Of the following supplies, a(n) _____ is NOT necessary to answer the telephone efficiently.
   A. patient's chart
   B. message pad or notebook
   C. pen/pencil
   D. appointment book

4. Of the following, which ending of a telephone conversation is most appropriate?
   A. Bye bye
   B. Talk to ya later
   C. Ciao
   D. Thank you for calling, Ms. Jones

5. When speaking with a caller, a medical assistant should NEVER _____.
   A. identify himself or herself
   B. use slang terms
   C. ask questions
   D. listen attentively

6. When placing a caller on hold, the medical assistant should _____.
   A. ask the caller if he or she minds being on hold for a moment and then wait for response
   B. say, "Just a minute," and put the caller on hold
   C. say, "I'm putting you on hold," and then push the hold button
   D. none of the above

7. Which one of the following is NOT a common type of call a medical assistant would receive on a routine basis?
   A. Emergency
   B. Payment or account balance information request
   C. Appointment
   D. Sales/telemarketing

8. Which one of the following would NOT be an acceptable outgoing telephone call a medical assistant would make as part of a routine day?
   A. Call to mother about dinner plans
   B. Call to make outpatient appointments
   C. Call to change or confirm a patient's appointment
   D. All of the above are calls a medical assistant would routinely make

9. Which medical office professional would professionally handle an incoming call regarding a patient who has been poisoned?
   A. Physician
   B. Medical assistant
   C. Medical administrative assistant
   D. Pharmaceutical sales representative

10. If another physician calls the office to speak to the physician, you should _____.
   A. take a message and send the message to the physician
   B. transfer the call to the clinical medical assistant
   C. transfer the call immediately to the physician in most circumstances
   D. none of the above

11. When an outside laboratory calls with lab results, you should _____.
   A. transfer the call to the physician
   B. transfer the call to the individual requested by the lab
   C. transfer the call to the business office manager
   D. take a message and return the call later

12. If a patient "no-shows" an appointment, the medical assistant should _____.
   A. erase the patient's name so another patient can be scheduled
   B. write in ink next to the patient's name that the appointment was a no-show and document the occurrence in the patient's chart
   C. do nothing
   D. never schedule the patient for another appointment

13. The appointment book is a legal document; therefore the medical assistant must use only _____ to write in the appointment book.
   A. green ink
   B. red ink
   C. black ink
   D. pencil

14. When a new patient calls the office for an appointment, you will need all of the following information EXCEPT _____.
   A. name
   B. address
   C. employer's name
   D. purpose of the visit

15. _____ gives each patient an appointment for a definite period of time.
   A. Wave scheduling
   B. Open-hour scheduling
   C. Cluster scheduling
   D. None of the above

16. Practices that schedule half of their patients on the hour and the other patients on the half-hour are using _____ scheduling.
   A. wave
   B. modified-wave
   C. cluster
   D. none of the above

17. _____ mail includes all sealed or unsealed letters up to and including 11 ounces.
    A. First class
    B. Second class
    C. Third class
    D. Fourth class

18. Which class of mail is used to send journals and magazines?
    A. First class
    B. Second class
    C. Third class
    D. Fourth class

19. When mailing an item that has a declared monetary value and is being sent first class, it is sent as _____ mail.
    A. certified
    B. insured
    C. registered
    D. restricted

20. Which one of the following describes how to correctly fold a letter for a size #10 envelope?
    A. Fold the letter in thirds face-up.
    B. Fold the letter in half and then into thirds face-down.
    C. Fold the letter in half face-up.
    D. Do not fold the letter.

21. Which one of the following does NOT apply when addressing an envelope?
    A. Use single spacing and block format.
    B. Use correct punctuation.
    C. Use the two-letter abbreviation for states.
    D. Use only capital letters to start words throughout the address.

22. When using letterhead, the _____ contains the name and address with zip code to whom the letter is written.
    A. salutation
    B. enclosure notation
    C. inside address
    D. copy notation

23. The _____ notation lists all of the people receiving the letter in addition to the addressee.
    A. enclosure
    B. copy
    C. reference
    D. salutation

24. Immediately following a surgical procedure, a(n) _____ is dictated by the surgeon about the procedure.
    A. H&P report
    B. consultation report
    C. pathology report
    D. operative report

25. A(n) _____ is a final progress note about a patient who is leaving the hospital.
    A. radiology report
    B. H&P report
    C. discharge summary
    D. pathology summary

26. A(n) _____ includes the preliminary diagnosis for a patient's cause of death.
    A. H&P report
    B. discharge summary
    C. progress note
    D. autopsy report

Sentence Completion

Complete each sentence or statement.

1. Using _____ allows the medical assistant to indicate the reason for an appointment without writing out the reason using complete words and sentences.

2. A(n) _____ is any patient who has been seen in the past 3 years by the physician or provider in the practice.

3. A(n) _____ helps patients remember their next appointment and can be given to the patient at the end of their current appointment.

4. A second method of reminding a patient about their appointment is to give them a(n)

   _____.

5. The _____ is a great resource for familiarization of postal laws, regulations, and procedures.

6. Letters marked _____ are separated from other mail and delivered unopened to the person to whom they are addressed.

7. When you need to call a person or company in a different state, it is important to know in which

   _____ the person or company is located.

8. Most offices establish a(n) _____ or develop some other format to block off time that is not to be used in patient scheduling.

9. In _____ scheduling, several appointments for similar types of examinations are grouped.

10. Before sending any written or keyed correspondence, you must _____ it to be certain the document is free of errors.

11. A(n) _____ is written for employees within the medical office setting to provide details about an upcoming event or meeting or to relay office policy decisions.

12. A(n) _____ is an article for a journal or other publication.

13. A(n) _____ is a person who listens to recorded dictation and converts it into a written document.

Short Answers

1. List the seven types of information documented when taking a telephone message.

   _____

   _____

   _____

   _____

   _____

2. Why is it important to know the reason for a patient's office visit when making an appointment over the telephone?

   _____

   _____

   _____

   _____

3. Briefly describe the process of putting a caller on hold if more than one line is ringing.

   _____

   _____

   _____

   _____

4. List three pieces of information needed when scheduling an appointment for an established patient.

   _____

   _____

   _____

5. Explain how to accommodate a patient who is habitually late for appointments.

   _____

   _____

   _____

   _____

6. List and describe the steps involved in preparing outgoing mail.

_____

_____

_____

_____

7. List the basic guidelines for effective written correspondence.

_____

_____

_____

_____

_____

8. List two complimentary closings in each of the following categories.

Great respect: _____

Formal: _____

Less formal: _____

Friendly: _____

Critical Thinking

It has been an incredibly busy Monday and the telephones have not stopped ringing. You currently have six callers on hold. Prioritize each caller by using a scale of 1 to 6, with 1 being the most important call to handle and 6 being the least important call to handle, and then write a brief summary of how each of the following callers should be handled.

_____ a. Dr. Jacobs is on line 1 and is waiting to speak to the physician.

_____ b. Hartley is on line 2 and would like to make an appointment for next month.

_____ c. Sara Raphael is on line 3 and would like her prescription of Vicodin refilled as she is still in a lot of pain. This is her third refill request.

_____ d. Porter is on line 4 and is calling to discuss his wife's pregnancy test results.

_____ e. Caria Thopher is on line 5 with a personal call for the clinical medical assistant Grace.

_____ f. The laboratory is on line 6 and would like to give someone test results.

Internet Research

Keywords: Telephone etiquette, medical appointment scheduling

Choose one of the following topics to research: telephone etiquette or various methods of medical appointment scheduling. Write a two-paragraph report supporting your topic. Cite your source. Be prepared to give a 2-minute oral presentation should your instructor assign you to do so.

What Would You Do?

If you have accomplished the objectives in this chapter, you will be able to make better choices as a medical assistant. Take a look at this situation and decide what you would do.

Tara is a new medical assistant at a physician's office. Dr. Vickers has hired her to answer the phone and to greet patients as they arrive, as well as to assist with making appointments as needed. On a particularly busy day, the phone is ringing with two lines already on hold, and a new patient arrives at the reception desk. Steve, the physician's assistant, asks Tara to make an appointment for another patient to see Dr. Vickers as soon as possible. Since the office makes appointments in a modified wave, Steve tells the patient to wait to be seen because Tara has found an opening in about a half-hour. In all the confusion Tara does not return to the patients who are on hold for several minutes, and one of the calls is an emergency. Furthermore, Tara is short-tempered with the new patient who has arrived at the office. Tara's frustration about the busy schedule she is expected to keep shows, and the new patient states that she is not sure that she has chosen the best physician's office for her medical care.

What effect will Tara's frustration have on this medical office? How would you have handled the situation differently?

1. Why is the role of the receptionist so important in putting a patient at ease?

_____

_____

2. When answering the phone, what are the voice qualities that are important in making a good impression?

_____

_____

3. What are the guidelines necessary in answering multiline calls?

_____

_____

_____

_____

4. What information should be obtained from a patient when making appointments?

_____

_____

_____

5. Why is a patient information booklet important for a new patient?

_____

_____

_____

_____

6. What is modified-wave appointment scheduling? What are the problems with this type of scheduling?

_____

_____

_____

_____

7. How should Tara have handled the callers placed on hold?

_____

_____

_____

Chapter Quiz

Multiple Choice

Identify the letter of the choice that best completes the statement or answers the question.

1. A patient who has not been seen in the medical office for _____ is considered a new patient.
   A. 6 months
   B. 12 months
   C. 3 years
   D. 5 years

2. A letter that has all lines flush with the left margin, except for the first line of a new paragraph and date, closing, and signature lines, is in _____ format.
   A. modified-block
   B. full-block
   C. abstract
   D. manuscript

3. A _____ is a document used for formal publication.
   A. matrix
   B. memo
   C. progress notes
   D. manuscript

4. The importance of a triage manual is which one of the following?
   A. Helps the receptionist screen incoming calls and determine the level of urgency
   B. Provides the receptionist with information about the practice's policies and services
   C. Provides a list of routine questions to ask a patient scheduling an appointment
   D. None of the above

5. Which one of the following is not a piece of information you need to obtain when taking a telephone message?
   A. Caller's name
   B. Caller's telephone number
   C. Callers date of birth
   D. Caller's message

6. In which one of the following types of schedules does every patient have an appointment for a definite time?
   A. Wave scheduling
   B. Time-specified scheduling
   C. Modified-wave scheduling
   D. Cluster scheduling

7. A _____ is used for interoffice communication.
   A. manuscript
   B. formal business letter
   C. memo
   D. journal

8. _____ help(s) the medical assistant see what needs to be corrected before sending out correspondence.
   A. Proofreader marks
   B. Dictionary
   C. Spell-check
   D. All of the above

9. _____ reports are initiated by the medical office before treatment begins.
   A. Radiology
   B. Consultation
   C. Discharge summary
   D. History and physical

10. _____ describes the surgical procedure and includes pathological specimens, results, and personnel involved.
    A. H&P
    B. OP report
    C. Autopsy
    D. Discharge summary

11. _____ requires that someone listen to recorded information and produce the information in a written document.
    A. Dictation
    B. Proofreading
    C. Shorthand
    D. Transcription

12. _____ mail is used when it is necessary to prove that a letter was delivered.
    A. Registered
    B. Certified
    C. Express
    D. Overnight

13. _____ is(are) special services offered by both the U.S. Postal Service and Western Union.
   A. Air mail
   B. Telegram
   C. Mailgrams
   D. Express mail

14. If a patient calls the office with a question about an insurance payment, the _____ would typically handle the call.
   A. Physician
   B. Clinical medical assistant
   C. Administrative medical assistant
   D. None of the above

15. The abbreviation used on the appointment book for a complete physical exam is which one of the following?
   A. CPE
   B. CPX
   C. CPR
   D. None of the above

16. The abbreviation S/R noted in the appointment book means the patient is being seen for _____.
   A. Surgery
   B. Superficial reattachment
   C. Suture removal
   D. Sinus/respiratory disorder

17. Scheduling in which more than one patient is booked for the same time slot on the schedule is called _____.
   A. cluster scheduling
   B. double booking
   C. modified-wave scheduling
   D. open-hour booking

18. Your physician just called the office; she is going to be 2 hours late to see patients this morning because of an emergency with a patient at the hospital. Which one of the following is the best way to handle this situation?
   A. Call the scheduled patients, explain the situation, and offer to reschedule their appointments.
   B. Call the scheduled patients and explain the situation and that it would be best if they could arrive at their scheduled times, as it will be a first-come first-serve basis when the physician arrives.
   C. Inform the patients of the delay, ask them to wait patiently, and offer them a beverage.
   D. None of the above

19. When scheduling a patient for a hospital admission, you must have a written order from the physician.
   A. True
   B. False

20. If the physician receives a letter marked "Personal," you should open it immediately, annotate it, and place on the physician's desk.
   A. True
   B. False

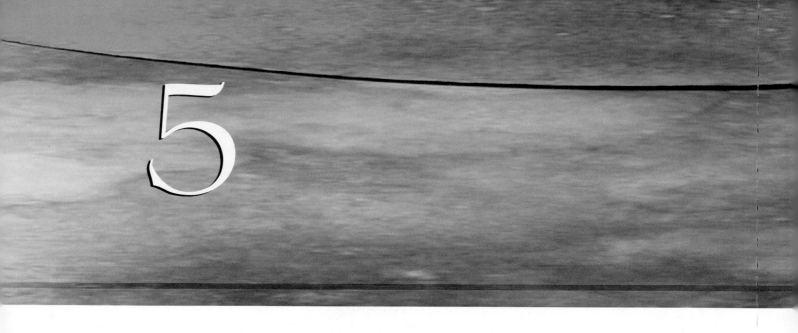

5

"A beautiful eye makes silence eloquent, a kind eye makes contradiction an assent, an enraged eye makes beauty deformed. This little member gives life to every part about us."
—Joseph Addison

OBJECTIVES

1. Recognize and use terms related to the anatomy and physiology of the eyes and ears.
2. Recognize and use terms related to the pathology of the eyes and ears.
3. Recognize and use terms related to the diagnostic procedures for the eyes and ears.
4. Recognize and use terms related to the therapeutic interventions for the eyes and ears.

MEDICAL TERMINOLOGY OF THE SPECIAL SENSES: EYE AND EAR

CHAPTER AT A GLANCE

ANATOMY AND PHYSIOLOGY: THE EYE

accommodation	fovea	meibomian gland	retina
aqueous humor	iris	optic disk	rods
cones	lacrimal gland	orbit	sclera
conjunctiva	lacrimation	palpebral fissure	uvea
cornea	lens	pupil	vitreous humor
extraocular muscle	macula lutea	refraction	

KEY WORD PARTS

PREFIXES	SUFFIXES	COMBINING FORMS	
bi-, bin-	-ia	blephar/o	ocul/o
extra-	-metry	choroid/o	ophthalm/o
	-opia	conjunctiv/o	opt/o, optic/o
	-scopy	cor/o, core/o	palpebr/o
		corne/o	papill/o
		cycl/o	phac/o, phak/o
		dacry/o	pupill/o
		ir/o, irid/o	retin/o
		kerat/o	scler/o
		lacrim/o	uve/o
		lent/i	vitre/o
		macul/o	

KEY TERMS

amblyopia	conjunctivitis	goniotomy	nyctalopia
age-related macular degeneration (ARMD)	corneal ulcer	hordeolum	ophthalmoscopy
	diabetic retinopathy	hyphema	otitis media (OM)
aphakia	diplopia	intraocular pressure (IOP)	presbyopia
astigmatism (Astigm, As, Ast)	exophthalmia	keratitis	strabismus
blepharoptosis	exotropia	keratoplasty	tonometry
cataract	glaucoma	myopia (MY)	xerophthalmia

CHAPTER AT A GLANCE–cont'd

ANATOMY AND PHYSIOLOGY: THE EAR

auricle	external auditory canal	malleus	saccule
cerumen	external auditory meatus	organ of Corti	stapes
cochlea	incus	ossicular chain	tympanic membrane
crista ampullaris	labyrinth	oval window	utricle
eustachian tube	macula	pinna	vestibule

KEY WORD PARTS

PREFIXES
ana-
macro-
micro-
presby-

SUFFIXES
-acusis
-metry
-plasty
-scopy
-stomy

COMBINING FORMS

acous/o	ossicul/o
audi/o	ot/o
aur/o, auricul/o	rhin/o
cerumin/o	salping/o
cochle/o	staped/o
labyrinth/o	tempor/o
myring/o	tympan/o

KEY TERMS

anacusis	myringostomy	otoscopy	tinnitus
audiometry	otalgia	paracusis	tympanoplasty
infectious myringitis	otitis media (OM)	presbycusis	vertigo
Meniere disease	otoplasty	stapedectomy	

FUNCTIONS OF THE SPECIAL SENSES

When we want to relate our understanding of how someone is feeling, we say, "I hear you" or even "I see what you're saying!" Our experience in the world is filtered through our senses and our interpretations of them.

The senses include vision, hearing, taste, smell, and touch. They allow us to experience our environment through specific nervous tissue that transmits, processes, and then acts on our perceptions. This chapter covers the eyes and ears.

THE EYE

ANATOMY AND PHYSIOLOGY

The eye can be divided into the ocular adnexa—the structures that surround and support the function of the eyeball—and the structures of the globe of the eye itself.

Ocular Adnexa

Each of our paired eyes is encased in a protective, bony socket called the **orbit.** Our **binocular** vision sends two slightly different images to the brain that produce depth of vision. The right eye is called the *oculus dextra,* the left eye is called the *oculus sinistra,* and the term for "each eye" is *oculus uterque.* Within the orbit, the eyeball is protected by a cushion of fatty tissue. The **eyebrows** mark the supraorbital area and provide a modest amount of protection from perspiration and sun glare. Further protection is provided by the upper and lower eyelids and the eyelashes that line their edges (Fig. 5-1).

The corners of the eyes are referred to as the **canthi** (KAN thy) (*sing.* canthus); the inner canthus is termed *medial* (toward the middle of the body), and the outer canthus is *lateral.* The area where the upper and lower eyelids meet is referred to as the **palpebral fissure** (PAL puh brul FISH ur). This term comes from the function of blinking, called **palpebration** (pal puh BRAY shun). The eyelids are lined with a protective, thin mucous membrane called the **conjunctiva** (kun jungk TYE vuh) (*pl.* conjunctivae) that spreads to coat the anterior surface of the eyeball as well.

> ### ⊠ BE CAREFUL!
>
> The abbreviations for the eye, OD (right eye), OS (left eye), and OU (each eye), are considered to be "dangerous" abbreviations by the Joint Commission. They have the potential to be confused with similar abbreviations for the ear: AD (right ear), AS (left ear), and AU (each ear). Suggested safe medical practice is to write out right eye, left eye, etc., to prevent confusion.

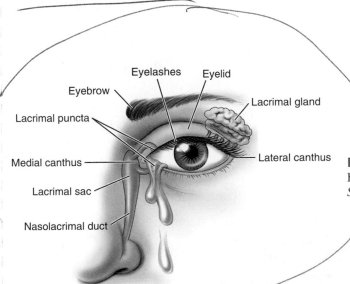

Eyelashes Eyelid
Eyebrow
Lacrimal gland
Lacrimal puncta
Medial canthus
Lateral canthus
Lacrimal sac
Nasolacrimal duct

Fig. 5-1 Ocular adnexa. (*From Herlihy B, Maebius NK: The human body in health and illness, ed 2, Philadelphia, 2003, Saunders.*)

⊗ BE CAREFUL!

The term *palpebrate* means to blink or wink. Do not confuse this with the terms *palpate* or *palpitate*.

Also surrounding the eye are two types of glands. Sebaceous glands in the eyelid secrete oil to lubricate the eyelashes, and lacrimal glands above the eyes produce tears. The sebaceous glands for the eyelashes are called **meibomian** (mye BOH mee un) **glands.** These glands can be a source of complaint when they become blocked or infected. The other type of gland, the **lacrimal** (LACK rih mul) **gland,** or tear gland, provides a constant source of cleansing and lubrication for the eye. The process of producing tears is termed **lacrimation** (lack rih MAY shun). The lacrimal glands are located in the upper outer corners of the orbit. The constant blinking of the eyelids spreads the tears across the eyeball. They then drain into two small holes (the lacrimal puncta) in the medial canthus, into the lacrimal sacs, and then into the **nasolacrimal ducts,** which carry the tears to the nasal cavity.

The **extraocular** (eck strah OCK yoo lur) **muscles** attach the eyeball to the orbit and, on impulse from the cranial nerves, move the eyes. These six voluntary (skeletal) muscles are made up of four rectus (straight) and two oblique (diagonal) muscles.

COMBINING FORMS FOR ACCESSORY EYE STRUCTURES

MEANING	COMBINING FORM
conjunctiva	conjunctiv/o
eye	ophthalm/o, ocul/o
eyelids	palpebr/o, blephar/o
tear	lacrim/o, dacry/o
vision	opt/o, optic/o

PREFIXES FOR ACCESSORY EYE STRUCTURES

PREFIX	MEANING
bi-, bin-	two
extra-	outside
supra-	above

◆ Exercise 5-1: ACCESSORY EYE STRUCTURES

Match the term with its correct combining form or prefix. More than one answer may be correct.

_____ 1. membrane that lines eyelids and covers the surface of the eyes

_____ 2. eyelid

_____ 3. tear

_____ 4. vision

_____ 5. two

_____ 6. eye

_____ 7. outside

_____ 8. above

A. lacrim/o
B. conjunctiv/o
C. optic/o, opt/o
D. ophthalm/o
E. palpebr/o
F. ocul/o

G. blephar/o
H. bin-
I. dacry/o
J. supra-
K. extra-

Circle the correct answer.

9. The eyeball is located in a bony structure termed the *(adnexa, orbit).*
10. The corners of the eyes are referred to as the medial and lateral *(canthi, fissures).*
11. The process of blinking is called *(palpitation, palpebration).*
12. The sebaceous glands for the eyelashes are called *(meibomian, Bartholin)* glands.
13. The process of producing tears is called *(lacrimation, lactation).*
14. The eyes move as the result of six voluntary *(intra-, extra-)* ocular muscles.

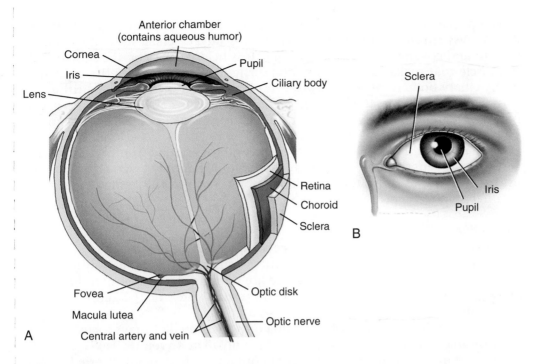

Fig. 5-2 A, The eyeball viewed from above. **B,** The anterior view of the eyeball.

The Eyeball

The anatomy of the eyeball itself is traditionally explained in three layers or **tunics** (TOO nicks) (Fig. 5-2). The outer layer, or **fibrous tunic,** consists of the **sclera** (SKLIR uh) and **cornea** (KOR nee uh). The middle layer, or **vascular tunic,** consists of the **uvea** (YOO vee uh), which is made up of the **choroid** (KOR oyd), **ciliary** (SILL ih air ee) **body,** and **iris** (EYE ris). The inner layer, or **nervous tunic,** consists of the **retina** (RET in uh). These three layers are essential to the process of seeing. All parts work together with impressive harmony. The eye muscles coordinate their movements with one another; the cornea and pupil control the amount of light that enters the eye; the lens focuses the image on the retina; and the optic nerve transmits the image to the brain.

Two important mechanisms also contribute to the ability to see. As light hits the eye, it passes first through the cornea, which bends the rays of light **(refraction)** so that they are projected properly onto receptor cells in the eye. Then, muscles in the ciliary body adjust the shape of the lens to aid in this refraction. The lens flattens to adjust to something seen at a distance, or thickens for close vision—a process called **accommodation.** Errors of refraction are the most common reason for lens prescriptions.

The Sclera

The outermost lateral and posterior portion of the eye, the white of the eye, is called the **sclera,** which means *hard.* The portion of the sclera that covers the anterior section of the eye is transparent and is called the **cornea.** The border of the cornea, between it and the sclera, is called the **limbus** (LIM bus). The cornea is where refraction (the bending of light) begins.

The Uvea

The **uvea** is the middle, highly vascular layer of the eye. It includes the **iris,** the **ciliary body,** and the **choroid.** The iris (*pl.* irides), pupil, lens (*pl.* lenses), and ciliary body are located directly behind the cornea. The iris is a smooth muscle that contracts and relaxes to moderate the amount of light that enters the eye. In most individuals, this is the colored part of the eye (brown, gray, hazel, blue) because of its pigmentation. Individuals with albinism, however, have reddish-pink irides (*sing.* iris) because a lack of pigment makes visible the blood cells traveling through the vessels supplying the iris.

> ⊠ BE CAREFUL!
>
> *Core/o,* meaning pupil of the eye, and *corne/o,* meaning cornea, are easy to confuse.

The **pupil** is the dark area in the center of the iris where the light continues its progress through to the lens. The **lens** is an avascular structure made of protein and covered by an elastic capsule. It is held in place by the thin strands of muscle that make up the ciliary body. The fluid produced by the capillaries of the ciliary body is called the **aqueous** (AY kwee us) **humor.** It nourishes the cornea, gives shape to the anterior eye, and maintains an optimal intraocular pressure. It normally drains through tiny veins called the canals of Schlemm's. The aqueous humor circulates in both the anterior chamber, between the cornea and the iris, and the posterior chamber, behind the iris and in front of the lens. Between the lens and the retina is a jelly-like substance, the **vitreous** (VIT ree us) **humor,** which holds the choroid membrane against the retina to ensure an adequate blood supply.

The Retina

The inner layer of the eye, called the **retina,** contains the sensory receptors for the images carried by the light rays. These sensory receptors are either **rods,** which appear throughout the retina and are responsible for vision in dim light, or **cones,** which are concentrated in the central area of the retina and are responsible for color vision.

During daylight, the area of the retina on which the light rays focus is called the **macula lutea** (MACK yoo lah LOO tee uh). The **fovea** (FOH vee uh) centralis is an area within the macula that contains only cones and provides the sharpest image. The area that allows a natural blind spot in our vision is the **optic disk,** where the optic nerve leaves the retina to travel to the brain. There are no light receptors there.

DID YOU KNOW?

The combining form *kerat/o* means hard or horny and refers to both the skin and the cornea. This is because the cornea is formed from the same tissue as the epidermis.

COMBINING FORMS FOR THE EYEBALL

MEANING	COMBINING FORM	MEANING	COMBINING FORM
choroid	choroid/o	optic disk	papill/o
ciliary body	cycl/o	pupil	pupill/o, cor/o, core/o
cornea	kerat/o, corne/o	retina	retin/o
iris	ir/o, irid/o	sclera	scler/o
lens	phac/o, phak/o, lent/i	uvea	uve/o
macula lutea	macul/o	vitreous body	vitre/o

◈ Exercise 5-2: THE EYEBALLS

Match the parts of the eye with the correct combining forms. More than one answer may be correct.

_____ 1. ir/o, irid/o

_____ 2. papill/o

_____ 3. retin/o

_____ 4. cor/o, core/o

_____ 5. pupill/o

_____ 6. macul/o

_____ 7. phac/o, phak/o

_____ 8. choroid/o

_____ 9. cycl/o

_____ 10. lent/i

_____ 11. uve/o

_____ 12. kerat/o

_____ 13. scler/o

_____ 14. corne/o

_____ 15. vitre/o

A. hard, outer covering of the eye
B. dark center of iris
C. substance between retina and lens
D. middle, highly vascular layer of the eye
E. choroid
F. ciliary body
G. transparent, anterior portion of sclera
H. lens
I. made up of rods and cones
J. pigmented muscle that allows light in eye
K. light focuses on this retinal structure
L. optic disk
M. inner layer of eye

Circle the correct answer.

16. The order of the layers of the eyes from outside to inside is fibrous → vascular → *(nervous, muscular)*.
17. The vascular tunic consists of the *(uvea, retina)*.
18. The tough outer covering is composed of the iris, ciliary body, and *(choroid membrane, sclera)*.
19. Optimal intraocular pressure is maintained by the *(aqueous, vitreous)* humor.
20. The sensory receptors of the retina responsible for color vision are the *(rods, cones)*.
21. The area within the macula lutea that provides the sharpest image is the *(optic disk, fovea)*.

PATHOLOGY

Terms Related to Eyelid Disorders

TERM	WORD ORIGIN	DEFINITION
Blepharedema bleff ah ruh DEE mah	*blephar/o* eyelid *-edema* swelling	Swelling of the eyelid.
Blepharitis bleff ah RYE tis	*blephar/o* eyelid *-itis* inflammation	Inflammation of the eyelid.
Blepharochalasis bleff ah roh KAL luh sis	*blephar/o* eyelid *-chalasis* relaxation, slackening	Hypertrophy of the skin of the eyelid.
Blepharoptosis bleff ah rop TOH sis	*blephar/o* eyelid *-ptosis* drooping	Drooping of the upper eyelid.
Ectropion eck TROH pee on	*ec-* out *trop/o* turning *-ion* process of	Turning outward (eversion) of the eyelid, exposing the conjunctiva (Fig. 5-3).
Entropion en TROH pee on	*en-* in *trop/o* turning *-ion* process of	Turning inward of the eyelid toward the eye (Fig. 5-4).

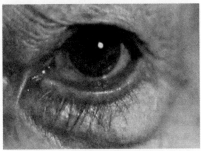

Fig. 5-3 Ectropion. *(From Seidel HM, Ball JW, Dains JI et al: Mosby's guide to physical examination, ed 5, St Louis, 2003, Mosby.)*

Fig. 5-4 Entropion. Note that this patient has undergone corneal transplantation. *(From Seidel HM, Ball JW, Dains JI et al: Mosby's guide to physical examination, ed 5, St Louis, 2003, Mosby.)*

Terms Related to Eyelash Disorders

TERM	WORD ORIGIN	DEFINITION
Chalazion kuh LAY zee on		Hardened swelling of a meibomian gland resulting from a blockage. Also called **meibomian cyst** (Fig. 5-5).
Hordeolum hor DEE uh lum		Stye; infection of one of the sebaceous glands of an eyelash (Fig. 5-6).

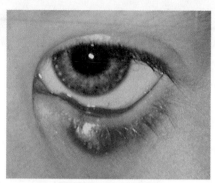

Fig. 5-5 Chalazion. *(From Zitelli RJ, Davis HN: Atlas of pediatric physical diagnosis, ed 4, St Louis, 2002, Mosby.)*

Fig. 5-6 Acute hordeolum of upper eyelid. *(From Seidel HM, Ball JW, Dains JI: Mosby's guide to physical examination, ed 5, St Louis, 2003, Mosby.)*

Terms Related to Tear Gland Disorders

TERM	WORD ORIGIN	DEFINITION
Dacryoadenitis dack ree oh add eh NYE tis	*dacry/o* tear *aden/o* gland *-itis* inflammation	Inflammation of a lacrimal gland.
Dacryocystitis dack ree oh sis TYE tis	*dacry/o* tear *cyst/o* sac *-itis* inflammation	Inflammation of a lacrimal sac.
Epiphora eh PIFF or ah		Overflow of tears; excessive lacrimation.
Keratoconjunctivitis sicca kair ah toh kun junk tih VYE tis SICK ah	*kerat/o* cornea *conjunctiv/o* conjunctiva *-itis* inflammation *sicca* dry	Dryness and/or inflammation of the cornea and conjunctiva caused by inadequate tear production. Usually the result of an immune disorder.
Xerophthalmia zeer off THAL mee ah	*Xer/o* dry *ophthalm/o* eye *-ia* condition	Dry eye; lack of adequate tear production to lubricate the eye. Usually the result of vitamin A deficiency.

Terms Related to Conjunctiva Disorders

TERM	WORD ORIGIN	DEFINITION
Conjunctivitis kun junk tih VYE tis	*conjunctiv/o* conjunctiva *-itis* inflammation	Inflammation of the conjunctiva, commonly known as **pinkeye,** a highly contagious disorder (Fig. 5-7).
Ophthalmia neonatorum off THAL mee uh nee oh nay TORE um	*Ophthalm/o* eye *-ia* condition *neo-* new *nat/o* born	Severe, purulent conjunctivitis in the newborn, usually due to gonorrheal or chlamydial infection. Routine introduction of an antibiotic ophthalmic ointment (erythromycin) prevents most cases.

Terms Related to Eye Muscle and Orbital Disorders

TERM	WORD ORIGIN	DEFINITION
Amblyopia am blee OH pee ah	*ambly/o* dull, dim *-opia* vision	Dull or dim vision due to disuse.
Diplopia dih PLOH pee ah	*dipl/o* double *-opia* vision	Double vision. **Emmetropia** means normal vision.
Esotropia eh soh TROH pee ah	*eso-* inward *trop/o* turning *-ia* condition	Turning inward of one or both eyes.
Exophthalmia eck soff THAL mee ah	*ex-* out *ophthalm/o* eye *-ia* condition	Protrusion of the eyeball from its orbit; may be congenital or the result of an endocrine disorder (Fig. 5-8). *Bulging*
Exotropia eck so TROH pee ah	*exo-* outward *trop/o* turning *-ia* condition	Turning outward of one or both eyes.
Strabismus strah BISS mus		General term for a lack of coordination between the eyes, usually due to a muscle weakness or paralysis. Sometimes called a "squint," which refers to the patient's effort to correct the disorder.

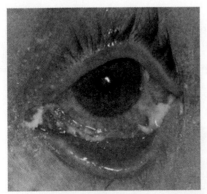

Fig. 5-7 Acute purulent conjunctivitis. *(From Seidel HM, Ball JW, Dains JI: Mosby's guide to physical examination, ed 5, St Louis, 2003, Mosby.)*

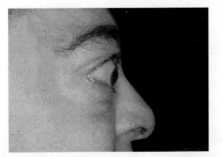

Fig. 5-8 Exophthalmia. *(From Seidel HM, Ball JW, Dains JI: Mosby's guide to physical examination, ed 5, St Louis, 2003, Mosby.)*

⌧ BE CAREFUL!

Do not confuse these similar terms: *esotropia, exotropia, entropion,* and *ectropion.*

◆ Exercise 5-3: DISORDERS OF THE OCULAR ADNEXA

Matching.

_____ 1. epiphora   _____ 6. blepharoptosis

_____ 2. xerophthalmia   _____ 7. chalazion

_____ 3. hordeolum   _____ 8. exotropia

_____ 4. ectropion   _____ 9. conjunctivitis

_____ 5. diplopia   _____ 10. exophthalmia

A. double vision
B. eversion of the eyelid
C. pinkeye
D. excessive lacrimation
E. drooping of an upper eyelid
F. stye
G. meibomian cyst
H. outward protrusion of the eyeball
I. dry eye
J. outward turning of the eye

Circle the correct answer.

11. Normal vision is called *(amblyopia, emmetropia)*.
12. A turning inward of one or both eyes is called *(esotropia, entropion)*.
13. A swelling of an eyelid is called *(blepharitis, blepharedema)*.
14. An inflamed lacrimal sac is called *(dacryoadenitis, dacryocystitis)*.
15. Dryness and inflammation of the cornea and conjunctiva caused by inadequate tear production is called *(ophthalmia neonatorum, keratoconjunctivitis sicca)*.

Terms Related to Refraction and Accommodation Disorders

TERM	WORD ORIGIN	DEFINITION
Asthenopia as thuh NOH pee ah	*a-* lack of *sthen/o* strength *-opia* vision	Visual impairment due to weakness of ocular or ciliary muscles.
Astigmatism ah STIG mah tiz um		Malcurvature of the cornea leading to blurred vision. If uncorrected, asthenopia may result (Fig. 5-9, *A*).
Hyperopia hye pur OH pee ah	*hyper-* excessive *-opia* vision	Farsightedness; refractive error that does not allow the eye to focus on nearby objects (Fig. 5-9, *B*). Also called hypermetropia.
Myopia mye OH pee ah	*my/o* muscle *-opia* vision	Nearsightedness; refractive error that does not allow the eye to focus on distant objects (Fig. 5-9, *C*).
Presbyopia press bee OH pee ah	*presby/o* old age *-opia* vision	Progressive loss of elasticity of the lens (usually accompanies aging), resulting in hyperopia.

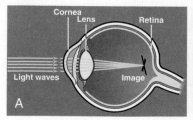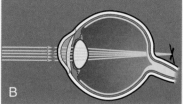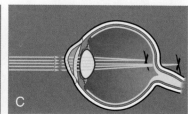

Fig. 5-9 Refraction errors. **A,** Myopia (nearsightedness). **B,** Hyperopia (farsightedness). **C,** Astigmatism. *(From Herlihy B, Maebius NK: The human body in health and illness, ed 2, Philadelphia, 2003, Saunders.)*

Terms Related to Sclera Disorders

TERM	WORD ORIGIN	DEFINITION
Corneal ulcer	*corne/o* cornea *-al* pertaining to	Trauma to the outer covering of the eye, resulting in an abrasion.
Keratitis kair uh TYE tis	*kerat/o* cornea *-itis* inflammation	Inflammation of the cornea.
Keratoconus kair uh toh KOH nus	*kerat/o* cornea *con/o* cone	Malformation of the cornea that appears as a protrusion of the center of the cornea. More prevalent in females than males, this condition may cause astigmatism.

Terms Related to Uvea Disorders

TERM	WORD ORIGIN	DEFINITION
Anisocoria an nye soh KORE ee ah	*an-* not *is/o* equal *cor/o* pupil *-ia* condition	Condition of unequally sized pupils, sometimes due to pressure on the optic nerve as a result of trauma or lesion (Fig. 5-10).
Hyphema hye FEE mah	*hypo-* under *hem/o* blood *-a* noun ending	Blood in the anterior chamber of the eye as a result of hemorrhage due to trauma.
Iritis eye RYE tis	*ir/o* iris *-itis* inflammation	Inflammation of the iris.
Uveitis yoo vee EYE tis	*uve/o* uvea *-itis* inflammation	Inflammation of the uvea (iris, ciliary body, and choroids).

 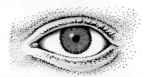

Fig. 5-10 Anisocoria. *(From NAEMT:* PHTLS basic and advanced prehospital trauma life support, *ed 5, St Louis, Mosby.)*

Terms Related to Lens Disorders

TERM	WORD ORIGIN	DEFINITION
Aphakia ah FAY kee ah	*a-* without *phak/o* lens *-ia* condition	Condition of no lens, either congenital or acquired.
Cataract KAT ur ackt		Progressive loss of transparency of the lens of the eye (Fig. 5-11).
Glaucoma glah KOH mah	*glauc/o* gray, bluish green *-oma* mass, swelling	Abnormal intraocular pressure due to the obstruction of the outflow of the aqueous humor. **Chronic** or **primary open-angle glaucoma** (Fig. 5-12) is characterized by an open anterior chamber angle. **Angle-closure** or **narrow-angle glaucoma** is characterized by an abnormally narrowed anterior chamber angle.
Synechia sin ECK kee ah		Adhesion of the iris to the lens and the cornea.

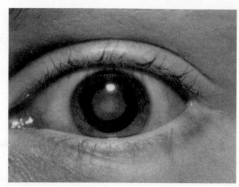

Fig. 5-11   The cloudy appearance of a lens affected by a cataract. *(From Black JM, Hawks JH, Keene A: Medical-surgical nursing: clinical management for positive outcomes, ed 7, Philadelphia, 2005, Saunders.)*

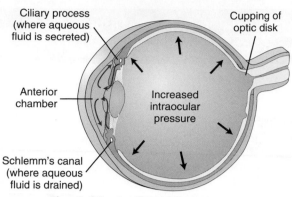

Fig. 5-12   Open-angle glaucoma.

Terms Related to Retina Disorders

TERM	WORD ORIGIN	DEFINITION
Achromatopsia ah kroh mah TOPE see ah	*a-* without *chromat/o* color *-opsia* vision	Impairment of color vision. Inability to distinguish between certain colors because of abnormalities of the photopigments produced in the retina. Also called **color blindness**.
Age-related macular degeneration (ARMD or AMD)		Progressive destruction of the macula, resulting in a loss of central vision. This is the most common visual disorder after the age of 75 (Fig. 5-13).
Diabetic retinopathy dye ah BET ick ret in OP ah thee	*retin/o* retina *-pathy* disease	Damage of the retina due to diabetes; the leading cause of blindness (Fig. 5-14).
Hemianopsia hem ee an NOP see ah	*hemi-* half *an-* without *-opsia* vision	Loss of half the visual field, often the result of a cerebrovascular accident.
Nyctalopia nick tuh LOH pee ah	*nyctal/o* night blindness *-opia* vision	Inability to see well in dim light. May be due to a vitamin A deficiency, retinitis pigmentosa, or choroidoretinitis.
Retinal tear, retinal detachment		Separation of the retina from the choroid layer. May be due to trauma, inflammation of the interior of the eye, or aging. A hole in the retina allows fluid from the vitreous humor to leak between the two layers.
Retinitis pigmentosa ret in EYE tis pig men TOH sah	*retin/o* retina *-itis* inflammation	Hereditary, degenerative disease marked by nyctalopia and a progressive loss of the visual field.
Scotoma skoh TOH mah	*scot/o* darkness *-oma* mass, tumor	Area of decreased vision in the visual field. Commonly called a **blind spot**.

Fig. 5-13   Macular degeneration.

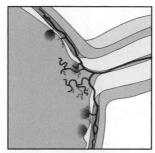

Fig. 5-14   Diabetic retinopathy.

Terms Related to Optic Nerve Disorders

TERM	WORD ORIGIN	DEFINITION
Nystagmus nye STAG mus		Involuntary, back-and-forth eye movements due to a disorder of the labyrinth of the ear and/or parts of the nervous system associated with rhythmic eye movements.
Optic neuritis OP tick nyoo RYE tis	*opt/o* vision *-ic* pertaining to *neur/o* nerve *-itis* inflammation	Inflammation of the optic nerve resulting in blindness; often mentioned as a predecessor to the development of multiple sclerosis.

◆ **Exercise 5-4: DISORDERS OF THE EYEBALL**

Matching.

_____ 1. cataract

_____ 2. ARMD

_____ 3. glaucoma

_____ 4. anisocoria

_____ 5. aphakia

_____ 6. myopia

_____ 7. hyperopia

_____ 8. corneal ulcer

_____ 9. astigmatism

_____ 10. hyphema

A.   abrasion of the outer eye
B.   farsightedness
C.   lack of a lens
D.   hemorrhage within the eye
E.   malcurvature of the cornea
F.   increased intraocular pressure
G.   unequally sized pupils
H.   nearsightedness
I.   loss of central vision
J.   loss of transparency of the lens

Circle the correct answer.

11. Patients with an inflammation of the cornea have *(keratitis, uveitis)*.
12. An impairment of color vision is called *(scotoma, achromatopsia)*.
13. The inability to see well in dim light is called *(amblyopia, nyctalopia)*.
14. Adhesion of the iris to the lens and cornea is called *(synechia, macular degeneration)*.
15. Loss of half of the visual field is called *(optic neuritis, hemianopsia)*.

Terms Related to Malignant Neoplasms

TERM	WORD ORIGIN	DEFINITION
Intraocular melanoma in trah OCK you lahr mell ah NOH mah	*intra-* within *ocul/o* eye *-ar* pertaining to *melan/o* dark, black *-oma* tumor, mass	Malignant tumor of the choroid, ciliary body, or iris that usually occurs in individuals in their 50s or 60s.
Retinoblastoma reh tin oh blass TOH mah	*retin/o* retina *blast/o* embryonic, immature *-oma* tumor, mass	An inherited condition present at birth that arises from embryonic retinal cells (Fig. 5-15).

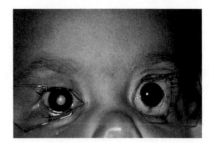

Fig. 5-15 Retinoblastoma. White pupil is a classic sign. *(From Damjanov I, Linder J:* Anderson's pathology, *ed 10, St Louis, 1996, Mosby.)*

◆ Exercise 5-5: NEOPLASMS

Fill in the blank.

1. What is an inherited malignant condition of the eye? _____

2. What is a malignant tumor of the choroids, iris, or ciliary body? _____

 Age Matters

Pediatrics

The most prevalent disorder of the eyes is conjunctivitis, which accounts for a large number of pediatric visits. Because it is highly contagious, entire classrooms may be infected as a result of one student's infection. Routine introduction of erythromycin has severely limited the number of cases of ophthalmia neonatorum, conjunctivitis of the newborn that is usually due to gonorrhea or chlamydial infection.

Geriatrics

Age-related macular degeneration and cataracts are the most common causes of blindness in the elderly, although there are several successful procedures to treat cataracts. Currently there are no treatments to cure ARMD. Diabetic retinopathy is the most common cause of blindness but may also occur much earlier in life. Presbyopia is a visual disorder that usually accompanies aging, resulting in farsightedness.

≋ DIAGNOSTIC PROCEDURES

Terms Related to Diagnostic Procedures

Term	Word Origin	Definition
Amsler grid		Test to assess central vision and to assist in the diagnosis of age-related macular degeneration.
Diopters DYE op turs		Level of measurement that quantifies **refraction errors,** including the amount of nearsightedness (negative numbers), farsightedness (positive numbers), and astigmatism.
Fluorescein angiography FLOO res seen an jee AH gruh fee	*angi/o* vessel *-graphy* process of recording	Procedure to confirm suspected retinal disease by injection of a fluorescein dye into the eye and use of a camera to record the vessels of the retina.
Fluorescein staining		Use of a dye dropped into the eyes that allows differential staining of abnormalities of the cornea.
Gonioscopy goh nee AH skuh pee	*goni/o* angle *-scopy* visual exam	Visualization of the angle of the anterior chamber of the eye; used to diagnose glaucoma and inspect ocular movement.
Ophthalmic ultrasonography	*ophthalm/o* eye *-ic* pertaining to *ultra-* beyond *son/o* sound *-graphy* process of recording	Use of high-frequency sound waves to image the interior of the eye when opacities prevent other imaging techniques. May be used for diagnosing retinal detachments, inflammatory conditions, vascular malformations, and suspicious masses.
Ophthalmoscopy off thal MAH skuh pee	*ophthalm/o* eye *-scopy* visual exam	Any visual examination of the interior of the eye with an ophthalmoscope.
Schirmer tear test		Test to determine the amount of tear production; useful in diagnosing dry eye (xerophthalmia).
Slit lamp examination		Part of a routine eye examination; used to examine the various layers of the eye. Medications may be used to dilate the pupils (mydriatics), numb the eye (anesthetics), or dye the eye (fluorescein staining).
Tonometry toh NAH meh tree	*ton/o* tone, tension *-metry* process of measurement	Measurement of intraocular pressure; used in the diagnosis of glaucoma. In **Goldmann applanation tonometry,** the eye is numbed and measurements are taken directly on the eye. In **air-puff tonometry,** a puff of air is blown onto the cornea.
Visual acuity (VA) assessment		Test of the clearness or sharpness of vision; also called the **Snellen test.** Normal vision is described as being 20/20. The top figure is the number of feet the examinee is standing from the Snellen chart (Fig. 5-16); the bottom figure is the number of feet a normal person would be from the chart and still be able to read the smallest letters. Thus if the result is 20/40, the highest line that the individual can read is what a person with normal vision can read at 40 feet.
Visual field (VF) test		Test to determine the area of physical space visible to an individual. A normal visual field is 65 degrees upward, 75 degrees downward, 60 degrees inward, and 90 degrees outward (Fig. 5-17).

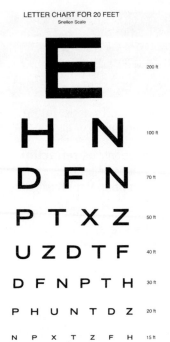

LETTER CHART FOR 20 FEET
Snellen Scale

Fig. 5-16   Snellen chart. *(From Ignatavicius DD, Workman ML:* Medical-surgical nursing: critical thinking for collaborative care, *ed 5, Philadelphia, 2005, Saunders.)*

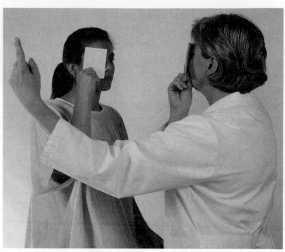

Fig. 5-17   Assessment of visual fields. *(From Black JM, Hawks JH, Keene A:* Medical-surgical nursing: clinical management for positive outcomes, *ed 7, Philadelphia, 2005, Saunders.)*

◈ Exercise 5-6: DIAGNOSTIC PROCEDURES

Matching.

_____ 1. measure of the area of physical space visible to an individual

_____ 2. examination of intraocular pressure

_____ 3. visual examination of interior of eye

_____ 4. test of sharpness of vision

_____ 5. visualization of angle of anterior chamber

_____ 6. test to measure central vision

_____ 7. test to determine amount of tear production

_____ 8. examination of abnormalities of cornea

_____ 9. part of routine eye examination of layers of the eye

_____ 10. use of injected dye to record suspected retinal disease

_____ 11. measurement units used to determine refraction errors

A. slit lamp examination
B. VA test
C. Schirmer test
D. fluorescein staining
E. VF test
F. ophthalmoscopy
G. Amsler grid
H. tonometry
I. gonioscopy
J. fluorescein angiography
K. diopters

≋ THERAPEUTIC INTERVENTIONS

Terms Related to Interventions of the Eyeball and Adnexa

TERM	WORD ORIGIN	DEFINITION
Blepharoplasty bleff OR uh plas tee	*blephar/o* eyelid *-plasty* surgical repair	Surgical repair of the eyelids. May be done to correct blepharoptosis or blepharochalasis.
Blepharorrhaphy BLEFF ar oh rah fee	*blephar/o* eyelid *-rrhaphy* suture	Suture of the eyelids.
Enucleation of the eye eh noo klee AY shun		Removal of the entire eyeball.
Evisceration of the eye eh vis uh RAY shun		Removal of the contents of the eyeball, leaving the outer coat (the sclera) intact.
Exenteration of the eye eck sen tur RAY shun		Removal of the entire contents of the orbit.

Terms Related to Refractive Surgery

TERM	WORD ORIGIN	DEFINITION
Astigmatic keratotomy (AK) as tig MAT ick kair uh TAH tuh mee	*kerat/o* cornea *-tomy* incision	Corneal incision process that treats astigmatism by effecting a more rounded cornea.
Corneal incision procedure		Any keratotomy procedure in which the cornea is cut to change shape, correcting a refractive error (AK, RK, PRK).
Flap procedure		Any procedure in which a segment of the cornea is cut as a means of access to the structures below (LASIK, LASEK).
Laser-assisted in-situ keratomileusis (LASIK) kair uh toh mih LOO sis	*kerat/o* cornea	Flap procedure in which an excimer laser is used to remove material under the corneal flap. Corrects astigmatism, myopia, and hyperopia (Fig. 5-18).
Laser epithelial keratomileusis (LASEK)	*kerat/o* cornea	Flap procedure that differs from the LASIK procedure only in the amount of tissue cut. LASEK incises the epithelium and only part of the stroma, with an advantage of the opportunity for more easily treated possible infections.
Photoablation foh toh ah BLAY shun	*photo-* light *ablation* removal	Use of ultraviolet radiation to destroy and remove tissue from the cornea.
Photorefractive keratectomy (PRK) foh toh ree FRACK tiv kair uh TECK tuh mee	*kerat/o* cornea *-ectomy* removal	Treatment for astigmatism, hyperopia, and myopia that uses an excimer laser to reshape the cornea.
Radial keratotomy (RK) RAY dee ul Kair uh TAH tuh mee	*radi/o* rays *-al* pertaining to *kerat/o* cornea *-tomy* incision	Corneal incision process that treats myopia by incising the cornea in a spokelike pattern.

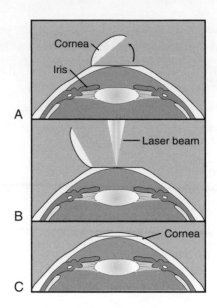

Fig. 5-18 LASIK surgery. **A,** A microkeratome is used to create a hinged cap of tissue, which is lifted off the cornea. **B,** An excimer laser is used to vaporize and reshape underlying tissue. **C,** Tissue cap is replaced.

Terms Related to Limbal, Scleral, and Corneal Procedures

TERM	WORD ORIGIN	DEFINITION
Anterior ciliary sclerotomy (ACS) sklair AH tuh mee	*scler/o* sclera *-tomy* incision	Incision in the sclera to treat presbyopia.
Corneal transplant		Transplantation of corneal tissue from a donor or the patient's own (autograft) cornea. May be either full- or partial-thickness grafts; also called **keratoplasty** (KAIR uh toh plas tee).
Epikeratophakia eh pee kair uh toh FAY kee ah	*epi-* above *kerat/o* cornea *phak/o* lens *-ia* condition	Replacement of lens function with the use of a donor corneal graft. May be used for myopia, hyperopia, astigmatism, and, occasionally, keratoconus.
Implantation of corneal ring segments		Procedure to correct myopia with the addition of pieces to the cornea.
Laser thermal keratoplasty (LTK)	*therm/o* heat *-al* pertaining to *kerat/o* cornea *-plasty* surgical repair	Use of heat and a holmium laser to treat hyperopia in patients over 40.
Limbal relaxing incision (LRI)		Incision of the limbus to treat astigmatism.

Terms Related to Lens Interventions

TERM	WORD ORIGIN	DEFINITION
Extraction of the lens		Removal of the lens to treat cataracts. May be **intracapsular**, in which the entire lens and capsule are removed, or **extracapsular**, in which the lens capsule is left in place (Fig. 5-19).
Implantable contact lenses (ICL)		Use of an artificial lens implanted behind the iris and in front of the natural abnormal lens to treat myopia and farsightedness.
Phacoemulsification and aspiration of cataract fay koh ee MULL sih fih KAY shun	*phac/o* lens	Vision correction accomplished through the destruction and removal of the contents of the capsule by breaking it into small pieces and removing them by suction.

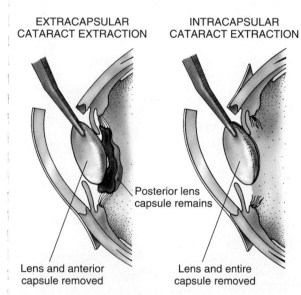

EXTRACAPSULAR CATARACT EXTRACTION

INTRACAPSULAR CATARACT EXTRACTION

Posterior lens capsule remains

Lens and anterior capsule removed

Lens and entire capsule removed

Fig. 5-19 Lens removal. *(From Ignatavicius DD, Workman ML: Medical-surgical nursing: critical thinking for collaborative care, ed 5, Philadelphia, 2005, Saunders.)*

Terms Related to Iris Interventions

TERM	WORD ORIGIN	DEFINITION
Coreoplasty kore ee oh PLAS tee	*core/o* pupil -*plasty* surgical repair	Surgical repair to form an artificial pupil.
Goniotomy goh nee AH tuh mee	*goni/o* angle -*tomy* incision	Incision of Schlemm's canal to correct glaucoma by providing an exit for the aqueous humor.
Iridotomy eye rih DOT tuh mee	*irid/o* iris -*tomy* incision	Incision of the iris to treat postoperative glaucoma or to gain access for cataract surgery.
Trabeculotomy truh beck kyoo LAH tuh mee		External incision of the eye to promote intraocular circulation.

Terms Related to Retina Interventions

TERM	WORD ORIGIN	DEFINITION
Retinal photocoagulation RET in ul foh toh koh agg yoo LAY shun	*retin/o* retina *-al* pertaining to *phot/o* light *coagulation* to clot	Destruction of retinal lesions using light rays to solidify tissue.
Scleral buckling SKLAIR ul BUCK ling	*scler/o* sclera *-al* pertaining to	Reattachment of the retina with a cryoprobe and the use of a silicone sponge to push the sclera in toward the retinal scar; includes the removal of fluid from the subretinal space (Fig. 5-20).
Vitrectomy vih TRECK tuh mee	*vitr/o* vitreous humor, glassy *-ectomy* removal	Removal of part or all of the vitreous humor.

◆ Exercise 5-7: THERAPEUTIC INTERVENTIONS

Matching.

_____ 1. suture of the eyelids

_____ 2. removal of vitreous humor

_____ 3. surgical repair of a pupil defect

_____ 4. destruction of retinal lesions with light

_____ 5. incision of Schlemm's canal to correct glaucoma

_____ 6. incision of the iris to treat glaucoma

_____ 7. removal of contents of eyeball, except for outer coat

_____ 8. any keratotomy procedure to correct a refractive error

_____ 9. procedure to cut cornea to access deeper structures

_____ 10. use of UV radiation to destroy tissue

_____ 11. corneal transplant

_____ 12. removal of entire orbital contents

_____ 13. reattachment of retina

_____ 14. removal of entire eyeball

_____ 15. surgical repair of eyelids

A. retinal photocoagulation
B. blepharoplasty
C. scleral buckling
D. enucleation of eye
E. corneal incision procedure
F. exenteration of the eye
G. flap procedure
H. vitrectomy
I. blepharorrhaphy
J. iridotomy
K. goniotomy
L. photoablation
M. evisceration of eye
N. coreoplasty
O. keratoplasty

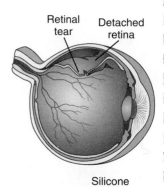

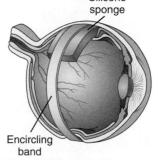

Fig. 5-20 Scleral buckling procedure. *(From Ignatavicius DD, Workman ML: Medical-surgical nursing: critical thinking for collaborative care, ed 5, Philadelphia, 2005, Saunders.)*

PHARMACOLOGY

Antibiotics: A term commonly misused to refer to medications used to treat bacterial infections. Examples include gentamicin (Garamycin) and ciprofloxacin (Cipro) which are referred to as anti-infectives.

Antihistamines: Drugs used to treat allergic conditions such as itchy or watery eyes. Diphenhydramine (Benadryl) is a common over-the-counter product used to treat allergies.

Cycloplegics: Pharmaceutical agents that induce paralysis of the ciliary body to allow examination of the eye.

Lubricants: Medications that keep the eyes moist, mimicking natural tears.

Medications to treat glaucoma: Medications used to decrease the intraocular pressure by decreasing the amount of fluid in the eye or increasing the drainage include carbonic anhydrase inhibitors (dorzolamide), cholinergics (pilocarpine), prostaglandin agonists (latanoprost), beta blockers (levobunolol), and alpha-2 agonists (brimonidine).

Miotics: Drugs that cause the pupils to constrict; often used to treat glaucoma.

Mydriatics: Drugs that cause the pupils to dilate; used in diagnostic and refractive examination of the eye.

Ophthalmics: Drugs applied directly to the eye. These may be in the form of solutions or ointments.

Topical anesthetics: Medications used to temporarily anesthetize the eye for the purpose of examination.

DID YOU KNOW?

Photophobia may mean *sensitivity to light* when used to describe the eyes, or *fear of light* when used to describe a psychiatric condition.

DID YOU KNOW?

The term *mydriatic* comes from a Greek word meaning *hot mass.* The Greeks thought that grasping something hot would cause one's pupils to widen.

◇ Exercise 5-8: PHARMACOLOGY

Matching.

_____ 1. used to treat allergic conditions

_____ 2. used to constrict pupils

_____ 3. used to allow examination of eye by paralyzing ciliary body

_____ 4. used to dilate pupils

_____ 5. used to keep eyes moist

A. mydriatics
B. cycloplegics
C. antihistamines
D. lubricants
E. miotics

Morgan Ophthalmology Associates
789 Henry Ave.
Philadelphia, PA 19118

OPERATIVE REPORT

Patient is a 75-year-old gentleman with a visually significant cataract of the right eye. He was seen pre-operatively by his family physician and cleared for local anesthetic. Patient was brought into the outpatient surgical suite and underwent uncomplicated phacoemulsification and posterior lens implant of the right eye under local standby using topical anesthetic.

He was taken to the recovery room in good condition.

Adam Westgate, MD

 Exercise 5-9: OPERATIVE REPORT

Using the operative report above, answer the following questions.

1. What is the condition that the procedure is intended to correct? _____

2. When was he seen by his family physician? _____

3. Phacoemulsification means that the lens was _____.

4. How do you know that he received a new lens? _____

5. What type of anesthetic was used during the surgery? _____

Abbreviations

Abbreviation	Meaning	Abbreviation	Meaning
Acc	Accommodation	MY	Myopia
ARMD, AMD	Age-related macular degeneration	NVA	Near visual acuity
Astigm, As, Ast	Astigmatism	Ophth	Ophthalmology
c̄ gl	Correction with glasses	PERRLA	Pupils equal, round, reactive to light and accommodation
ECCE	Extracapsular cataract extraction		
EM, Em	Emmetropia	PRK	Photorefractive keratectomy
EOM	Extraocular movements	RK	Radial keratotomy
ICCE	Intracapsular cataract extraction	s̄ gl	Correction without glasses
IOL	Intraocular lens	VA	Visual acuity
IOP	Intraocular pressure	VF	Visual field
L & A	Light and accommodation	WNL	Within normal limits
LASIK	Laser-assisted in-situ keratomileusis		

Exercise 5-10: ABBREVIATIONS

Write out the following abbreviations.

1. Jonathan Sobel was diagnosed with MY in his left eye.

   _____

2. Marlena decided to consider the merits of LASIK and PRK before she had her prescription filled.

   _____

3. Katsuko's vision was described as 20/300 on his VA test.

   _____

4. The patient had AMD. _____

5. Arielle was referred to Ophth. _____

6. The patient's IOP is described as being WNL. _____

7. An Amsler grid is used to test the patient's VF. _____

THE EAR

 ### ANATOMY AND PHYSIOLOGY

The ear is regionally divided into the outer, middle, and inner ear (Fig. 5-21). Sound is conducted through air, bone, and fluid through these divisions. The majority of the ear is contained within the **petrous** (PEH trus) portion of the temporal bone.

Outer (External) Ear

Sound waves are initially gathered by the flesh-covered cartilage of the outer ear called the **pinna** (PIN nuh), or **auricle** (ORE ick kul). The gathered sound is then funneled into the **external auditory canal.** Earwax, or **cerumen** (sih ROO mun), is secreted by modified sweat glands within the external auditory canal and protects the ear with its antiseptic property and its stickiness, trapping foreign debris and moving it out of the ear. The opening of the outer ear is the **external auditory meatus** (AH dih tor ee mee AY tus). The **tympanic** (tim PAN ick) **membrane,** or eardrum, marks the end of the external ear and the beginning of the middle ear.

Middle Ear

The eardrum conducts sound to three tiny bones in the middle ear called the **ossicles** (AH sick kuls), or the **ossicular chain.** These ossicles are named for their shapes: the **malleus** (MAL ee us), or hammer; the **incus** (ING kus), or anvil; and the **stapes** (STAY peez) (*pl.* stapedes), or stirrup. The ossicles transmit the sound to the **oval window** through the stapes. Within the middle ear is

 ### BE CAREFUL!

The abbreviations for the ear, AD (right ear), AS (left ear), and AU (each ear), share the same "dangerous" abbreviation status as the ones for the eyes (OD, OS, and OU). The Joint Commission recommends that the full term be written out to avoid any confusion.

BE CAREFUL!

The combining form *salping/o* means both fallopian tube and eustachian tube.

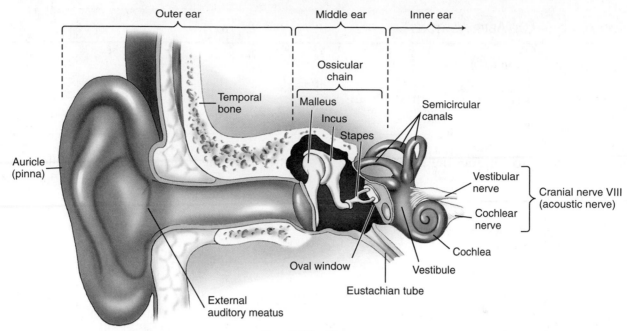

Fig. 5-21   The ear.

the opening for the **eustachian** (yoo STAY shun) **tube,** also called the auditory tube, a mucous membrane–lined connection between the ears and the throat that equalizes pressure within the middle ear.

Inner Ear

Once sound is conducted to the oval window, it is transmitted to a structure called the **labyrinth** (LAB uh rinth), or the inner ear. A membranous labyrinth is enclosed within a bony labyrinth. Between the two, and surrounding the inner labyrinth, is a fluid called **perilymph** (PAIR ee limf). Within the membranous labyrinth is a fluid called **endolymph** (EN doh limf). Hair cells within the inner ear fluids act as nerve endings that function as sensory receptors for hearing and equilibrium. The outer, bony labyrinth is composed of three parts: the vestibule, the semicircular canals, and the cochlea. The **vestibule** (VES tih byool) and **semicircular canals** function to provide information about the body's sense of equilibrium, whereas the **cochlea** (KAH klee ah) is an organ of hearing.

Within the vestibule, two structures called the **utricle** (YOO trick ul) and the **saccule** (SACK yool) function to determine the body's static equilibrium. A specialized patch of epithelium called the **macula** (MACK yoo lah), found in both the utricle and the saccule, provides information about the position of the head and a sense of acceleration and deceleration. The semicircular canals detect dynamic equilibrium, or a sense of sudden rotation, through the function of a structure called the **crista ampullaris** (KRIS tah am pyoo LAIR is).

The cochlea receives the vibrations from the perilymph and transmits them to the cochlear duct, which is filled with endolymph. The transmission of sound continues through the endolymph to the **organ of Corti,** where the hearing receptor cells (hairs) stimulate a branch of the eighth cranial nerve, the vestibulocochlear nerve, to transmit the information to the temporal lobe of the brain.

✖ BE CAREFUL!

Malleus means an ossicle. *Malleolus* means one of the processes on the distal tibia and fibula.

✖ BE CAREFUL!

Do not confuse *oral,* meaning by mouth, with *aural,* meaning by ear.

COMBINING FORMS FOR ANATOMY OF THE EAR

MEANING	COMBINING FORM	MEANING	COMBINING FORM
ear	ot/o, aur/o, auricul/o	inner ear	labyrinth/o
eardrum	tympan/o, myring/o	nose	rhin/o
earwax	cerumin/o	ossicles	ossicul/o
eustachian tube	salping/o	stapes	staped/o, stapedi/o
hearing	audi/o, acous/o	temporal bone	tempor/o

◆ Exercise 5-11: ANATOMY OF THE EAR

Match the combining forms with the correct parts of the ear. More than one letter may be correct.

_____ 1. eardrum

_____ 2. bones of the ear

_____ 3. earwax

_____ 4. inner ear

_____ 5. hearing

_____ 6. eustachian tube

_____ 7. ear

_____ 8. stirrup-shaped ear bone

_____ 9. temporal bone

A. tempor/o
B. labyrinth/o
C. ossicul/o
D. cerumin/o
E. staped/o
F. myring/o
G. salping/o
H. ot/o
I. audi/o
J. tympan/o
K. aur/o

Fill in the blanks.

10. Fill in the missing structures. Pinna → _____ → tympanic membrane → _____

    → oval window → _____ → eighth cranial nerve

11. Name the three bones in the ossicular chain. _____

12. Which structure of the labyrinth is responsible for hearing? _____

13. Which structures of the labyrinth are responsible for equilibrium? _____

≋ PATHOLOGY

Terms Related to Symptomatic Disorders

TERM	WORD ORIGIN	DEFINITION
Otalgia oh TAL juh	ot/o ear -algia pain	Earache, pain in the ear; also called **otodynia** (oh toh DIN nee ah).
Otorrhea oh tuh REE ah	ot/o ear -rrhea discharge	Discharge from the auditory canal; may be serous, bloody, or purulent.

Continued

Terms Related to Symptomatic Disorders—cont'd

TERM	WORD ORIGIN	DEFINITION
Tinnitus tin EYE tis		Abnormal sound heard in one or both ears caused by trauma or disease; may be a ringing, buzzing, or jingling.
Vertigo VUR tih goh		Dizziness. Abnormal sensation of movement when there is none, either of one's self moving or of objects moving around oneself. May be caused by middle ear infections or the toxic effects of alcohol, sunstroke, and certain medications.

Terms Related to Outer Ear Disorders

TERM	WORD ORIGIN	DEFINITION
Impacted cerumen		Blockage of the external auditory canal with cerumen.
Macrotia mah KROH sha	*macro-* large *ot/o* ear *-ia* condition	Condition of abnormally large auricles; greater than 10 cm.
Microtia mye KROH sha	*micro-* small *ot/o* ear *-ia* condition	Condition of abnormally small auricles; less than 4 cm.
Otitis externa oh TYE tis eck STER nah	*ot/o* ear *-itis* inflammation *externa* outer	Inflammation of the outer ear.

Terms Related to Middle Ear Disorders

TERM	WORD ORIGIN	DEFINITION
Cholesteatoma koh less tee ah TOH mah	*chol/e* bile *steat/o* fat *-oma* tumor	Cystic mass composed of epithelial cells and cholesterol. Mass may occlude middle ear and destroy adjacent bones.
Infectious myringitis meer in JYE tis	*myring/o* eardrum *-itis* inflammation	Inflammation of the eardrum due to a bacterial or viral infection.
Otitis media (OM) oh TYE tis MEE dee ah	*ot/o* ear *-itis* inflammation *media* middle	Inflammation of the middle ear. Common in young children, it is usually secondary to an upper respiratory infection. Treatment usually includes administration of antibiotics (Fig. 5-22).
Otosclerosis oh toh sklair ROH sis	*ot/o* ear *-sclerosis* condition of hardening	Development of bone around the oval window with resulting ankylosis of the stapes to the oval window; usually results in progressive deafness.

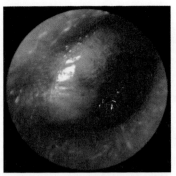

Fig. 5-22 Otitis media. Tympanic membrane is erythematous, opaque, and bulging. *(From Zitelli BJ, Davis HW: Atlas of pediatric physical diagnosis, ed 4, St Louis, 2002, Mosby.)*

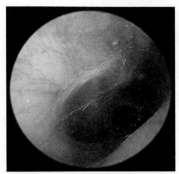

Fig. 5-23 Tympanic membrane perforation. *(From Zitelli BJ, Davis HW: Atlas of pediatric physical diagnosis, ed 4, St Louis, 2002, Mosby.)*

Terms Related to Inner Ear Disorders

TERM	WORD ORIGIN	DEFINITION
Acoustic neuroma ah KOO stick noo ROH mah	*acous/o* hearing *-tic* pertaining to *neur/o* nerve *-oma* tumor	Benign tumor that grows in the auditory canal; may result in hearing loss, dizziness, and unsteady gait.
Labyrinthitis lab uh rinth EYE tis	*labyrinth/o* labyrinth *-itis* inflammation	Inflammation of the inner ear that may be due to infection or trauma; symptoms may include vertigo, nausea, and nystagmus.
Meniere disease may nee URZ		Chronic condition of excess fluid in the inner ear characterized by vertigo, hearing loss, and tinnitus. The cause is unknown.
Ruptured tympanic membrane		Tear (perforation) of the eardrum due to trauma or disease process (Fig. 5-23).

Terms Related to Hearing Loss Disorders

TERM	WORD ORIGIN	DEFINITION
Anacusis an uh KYOO sis	*an-* without *-acusis* hearing	General term for hearing loss or deafness.
Conductive hearing loss		Hearing loss resulting from damage to or malformation of the middle or outer ear.
Paracusis pair uh KYOO sis	*para-* abnormal *-acusis* hearing	Abnormality of hearing.
Presbycusis prez bee KYOO sis	*presby/o* old age *-acusis* hearing	Loss of hearing common in old age.
Sensorineural hearing loss Sen suh ree NOOR ul		Hearing loss resulting from damage to the inner ear (cochlea) or the auditory nerve.

◈ Exercise 5-12: PATHOLOGY

Matching.

_____ 1. cholesteatoma   _____ 7. tinnitus   A. cystic mass in the middle ear composed of
                                                        cholesterol
_____ 2. vertigo   _____ 8. presbycusis   B. ringing in the ears
                                                     C. earache
_____ 3. otorrhea   _____ 9. otalgia   D. loss of hearing typical of aging
                                                     E. hearing loss
_____ 4. macrotia   _____ 10. anacusis   F. inflammation of inner ear
                                                     G. abnormally large auricles
_____ 5. labyrinthitis   _____ 11. otitis externa H. abnormal sense of movement
                                                     I. middle ear infection
_____ 6. otitis media   _____ 12. paracusis   J. inflammation of outer ear
                                                     K. discharge from the ear
                                                     L. abnormality of hearing

Circle the correct answer.

13. Hearing loss caused by damage to the inner ear or auditory nerve is *(conductive hearing loss, sensorineural hearing loss)*.
14. Blockage of the external auditory canal with earwax is called *(impacted cerumen, otosclerosis)*.
15. A patient who exhibits a chronic condition of the inner ear characterized by ringing in the ear, hearing loss, and vertigo may have *(infectious myringitis, Meniere disease)*.

Terms Related to Benign Neoplasms

TERM	WORD ORIGIN	DEFINITION
Acoustic neuroma	*acous/o* hearing *-tic* pertaining to *neur/o* nerve *-oma* tumor, mass	A benign tumor of the eighth cranial nerve (vestibulocochlear) that causes tinnitus and vertigo.
Ceruminoma	*cerumin/o* cerumen, earwax *-oma* tumor, mass	A benign adenocarcinoma of the glands that produce earwax.
Cholesteatoma	*chol/e* bile *steat/o* fat *-oma* tumor, mass	A mass of epithelial cells and cholesterol in the middle ear usually resulting from chronic otitis media.

◈ Exercise 5-13: NEOPLASMS

Fill in the blank.

1. What is a benign tumor of the eighth cranial nerve? _____

2. What is a benign growth that usually results from chronic otitis media? _____

3. What is a benign adenocarcinoma of the glands that produce earwax? _____

Godfrey Medical Assoc.
3122 Shannon Ave.
Fort Augustus, AZ 86534

PROGRESS NOTE

Date:	09/01/XX	**Vital Signs:**	T	R
Chief Complaint:	Temperature		P	BP

09/01/XX	This 3-year-old male comes in with a temperature of 100.5° F. Denies any pain, but mother has noted him to be lethargic. Patient has had frequent ear infections in the past. He also has history of strep throat.
	PHYSICAL EXAM: Alert male, lethargic, but responsive
	Not in acute respiratory distress
	Temperature: 101, Pulse 120, BP 120/80
	Neck: No lymphadenopathy or stiffness. Full ROM
	Lungs: Clear with upper respiratory sounds, but no wheezing
	Cardiac: Regular rate and rhythm
	HEENT: Reveals dull red right TM. Oropharyngeal exam normal.
	ASSESSMENT: Right otitis media
	Treat with Zithromax 200 per 5. Given Auralgan suspension, 3 drops to right ear.
	Felix Washington MD

		Patient Name: John Roberts
		DOB: 4/1/XX
		MR/Chart #: 65487

◆ **Exercise 5-14: PROGRESS NOTE**

Using the progress note above, answer the following questions.

1. How do you know that the patient had no disease of his lymph glands? _____

2. What term tells you that the patient did not exhibit a whistling sound made during breathing?

   _____

3. The patient's right eardrum is examined and found to be dull and red. What do you think TM stands

   for? _____

4. What area of the throat appears normal on examination? _____

5. The diagnosis is an inflammation of the middle ear. What is the term? _____

Age Matters

Pediatrics

Although very few babies are born with a hearing loss, the Universal Newborn Hearing Screening test is a means to detect deafness in infancy. Once given the diagnosis, the parents can begin to plan for how to best handle the condition.

Otitis media is the most frequently diagnosed childhood ear disease.

Geriatrics

Hearing loss that may accompany the aging process is termed *presbycusis*.

≋ DIAGNOSTIC PROCEDURES

Terms Related to Hearing Tests

TERM	WORD ORIGIN	DEFINITION
Audiometric testing	*audi/o* hearing *-metric* pertaining to measurement	Measurement of hearing, usually with an instrument called an **audiometer** (ah dee AH met tur). The graphic representation of the results is called an **audiogram** (Fig. 5-24).
Electrocochleography ee lek troh koh klee OG rah fee	*electr/o* electricity *cochle/o* cochlea *-graphy* process of recording	Measurement of function of the eighth cranial nerve.
Otoscopy oh TAH skuh pee	*ot/o* ear *-scopy* process of visual examination	Visual examination of the external auditory canal and the tympanic membrane using an **otoscope**.
Pure tone audiometry	*audi/o* hearing *-metry* process of measurement	Measurement of perception of pure tones with extraneous sound screened out.
Rinne tuning fork test RIH nuh		Method of distinguishing conductive from sensorineural hearing loss.
Speech audiometry	*audi/o* hearing *-metry* process of measurement	Measurement of ability to hear and understand speech.
Tympanometry tim pan NAH muh tree	*tympan/o* eardrum *-metry* process of measurement	Measurement of the condition and mobility function of the eardrum. The resultant graph is called a **tympanogram.**
Universal Newborn Hearing Screening (UNHS) test		Test that uses **otoacoustic emissions (OAEs)** measured by the insertion of a probe into the baby's ear canal and **auditory brain stem response (ABR),** which involves the placement of four electrodes on the baby's head to measure the change in the electrical activity of the brain in response to sound while the baby is sleeping.
Weber tuning fork test WEB ur		Method of testing auditory acuity.

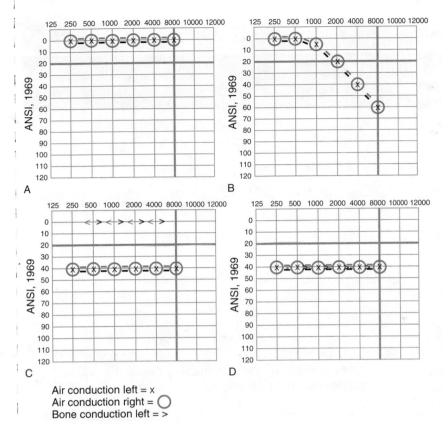

Fig. 5-24 Audiograms. **A,** Normal hearing. **B,** Conductive hearing loss. **C,** High-frequency hearing loss. **D,** Sensorineural hearing loss. *(From Black JM, Hawks JH, Keene A: Medical-surgical nursing, clinical management for positive outcomes, ed 7, Philadelphia, 2005, Saunders.)*

Air conduction left = x
Air conduction right = ◯
Bone conduction left = >
Bone conduction right = <

◈ Exercise 5-15: DIAGNOSTIC PROCEDURES

Matching.

_____ 1. instrument to measure hearing

_____ 2. test of auditory acuity

_____ 3. record of function of eardrum

_____ 4. instrument to visually examine the ears

_____ 5. test to distinguish between conductive and sensorineural hearing loss

_____ 6. measurement of ability to hear and understand speech

A. otoscope
B. Rinne tuning fork test
C. speech audiometry
D. Weber tuning fork test
E. audiometer
F. tympanogram

≋ THERAPEUTIC INTERVENTIONS

Terms Related to Therapeutic Interventions

TERM	WORD ORIGIN	DEFINITION
Cochlear implant KAH klee ur	*cochle/o* cochlea *-ar* pertaining to	Implanted device that assists those with hearing loss by electrically stimulating the cochlea (Fig. 5-25).
Hearing aid		Electronic device that amplifies sound.
Otoplasty oh toh plas tee	*ot/o* ear *-plasty* surgical repair	Surgical or plastic repair and/or reconstruction of the external ear.
Stapedectomy stay puh DECK tuh mee	*staped/o* stapes *-ectomy* removal	Removal of the third ossicle, the stapes, from the middle ear.
Tympanoplasty tim pan oh plas tee	*tympan/o* eardrum *-plasty* surgical repair	Surgical repair of the eardrum, with or without ossicular chain reconstruction. Some patients may require a prosthesis (an artificial replacement) for one or more of the ossicles.
Tympanostomy tim pan AH stuh mee	*tympan/o* eardrum *-stomy* new opening	Surgical creation of an opening through the eardrum to promote drainage and/or allow the introduction of artificial tubes to maintain the opening (Fig. 5-26); also called a **myringostomy** (mir ring AH stoh mee).
Tympanotomy tim pan AH tuh mee	*tympan/o* eardrum *-tomy* incision	Incision of an eardrum; also called a **myringotomy** (mir ring AH toh mee).

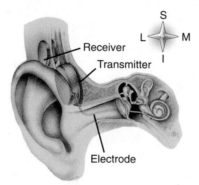

Fig. 5-25 Cochlear implant. *(From Thibodeau GA, Patton KT:* Anatomy and physiology, *ed 5, St Louis, 2002, Mosby.)*

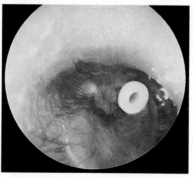

Fig. 5-26 Tympanostomy tube in place. *(From Zitelli BJ, Davis HW:* Atlas of pediatric physical diagnosis, *ed 4, St Louis, 2002, Mosby.)*

◈ Exercise 5-16: THERAPEUTIC INTERVENTIONS

Matching.

_____ 1. incision of eardrum

_____ 2. surgical reconstruction of the external ear

_____ 3. surgical creation of a new opening through the eardrum

_____ 4. device implanted in inner ear to stimulate hearing

_____ 5. excision of ossicle that strikes the oval window

A. cochlear implant
B. otoplasty
C. tympanostomy
D. stapedectomy
E. myringotomy

PHARMACOLOGY

Antibiotics: A term commonly misused to refer to drugs used to treat bacterial infections. A commonly used oral agent to treat ear infections is amoxicillin (Amoxil), an anti-infective.

Ceruminolytics: Medications used to soften and break down earwax. An example is carbamide peroxide (Debrox, Murine earwax drops).

Decongestants: Drugs used to relieve congestion associated with a cold, allergy, or sinus pressure. These drugs may be available as eye drops, a nasal spray, or an oral product. Examples include pseudoephedrine (Sudafed) and oxymetazoline (Afrin, Visine LR).

Otics: Drugs applied directly to the external ear canal. These may be in the form of solutions, suspensions, or ointments.

◈ Exercise 5-17: PHARMACOLOGY

Matching.

_____ 1. otics

_____ 2. ceruminolytics

_____ 3. antibiotics

_____ 4. decongestants

A. drugs used to treat infections
B. drugs used to relieve congestion
C. drugs applied to the external ear canal
D. medications to soften and break down earwax

Abbreviations

Abbreviation	Meaning	Abbreviation	Meaning
ABR	Auditory brain response	OAE	Otoacoustic emission
AC	Air conduction	OM	Otitis media
ASL	American sign language	Oto	Otology
BC	Bone conduction	PHL	Permanent hearing loss
ENT	Ear, nose, throat		

◈ Exercise 5-18: ABBREVIATIONS

Matching.

_____ 1. OM

_____ 2. ASL

_____ 3. BC

_____ 4. ENT

_____ 5. OAE

A. bone conduction
B. otoacoustic emission
C. American sign language
D. ear, nose, throat
E. otitis media

Careers

Optometrist

Optometrists monitor the visual health of their patients by diagnosing vision disorders. When the disorder is a refractive one, they may prescribe corrective lenses (either glasses or contacts) or discuss possible surgical interventions. Increasingly, optometrists are given the responsibility of prescribing medications for nonrefractive types of visual disorders.

To be an optometrist, a student must complete at least 3 years of college, taking courses in biology, chemistry, physics, mathematics, and English. Application to one of the accredited schools in optometry requires the completion of the Optometric Admissions Test. On graduation from optometric school (4 years), the graduate becomes a Doctor of Optometry. Before beginning to practice, the optometrist must take a written and clinical state board examination to be licensed to work in any of the states or the District of Columbia.

The job outlook for optometrists is good; opportunities are expected to increase as fast as the average for health care. The competing factors influencing the outlook are an aging population with more visual impairments versus improved technology allowing the quicker treatment of a greater number of patients. Optometrists are currently able to provide pre-operative and post-operative care for patients who have the different types of laser surgery, and although the number of prescriptions for glasses may decrease, it is expected that surgical intervention will increase.

For more information, contact the following: the Association of Schools and Colleges of Optometry at http://wwww.opted.org and the American Optometric Association at http://www.aoanet.org.

Orthoptist

Orthoptists evaluate and treat visual disorders in children and adults and work in conjunction with an ophthalmologist. They perform diagnostic tests on patients with conditions such as strabismus, diplopia, and amblyopia. A large part of a normal practice includes children with physical, mental, or emotional disabilities, so individuals interested in this field should be comfortable working with children. Training is 2 years of postgraduate study with extensive clinical experience and research. Courses include anatomy, ophthalmic optics, and clinical research methods. For more information, visit the website of the American Association of Certified Orthoptists at http://www.orthoptics.org.

Audiologist

Audiologists work with patients who have hearing and balance problems. They are responsible for measuring an individual's hearing loss and devising a treatment plan to deal with the diagnosis.

The number of audiologists needed is expected to grow much faster than average for all occupations through 2010 because of the increasing proportion of middle-aged and older adults. Most of those interested in this profession will need to pursue a graduate-level degree and licensure. Courses may include anatomy and physiology, genetics, math, physics, communication development, auditory balance and neural systems assessment and treatment, audiological rehabilitation, and ethics.

If interested, visit the website for the American Academy of Audiology at http://www.audiology.org and the American Speech-Language-Hearing Association at http://professional.asha.org.

Speech-Language Pathologist

Speech-language pathologists (SLPs), also called *speech therapists,* diagnose and treat communication disorders and dysphagia in adults and children and feeding disorders in infants. They work with individuals who have problems such as stuttering, problems understanding and producing language, and voice quality problems. Approximately half of the jobs held by SLPs are in educational settings, whereas the others are in health care settings and private practice. A master's degree is currently required by most states. Certification in the field can be gained through the American Speech-Language-Hearing Association. This profession is expected to grow faster than average because of the health problems of the baby boomers and the increase in the number of premature births. For more information, visit the American Speech-Language-Hearing Association at http://www.asha.org.

Chapter Review

A. Functions, Anatomy, and Physiology of Eyes and Ears

1. What is the term for the process of blinking? _____

2. What is the term for the production of tears? _____

3. Kerat/o is the combining form for which structure of the eye? _____

4. The muscles that hold the eye in place are the _____ muscles.

5. What type of error is due to an inability of the lens to focus accurately? _____

6. The eardrum is called the _____.

7. The ossicular chain is made up of the _____.

8. The part of the inner ear that is responsible for hearing is the _____.

9. Which part of the middle ear strikes the oval window? _____

10. The combining form for the temporal bone is _____.

B. Pathology

11. The term for nearsightedness is _____.

12. Label the following illustrations, including combining forms.

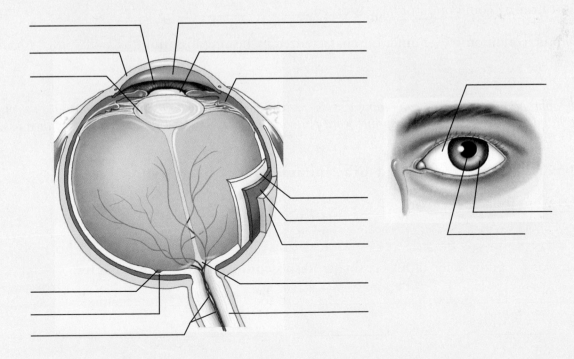

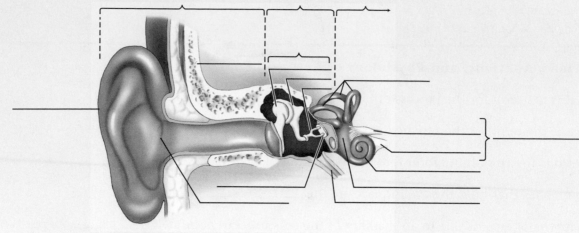

13. The other term for a stye is _____.

14. An overflow of tears is called _____.

15. Disease of the retina caused by diabetes is termed _____.

16. Ringing in the ears is called _____.

17. The term for a blockage of the external auditory canal with earwax. _____

18. Inflammation of the outer ear is called _____.

19. Development of bone around the oval window resulting in an ankylosis of the stapes is called

_____.

20. Loss of hearing common in old age is called _____.

21. A chronic condition of the inner ear characterized by hearing loss, tinnitus, and vertigo is called

_____.

Choose the appropriate word roots, combining vowels, prefixes, and suffixes to build terms that take the place of the phrase in bold. First, write the appropriate word parts in the space provided next to their type, then assemble the term on the line after the parentheses.

Ex: The 3-month-old infant was treated for an **inflammation of her eyelids**.

(*blephar* word root/*-itis* suffix)

blepharitis

22. Roger was teased by some of his classmates for his **condition of large auricles.**

(_____ prefix/ _____ word root/ _____ suffix)

_____

23. The patient called for an appointment for her **pain in the ear.**

(_____ word root/ _____ suffix)

_____

24. The triage nurse noted a **discharge from the ear** in the infant she was examining.

(_____ word root/ _____ combining vowel/ _____ suffix)

_____

25. Melissa always carried eyedrops because of her **condition of dry eyes.**

(_____ word root/ _____ word root/ _____ suffix)

_____

26. The patient reported a **condition of double vision** after being hit in the head while playing hockey.

(_____ word root/ _____ suffix)

_____

Decode the medical terms by writing the meaning of the word part in the space provided, then using the parts to form a definition.

Ex: **amblyopia**

(ambly/o *dull, dim* + -opi *vision*)

dim vision _____

27. **anisocoria**

(an- _____ + is/o _____ + cor/o _____ + -ia _____)

_____

28. **otitis media**

(ot/o _____ + -itis _____ + media _____)

_____

29. **paracusis**

(para- _____ + -acusis _____)

_____

30. **aphakia**

(a- _____ + phak/o _____ + -ia _____)

_____

31. **achromatopsia**

   (a- _____ + chromat/o _____ + -opsia _____)

   _____

C. Diagnostic Procedures

32. Term for the use of high-frequency sound waves to image the interior of the eye. _____

33. What is a test of the clearness of vision? _____

34. What is a visualization of the angle of the anterior chamber of the eye? _____

35. What test is used to screen for ARMD? _____

36. What is the term for the visual examination of the interior of the eye with an ophthalmoscope?

   _____

37. What is the measurement of intraocular pressure called? _____

38. What is a method of testing auditory acuity? _____

39. What is a measurement of the condition and mobility function of the eardrum? _____

40. What is a test of an individual's ability to hear and understand speech? _____

41. What is the term for placement of electrodes on babies to measure their response to sound?

   _____

D. Therapeutic Interventions

42. What is a suture of the eyelids? _____

43. What is the abbreviation for the use of an excimer laser to remove material under a corneal flap?

   _____

44. What is the removal of the entire contents of the orbit called? _____

45. What is the replacement of lens function by the use of a donor corneal graft? _____

46. Term for removal of the entire lens and its capsule. _____

47. Term for an incision of the eardrum. _____

48. Term for surgical repair of the external ear. _____

49. What is an opening of the eardrum to insert tubes called? _____

50. What is an implanted device that assists those with hearing loss? _____

Choose the appropriate word roots, combining vowels, prefixes, and suffixes to build terms that take the place of the phrase in bold. First, write the appropriate word parts in the space provided next to their type, then assemble the term on the line after the parentheses.

51. Shawna's great aunt was being evaluated for a possible correction to her **relaxation of the eyelids.**

    (_____ word root/ _____ combining vowel/ _____ suffix)

    _____

52. An **incision of the iris** was done to treat Mrs. Walter's glaucoma.

    (_____ word root/ _____ combining vowel/ _____ suffix)

    _____

53. After his CVA, Rosa's grandfather had **lost half of his visual field.**

    (_____ prefix/ _____ prefix/ _____ suffix)

    _____

Decode the medical term by writing the meaning of the word part in the space provided, then using the parts to form a definition.

54. **keratotomy**

    (kerat/o _____ + -tomy _____)

    _____

55. **blepharoplasty**

    (blephar/o _____ + -plasty _____)

    _____

56. **stapedectomy**

    (staped/o _____ + -ectomy _____)

    _____

E. Pharmacology

57. What class of medications keeps the eyes moist? _____

58. What class of medications is used to dilate the pupils? _____

59. What class of medications temporarily numbs the eyes? _____

60. What class of medications paralyzes the ciliary muscle? _____

61. What disorder is treated with carbonic anhydrase inhibitors, osmotics, anticholinergics, beta blockers, and alpha agonists? _____

62. What type of medication is used to dissolve earwax? _____

63. What type of drug is applied directly to the ear? _____

64. What type of medication is used to relieve congestion? _____

65. What type of medication is used to reduce infection? _____

66. What type of medication is used to constrict the pupils? _____

F. Abbreviations

67. What is the abbreviation for correct vision? _____

68. What is the abbreviation for accommodation? _____

69. A patient with a diagnosis of As has _____.

70. Eulalia had a notation in her chart that said PERRLA. What does this mean?

_____

71. The ophthalmologist measures a patient's IOP. What exactly is he or she measuring?

_____

72. What is the abbreviation for myopia? _____

73. What is the diagnosis for a patient with OM? _____

74. What is the abbreviation for the study of the ear? _____

75. A patient has her hyperopia c̄ gl. What does this mean? _____

76. What does the Snellen test measure? _____

G. Singulars and Plurals

Change the following singular terms to plural.

77. pinna _____

78. stapes _____

79. malleus _____

80. iris _____

81. canthus _____

82. conjunctiva _____

83. sclera _____

84. cornea _____

H. Translations

Rewrite the following sentences in your own words.

85. Maria appeared at the ED complaining of <u>photophobia</u>, <u>epiphora</u>, and <u>conjunctivitis</u>.

_____

86. The baby appeared inconsolable when her mother brought her to the pediatrician for what was diagnosed as <u>otitis media</u>.

_____

87. An auto accident victim came to the ED with <u>anisocoria</u>, <u>hyphema</u>, and a closed ear injury after being thrown from his vehicle.

_____

88. When the child had his first full eye examination, it was discovered that he had slight red/green <u>achromatopsia</u> and <u>emmetropia</u>.

_____

89. The 80-year-old patient evaluated by an <u>audiologist</u> was found to have <u>presbycusis</u>.

_____

90. The patient with <u>glaucoma</u> was tested with <u>tonometry</u> to measure her intraocular pressure.

_____

I. Be Careful

91. What is the difference between oral and aural?

_____

92. What is the difference between exotropia and esotropia?

_____

93. Photophobia, as a symptom of a corneal abrasion, means _____.

94. Give two meanings for the combining form salping/o.

_____

95. Explain the difference between palpebrate, palpate, and palpitate.

_____

96. What is the difference between malleus and malleolus?

_____

Case Study With Accompanying Medical Report

Mary Ellen Wright has had moderate vision problems for much of her life. She has worn glasses since she was 10 years old. She tried contacts a couple of times, but could not get used to them. Today she is visiting her optometrist, Dr. Roland O'Connor, for her annual checkup. She is planning to ask him if he thinks she is a candidate for LASIK surgery.

Mary Ellen has astigmatism. Because it has always been diligently treated with eyeglasses, she has no asthenopia, or muscle weakening, but her blurred vision is beginning to get worse. Dr. O'Connor performs routine ophthalmoscopy and slit lamp examination on Mary Ellen. Then the doctor uses fluorescein staining to visualize the abnormalities on Mary Ellen's cornea.

After a thorough examination, Dr. O'Connor talks to Mary Ellen about LASIK. He thinks she is an excellent candidate for such a procedure. He gives her a list of recommended doctors that perform LASIK and other procedures. Mary Ellen has the procedure done and very soon is seeing 20/20 again. She gratefully donates her glasses to charity.

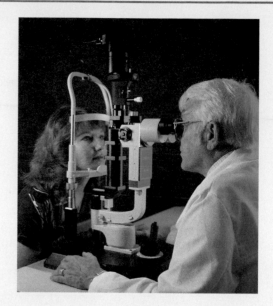

K. Health Care Report

Using the health care report on p. 197, answer the following questions.

97. Mary Ellen denies diplopia, asthenopia, and cephalgia. Explain these terms.

_____

_____

98. Mary Ellen has been diagnosed with myopic astigmatism. In your own words, explain this visual disorder.

_____

99. What is the name of the test for glaucoma? _____

100. Explain the term *paralimbal.* _____

O'Connor Eye Associates
456 Humphrey St.
Philadelphia, PA 19117

Morgan Ophthalmology Associates
789 Henry Ave.
Philadelphia, PA 19118

August 12, 200X

Re: Mary Ellen Wright, DOB: 4/1/1970

Dear Dr. Morgan:

I have had the pleasure of treating Mary Ellen Wright for the past 11 years. She has asked me to summarize her treatment for you.

Ms. Wright had received comprehensive optometric care from her previous optometrist from 1985 to 1991. Her previous records reflected good binocular oculomotor function and good ocular health, including the absence of posterior vitreous detachment, retinal breaks, or peripheral retinal degeneration either eye. She specifically denies any incidence of trauma, diplopia, asthenopia, or cephalgia. She also denies any personal or family history of glaucoma, strabismus, retinal disease, diabetes, hypertension, heart disease, or breathing problems. She is on no medications. Entrance tests, such as EOMs, pupils, color vision, confrontation fields, and cover test appeared unchanged from previously reported exams. Refractive correction for compound myopic astigmatism contained the following parameters:

Spectacle Correction: Right eye −7.50 − 1.00 × 165 20/20
                                      Left eye −7.50 − 1.00 × 180 20/20
Contact Lenses: Right eye 20/15; OS 20/15

The contact lens fit showed a stable paralimbal soft lens fit with good centration, 360 degree corneal coverage, and 0.50 mm movement each eye. Each lens surface contained a trace amount of scattered protein deposits.

She came for her last comprehensive examination without any visual or ocular complaints. She desired a new supply of disposable contact lenses. She reported clear and comfortable vision at distance, intermediate, and near with both her glasses and contact lenses.

Eye Health Assessment: Slit lamp examination revealed clean lids with good tonicity and apposition to the globe. The lashes and lid margins were clear of debris. There was no discharge from either eye. The corneas were clear with no fluorescein staining either eye. Pupils were equal, round, and reactive to light and accommodation without afferent defect. Intraocular pressures measured 10 mm Hg right eye, left eye at 1:30 p.m. with Goldmann applanation tonometry.

If any further information is needed, please feel free to contact me regarding this patient.

Sincerely,

Roland O'Connor, OD

Reference

Quotation from http://www.quoteablequotes.net.

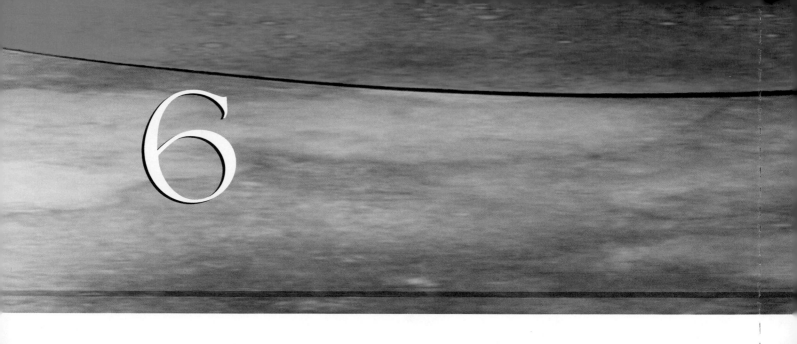

6

OBJECTIVES

You will be able to do the following after completing this chapter:

Key Terms
1. Define, appropriately use, and spell all the Key Terms for this chapter.

Sensory System
2. Explain the purpose of the sensory system.
3. List and describe the five main senses.
4. List the five general sensations.
5. Name the organs and structures of the sensory system and describe the function of each.

Eye Structure and Function
6. List and describe seven common signs and symptoms of eye disease.
7. List six diagnostic tests and procedures for eye disease and explain the use of each.
8. List 12 eye diseases and describe the etiology, signs and symptoms, diagnosis, therapy, and interventions for each.

Eye Treatments
9. Demonstrate the correct procedure for irrigating a patient's eye to remove foreign particles.
10. Demonstrate the procedure for properly instilling prescribed medication in an affected eye.
11. Explain why the medical assistant should be careful not to touch the surface of the eye with the tip of the irrigating syringe, the tip of the eyedropper, or the finger.

Ear Structure and Function
12. List and describe four signs and symptoms of ear disorders.
13. List four tests for ear disorders and explain the use of each.
14. List seven ear disorders and describe the etiology, signs and symptoms, diagnosis, therapy, and interventions for each.

Hearing Acuity Tests
15. List the three types of hearing acuity tests and state the purpose of each.

Ear Treatments
16. Demonstrate the correct procedure for irrigating the external ear canal to remove cerumen or foreign objects.
17. Demonstrate the procedure for properly instilling prescribed medication in an affected ear.
18. Explain why extreme care must be taken when working with a patient's infected ear.

ANATOMY AND PHYSIOLOGY OF THE SPECIAL SENSES

Patient-Centered Professionalism

19. Analyze a realistic medical office situation and apply your understanding of the special senses to determine the best course of action.
20. Describe the impact on patient care when medical assistants have a solid understanding of the structure and function of the special senses.

KEY TERMS

The Key Terms for this chapter have been organized into sections so that you can easily see the terminology associated with each aspect of the nervous system.

Sensory System

equilibrium Sense of balance.
olfaction Sense of smell.
proprioception Awareness of body position.
tactile Pertaining to the sense of touch.

Taste

gustatory receptors Receptors in the taste buds that relay impulses of taste to the brain.
papillae Small projections on the tongue that contain taste buds.

Vision

accommodation Visual adjustment that allows for vision at various distances.
optic nerve Nerve that carries visual impulses from the retina to the brain; second cranial nerve.
refraction Bending of light rays as they pass from one medium to another.
Eyeball
anterior cavity Space in front of the lens between the cornea and iris.
aqueous humor Fluid portion of anterior chambers of the eye.
choroid Middle vascular part of the eye; supplies oxygen and nutrients to the eye.

ciliary body Blood-rich ringed structure surrounding the lens and adjusting its shapes for near and far vision.
cones Receptors of color.
cornea Anterior portion of the sclera; transparent (allows light through).
fovea centralis Depression in the retina; point of sharpest vision.
iris Colored portion of the eye between the lens and cornea that regulates the amount of light entering the pupil; separates anterior and posterior chambers.
lens Transparent structure in the anterior portion of the eye; focuses images on the eye.
macula lutea Yellowish spot in the retina that contains the fovea.
opaque Not clear; cloudy.
ophthalmoscope Instrument used to view the retina.
optic disk (blind spot) Area of no visual reception (no rods or cones) where the optic nerve joins the retina.
posterior cavity Space between the iris and lens.
pupil Opening at the center of the iris that regulates the entrance of light.
retina Innermost layer containing the cones, rods, and blood vessels.
rods Receptors for black and white and peripheral vision.
sclera White of the eye; tough outer layer.
vitreous humor Jelly-like substance in the posterior chamber that gives the eyeball its shape.
Eye Muscles
extrinsic muscles Six skeletal muscles that allow the eye to move and hold it to the orbit.

KEY TERMS—cont'd

intrinsic muscles Smooth muscles in the iris that control the amount of light entering the eye.

oblique Angled.

rectus Straight.

suspensory ligament Ligament that holds the lens in place.

Accessory Organs

canthus Angle at either side of the slit between the eyelids.

conjunctiva Mucous membrane that lines the eyelids and anterior portion of the eyeball; keeps the eye moist.

Eye Diseases

astigmatism Refraction error caused by the abnormal curvature of the cornea and lens.

cataract Opacity of the lens.

chalazion Small mass on the eyelid caused by inflammation and blockage of a gland.

conjunctivitis (pinkeye) Inflamed conjunctiva.

glaucoma Condition resulting when aqueous humor does not drain properly, increasing intraocular pressure, compressing choroid layer, and diminishing blood supply to the retina.

hordeolum (stye) Localized bacterial infection in the eyelid.

hyperopia (farsightedness) Light rays form behind the retina.

myopia (nearsightedness) Light rays focus in front of the retina.

nystagmus Rapid, involuntary, rhythmic movement of the eyeball.

ophthalmologist Specialist in the treatment of eye disorders.

presbyopia (old eyes) Lens loses its ability to change shape during accommodation for close objects.

ptosis Drooping (e.g., upper eyelid is unable to remain open).

slit-lamp examination Examination of various layers of the eye.

strabismus (cross-eye) Movements of the eyeball are not coordinated because of a congenital weakness of external eye muscles.

tonometry Measurement of intraocular pressure (glaucoma).

Hearing

auditory Hearing.

inner ear Part of the ear that contains receptors for sound waves, maintaining equilibrium.

middle ear Cavity in the temporal bone filled with air that is connected to the throat.

outer ear External ear, including the pinna, external auditory canal, and tympanic membrane.

Outer Ear

cerumen Earwax; yellow or brown substance produced by sweat glands in the external ear.

external auditory canal Path that leads from the pinna to the middle ear.

pinna (auricle) External portion of the ear (flap).

tympanic membrane (eardrum) Structure that transmits sound waves to the ossicles of the middle ear.

Middle Ear

eustachian tube Tube that connects the middle ear with the nasopharynx and acts to equalize pressure between the outer ear and middle ear.

incus (anvil) Part of the middle ear that transmits sound vibrations from the malleus to the stapes.

malleus (hammer) One of the three bones of the middle ear responsible for producing sound; connected to the tympanic membrane and transmits vibrations to the incus.

ossicles Small bones of the middle ear, including the malleus, incus, and stapes.

oval window Opening in the inner ear that is in contact with the stapes.

round window Area below the oval window that separates the middle ear and inner ear.

stapes (stirrup) Part of the middle ear that transmits sound vibrations from the incus to the internal ear; smallest bone in the body.

Inner Ear

cochlea Coiled portion of the inner ear that contains the receptors for hearing.

labyrinth Bones and membranes of the inner ear that contain receptors for sound waves and maintain balance (equilibrium).

organ of Corti Receptor of hearing located in the cochlea.

Sound

audiometry Test that measures sounds heard by the human ear.

decibels (dB) Measurement of loud or soft sounds.

pitch Pertains to high or low sound created by sound waves.

Ear Disorders

deafness Interference with the passage of sound waves from the outside to the inner ear; complete or partial inability to hear.

mastoiditis Inflammation of the lining of mastoid cells.

Meniere disease Buildup of excess fluid in the semicircular canals, which places excess pressure on the canals, vestibule, and the cochlea, causing dizziness, ringing in the ears, and a sensation of fullness.

otitis externa (swimmer's ear) Inflammation of the outer ear.

otitis media Inflammation of the middle ear.

otolaryngologist Specialist in the treatment of ear, nose, and throat diseases.

otosclerosis Hardening of the ear bones.

otoscopy Views the tympanic membrane and various parts of the outer ear.

presbycusis Progressive hearing loss occurring in old age.

tinnitus Ringing in the ears.

Equilibrium

motion sickness Excessive stimulation to the vestibular apparatus, causing a feeling of nausea.

semicircular canals Inner ear structures that control equilibrium and detect motion.

KEY TERMS—*cont'd*

vestibular apparatus Portion of the inner ear that handles equilibrium; consists of the vestibule and semicircular canals.

vestibule Inner ear structure behind the cochlea that controls the sense of position in space.

Hearing Tests

audiogram Record produced by an audiometer.

audiologist Specialist in audiology or hearing disorders.

audiometry Measurement of hearing ability.

conduction Ability to move from one area to another, as in hearing with transmission of sound through nervous tissue.

hearing acuity tests Tests used to check for hearing loss.

Rinne test Test that uses a tuning fork to compare bone conduction and air conduction of sound.

tuning fork Instrument used to test for hearing using vibration through bone conduction.

Weber test Test to determine whether a hearing loss is conductive or sensorineural.

Eye and Ear Treatments

instillation Process of placing medication into an area as prescribed by a physician.

irrigation Washing or rinsing out an area to remove foreign matter.

What Would You Do?

The senses allow the body to respond to both internal and external stimuli. Senses are needed to maintain homeostasis, protect the body from harm, and conduct pleasure or pain. Each sense (e.g., taste, vision, smell) has a sensory system with receptors that allow it to transmit impulses to the central nervous system (CNS) for interpretation. The main senses include taste, smell **(olfaction),** vision, hearing, and balance. General sensations include pain, touch **(tactile),** pressure, temperature, and **proprioception** (Box 6-1 and Fig. 6-1).

SENSORY SYSTEM

TASTE

The tongue is a movable muscular organ and consists of two halves united in the center. **Papillae** cover the tongue and contain capillaries and nerves. The taste buds are distributed on the surface of the tongue and throughout the mouth, especially the soft palate. Each taste bud is made up of **gustatory receptors** that relay impulses to the brain. They are stimulated only if the substance to be tasted is in a solution. The four different kinds of taste buds have separate locations on the tongue (Fig. 6-2), as follows:

1. *Sweet* taste: located near the tip of the tongue.
2. *Sour* taste: located on both sides of the tongue.
3. *Salty* taste: located near the tip of the tongue.
4. *Bitter* taste: located at the back of the tongue.

BOX 6-1   General Sensations*

- *Pain* is a reaction to tissue damage and therefore acts as a protective function of the body. Pain receptors are distributed throughout the body and react to release of chemicals when the tissue is damaged, when oxygen fails to reach tissue, or when tissues are stretched or deformed.
- *Touch* and *pressure* (tactile) receptors are located in the skin, subcutaneous tissue, and deep tissue and respond to pressure and vibration. Tactile receptors are most concentrated in the lips and fingers.
- *Temperature* receptors detect hot and cold. Cold receptors are stimulated at 10° to 25° C and heat receptors at 25° to 45° C. Both types of receptors adapt to the heat or cold, and therefore the sensation fades after 20 to 30 minutes (*accommodation*).
- *Proprioception* receptors are found in muscles, tendons, joints, and inner ear and function to maintain balance and to create awareness of one's sense of position in space.

*See also Fig. 6-1.

≋ SMELL

The sense of smell is accomplished by the olfactory nerve. Branches containing receptors are located throughout the upper part of the nasal cavity and the upper third of the septum (Fig. 6-3). Nasal sensations of cold, heat, pain, and pressure are produced by the trigeminal nerve.

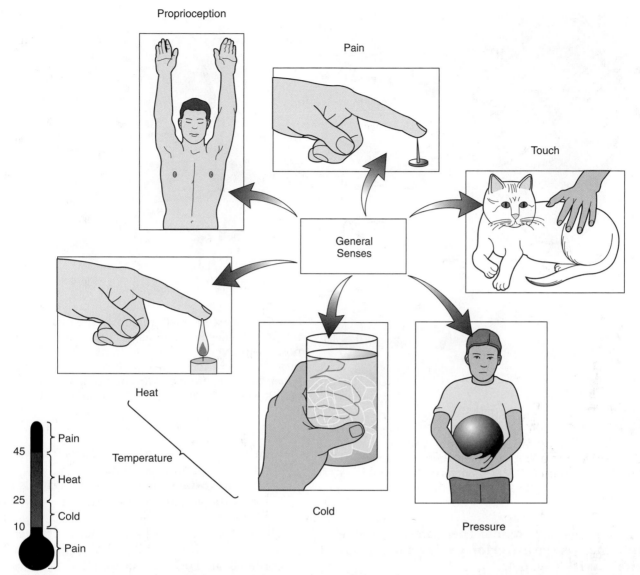

Fig. 6-1 General senses: pain, touch, pressure, temperature, and proprioception. *(From Herlihy B, Maebius NK: The human body in health and illness, ed 2, Philadelphia, 2003, Saunders.)*

The sense of smell is closely related to the sense of taste. When the sense of smell is decreased (e.g., person has a cold), the sense of taste also diminishes. Olfactory nerves become less sensitive after detecting the same odor over time, which is why it is harder to smell your laundry soap, bath soap, or shampoo if you use the same type over a long period.

PATIENT CENTERED PROFESSIONALISM

- How does being knowledgeable about the sensory system and diseases affecting this system make the medical assistant a valuable asset in the medical office?

VISION

The eye and other organs work together to provide vision.

Eye Structure and Function

The eye is the receptor organ of vision, providing us with three-dimensional sight. The eye receives light rays and sends the impulses to the **optic nerve.** The optic nerve carries impulses to the brain, where they are interpreted for sight. Each eye is located in a bony orbital cavity within the skull for protection.

Eyeball

The eyeball is a round, hollow structure about an inch in diameter. It is composed of three layers: the

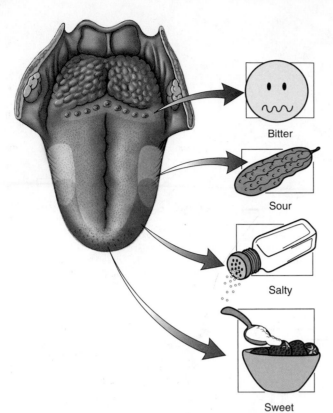

Fig. 6-2 Sense of taste in the tongue (gustatory sense). Taste buds located on specific areas of tongue identify four taste sensations: bitter, sour, salty, and sweet. *(From Herlihy B, Maebius NK: The human body in health and illness, ed 2, Philadelphia, 2003, Saunders.)*

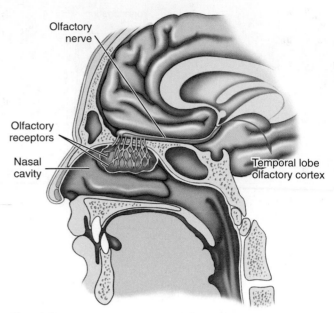

Fig. 6-3 Sense of smell: the nose. The olfactory (smell) receptors are chemoreceptors and are located in the upper nose. Sensory information is transmitted through the olfactory nerve to the temporal lobe of the cerebrum. *(From Herlihy B, Maebius NK: The human body in health and illness, ed 2, Philadelphia, 2003, Saunders.)*

sclera, choroid, and retina. There are two cavities within the eye: the **anterior cavity** and the **posterior cavity** (Fig. 6-4, *A*).

1. The **sclera** is the outermost layer, or white of the eye. It is a fibrous protective tissue that maintains the shape of the eye, is the attachment site for the extrinsic eye muscles, and protects the other layers. The **cornea** is avascular and does not contain blood vessels, so light rays are allowed to penetrate.
2. The **choroid** is the middle layer and is **opaque.** It contains many blood vessels and is attached to the retina. The other parts of the middle layer are the iris and the ciliary body.
   - The **iris** lies beneath the cornea and is in front of the **lens.** The opening in the center of the iris is the **pupil.** The iris contains the eye color, and the pupil is a radial muscle that dilates or constricts to regulate the amount of light that enters the eye.
   - The **ciliary body** contains the ciliary muscle, which controls the shape or

curvature of the lens and allows for near and far vision, a process called **accommodation.** The ciliary body also forms the aqueous humor that flows in front of the eye.
3. The **retina,** the third and innermost layer, lines the interior of the eyeball. The retina contains the **rods** and **cones** that are photoreceptors sensitive to light. Proper sight requires that light rays bend **(refraction)** as they pass through the eye structures to the retina. The optic nerve branches out within the retina to collect the impulses given off by the rods and cones and transmits them to the brain.
   - The rods are responsible for sight in dim light and peripheral vision and are sensitive to black and white.
   - The cones are responsible for sight in bright light and are sensitive to color.

Between the cornea and the iris and between the iris and the lens is the anterior cavity and posterior cavity (Fig. 6-4, *B* and *C*) filled with fluid (humor). The **aqueous humor** helps to maintain a constant pressure within the eye in the anterior cavity.

Directly behind the lens is the posterior chamber filled with **vitreous humor,** a clear, jelly-like substance that maintains the shape of the eye and gives

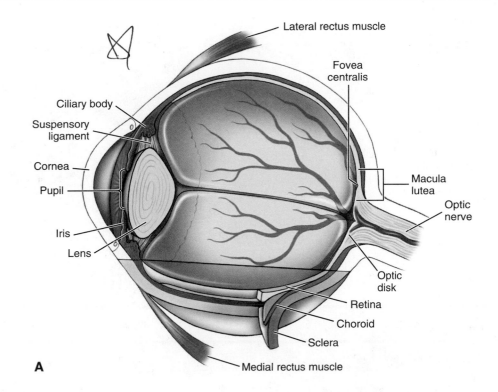

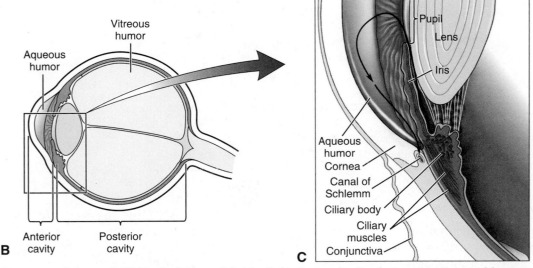

Fig. 6-4 **A,** Structure of the eyeball. **B,** Cavities and fluids. Posterior cavity lies between retina and lens; it is filled with vitreous humor. Anterior cavity lies between lens and cornea. **C,** Note flow of aqueous humor from ciliary body to canal of Schlemm *(arrow)*. *(From Herlihy B, Maebius NK: The human body in health and illness, ed 2, Philadelphia, 2003, Saunders.)*

the retina support. Together the lens, vitreous humor, and the aqueous humor allow light rays to bend (refract) (Fig. 6-4, *B*).

When the physician views the retina through the **ophthalmoscope,** a yellow disk **(macula lutea)** is seen. Within the disk is the **fovea centralis** that contains only the cones for color vision. To the side of the fovea is a pale disc called the **optic disk,** or **blind spot.** There are no rods or cones in this area and thus no visual reception.

Eye Muscles

Six different **extrinsic** skeletal muscles allow the eye to move and anchor the eye in place. There are four **rectus** (straight) muscles—superior, inferior, medial, and lateral—and two **oblique** (angled) muscles, superior and inferior (Fig. 6-5 and Table 6-1). The **intrinsic muscles** within the iris are smooth involuntary muscles, and this controls the amount of light entering the pupil and allows for close vision.

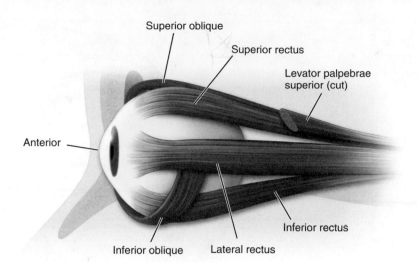

Fig. 6-5 Muscles of the eye. *(Modified from Chester GA: Modern medical assisting, Philadelphia, 1999, Saunders.)*

TABLE 6-1	Eye Muscles	
Muscle	**Function**	**Cranial Nerve**
Extrinsic		
Superior rectus	Elevates or rolls the eyeball upward	III
Inferior rectus	Depresses or rolls the eyeball downward	III
Medial rectus	Moves or rolls the eyeball toward the middle	III
Lateral rectus	Moves or rolls the eyeball to the side or laterally	VI
Superior oblique	Depresses or rolls the eyeball to the side or laterally	IV
Inferior oblique	Elevates or rolls the eyeball upward	III
Intrinsic		
Ciliary	Allows the **suspensory ligament** to relax and the lens to become more convex for close vision	III
Iris, circular	Constricts the pupil to allow less light to enter the eye	III
Iris, radial	Dilates the pupil to allow more light to enter the eye	III

Accessory Organs

Besides the eye, additional organs help us to see. The visual accessory organs include the eyebrows, eyelids, eyelashes, lacrimal apparatus, and extrinsic eye muscles (Fig. 6-6).

- The *eyebrows* are small patches of coarse hair above the eyes. The brows shade the eyes from sunlight and keep perspiration (sweat) from falling into the eyes.
- The *eyelids* are protective folds covering the eyes. The lids protect the eye from excessive light and foreign matter by blinking. The angles at the ends of the area where the upper and lower lids meet are called the **canthi** (sing., canthus). The **conjunctiva** is a mucous membrane that lines the underside of the eyelid and protects the exposed area of the eyeball.

- The *eyelashes* line the edge of the eyelid and serve to trap foreign objects (e.g., dust). The lashes protrude from oil-producing sebaceous glands on the edge of the lid.
- The *lacrimal apparatus* is composed of the lacrimal gland and tear ducts. The lacrimal gland secretes tears that drain into nasolacrimal ducts. Tears function to lubricate, cleanse the eye surface, and keep the eye from becoming dry.
- The *extrinsic eye muscles* are discussed previously (see Table 6-1).

Eye Diseases

Diseases of the eye may be present at birth or may appear as the body ages. An **ophthalmologist** treats disorders of the eye. Drugs may be prescribed to treat diseases of the eye (Table 6-2).

TABLE 6-2 Eye Drug Classifications

Drug Classification	Common Generic (Brand) Drugs
Antifungals Reduce effects of fungal infection	natamycin (Natacyn)
Anti-infectives Destroy bacteria	gentamicin (Garamycin) tetracycline (Achromycin)
Anti-inflammatories Reduce inflammation	ketorolac (Acular) dexamethasone (Decadron)
Antiseptics Prohibit growth of bacteria (prophylaxis)	silver nitrate 1% boric acid (Blinx)
Antivirals Treat infections of the eye	vidarabine (Vira-A) trifluridine (Viroptic)
Antiglaucoma agents Reduce intraocular pressure by increasing drainage of aqueous humor or decreasing its production	pilocarpine (Pilocar) apraclonidine (Lopidine)
Topical anesthetics Prevent eye pain	tetracaine (Pontocaine) proparacaine (Kainair)

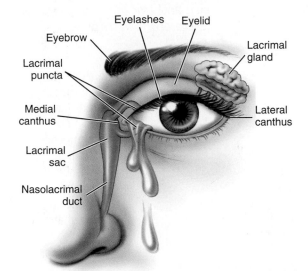

Fig. 6-6 Visual accessory organs: eyebrows, eyelids, eyelashes, and lacrimal apparatus. Tears are secreted by the lacrimal gland, wash over the surface of the eye, and drain into the lacrimal sac and finally into the nasolacrimal duct. Crying floods the system, causing tears to flow. *(From Herlihy B, Maebius NK: The human body in health and illness, ed 2, Philadelphia, 2003, Saunders.)*

Medical assistants need to be able to recognize the common signs and symptoms of and diagnostic tests for the different types of eye disorders.

- Study Box 6-2 to familiarize yourself with the common signs and symptoms.
- Study Box 6-3 to learn about common diagnostic tests.
- Study Table 6-3 to understand the diseases that affect the eye.

BOX 6-2 Common Signs and Symptoms of Eye Disorders

Amblyopia	Dull or dim vision caused by disease
Diplopia	Seeing double
Dacryoadenitis	Inflammation of lacrimal gland
Esotropia	Turning inward of one or both eyes
Exophthalmia	Protrusion of the eyeballs
Exotropia	Turning outward of one or both eyes
Xerophthalmia	Dry eye

BOX 6-3 Diagnostic Tests and Procedures for the Eye

Amsler grid	Assesses central vision (macular degeneration)
Fluorescein angiography	Traces pathway through vessels of retina after injection of dye
Fluorescein staining	Assesses for abnormalities of cornea after drops of dye instilled into eye
Gonioscopy	Visualizes angle of anterior chamber (glaucoma)
Slit-lamp examination	Examines various layers of the eye
Tonometry	Measures intraocular pressure (glaucoma)

TABLE 6-3	Diseases and Disorders of the Eye				
Disease and Description	**Etiology**	**Signs and Symptoms**	**Diagnosis**	**Therapy**	**Interventions**
Cataract Opacity of lens of eye	*Senile cataracts:* in elderly; chemical changes in lens *Congenital cataracts:* in newborns; errors of metabolism *Traumatic cataracts:* trauma allows humor to invade lens capsule	Complaints of gradual vision loss; glare or poor vision in bright sunlight or night driving	Visual acuity test that supports complaint of vision loss; **slit-lamp examination** that identifies lens opacity and apparent cloudy lens on examination	Surgical lens extraction and lens implant to correct vision	Avoid activities after eye surgery that would increase eye pressure (e.g., bending over, straining with coughing, bowel movements, or lifting)
Chalazion Small mass on eyelid caused by inflammation and blockage of gland	Obstruction of gland duct in eyelid	Nontender, small cyst on eyelid	Visual examination	Warm compresses to open gland and antibiotic eye drops to prevent infection	Provide proper instructions for using warm compresses to prevent cross-contamination
Conjunctivitis (pinkeye) Conjunctiva becomes inflamed (Fig. 6-7, C)	Irritation caused by allergies or viral or bacterial infection	Complaints of eye pain, photophobia, burning, itching, and crusting	Inspection of eye shows discharge, tearing, and hyperemia*; culture and sensitivity tests of discharge identify organism	Topical antibiotic	Illustrate proper handwashing techniques to minimize spread of infection to family members; emphasize importance of not sharing towels, washcloths, or pillows
Glaucoma Aqueous humor does not drain properly, and intraocular pressure increases and compresses choroid layer, diminishing blood supply to retina	Can be found in families because of narrow channel between iris and cornea	May be insidious and progress slowly, therefore asymptomatic; dull morning headache, aching in eyes, loss of peripheral vision, seeing halos around lights, decrease in visual acuity; may also be acute with severe eye pain	**Tonometry** is used to measure intraocular pressure; slit-lamp examination for anterior eye structures	Medications to reduce aqueous humor production and promote outflow of humor; in extreme cases, laser surgery to enhance aqueous humor outflow	Encourage following treatment regimen to decrease risk of total blindness

TABLE 6-3	Diseases and Disorders of the Eye—cont'd				
Disease and Description	**Etiology**	**Signs and Symptoms**	**Diagnosis**	**Therapy**	**Interventions**
Hordeolum (stye) Localized infection in eyelid (Fig. 6-7, *B*)	Hair follicle in eyelid becomes infected with staphylococcal organism	Painful swelling of eyelid	Culture and sensitivity of exudate	Warm compresses 4 times daily; ophthalmic antibiotic drops or ointment	Instruct patient to use clean compress for each application; dispose of or launder it separately; caution not to squeeze stye or rub eye (could spread infection)
Ptosis Upper eyelid unable to remain open (Fig. 6-7, *A*)	*Congenital:* levator muscles fail to develop *Acquired:* age, swelling, neurogenic factors, thiamine deficiency (alcoholism)	One eyelid covers iris partially or completely	Clinical inspection to determine cause may include glucose tolerance test to verify presence of diabetes, ophthalmic examination to rule out trauma or foreign body	If severe ptosis exists, surgical intervention is needed to resect levator muscles	Ensure patient is aware of increased risk for injury and perceptual and sensory alterations
Strabismus (cross-eye) Movements of eyeball not coordinated (Fig. 6-7, *D*)	May occur from trauma or eye muscle imbalance	Eyes deviate inward, upward, or outward	Neurological examination to determine if cause is muscular or neurological	Patching normal eye to force affected eye to focus straight, strengthening muscle; surgical intervention to shorten muscle	Emphasize need for follow-up care; patient teaching for instilling eye medications if used after surgery

Additional Eye Conditions

Astigmatism: Refraction error caused by abnormal curvature of cornea and lens (Fig. 6-8, *C*)

Hyperopia (farsightedness): Occurs when light rays form behind retina (Fig. 6-8, *B*)

Myopia (nearsightedness): Occurs when light rays focus in front of retina (Fig. 6-8, *A*)

Nystagmus: Rapid, involuntary, rhythmic movement of the eyeball

Presbyopia (old eyes): Occurs when the lens loses its ability to change shape during accommodation for close objects

*Hyperemia engorgement, excessive blood in tissues.

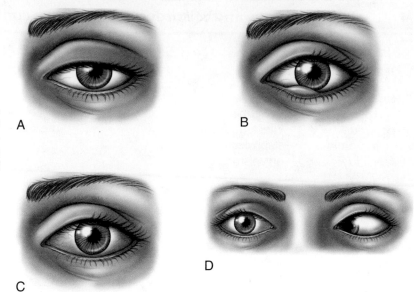

Fig. 6-7 **A**, Ptosis of eyelid; droopy eyelid. **B**, Hordeolum, or stye. **C**, Conjunctivitis, or pinkeye. **D**, Strabismus. Note that eyeball deviates from the midline. *(From Herlihy B, Maebius NK:* The human body in health and illness, *ed 2, Philadelphia, 2003, Saunders.)*

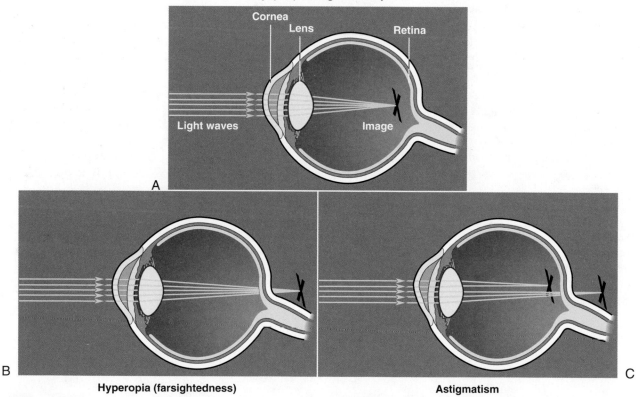

Fig. 6-8 **A**, Myopia, or nearsightedness. **B**, Hyperopia, or farsightedness. **C**, Astigmatism. *(From Herlihy B, Maebius NK:* The human body in health and illness, *ed 2, Philadelphia, 2003, Saunders.)*

Eye Treatments

Eye treatments are also performed in the medical office. Eye irrigation and eye instillation are two procedures that medical assistants must be able to perform.

Eye Irrigation

Eye irrigations are performed to rinse irritants or discharge away from affected eyes. Irritants and discharge can cause damage to the exterior eye. Rinsing them away minimizes tissue damage and soothes the irritated tissue. Procedure 6-1 describes the process of performing eye irrigation.

Procedure 6-1 Perform an Eye Irrigation

TASK: Irrigate the patient's eye(s) to remove foreign particles (by flushing irritants from the eye) and to soothe irritated tissue.

EQUIPMENT AND SUPPLIES
- Sterile irrigating solution
- Sterile container to hold the solution
- Sterile rubber bulb syringe or bottled solution
- Disposable gloves (powder free)
- Basin for the returned solution
- Sterile gauze squares
- Disposable moisture-resistant towel
- Biohazardous waste container
- Patient's medical record
- Tissues

SKILLS/RATIONALE

STANDARD PRECAUTIONS ARE TO BE FOLLOWED.

1. **Procedural Step. Sanitize the hands.**
   An alcohol-based hand rub may be used instead of washing hands with soap and water, unless hands are visibly soiled.
   Rationale. Hand sanitization promotes infection control.

2. **Procedural Step. Assemble equipment and supplies.**
   Rationale. It is important to have all supplies and equipment ready and available before starting any procedure to ensure efficiency.

3. **Procedural Step. Verify the physician's order.**
   Typically the physician will order normal saline as the irrigating solution. Check the expiration date of the solution. As with all medications, ensure that the correct preparation is being used by reading the label three times: the first time when the medication is taken from the cupboard; the second time while you are preparing the medication; and the third time just before returning the solution to the cupboard.
   NOTE: If both eyes are to be irrigated, two separate sets of supplies and equipment must be used to prevent cross-infection from one eye to the other.
   Rationale. The solution should be carefully compared with the physician's instructions to prevent an error. If the solution is outdated, consult the physician; it may produce undesirable effects.
   Rationale. If the solution is too cold or too warm, it will be uncomfortable for the patient.

4. **Procedural Step. Obtain the patient's medical record.**

5. **Procedural Step. Escort the patient to the examination room, greet and identify the patient, and ask the patient to have a seat on the end of the examination table.**
   Rationale. Identifying the patient ensures the procedure is performed on the correct patient.

6. **Procedural Step. Explain the procedure to the patient.**
   Rationale. Explaining the procedure to the patient promotes cooperation and provides a means of obtaining implied consent.

7. **Procedural Step. Warm the irrigating solution to body temperature by running the container under warm running tap water (98.6° to 100° F).**

8. **Procedural Step. Position the patient.**
   Place the patient in a supine position. Ask the patient to tilt the head toward the affected eye. A moisture-resistant towel should be placed on the patient's shoulder to protect the patient's clothing. Position a basin tightly against the patient's cheek under the affected eye to catch the irrigating solution.
   Rationale. The patient is positioned to prevent solution from the affected eye from flowing into the unaffected eye and causing cross-contamination.

9. **Procedural Step. Put on disposable powder-free gloves.**
   Rationale. Using powdered gloves may irritate the patient's eyes if powder from the outside of the glove comes in contact with the eye.

10. **Procedural Step. Remove any debris or discharge from the patient's eyelid.**
    Moisten three or four gauze squares with the irrigating solution, and wipe the eyelids and eyelashes from the inner canthus (next to the nose) to the outer canthus. Use each cotton ball or gauze square to wipe the eyelid only once and then discard.
    Rationale. The eyelids must be cleaned to prevent any foreign particles from entering the eye during the irrigation. Cleansing from the inner to the outer canthus prevents cross-infection.

11. **Procedural Step. Prepare the irrigation syringe.**
    Remove the cap from the sterile irrigating solution bottle, being careful not to touch the tip of the bottle and keeping the inside of the cap up to prevent contamination. If you are

Continued

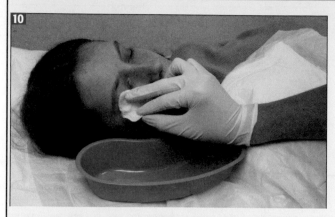

using an irrigating syringe instead of using the solution directly from the sterile bottle, pour the warmed solution into the sterile basin. Fill the irrigating syringe by squeezing and releasing the bulb until the ordered amount of solution fills the syringe.

12. **Procedural Step. Expose the lower conjunctiva by separating the eyelids with the gloved index finger and thumb, and ask the patient to stare at a fixed spot.**

    Rationale. Staring at a fixed spot limits the patient's eye movement during the irrigation. The patient will naturally want to close the eye during the irrigation, so it must be held open.

13. **Procedural Step. Irrigate the affected eye(s).**

    Rest the syringe or irrigating solution bottle on the bridge of the patient's nose, being extremely careful not to touch the eye or conjunctiva with the tip. Gently release the solution, at an even flow rate and directed at the lower conjunctiva, from the inner canthus toward the outer canthus.

    NOTE: If both eyes are being treated, two medical assistants may be required to perform

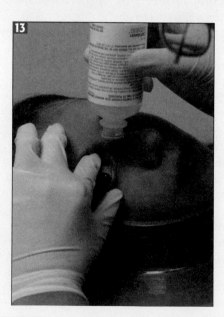

the procedure or one eye may be irrigated at a time. Provide a gown and ask the patient to change clothes. Prepare two sets of supplies. Place the patient in a supine position, and ask the patient to stare up at the ceiling. Place a towel under the patient's shoulders. A basin should be provided for both sides. Follow Steps 9 through 13, being certain that the irrigating solution runs from the inner to the outer canthus of both eyes.

Rationale. Directing the solution away from the unaffected eye prevents cross-contamination. The irrigating solution must be directed at the lower conjunctiva to prevent injury to the sensitive cornea.

14. **Procedural Step. Continue with the irrigation until the correct amount of solution has been used or as ordered by the physician.**

    You may be required to refill the irrigating syringe or to open a second bottle of sterile normal saline. The amount of the solution ordered will vary according to the purpose of the irrigation.

15. **Procedural Step. When the correct amount of irrigating solution has been used, dry the eyelids from the inner to the outer canthus (as in Step 10) using dry gauze squares.**

16. **Procedural Step. Provide the patient with tissue to wipe the face and neck as needed. Inform the patient that the eye(s) may be red and irritated.**

17. **Procedural Step. Remove gloves and sanitize the hands.**

    Always sanitize the hands after every procedure or after using gloves.

18. **Procedural Step. Provide follow-up instructions.**

19. **Procedural Step. Document the procedure.**

    Include the date and time; which eye was irrigated; type, strength, and amount of solution used; and any significant observations and patient reactions.

20. **Procedural Step. Clean the equipment and examination room.**

    Discard all used supplies in an appropriate waste container. If discharge or exudate was present, discard contaminated supplies in the biohazardous waste container.

Charting Example	
Date	
12/3/xx	11:00 a.m. right eye irrigated c̄ 100 mL sterile normal saline to remove foreign particles. Several small brown flecks returned. Patient tolerated procedure well. No complaints of discomfort.
	—— C. Arundel, CMA (AAMA)

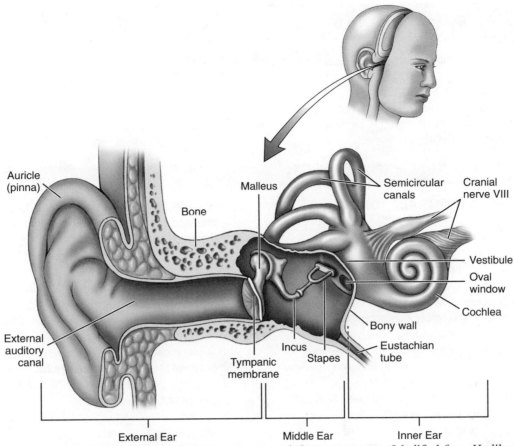

Fig. 6-9   Three divisions of the ear (external, middle, inner) and their structures. *(Modified from Herlihy B, Maebius NK: The human body in health and illness, ed 2, Philadelphia, 2003, Saunders.)*

All irrigating solutions must be sterile. When performing eye irrigation, the medical assistant must be careful not to touch the surface of the eye or the finger with the tip of the irrigating syringe. Contact with either of these will contaminate the tip of the irrigating syringe and therefore anything else the tip contacts. Always irrigate with the patient's head tilted away from the unaffected eye to prevent cross-contamination.

Eye Instillation

Eye instillation is the application of prescribed medication to the eye. Eye medications are either a liquid or an **ointment.** Procedure 6-2 describes the process of performing eye instillation.

As with eye irrigation, be careful not to touch the surface of the eye with the tip of the eyedropper or the finger to prevent cross-contamination.

HEARING

The ear is the major organ of hearing. It picks up sound waves and sends the impulses to the **auditory** center of the brain in the temporal region. The transmission of sound waves in the **outer ear** occurs through air, in the **middle ear** occurs

through bone, and in the **inner ear** occurs through fluid. The inner ear also functions to maintain balance, **equilibrium,** and awareness of position.

Ear Structure and Function

The ear consists of three parts: the outer ear, middle ear, and inner ear (Fig. 6-9).

Outer (External) Ear

The outer ear is the visible part of the ear and a canal that connects to the middle ear.

- The **pinna,** or **auricle,** is the projecting part of the ear. It is the flap of skin and cartilage on the outside of the head.
- The **external auditory canal** extends from the auricle to about 4 cm into the skull and ends at the tympanic membrane. Air vibrations are guided through the canal to the tympanic membrane.
- The **tympanic membrane,** or **eardrum,** is a thin membrane that completely separates the outer ear from the middle ear, with skin on the outside and a mucous membrane on the inside. The eardrum vibrates when struck by sound waves.

Procedure 6-2 Perform an Eye Instillation

TASK: Properly instill prescribed medication in the affected eye(s).

EQUIPMENT AND SUPPLIES

- Ophthalmic drops with sterile eyedropper or ophthalmic ointment ordered by physician
- Sterile gauze squares
- Tissues
- Disposable gloves (powder free)
- Patient's medical record

SKILLS/RATIONALE

STANDARD PRECAUTIONS ARE TO BE FOLLOWED.

1. **Procedural Step. Sanitize the hands.**
An alcohol-based hand rub may be used instead of washing hands with soap and water, unless hands are visibly soiled.
Rationale. Hand sanitization promotes infection control.

2. **Procedural Step. Assemble equipment and supplies.**
Rationale. It is important to have all supplies and equipment ready and available before starting any procedure to ensure efficiency.

3. **Procedural Step. Obtain the patient's medical record and verify the physician's order.**
The medication should bear the word "ophthalmic." Check the expiration date. As with all medications, ensure that the correct preparation is being used by reading the label three times: (a) when the medication is taken from the cupboard, (b) while you are drawing the medication into the dropper, and (c) just before returning the solution to the cupboard.
Rationale. The medication should be carefully compared with the physician's instructions to prevent a drug error. Any medication instilled into the eye should contain the word "ophthalmic." Medication without "ophthalmic" should never be placed in the eye because it could result in serious injury. If the medication is outdated, consult the physician; it may produce undesirable effects.

4. **Procedural Step. Escort the patient to the examination room, greet and identify the patient, and ask the patient to have a seat on the end of the examination table.**
Rationale. Identifying the patient ensures the procedure is performed on the correct patient.

5. **Procedural Step. Explain the procedure to the patient.**
Rationale. Explaining the procedure to the patient promotes cooperation and provides a means of obtaining implied consent.

6. **Procedural Step. Place the patient in a sitting or supine position, and ask the patient to stare at a fixed spot during the instillation.**

7. **Procedural Step. Put on disposable powder-free gloves and prepare the medication.**
If the medication bottle feels cold to the touch, gently roll it back and forth between your hands to warm the medication.
Eyedrops: Withdraw the medication into the dropper.
Eye ointment: Remove the cap from the tip of the tube.
Rationale. If the medication bottle feels cold, the medication itself is probably cold. Cold medication may cause discomfort to the patient.

8. **Procedural Step. Prepare the eye for instillation.**
a. Ask the patient to look up to the ceiling, keeping both eyes open.
b. Expose the lower conjunctival sac of the affected eye.
c. Use the fingers of your nondominant hand to place a gauze square or tissue on the patient's cheek under the affected eye.
d. Gently pull the skin of the cheek downward.
Rationale. Looking up with both eyes open helps keep the patient from blinking during the instillation and the dropper from touching the cornea. The gauze square or tissue placed on the cheek helps to prevent the fingers from slipping.

9. **Procedural Step. Instill the medication.**
Place the correct number of eyedrops in the center of the lower conjunctival sac of the affected eye, or place a thin ribbon of ointment along the length of the lower conjunctival sac from inner to outer canthus. Use a twisting motion to end the ribbon of ointment to help keep the ointment in the eye. The tip of the dropper or ointment tube should be held approximately 1/2 inch above the eye sac and must never touch the eye.
Rationale. Medication instilled into the eye must never be placed directly on the eye because it may cause damage to the cornea. Touching the dropper or tube to the eye results in contamination of these items.

10 **Procedural Step. Discard any unused solution from the eyedropper, and replace the dropper into the bottle.**
Be careful not to let the dropper touch the outside of the bottle when replacing it. When using ointments, replace the cap on the tube.

Continued

Procedure 6-2 Perform an Eye Instillation—cont'd

Rationale. Unused solution must not be returned to the bottle because it will contaminate the medication remaining in the bottle. Touching the dropper to the outside of the bottle contaminates the dropper; if this occurs, the entire bottle must be discarded.

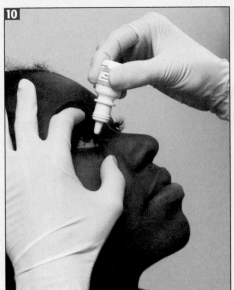

11. **Procedural Step. Instruct the patient about the instillation.**
    a. Ask the patient to close the eyes gently and rotate the eyeballs.
    b. Advise the patient not to squeeze the eyelids because this will discharge the medicine.
    c. Explain that the patient's vision may be temporarily blurred.
    Rationale. Rotating the eyeballs helps distribute the medication over the entire eye. If the eyes are shut tightly, the drops or ointment may be pushed out. If the instillation blurs the patient's vision, arrangements must be made in advance for

transportation, because the patient must not be permitted to drive until vision is clear.

12. **Procedural Step. Blot-dry the eyelid from the inner to the outer canthus with a dry gauze square to remove any excess medication.**
    Provide the patient with a separate tissue for each eye. Apply gentle pressure to the inner canthus for 1 to 3 minutes.
    Rationale. Applying pressure to the inner canthus prevents eyedrops from going down the nasolacrimal sac. Advise the patient not to wipe the eyes with tissue but to blot any medication that may run out.

13. **Procedural Step. Remove gloves and sanitize the hands.**

14. **Procedural Step. Provide verbal and written follow-up instructions.**
    Always sanitize the hands after every procedure or after using gloves.

15. **Procedural Step. Document the procedure.**
    Include the date and time, name and strength of the medication, number of drops or amount of ointment, which eye(s) received the instillation, any observations noted, and the patient's reaction.

16. **Procedural Step. Clean the equipment and examination room.**
    Discard all used supplies in an appropriate waste container.

Charting Example

Date	
12/5/xx	11:00 a.m. Chloromycetin 1%, gtts iii instilled both eyes. No discharge present. Patient tolerated procedure well with no c/o pain or discomfort.————— S. Gilstrap, CMA (AAMA)

Middle Ear

The middle ear is a cavity in the temporal bone that is full of air. It is connected to the nasopharynx (throat) by the eustachian tube. The middle ear contains three small bones, or **ossicles,** that conduct sound waves. Because of their shapes, these bones form a movable chain between the eardrum and the **oval window.**

The **malleus (hammer), incus (anvil),** and **stapes (stirrup)** amplify sound waves across the middle ear to the inner ear when the eardrum vibrates. The oval window permits the passage of the sound waves from the ossicles to the inner ear. The

round window is located below the oval window and separates the middle and inner ear. The round window bends as the stapes pushes the oval window, preventing pressure buildup in the inner ear.

The **eustachian tube** that links the ear and the nasopharynx regulates pressure in the middle ear to equalize the pressure on both sides of the eardrum. When sudden pressure changes occur (e.g., flying), swallowing helps to equalize the pressure. Children are more prone to ear infection because the eustachian tube connects to the throat horizontally. As a child grows, the angle increases, leaving less access for bacteria to enter the ear from the throat.

Inner Ear

The inner ear contains receptors for sound waves to permit hearing and maintain equilibrium. The inner ear, called the **labyrinth,** is composed of a bony outer shell and a membranous lining. Three major structures contain receptors for sound waves for hearing and for maintaining equilibrium.

1. The **cochlea** lies below the vestibule and is shaped like a snail shell. On the floor is the receptor for hearing, the **organ of Corti.** This receptor is made of tiny hairs. As fluid moves through the cochlea, the hairs move and initiate sensory nerve impulses (sound waves) that travel through the cochlear nerve to the acoustic nerve.
2. The **vestibule** controls the sense of position. It is a small chamber separated from the middle ear by the oval window. The stapes rests against the window, and when the sound waves are picked up, they are sent through the fluid in the inner ear by vibrating against the window.
3. The **semicircular canals,** located above the vestibule, control equilibrium. The canals contain liquid and hairlike cells that bend when the fluid is set in motion by body and head movements. The impulses are sent to the brain to help maintain equilibrium, or body balance.

Sound

When sound waves vibrate, they create a **pitch.** The number of times a sound wave vibrates is referred to as *frequency,* and from this pitch is determined. The greater and higher the frequency of sound waves, the higher is the pitch. The loudness of a sound is determined by the height of the sound waves and intensity of the vibration. Sound is measured in **decibels (dB).** The human ear hears up to 140 dB. If sound is higher than this, pain is experienced. **Audiometry** measures sounds heard by the human ear.

Ear Disorders

Disorders of the ear may occur at birth or may be associated with heredity, noise pollution, or age. A common problem seen in the medical office, especially in children and elderly patients, is a buildup of earwax **(cerumen)** in the external ear. Cerumen is produced by the sweat glands of the external ear to aid in protecting the canal. If too much cerumen accumulates, hearing can be impaired. An **otolaryngologist** can treat disorders of the ears, and an *audiometrist* evaluates hearing loss. Drugs may be prescribed to treat conditions of the ear (Table 6-4).

Medical assistants need to be able to recognize the common signs and symptoms of and diagnostic tests for the different types of ear disorders.

- Study Box 6-4 to familiarize yourself with the common signs and symptoms of auditory disorders.
- Study Box 6-5 to learn about common diagnostic tests and procedures.

TABLE 6-4	Ear Drug Classifications	
Drug Classification	**Common Generic (Brand) Drugs**
Anti-infectives Treat bacterial infections *Ceruminolytics* Soften and break down earwax	neomycin, polymyxin B (Cortisporin) chloramphenicol (Pentamycetin) carbamide peroxide (Murine ear drops; Cerumenex)

BOX 6-4	Common Signs and Symptoms of Ear Disorders
Otalgia	Ear pain
Otorrhea	Discharge from the auditory canal
Tinnitus	Ringing in the ears
Vertigo	Dizziness

BOX 6-5	Diagnostic Tests and Procedures for the Ear
Audiometry	Measures how well a person hears various frequencies of sound
Otoscopy	Views the tympanic membrane and various parts of the outer ear
Rinne test	Compares bone conduction and air conduction of sound using a tuning fork
Weber test	Determines if a hearing loss is caused by conductive loss or sensorineural loss

TABLE 6-5	Diseases and Disorders of the Ear				
Disease and Description	**Etiology**	**Signs and Symptoms**	**Diagnosis**	**Therapy**	**Interventions**
Meniere disease Buildup of excess fluid in semicircular canals, with excess pressure on canals, vestibule, and cochlea	Unknown	Hearing loss, vertigo, **tinnitus**	Series of hearing tests; diuretic between tests reduces pressure in ear; if patient improves, diagnosis is confirmed; electrocochleography and MRI to rule out brain lesions	Medications, including diuretic and antivertigo drugs; in severe cases, shunt used to drain excess fluid to cerebrospinal fluid	Encourage a diet low in sodium. Instruct patient to avoid sudden position changes
Mastoiditis Inflammation of lining of mastoid cells	Bacterial infection; often a complication of otitis media	Dull earache, low-grade fever, swelling of ear canal, discharge, hearing loss	X-rays confirm the diagnosis, and audiometric testing confirms hearing loss	Antibiotic therapy	Answer patient's questions and concerns about hearing loss; encourage compliance with prescribed treatment
Deafness *Conduction* Interference with passage of sound waves from outside to inner ear	Impacted cerumen; foreign bodies; inflammation; damage to tympanic membranes (chronic otitis media)	Inability to respond to external stimuli from outer ear; tinnitus may be first symptom noticed by patient	Patient history, audiometry testing	Remove source	Answer patient's questions and concerns about hearing loss; provide information on support groups available
Sensorineural Loss of function of cochlea or acoustic nerve	Brain tumor; **otosclerosis** (loss of vibrations) due to damaged ossicles; nerve damage; loud noise	Inability to respond to external stimuli from outer ear; tinnitus may be first symptom noticed by patient	Patient history, audiometry testing	Reduce further damage by removing source if known; use of ear protectors in areas with high noise levels	Answer patient's questions and concerns about hearing loss; provide information on support groups available

Continued

TABLE 6-5	Diseases and Disorders of the Ear—cont'd				
Disease and Description	Etiology	Signs and Symptoms	Diagnosis	Therapy	Interventions
Otitis externa (swimmer's ear) Inflammation of outer ear	Common causes: allergy, bacteria, fungi, viruses, trauma	Pain or itching and swelling in ear canal	Direct examination of ear canal; culture of drainage	Analgesics for discomfort; antibiotics for causative agent	Encourage proper cleaning and drying of external ear and avoidance of allergic substance
Otitis media Inflammation of middle ear	Bacterial or viral infection	Complaint of severe earache; fever, vomiting, fullness in ears	Clinical evaluation: erythematous (redness) eardrum on examination	Possible surgery to insert tubes to drain fluid from eardrum if bulging; antibiotics to control infective agent; antihistamines to reduce fluids; antipyretics for fever and pain	Encourage general cleaning of ears to prevent buildup of moisture that can harbor microorganisms

Presbycusis: Progressive hearing loss occurring in old age

MRI, Magnetic resonance imaging.

- Study Table 6-5 to understand the diseases that affect the ear.

Equilibrium

As mentioned, our sense of equilibrium is controlled by the semicircular canals located above the vestibule in the inner ear. The **vestibular apparatus** is involved in body balance, or equilibrium. Balance is related to maintaining the position of the body (mainly the head) with respect to gravity and sudden movements. **Motion sickness** is caused by excessive stimulation of the vestibular apparatus.

Hearing Acuity Tests

Hearing acuity tests are used to detect hearing loss and to look for **conduction** defects or nerve impairment. The Weber and Rinne tests both require a **tuning fork.** The Weber test checks that the loudness of the sound is heard the same in both ears, whereas the Rinne test compares air conduction with bone conduction. Audiometry is used to measure the degree of hearing.

Weber Test

The **Weber test** assesses hearing loss in both ears at once. The tuning fork is held by its base and struck against the palm of the opposite hand or the knee. The base of the vibrating fork is placed on the center of the patient's head (Fig. 6-10). If hearing is normal, the patient will hear the sound equally in both ears.

The physician often performs the Weber and Rinne tests but can train and provide instructions for the medical assistant to perform these tests just as efficiently. If a patient has air conduction deafness, the patient will hear the sound better in the affected ear because bone will transmit sound directly to that ear.

Rinne Test

The **Rinne test** compares bone and air conduction by placing the base of the vibrating tuning fork to the patient's mastoid bone behind each ear (Fig. 6-11). The patient is asked to report when the sound is no longer heard. The tuning fork is then held beside the ear, and the patient is asked if he or she can hear it. If the patient can, the hearing is

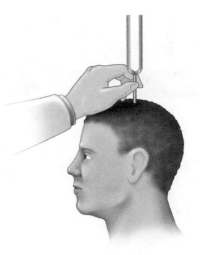

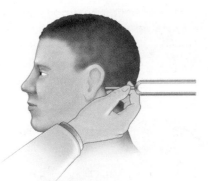

Bone conduction

Normal hearing
The patient hears the sound equally
in both ears or in the center of the head.

Conductive hearing loss
The patient hears the sound better in
the problem ear.

Sensorineural hearing loss
The patient does not hear the sound as
well in the problem ear.

Fig. 6-10 Weber test. *(Modified from Bonewit-West
K: Clinical procedures for medical assistants, ed 6,
Philadelphia, 2004, Saunders.)*

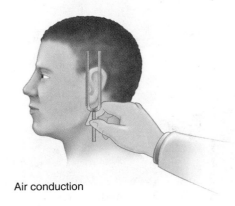

Air conduction

Normal hearing
The patient hears the sound at least
twice as long through air conduction as
through bone conduction.

Conductive hearing loss
The patient hears the sound longer by
bone conduction than by air conduction.

Sensorineural hearing loss
The sound is reduced. The patient will
also hear the sound longer through air
conduction than through bone
conduction but not twice as long.

Fig. 6-11 Rinne test. *(Modified from Bonewit-West
K: Clinical procedures for medical assistants, ed 6,
Philadelphia, 2004, Saunders.)*

normal. Normal results occur when air conduction hearing is greater than bone conduction hearing.

Audiometry

Audiometry is the measurement of hearing ability with an *audiometer* (Fig. 6-12). The audiometer measures hearing sensitivity by producing an **audiogram,** which shows hearing loss as a function of tone frequency. The medical assistant can perform this test after receiving additional technical training, which is usually provided by the manufacturer or by an **audiologist.**

In audiometric testing, measurements are taken in decibels (dB). Most sounds that are associated with normal speech patterns fall in the range of 20 to 50 dB. An adult with normal hearing should be able to detect tones between 0 and 20 dB.

To perform audiometry, the room must be quiet to prevent outside interference. Headphones are provided to the patient, and when the audiometer sends a frequency, the patient is asked to signal when he or she hears the sound. The frequencies begin low and progress to high.

PATIENT-CENTERED PROFESSIONALISM

• What role does the medical assistant have in hearing acuity tests?

Ear Treatments

Ear treatments are performed in the medical office, often as a part of an ear examination. Ear irrigation and ear instillation are two procedures that medical assistants need to understand and be able to perform.

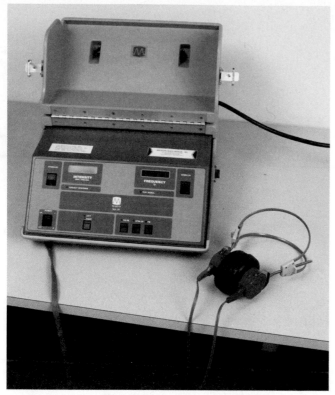

Fig. 6-12 Audiometer.

Ear Irrigation

Before examining the ear, the physician may request that ear **irrigation** be performed to remove an accumulation of impacted **cerumen** (earwax). This procedure may also be ordered to remove a foreign object. Procedure 6-3 explains how to perform ear irrigation.

When irrigating the ear, it is important to instill the solution toward the roof of the canal. Avoid using a solution that is cold or too warm, blowing air into the ear, or in any way touching the eardrum. When irrigating (flushing) the ear canal, the ear syringe must never block the canal because this will place pressure on the eardrum and could cause damage to the membrane. The medical assistant must be aware that the patient may experience dizziness after ear irrigation, and the assistant should assist the patient as needed.

Ear Instillation

Ear **instillation** is the process of administering medication to an affected ear. Before medication can be put into the ear, the ear canal must be **patent** (open). Procedure 6-4 explains the process of instilling prescribed medication to an affected ear. The medical assistant must take extreme care when working with a patient who has an infected ear. The inside of the ear is naturally sensitive, and it becomes very painful when infected.

PATIENT-CENTERED PROFESSIONALISM

- Why is it important for the medical assistant to understand the purpose of and be knowledgeable about eye and ear treatments?

SUMMARY

Reinforce your understanding of the material in this chapter by reviewing the curriculum objectives and key content points below.

1. Define, appropriately use, and spell all the Key Terms for this chapter.
   - Review the Key Terms if necessary.
2. Explain the purpose of the sensory system.
   - The senses allow the body to respond to both internal and external stimuli.
   - The senses protect the body from harm, maintain the body in homeostasis, and transmit pleasure and pain.
3. List and describe the five main senses.
   - The five main senses are taste, smell, vision, hearing, and balance (equilibrium).
4. List the five general sensations.
   - General sensations include pain, touch (tactile), pressure, temperature, and proprioception.
5. Name the organs and structures of the sensory system and describe the function of each.
   - Papillae in the mouth allow us to taste sweet, sour, salty, and bitter.
   - The nose filters the air we breathe and transmits perceived fragrance and odor. The sense of smell is closely related to the sense of taste.
   - The eye refracts light for visual perception.

Text continued on p. 227

Procedure 6-3 Perform an Ear Irrigation

TASK: Irrigate the external ear canal to remove cerumen.

EQUIPMENT AND SUPPLIES
- Irrigating solution (may use warm tap water)
- Container to hold irrigating solution (sterile)
- Irrigating syringe or Reiner's ear syringe
- Ear basin for drainage
- Disposable barrier drape
- Disposable gloves
- Otoscope with probe cover
- Biohazardous waste container
- Gauze squares
- Patient's medical record

SKILLS/RATIONALE

STANDARD PRECAUTIONS ARE TO BE FOLLOWED.

1. **Procedural Step. Sanitize the hands.**
   An alcohol-based hand rub may be used instead of washing hands with soap and water, unless hands are visibly soiled.
   Rationale. Hand sanitization promotes infection control.

2. **Procedural Step. Assemble equipment and supplies.**
   Rationale. It is important to have all supplies and equipment ready and available before starting any procedure to ensure efficiency.

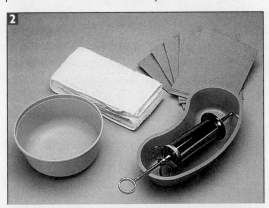

3. **Procedural Step. Obtain the patient's medical record, verify the physician's order, and obtain correct solution.**
   If a prepared irrigating solution is to be used, check the expiration date of the solution. As with all medications, ensure that the correct preparation is being used by reading the label three times: the first time when the irrigating solution is taken from the cupboard; the second

time while you are pouring the solution into the basin; and the third time just before returning the solution to the cupboard.
   NOTE: All medications must be returned to storage before patient use.

4. **Procedural Step. Escort the patient to the examination room, greet and identify the patient, and ask the patient to have a seat on the end of the examination table.**
   Rationale. Identifying the patient ensures the procedure is performed on the correct patient.

5. **Procedural Step. Explain the procedure to the patient.**
   Explain that the procedure usually is not painful but that the patient may feel some discomfort or a sense of pressure. Some patients may feel dizzy or nauseated. The patient may have a sensation of warmth or even burning as the solution comes in contact with the tympanic membrane.
   Rationale. Explaining the procedure to the patient promotes cooperation and provides a means of obtaining implied consent. Although it is important to inform the patient of all outcomes of a procedure, it is equally as important not to alarm the patient. If patients are told that a procedure is going to feel a certain way or that they can expect to feel dizzy or nauseated, they may experience these discomforts simply because they were told they would.

6. **Procedural Step. Warm the irrigating solution to body temperature by running the container under warm tap water.**
   The physician may order that warm tap water be used as the irrigating solution. For patient

Continued

Procedure 6-3 Perform an Ear Irrigation—cont'd

comfort, the water should be between 98.6° to 100° F.

Rationale. The solution must be carefully compared with the physician's instructions to prevent an error. Outdated solutions must be discarded because they may cause adverse effects. If the solution is too cold or too warm, the patient may become dizzy or nauseated as a result of overstimulation of the inner ear.

7. **Procedural Step. Put on disposable gloves.**
   Rationale. This prevents the spread of infection.

8. **Procedural Step. Examine the ear.**
   Place a new probe cover on the otoscope and gently pull the auricle upward and back (if an adult patient) in order to straighten the external auditory canal. Insert the otoscope and examine the external auditory canal and the tympanic membrane with the otoscope.
   Rationale. Viewing the external auditory canal and tympanic membrane before the irrigation provides a baseline for comparison on completing the irrigation. You may also be able to visualize the placement of excessive cerumen or a foreign body that needs to be dislodged.

9. **Procedural Step. Position the patient.**
   a. Ask the patient to tilt the head slightly forward and toward the affected ear.
   b. Place a water-resistant disposable barrier on the patient's shoulder on the affected side.
   c. Provide an ear basin, and ask the patient to hold the basin snugly against the head underneath the affected ear.
   Rationale. The water-resistant disposable barrier protects the patient's clothing and prevents water from running down the patient's neck, chest, and back. The patient is positioned so that gravity aids the flow of the solution out of the ear and into the basin. The basin is used to catch the irrigating solution, any drainage, and cerumen. A gown may be offered to the patient before the procedure to protect the clothing from accidents.

10. **Procedural Step. Using the solution ordered to perform the irrigation, moisten 2 × 2–inch gauze squares and clean the outer ear (auricle, pinna).**
    Rationale. This will remove any discharge or other debris that may be present. Debris or foreign particles should not be introduced into the ear during the irrigation.

11. **Procedural Step. Pour the warmed solution into the sterile basin.**

12. **Procedural Step. Fill the ear-irrigating syringe with the ordered solution.**

If air has been drawn into the syringe during this process, it must be expelled before the irrigation.

Rationale. Air forced into the ear is uncomfortable for the patient, and, if introduced too forcefully, air can cause severe damage to the tympanic membrane.

13. **Procedural Step. Position the ear.**
    Straighten the external ear canal by gently pulling the ear upward and backward for adults and children older than 3 years old, or downward and backward for children 3 years and younger.
    Rationale. The ear canal must be straightened to ensure the irrigating solution reaches all areas of the external auditory canal.

14. **Procedural Step. Irrigate the ear.**
    An ear irrigation may be ordered to remove a foreign body, soothe inflamed membranes, remove impacted cerumen, or clear discharge. The reason the irrigation was ordered will determine the length of irrigation.

    Insert the tip of the irrigating syringe into the ear canal and gently inject the irrigating solution toward the roof of the canal. It is important that the tip of the syringe not be inserted too deeply and that the solution is injected toward the roof of the canal to prevent damage to the tympanic membrane. The tip of the syringe must not obstruct the opening to the ear canal; the irrigating solution must be able to flow freely out of the canal.
    Rationale. The irrigating solution should not be injected too forcefully and should not be directed at the tympanic membrane, or damage to the tympanic membrane can occur. Directing the solution toward the roof of the external ear canal also helps when trying to dislodge foreign bodies; the stream of the solution will flow in over the top of the object, back behind it, and then out from the bottom, loosening the trapped particle. If the tip of the syringe is inserted too deeply, the patient will experience discomfort, and the tympanic membrane may be damaged. Patients often experience the most discomfort when the solution is injected directly at the tympanic membrane.

15. **Procedural Step. Continue irrigating until all the solution has been used or until the desired results have been achieved.**
    a. Refill the syringe as needed.
    b. If requested by the physician, periodically examine the ear canal with the otoscope to

Procedure 6-3 Perform an Ear Irrigation—cont'd

check the progress of the procedure, especially if the procedure has been ordered to remove cerumen or a foreign body.

c. Observe the returning solution, and note the type of material present (e.g., cerumen, discharge, or foreign object) and the amount (small, moderate, large).

Rationale. All dislodged materials in the returning solution and the amount of the substance must be noted for the patient's medical record.

16. Procedural Step. Conclude the irrigation.

a. Examine the ear canal with the otoscope at the end of the procedure.

b. Gently dry the outside of the ear with a cotton ball or 2 × 2 gauze squares.

c. Explain to the patient that the ear may feel sensitive for a few hours. Ask the patient to lie on the examination table with the affected ear down for approximately 15 minutes. A moistened cotton ball may be placed in the ear at the physician's request.

Rationale. Lying on the examination table with the affected ear down allows any solution remaining in the ear to drain out. Placing a moist cotton ball in the ear canal provides a barrier and helps to alleviate discomfort or any sensitivity the patient may feel after the procedure.

17. Procedural Step. Remove gloves and sanitize the hands.

Always sanitize the hands after every procedure or after using gloves.

18. Procedural Step. The physician will examine the ear and provide follow-up instructions to the patient.

The physician may ask to examine the returned irrigating solution and will require the otoscope to examine the ear canal. Instructions are provided to the patient both verbally and in writing.

19. Procedural Step. Ask if the patient has any questions or would like clarification on any instructions. Thank the patient, and escort the patient to the reception area for payment or scheduling follow-up appointment(s).

20. Procedural Step. Document the procedure.

Include the following: date and time; which ear was irrigated; type, strength, and amount of solution used; amount and type of material returned in the irrigating solution; any significant observations; patient instructions; and patient reactions.

21. Procedural Step. Clean the equipment and examination room.

Discard all used supplies in an appropriate waste container. If an item is contaminated with blood, it must be discarded in a biohazardous waste container.

NOTE: Wear protective gloves when cleaning equipment and the examination room.

Charting Example

Date	
12/3/xx	1:20 p.m. Irrigated right ear c̄ 250 mL sterile normal saline. Large amount of soft, brown, stringy cerumen removed. Patient tolerated procedure well. No complaints of dizziness, nausea, or pain.
	S. Cline, CMA (AAMA)

Photos from Young AP, Kennedy DB: *Kinn's the medical assistant*, ed 9, Philadelphia, 2003, Saunders.

Procedure 6-4 Perform an Ear Instillation

TASK: Properly instill prescribed medication to the affected ear.

EQUIPMENT AND SUPPLIES
- Otic drops with sterile dropper
- Cotton balls
- Disposable gloves
- Patient's medical record

SKILLS/RATIONALE

STANDARD PRECAUTIONS ARE TO BE FOLLOWED.

1. **Procedural Step. Sanitize the hands.**
   An alcohol-based hand rub may be used instead of washing hands with soap and water, unless hands are visibly soiled.
   Rationale. Hand sanitization promotes infection control.

2. **Procedural Step. Assemble equipment and supplies.**
   Rationale. It is important to have all supplies and equipment ready and available before starting any procedure to ensure efficiency.

3. **Procedural Step. Verify the physician's order.**
   Any medication that is instilled in the ear must be labeled with the word "otic." Check the expiration date of the solution. As with all medications, ensure that the correct preparation is being used by reading the label three times: (a) when the medication is taken from the cupboard, (b) while you are drawing the medication into the dropper, and (c) just before returning the solution to the cupboard.
   NOTE: All medications must be returned to storage before patient use.
   Rationale. The solution must be carefully compared with the physician's instructions to prevent an error. Outdated solutions must be discarded because they may produce adverse effects. Medications without the word "otic" must not be used in the ear because they could result in injury to the ear.

4. **Procedural Step. Obtain the patient's medical record.**

5. **Procedural Step. Escort the patient to the examination room, greet and identify the patient, and ask the patient to have a seat on the end of the examination table.**
   Rationale. Identifying the patient ensures the procedure is performed on the correct patient.

6. **Procedural Step. Explain the procedure to the patient.**
   Rationale. Explaining the procedure to the patient promotes cooperation and provides a means of obtaining implied consent.

7. **Procedural Step. Put on disposable gloves.**
   Rationale. This prevents the spread of infection.

8. **Procedural Step. Warm the medication, if necessary, and draw the medication into the dropper.**
   If the medication bottle feels cold to the touch, gently roll it back and forth between your hands to warm it.
   Rationale. If the medication bottle feels cold, the medication itself is probably cold. Cold medication may cause discomfort to the patient.

9. **Procedural Step. Ask the patient to tilt the head in the direction of the unaffected ear.**
   Rationale. In this position, gravity helps the medication to flow into the ear canal and to be retained for the required time.

10. **Procedural Step. Position the ear.**
    Straighten the external ear canal by gently pulling the ear upward and backward for adults and children older than 3 years old, or downward and backward for children 3 years and younger.
    Rationale. Straightening the ear canal permits the medication to reach all areas of the external auditory canal.

11. **Procedural Step. Place the medication in the ear.**
    Insert the tip of the dropper into the ear canal, making sure the dropper never touches the ear canal. Instill the correct amount of medication (number of drops) ordered by the physician by squeezing the bulb of the dropper gently. Medication should be instilled drop by drop along the side of the canal.

12. **Procedural Step. Discard any unused medication in the dropper.**
    Unused medication must be discarded before returning the dropper to the bottle. The dropper must never touch the patient or the outside of the bottle; if it does, the dropper must be discarded.
    Rationale. Unused solution must never be returned to the bottle because it would contaminate the remaining solution. Touching the dropper to the patient or the outside of the bottle contaminates the dropper.

13. **Procedural Step. Instruct the patient to rest on the unaffected side for approximately 5 minutes.**
    Rationale. Resting with the unaffected side down for 5 minutes allows the medication to distribute completely throughout the ear canal. If the patient sits up

Procedure 6-4 Perform an Ear Instillation—cont'd

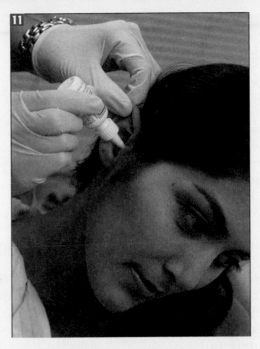

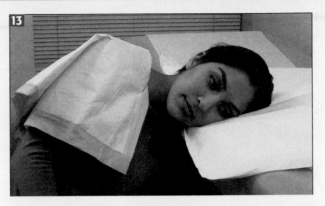

straight, the medication may run out, and the patient will not receive the full benefit of the instillation.

14. **Procedural Step. If the physician orders it, loosely place a cotton ball moistened with petroleum jelly in the ear canal for 15 minutes.**
    Rationale. The moistened cotton ball prevents the medication from running out when the patient is upright. Moistening the cotton ball with petroleum jelly prevents the cotton ball from absorbing the medication.

15. **Procedural Step. Remove gloves and sanitize the hands.**
    Always sanitize the hands after every procedure or after using gloves.

16. **Procedural Step. Provide the patient with verbal and written follow-up instructions.**

17. **Procedural Step. Escort the patient to the reception area.**

18. **Procedural Step. Document the procedure.**
    Include the date and time, the name and strength of the medication, number of drops, which ear(s) received the instillation, any significant observations, and the patient's reaction.

19. **Procedural Step. Clean the equipment and examination room.**
    Discard all used supplies in an appropriate waste container.

Charting Example

Date	
12/4/xx	1:30 p.m. Ofloxacin, gtts v instilled, right ear. No discharge present. Pt tolerated the procedure well with no complaint of pain, dizziness, or nausea.
	———— S. Davis, CMA (AAMA)

- The ear is responsible for both sound and equilibrium.

6. List and describe seven common signs and symptoms of eye disease.
   - Refer to Box 6-2 for the eye.

7. List six diagnostic tests and procedures for eye disease and explain the use of each.
   - Refer to Box 6-3 for the eye.

8. List 12 eye diseases and describe the etiology, signs and symptoms, diagnosis, therapy, and interventions for each.
   - Refer to Table 6-3 for eye diseases.

9. Demonstrate the correct procedure for irrigating a patient's eye to remove foreign particles.
   - Review Procedure 6-1.

10. Demonstrate the procedure for properly instilling prescribed medication in an affected eye.
    - Review Procedure 6-2.

11. Explain why the medical assistant should be careful not to touch the surface of the eye with the tip of the irrigating syringe, the tip of the eyedropper, or the finger.
    - Touching the surface of the affected eye could contaminate the syringe or eyedropper. This can result in cross-contamination if the contaminated items come into contact with other areas.

12. List four signs and symptoms of ear disorders.
    - Refer to Box 6-4 for the ear.

13. List four tests for ear disorders and explain the use of each.
    - Refer to Box 6-5 for the ear.
14. List seven ear disorders and describe the etiology, signs and symptoms, diagnosis, therapy, and interventions for each.
    - Refer to Table 6-5 for ear diseases.
15. List the three types of hearing acuity tests and state the purpose of each.
    - The Weber test assesses hearing loss using a vibrating tuning fork on the center of the patient's head to determine if sound is heard equally in both ears.
    - The Rinne test compares bone and air conduction by placing the base of the vibrating tuning fork to the patient's mastoid bone behind each ear to determine when the sound is no longer heard.
    - Audiometry tests hearing ability with an audiometer by measuring hearing sensitivity with tones.
16. Demonstrate the correct procedure for irrigating the external ear canal to remove cerumen or foreign objects.
    - Review Procedure 6-3.
17. Demonstrate the procedure for properly instilling prescribed medication in an affected ear.
    - Review Procedure 6-4.
18. Explain why extreme care must be taken when working with a patient's infected ear.
    - When an ear is infected it becomes very painful and the tympanic membrane may be bulging and could rupture if care is not taken.
19. Analyze a realistic medical office situation and apply your understanding of the special senses to determine the best course of action.
    - By understanding the special senses, you are more prepared to understand patients' perceptions and tailor education to their ability to comprehend.
20. Describe the impact on patient care when medical assistants have a solid understanding of the structure and function of the special senses.
    - With effective communication and a good understanding of the physiology of the special senses, the medical assistant can successfully encourage patients to follow their prescribed treatment plan.

WORD PARTS: SPECIAL SENSES

Sensory System
Suffixes

-algesia	pain
-esthesia	sensation
-geusia	sense of taste
-osmia	sense of smell

Vision
Combining Forms

blephar/o	eyelid
choroid/o	choroid
corne/o	cornea
cycl/o	ciliary body, ciliary muscle
dacry/o	tear; lacrimal apparatus
ir/o, irid/o	iris
kerat/o	cornea; horny tissue
lacrim/o	tear; lacrimal apparatus
lent/i	lens
ocul/o, ophthalm/o	eye
opt/o, optic/o	vision
phak/o, phac/o	lens
pupill/o	pupil
retin/o	retina
scler/o	sclera

Suffix

-opia	vision

Hearing
Combining Forms

audi/o	hearing
acous/o	sound, hearing
cochle/o	cochlea
labyrinth/o	labyrinth
myring/o	tympanic membrane
ot/o	ear
staped/o, stapedi/o	stapes
tympan/o	tympanic membrane
vestibul/o	vestibule

Suffixes

-acusis	hearing
-otia	ear condition

Abbreviations: Special Senses

ENT	ear, nose, throat
EENT	eyes, ears, nose, throat

Chapter Review

Vocabulary Review

Matching

Match each term with the correct definition.

_____ 1. Pertains to the sense of touch

_____ 2. Loud/soft measurement of sound

_____ 3. Instrument used to view the retina

_____ 4. Small bones of the middle ear

_____ 5. Controls equilibrium

_____ 6. Adjustment that allows for vision at various distances

_____ 7. Yellow-brown substance produced by the sweat glands in the external ear

_____ 8. Dizziness

_____ 9. Specialist in the treatment of ear, nose, and throat diseases

_____ 10. Tube that connects the middle ear with the nasopharynx and acts to equalize pressure between the outer and middle ear

_____ 11. Balance

_____ 12. Process of placing medication into an area as prescribed by a physician

_____ 13. Washing of or rinsing out of an area to remove foreign matter

_____ 14. Tests used to check for hearing loss

_____ 15. Ability to move from one area to another, as in hearing with transmission of sound through nervous tissue

A. equilibrium
B. vertigo
C. tactile
D. accommodation
E. ophthalmoscope
F. cerumen
G. eustachian tube
H. ossicles
I. decibels
J. otolaryngologist
K. semicircular canals
L. instillation
M. irrigation
N. conduction
O. hearing acuity tests

Theory Recall

True/False

Indicate whether the sentence or statement is true or false.

_____ 1. An ophthalmologist treats disorders of the eye.

_____ 2. Antiseptics are used to reduce growth of bacteria in the eye.

_____ 3. Ear treatments are never performed as part of an ear examination.

_____ 4. All irrigation solutions must be sterile.

Multiple Choice

Identify the letter of the choice that best completes the statement or answers the question.

1. The suffix for "hearing" is _____.
   A. -acusis
   B. -geusia
   C. -kinesia
   D. -otia

2. _____ soften and break down ear wax.
   A. Anti-infectives
   B. Vasodilators
   C. Ceruminolytics
   D. Anxiolytics

3. The _____ nerve controls salivation, swallowing, and taste.
   A. olfactory
   B. trochlear
   C. glossopharyngeal
   D. hypoglossal

4. Which one of the following is NOT an extrinsic eye muscle?
   A. Superior rectus
   B. Lateral rectus
   C. Superior oblique
   D. Ciliary

5. Which eye muscle elevates or rolls the eyeball upward?
   A. Inferior rectus
   B. Medial rectus
   C. Superior oblique
   D. Inferior oblique

6. _____ is used to measure intraocular pressure.
   A. Amsler grid
   B. Gonioscopy
   C. Tonometry
   D. All of the above

7. _____ occurs when the aqueous humor does not drain properly and the intraocular pressure increases and compresses the choroid layer, diminishing blood supply to the retina.
   A. Cataract
   B. Glaucoma
   C. Strabismus
   D. Myopia

8. _____ is a refraction error caused by the abnormal curvature of the cornea and lens.
   A. Astigmatism
   B. Ptosis
   C. Strabismus
   D. Hyperopia

9. _____ is a buildup of excess fluid in the semicircular canals, which places excess pressure on the canals, vestibule, and cochlea.
   A. Otosclerosis
   B. Mastoiditis
   C. Meniere disease
   D. None of the above

10. An _____ is a record produced by an audiometer.
    A. audiogram
    B. audiologist
    C. audiometry
    D. none of the above

11. Rinne and Weber tests are types of _____.
    A. blood tests
    B. hearing tests
    C. postpartum tests
    D. prenatal tests

12. When performing eye irrigation, the medical assistant should rinse _____.
    A. toward the center of the eye
    B. toward the inner corner of the eye
    C. toward the outer corner of the eye
    D. with patient's head tilted forward

13. When instilling eardrops, it is important to remember to instill the drops toward the _____ of the canal.
    A. bottom
    B. center
    C. roof
    D. It does not matter which way the drops are instilled.

14. When irrigating an ear of an adult patient, the medical assistant should straighten the ear canal by gently pulling the ear _____.
    A. upward and backward
    B. downward and forward
    C. upward and forward
    D. downward and backward

15. An ear irrigation is performed to _____.
    A. introduce medication into the ear canal
    B. dislodge materials such as insects and earwax
    C. chill the tympanic membrane
    D. all of the above

Sentence Completion

Complete each sentence or statement.

1. _____ is the progressive hearing loss occurring in old age.

2. A(n) _____ test compares bone conduction and air conduction of sound using a tuning fork.

3. The _____ test assesses the hearing in both ears at once.

4. _____ is the medical name for "earwax."

Short Answers

1. Explain the purpose of the sensory system.

   _____

   _____

   _____

   _____

Critical Thinking

Jason Ball is a 56-year-old patient who comes to the clinic today with a complaint of gradual hearing loss. The physician wants you to get Jason ready for hearing acuity tests. What tests does the physician want to perform and how are they performed?

Application of Skills

Wear a blindfold for 2 hours to completely block your vision. Participate in all of your regular activities—get dressed, brush your teeth, do household chores, etc. Write one paragraph describing your experience. Identify the points that you can now share with a recently blind patient or a patient who is losing his or her eyesight.

Internet Research

Keyword: (Use the name of the condition or disease you select to write about)

Select one condition or disease from Tables 6-3 and 6-5. Write a two-paragraph report regarding the condition or disease you selected listing the etiology, signs and symptoms, diagnosis, therapy, and interventions. Cite your source. (You may not use the information on the tables exclusively for your report.) Be prepared to give a 2-minute oral presentation should your instructor assign you to do so.

What Would You Do?

If you have accomplished the objectives in this chapter, you will be able to make better choices as a medical assistant. Take a look at this situation and decide what you would do.

A multispecialty practice has medical assistants who work with each of the specialists. Allene, a medical assistant who has not had the benefit of training, works with Dr. Sumar, an ophthalmologist. The ophthalmologist and the otolaryngologist share the same examination room, but they use it on different days. Allene is not very busy one day, so she decides to clean the medicine cabinet and rearrange the drugs. She moves the ophthalmic medications to the spot where the otic medications are usually stored, and vice versa.

When Dr. Sumar treats a patient with conjunctivitis the next day, Allene hands him an otic preparation for the eye instillation. Luckily, Dr. Sumar reads the label on the medication before instilling the drops into the patient's eye. Later in the day, Dr. Sumar reprimands Allene for handing him the otic drops.

Would you be able to step into the role of Allene and perform her duties successfully?

1. Why is it important for ophthalmic and otic preparations to remain in the same storage places?

_____

_____

_____

2. What is the danger of placing otic medications into the patient's eye?

_____

_____

_____

3. Would the ear patient have a problem if the ophthalmic preparation had been used for the ear instillation?

_____

_____

_____

4. What reasons do you believe led to Allene's reprimand? What actions during the cleaning process could have caused the medication error?

_____

_____

_____

_____

_____

Chapter Quiz

Multiple Choice

Identify the letter of the choice that best completes the statement or answers the question.

1. The _____ is the anterior portion of the sclera; also means "transparent—allows light through."
   A. iris
   B. chorioid
   C. lens
   D. cornea

2. Which one of the following is NOT a muscle of the eye?
   A. Oblique
   B. Canthus
   C. Rectus
   D. All of the above are muscles of the eye

3. _____ occurs when the lens loses its ability to change shape during accommodation for close objects.
   A. Presbycusis
   B. Strabismus
   C. Presbyopia
   D. Hyperopia

4. The _____ is the external flap of the ear.
   A. pinna
   B. auricle
   C. both A and B
   D. none of the above

5. The medical term for pinkeye is _____.
   A. chalazoin
   B. conjunctivitis
   C. strabismus
   D. hordeolum

6. _____ is a buildup of excess fluid in the semicircular canals, which places excess pressure on the canals, vestibule, and cochlea.
   A. Meniere disease
   B. Vertigo
   C. Otosclerosis
   D. Presbycusis

7. Ringing in the ears is a symptom called:
   A. tinnitus
   B. vertigo
   C. otorrhea
   D. otalgia

8. The _____ of the ear lies below the vestibule and is shaped like a snail shell.
   A. labyrinth
   B. eustachian tube
   C. organ of Corti
   D. cochlea

9. When performing an eye irrigation, the medical assistant _____.
   A. irrigates from the back of the patient with the patient's head tilted back toward you
   B. has patient tilt head away from affected eye
   C. has patient tilt head away from the unaffected eye
   D. uses slightly warm tap water for irrigation

10. All of the following are taste buds except:
    A. sweet
    B. sour
    C. spicy
    D. bitter

11. The auditory ossicles include:
    A. the malleus
    B. the incus
    C. the stapes
    D. all of the above

12. Which of the following structures is not a part of the external ear?
    A. auricle
    B. tympanic membrane
    C. eustachian tube
    D. external auditory canal

13. Blood vessels are found in which part of the eye?
    A. sclera
    B. lens
    C. choroid
    D. aqueous humor

14. What part of the eye consists of nervous tissue?
    A. sclera
    B. choroid
    C. iris
    D. retina

15. The vitreous humor maintains the shape of the eye and _____.
    A. refracts light
    B. provides support to the retina
    C. secretes tears
    D. allows for near and far vision

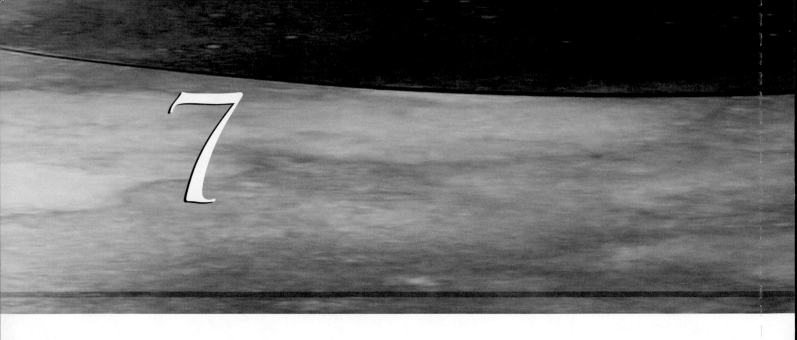

CURRICULUM OBJECTIVES

You will be able to do the following after completing this chapter:

Key Terms
1. Define, appropriately use, and spell all the Key Terms for this chapter.

Sections of the Medical History
2. Demonstrate the correct procedure for completing a medical history form.
3. List seven sections of the medical history and briefly explain what type of information is collected in each.
4. Distinguish between *objective* and *subjective* data.

Interviewing Skills
5. State two positive outcomes of interviewing a patient effectively.
6. Explain the importance of maintaining the patient's privacy during and after the interview.
7. Explain the need for effective communication skills during a patient interview.
8. Demonstrate the correct procedure for recognizing and responding to nonverbal communication.

Charting
9. Explain the importance of charting patient statements and observations accurately.
10. Differentiate between "specific" and "general" patient statements and know when to obtain more detail.
11. Accurately record observations made during a patient interview.
12. Recognize judgmental statements in charting and explain the need for nonjudgmental documentation.
13. List seven guidelines for effective charting.

Patient-Centered Professionalism
14. Analyze a realistic medical office situation and apply your understanding of medical history taking to determine the best course of action.
15. Describe the impact on patient care when medical assistants understand how to take a patient's medical history appropriately and accurately.

MEDICAL HISTORY TAKING

KEY TERMS

charting Documenting what is observed or what is told by the patient.

chief complaint (CC) Reason that the patient wants to see the physician.

demographic Biographical data; personal information.

diagnosis (Dx) Identification of a disease or condition based on review of signs and symptoms, laboratory reports, history, and procedures.

familial Within the family; genetically acquired.

family history (FH) Health inventory of a patient's immediate family.

Health Insurance Portability and Accountability Act (HIPAA) Government act mandating that appropriate measures be taken to protect patients' personal information.

hereditary Acquired through genetic makeup.

objective Able to be seen or measured.

open-ended questions Questions that require more than a "yes" or "no" answer.

past history (PH) Summary of a patient's prior health.

present illness (PI) Expansion of a patient's chief complaint.

"release of information" form Legal form signed by a patient that indicates who can see the patient's health records.

review of systems (ROS) Step-by-step review of each body system.

signs Observable evidence that can be seen or measured; objective data.

social history (SH) Overview of a patient's lifestyle, including smoking, education, exercise, occupation, and other environmental factors.

subjective Not able to be seen or measured.

symptoms Subjective data reported by the patient.

What Would You Do?

A patient's medical and health history provides valuable information about the patient's present and past health and medical treatment. The physician uses this information to diagnose current illnesses or injuries and to monitor the patient's health as he or she ages. Because this information is so important, a complete medical history is taken for each new patient in the medical office.

The patient can provide some of the information needed for the health history in advance. The medical assistant or the physician must obtain other medical information during the office visit. In some cases the medical assistant takes much of this information in a patient interview. Taking a patient's medical history requires knowledge of the medical history form, good interviewing skills, and the ability to chart accurately.

≋ SECTIONS OF THE MEDICAL HISTORY

A medical history form provides data or information about a patient that the physician can use to correlate the patient's symptoms and formulate a treatment plan. The medical history form is considered the foundation for understanding a patient's health status. These forms can be very comprehensive depending on the specialty (Fig. 7-1). Simple one-page or two-page documents may also be used (Fig. 7-2).

The sections of the medical history include personal data, chief complaint, present illness, past history, family history, social history, and review of systems. Procedure 7-1 describes the steps in completing a medical history form.

Personal Data

The personal data section requests basic information about the patient. This **demographic** material is completed by the patient and includes the patient's name, address, date of birth (DOB), gender, telephone number, insurance information, marital status, and occupation. The medical assistant should be ready to help patients who have difficulty completing this part of the medical history.

Chief Complaint

The **chief complaint (CC)** is the reason the patient wants to see the physician. The medical assistant should chart the CC concisely but with as much important information as possible and in the patient's own words. The CC is a brief statement of only one or two **signs** or **symptoms,** body location, character, severity of precipitating events (e.g., "what caused the problem"), aggravating or reliev-

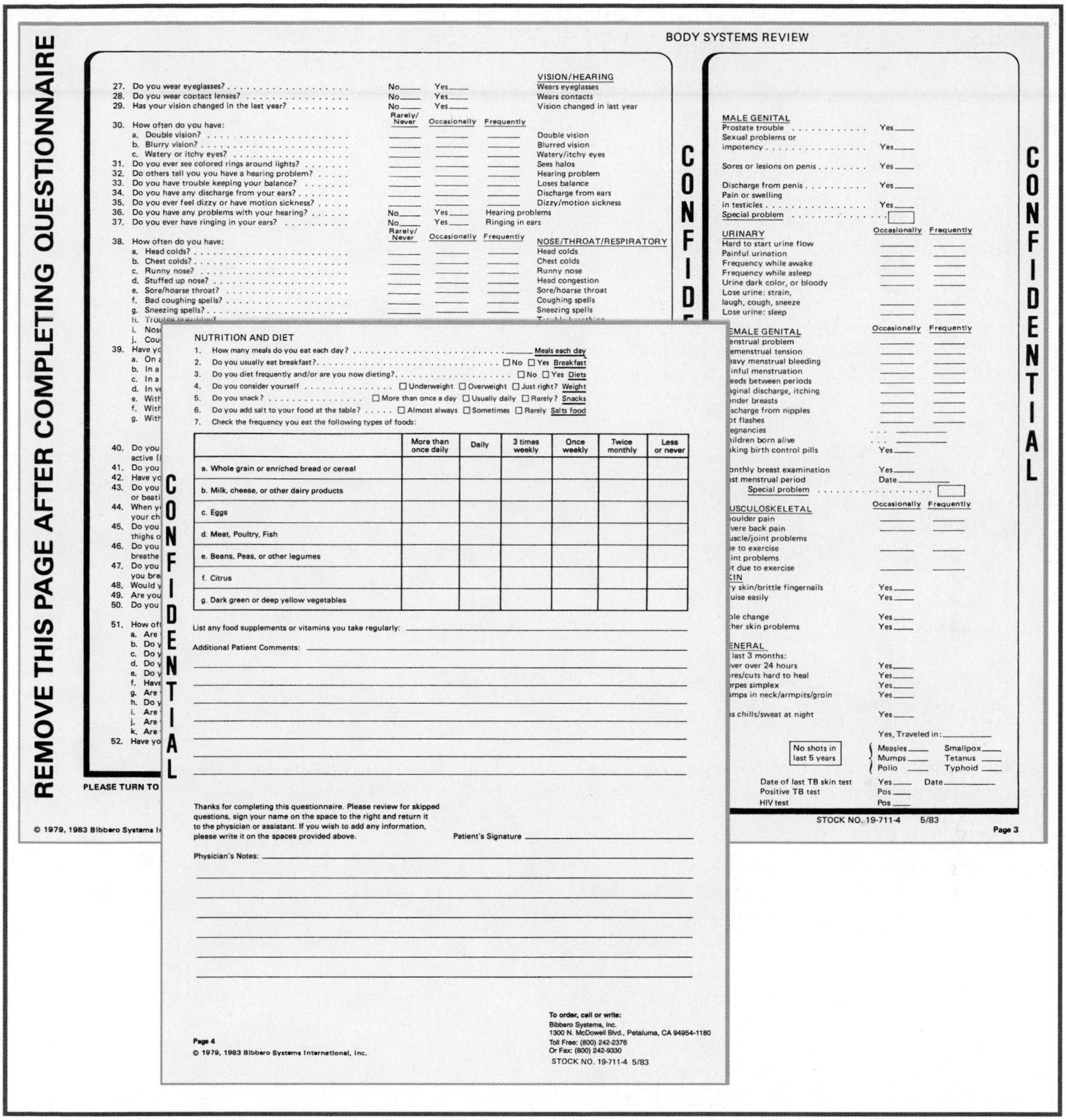

Fig. 7-1 Comprehensive medical history form. *(Courtesy Bibbero System, Inc., Petaluma, Calif., (800) 242-2376; Fax (800) 242-9330; www.bibbero.com.)*

ing factors, and the duration (length of time) of the problem.

Symptoms that cannot be measured or seen are referred to as **subjective** information. If a patient states she has felt dizzy for the past 3 days, for example, this is subjective because dizziness cannot be measured or observed. **Objective** information can be measured or observed. For example, elevated blood pressure can be measured and reported (e.g.,

$^{160}/_{100}$ mm Hg), so this is an objective symptom. Box 7-1 provides more examples of objective and subjective data as listed in the sections of the medical health history.

When gathering information, the medical assistant should try and pinpoint the CC to a particular body system, time frame (onset, duration, frequency), degree of discomfort, and way in which it affects daily activities. Fig. 7-3 provides

FORM 8184   MEDICAL RECORD

NAME			AGE	SEX	S M D W
ADDRESS		PHONE		DATE	
SPONSOR		ADDRESS			
OCCUPATION		REF BY		ACKN	

CHIEF COMPLAINT

PRESENT ILLNESS

FAMILY HISTORY			URINARY TRACT	
MOTHER	FATHER		NOCTURIA	FREQUENCY
BROTHERS			PAIN	BURNING
SISTERS			BLEEDING	INFECTION
TB	DIAB	MALIG	INCONTINENCE	
HT DIS	NEPH	EPILEP	GENITAL TRACT	
PSYCH			AGE AT MENST	TYPE PERIOD
PAST HISTORY — GENL HEALTH			INTERMEN BLEEDING	
			AMENORRHEA	DYSMENORRHEA
CHILDHOOD DISEASES			VAG DISCH	IRRITATION
SC FEV	RHEUM FEV	ALLERGY	PAINFUL PERIOD	
OTHER			L M P	
USUAL WEIGHT			CHILDREN — L	D S B
ACCIDENTS			MARRIED YRS.	YOUNGEST CHILD

HABITS COFFEE TOBACCO ALCOHOL	NEUROMUSCULAR	
REVIEW OF SYSTEMS	STRENGTH	NERVOUSNESS
E E N T — EYES	SLEEP	WORRY
EARS	MUSCULAR PAIN	
NOSE	JOINT PAIN	
THROAT	ABNORMAL SENSATIONS	
NECK	DEFORMITIES	
BREASTS		

HEART — LUNGS		OPERATIONS
PAIN	COUGH	
BLEEDING	DYSPNEA	
IRREG	EDEMA	
GASTROINTESTINAL		TREATMENTS
APPETITE	DIET	
INDIGESTION	PAIN	
NAUSEA	VOMITING	
JAUNDICE	BLEEDING	COMMENTS
BOWEL HABITS		
HEMORRHOIDS		
PAIN WITH STOOL	ITCHING	
OTHER		
OTHER		

FORM 8184 COLWELL SYSTEMS, CHAMPAIGN, ILL.

Fig. 7-2 General medical history form. *(Courtesy Colwell Systems, Champaign, Ill.)*

Procedure 7-1 Complete a Medical History Form

TASK: Obtain and record a patient's medical history using verbal and nonverbal communication skills and applying the principles of accurate documentation in the patient's medical record.

EQUIPMENT AND SUPPLIES
- Medical history form
- Patient's medical record
- Pens (red and black ink)
- Clipboard
- Quiet, private area

SKILLS/RATIONALE

1. **Procedural Step. Assemble necessary supplies.**
   Rationale. It is important to have all supplies ready and available before starting any procedure to ensure efficiency.

2. **Procedural Step. Greet and identify the patient.**
   Rationale. Identifying the patient ensures the right patient is being interviewed.

3. **Procedural Step. Escort the patient to a quiet, comfortable room that is well lit to conduct the interview.**

4. **Procedural Step. Explain why information is required, and reassure the patient that the information gathered will be kept confidential.**
   NOTE: It is important to explain to the patient that your purpose for reviewing the forms is to be sure that the physician has all the relevant information about the patient's health history.
   Rationale. Patients are more comfortable and cooperative when they understand the reason for obtaining and recording their medical history.

5. **Procedural Step. Seat the patient, then sit down next to the patient at eye level for questioning.**
   Rationale. The patient feels less intimidated if the medical assistant is sitting rather than standing.

6. **Procedural Step. Review the completed portion of the medical history form with the patient, looking for omissions or incomplete answers.**
   Obtain any missing information from the patient by asking the appropriate questions.

7. **Procedural Step. Speak clearly and distinctly and maintain eye contact (if appropriate) with the patient.**
   Rationale. The patient should feel at ease to speak freely about the medical history; maintaining eye contact can assure the patient that you care and are listening. (However, keep in mind that some cultures consider eye contact to be inappropriate.)

8. **Procedural Step. Once the medical history form has been reviewed, ask the patient to state the reason for today's visit.**
   This is the patient's "chief complaint," or current medical problem. Ask open-ended questions requiring more than a "yes" or "no" answer to obtain the patient's chief complaint. The chief complaint should be limited to one or two symptoms and should refer to specific, rather than general or "vague," symptoms.

9. **Procedural Step. Record the information briefly and concisely, using the patient's own words as much as possible.**
   Use "c/o" for "complains of" and quotation marks when quoting the patient. Include the duration of the symptoms. Avoid using names of diseases or diagnostic terms. Use medical terminology to describe locations on the body but not disease processes.
   Rationale. This information is needed by the physician to make an accurate assessment and diagnosis. The physician usually completes the systems review during the pre-examination interview.

10. **Procedural Step. Ask the patient about prescription, over-the-counter (OTC), and herbal medications; record all medications the patient is taking.**
    If the patient is not taking any medications, write "none" in the medication section of the medical history form. Be sure to ask if the patient is taking vitamin supplements or nonprescription (OTC) medications such as pain relievers. Many patients will forget to mention such medications because they do not consider these to be drugs.
    Rationale. It is important that the physician have a complete list of medications because many medications have interactions with other medications.

11. **Procedural Step. Inquire about allergies to medications, foods, and other substances, and record any allergies in red ink on every page of the history form.**

Continued

Procedure 7-1 Complete a Medical History Form—cont'd

If the patient does not have allergies, write "NKA" ("no known allergies") or "NKDA" ("no known drug allergies") in the record.
Rationale. This will alert the physician and all caregivers to the patient's allergies. The presence of an allergy may alter medication and treatment procedures as planned by the physician. Writing "NKA" or "NKDA" in the record informs the physician that you asked the question.

12. **Procedural Step. Review and record information in all the following sections of the medical history form:**
    - Family history
    - Social history
    - Past history
    - Hospitalizations
    - Surgeries
    - Injuries

13. **Procedural Step. Record all information legibly and neatly in black ink.**
    Rationale. Recording in ink maintains a medical record that is understandable and defensible in court and prevents alterations to documentation.

14. **Procedural Step. Thank the patient for providing the information.**

15. **Procedural Step. Review the record for errors before giving it to the physician.**
    Ask about any areas where further clarification may be needed.

16. **Procedural Step. Use the information to complete the patient's record as directed by office policy.**
    All information about the patient must remain confidential and can be discussed only with the physician or health care member responsible for the patient's care.

BOX 7-1 Medical Health History: Objective and Subjective Data

Subjective

Personal Data
Name, date of birth, marital status.

Chief Complaint
Patient symptoms and duration, self-medication (e.g., throbbing headache for 3 days with no relief from aspirin).

Past History
Past illnesses, past surgeries (e.g., gallbladder removed).

Family History
Causes of death, past or present diseases or illnesses (e.g., both parents died of heart disease; brother has high blood pressure).

Social History
Patient's lifestyle, to include smoking, drinking, and occupation (e.g., worked in coal mine for 30 years).

Objective

Systems Review
Physician records, past history, current findings.

Laboratory and Radiology Reports
Lab reports include complete blood count (CBC) and wound cultures. Radiology reports include x-ray series and magnetic resonance imaging (MRI).

Diagnosis
Based on prior health history, signs and symptoms, and physical examination.

Treatment
Instructions for follow-up.

Progress Notes
Documentation of patient's care.

---

examples of charting the CC based on the patient interview.

Present Illness

The **present illness (PI)** section provides an expansion of the CC. The PI contains more descrip-tion about the current illness or injury, including the severity of the pain, whether symptoms have improved or worsened, and whether other minor symptoms are present. For example, a patient may state that he tripped on the stairs that morning and fell on his right arm, which is now swollen and painful: this would be the CC. If he went on to

Patient Interview #1

Medical Assistant:	What is the reason for your visit today?
Patient:	My throat has been sore since Tuesday.
Medical Assistant:	That's three days now isn't it? Have you had any fever?
Patient:	I don't know. I don't think so.

Sample charting

6/12/99	c/o sore throat x 3 days —————————————— S. Williams, CMA

Patient Interview #2

Medical Assistant:	Why have you come to see the doctor today?
Patient:	I have had terrible stomach pain all morning.
Medical Assistant:	Can you show me where it hurts?
	Patient points to area 3 inches below belly button in the middle.
Medical Assistant:	Have you taken anything to relieve the pain?
Patient:	I took Maalox but it didn't help.
Medical Assistant:	When did you take it?
Patient:	At 9:30 this morning.

Sample charting

6/12/99	Pt. c/o severe midline abdominal pain since this AM. Took Maalox at
	9:30 AM c̄ relief. ————————————— S. Williams, CMA

Patient Interview #3

Medical Assistant:	What is the reason for your visit today?
Patient:	I have been having really bad headaches.
Medical Assistant:	When did the headaches begin?
Patient:	Well, I always have headaches occasionally, but lately I've had two or three a week, like for the last two weeks.
Medical Assistant:	Are they in the front or back, can you show me?
Patient:	They are all over. It feels like someone is hammering my head.
Medical Assistant:	On both sides?
Patient:	Yes.
Medical Assistant:	What do you do when you have one?
Patient:	I have to lie down. I've been taking ibuprofen but it doesn't help. When I have one I'm too sick to do anything.
Medical Assistant:	Do you have any nausea or see flashing lights?
Patient:	No.
Medical Assistant:	Have you been sick or had any other problems?
Patient:	Not really.

Sample charting

6/12/99	Pt. c/o severe generalized headaches x 2 weeks, about 2-3 per week.
	Describes as "it feels like someone is hammering my head." Pain is not
	relieved by ibuprofen. Denies other symptoms or illness.—————
	————————————— S. Williams, CMA

Fig. 7-3 Sample patient interview and charting of the chief complaint. *(From Hunt SA:* Saunders fundamentals of medical assisting, *Philadelphia, 2002, Saunders.)*

explain in the interview that he applied ice to the right arm and took two Tylenol tablets with no relief, this information would go in the PI.

Sometimes the PI is based on a past medical problem. A patient's past illness may have been treated elsewhere. For example, if a patient with diabetes has moved from Ohio to Florida, the patient's new physician would want to see documentation of the patient's previous care. For this to occur, the patient or the legal guardian must complete a **"release of information" form** (Fig. 7-4), then sign and date it, so that the release can be sent to the former physician to obtain the patient's medical records.

Past History

Past history (PH) is a summary of the patient's prior health. This information is needed to assist the physician in treating the patient's current problem. Past diseases, conditions, or injuries can affect a person's present state of health. As part of a PH, information is gathered about the following:

- Childhood diseases
- Major or chronic illnesses
- Surgeries
- Hospitalizations
- Allergies
- Accidents or injuries

```
┌─────────────────────────────────────────────────────────────┐
│  RECORDS RELEASE                         Date _____   │
│                                                               │
│  To _____│
│                           DOCTOR                              │
│                                                               │
│  _____│
│                           ADDRESS                             │
│                                                               │
│  I hereby authorize and request you to release                │
│                                                               │
│  to _____│
│                           DOCTOR                              │
│                                                               │
│  _____│
│                           ADDRESS                             │
│                                                               │
│  the complete medical records in your possession, concerning  │
│  my illness and/or treatment during                           │
│                                                               │
│  the period from _____ to _____  │
│                                                               │
│                             Signed _____  │
│                                     (PATIENT OR NEAREST RELATIVE) │
│                                                               │
│  _____ Relationship _____  │
│           WITNESS                                             │
└─────────────────────────────────────────────────────────────┘
```

Fig. 7-4 "Release of information" request form ("records release" form).

- Last examination date
- Current and past medications (prescription and nonprescription); over-the-counter medications and herbal supplements
- Immunizations

Family History

Family history (FH) includes a health inventory of the patient's immediate blood relatives. Health information is gathered about the patient's mother, father, brothers, sisters, and both maternal and paternal grandparents. The FH includes information about relatives' current state of health, significant health issues, and causes of death. The physician will reference the FH when studying a patient's current symptoms. Some diseases are **hereditary** (e.g., sickle cell anemia, hemophilia, muscular dystrophy), or **familial,** meaning they are passed down from a parent. Diabetes mellitus is a common example of a familial disease, as are hypertension, heart disease, and allergies.

Social History

Social history (SH) presents an overview of the patient's lifestyle, including eating, drinking, smoking, education, exercise habits, past and present occupations, and (when applicable) sexual habits. Although this information is sometimes awkward to obtain, it is important because it is helpful to the physician. The SH may provide insight regarding the patient's ability to comply with the course of treatment. In addition, it may help the physician pinpoint the etiology of the disease. For example, a person's occupational history would include emotional demands and environmental conditions such as chemical exposure and dust (e.g., coal, asbestos).

Review of Systems

The **review of systems (ROS),** also called the *systems review,* is a step-by-step review of each body system, past and present. The physician usually completes the ROS while doing a physical assessment of the patient. If these questions are included on a health history questionnaire completed by the patient, the medical assistant should go over these questions to ensure all the information is correct and was understood by the patient. One disease may affect another system without the patient's awareness. For example, a patient with severe back pain may think she has pulled a muscle, but the full ROS may detect a urinary tract infection (UTI).

An ROS starts at the head and moves downward. Table 7-1 provides typical information recorded by the physician. Using the patient's prior health history and reviewing symptoms related to the system, the physician can make a "tentative" (clinical) **diagnosis (Dx).** Fig. 7-5 is an example of a medical report completed by a physician. Box 7-2 describes the three major types of diagnoses.

TABLE 7-1	Review of Systems (ROS): Examples of Patient Signs and Symptoms*	
Body Part	**Signs**	**Symptoms**
Head	Fainting	Dizziness, headaches, pain
Eyes	Redness, discharge, swelling, excessive tearing	Pain, double vision, vision changes
Ears	Redness, discharge, hearing loss	Pain, ringing in ears, dizziness
Nose	Nosebleeds, discharge, obstruction	Altered smell, frequency of colds
Neck	Swelling, lumps	Tenderness, pain on movement
Mouth and throat	Swelling of gums, loose teeth, bleeding gums, yellow or white patches on mucous membranes, hoarseness, voice changes	Burning of tongue, sore throat
Chest	Cough, wheezing, shortness of breath, sputum production (color, quantity)	Pain with breathing, tightness
Cardiac	Palpitations, shortness of breath on exertion	Pain, tenderness of heart area
Abdomen	Swelling, bowel sounds	Pain, tenderness
Skin	Rashes, hives, itching, dryness, bruises, changes in skin color and texture of hair and nails	Burning, sensitive to touch, itching
General appearance	Fever, change in weight, night sweats, muscle weakness	Chills, fatigue

***Signs** provide objective information, whereas **symptoms** are subjective complaints.

BOX 7-2	Types of Diagnoses

Clinical Diagnosis

Physician uses patient's health history, chief complaint (CC), and physical examination (PE).

Example: CC: joint pain, headache, irritability, weight loss. Patient history: unremarkable. PE: limited range of motion; other systems WNL.

Laboratory tests ordered: CBC with diff, Sed rate, Rheumatoid factor (RF)

Dx: Arthritis

Final Diagnosis

Physician uses patient's health history, chief complaint, physical examination, laboratory test results, and results of diagnostic procedures.

Test results: Moderate anemia, decreased WBC, increased sed rate, RF increased

Dx: Rheumatoid arthritis

Differential Diagnosis

Once treatment occurs, the patient is re-evaluated to determine if the clinical diagnosis has changed. If it has changed, treatment is altered, and additional tests may be ordered.

Example: Patient is not responding to treatment. Developed skin lesions on the face, scalp, and neck. Rash appears on the face and the bridge of the nose. New symptoms and nonresponsiveness to treatment; additional tests ordered.

Dx: Lupus erythematosus

CBC, Complete blood count; *WBC,* white blood cells (count); *WNL,* within normal limits.

PATIENT-CENTERED PROFESSIONALISM

- Why must the medical assistant be certain all information is completed in each section of the patient medical history form?
- Why must the medical assistant record the chief complaint concisely and in the patient's own words?

INTERVIEWING SKILLS

Medical assistants often interview patients to obtain their history. As this is done, the medical assistant can observe and assess the patient's alertness, level of orientation, grooming, and comfort. In addition, this is a good opportunity to establish a trusting relationship with the patient. The patient will often

---

MEDICAL HISTORY AND REVIEW OF SYSTEMS

Ivan Shapiro
07/14/XX

HISTORY OF PRESENT ILLNESS	This 55-year-old white male presents with a history of chest tightness when exercising for the past month, which has increased in frequency during the last week. The tightness across the chest was first noticed when mowing the lawn. The episodes have been increasing in frequency until there are about one or two episodes per day, usually associated with exercise and all relieved by rest. Has taken antacids once or twice thinking that the pain might be due to indigestion without noticeable relief. Otherwise in good health.
MEDICATIONS	Not taking any prescription medications, but occasionally uses ibuprofen for relief of muscle pain; takes multivitamin daily.
ALLERGIES	Allergic to penicillin which results in urticaria. Has not taken penicillin for past 30 years.
PAST HISTORY	Had usual childhood diseases including mumps, measles, German measles, chicken pox. T&A when 6 years old. Fracture of left fibula at age 13; healed without problems. No other surgeries or medical problems.
FAMILY HISTORY	Father died at age 64 of MI. Mother living, has NIDDM, also being treated for hypertension. Siblings living and well. Has three children, all in good health. No other significant family history.
SOCIAL HISTORY	Smokes 20 cigarettes per day for the past 25 years. Social drinker. Drinks two cups of coffee daily.
OCCUPATIONAL HISTORY	Has been a carpenter for about 20 years. Worked on a farm for a few years after high school. No significant injuries due to occupation.
REVIEW OF SYSTEMS	Denies radiation of chest pain, has occasional indigestion, increasing in the past 6 months. Other than occasional muscle pain following physical exertion and recent chest pain, denies physical symptoms.

Joanne Hughes, MD

Fig. 7-5 Sample medical report, including the patient history and review of systems. *(From Hunt SA: Saunders fundamentals of medical assisting, Philadelphia, 2002, Saunders.)*

provide the medical assistant with information that the patient is reluctant to tell the physician.

For the interview to be effective, the medical assistant must present a feeling of genuine concern for the patient's well-being and show respect for the patient's concerns. In addition, it is important to consider the patient's privacy and to remember good communication skills.

Patient Privacy

The first step in interviewing any patient is to ensure the interview area is private and free from interruptions. A sense of confidentiality must be clearly demonstrated to the patient. This can be accomplished by going to a separate room and closing the door. When assured that the area is private, the patient will feel more comfortable being open about health details of a personal nature.

The **Health Insurance Portability and Accountability Act (HIPAA)** mandates, among other regulations, that appropriate measures be taken to protect personal information. Besides being the law, the patient has a right to expect privacy. Only individuals directly involved in the patient's care are allowed access to the patient's medical record. All information provided by the patient (e.g., FH, SH) must be kept in strictest confidence.

Effective Communication

Effective communication enables the medical assistant to obtain the necessary information about the patient's medical history. As will be discussed in Chapters 9 and 10, remember to (1) make eye contact (unless this has cultural implications), (2) be a good listener (silent periods allow the patient time to express feelings), and (3) acknowledge the patient (positive facial expressions show you are listening).

Convey sensitivity toward the patient's needs and feelings by leaning toward the patient to show interest and by nodding your head to encourage the patient to continue. This approach supports the patient and provides insight into the patient's attitudes about health and illness. Do not react to personal or "shocking" details the patient may reveal. It is important to be respectful and nonjudgmental, not reactive. Procedure 7-2 provides more information about recognizing and responding to nonverbal communication.

Explaining the reason for the health history form gives the patient confidence in the medical assistant's abilities because the patient can see that the assistant understands the need for the information. The patient feels more confident about providing information to a medical assistant who shows competence and professionalism.

PATIENT-CENTERED PROFESSIONALISM

- Why must the medical assistant apply good communication skills when conducting the patient interview?
- What are some advantages of the medical assistant interviewing the patient while obtaining the medical history versus the patient filling out a health questionnaire?

CHARTING

Medical assistants are responsible for **charting** the information they obtain when taking the patient history. Charting must be clear, concise, objective (nonjudgmental), and correct.

Patient Statements

Charting patient statements that pertain to their health is key in providing a good database for the patient's physical examination. Having the patient pinpoint specific symptoms rather than make generalizations is most helpful. Always use quotation marks when charting the patient's words.

Example of general statements vs. specific symptoms

General: "My hand seems to go numb all the time."
Specific: "When I am working on the computer for more than 15 minutes, my right hand gets numb."

Allow patients to describe the reason for the visit or complaint in their own words. The medical assistant might have the tendency to make assumptions. Avoid using "yes" or "no" questions because patients tend to answer them with simply "yes" or "no" without elaborating. This can result in the medical assistant forming an incorrect assumption because of oversimplification or misinterpretation of the patient's meaning. Using **open-ended questions** encourages patients to explain fully what they mean.

Example of yes-no questions vs. open-ended questions

Yes-no: "Do you mean your foot is falling asleep?"
Open ended: "Tell me about the numbness in your foot."

Observations

In addition to what the patient says, the medical assistant must report what is seen, heard, felt, or smelled. Observations are based on the following areas:

- *Physical appearance* (e.g., patient's face is flushed; patient's clothes are loose fitting; patient is wearing long sleeves in hot weather)
- *Body structure* (e.g., poor posture, deformity)
- *Mobility* (e.g., gait slow, range of motion diminished)
- *Behavior* (e.g., answering questions inappropriately, disoriented, unresponsive to questions)

Charting Tips

The medical assistant's notes should be concise. Only important information should be recorded.

Charting can be done in several forms. Box 7-3 reviews the necessary criteria for charting the patient's chief complaint and information about the present illness. Regardless of the form of charting used, the medical assistant should remember the following simple rules:

1. Always check the name on the chart and at the top of the page to be certain the correct patient is being charted.
2. Use black ink because it photocopies better than blue.

Procedure 7-2 Recognize and Respond to Verbal and Nonverbal Communication

TASK: Recognize and respond to basic verbal and nonverbal communication.

EQUIPMENT AND SUPPLIES
None.

SKILLS/RATIONALE

1. **Procedural Step. Greet the patient, smile to welcome the patient, and introduce yourself.**
2. **Procedural Step. Verify the patient's name and use it with a courtesy title, such as Mr. or Mrs., unless otherwise instructed by the patient.**
   Rationale. This ensures you are speaking to the correct patient, demonstrates a personal interest, and shows respect.
3. **Procedural Step. Establish a comfortable physical environment.**
   Establish an appropriate social distance, position yourself on the same level as the patient (not above or below), make eye contact (if culturally appropriate), reduce any physical noise (e.g., loud fans, sounds from nearby rooms), and provide privacy.
   Rationale. A comfortable environment free from distractions is required by the Health Insurance Portability and Accountability Act of 1996 (HIPAA).
4. **Procedural Step. Verify that the patient feels comfortable.**
5. **Procedural Step. Establish the topic of discussion.**
   If you need to introduce the topic, tell the patient what it is and why you will discuss it. If the patient will introduce the topic, ask the patient what he or she would like to discuss.
6. **Procedural Step. Observe the patient for nonverbal communication cues.**
   Nonverbal communication is communication without the use of words. It includes gestures, posture, facial expressions, eye contact, and physical touch. A medical assistant must be fully aware of any body language exhibited by the patient and report it, if necessary, according to the outcome of the response. The medical assistant must also be aware of his or her own body language when questioning a patient about sensitive material.

   Rationale. Observing the patient will help you become more sensitive to what the patient is saying without using words. This is especially important when discussing social habits like smoking, alcohol consumption, or drug usage. Eye contact is important to show confidence in asking the types of questions that may be required.
7. **Procedural Step. Verify that the patient understands; ask open-ended questions that request the patient to explain his or her understanding.**
   Rationale. An open-ended question can generate many different responses; it cannot be answered with a one-word response. Thus the information you receive from the patient will be more complete and accurate.
8. **Procedural Step. Practice active listening; provide feedback.**
   Active listening means focusing on the patient, what the patient is saying, how he or she is saying it, and what nonverbal messages he or she is sending. It also includes using the patient's verbal and nonverbal cues to ask follow-up questions. In active listening, it is important to verify your understanding of the message; a common approach is to "paraphrase," or repeat the message in a slightly different way. Another important part of active listening is eye contact.
   Rationale. This makes the patient feel that you are listening attentively and may help the patient to "open up."
9. **Procedural Step. Near the end of the discussion, provide the patient with the opportunity to ask additional questions or to provide further clarification.**
10. **Procedural Step. Thank the patient for his or her comments and signal the end of the discussion.**
    When possible, indicate what will happen next so that the patient knows what to expect.

BOX 7-3 Charting "Chief Complaint" and "Present Illness" Information

Before you chart the chief complaint, the following information is needed:

1. Date
2. Time
3. **Chief Complaint (CC)** (What brings you to the office today?)
   - **Signs and symptoms** (Patient's own words)
   - **Specific location of** symptoms or pain
   - **Onset** (When did it begin? or When did you first notice the symptoms?)
   - **Intensity** (How severe is it?)
   - **Precipitating factor** (What caused it to happen? What activities, situations, or positions make the pain worse or better?)
   - **Duration** (How long have you had these symptoms? Is it constant or intermittent? Does it come and go?)
   - **Remedies** (What has the patient done prior to seeking medical attention?)
4. Proper signature and credential

Descriptive Terms

For Pain
Aching, sharp, throbbing, burning, cramplike, nagging

For Duration
Sudden, constant, intermittent, sporadic

For Intensity
Intense, moderate, mild; "On a scale of 0 to 10, with 0 being less severe and 10 most severe, describe your pain." (Use an assessment scale)

3. Ensure that writing is clear and legible.
4. Always begin charting with the date and time. Then make the entry, and end with your first initial, last name, and credential (Fig. 7-6).
5. Do not leave any space between the end of the entry and the signature.
6. Ensure accuracy with regard to information, spelling, abbreviations, and symbols. Credibility is ruined if words are misspelled or proper abbreviations are not used.
7. Use proper technique for correcting errors (Fig. 7-7).

Review your handbook for common abbreviations in charting and correcting errors in medical records.

As mentioned previously, charting the patient's responses clearly and without judgment provides the physician with a foundation on which to build a treatment plan for the patient. Notes should never include judgmental statements. The medical assistant should not record his or her opinions, only observations and statements from the patient.

Example of judgmental vs. nonjudgmental charting

Judgmental: Lack of good hygiene has caused the patient to have an infected toe.

Nonjudgmental: Patient states foot has been sore for several days.

Judgmental: The patient appears upset.

Nonjudgmental: The patient is crying and wringing her hands.

PATIENT-CENTERED PROFESSIONALISM

- Why must medical assistants chart only what they observe, hear, and see?

Fig. 7-6 Charting example. *(From Bonewit-West K: Clinical procedures for medical assistants, ed 6, Philadelphia, 2004, Saunders.)*

Charting Example	
Date	
6/30/05	3:15 p.m. CC: Intense pain in the ⓛ ear for the past 2 days. States
	pain is sharp and continuous. Noted sl yellow discharge from ⓛ ear.
	Fever of 101° F began last night about 9 p.m. Took Tylenol 2 tabs at 8 a.m.
	———————————————————— D. Bennett, CMA

Fig. 7-7 The proper way to correct an error in the patient's record. *(From Bonewit-West K: Clinical procedures for medical assistants, ed 6, Philadelphia, 2004, Saunders.)*

	error 10/15/05 ———————— D.Bennett, CMA
10/15/05	9:30 a.m. Tubersol Mantoux test: Ømm induration. ————————
	————————————— 12 ————————— D. Bennett, CMA

CONCLUSION

The medical history form is a key information tool used in treating the patient. Each section assists in answering questions about a patient's current state of health. The medical assistant can begin establishing rapport with the patient if the assistant is involved in the process of completing the health history. Charting should provide the physician with a "snapshot" explanation of why the patient is seeking treatment.

Effective listening and communication skills should be used when conducting a patient interview. Putting the patient at ease and demonstrating competence and professionalism give the patient confidence and a sense of security about sharing personal health information. Obtaining the necessary health and medical history information and documenting it accurately help establish a foundation for effective, quality patient care.

SUMMARY

Reinforce your understanding of the material in this chapter by reviewing the curriculum objectives and key content points below.

1. Define, appropriately use, and spell all the Key Terms for this chapter.
   - Review the Key Terms if necessary.
2. Demonstrate the correct procedure for completing a medical history form.
   - Review Procedure 7-1.
3. List seven sections of the medical history and briefly explain what type of information is collected in each.
   - Demographic material: name, address, DOB, insurance information.
   - Chief complaint: main reason the patient wants to see the physician.
   - Present illness: expansion of the chief complaint.
   - Past history: summary of the patient's prior health.
   - Family history: inventory of the patient's immediate blood relatives.
   - Social history: overview of the patient's lifestyle, including smoking, drinking, education, and exercise.
   - Review of systems: step-by-step review of each body system.
4. Distinguish between *objective* and *subjective* data.
   - Objective data (signs) can be observed or measured.

   - Subjective data (symptoms) include patient complaints and feelings.
5. State two positive outcomes of interviewing a patient effectively.
   - The patient's alertness, level of orientation, grooming, and comfort level can be observed during an interview.
   - The interview is a good opportunity to establish a trusting relationship with the patient.
6. Explain the importance of maintaining the patient's privacy during and after the interview.
   - Patients are more likely to open up to the medical assistant when their privacy is maintained.
   - HIPAA mandates that measures be taken to protect patient privacy.
   - Patients have a *right* to expect that their confidential information is being protected.
7. Explain the need for effective communication skills during a patient interview.
   - Effective communication encourages the patient to provide all the necessary information and allows the interviewer to receive and understand it.
   - Effective communication helps patients explain the situation completely without being influenced by the interviewer.
8. Demonstrate the correct procedure for recognizing and responding to nonverbal communication.
   - Review Procedure 7-2.
9. Explain the importance of charting patient statements and observations accurately.
   - The physician's treatment plan is based on the information gathered during history taking and the physician's examination of the patient.
   - Accurate documentation provides a thorough record of the office visit.
10. Differentiate between "specific" and "general" patient statements and know when to obtain more detail.
    - Encourage patients to provide detailed information with specific statements (e.g., "four days" vs. "a few days").
    - If patients do make general statements, ask questions to clarify the details.
11. Accurately record observations made during a patient interview.
    - Medical assistants should make note of what they see, hear, feel, and smell, in addition to what the patient says.
12. Recognize judgmental statements in charting and explain the need for nonjudgmental documentation.

- Charting should be done using nonjudgmental statements (e.g., "the patient reports feeling sad much of the time and experiences constant fatigue" vs. "the patient seems depressed").
- Nonjudgmental statements provide the physician with a solid foundation on which to build a treatment plan for the patient.

13. List seven guidelines for effective charting.
- The chart should first be checked to make sure it is the correct patient's record.
- Black ink should always be used.
- Writing should be clear and legible.
- Chart notes should include date and time and should be properly signed with first initial, last name, and credential.
- No space should be left between the end of an entry and the signature.
- No lines should be left between entries.
- Charting should be done accurately, using correct information, spelling, abbreviations, and symbols.
- Proper technique should be used for correcting errors.

14. Analyze a realistic medical office situation and apply your understanding of medical history taking to determine the best course of action.
- Effective communication skills must be used to take the patient's history.

- History taking is an opportunity for the medical assistant to build trust and rapport with the patient.

15. Describe the impact on patient care when medical assistants understand how to take a patient's medical history appropriately and accurately.
- The medical history provides information about the patient's past and present, and proper collection of the data is necessary to formulate a diagnosis.
- Properly collected data provide the physician with the necessary tools to make a diagnosis and treat the patient.

FOR FURTHER EXPLORATION

Research interviewing techniques. When interviewing techniques are used effectively, time is saved and credibility with the patient is developed. The medical assistant can benefit from additional training to improve interviewing skills.

Keywords: Use the following keywords in your search: interviewing techniques, communication skills, interviewing skills.

Chapter Review

Vocabulary Review

Matching

Match each term with the correct definition.

_____ 1. Step-by-step review of each body system

_____ 2. Biographical data; personal information

_____ 3. Subjective data reported by the patient

_____ 4. Able to be seen or measured

_____ 5. Summary of a patient's prior health

_____ 6. Found in family member

_____ 7. Overview of a patient's lifestyle

_____ 8. Documenting what is observed or what is told by the patient

_____ 9. Not able to be seen or measured

_____ 10. Government act mandating that appropriate measures be taken to protect a patient's personal information

_____ 11. Legal form signed by a patient that indicates who can see the patient's health records

_____ 12. Acquired through genetic makeup

_____ 13. Reason that the patient wants to see the physician

_____ 14. Questions that require more than a "yes" or "no" answer

_____ 15. Observable evidence that can be seen or measured

A. charting
B. demographics
C. familial
D. Health Insurance Portability and Accountability Act (HIPAA)
E. hereditary
F. objective information
G. past history
H. release of information
I. review of systems
J. social history
K. subjective information
L. symptoms
M. chief complaint
N. open-ended questions
O. signs

Theory Recall

True/False

Indicate whether the sentence or statement is true or false.

_____ 1. The first step in interviewing any patient is to ensure the interview is private and free of interruptions.

_____ 2. Information that can be measured or observed is called objective information.

_____ 3. Effective communication slows down the medical assistant in her or his search for necessary information.

_____ 4. It is important to be reactive to shocking details the patient tells the medical assistant.

_____ 5. The medical assistant must report what is seen, heard, felt, and smelled.

Multiple Choice

Identify the letter of the choice that best completes the statement or answers the question.

1. Charting must be _____.
   A. clear
   B. correct
   C. nonjudgmental
   D. all of the above

2. Personal data section of a medical history is completed by the _____.
   A. physician
   B. medical assistant
   C. patient
   D. insurance company
   E. either B or C

3. Symptoms that cannot be seen are referred to as _____ information.
   A. assessment
   B. objective
   C. subjective
   D. present illness

4. The medical assistant should start the charting with _____.
   A. a clean progress note sheet
   B. the date and time
   C. a pen, blue ink only
   D. a bottle of white-out in hand to make necessary corrections

5. When interviewing the patient, the medical assistant should _____.
   A. be quick, efficient, and to the point
   B. relay personal stories to make the patient feel more at ease
   C. show genuine concern for the patient
   D. make assumptions as to the patient's answers

6. The _____ section contains more description about the current illness.
   A. social history
   B. present illness
   C. past history
   D. family history

7. The review of systems starts _____.
   A. as the patient walks in the door
   B. at the patient's feet and moves upward
   C. at the patient's head and moves downward
   D. none of the above

8. The medical assistant should ask _____.
   A. only the 13 standard questions of a physical examination
   B. yes or no questions
   C. open-ended questions
   D. direct questions

9. _____ is a brief statement of only one or two signs or symptoms.
   A. CC
   B. PH
   C. SH
   D. PI

10. _____ statements that pertain to the patient are key to providing a good database for the patient's physical examination.
    A. Encoding
    B. Charting
    C. Expanding on
    D. None of the above

11. The physician's treatment plan is based on _____.
    A. latest trends in technology
    B. laboratory findings only
    C. information gathered during history taking and physical examination
    D. physical examination only

12. Patients have _____ to expect that their confidential information is being protected.
    A. the right
    B. the privilege
    C. guarantees
    D. laws

Sentence Completion

Complete each sentence or statement.

1. _____ is an inventory of a patient's immediate family.

2. _____ information includes the patient's name, address, date of birth, and telephone number.

3. _____ is an expansion of the patient's chief complaint.

4. _____ must be completed before a patient's chart can be shared with another physician.

5. _____ presents an overview of the patient's lifestyle.

Short Answers

1. List six pieces of information that need to be included when gathering the patient's past history.

_____

_____

_____

2. List the four areas on which observations are based.

_____

_____

_____

3. List the seven sections of the medical history form.

_____

_____

_____

4. List five items the medical assistant should remember about charting.

_____

_____

_____

_____

Critical Thinking

Melinda was your eighth patient after lunch. The last thing you felt like doing was taking Melinda back to the examination room. Melinda always had a zillion questions and a story for everything. Trying to get to the reason Melinda was in to see the physician was always a challenge.

"Hey, Claire, will you take Melinda back?"

"No way. It's your turn," replied Claire. "I did it last week; it is your turn."

"Oh, all right." "Good afternoon, Melinda. How are you today?" Cindy asked as she went to retrieve Melinda from the waiting area.

"I'm fine, and you?" Melinda wasn't even smiling. She was shuffling her feet and staring at the ground all the way back to the examination room.

"What's wrong, Melinda? You don't seem to be yourself today."

"No, dear, I'm just fine; don't you worry."

But Cindy was worried that what Melinda was saying did not coincide with how she was acting.

1. Describe what verbal and nonverbal communication is occurring between Cindy and Melinda.

2. If you had to guess, what do you think is going on with Melinda, based just on the brief exchange given here.

Internet Research

Keyword: Verbal and nonverbal communication

Choose one of the following topics to research: effective communication or what nonverbal communication tells the health care provider. Cite your source. Be prepared to give a 2-minute oral presentation should your instructor assign you to do so.

What Would You Do?

If you have accomplished the objectives in this chapter, you will be able to make better choices as a medical assistant. Take another look at this situation and decide what you would do.

Dr. Walker, an obstetrician/gynecologist and internal medicine physician, has hired Jenny to assist with taking medical histories for his patients. Dr. Walker sees many patients who have high-risk pregnancies because of an infectious disease. Sarah, a new patient who is 4 months pregnant, has been referred to Dr. Walker because she is at risk for several infectious diseases. Jenny goes to the waiting room and starts to ask Sarah questions about her pregnancy and her past medical history. Sarah tells Jenny that she does not want to discuss this with a medical assistant and would rather give the information to Dr. Walker. Jenny adamantly tells Sarah that if she does not want to cooperate, Dr. Walker will not see her as a patient. Sarah begins to cry but starts telling her history to Jenny. Trying to impress Sarah during the interview, Jenny uses medical terminology to ask questions, and she never looks at Sarah or makes any observations about Sarah's remarks. After the history taking, Sarah is escorted to the examination room, where her vital signs are taken. After discussing her previous illnesses and family history, Dr. Walker examines Sarah and orders several laboratory tests, including tests for HIV and for syphilis. His tentative diagnosis is "possible HIV infection," and he confirms her pregnancy of 4 months. On leaving the office, Sarah makes an appointment for 2 weeks to discuss her test results and final diagnosis with Dr. Walker.

What should Jenny have done differently as a medical assistant initially taking Sarah's history?

1. Did Jenny handle the taking of the medical history correctly? Where should the history have been taken?

_____

_____

_____

_____

2. What actions would cause Sarah to think that Jenny is incompetent in taking a medical history?

_____

_____

_____

_____

3. Why is effective communication between the patient and the medical assistant so important when taking a medical history?

_____

_____

_____

_____

4. What is the "chief complaint," and how should it be documented?

_____

_____

_____

_____

5. What are signs? What are symptoms?

_____

_____

_____

_____

_____

6. What is the correct name for the "tentative diagnosis"? What is the difference between this diagnosis and the "final diagnosis"?

_____

_____

_____

_____

7. Why would it be incorrect for the insurance coder to use the tentative diagnosis on the insurance claim form? What could be the repercussions if the laboratory tests are negative?

_____

_____

_____

_____

_____

8. Why would it have been important for Jenny to observe Sarah during the taking of the medical history?

_____

_____

_____

_____

Chapter Quiz

Multiple Choice

Identify the letter of the choice that best completes the statement or answers the question.

1. The medical assistant must ensure _____ in order to obtain a good interview with a patient.
   A. confidentiality
   B. privacy
   C. an interruption-free environment
   D. all of the above

2. Symptoms that cannot be measured are known as (the) _____.
   A. chief complaint
   B. objective information
   C. present illness
   D. subjective information

3. A release of information form must be on file in order for a patient's information to be released to another physician.
   A. True
   B. False

4. _____ gives an overview of the patient's eating, drinking, smoking, and exercise habits.
   A. Family history
   B. Past history
   C. Review of systems
   D. Social history

5. _____ provide(s) observable information that can be measured.
   A. Chief complaint
   B. Signs
   C. Symptoms
   D. Past history

6. When charting, the medical assistant must be _____.
   A. clear and concise
   B. judgmental and critical
   C. selective and indecisive
   D. quick and decisive

7. _____ information includes a patient's name, address, date of birth, and gender.
   A. Familial
   B. Social
   C. Demographic
   D. Past history

8. The ROS starts with the _____.
   A. feet
   B. head
   C. when the patient walks in the door
   D. none of the above

9. The medical assistant has to report only what he or she hears to the physician.
   A. True
   B. False

10. Identification of a disease or condition based on review of signs and symptoms, laboratory reports, history, and procedures is known as the _____.
    A. chief complaint
    B. diagnosis
    C. objective information
    D. past history

11. _____ should be held in the strictest confidence.
    A. Family history
    B. Social history
    C. Past history
    D. All of the above

12. A medical assistant is allowed to chart his or her opinions about the patient's present history.
    A. True
    B. False

13. Information that can be measured or observed is _____.
    A. objective
    B. subjective
    C. assessment
    D. social history

14. _____ are observable evidence that can be seen or measured.
    A. Signs
    B. Symptoms

15. _____ is acquired through genetic makeup.
    A. Heredity
    B. Social history
    C. Environmental history
    D. None of the above

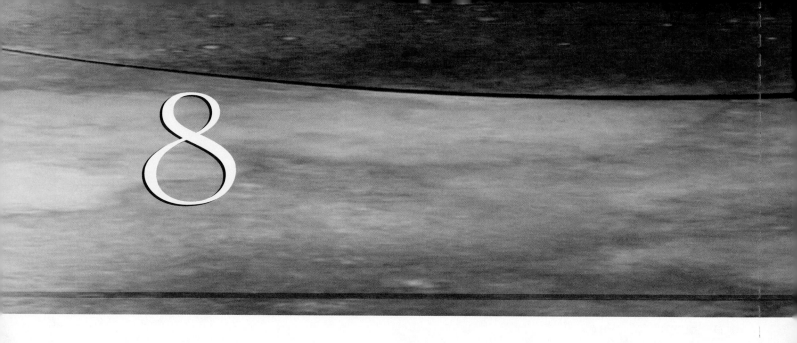

OBJECTIVES

You will be able to do the following after completing this chapter:

Key Terms
1. Define, appropriately use, and spell all the Key Terms for this chapter.

Preparing the Patient
2. List the three main responsibilities of the medical assistant in preparing a patient for a physical examination.
3. List three responsibilities of the medical assistant in assisting the patient to disrobe for an examination.
4. Demonstrate the correct procedure for providing the physician and the patient with items needed to perform a complete physical examination.
5. Explain what a "consent-to-treat form" involves and when formal consent is needed for an examination.

Positioning and Draping the Patient
6. Explain the importance of draping the patient appropriately for an examination or procedure.
7. List the three criteria for selecting the position to be used for an examination.
8. List eight examination positions and briefly explain what types of examinations are performed using each position.
9. Demonstrate the correct procedure for properly positioning and draping a patient in the sitting position.
10. Demonstrate the correct procedure for properly positioning and draping a patient in the recumbent position.
11. Demonstrate the correct procedure for properly positioning and draping a patient in the Sims' position.
12. Demonstrate the correct procedure for properly positioning and draping a patient in the prone position.
13. Demonstrate the correct procedure for properly positioning and draping a patient in the knee-chest position.
14. Demonstrate the correct procedure for properly positioning and draping a patient in the Fowler's and semi-Fowler's positions.

Examination Methods
15. List the four primary methods of examining used during a physical examination and briefly explain what occurs in each.

Vision Testing
16. State the purpose of a Snellen chart, and explain when each of the three types of Snellen charts should be used.
17. Demonstrate the correct procedure for accurately measuring and recording a patient's visual acuity with a Snellen chart.
18. List five types of common visual defects that are correctable by lenses or surgery.
19. Demonstrate the correct procedure for accurately measuring and recording a patient's color visual acuity with the Ishihara test.

ASSISTING WITH THE PHYSICAL EXAMINATION

20. Demonstrate the correct procedure for accurately measuring and recording a patient's near visual acuity with a Jaeger reading card.

Ear Examination

21. Differentiate between an ophthalmoscope and an otoscope and explain how each is used in the physical examination.

Patient-Centered Professionalism

22. Analyze a realistic medical office situation and apply your understanding of assisting with a physical examination to determine the best course of action.
23. Describe the impact on patient care when medical assistants understand how to assist the physician with the physical examination.

KEY TERMS

accommodation Ability of the eye to see objects in the distance and then adjust to a close object.

auscultation Listening for body sounds (e.g., heart, breathing, bowel), usually with a stethoscope.

body mechanics Use of appropriate body movements to perform a physical activity.

BPH Benign prostatic hypertrophy.

bruit Blowing sound heard in narrowing arteries.

BSE Breast self-examination.

consent Patient's permission for physician to proceed with an examination or procedure.

crepitus Crackling sound heard in the lungs or joints.

cyanosis Bluish discoloration of the skin caused by lack of oxygen.

diaphoresis Excessive perspiration.

distention Swollen.

dorsal recumbent position Patient is flat on the back with the knees and hips bent sharply and the feet flat on the table.

erythema Reddish discoloration of the skin.

Fowler's position Patient is in a supine position with the head of the table either at a 45-degree (semi-Fowler's position) or a 90-degree angle (full-Fowler's position).

gingivitis Inflammation of the gums.

goniometer Device used to measure joint movements and angles.

HEENT Head, eyes, ears, nose, and throat.

herpes simplex 1 Viral infection of the lip-skin junction; cold sore.

horizontal recumbent position Patient lies flat on the back; supine position.

inspection Visual viewing of body parts.

jaundice Yellowish appearance to the skin and eyes.

knee-chest position Patient begins in the prone position, then moves into a kneeling position with the buttocks elevated and the chest on the table.

LMP Last menstrual period.

macrotia Ears larger than 10 cm.

microtia Ears smaller than 4 cm.

murmur Humming or low-pitched fluttering sound of the heart heard on auscultation.

ophthalmoscope Hand-held instrument used for viewing the internal structure of the eye, especially the retina, optic nerve, and blood vessels.

otoscope Hand-held instrument used to visualize at the internal structures of the ear, ear canal, and eardrum.

pallor Paleness.

KEY TERMS—*cont'd*

palpation Touching or feeling of body organs, lymph nodes, and tissue.

patent Open; not obstructed.

percussion Tapping to check for reflexes or sounds of body cavities.

perforation Tear or hole in an organ or body part (e.g., eardrum rupture, perforated bowel).

PERRLA Pupils equal, round, and react to light and accommodation.

positioning Placing a patient in a particular posture.

presbycusis Decrease in hearing ability resulting from aging.

prone position Patient lies on the abdomen with the head turned slightly to the side.

rales Crackling sounds heard in the lungs, usually at the base.

rhonchi Rattling sounds heard in the lungs, usually in the upper bronchi and airway.

Rinne test Test that compares air conduction to bone conduction in the hearing response.

ROM Range of motion.

Sims' position Patient is first in the supine position, then turns onto the left side with the right leg sharply bent upward.

sitting position Patient's body is at a 90-degree angle.

standing position Erect; a position where the body is in an upright position.

supine position Patient's back is on the table; horizontal recumbent position.

thrill Palpable vibration.

tinnitus Ringing in the ears.

TSE Testicular self-examination.

turgor Skin resiliency.

vertigo Dizziness.

visual acuity Ability to see at different distances.

Weber test Test used to evaluate hearing quality in both ears by placing a vibrating tuning fork stem on the center of the skull and determining if sound is equal in both ears.

What Would You Do?

Read the following scenario and keep it in mind as you learn about assisting with the physical examination.

Beth is a medical assistant in the office of Dr. Havidiz, a family practitioner. Dr. Havidiz treats many low-income families, and many women in the community see him for gynecological visits. Holly, a new patient, comes to see Dr. Havidiz for a possible vaginal infection. Her demeanor shows her fear of the doctor's office, especially since this is the first time she has seen Dr. Havidiz. Dr. Havidiz was called to the hospital to see a critically ill patient earlier in the day, so appointments are delayed.

There is an available examination room when Holly arrives, so Beth takes her to the room and tells her to undress completely. Beth does not tell Holly how to put on the gown, but she stands in the room and watches Holly undress. While Holly is undressing, Beth asks the questions necessary to obtain the medical history. Beth then places Holly on the examination table in the dorsal recumbent position and immediately leaves the room, giving the impression that she is in a great hurry. After 15 minutes, Holly has discomfort in her back but dares not move from the position because she does not want to delay the examination. After 30 minutes, Holly wonders just how much longer it will take for Dr. Havidiz to come and check her. Finally, Dr. Havidiz arrives and the examination begins.

During the examination, Beth leaves the room to answer a personal phone call, leaving Dr. Havidiz and Holly alone. As Holly leaves the office, she is in tears from back pain and appears to be very upset. Beth shows no sympathy or empathy for Holly. Two days later, Holly asks that her records be transferred to another physician and tells Dr. Havidiz that she has never been treated as rudely as she was in his office.

How might this situation have been avoided?

A patient may come to the medical office for many reasons. The person may be ill or injured, may be due for a general physical checkup, or may have been referred by another physician for a special procedure. The main purpose of a physical examination is for the physician to assess the status of the patient's health. Although the physician performs the examination and makes diagnoses, the medical assistant plays an important role in the physical examination.

The medical assistant's role is to prepare the examination room, prepare the patient for the examination, and then to assist the physician. Keep in mind that patients may be nervous or anxious. The manner in which the medical assistant handles the patient from the beginning of the office visit establishes the "mood" for the remainder of the visit. If the medical assistant makes the patient feel comfortable and at ease about the upcoming examination or procedure, the patient will be cooperative and comfortable with the physician.

Important aspects of assisting with the physical examination include giving the patient instructions, positioning the patient, knowing the methods of examination, and understanding what happens in vision and hearing examinations.

PREPARING THE PATIENT

Once the medical history has been completed and the patient's vital signs taken, the patient is ready for the examination. The medical assistant's major role in preparing a patient for the complete physical examination (CPX) is to have the patient gowned, appropriately positioned, and draped for the physician to perform the examination, and to assist the physician as necessary (Procedure 8-1). It is also important to consider whether informed consent is needed for an examination or procedure and to explain the examination or procedure completely to the patient. Answer questions and put the patient at ease before the examination begins.

Disrobing and Gowning the Patient

It is usually necessary for the patient to remove articles of clothing and put on a gown that can open to expose only the body part to be examined. The medical assistant must (1) choose the right type of gown for the procedure to be performed, (2) provide clear instructions for disrobing and gowning,

Procedure 8-1 Assist with the Physical Examination

TASK: Prepare a patient and assist the physician or health care practitioner with a general physical examination.

EQUIPMENT AND SUPPLIES
- Examination table
- Table paper
- Patient gown
- Drape
- Urine specimen container
- Snellen chart
- Patient's medical record
- Balance scale
- Tongue depressor
- Plastic-backed paper towel
- Stethoscope
- Sphygmomanometer
- Otoscope
- Ophthalmoscope
- Disposable gloves

SKILLS/RATIONALE

STANDARD PRECAUTIONS ARE TO BE FOLLOWED.

1. **Procedural Step. Sanitize the hands.**
   An alcohol-based hand rub may be used instead of washing hands with soap and water, unless hands are visibly soiled.
   Rationale. Hand sanitization promotes infection control.

2. **Procedural Step. Assemble equipment and supplies.**
   Line the stainless steel instrument tray with a plastic-backed paper towel. Lay out the instruments and supplies for a general physical examination, making sure the items do not overlap. The instruments include the following:
   - Otoscope/ophthalmoscope (unless mounted on wall)
   - Nasal speculum

   - Penlight
   - Percussion hammer
   - Tuning fork
   - Tape measure

   Other items that may be added to the tray include gloves, tongue depressor, gauze squares, cotton balls, safety pins, water-based lubricant, tissue, cotton-tipped applicators, and laboratory supplies.
   Rationale. It is important to have all supplies and equipment ready and available before starting any procedure to ensure efficiency.

3. **Procedural Step. Obtain the patient's medical record.**

4. **Procedural Step. Greet and identify the patient.**
   Rationale. Identifying the patient ensures the procedure is performed on the correct patient.

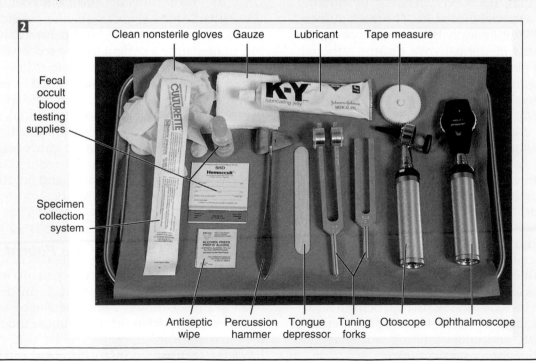

Procedure 8-1 Assist with the Physical Examination—cont'd

5. **Procedural Step. Explain the procedure to the patient.**
   Rationale. Explaining the procedure to the patient promotes cooperation and provides a means of obtaining implied consent.
6. **Procedural Step. Measure the patient's weight and height, and chart the results.**
7. **Procedural Step. Measure the patient's visual acuity, and chart the results.**
8. **Procedural Step. Have the patient provide a urine sample (if required).**
   Depending on the type or extent of the physical examination, a urine sample may be tested.
   Rationale. Having the patient void before the physical examination will ensure the patient is more comfortable during the examination.
9. **Procedural Step. Escort the patient to the examination room.**
10. **Procedural Step. Measure the patient's vital signs, and chart the results, if not done previously.**
11. **Procedural Step. Provide a gown and drape the patient.**
    Instruct the patient to change from street clothes into a patient gown. The gown should open in the back. Most male patients will not require a gown, but a drape should be provided to place over the patient's lap once seated on the examination table. Elderly patients may require assistance in changing into the gown and stepping up to sit on the examination table. Be sure to give the patient a few minutes to change into the gown. Protect your patient's right to privacy at all times. Knock on the door before entering once the patient has begun to change into the patient gown.
    Rationale. A drape provides for the patient's modesty and warmth.
12. **Procedural Step. Allow the patient to change into the gown, inform the physician that the patient is ready, and make the patient's record available to the physician.**
    Instruct the patient to have a seat on the end of the examination table when ready.
    NOTE: Never leave an elderly patient or a patient who has symptoms of dizziness sitting alone on an examination table because of the danger of falling or injury.
13. **Procedural Step. Assist the physician with the examination of the body systems.**
    The patient is generally placed in a sitting position for an examination of the upper body.
14. **Procedural Step. Assist the physician with the eye examination.**

Hand the physician the ophthalmoscope. Dim the lights when the physician is ready to use it.
Rationale. Dimming the lights during examination of the eyes will help dilate the patient's pupils, thereby providing the physician with better visualization of the interior of the eye.
15. **Procedural Step. Assist the physician with the ear examination.**
    Hand the physician the otoscope. A disposable otoscope speculum should be attached to the otoscope before it is passed to the physician in working position (handle first). Dispose of the otoscope speculum in a regular waste container on completion of this portion of the examination, unless there are obvious signs of contamination from blood (in which case you should dispose of it in a biohazardous waste container).
16. **Procedural Step. Hand the tuning fork to the physician in working position (handle first).**
    The physician will test the patient's ability to hear sound conducted first through the air, then through the bone of the skull.
17. **Procedural Step. Assist the physician with the nose examination.**
    Pass the nasal speculum and penlight to the physician in working position (handle first). The physician will examine the patient's nasal cavities for nasal congestion, excessive nasal drainage from the sinuses, or the presence of abnormal growths.
18. **Procedural Step. Assist the physician with the throat examination.**
    Hold the tongue depressor at the center when transferring it to the physician. Discard the tongue depressor in a biohazardous waste container when this portion of the examination has been completed, by either stepping on the foot pedal and allowing the physician to drop it directly into the container or by taking it from the physician by holding it at the center and throwing it away.
    Rationale. The tongue depressor is passed by holding it in the middle so that the end inserted into the patient's mouth is not handled before or after use. This prevents contact with the patient's secretions, which may contain pathogens.
19. **Procedural Step. Assist the physician with the lung and heart examination.**
    Hand the physician a stethoscope if he or she does not already have one. (Most physicians keep their own stethoscope in a pocket or around the neck.)

Continued

Procedure 8-1 Assist with the Physical Examination—cont'd

20. **Procedural Step. Assist the physician with the examination of the upper extremity reflexes.**
Hand the physician the percussion hammer in working position (handle first).

21. **Procedural Step. Position the patient as required for examination of the remaining body systems.**
This assessment includes palpation of the organs of the abdomen, strength and reflex testing of the lower extremities, auscultation of the abdomen for bowel sounds with a stethoscope, abnormalities that can be visualized, and observation of any abnormal smells.
Rationale. Certain patient positions are required so that the physician can examine a particular part of the body.

22. **Procedural Step. Assist the patient off the examination table as needed, to prevent the patient from falling.**
Rationale. Elderly patients frequently become dizzy after being positioned on the examining table, and they often need assistance.

23. **Procedural Step. Allow the patient time to change from the patient gown back into street clothes.**
Provide assistance to the patient as needed. Tell the patient about the next steps of the examination. Allow adequate time for the patient to change clothes.
Rationale. It is important to inform patients that they may change back into their clothes; otherwise, patients may remain in the patient gown.

24. **Procedural Step. Allow time for further discussion between the physician and patient regarding prescriptions, medications, and a return visit. Ask the patient if he or she has any questions.**
Rationale. Answers and instructions given by the medical assistant involving medical care should be explained in terms the patient can understand. The medical assistant should answer questions within the scope of practice and refer other questions to the physician as necessary.

25. **Procedural Step. Document any instructions given to the patient in the medical record.**

26. **Procedural Step. Clean the examination room according to Standard Precautions before the next patient arrives.**
Put on disposable gloves before cleaning the examination room. Cleaning the examination room includes the following:
   - Disposing of the patient gown and drape.
   - Changing the crumpled or soiled table paper.
   - Disposing of any waste materials in the appropriate container.
   - Removing soiled instruments.
   - Wiping down the examination table and counters.
   - Replenishing supplies as needed.

   Always clean the examination room immediately after the patient has left. Never bring a patient into a room with crumpled table paper and used instruments. Never clean a room in front of a patient. If the room has not been cleaned and you inadvertently bring the next patient into the examination room, apologize to the patient immediately. This is the only circumstance when cleaning a room in front of a patient would be acceptable. However, take steps to ensure this does not occur again.

27. **Procedural Step. Sanitize the hands.**
Always sanitize the hands after every procedure or after using gloves.

From Bonewit-West K: *Clinical procedures for medical assistants*, ed 6, Philadelphia, 2004, Saunders.

---

and (3) assist patients who need help disrobing (e.g., elderly patient, patient with a disability). Remember, always respect the dignity of the patient by asking if he or she would like assistance.

The purpose or type of procedure will determine how much clothing the patient will need to remove. An upper respiratory complaint requires that only clothing from the waist up be removed, whereas a "well-woman visit" requires removal of all clothing except the socks. The physician's preference and need for accessibility will dictate whether the gown opening should be in the front or back. Gowns can be either *full length*, which covers the patient's body to the knees, or *half-length* (partial), which covers only the shoulders, chest, and back.

A medical assistant must respect the patient's right to privacy when the patient is to disrobe. Before leaving the room, make certain the patient understands what is to be done, how to wear the gown, how far to disrobe, and where to place their clothes. Assure the patient the physician will be arriving shortly. If the physician is delayed, be honest with the patient about the approximate waiting time.

CONSENT TO TREAT FORM

I, _____, hereby consent to have

Dr. _____ perform _____ .

I have been fully informed of the following by my physician:

1. The nature of the procedure: _____
2. Purpose of the procedure: _____
3. An explanation of risks involved with the procedure to include: _____
4. Alternative treatments or procedures available: _____
5. The risks involved with declining or delaying the procedure: _____

My physician has offered to answer all questions concerning the proposed procedure.

I am aware that the practice of medicine and surgery is not an exact science, and I acknowledge that no guarantees have been made to me about the results of the procedure.

Patient or Guardian _____ Date _____

Witness _____ Date _____

Fig. 8-1 Patient consent form to have procedure performed.

Securing Consent

For a procedure that is beyond the basic wellness examination, it is necessary to obtain the patient's informed **consent**. A consent-to-treat form (procedure consent form) must be signed, dated, and witnessed (Fig. 8-1). The physician must explain all details concerning the procedure, but the medical assistant can act as a witness. The consent-to-treat form must be included in the patient's chart before the procedure is performed. Remember that *implied* consent is only good for basic common procedures (e.g., ECGs, blood tests), whereas other procedures require written consent.

Failure to secure consent for procedures such as a colonoscopy or a stress test is considered assault and battery. Patients have the right to refuse treatments and procedures. In addition, patients can withdraw their consent at any time.

PATIENT-CENTERED PROFESSIONALISM

- Why must the medical assistant demonstrate competence when assisting the patient for a physical examination?

BODY MECHANICS

Body mechanics means using appropriate body movements to perform certain functions in a manner that protects the medical assistant's muscles and skeletal system from injury. Using correct techniques protects you from injury by aligning body segments to one another. By standing up straight, the main parts of the body (head, chest, and pelvis) are properly aligned one over the other to maintain good balance. Using good body mechanics reduces muscle fatigue and prevents strain on the spine by making the spine work with you to maximize body strength when lifting or moving objects. Using good body mechanics also provides balance and stability.

Remember, your feet are your support base, and your strongest and largest muscles in your body are those of the shoulders, upper arms, hips, and thighs. This is why we use these muscles to lift and move heavy objects. Before lifting, you must stand up straight with your feet slightly apart (about 18 inches), with one foot slightly ahead of the other (Fig. 8-2). This position helps provide better stability, and this stability prevents the medical assistant from becoming overbalanced, as when assisting a patient out of a wheelchair, for example.

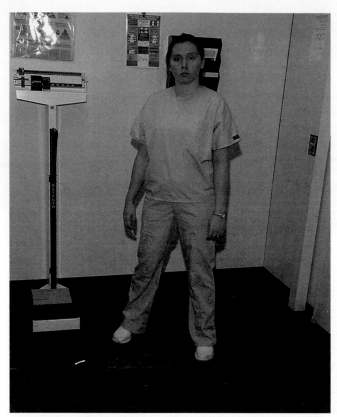

Fig. 8-2 Proper stance prior to lifting a heavy object.

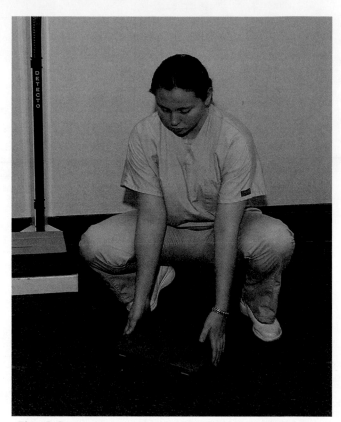

Fig. 8-3 Proper position when lifting a heavy object.

When lifting, get close to whatever is being lifted instead of reaching for it. Keep your back straight; bend at the hip and knees (Fig. 8-3). Straighten your legs and use your upper arm and leg muscles to lift. When an activity requires a physical effort, use as many muscles as possible (e.g., use both hands to pick up a heavy object, not just one hand). When picking something up off the floor, squat down rather than bending over at the waist, thus reducing the strain on the spine. Always carry objects close to the midline of the body, thus keeping the body in alignment.

≈ POSITIONING AND DRAPING THE PATIENT

Another responsibility of the medical assistant is to position and drape patients appropriately for the procedures being performed. When **positioning** and draping, always consider the patient's comfort and minimize exposure of nonessential body parts.

Many types of positions are used for various procedures. Selection of a position depends on the examination or procedure to be performed. A patient's chief complaint and age are also important criteria to consider when choosing the best position. Medical assistants should be familiar with

eight examination positions: sitting, standing, horizontal recumbent, dorsal recumbent, Sims', prone, knee-chest, and Fowler's positions.

Regardless of what position the patient will assume, it is the medical assistant's responsibility to explain to the patient the reason for the position and to provide clear instructions on assuming the position. Patient safety must be the prime consideration for the medical assistant during positioning (Box 8-1).

Sitting

The **sitting position** has the patient in an upright position at the end of the examination table, using the footrest for support (since the feet should not be left dangling for long periods). As needed, the drape extends from the waist and over the legs. Procedure 8-2 presents proper positioning and draping for the sitting position.

The sitting position is used most often to begin the physical examination because the upper extremities are clearly accessible. The neurological reflexes (knee, elbow, wrist, and ankle) can be tested in this position, and sitting provides the most comfort for the patient. Heart and lung sounds can be detected because sitting allows for maximal lung expansion, and sitting patients can easily answer questions for the physician concerning their state of health.

BOX 8-1 Safety and Comfort in Patient Positioning

The medical assistant is responsible for patient safety. When positioning a patient, the medical assistant is responsible for ensuring that the patient is free from harm. For example, an elderly patient who is unsteady should never be left sitting on the examination table without someone in the room. If the medical assistant must leave the room, a family member or other caregiver must be present.

It takes time and practice to learn proper positioning techniques. A priority is to avoid causing additional discomfort or inflicting discomfort on the patient. When a male physician examines a female patient (or when a female physician examines a male patient), for the physician's legal protection, a medical assistant should be present. This provides support for the physician if the female (or male) patient complains of inappropriate touching, and it provides support for the female (or male) patient in an uncomfortable situation.

Standing

The physician may need to evaluate coordination and balance by observing the patient in the **standing position** (erect) for seconds to minutes. No special draping is needed, but the gown must be able to cover the patient's whole body if this type of observation is performed.

Horizontal Recumbent (Supine)

In the **horizontal recumbent position,** or **supine position**, the patient is lying flat on his or her back with the arms to the sides and the head elevated with a pillow. The drape starts just under the arms and extends to the feet (Procedure 8-3).

Examination of the chest, abdomen, and lower extremities can be performed with the patient in the horizontal recumbent position.

Dorsal Recumbent

In the **dorsal recumbent position,** the patient is in a supine position, but the knees are flexed

Procedure 8-2 Sitting Position

TASK: Properly position and drape the patient for examination of the head, neck, chest, and upper extremities and measurement of vital signs.

EQUIPMENT AND SUPPLIES
- Examination table
- Table paper
- Patient gown
- Drape

SKILLS/RATIONALE

STANDARD PRECAUTIONS ARE TO BE FOLLOWED.

1. **Procedural Step. Sanitize the hands.**
   An alcohol-based hand rub may be used instead of washing hands with soap and water, unless hands are visibly soiled.
   Rationale. Hand sanitization promotes infection control.

2. **Procedural Step. Assemble equipment and supplies.**
   Rationale. It is important to have all supplies and equipment ready and available before starting any procedure to ensure efficiency.

3. **Procedural Step. Greet and identify the patient.**
   Rationale. Identifying the patient ensures the procedure is performed on the correct patient.

4. **Procedural Step. Explain the procedure to the patient.**
   Rationale. Explaining the procedure to the patient promotes cooperation and provides a means of obtaining implied consent.

5. **Procedural Step. Provide a gown for the patient.**
   Instruct the patient to remove the appropriate clothing for the type of examination being performed. The gown typically opens in the back. Allow the patient to have privacy while changing. Assist the patient as appropriate.

6. **Procedural Step. Pull out the footrest of the table, and assist the patient to a sitting position.**

Continued

Procedure 8-2 Sitting Position—cont'd

7 **Procedural Step. Drape the patient.**
Draping will vary depending on the required exposure of the patient.
Rationale. Draping provides warmth and modesty to the patient while still allowing the health care provider access to the body areas to be examined.

8. **Procedural Step. When the examination is complete, assist the patient from the table.**
   a. Return the footrest to its original position.
   b. Instruct the patient to dress; assist as needed.
9. **Procedural Step. Clean the examination room according to Standard Precautions.**
   Always clean the examination room immediately after the patient has left. Never bring the next patient into an unclean room.
10. **Procedural Step. Sanitize the hands.**
   Always sanitize the hands after every procedure or after using gloves.

Procedure 8-3 Recumbent Position

TASK: Properly position and drape the patient for catheter insertion, examinations of the abdomen, and general examination procedures.

EQUIPMENT AND SUPPLIES
- Examination table
- Table paper
- Patient gown
- Drape

SKILLS/RATIONALE

STANDARD PRECAUTIONS ARE TO BE FOLLOWED.

1. **Procedural Step. Sanitize the hands.**
   An alcohol-based hand rub may be used instead of washing hands with soap and water, unless hands are visibly soiled.
   Rationale. Hand sanitization promotes infection control.
2. **Procedural Step. Assemble equipment and supplies.**
   Rationale. It is important to have all supplies and equipment ready and available before starting any procedure to ensure efficiency.
3. **Procedural Step. Greet and identify the patient.**
   Rationale. Identifying the patient ensures the procedure is performed on the correct patient.

4. **Procedural Step. Explain the procedure to the patient.**
   Rationale. Explaining the procedure to the patient promotes cooperation and provides a means of obtaining implied consent.
5. **Procedural Step. Provide a gown for the patient.**
   Instruct the patient to remove clothing appropriate for the type of examination being performed. The gown typically opens in the back. Allow the patient to have privacy while changing. Assist the patient as needed.
6. **Procedural Step. Place the patient in the recumbent position.**
   a. Pull out the footrest of the table, and assist the patient to a sitting position.

Procedure 8-3 Recumbent Position—cont'd

b. Have the patient move back on the table, and pull out the table extension supporting the patient's lower extremities.

c Assist the patient to lie down on his or her back with the head slightly elevated with a pillow. The arms can be placed above the head or alongside the body; this is the *horizontal recumbent* or *supine* position.

d To place the patient in a *dorsal recumbent* position, have the patient bend the knees and place each foot at the edge of the table.

e. Push in the table extension and footrest.

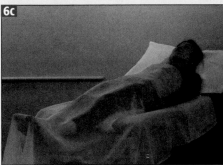

7. **Procedural Step. Drape the patient.**
   a. The *horizontal* recumbent or supine drape is placed over the patient.
   b. The *dorsal* recumbent drape should be positioned diagonally.
   Rationale. Draping is designed to provide modesty to the patient while still allowing the health care provider access to the body areas to be examined.

8. **Procedural Step. When the examination is complete, assist the patient from the recumbent position and into a sitting position.**

9. **Procedural Step. Assist the patient from the examination table.**
   a. Return the footrest to its original position.
   b. Instruct the patient to dress; assist as needed.

10. **Procedural Step. Clean the examination room according to Standard Precautions.**
    Always clean the examination room immediately after the patient has left. Never bring the next patient into an unclean room.

11. **Procedural Step. Sanitize the hands.**
    Always sanitize the hands after every procedure or after using gloves.

(bent) sharply with the feet flat on the table. Bending the knees takes pressure away from the lower back and is more comfortable than the supine position. The drape is placed in a diamond shape, with the lower corner over the pubic area. When the physician wants to examine the pubic area, the corner is lifted up to expose the genitals.

The dorsal recumbent position allows for the examination of the vagina and rectal areas on the female and the rectal area on the male.

Sims'

For the **Sims' position,** the patient first assumes the supine position and then moves to the left, side-lying position. The left arm is kept behind the body, and the right arm is up, flexed, and forward. Both legs are bent at the knee, with the right leg sharply

bent to expose the anal area. The drape is positioned to cover the back from under the arms to the toes. Extra pillows may be needed for positioning purposes (Procedure 8-4). When the anal area is examined, the drape is adjusted.

The Sims' position can be used for rectal examinations and enema administration.

Prone

In the **prone position,** the patient is lying on the abdomen with the head slightly turned to the side and the arms above the head or alongside the body. The drape starts just under the arms to the feet and is adjusted as needed during the examination (Procedure 8-5).

The back and lower extremities can be examined in the prone position.

Procedure 8-4 Sims' Position

TASK: Properly position and drape the patient for a vaginal or rectal examination.

EQUIPMENT AND SUPPLIES
- Examination table
- Table paper
- Patient gown
- Drape

SKILLS/RATIONALE

STANDARD PRECAUTIONS ARE TO BE FOLLOWED.

1. **Procedural Step. Sanitize the hands.**
   An alcohol-based hand rub may be used instead of washing hands with soap and water, unless hands are visibly soiled.
   Rationale. Hand sanitization promotes infection control.

2. **Procedural Step. Assemble equipment and supplies.**
   Rationale. It is important to have all supplies and equipment ready and available before starting any procedure to ensure efficiency.

3. **Procedural Step. Greet and identify the patient.**
   Rationale. Identifying the patient ensures the procedure is performed on the correct patient.

4. **Procedural Step. Explain the procedure to the patient.**
   Rationale. Explaining the procedure to the patient promotes cooperation and provides a means of obtaining implied consent.

5. **Procedural Step. Provide a gown for the patient.**
   Instruct the patient to remove the appropriate clothing for the type of examination being performed. The gown typically opens in the back. Allow the patient to have privacy while changing. Assist the patient as needed.

6. **Procedural Step. Place the patient in the supine position.**
   a. Pull out the footrest of the table, and assist the patient to a sitting position.
   b. Have the patient move back on the table, and pull out the table extension supporting the patient's lower extremities.
   c. Assist the patient to lie down on his or her back with the head slightly elevated with a pillow. The arms can be placed above the head or alongside the body.

7. **Procedural Step. Drape the patient.**
   The drape should be placed diagonally from under the arms to below the knees.
   Rationale. Draping is designed to provide modesty to the patient while still allowing the health care provider access to the body areas to be examined.

8. **Procedural Step. Place the patient in the Sims' position.**
   a. Have the patient turn to the left side.
   b. Have the patient place the left arm behind the body and the right arm forward and bent at the elbow.
   c. The right leg is sharply flexed upward and the left leg bent slightly.
   d. Position the buttocks at the edge of the table.

9. **Procedural Step. Adjust the drape as the physician examines the anal area.**

10. **Procedural Step. When the examination is complete, assist the patient to the supine position and then to the sitting position.**

11. **Procedural Step. Assist the patient from the examination table.**
    a. Push in the table extension while supporting the lower extremities.
    b. Pull out the footrest, and help the patient from the table as needed.
    c. Return the footrest to its original position.
    d. Instruct the patient to dress; assist as needed.

12. **Procedural Step. Clean the examination room according to Standard Precautions.**
    Always clean the examination room immediately after the patient has left. Never bring the next patient into an unclean room.

13. **Procedural Step. Sanitize the hands.**
    Always sanitize the hands after every procedure or after using gloves.

Procedure 8-5 Prone Position

TASK: Properly position and drape the patient for examination of the back.

EQUIPMENT AND SUPPLIES
- Examination table
- Table paper
- Patient gown
- Drape

SKILLS/RATIONALE

STANDARD PRECAUTIONS ARE TO BE FOLLOWED.

1. **Procedural Step. Sanitize the hands.**
   An alcohol-based hand rub may be used instead of washing hands with soap and water, unless hands are visibly soiled.
   Rationale. Hand sanitization promotes infection control.

2. **Procedural Step. Assemble equipment and supplies.**
   Rationale. It is important to have all supplies and equipment ready and available before starting any procedure to ensure efficiency.

3. **Procedural Step. Greet and identify the patient.**
   Rationale. Identifying the patient ensures the procedure is performed on the correct patient.

4. **Procedural Step. Explain the procedure to the patient.**
   Rationale. Explaining the procedure to the patient promotes cooperation and provides a means of obtaining implied consent.

5. **Procedural Step. Provide a gown for the patient.**
   Instruct the patient to remove the appropriate clothing for the type of examination being performed. The gown typically opens in the back. Allow the patient to have privacy while changing. Assist the patient as needed.

6. **Procedural Step. Place the patient on his or her back.**
   a. Pull out the footrest of the table, and assist the patient to a sitting position.
   b. Have the patient move back on the table, and pull out the table extension supporting the patient's lower extremities.
   c. Assist the patient to lie down on his or her back.

7. **Procedural Step. Drape the patient.**
   Drape the patient before turning to protect the patient's modesty since the gown is open in the back.
   a. The drape should be placed over any exposed area not being examined.
   b. For a female patient, the gown should extend high enough to cover the breasts, because she may be required to turn over and be positioned in the lithotomy or dorsal recumbent position later in the examination.
   Rationale. Draping is designed to provide modesty to the patient while still allowing the health care provider access to the body areas to be examined.

8. **Procedural Step. Place the patient in the prone position.**
   a. Have the patient turn onto his or her abdomen with the legs together by rolling toward you.
   b. Ask the patient to turn his or her head to one side.
   c. The patient's arms can be positioned above the head or alongside the body.

9. **Procedural Step. When the examination is complete, assist the patient to the supine position and then to the sitting position.**

10. **Procedural Step. Assist the patient from the examination table.**
    a. Push in the table extension while supporting the lower extremities.
    b. Pull out the footrest, and help the patient from the table as needed.
    c. Return the footrest to its original position.
    d. Instruct the patient to dress; assist as needed.

11. **Procedural Step. Clean the examination room according to Standard Precautions.**
    Always clean the examination room immediately after the patient has left. Never bring the next patient into an unclean room.

12. **Procedural Step. Sanitize the hands.**
    Always sanitize the hands after every procedure or after using gloves.

Knee-Chest

The **knee-chest position** begins with the patient in the prone position. The patient is assisted into a kneeling position, with the buttocks elevated and the head and chest lowered onto the table. The arms are above the head and bent at the elbow. For patient comfort, a pillow can be placed under the chest area (Procedure 8-6).

The patient is not placed in the knee-chest position until the physician is ready. The patient should never be left unattended in this position. The knee-chest position is most often used for sigmoidoscopy.

Procedure 8-6 Knee-Chest Position

TASK: Properly position and drape the patient for a proctological examination.

EQUIPMENT AND SUPPLIES
- Examination table
- Table paper
- Patient gown
- Drape
- Tissue

SKILLS/RATIONALE

STANDARD PRECAUTIONS ARE TO BE FOLLOWED.

1. **Procedural Step. Sanitize the hands.**
   An alcohol-based hand rub may be used instead of washing hands with soap and water, unless hands are visibly soiled.
   Rationale. Hand sanitization promotes infection control.

2. **Procedural Step. Assemble equipment and supplies.**
   Rationale. It is important to have all supplies and equipment ready and available before starting any procedure to ensure efficiency.

3. **Procedural Step. Greet and identify the patient.**
   Rationale. Identifying the patient ensures the procedure is performed on the correct patient.

4. **Procedural Step. Explain the procedure to the patient.**
   Rationale. Explaining the procedure to the patient promotes cooperation and provides a means of obtaining implied consent.

5. **Procedural Step. Provide a gown for the patient.**
   Instruct the patient to remove the appropriate clothing for the type of examination being performed. The gown typically opens in the back. Allow the patient to have privacy while changing. Assist the patient as needed.

6. **Procedural Step. Place the patient in the prone position.**
   a. Pull out the footrest of the table, and assist the patient to a sitting position.
   b. Have the patient move back on the table, and pull out the table extension supporting the patient's lower extremities.

7. **Procedural Step. Drape the patient.**
   The drape should be placed diagonally.
   Rationale. Draping is designed to provide modesty to the patient while still allowing the health care provider access to the body areas to be examined.

8. **Procedural Step. Assist the patient to lie down in the supine position, then the prone position.**

9. **Procedural Step. Have the patient bend the arms at the elbows and rest them alongside the head.**

10. **Procedural Step. Place the patient in the knee-chest position.**
    a. Ask the patient to raise the buttocks by moving up onto the knees while keeping the back straight.
    b. The patient may turn the head to either side.
    c. The patient should relax the upper body down onto the chest, supporting the majority of the body's weight and taking the strain off the knees.

11. **Procedural Step. Adjust the drape as the physician examines the anal area.**

12. **Procedural Step. When the examination is complete, assist the patient to the prone position,**

Procedure 8-6 Knee-Chest Position—cont'd

then to the supine position, and then to the sitting position.

13. **Procedural Step. Push in the table extension while supporting the lower extremities and pull out the footrest.**

14. **Procedural Step. Allow the patient time to rest, then assist the patient from the examination table.**

    a. Hand the patient tissues and help the patient from the table, *or* assist the patient in cleaning up, then help the patient from the table.

    b. Return the footrest to its original position.

    c. Instruct the patient to dress; assist as needed.

15. **Procedural Step. Clean the examination room according to Standard Precautions.**
    Always clean the examination room immediately after the patient has left. Never bring the next patient into an unclean room.

16. **Procedural Step. Sanitize the hands.**
    Always sanitize the hands after every procedure or after using gloves.

Fowler's

In the **Fowler's position,** the patient is lying in a supine position with the back of the table drawn up at either a 45-degree angle (*semi-Fowler's position*) or a 90-degree angle (*Fowler's or full Fowler's position*). The patient's legs are only slightly bent (Procedure 8-7).

Fowler's position helps the patient breathe easier and is used for examination of the upper extremities.

PATIENT-CENTERED PROFESSIONALISM

- Why is it important for the medical assistant to have the patient in the correct position and well supported during the physical examination?

⠿ EXAMINATION METHODS

The overall purpose of the physical examination is to examine the patient completely and to help the physician form a conclusion about the patient's health status. The medical assistant begins the assessment process by observing the patient (inspection) as soon as he or she greets the patient, and the physician carries the assessment through the physical examination. The patient's weight, height, and vital signs are taken before the physician begins the assessment. The physician uses the following assessment techniques to complete the physical examination:

- **Inspection** is a visual viewing of all body parts and surface areas for symmetry. The condition of the skin and its color, body movements (**ROM**, or range of motion), and body contours are observed (Fig. 8-4, *A*).

- **Palpation** involves the physician using the hand to locate and touch major organs and lymph nodes and to detect tenderness in an area. Taking a patient's pulse is done by palpation (Fig. 8-4, *B*).

- **Percussion** is used to check the nervous system and respiratory system. A percussion hammer is used to check for reflex action by tapping a tendon (Fig. 8-5). The physician uses the fingers to tap the patient's chest, back, and abdominal area while listening for distinctive sounds (Fig. 8-4, *C*).

- **Auscultation** involves use of a stethoscope to detect the sounds of the heart, respiratory system, and intestines (bowels). Taking an apical pulse and recording blood pressure are other examples of this process (Fig. 8-4, *D*).

These methods of assessment use the basic senses of sight, touch, smell, and hearing and require attention to detail.

PATIENT-CENTERED PROFESSIONALISM

- Why must the medical assistant understand the function of the various examination methods or assessment techniques?

⠿ VISION TESTING

Vision tests are performed in the physician's office for a variety of reasons, including changes in visual acuity, blurred vision, and loss of vision. Vision tests may also be performed as part of a general physical examination. Most vision changes or visual defects are correctable with either eyeglasses or contact lenses (Table 8-1). As a person ages, the

Procedure 8-7 Fowler's Position

TASK: Properly position and drape the patient for examination of the head, chest, abdomen, and extremities.

EQUIPMENT AND SUPPLIES
- Examination table
- Table paper
- Patient gown
- Drape

SKILLS/RATIONALE

STANDARD PRECAUTIONS ARE TO BE FOLLOWED.

1. **Procedural Step. Sanitize the hands.**
   An alcohol-based hand rub may be used instead of washing hands with soap and water, unless hands are visibly soiled.
   Rationale. Hand sanitization promotes infection control.

2. **Procedural Step. Assemble equipment and supplies.**
   Rationale. It is important to have all supplies and equipment ready and available before starting any procedure to ensure efficiency.

3. **Procedural Step. Greet and identify the patient.**
   Rationale. Identifying the patient ensures the procedure is performed on the correct patient.

4. **Procedural Step. Explain the procedure to the patient.**
   Rationale. Explaining the procedure to the patient promotes cooperation and provides a means of obtaining implied consent.

5. **Procedural Step. Provide a gown for the patient.**
   Instruct the patient to remove the appropriate clothing for the type of examination being performed. The gown typically opens in the back. Allow the patient to have privacy while changing. Assist the patient as needed.

6. **Procedural Step. Place the patient in Fowler's position.**
   a. Pull out the footrest of the table, and assist the patient to a sitting position.
   b. Have the patient move back on the table, and pull out the table extension supporting the patient's lower extremities.
   c. Have the patient lean back against the head of the table with a pillow under the head.
   d. For *semi-Fowler's* position, the angle should be 45 degrees.
   e. For *full Fowler's* position, the angle is 90 degrees.

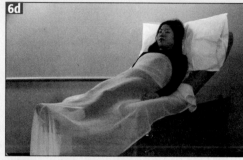

7. **Procedural Step. Drape the patient.**
   The drape should be placed over any exposed area not being examined.
   Rationale. Draping is designed to provide modesty to the patient while still allowing the health care provider access to the body areas to be examined.

8. **Procedural Step. When the examination is complete, assist the patient to the supine position and then to the sitting position.**

9. **Procedural Step. Assist the patient from the examination table.**
   a. Push in the table extension while supporting the lower extremities.
   b. Pull out the footrest and help the patient from the table as needed.
   c. Return the head of the table to its normal position.

Procedure 8-7 Fowler's Position—cont'd

10. **Procedural Step. Return the footrest to its original position. Allow the patient to get dressed; assist as needed.**

11. **Procedural Step. Clean the examination room according to Standard Precautions.**
    Always clean the examination room immediately after the patient has left. Never bring the next patient into an unclean room.

12. **Procedural Step. Sanitize the hands.**
    Always sanitize the hands after every procedure or after using gloves.

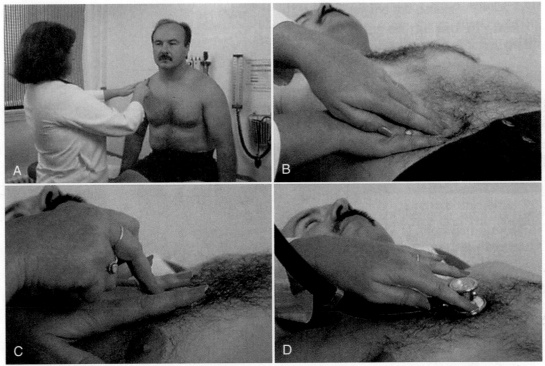

Fig. 8-4 Methods of physical examination. **A,** Inspection. **B,** Palpation. **C,** Percussion. **D,** Auscultation. *(From Zakus SM: Clinical skills for medical assistants, ed 4, St Louis, 2001, Mosby.)*

structure and function of the eyes change. The lens loses its ability to adjust, which changes a person's field of vision (presbyopia).

The physician examines the interior of the eye with the **ophthalmoscope** (Fig. 8-6). This instrument allows the physician to look at the condition of the retina, optic nerve, and the blood vessels of the eye. The medical assistant needs to make certain the light of the ophthalmoscope is working properly and he or she may be asked to dim the lights when the physician is using this instrument. Extra bulbs and batteries should always be accessible in case of a malfunction.

The medical assistant is often responsible for testing the patient's **visual acuity** (ability to see)

and color vision. Common tests include the Snellen eye chart, Ishihara color plates, and Jaeger reading card. Box 8-2 reviews the necessary criteria for charting visual testing procedures.

Snellen Eye Chart

The visual acuity test most often used in the medical office is performed with the use of a Snellen eye chart. The Snellen eye chart is a screening device and measures a patient's ability to view letters or images at a distance. Each row decreases in size to measure the patient's ability to see at a measured distance. Available visual acuity charts include the following:

TABLE 8-1   Correctable Visual Defects

Defect	Description
Hypermetropia or hyperopia (farsightedness)	Patient has trouble seeing objects clearly when they are close. Contour of crystalline lens is distorted.
Myopia (nearsightedness)	Patient has trouble seeing objects far away. Contour of crystalline lens is distorted.
Presbyopia ("old eye")	As people age, they are less able to see close objects clearly. Crystalline lens loses ability to adapt.
Astigmatism	Patient has trouble focusing; vision is blurred. Shape of cornea or lens prevents light from projecting on retina.
Strabismus (e.g., esotropia, or "cross-eye")	Eyes do not focus on an object at the same time. Main problem is muscle coordination. Eye exercises, surgery, and glasses can improve the various forms of strabismus.

Fig. 8-5   Percussion hammer.

Fig. 8-6 Ophthalmoscope. *(From Jarvis C:* Physical examination and health assessment, *ed 4, Philadelphia, 2004, Saunders.)*

BOX 8-2   Documentation when Charting Visual Testing Procedures

1. Date
2. Time
3. Name of visual test performed:
   • Snellen test
   • Jaeger test
   • Ishihara test
4. Results, indicating which eye was tested
5. Patient reaction, if any
6. Proper signature and credential

- *Alphabet chart* is for English-speaking patients who know their alphabet (Fig. 8-7, *A*).
- *Rotating "E" chart* is for non–English-speaking patients. The letter "E" is rotated in various positions (points in different directions) on the chart, and each row decreases in size (Fig. 8-7, *B*).
- *Object chart* works well with preschoolers because it shows pictures of familiar objects that children can identify (Fig. 8-7, *C*). Be sure the child understands what the picture depicts.

The alphabet Snellen eye chart has rows of letters. Each row has a fraction listed on the left side. The top number of the fraction is always 20 feet. This means that the patient is standing 20 feet from the chart. The bottom number indicates the distance at which people with normal vision could read the row (e.g., 20/20 would mean the patient can read

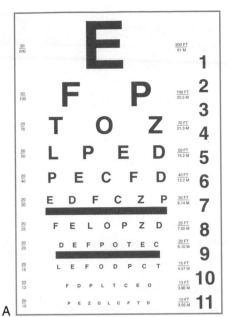
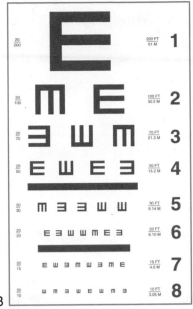

Fig. 8-7 Snellen visual acuity charts. **A,** Alphabet eye chart. **B,** Snellen rotating "E" ("Big E") eye chart. **C,** Objects eye chart for testing preschoolers. *(From Young AP, Kennedy DB:* Kinn's the medical assistant, *ed 9, Philadelphia, 2003, Saunders.)*

the 20 line at 20 feet for a given eye).

Each eye can be different with respect to its visual ability. Because of this, each eye must be tested independently and then both eyes together. Procedure 8-8 explains the process of accurately measuring and recording a patient's visual acuity using a Snellen chart.

Ishihara Color Vision Plates

Color vision is tested with Ishihara color vision plates (Fig. 8-8). People with certain occupations, such as cosmetologists and airline pilots, are tested before schooling (Procedure 8-9).

Jaeger Reading Card

The Jaeger reading card (or chart) is used to test a person's ability to read at a prescribed distance. This test is conducted with a card containing sentences or phrases. The patient reads the card at varying distances, with each eye measured separately (Procedure 8-10).

PATIENT-CENTERED PROFESSIONALISM

- What are the responsibilities of the medical assistant in vision testing?

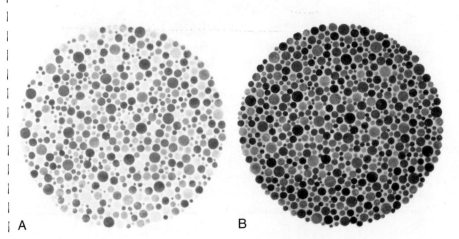

Fig. 8-8 Ishihara color plates. **A,** Person with normal color vision reads 74, but red-green color-blind person reads 21. **B,** Red-blind person reads 2, but green-blind person reads 4. Normal-vision person reads 42. *(From Ishihara J:* Tests for color blindness, *Tokyo, 1920, Kanehara.)*

Procedure 8-8 Assess Distance Visual Acuity Using a Snellen Chart

TASK: Accurately measure visual acuity using a Snellen eye chart, and document the procedure in the patient's medical record.

EQUIPMENT AND SUPPLIES
- Snellen eye chart
- Eye occluder (or index card, paper cup)
- Well-lit examination room
- Floor mark (20 feet from eye chart)
- Patient's medical record
- Pen

SKILLS/RATIONALE

STANDARD PRECAUTIONS ARE TO BE FOLLOWED.

1. **Procedural Step. Sanitize the hands.**
   An alcohol-based hand rub may be used instead of washing hands with soap and water, unless hands are visibly soiled.
   Rationale. Hand sanitization promotes infection control.

2. **Procedural Step. Assemble equipment and supplies.**
   Disinfect the occluder and allow it to dry completely.
   Rationale. It is important to have all supplies and equipment ready and available before starting any procedure to ensure efficiency. You should sanitize the occluder (if it is not disposable) between patients to prevent cross-contamination. It is important that the occluder dry completely before use; fumes from the antiseptic may burn the eyes, causing them to water and vision to blur.

3. **Procedural Step. Greet and identify the patient.**
   Rationale. Identifying the patient ensures the procedure is performed on the correct patient.

4. **Procedural Step. Explain the procedure to the patient.**
   NOTE: For this procedure, the Snellen *alphabet* chart is used.
   The patient should be told that he or she will be asked to read several lines of letters. The patient should **not** have an opportunity to study or memorize the letters before beginning the test. The patient should be instructed not to squint during the test because squinting temporarily improves vision.
   Rationale. Explaining the procedure to the patient promotes cooperation and provides a means of obtaining implied consent. If the patient squints during the test, the results may be inaccurate.

5. **Procedural Step. Ask the patient if he or she is wearing contact lenses, and observe for eyeglasses.**

The patient may be told to keep contacts in or glasses on during the test.
Rationale. Most physicians prefer that corrective lenses be kept in place because this is a screening test.

6. **Procedural Step. Place the patient in a comfortable position 20 feet from the chart.**
   The patient may sit or stand.

7. **Procedural Step. Select the appropriate Snellen chart for the patient. (In this case the Snellen alphabet chart is used.)**
   Rationale. Selection of the chart is typically based on age and comprehension levels of the patient.

8. **Procedural Step. Position the center of the Snellen chart at the patient's eye level, and stand next to the chart during the test to indicate to the patient the line to be identified.**

9. **Procedural Step. Ask the patient to cover the left eye with the eye occluder, but to keep the eye open.**
   Rationale. Keeping the left eye open prevents squinting of the right eye, which would increase visual acuity.

10. **Procedural Step. Measure the visual acuity of the right eye first.**
    NOTE: You should develop the routine of following the same steps with every patient,

Procedure 8-8 Assess Distance Visual Acuity Using a Snellen Chart—cont'd

such as starting with the right eye first each time, because it reduces the opportunity for errors.

11. **Procedural Step. Ask the patient to identify verbally each letter (or picture or rotating "E" direction) in the row on the Snellen chart, starting with the 20/70 line.**
    Rationale. It is best to start at a line that is above the 20/20 line to give the patient a chance to gain confidence and to become familiar with the test procedure.

12. **Procedural Step. Proceed up or down the chart as necessary.**
    a. If the patient is able to read the 20/70 line, proceed down the chart until the patient can read the smallest line of letters with two errors or fewer.
    b. If the patient is unable to read the 20/70 line, proceed up the chart until the patient again can read the smallest line of letters with two errors or fewer.
    c. All errors are recorded in the patient's medical record with a minus sign (e.g., right eye 20/40–1).

13. **Procedural Step. Observe the patient for any unusual symptoms while he or she is reading the letters, such as squinting, tilting the head, or watering eyes.**

Rationale. These symptoms may indicate that the patient is having difficulty identifying the letters.

14. **Procedural Step. Repeat the procedure to test the left eye by covering the right eye.**

15. **Procedural Step. Repeat the procedure without covering either eye.**

16. **Procedural Step. Chart the procedure.**
    a. Include the date and time, the name of the test (Snellen test), and the visual acuity results.
    b. The results must be charted as two numbers, or the number (fraction) on the left side of the chart next to the row read most accurately (e.g., right eye 20/20).
    c. Any unusual symptoms the patient may have exhibited during the test must be charted.
    d. Chart whether or not the patient was wearing corrective lenses during the test (e.g., left eye 20/40 w/contacts).

17. **Procedural Step. Sanitize the hands.**
    Always sanitize the hands after a procedure or after using gloves.

Charting Example

Date	
1/6/xx	9:30 a.m. Snellen test: right eye 20/20–1; left eye 20/40 —————— M. Jones, SMA

Procedure 8-9 Assess Color Vision Using the Ishihara Test

TASK: Measure color visual acuity accurately using the Ishihara color-blindness test.

EQUIPMENT AND SUPPLIES
- Ishihara color plate book
- Cotton swab
- Well-lit examination room (natural light preferred)
- Watch with second hand
- Patient's medical record
- Pen or pencil

SKILLS/RATIONALE

STANDARD PRECAUTIONS ARE TO BE FOLLOWED.

1. **Procedural Step. Sanitize the hands.**
   An alcohol-based hand rub may be used instead of washing hands with soap and water, unless hands are visibly soiled.
   Rationale. Hand sanitization promotes infection control.

2. **Procedural Step. Assemble equipment and supplies.**
   Rationale. It is important to have all supplies and equipment ready and available before starting any procedure to ensure efficiency.

3. **Procedural Step. Greet and identify the patient.**

Continued

Procedure 8-9 Assess Color Vision Using the Ishihara Test—cont'd

Rationale. Identifying the patient ensures the procedure is performed on the correct patient.

4. **Procedural Step. Explain the procedure to the patient.**

   Rationale. Explaining the procedure to the patient promotes cooperation and provides a means of obtaining implied consent.

5. **Procedural Step. Identify the light source that will be used during the test.**

   Rationale. The Ishihara color-blindness test is most accurate when the test is given in a quiet room illuminated by natural daylight. Using artificial light may change the appearance of the shades of color on the plates, leading to inaccurate test results.

6. **Procedural Step. Use the first plate in the book as an example, and instruct the patient on how the examination will be conducted using this plate.**

   Explain to the patient that he or she will have 3 seconds to identify numbers verbally or to trace a winding path formed by colored dots on each plate.

   Rationale. The first plate is designed to be read correctly by all individuals and is used to explain the procedure to the patient.

7. **Procedural Step. Hold the color plates 30 inches from the patient.**

   The plate should be held at a right angle to the patient's line of vision. Both eyes should be kept open during the test.

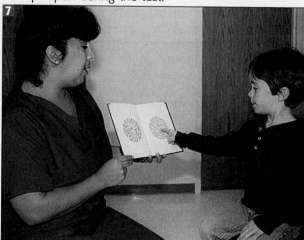

8. **Procedural Step. Ask the patient to identify the number on the plate or, using a cotton-tipped swab, to trace the winding path.**

   In some cases, a patient may be asked to trace the numbers.

   Rationale. Tracing ensures the number is read and not previously memorized. A swab is used because

using the fingers would leave body oil on the paper and damage the plate.

9. **Procedural Step. Record the results after each plate, and continue until the patient has viewed and responded to all 11 plates.**

10. **Procedural Step. Record the results in the patient's medical record.**

    Three methods are typically used to record the results in the patient's medical record:

    a. The first method is "pass/fail." The plate number is recorded, and if the patient was able to identify the number, "pass" is written next to it (e.g., Plate 2 = pass). If the patient cannot identify the number, an "X" is placed next to the plate number (e.g., Plate 4 = X).

    b. The second method of charting is similar to the first. Instead of "pass/fail," however, if the patient correctly identifies the number, the *number viewed* is placed next to the plate number (e.g., Plate 5 = 21). If the patient is unable to identify a number, an "X" is recorded to indicate that the patient could not read the plate in the same manner as the first example.

    c. The third method of charting requires that only the plate number with an "X" be recorded for the plates not read by the patient (e.g., Plate 4 = X, all other plates read correctly).

11. **Procedural Step. Chart the results in the patient's medical record.**

    a. Include the date and time, the name of the test (Ishihara test), and color vision results.

    b. Report any unusual symptoms that the patient may have exhibited during the test, such as squinting or rubbing the eyes.

12. **Procedural Step. Return the Ishihara book to its proper place.**

    Rationale. The book of color plates must be stored in a closed position to protect it from light. Exposing the plates to excessive and unnecessary light results in fading of the color.

13. **Procedural Step. Sanitize the hands.**

    Always sanitize the hands after every procedure or after using gloves.

Charting Example

Date	
3/13/xx	2:30 p.m. Ishihara plates: all plates read correctly ———————— D. Done, SMA

Procedure 8-10 Assess Near Vision Using a Jaeger Card

TASK: Measure near visual acuity accurately using the Jaeger near-vision acuity card. Document the procedure in the patient's medical record.

EQUIPMENT AND SUPPLIES
- Jaeger card
- Well-lit examination room
- Patient's medical record
- Pen
- 18-inch ruler or tape measure

SKILLS/RATIONALE

STANDARD PRECAUTIONS ARE TO BE FOLLOWED.

1. **Procedural Step. Sanitize the hands.**
   An alcohol-based hand rub may be used instead of washing hands with soap and water, unless hands are visibly soiled.
   Rationale. Hand sanitization promotes infection control.

2. **Procedural Step. Assemble equipment and supplies.**
   Rationale. It is important to have all supplies and equipment ready and available before starting any procedure, to ensure efficiency.

3. **Procedural Step. Greet and identify the patient.**
   Rationale. Identifying the patient ensures the procedure is performed on the correct patient.

4. **Procedural Step. Explain the procedure to the patient.**
   Rationale. Explaining the procedure to the patient promotes cooperation and provides a means of obtaining implied consent.

5. **Procedural Step. Have the patient sit in a comfortable position.**

6. **Procedural Step. Provide the patient with the Jaeger card.**

7. **Procedural Step. Instruct the patient to hold the card 14 to 16 inches away from the eyes. Measure the distance for accuracy.**

8. **Procedural Step. Ask the patient to read out loud the paragraphs on the card.**
   The patient should read the card starting at the top and reading down to the smallest print the patient can read. As with the Snellen test, the near-vision acuity test is performed on each eye starting with the right eye.

9. **Procedural Step. Document the number at which the patient stopped reading for each eye.**
   Record the results and any problems experienced by the patient (e.g., squinting) in the medical record.

10. **Procedural Step. Return the Jaeger card to its proper storage place.**

11. **Procedural Step. Sanitize the hands.**
    Always sanitize the hands after every procedure or after using gloves.

Charting Example

Date	
12/10/xx	10:15 a.m. Jaeger card: successfully read No. 7 (1.50M) c̄ contacts
	M. Lamb, SMA

Continued

Procedure 8-10 Assess Near Vision Using a Jaeger Card—cont'd

6

No. 1.
.37M

In the second century of the Christian era, the empire of Rome comprehended the fairest part of the earth, and the most civilized portion of mankind. The frontiers of that extensive monarchy were guarded by ancient renown and disciplined valor. The gentle but powerful influence of laws and manners had gradually cemented the union of the provinces. Their peaceful inhabitants enjoyed and abused the advantages of wealth.

No. 2.
.50M

fourscore years, the public administration was conducted by the virtue and abilities of Nerva, Trajan, Hadrian, and the two Antonines. It is the design of this, and of the two succeeding chapters, to describe the prosperous condition of their empire; and afterwards, from the death of Marcus Antoninus, to deduce the most important circumstances of its decline and fall; a revolution which will ever be remembered, and is still felt by

No. 3.
.62M

the nations of the earth. The principal conquests of the Romans were achieved under the republic; and the emperors, for the most part, were satisfied with preserving those dominions which had been acquired by the policy of the senate, the active emulations of the consuls, and the martial enthusiasm of the people. The seven first centuries were filled with a rapid succession of triumphs; but it was

No. 4.
.75M

reserved for Augustus to relinquish the ambitious design of subduing the whole earth, and to introduce a spirit of moderation into the public councils. Inclined to peace by his temper and situation, it was very easy for him to discover that Rome, in her present exalted situation, had much less to hope than to fear from the chance of arms; and that, in the prosecution of

No. 5.
1.00M

the undertaking became every day more difficult, the event more doubtful, and the possession more precarious, and less beneficial. The experience of Augustus added weight to these salutary reflections, and effectually convinced him that, by the prudent vigor of

No. 6.
1.25M

his counsels, it would be easy to secure every concession which the safety or the dignity of Rome might require from the most formidable barbarians. Instead of exposing his person or his legions to the arrows of the Parthinians, he obtained, by an honor-

No. 7.
1.50M

able treaty, the restitution of the standards and prisoners which had been taken in the defeat of Crassus. His generals, in the early part of his reign, attempted the reduction of Ethiopia and Arabia Felix. They marched near a thou-

No. 8.
1.75M

sand miles to the south of the tropic; but the heat of the climate soon repelled the invaders, and protected the unwarlike natives of those sequestered regions

No. 9.
2.00M

The northern countries of Europe scarcely deserved the expense and labor of conquest. The forests and morasses of Germany were

No. 10.
2.25M

filled with a hardy race of barbarians who despised life when it was separated from freedom; and though, on the first

No. 11.
2.50M

attack, they seemed to yield to the weight of the Roman power, they soon, by a signal

---

≋ EAR EXAMINATION

The physician also examines the patient's ears in the CPX. Patient complaints involving the ear often include pain, discharge, hearing loss, ringing (**tinnitus**), or dizziness (**vertigo**). As a person ages, loss of hearing (**presbycusis**) occurs first as an inability to hear high-pitched sounds, then progresses to lower-pitched sounds.

The physician uses an **otoscope** to check the appearance of the ear canal and the eardrum or tympanic membrane (Fig. 8-7). The otoscope uses a disposable *speculum* that fits the external ear canal of the patient. An adult's ear is examined by pulling the auricle upward and backward. A child's ear is examined by pulling the auricle downward and backward (up to age 3 years) to straighten the ear

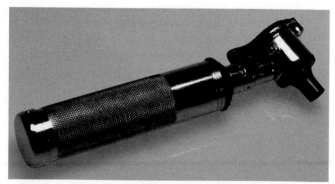

Fig. 8-9 Otoscope.

canal. Children are prone to ear infections because the eustachian tube is parallel with the pharynx. After visualizing the ear, the physician discards the speculum (most medical offices now use disposable specula).

CONCLUSION

The medical assistant is responsible for having the patient ready for the physician. This includes taking the vital signs and preparing the patient for an examination or a procedure. Having a patient in a gown and positioned properly allows the physician to begin the examination. The medical assistant should consider the patient's comfort level and safety at all times.

Understanding the proper methods for preparing the examination room and the patient, and for assisting the physician, will help the patient appointment proceed smoothly and efficiently. This helps save both the physician's time and the patient's time. It also demonstrates professionalism and competence by conveying to the patient that he or she is in good hands.

Table 8-2 provides an overview of positions, body areas, assessment methods, abbreviations and medical terminology, and instruments and supplies needed for a physical examination.

PATIENT-CENTERED PROFESSIONALISM

- What are the responsibilities of the medical assistant in ear examinations?

TABLE 8-2   Physical Examination Overview

Position	Body Area	Assessment Technique	Common Terms and Abbreviations	Instruments Used
Sitting	Skin	**Inspection:** Color and pigmentation Change in surface texture **Palpation:** Temperature Edema, tenderness Moisture	**Pallor** **Erythema** **Cyanosis** **Jaundice** **Turgor** **Diaphoresis**	
	Head and neck	**Inspection:** Contour, shape, deformities Facial expression Scalp, hair **Palpation:** Swelling, tenderness (lymph node, thyroid) Temporal artery, temporomandibular joint	**HEENT** (head, eyes, ears, nose, and throat)	
		Auscultation: Carotid pulse	**Bruit**	Stethoscope with bell
	Eyes	**Inspection:** Extraocular (EOM) function Pupillary light reflex Optic disk/retina/macula Color vision Visual acuity	**PERRLA** (pupils equal, round, react to light, and **accommodation**)	Penlight Ophthalmoscope Ishihara color plates, Snellen chart
	Ears	**Inspection:** Size, shape, color, redness, position, head alignment Eardrum (tympanic membrane): color, intact, position (flat, bulging) Hearing acuity	**Microtia** **Macrotia** **Perforation** **Weber test** **Rinne test**	Otoscope with ear speculum Tuning fork or audiometer

Continued

TABLE 8-2	Physical Examination Overview—cont'd

Position	Body Area	Assessment Technique	Common Terms and Abbreviations	Instruments Used
	Nose, mouth, and throat	**Inspection:** Symmetry, lesions Color and intact nasal mucosa Polyps, swelling	**Patent** **Herpes simplex 1** **Gingivitis**	Otoscope with short, wide-tipped nasal speculum *or* nasal speculum and penlight Penlight, tongue depressor, disposable glove
		Palpation: Sinus areas		
		Inspection: *Lips:* color, cracking, lesions *Teeth, gums, tongue, mucosa:* color, lesions, breath odor, gag reflex		
		Palpation: *Mouth:* tenderness, lumps		
	Breast	**Inspection:** Symmetry of size and shape		
Supine	Breast and axillae	**Palpation:** Lymph nodes Breast tissue	**BSE** (breast self-examination)	Small pillow, tape measure
Sitting	Chest	**Inspection:** Rib cage and vertebrae for deformities	"Barrel chest": protrusion of chest caused by hyperinflation of the lungs	
		Palpation: Lumps, tenderness Chest expansion		
		Percussion: Over lungs		
		Auscultation: Breath sounds	**Crepitus** **Rales** **Rhonchi**	Stethoscope
	Heart	**Auscultation:** Rate and rhythm	**Murmur** **Thrill**	Stethoscope with diaphragm and bell end pieces
Supine	Abdomen	**Inspection:** Contour; masses or bulges	**Distention** RLQ (right lower quadrant) LLQ (left lower quadrant)	
		Auscultation: Bowel sounds Vascular sounds (aorta, renal and femoral arteries)		Stethoscope
		Palpation: All quadrants Liver, spleen, kidneys Tenderness		
		Percussion: All quadrants Liver and spleen		

TABLE 8-2   Physical Examination Overview—cont'd

Position	Body Area	Assessment Technique	Common Terms and Abbreviations	Instruments Used
	Arms and legs	**Inspection:** Color, size, lesions **Palpation:** *Pulses:* radial, brachial, femoral, popliteal, dorsalis pedis Inguinal nodes Temperature of feet and legs Muscle tone, tenderness, and masses ROM (range of motion) **Percussion:** Biceps, triceps, abdominal, patellar, Achilles, plantar reflexes	Reflex findings: 0: No response 1+: Low normal 2+: WNL* 3+: Above normal 4+: Hyperactive	Goniometer Percussion hammer
Lithotomy	Female genitalia	**Inspection:** External genitalia Vagina and cervix (obtain specimens) **Palpation:** Labia, Skene and Bartholin glands	**LMP** (last menstrual period)	Vaginal speculum, glove, slide, fixative or Thin Prep solution, cervical brush and spatula
	Anal canal	**Inspection:** Rectum **Palpation:** Rectum		Glove and lubricant
Standing	Male genitalia	**Inspection:** Penis, scrotum and testes	**TSE** (testicular self-examination) **BPH** (benign prostatic hypertrophy)	Glove Lubricant
	Anal canal	Anus **Palpation:** Penis, scrotum and testes Inguinal hernia Prostate Rectum		

*Within normal limits.

SUMMARY

Reinforce your understanding of the material in this chapter by reviewing the curriculum objectives and key content points below.

1. Define, appropriately use, and spell all of the Key Terms for this chapter.
   - Review the Key Terms if necessary.
2. List the three main responsibilities of the medical assistant in preparing a patient for a physical examination.
   - The medical assistant is responsible for having the patient gowned, appropriately positioned, and draped for the physician to perform the physical examination.
3. List three responsibilities of the medical assistant in assisting the patient to disrobe for an examination.
   - The medical assistant must choose the right type of gown for the given procedure, provide clear instructions for disrobing and gowning, and assist patients who need help disrobing.
4. Demonstrate the correct procedure for providing the physician and the patient with items needed to perform a complete physical examination.

- Review Procedure 8-1.
5. Explain what a "consent-to-treat form" involves and when formal consent is needed for an examination.
   - For invasive procedures beyond the basic examination, such as biopsies, the patient must sign a consent-to-treat form.
   - The form must be signed before the procedure is performed.
6. Explain the importance of draping the patient appropriately for an examination or procedure.
   - Draping the patient provides warmth, comfort, and modesty.
7. List the three criteria for selecting the position to be used for an examination.
   - The position used depends on the procedure to be performed, the patient's chief complaint, and the patient's age.
8. List nine examination positions and briefly explain what types of examinations are performed using each position.
   - Sitting position is used to begin the physical examination because the upper extremities are easily accessible.
   - Standing position is used to evaluate coordination and balance.
   - Horizontal recumbent, or supine, position is used for examination of the chest, abdomen, and lower extremities.
   - Dorsal recumbent position is used for examination of the vaginal area for females and the rectal area for both males and females.
   - Lithotomy position is used for the pelvic examination in females.
   - Sims' position is used for rectal examinations, enema administration, and sigmoidoscopy.
   - Prone position is used to examine the back and lower extremities.
   - Knee-chest position is used for sigmoidoscopies.
   - Fowler's position helps the patient breathe easier and is used to examine the upper extremities.
9. Demonstrate the correct procedure for properly positioning and draping a patient in the sitting position.
   - Review Procedure 8-2.
10. Demonstrate the correct procedure for properly positioning and draping a patient in the recumbent position.
    - Review Procedure 8-3.
11. Demonstrate the correct procedure for properly positioning and draping a patient in the Sims' position.
    - Review Procedure 8-4.

12. Demonstrate the correct procedure for properly positioning and draping a patient in the prone position.
    - Review Procedure 8-5.
13. Demonstrate the correct procedure for properly positioning and draping a patient in the knee-chest position.
    - Review Procedure 8-6.
14. Demonstrate the correct procedure for properly positioning and draping a patient in the Fowler's and semi-Fowler's positions.
    - Review Procedure 8-7.
15. List the four primary methods of examining used during a physical examination and briefly explain what occurs in each.
    - Inspection is the visual viewing of all body surfaces for abnormalities and signs of disease.
    - Palpation uses touch to detect abnormalities.
    - Percussion uses the fingers to tap the body surfaces while listening for sounds.
    - Auscultation is accomplished by using a stethoscope to listen for body sounds.
16. State the purpose of a Snellen chart, and explain when each of the three types of Snellen charts should be used.
    - Vision testing done in the medical office includes using the Snellen chart for distance viewing.
    - The alphabetic chart can be used for English-speaking patients.
    - The rotating "E" chart can be used for non–English-speaking patients.
    - The object chart can be used for preschoolers.
17. Demonstrate the correct procedure for accuracy in measuring and recording a patient's visual acuity with a Snellen chart.
    - Review Procedure 8-8.
18. List five types of common visual defects that are correctable by lenses or surgery.
    - Hyperopia (farsightedness), myopia (near-sightedness), presbyopia ("old eyes"), astigmatism, and strabismus (e.g., "cross-eye") can be corrected.
19. Demonstrate the correct procedure for accurately measuring and recording a patient's color visual acuity with the Ishihara test.
    - Review Procedure 8-9.
20. Demonstrate the correct procedure for accurately measuring and recording a patient's near visual acuity with a Jaeger reading card.
    - Review Procedure 8-10.
21. Differentiate between an ophthalmoscope and an otoscope and explain how each is used in the physical examination.

- An ophthalmoscope is used to look at the inner structures of the eye.
- An otoscope is used to examine the external ear canal, tympanic membrane, and middle ear.

22. Analyze a realistic medical office situation and apply your understanding of assisting with a physical examination to determine the best course of action.
   - Care must be taken to treat the patient with dignity and respect during the physical examination.
   - The patient's safety and comfort are the primary concerns.

23. Describe the impact on patient care when medical assistants understand how to assist the physician with the physical examination.
   - Patient care is enhanced when the medical assistant is organized.

- Patients have more confidence in their treatment plan when the medical assistant demonstrates competency and a caring attitude about their safety.

FOR FURTHER EXPLORATION

Research the concept of *periodic* health examination versus the *annual* examination. Replacing the annual examination with the periodic examination was done to promote the detection and prevention of specific diseases. Detecting a problem in its early stages can result in long-term benefits.

Keywords: Use the following keywords in your search: preventive medicine, health examination, physical examination.

Chapter Review

Vocabulary Review

Matching

Match each term with the correct definition.

A. accommodation

B. auscultation

C. BSE

D. crepitus

E. diaphoresis

F. distention

G. erythema

H. gingivitis

I. goniometer

J. herpes simplex

K. jaundice

L. macrotia

M. murmur

N. pallor

O. patent

P. percussion

Q. perforation

R. PERRLA

S. presbycusis

T. prone position

U. rhonchi

V. Sims' position

W. supine position

_____ 1. Patient's back is on the table; horizontal recumbent position

_____ 2. Crackling sound heard in the lungs or joints

_____ 3. Paleness

_____ 4. Humming or low-pitched fluttering sound of the heart heard on auscultation

_____ 5. Viral infection of the lip-skin junction; cold sore

_____ 6. Rattling sounds heard in the lungs, usually at the base

_____ 7. Ability of the eye to see objects in the distance and then adjust to a close object

_____ 8. Ability to see at different distances

_____ 9. Decrease in hearing ability resulting from aging

_____ 10. Swollen

_____ 11. Tapping to check for reflexes or sounds of body cavities

_____ 12. Ringing in the ears

_____ 13. Listening for signs using a stethoscope

_____ 14. Open; not obstructed

_____ 15. Patient is first in the supine position, then turns onto left side with the right leg sharply bent upward

_____ 16. Skin resiliency

_____ 17. Ears larger than 10 cm

X. thrill

Y. tinnitus

Z. turgor

AA. vertigo

BB. visual acuity

CC. sitting position

_____ 18. Yellowish appearance to the skin and eyes

_____ 19. Pupils equal, round, and reactive to light and accommodation

_____ 20. Excessive perspiration

_____ 21. Palpable vibration

_____ 22. Device used to measure joint movements and angles

_____ 23. Breast self-examination

_____ 24. Dizziness

_____ 25. Inflammation of the gums

_____ 26. Tear or hole in an organ or body part

_____ 27. Reddish discoloration of the skin

_____ 28. Patient lies on the abdomen with the head turned slightly to the side

_____ 29. Patient's body is at a 90-degree angle

Theory Recall

True/False

Indicate whether the sentence or statement is true or false.

_____ 1. When the medical assistant is positioning and draping the patient, he or she should always consider the patient's comfort and minimize the area of exposure.

_____ 2. When a patient is in semi-Fowler's position, the table must be at a 90-degree angle.

_____ 3. The medical assistant must assist the elderly patient with disrobing.

_____ 4. The receptionist is responsible for having the patient ready in a room for the medical assistant.

_____ 5. A patient can withdraw consent for an examination after the form has been put into the chart.

Multiple Choice

Identify the letter of the choice that best completes the statement or answers the question.

1. The _____ position helps the patient breathe easier.
   A. dorsal recumbent
   B. knee-chest
   C. Fowler's
   D. Sims'

2. _____ is the medical term for "ringing of the ears."
   A. Crepitus
   B. Tinnitus
   C. Presbycusis
   D. Vertigo

3. A _____ must be provided if the examination is beyond a wellness physical.
   A. chaperone
   B. gown
   C. patient's informed consent
   D. none of the above

4. Failure to secure consent for a procedure such as a colonoscopy is considered _____.
   A. assault and battery
   B. an OSHA violation
   C. dangerous
   D. consent is not required for a colonoscopy

5. The _____ position is most often used to begin a physical examination because the upper extremities are clearly accessible.
   A. horizontal recumbent
   B. sitting
   C. Sims'
   D. standing

6. When a patient is in full-Fowler's position, the table will be at a _____ -degree angle.
   A. 30
   B. 45
   C. 60
   D. 90

7. The _____ position can be used for rectal examination and enema administration.
   A. knee-chest
   B. prone
   C. Sims'
   D. supine

8. The physician uses a(n) _____ to examine the interior of the eye.
   A. otoscope
   B. ophthalmoscope
   C. speculum
   D. none of the above

9. The _____ chart is used to test a person's ability to read at a prescribed near distance.
   A. Jaeger
   B. Ishihara
   C. Snellen
   D. rotating E chart

10. When using the Snellen eye chart, the patient should be _____ feet from the chart.
    A. 10
    B. 15
    C. 20
    D. 25

11. The patient's type of gown will be decided by the _____.
    A. patient's preference
    B. procedure to be performed
    C. AMA
    D. all of the above

12. Patients have the right to refuse treatment.
    A. True
    B. False

13. _____ is a yellowish discoloration of the skin and eyes.
    A. Bruit
    B. Cyanosis
    C. Jaundice
    D. Erythema

14. _____ is a low-pitched fluttering sound made by the heart.
    A. Rales
    B. Thrill
    C. Turgor
    D. Murmur

15. _____ is the touching or feeling of body organs, lymph nodes, and tissue.
    A. Auscultation
    B. Palpation
    C. Percussion
    D. Turgor

16. Patient _____ must be the prime consideration for the medical assistant during positioning of the patient.
    A. safety
    B. ethnicity
    C. body size
    D. modesty

17. The _____ eye chart has rows of letters.
    A. Jaeger
    B. Ishihara
    C. Snellen
    D. none of the above

18. The _____ position is most often used for nonflexible sigmoidoscopy.
    A. Sims'
    B. Fowler's
    C. knee-chest
    D. dorsal recumbent

19. When a physician needs to determine the patient's coordination and balance through observation, the patient would be in the _____ position.
    A. dorsal recumbent
    B. sitting
    C. prone
    D. standing

20. _____ is a visual viewing of all body parts and surface areas for symmetry.
    A. Palpation
    B. Auscultation
    C. Inspection
    D. Percussion

21. _____ is when a patient has trouble focusing and vision is blurred. The shape of the cornea or lens prevents light from projecting onto the retina.
    A. Hypermetropia
    B. Myopia
    C. Presbyopia
    D. Astigmatism

22. Which method of vision testing works best for preschoolers?
    A. Jaeger
    B. Ishihara
    C. Snellen
    D. None of the above

23. Of the following, which item would NOT be used for a distance visual acuity test?
    A. Eye occluder
    B. Snellen eye chart
    C. Ophthalmoscope
    D. All would be used

24. The medical assistant's major role in preparing a patient for a _____ is to have the patient gowned, appropriately positioned, and draped for the physician.
    A. CPX
    B. BMI
    C. CXR
    D. PXR

25. Which one of the following items is NOT required for a routine physical examination?
    A. Tape measure
    B. Vaginal speculum
    C. Percussion hammer
    D. Tuning fork

Sentence Completion

Complete each sentence or statement.

1. _____ involves the use of a stethoscope to detect sounds of the heart, respiratory system, and intestines.

2. The _____ position is the best position for breathing difficulties.

3. _____ involves the use by the physician of his or her hands to locate and touch major organs and lymph nodes to detect tenderness in an area.

4. The _____ eye chart tests for distant visual acuity.

5. The _____ aids physicians in checking the appearance of the eardrum and ear canal.

Short Answers

1. List the eight examination positions with which a medical assistant should be familiar.

_____

_____

_____

_____

2. Describe the three types of the Snellen charts, and give one example of why each would be used.

_____

_____

_____

_____

_____

_____

3. Explain the difference between implied and informed consent.

_____

_____

_____

_____

_____

Critical Thinking

Magdalena Jimenez has recently moved to the United States; her mother is enrolling her in school and has made an appointment for a school physical. Magdalena does not speak English, and her mother speaks very little. You do not speak Spanish. Describe how you would proceed with Magdalena's physical examination. Which Snellen chart would you use to assess Magdalena's visual acuity?

Internet Research

Keywords: Visual acuity testing, physical exams

Based on your Internet research, write a one-page paper on your topic of choice. Cite your source. Be prepared to give a 2-minute oral presentation should your instructor assign you to do so.

What Would You Do?

If you have accomplished the objectives in this chapter, you will be able to make better choices as a medical assistant. Take a look at this situation and decide what you would do.

Beth is a medical assistant in the office of Dr. Havidiz, a family practitioner. Dr. Havidiz treats many low-income families, and many women in the community see him for gynecological visits. Holly, a new patient, comes to see Dr. Havidiz for a possible vaginal infection. Her demeanor shows her fear of the doctor's office, especially since this is the first time she has seen Dr. Havidiz. Dr. Havidiz was called to the hospital to see a critically ill patient earlier in the day, so appointments are delayed.

There is an available examination room when Holly arrives, so Beth takes her to the room and tells her to undress completely. Beth does not tell Holly how to put on the gown, but she stands in the room and watches Holly undress. While Holly is undressing, Beth asks the questions necessary to obtain the medical history. Beth then places Holly on the examination table in the dorsal recumbent position and immediately leaves the room, giving the impression that she is in a great hurry. After 15 minutes, Holly has discomfort in her back but dares not move from the position because she does not want to delay the examination. After 30 minutes, Holly wonders just how much longer it will take for Dr. Havidiz to come and check her. Finally, Dr. Havidiz arrives and the examination begins.

During the examination, Beth leaves the room to answer a personal phone call, leaving Dr. Havidiz and Holly alone. As Holly leaves the office, she is in tears from back pain and appears to be very upset. Beth shows no sympathy or empathy for Holly. Two days later, Holly asks that her records be transferred to another physician and tells Dr. Havidiz that she has never been treated as rudely as she was in his office.

How might this situation have been prevented?

1. How did Beth invade Holly's privacy?

_____

_____

_____

2. Under what conditions should Beth have taken Holly's history?

_____

_____

3. Why was it important to tell Holly how to put on the gown for the examination? How should the drape have been applied?

_____

_____

_____

_____

4. What examination methods would you expect the medical assistant to use while preparing Holly for an examination?

_____

_____

_____

_____

5. What methods of examination would you expect the physician to use during the examination?

_____

_____

_____

_____

6. What positions should have been used for Holly while she was waiting for the pelvic examination? What positions are inappropriate for a long wait? What explanation should Beth have given when placing Holly in the position?

_____

_____

_____

_____

_____

7. How should Beth have handled the delay?

_____

_____

_____

8. Why is it unethical for Beth to leave the room during the physical examination?

_____

_____

_____

9. Do you think that Holly had a legitimate complaint to Dr. Havidiz about her treatment? Explain your answer.

_____

_____

_____

_____

Chapter Quiz

Multiple Choice

Identify the letter of the choice that best completes the statement or answers the question.

1. _____ is the position that helps the patient breathe better when in respiratory distress.
   A. Dorsal recumbent
   B. Standing
   C. Fowler's
   D. Sims'

2. _____ is used by the physician to check the nervous system.
   A. Auscultation
   B. Palpation
   C. Percussion
   D. Inspection

3. The medical assistant must choose the right type and size of gown for the examination being performed.
   A. True
   B. False

4. _____ is another name for "ringing in the ears."
   A. Crepitus
   B. Turgor
   C. Tinnitus
   D. Vertigo

5. Listening for body sounds, usually with a stethoscope, is called _____.
   A. auscultation
   B. inspection
   C. palpation
   D. thrill

6. Patients cannot withdraw their consent once it has been given and documented in their chart.
   A. True
   B. False

7. Bluish coloration of the skin due to lack of oxygen is called _____.
   A. bruit
   B. cyanosis
   C. jaundice
   D. gingivitis

8. _____ is(are) crackling sounds heard in the lungs, usually at the base.
   A. Bruit
   B. Crepitus
   C. Rales
   D. Rhonchi

9. Taking a patient's pulse is done by palpation.
   A. True
   B. False

10. The _____ position is most often used for a colonoscopy.
    A. dorsal recumbent
    B. knee-chest
    C. Fowler's
    D. prone

11. Color vision is tested with the _____ test.
    A. Ishihara
    B. Jaeger
    C. Snellen
    D. rotating E chart

12. A patient in the supine position whose head is at a 45-degree angle is in the _____ position.
    A. dorsal recumbent
    B. full-Fowler's
    C. semi-Fowler's
    D. supine

13. The physician uses a(n) _____ to visualize the eardrum or tympanic membrane.
    A. ophthalmoscope
    B. otoscope
    C. speculum
    D. none of the above

14. Ears smaller than 4 cm are known as macrotia.
    A. True
    B. False

15. The back and lower extremities can be examined with the patient in the _____ position.
    A. lithotomy
    B. prone
    C. sitting
    D. standing

16. Observation of the reaction of the pupils to the exposure of direct light is documented using which one of the following acronyms?
    A. PUPIL
    B. PERRLA
    C. AAOLX3
    D. None of the above

17. A device used to measure joint movements and angles is called a _____.
    A. flexible cloth tape measure
    B. yardstick
    C. goniometer
    D. pelvimeter

18. Decrease in hearing ability resulting from aging is called _____.
    A. myopia
    B. presbyopia
    C. presbycusis
    D. tinnitus

19. The medical term for "dizziness" is _____.
    A. tinnitus
    B. turgor
    C. macrotia
    D. vertigo

20. The medical term for "excessive sweating" is _____.
    A. diaphoresis
    B. crepitus
    C. gingivitis
    D. turgor

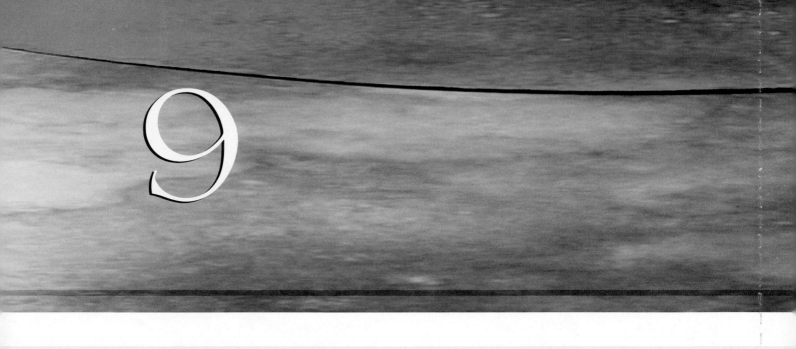

9

Objectives

You will be able to do the following after completing this chapter:

Key Terms
1. Define, appropriately use, and spell all the Key Terms for this chapter.

The Communication Process
2. State the goal of the communication process.
3. List and describe the three components of the communication process.

Effective Verbal Communication
4. List and describe the four steps in sending a message that will be understood.
5. List the three types of distracters that can prevent a message from being sent or received.
6. Explain how a verbal message can be misinterpreted.
7. Explain the process of sending a verbal message and evaluating its receipt.

Effective Nonverbal Communication
8. List and describe three ways that people communicate nonverbally.
9. Explain how a nonverbal message can be misinterpreted.

Effective Listening
10. List the three components of effective listening.
11. Compare and contrast active and passive listening and give an example of each.
12. State six steps to becoming a better listener.

Effective Written Communication
13. Recognize the parts of speech and give an example of each.
14. Demonstrate correct use of punctuation.
15. Explain the importance of choosing the correct words.
16. List six words that are frequently misspelled in the medical office.

Effective Communication Using Electronic Technology
17. Explain the importance of understanding how to communicate effectively using electronic technology.
18. List the different types of electronic technology used for communication in a medical office.
19. List six guidelines for e-mail etiquette.

EFFECTIVE COMMUNICATION

Patient-Centered Professionalism

20. Analyze a realistic medical office situation and apply your understanding of effective communication to determine the best course of action.
21. Describe the impact on patient care when medical assistants consistently apply the principles of effective communication.

KEY TERMS

active listening Occurs when a listener maintains eye contact and provides responses to the speaker.

adjective A word used to describe a noun or pronoun.

adverb A word used to describe a verb, adjective, or another adverb.

body language Nonverbal signals using body motions.

communication The exchange of information between a sender and receiver.

conjunction A word used to join words or groups of words.

distracter Something that causes the sender or receiver not to give full attention to the message.

fax (facsimile) Method of communication in which written material is converted into electronic impulses transmitted by telephone lines.

feedback Verbal or nonverbal indication that a message was received.

grammar Study of words and their relationship to other words in a sentence.

interjection A word used to express strong feelings or emotion.

nonverbal Without using words (e.g., nonverbal communication).

noun A word used to name things, including people, places, objects, and ideas.

passive listening Hearing what the speaker is saying but not fully concentrating on the conversation.

prejudice Negative opinion(s) toward an individual because of the individual's affiliation with a specific group.

preposition A word used to begin a prepositional phrase.

pronoun A word used to take the place of a noun.

punctuation Marks within and between sentences that separate, emphasize, and clarify the different ideas within a sentence or group of sentences.

sentence Group of words that express a complete thought.

stereotyping Holding the belief that all members of a culture or group are the same.

subject Part of a sentence that identifies who or what is being discussed.

verb A word in a sentence that expresses action or a state of being.

What Would You Do?

Read the following scenario and keep it in mind as you learn about the principles of effective communication in this chapter.

Panina is a former resident of the Middle East who moved to the United States with her husband, Abed, 6 months ago. Naturally, she brings the cultural and ethnic contexts of her homeland with her. Panina awakens one morning with a pain in her breast. She becomes concerned and calls a physician's office for an appointment. Because she has difficulty understanding the English language, she misunderstands the appointment time, and Panina and Abed arrive at the office an hour late. Abed demands to accompany his wife to the examining room. Therese, the medical assistant, tells Abed that they are late for the appointment and that he must stay in the waiting room while Panina is being examined. Panina, refusing eye contact with Therese, begins to cry. Abed becomes upset and tells Therese that the only way Panina will be examined is if he accompanies her to the room to explain to the male doctor what is wrong with her. Therese refuses, and Panina and Abed leave the office, threatening to tell all their friends how this office "just does not care about patients at all."

Effective communication helps eliminate misunderstandings. If you were the medical assistant in this situation, how could you have used your understanding of effective communication skills to help?

Communication is the process of sharing information, including ideas, thoughts, opinions, facts, and feelings. In order for people to satisfy their needs and help satisfy the needs of others, those needs must be known. For instance, if you need help, you have to communicate this to someone before that person will help you. Whether at home or in a medical setting, effective communication helps people build good relationships. In the same way, poor communication can cause misunderstandings that harm relationships. Effective communication helps medical assistants establish trust, obtain and provide important information, build positive relationships, and carry out their duties in an efficient, professional way.

You can become an effective communicator by learning and practicing good verbal communication skills, nonverbal communication skills, listening skills, writing skills, and communication using electronic technology.

THE COMMUNICATION PROCESS

The goal of **communication** is the clear exchange of information between a *sender* (the person sending information) and a *receiver* (the person receiving information). The three components of the communication process are the sender, the receiver, and the *message* (the information being exchanged). The process can be done either *verbally*, when words are exchanged, as in speaking or writing, or *nonverbally*, when expressions, gestures, and body movement are used to send the message (Fig. 9-1).

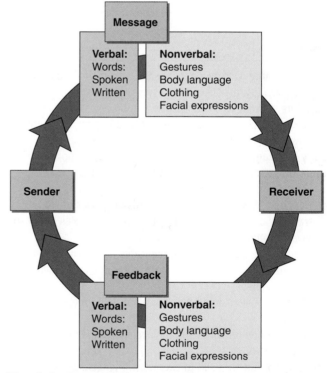

Fig. 9-1 Process of communication. *(From Hunt SA: Saunders fundamentals of medical assisting, Philadelphia, 2002, Saunders.)*

Never underestimate the power of nonverbal communication. When we communicate directly with another person, we send our message as follows:

- 10% is verbal.
- 40% is through our tone.
- 50% is through our body language.

Based on these statistics, 90% of person-to-person communication is nonverbal. Your words may be saying one thing, but is your nonverbal communication saying the same thing? To be an effective communicator, both verbal (spoken and written) and nonverbal (tone, body language) communication must be clear.

PATIENT-CENTERED PROFESSIONALISM

The way you communicate shows your respect for patients. Speaking with patients in a way that reflects your understanding of their feelings and fears not only shows respect for the patients but also promotes goodwill for the practice. How could each of the following remarks be changed to show more respect for patients?

- "Hold."
- "No, I can't give you an appointment today."
- "Fill out this form."
- "Doctor's busy."

≋ EFFECTIVE VERBAL COMMUNICATION

Although only 10% of all communicating is done verbally, words are powerful and must be chosen carefully. We have all been hurt by unkind or thoughtless words. You have learned how using labels can affect understanding and communication. Verbal communication is an important part of every medical assistant's day. You need to be able to communicate effectively with both co-workers and patients to provide effective care. Effective verbal communication involves (1) organizing a message, (2) prioritizing information, (3) sending the message, and (4) evaluating whether the message was received.

Organize

To ensure that the message being sent is focused on what the receiver wants or needs to know, the situation must be assessed and planning done. Consider the following when organizing verbal messages:

1. *Best organization of information to convey the information.* Is a lengthy explanation necessary or a brief summary? Would an example help clarify the idea?
2. *Time frame for communicating the message.* Is it something that must be conveyed immediately, or should it wait awhile?

3. Most important, *ability of the recipient to receive the message.* Will the person understand what you mean? How can you modify your communication based on the person's characteristics, abilities, and condition?

To be understandable, the message must be clear, concise, and in words that both the sender and the receiver can understand. For example, you could ask an adult patient to "urinate in the cup," but you may have to ask a child to "pee in the cup." Both these requests communicate the same message, but the wording has been adjusted to fit the understanding of the different receivers (adult and child).

Prioritize

Information being sent must be categorized and arranged in a logical order. What is it that you want the listener to hear first? A disorganized message is not likely to be understood by the listener.

Transmit

The sender must choose an appropriate way to transmit (send) the message. Depending on the information to be conveyed, the sender may transmit the message over the phone, in person, or by electronic mail (Fig. 9-2).

Delivery

The way a message is delivered is just as important as the message itself. Keep in mind the following about the delivery of messages:

Fig. 9-2 This medical assistant is sending a message to a patient when she confirms an appointment.

- Choose your words carefully and accurately; do not use slang terms or terminology the patient cannot understand.
- Be aware of the rate of your speech. If you talk too fast, your enunciation may become slurred, and the receiver may not be able to understand or hear all your words.
- Ensure that your message is clear and concise. Avoid a monotone voice. Vary your inflection (volume) when making points.
- Match your tone to the message you are sending. For example, use a serious tone for serious messages. Consider your volume as well; if your voice is too loud or too soft, the receiver may ignore the message.
- Give full attention to the listener. Maintain appropriate eye contact, use the listener's name, and smile if appropriate.

Distracters

A **distracter** is anything that causes the sender or receiver not to give full attention to the message. Distracters cause either the receiver to miss information provided or the sender to miscommunicate the message. For example, a person looking at her watch during an exchange of information gives the impression she wants to be someplace else. A person who constantly interrupts implies that the information being given is not important. Three major distracters you need to be aware of are the environment, your use of good grammar, and the physical well-being of the receiver.

Environment

The following environmental situations can distract a receiver and can prevent messages from being communicated:

- A noisy room with side conversations, a ringing telephone, or a TV in the background
- An uncomfortable room temperature (e.g., too warm or too cold)
- A room with either poor lighting or lights that are too bright or flickering

In each of these situations, the environment causes the receiver to pay more attention to the surroundings than to the message. When communicating, you must try to reduce the amount of *environmental interference*. For example, if you are trying to give instructions to a mother about her child and the child is misbehaving, the mother's focus is on the child and not the information being given. In this situation, you need to be patient and repeat the information when the mother is ready to listen to what you are saying. Providing written instructions to a parent or guardian for home care is also helpful.

Use of Grammar

The second major factor that distracts receivers from the information being sent is the improper use of grammar. When the sender uses improper grammar, the receiver may misunderstand the message being sent. In addition, the receiver may form a negative opinion about the sender (e.g., "this person doesn't speak properly; is she capable of performing her medical assisting duties?"). Even if the receiver believes and understands the message, he or she may not accept it because of the manner in which it is spoken. Proper use of grammar helps ensure that a message is organized well and communicated clearly. It also helps inspire confidence in the sender. Avoid using slang terms; patients may see them as unprofessional or may misinterpret their meaning altogether. Keep the medical explanations simple; do not use terminology the patient may not completely understand.

Physical Well-Being

The third major distracter is the receiver's physical well-being. If the receiver is weak from illness, in pain, or heavily medicated, he or she may not hear the message or be able to interpret or recall what is being communicated. If a family member or caregiver is not present with the patient at this time, be sure to provide written instructions for the patient to take home.

Evaluate

Even after the message is sent and received, the sender still has work to do. The message sent must be evaluated to determine how effective it was at communicating the intended information. Consider the following when evaluating a message's effectiveness:

1. Did the receiver understand the message exactly as you intended?
2. Did you obtain the expected response from the receiver?
3. Did a relationship of mutual respect and trust develop between you and the receiver?

You can answer these questions through feedback and clarification.

Assess Feedback

Receiving **feedback** (an indication that the message was received) from the receiver allows you to determine if the message was understood the way it was intended. Feedback occurs when the receiver responds to the information.

When communicating face-to-face, the feedback is immediate; you need only to observe the person's expression to decide if the message was received the way it was intended. For example, if the receiver looks confused or is silent, there usually is a problem.

When seeking feedback, you must use statements or questions that are open ended. *Open-ended questions* encourage more than a "yes" or "no" response. Open-ended questions such as "Tell me about yourself" (rather than "How long have you lived here?") encourage dialogue and allow patients to express more about their feelings and perceptions. These questions also give medical assistants a chance to verify that the information is accurate. *Closed-ended questions* (e.g., "yes" or "no" questions) may make patients feel rushed. If you are doing an assessment and use too many closed-ended questions, the patient may mentally tune out and provide only minimal information. Allowing the patient to ask questions and seek clarification before continuing on with the information greatly facilitates the communication process.

Seek Clarification

In some cases, you may have to repeat the information and even demonstrate what is needed from the receiver. This process, called *echoing,* helps you clarify the patient's feedback. If you discover during evaluation that the patient does not understand your message, adjust the message to fit the patient and send it again. Evaluating the effectiveness of your messages helps ensure that you are communicating clearly with patients.

PATIENT-CENTERED PROFESSIONALISM

- What is the most effective way for the medical assistant to communicate to the patient concerning a plan of care? How does effectively communicating a plan of care to patients benefit the patient and the health care team?
- What are some of the ways distracters can reduce the quality of care a patient receives?

≋ EFFECTIVE NONVERBAL COMMUNICATION

Nonverbal communication is the exchange of messages or information without using words. Nonverbal communication can help or hinder the process of sending a message depending on how it is used. Nonverbal communication is sometimes unintentional and unconscious, but it is still important. Understanding nonverbal communication

will help you to interpret patients' nonverbal messages as well as consider the messages you are sending as you interact with others. Your physical presentation, which includes not only your personal appearance but also your posture, movements, gestures, and facial expression, gives the patient clear signals about you. Body language, posture and movement, and personal space and distance are all forms of nonverbal communication.

Body Language

Our body language is as important as our words. When communicating with patients, you must look for nonverbal signals as you listen to what they are saying (Fig. 9-3). Consider how body motions such as a nod of the head, shrug of the shoulders, or a toddler's shake of the head to indicate "no" can send a clear message. However, understand that body language can sometimes be misinterpreted. A patient may interpret a medical assistant's unsmiling facial expression as a lack of concern for the patient's well-being, when the medical assistant simply may be tired that day. Cultural differences in body language can also cause misunderstandings. Casual touching of some body parts (e.g., arms, shoulder, face) and standing too close to a person's face may be offensive to some patients.

Always be aware of the nonverbal messages you are sending to patients. To improve communication with patients, you must understand the nonverbal messages that can be sent with the eyes, mouth, hands, and touch.

Eyes

The eyes can tell a great deal about what people are feeling. One look into a patient's eyes could reveal pain, fear, anger, or withdrawal. Our eyes send the following common nonverbal signals:

Fig. 9-3 What is this patient trying to communicate?

- The size of the pupil increases when looking at something of interest. The stronger the interest, the larger the pupil becomes.
- In America, looking downward or away can be interpreted as submission, giving in, or wanting to avoid a situation. When a teacher asks for a volunteer or asks a question, have you ever looked away because you didn't want to be called on?
- The eyes help create facial expressions that signal many emotions, including surprise, fear, anger, disgust, happiness, and sadness.

Mouth

The mouth can also send signals about what a person is feeling.

- When people are surprised, their mouths often drop open unexpectedly.
- A smile may signal acceptance, friendliness, or appreciation.
- A firm or set jaw may signal anger, impatience, or stubbornness.

Hands

The movements of the hands can send many signals.

- How would you interpret a message from someone who was pointing his or her finger at you?
- What message does a "thumbs-up" gesture send in Western culture?
- People may snap their fingers when they think of an idea, want to emphasize something, or want to get someone's attention.

Touch

Touch can send many nonverbal signals to the receiver. How a touch is interpreted depends on many variables. The growth and developmental stages and experiences of a person are important. If someone comes from a family environment where hugging was an everyday expression, touch may be accepted and welcome. Someone growing up in a family that is not "touchy-feely" may be uncomfortable with touch. Common messages associated with touch follow:

- In America a handshake is a social expression and can be used when meeting someone for the first time. In Europe the handshake is an everyday greeting among women and men alike.
- Hugs are usually saved for close relationships (e.g., within families or between close friends).
- A hand on the arm, shoulder, or back can convey comfort, support, or congratulations (Fig. 9-4).

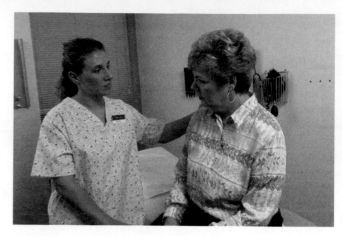

Fig. 9-4 A medical assistant lets the patient know she cares with a simple touch.

In the medical field touch can be used to express feelings of caring or concern. Touch is a basic form of communication for patients of all ages and does not require words or any previous experience or education to be effective. Medical assistants often use touch to offer support and to give positive reinforcement to patients. The patient's shoulders, arms, and hands are considered proper places for casual touch.

Posture and Movement

Posture and body movements are constantly sending messages. If you were speaking to a patient and his arms were folded over his chest, how would you interpret this? What might it mean if a patient turns her back to you? A patient's posture can tell you if the patient is tense or relaxed. In the same way that a patient's body movements and posture can send messages, the medical assistant's body movements and posture also send messages. For example, when questioning a patient, sitting instead of standing creates a more relaxed atmosphere and sends the message that you are taking your time.

Body movements can also imply many things. Fidgeting could signal that a patient is tired of waiting or anxious about something. Shivering could imply fear or feeling cold.

Space and Distance

When talking to another person, do you tend to stand very close to the person or farther away? The distance between people when communicating is often influenced by culture, race, gender, age, and personality. Different space considerations are as follows:

Public space (12 to 25 feet apart) is generally used when people are speaking to a group, or giving lectures or presentations. An example is a teacher speaking to an entire class.

Social space (2 to 4 feet apart) is mostly used in the workplace and similar situations. An example is a customer being helped by a salesperson at a store.

Personal space (arm's length distance, 1½ to 2½ feet) is used for personal conversations in soft to moderate tones. An example is two close friends "catching up on old times."

Intimate space (1 to 1½ feet apart) is used for those times of closeness. An example is a parent comforting a small child.

The distance between people when speaking depends on their feelings, what they are doing, and the nature of their relationship.

Other Nonverbal Considerations

Other factors that influence the interpretation of nonverbal communication include the following:

Time. How long it takes to send a message and how much time it takes to interpret it sends a nonverbal message.

Silence. Silence can be difficult to read, whether as acceptance, nonacceptance, or not understanding.

Sounds. Nonverbal communication can also be vocal. Examples include groans, sighs, or even screams when the patient is in pain.

Appearance. Just as your personal appearance as a medical assistant sends messages to patients, a patient's appearance sends messages as well. If a small child is not dressed warmly enough in cold weather, this might be interpreted as parental neglect.

Often, what you *don't* say is more important than what you do say. Make certain your actions reflect what you want sent to the receiver. By carefully observing the person, you can determine if the receiver has understood what you have said. Be careful that your facial expressions and body movements do not contradict your spoken words. Table 9-1 describes various behavioral styles of nonverbal communicators, and Box 9-1 defines some common American gestures.

PATIENT-CENTERED PROFESSIONALISM

- How can paying attention to a patient's body language improve communication between a medical assistant and the patient?
- What are some things that could happen if a patient's body language and nonverbal communication are ignored?
- Besides body language, what are some other nonverbal elements that could help you provide better care to patients?

EFFECTIVE LISTENING

Listening plays a key role in the communication process. Developing good listening skills takes practice. However, being a good listener will improve your skill in other areas of communication as well. When patients sense that you are listening to them, they become more relaxed and ready to communicate. This helps you establish rapport and prepares the patient for communicating with other members of the health care team. To listen effectively, you need to concentrate on the message, analyze the message, and provide feedback.

TABLE 9-1	Behavioral Styles of Nonverbal Communicators*		
	Confusion or Lack of Interest	**Understanding**	**Anger**
Gestures	Fidgeting	Reaching out	Pointing finger
Facial expressions	Blank look	Attentive	Frowning Rolling eyes
Eye contact	Downcast eyes	Direct	Glaring Staring
Posture	Slumped	Relaxed	Rigid
Tone	Weak or quiet	Appropriate volume	Loud
Rate of speech	Hesitant or slow	Matches situation	Fast Precise

*By carefully observing the nonverbal actions of the receiver, the sender of a message can decide how well it was understood and even if it has been accepted.

BOX 9-1 Common American Gestures

Greeting Gestures

- Handshake (firm, solid grip)
- Direct eye contact (when greeting and talking)
- Arm raised, and the open hand waves back and forth (signals "hello" or "goodbye"; also used in attempt to get someone's attention)

Beckoning Gestures

- Waving to another and then scooping the hand inward (signals a person to "come over")
- Raising the index finger toward one's face, and making a "curling" motion with that finger (beckons a person to "come closer")

Other Nonverbal Gestures

- Palm facing out with the index and middle fingers in a V shape (indicates a "victory" or "peace" sign)
- Closed fist with the thumb up (indicates approval ["good job," "way to go"] or hitchhiking)
- Whistling (indicates approval and recognition)
- Nodding or shaking the head (indicates "yes" or "no")

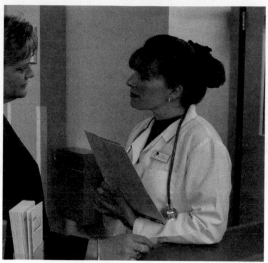

Fig. 9-5 A medical assistant listens carefully to a patient's concerns.

Concentrate on the Message

As a medical assistant, you will use your listening skills daily in all your routine activities. For example, one of your typical duties may be to listen and record why patients have come to the office (Fig. 9-5). You will also need to be a good listener when receiving oral instructions from the physician, co-workers, and patients. If you allow distracters to interfere with your listening, you will not obtain the information you need. This can affect the care that patients receive by causing confusion, miscommunication, and delays. Such communication mistakes can be costly in terms of time, money, goodwill, and reputation of the health care team.

Being a good listener as a medical assistant requires you to concentrate on the message being sent by the patient and its purpose. There are two types of listening: passive and active.

Passive listening involves hearing what the speaker is saying, but not listening with enough effort to become personally, intensely involved in what is being said. Examples of passive listening are cooking while listening to the television, doodling on paper while the teacher is talking in class, and looking through the patient's chart while the patient chats about the weather.

Active listening requires you to demonstrate listening by maintaining eye contact and providing responses (feedback) to indicate that you are listening and really thinking about what is being said. Unless you are listening actively to the patient, you may not hear or understand part of the message.

Analyze the Message

Active listeners analyze or evaluate the speaker's words as well as the person's posture, facial expressions, tone, mannerisms, and general appearance. Analyzing the message involves thinking on the part of the listener. To analyze a message, the following two conditions must be met:

1. The listener must be *able* to understand the message. This depends on the listener's vocabulary and attitudes. If you are listening and hear words you do not understand, ask for clarification. When patients are listening to you, confirm their understanding by paraphrasing, clarifying, validating, or encouraging them to repeat the message back to you. Use the patient's nonverbal clues to help you understand the meaning of the message while you are listening.
2. The listener must be *willing* to understand the message. A listener must want to grasp the meaning of the message and be willing to understand the speaker's point of view. As a health professional, you must overcome feelings of **prejudice** (negative opinion toward an individual because of his or her affiliation with a specific group) and avoid **stereotyping** (believing that all members of a culture or group are the same). Not accepting patients as

they are interferes with your ability to listen to what they are saying. When you stereotype or have feelings of prejudice toward patients, you make automatic assumptions about them that may or may not be true. If you consider a patient to be uncooperative, you may not accept the information the patient is giving you as true. This may cause you to respond incorrectly to the patient.

When listening to and responding to children, take special care to listen actively (Box 9-2). Children may not be as effective as adults at conveying their message because of their vocabulary level, or they may simply be uncomfortable or in pain.

As a medical assistant, you will need to listen in a variety of ways, both in person and on the phone. You can even apply active listening skills when reading written communication such as mail, faxes, letters, memos, and e-mail by "listening" between the lines to such factors as tone and perspective of the writer. You can become an active listener by practicing good listening skills and by always striving to concentrate on both the verbal and nonverbal messages being sent (Table 9-2).

Provide Feedback

Feedback is incredibly important. Feedback from the listener (receiver) helps the speaker (sender) know if the message has been received. The type of feedback given by a receiver affects the sender's message. Giving a quizzical glance, having an expression of confusion, or giving the appearance of boredom sends a message back to the sender. If a patient senses that the medical assistant is distracted or preoccupied while sending the message, the patient may tune out the message altogether.

The following factors influence a receiver's feedback and may cause roadblocks to effective communication:

- *Background of the receiver.* This includes the receiver's personality, life experiences, knowledge of the subject area being covered, and interest in hearing or motivation to listen to the message being sent. If the receiver is not interested, there will be minimal or no feedback.
- *Appearance of the sender or message being sent.* This can present roadblocks if the appearance is distracting or unprofessional. If the sender looks unkempt or does not speak clearly, or if a message contains bad grammar or spelling errors, the message is either lost to the receiver or seen as unimportant.
- *Skills of the sender and receiver.* The sender of a message needs to organize the message based on the receiver's vocabulary and

---

BOX 9-2	**Guidelines in Communicating with Children**

1. Be a good listener.
2. Let children speak at their own speed. Do not rush them or supply words. Let them complete their own thoughts and sentences.
3. Encourage self-talk.
4. Talk to children with words they can easily understand.
5. Be aware of situations that might be frightening to children, and try to reassure them.

TABLE 9-2	**Six Steps to Becoming a Better Listener**
L	1. Look at the entire delivery of the message. Read facial expression, posture, and gestures.
I	2. Interruptions should be avoided. Give your full attention to the speaker, and listen to his or her needs.
S	3. Stay involved. Do not think about other things you have to do. Remember, not everyone is a dynamic speaker, but all speakers have something important to say.
T	4. Transmit feedback based on your understanding of the message. Put yourself in the speaker's shoes. Ask probing questions and provide statements (without interrupting) that indicate your understanding. Listen until you have heard the entire message.
E	5. Evaluate the information thoroughly. Use all aspects of the communication process to draw your conclusions.
N	6. Neutralize bias and negative attitudes from your evaluation process. Treat the speaker with respect. Accept people for who they are, and do not let your attitudes interfere with listening carefully.

comprehension level. Ideally, the skills of the sender and receiver should match. A message that is "over the head" of a patient will not be understood. In the same way, using the wrong word (e.g., "Pacific" instead of "specific") changes the meaning of the intended message. A patient who understands the difference between these words may receive the impression that the medical assistant does not pay attention to detail and may even be careless about the patient's care. Even if the receiver understands the message, his or her impression of the sender is affected.

PATIENT-CENTERED PROFESSIONALISM

- How are relations with patients improved when medical assistants have good listening skills?
- How do poor listening skills interfere with a medical assistant's ability to provide quality patient care?
- How do prejudices and stereotyping interfere with the medical assistant's ability to communicate effectively with patients?
- How can effective use of feedback increase the likelihood that patients will communicate clearly and openly with the medical assistant?

EFFECTIVE WRITTEN COMMUNICATION

People judge a medical office by how its employees look, act, think, speak, and write. If a letter with grammatical and spelling errors is sent to a patient, the patient will have a negative feeling about the medical office and may not value the contents of the letter. Good writing skills are also needed to chart properly. Chart notes must be clear, concise, and precise when recording care given to the patient. Remember that written documentation serves as a permanent, legal record of care provided to a patient. If it is not documented or if the documentation is not clear, there is no proof that a procedure took place.

Rules and principles of grammar exist to help us write clearly and effectively. It is important to know the parts of speech used to create sentences, as well as the correct way to capitalize, use numbers, and use punctuation. Further, it is helpful to study words that are frequently misused and misspelled. This section covers the major areas that often cause problems in written communication.

Grammar

Grammar is the study of words and their relationship to other words in a sentence. A **sentence** is a group of words that expresses a complete thought. The different types of words that make up sentences are referred to as the "parts of speech." There are eight parts of speech: **nouns, pronouns, verbs, adjectives, adverbs, prepositions, conjunctions,** and **interjections.**

Parts of Speech

In order to express a complete thought, a sentence must contain a **subject** (what is being discussed) and a verb (action word) (Box 9-3). A subject is usually a noun or pronoun. Understanding the purpose of each part of speech will help you write sentences that are correct, clear, and professional (Table 9-3). Numbers may be used as nouns or adjectives. Take care to express them correctly when writing (Box 9-4).

Punctuation

Punctuation helps to separate, emphasize, and clarify the different ideas within sentences and between groups of sentences (Table 9-4). Incorrect punctuation marks can change the meaning of a sentence. Carefully proofread everything you write to be sure that you have used the correct punctuation.

Word Choice

Words that sound alike, look alike, or are pronounced exactly alike can be confusing and will

---

BOX 9-3 Sentence Structure

- A *sentence* is a group of words that expresses a *complete* thought.
- A *subject* is usually a noun or pronoun and indicates who is speaking or what the sentence involves. The subject often comes first in a sentence.
  Example: The patient has arrived. (*Patient* is the subject.)
- A *simple sentence* expresses only one thought.
  Example: The patient has arrived. (One thought is expressed.)
- A *compound sentence* expresses two or more thoughts, and the thoughts are joined by a conjunction.
  Example: The patient has arrived, and the physician is ready to see him. (Two thoughts are expressed: one about the patient and one about the physician.)

TABLE 9-3   Using the Parts of Speech Correctly

Part of Speech	What It Is	Examples	Function in Sentence	Sentence Examples
Noun	A word used to name things, including people, places, objects, and ideas.	Medical assistant, Calvin, phlebotomist, woman, Boston, city, store.	Often used as the subject, or the "thing" the sentence is talking about.	The *doctor* vacations in *Florida* every *year.* The *medical assistant* took his *blood pressure.*
Pronoun	A word used to take the place of a noun.	I, we, you, they, he, her, them, no one, someone, who, me, our.	Used as the subject of a sentence, to show ownership (e.g., his, hers, theirs, ours), or to talk about another person in the sentence.	Pete took *him* to the doctor's office. Give *me* my pencil.
Verb	A word or phrase used to express action, a condition, or a state of being.	Run, walk, eat, ask, is, has, was, seems, should have been.	Used to explain what is "happening" to the subject of the sentence.	The patient *came* to the office. He *is* a medical assistant. The child *seems to be* confused.
Adjective	A word used to describe a noun or pronoun.	Good, better, best, green, tall, heavy, nice, discolored, uneven, swollen.	Provides more information about a noun or pronoun (e.g., tells what kind, which one, or how many).	The *new* medical assistant started yesterday. There are *three* nurses in the office.
Adverb	A word used to describe a verb, adjective, or another adverb.	Quickly, evenly, carefully, well, too, very, soon, there, nearly.	Provides more information about how something happened or was done (e.g., tells where, when, how, why, or to what extent).	Put the chart *there.* *Carefully* remove the sutures. It is *too* late.
Preposition	A word used to begin a prepositional phrase.	*To* the left, *around* the corner, *over* the top, *before* the surgery.	Used to show the relationship between a noun and the rest of the sentence.	The request *from* the patient was *for* an afternoon appointment. The referral was received *after* lunch.
Conjunction	A word used to join words or groups of words.	And, or, but, nor, for, yet, since, if, because.	Connects related items or groups of words within a sentence; also used to join two short sentences to make one longer sentence.	The supplies *and* equipment arrived today. The patient would have been on time, *but* her car broke down.
Interjection	A word used to express strong feeling or emotion.	Wow! Yikes! Ouch! Oh.	Often used alone and followed by an exclamation point.	*Wow!* What an improvement. *Oh,* I forgot to leave a message.

TABLE 9-4 Using Punctuation Correctly

Punctuation	Symbol	How It Is Used	Sentence Examples
Period	.	To show where one statement or command ends and the next sentence begins.	The patient called for an appointment. Please pull the patient's records.
Question mark	?	To show where a question ends and the next sentence begins.	Will the doctor be available this afternoon? What is the fee for today's visit?
Exclamation mark	!	To add emphasis to the end of a sentence expressing strong feelings or emotion or to an interjection.	Congratulations! We are proud of you. You did it!
Comma	,	1. To separate two or more complete thoughts in a sentence joined by *and, but, or,* etc. 2. To separate items in a list or groups of words within a sentence. 3. To signal the reader to pause after an introductory word or group of words.	1. I left the patient with instructions, and I plan to follow up tomorrow. 2. The pens, pencils, and markers arrived with our order. 3. First, let me explain the procedure.
Semicolon	;	To join two or more complete thoughts in a sentence when *and, but, or,* or *nor* is not used.	The medical assistant has a new stethoscope; she prefers the other one. We have swabs; however, there may not be enough.
Colon	:	1. To introduce a list or an example or examples. 2. To add emphasis to a word.	1. We have the following: paper towels, antiseptic soap, and handrub. 2. There can be only one reason why she is late: illness.
Dash	—	To emphasize or separate something in a sentence.	This year's conference will be in Portland—be prepared for rain. He tried again—for the third time.
Apostrophe	'	1. To form contractions. 2. To show ownership.	1. It's been a great day. 2. Nate's lab coat is clean.
Parentheses	( )	To set off words that provide additional information or explanation.	The formula (see page 53) will help you make the calculation. Her aunt (the mayor) is visiting today.
Quotation marks	" "	1. To set off dialogue (conversations). 2. To signal use of the exact words of others. 3. To emphasize a term.	1. "Yes, it is," he replied. 2. The patient reports ". . . a bad feeling in my stomach, and a headache that has lasted for three days." 3. The term "fax" is often used to mean "facsimile."

BOX 9-4 Using Numbers in Writing*

- Numbers from one through nine should be spelled out; numbers 10 and up should be written numerically.
  Examples:
  The speaker has two hours to give the presentation.
  There are 26 pairs of nonsterile gloves left in the box.
- Numbers that begin sentences should be spelled out even if they are greater than nine.
  Example: Twenty people applied for the job.
- Fractions standing alone should be spelled out; when several fractions are being discussed, write them numerically.
  Examples:
  More than three fourths of the patients have medical insurance.
  Between $\frac{3}{4}$ and $\frac{7}{8}$ of all patients live within a 20-mile radius of the office.
- Ages are spelled out unless the age is being referred to as a statistic.
  Examples:
  Sue began working for the physician at the age of twenty-three.
  All patients over the age of 50 are sent for an annual colonoscopy.

*These general guidelines may vary according to the medical specialty and subject and the publisher and textbook, as in this text (e.g., 2 hours; age 23 years).

BOX 9-5 Words Frequently Misspelled in Medical Communication

abscess	concede	physician
accommodate	definitely	physiological
agglutinate	diarrhea	pneumonia
aggressive	embarrassing	questionnaire
analysis	fluctuation	rheumatism
benefited	forty	schedule
calendar	license	sphygmomanometer
canceled	negligence	stethoscope
clientele	ophthalmoscope	surgeon
committee	patients	vacuum

BOX 9-6 Spelling Hints

What Do You Do When Choosing "IE" Or "EI"?
Use "i" before "e" except after "c" ...

thief	chief
believe	friend
conceive	perceive

... or when it sounds like an "ay," as in "neighbor" and "weigh":

weigh	vein
eight	their

What Do You Do When Adding Endings To Words?
If a word ends in a consonant, repeat the consonant if it is preceded or followed by a vowel:

ship	shipped
bag	baggage

In words ending in a silent "e," the "e" is usually dropped if the ending begins with a vowel (e.g., "ing"):

use	using
decorate	decorating

cause miscommunication if not correctly applied. Medical assistants must choose the word that expresses the correct meaning for the situation. Study the words in Table 9-5 so that you will be able to use them correctly.

Spelling

Spelling words incorrectly not only creates an unprofessional impression but also can cause misunderstandings and mistakes in the treatment of patients. "Ilium" and "ileum" are pronounced the same way, but *ilium* refers to the hip area, whereas *ileum* refers to the intestinal area—the difference of one letter! Surgery on the incorrect body part (ilium or ileum) could be potential malpractice. Spelling problems often occur when there are double-letter combinations (e.g., accommodate, committee) and when trying to decide if a word is one word or two

(e.g., cannot, percent, all right). Box 9-5 shows other words that are frequently misspelled in medical communication. Study these words to reduce the chance of spelling them incorrectly. Box 9-6 provides hints to help you when spelling difficult words.

TABLE 9-5   Frequently Used Sound-Alike Words*

Word Pair	Definitions	Usage Examples
1. access	1. To gain admission (access) to; to get at	1. The door was locked, so he could not **access** the papers.
2. excess	2. Too much	2. **Excess** fat in one's diet is not good.
1. advise	1. To recommend	1. I **advise** you to hurry up.
2. advice	2. A helpful suggestion	2. I will take your **advice.**
1. affect	1. To change or influence (verb)	1. Your mood **affects** your behavior.
2. effect	2. Result; to bring out (noun)	2. The **effect** was positive.
1. already	1. Previously	1. We have **already** finished.
2. all ready	2. Prepared	2. We are **all ready** to go.
1. altogether	1. Entirely	1. It is **altogether** too time consuming.
2. all together	2. Everyone in a group	2. We were **all together** for Thanksgiving.
1. always	1. At all times	1. I **always** brush my teeth after meals.
2. all ways	2. All means or methods	2. Have you tried **all ways** possible to solve the problem?
1. anyway	1. In any case	1. He decided to go **anyway.**
2. any way	2. Any method	2. Is there **any way** you will reconsider?
1. assistance	1. To help	1. The doctor needs your **assistance.**
2. assistants	2. More than one person	2. All of the medical **assistants** were present.
1. awhile	1. For a short time	1. They talked **awhile** on the phone.
2. a while	2. A short period of time	2. In **a while,** we will close the office.
1. council	1. A group that advises	1. The national **council** meets each year.
2. counsel	2. To advise	2. The experienced medical assistant **counseled** the new assistant about a difficult situation.
1. disinterested	1. Unbiased	1. He is considered a **disinterested** voter because he favors neither candidate.
2. uninterested	2. Having no interest	2. The lecture was boring, so the listeners quickly became **uninterested.**
1. every day	1. Each day	1. Take some time for yourself **every day.**
2. everyday	2. Daily	2. Communication is an **everyday** occurrence.
1. farther	1. Physical distance (measurable)	1. She walked **farther** than she had ever gone.
2. further	2. Additional time or quantity	2. We will need **further** research to make the decision.
1. fewer	1. When items can be counted	1. We have **fewer** patients than last year.
2. less	2. When quantities cannot be counted	2. **Less** time should be wasted.
1. its	1. Shows possession	1. The dog dropped **its** bone.
2. it's	2. Contraction for "It is"	2. It looks like **it's** going to rain today.
1. patience	1. A sense of calm; waiting	1. Waiting takes **patience.**
2. patients	2. People seeking the care of a physician or other health care provider	2. There are 10 **patients** scheduled this morning.
1. principle	1. Doctrine	1. Follow the established ethics and **principles** of your profession.
2. principal	2. A person who is in a leading position	2. The **principal** called the teachers to a meeting.
1. rode	1. To have ridden	1. We **rode** the bus to work.
2. road	2. A path	2. The **road** was bumpy.
1. stationary	1. Not movable	1. The car that ran out of gas remained **stationary**.
2. stationery	2. Paper used to write letters	2. Use the office **stationery** to write the letter.

TABLE 9-5   Frequently Used Sound-Alike Words*—cont'd

Word Pair	Definitions	Usage Examples
1. than 2. then	1. Used in a comparison 2. Tells when	1. We need more **than** that amount. 2. First, get the towels; **then**, place them near the sink.
1. their 2. there 3. they're	1. Belonging to them 2. A location or direction 3. Contraction for "they are"	1. **Their** car is parked in the lot. 2. You can find the records over **there**. 3. **They're** leaving the office.
1. to 2. too 3. two	1. In the direction of 2. How much or to what degree 3. How many; number	1. The patient went **to** the office. 2. The patient's mother came, **too**. 3. The **two** walked to the door together.
1. your 2. you're	1. Belonging to you 2. Contraction for "you are"	1. You dropped **your** pen. 2. **You're** going to pass the test.

*To identify the correct word or meaning, decide how the word is used in the sentence.

PATIENT-CENTERED PROFESSIONALISM

- In what ways do the written communication skills of medical assistants influence patients' attitudes, confidence, and cooperation?
- Why is the use of good grammar so important when charting? How can improper grammar in charting affect patient care?

EFFECTIVE COMMUNICATION USING ELECTRONIC TECHNOLOGY

Just 10 to 20 years ago, no one would have ever considered using electronic technology to communicate in a medical office. Today, however, medical assistants and other health professionals must use electronic technology on a daily basis. Although most patients prefer speaking to "real people," and there is no replacement for in-person communication when discussing a health problem, electronic technology provides another way for patients to receive information and contact the medical office. As with all types of communication, care must be taken to communicate effectively and with confidentiality. Many of the same principles for effective verbal, nonverbal, and written communication apply when sending and receiving messages electronically.

To function in a modern medical office, medical assistants need to understand new and evolving technologies and develop the correct skills to use them effectively. Communicating through speaking or writing typically does not require special equipment. However, electronic information systems require properly functioning software, hardware, and processing equipment to be in place before the message can be sent. Four types of electronic technology used to send and receive messages in the medical office are voice mail systems, websites, fax machines, and electronic mail (e-mail).

Voice Mail

A *voice mail system* is an automated answering device. It allows the person calling on the phone to leave a voice message when the receiver is not available to take the call. The message is saved (stored) on a computer or an answering machine and can be retrieved later when it is convenient for the receiver to respond. In a medical office, voice mail should be retrieved at the same times each day (e.g., on arrival in the morning, after lunch hour). The voice mail system should provide callers with a time they can expect their call to be returned. The system should also provide instructions for emergency situations (e.g., "If this is an emergency, press '0,' call 911, or proceed to the emergency room"). The system is meant to help, not to replace, the receptionist. All incoming calls are immediately routed to the proper location (e.g., prescription refills, scheduling or billing department). Setting up a voice mail system can be done through the telephone company or by purchasing a software package.

Advantages

- People can call all day or at any hour to leave a message.
- Messages can be retrieved from other locations.
- Length of the message is reduced because communication is only one way.

Disadvantages

- Some people want to speak to a person immediately.
- Some messages may be incoherent.

Website

A *website* usually is created to provide information about the practice to patients and the community. Items that may be on a website include but are not limited to the following:

1. Directions to the practice
2. Hours of operation
3. Practice philosophy
4. Billing and insurance information
5. Information on the medical staff
6. Answers to the most frequently asked questions (FAQs)

Advantages

- Websites can answer some types of questions (e.g., hours, location, services) and save patients the time and effort of calling to ask.
- Websites can be quickly updated and are available 24 hours a day, 7 days a week.

Disadvantages

- All patients may not have access to the Internet.
- Providing a website may require staff members who can develop, program, and maintain the technical aspects of the website.

Fax Machine

A facsimile, or **fax,** machine converts written material or pictures into electronic impulses that are transmitted by telephone lines to other locations with similar equipment. Received messages are recorded magnetically and can be printed as a *hard copy* (on paper) by using a computer printer or fax machine. The material received is a duplicate of the original that was sent. Box 9-7 lists some important considerations for faxing materials.

Advantages

- Messages are sent and received rapidly.
- Faxing materials is often relatively inexpensive.
- Faxes are now considered forms of original and legal documents.

Disadvantages

- Extra care must be taken to maintain patient confidentiality when faxing.
- Not all patients have access to a fax machine.

BOX 9-7   Fax Transmission Protocol

- Health information should be faxed only when absolutely necessary.
- For any fax using thermal paper, the fax should be photocopied before filing in the patient's record because the print on thermal paper fades over time.
- Always use a cover sheet when faxing materials. Include the sender's and the receiver's telephone numbers, fax numbers, and the name of the contact person, as well as a confidentiality disclaimer.
- Ask for the receiving office to confirm receipt of the material.
- If information is confidential, arrange for the recipient to be available when the office will fax the documents.

Electronic Mail

- Written messages can be transmitted by electronic mail *(e-mail).* Messages are sent as electronic signals from one computer to another. E-mail is faster and less expensive than mailing a letter. Office e-mail messages should be answered at least once a day. E-mail is becoming more and more common. To communicate clearly and professionally, follow established "etiquette" guidelines (proper form and manners) when e-mailing (Box 9-8).

Advantages

- Messages can be sent to groups of people at one time (e.g., all Medicare patients).
- E-mail is available 24 hours a day.
- Messages are sent and received rapidly.
- Sender can verify that messages were received.
- Staff is not making multiple phone calls or stuffing letters.

PATIENT-CENTERED PROFESSIONALISM

- How are patients affected when medical assistants do not know and follow established guidelines when using electronic technology (e.g., voice mail, fax, e-mail)?
- How can you help ensure electronic technology is used in a way that provides convenience to patients but does not make them feel as if they are "just another patient"?

BOX 9-8 E-Mail Etiquette

1. Keep messages professional and to the point.
2. Do not type in "ALL CAPS." This creates the impression of shouting or yelling.
3. Use the "spell check" to create a professional document.
4. Respond to e-mail messages in a timely manner.
5. Be respectful to the receiver. Avoid sarcasm.
6. Do not forward copies of an e-mail to others unless instructed to do so by the sender.
7. Do not send confidential information.

Disadvantages

- It is easy to send a message to the wrong person and thus jeopardize patient confidentiality.
- Once a message is sent, it often cannot be "unsent" or canceled.
- All patients may not have access to e-mail.

CONCLUSION

A medical assistant relies on some form of communication every day to exchange information with patients. Communication must be clear, correct, and professional. The way you communicate creates an impression of you and the entire health care team. Communicating effectively and listening actively help to reduce misunderstandings and mistakes in the medical office. You improve your communication skills by understanding, applying, and practicing the principles of effective verbal, nonverbal, and written communication. Effective communication skills are an essential component of patient-centered professionalism.

SUMMARY

Reinforce your understanding of the material in this chapter by reviewing the curriculum objectives and key content points below.

1. Define, appropriately use, and spell all the Key Terms for this chapter.
   - Review the Key Terms if necessary.
2. State the goal of the communication process.
   - Communication is the sharing of information.
3. List and describe the three components of the communication process.

- The sender can be the patient or the medical assistant.
- The receiver can be the patient or the medical assistant.
- The message must be clearly conveyed by the sender and needs to be understood by the receiver.

4. List and describe the four steps in sending a message that will be understood.
   - To send a message that will be understood, the sender must organize the message, prioritize the information, transmit the message, and evaluate the effectiveness of the message.
5. List the three types of distracters that can prevent a message from being sent or received.
   - The environment, improper use of grammar, and physical well-being can be major distracters when sending or receiving a message.
6. Explain how a verbal message can be misinterpreted.
   - Improper grammar, lack of understanding on the part of the listener, and biased or negative attitudes can cause messages to be misinterpreted.
7. Explain the process of sending a verbal message and evaluating its receipt.
   - To be heard, the sender must organize a message logically and deliver it to the receiver in a manner that is easily understood.
   - After a message has been sent, the sender must evaluate the effectiveness of the transmission.
8. List and describe three ways that people communicate nonverbally.
   - Nonverbal communication includes body language, appearance, and the distance between two people when communicating.
9. Explain how a nonverbal message can be misinterpreted.
   - When analyzing a message being sent, the receiver must evaluate both verbal and nonverbal communications. When nonverbal communication does not match the verbal communication, conflicting messages are sent.
   - Patients of different cultures may have different beliefs and standards concerning body language.
10. List the three components of effective listening.
    - Effective listening requires that a listener concentrates, analyzes, and provides feedback.
11. Compare and contrast active and passive listening and give an example of each.

- Active listening requires the listener to respond to the speaker's message with some type of verbal or nonverbal feedback (e.g., answer to a direct question).
- Passive listening does not require the recipient's full attention (e.g., talking on the phone while watching TV).

12. State six steps to becoming a better listener.
    - Analyze or evaluate the speaker's words, posture, facial expressions, tone, mannerisms, and general appearance.
    - Refer to Table 9-2.

13. Recognize the parts of speech and give an example of each.
    - Every sentence must have a subject and a verb.
    - Words are classified into eight components, or parts of speech.
    - Refer to Table 9-3.

14. Demonstrate correct use of punctuation.
    - The way a sentence is written or spoken can alter the meaning of that sentence (e.g., "The panda eats shoots and leaves" vs. "The panda eats, shoots, and leaves").

15. Explain the importance of choosing the correct words.
    - Some words sound alike and can cause miscommunication if not used properly (e.g., *patients* vs. *patience*).
    - Miscommunication can lead to costly mistakes (e.g., *ilium* vs. *ileum*).

16. List six words that are frequently misspelled in the medical office.
    - Refer to Box 9-5.
    - Medical terminology must be spelled correctly or errors can occur in record keeping, billing, or even treatment.

17. Explain the importance of understanding how to communicate effectively using electronic technology.

- It is essential for medical assistants to be comfortable communicating with electronic technology because it is part of everyday life.

18. List the different types of electronic technology used for communication in a medical office.
    - Medical offices use voice mail systems, websites, fax machines, and e-mail to communicate with patients and other health professionals.

19. List six guidelines for e-mail etiquette.
    - Be just as courteous and professional in e-mail communication as you would on the phone, in a letter, or face-to-face. Never type in all-capital letters; you will appear to be yelling at the recipient.
    - Use "spell check" before you send e-mail.
    - Be concise and professional in tone.
    - Respond to e-mails in a timely manner.
    - Do not send confidential information via e-mail.

20. Analyze a realistic medical office situation and apply your understanding of effective communication to determine the best course of action.
    - Cultural and ethnic barriers can cause misunderstandings and miscommunication.
    - Make every attempt to understand what patients may be communicating with their actions and expressions in addition to what they say.

21. Describe the impact on patient care when medical assistants consistently apply the principles of effective communication.
    - When communication is effective, confusion or even dangerous mistakes can be prevented and patient care is not adversely affected.

FOR FURTHER EXPLORATION

1. **Research the topic of communication to improve your communication skills.** Communication skills are crucial to a successful patient–medical assistant relationship. Locate information on ways you can communicate more clearly with patients and help to establish good relationships.

   Keywords: Use the following keywords in your search: communicating with patients, communication techniques, communication.

2. **Research techniques for interpreting nonverbal communication.** Patients provide a wealth of information nonverbally about their feelings, beliefs, and comfort. Understanding how to interpret a patient's body language is important for effective communication.

   Keywords: Use the following keywords in your search: nonverbal communication, body language, patient body language.

3. **Research effective listening techniques to improve your listening skills.** Even if you are not a good listener, you can improve through learning and practice. Locate information and tips on how to be a better listener.

   Keywords: Use the following keywords in your search: listening skills, listening to patients.

4. **Research effective written communication to improve your writing skills.** As with listening, writing skills can be improved through learning and practice. Locate information and tips on how you can improve your writing skills.

   Keywords: Use the following keywords in your search: writing skills, writing styles, grammar, spelling.

5. **Research communication through electronic technology.** Current advances in technology allow patients or prospective patients to communicate with or gather information about the medical practice. Locate information and tips on how you can use electronic technology to communicate effectively in the medical office.

   Keywords: Use the following keywords in your search: website creation, facsimile, electronic mail, voice mail, computers in medical practice.

Chapter Review

Vocabulary Review

Matching

Match each term with the correct definition.

A. active listening

B. adjective

C. adverb

D. conjunction

E. distracter

F. feedback

G. grammar

H. interjection

I. noun

J. preposition

K. pronoun

L. punctuation

M. sentence

N. subject

O. verb

_____ 1. Verbal or nonverbal indication that a message was received

__B__ 2. Word used to describe a noun or pronoun

__J__ 3. Word used to begin a prepositional phrase

__H__ 4. Word used to express strong feelings or emotion

__O__ 5. Word in a sentence that expresses action or a state of being

_____ 6. Occurs when a listener maintains eye contact and provides responses to the speaker

__D__ 7. Word used to join words or groups of words

__L__ 8. Marks within and between sentences that separate, emphasize, and clarify the different ideas within a sentence or group of sentences

__G__ 9. Study of words and their relationship to other words in a sentence

__E__ 10. Something that prevents the sender or receiver from giving full attention to the message

__I__ 11. Word used to name things, including people, places, objects, and ideas

_____ 12. Word used to describe a verb, an adjective, or an another adverb

__K__ 13. Word used to take the place of a noun

__M__ 14. Group of words that express a complete thought

_____ 15. Part of a sentence that expresses action or a state of being

Theory Recall

True/False

Indicate whether the sentence or statement is true or false.

_____ 1. The goal of communication is to clearly exchange information between a sender and a receiver.

_____ 2. Public space is considered to be 2 to 4 feet apart.

_____ 3. Active listening involves hearing what the speaker is saying but not listening with enough effort to become personally, intensely involved in what is being said.

_____ 4. In order to express a complete thought, a sentence must contain at least one noun and one pronoun.

_____ 5. A fax machine converts written material or pictures into electronic impulses that are transmitted by telephone lines to other locations with similar equipment.

Multiple Choice

Identify the letter of the choice that best completes the statement or answers the question.

1. Nonverbal communication comprises approximately _____ percent of all communication.
   A. 10
   B. 40
   C. 75
   D. 90

2. Which one of the following is NOT an important part of delivering messages?
   A. Not using slang terms
   B. Rate of speech that is neither too fast nor too slow
   C. Voice inflection
   D. Ability to multitask while delivering the message

3. _____ is a communication distracter.
   A. Quiet environment
   B. Incorrect use of grammar
   C. Climate-controlled temperature
   D. Quiet music in the background

4. When communicating with a patient, it is best to ask _____ questions.
   A. open-ended
   B. closed-ended

5. Interpreting body language is an important part of _____ communication.
   A. verbal
   B. nonverbal

6. Two typical nonverbal signals that our eyes send are pupil size and _____.
   A. iris color
   B. direction of gaze
   C. posture
   D. both A and B

7. _____ is NOT a nonverbal response.
   A. Singing
   B. Smiling
   C. Physical appearance
   D. Both B and C

8. Numbers may be used as nouns or _____.
   A. verbs
   B. adjectives
   C. adverbs
   D. pronouns

9. _____ is an automated answering device.
   A. Voice mail system
   B. Facsimile
   C. E-mail
   D. None of the above

10. Which of the following is a disadvantage of voice mail?
    A. People can call all day or at any hour to leave a message.
    B. Length of message is reduced because communication is one-way.
    C. Some people want to speak to a person immediately.
    D. Messages can be retrieved from other locations.

11. Which of the following is NOT an item that can be included on a website?
    A. Practice philosophy
    B. Hours of operation
    C. Billing and insurance information
    D. All of the above could be included.

12. Advantages of a website include all of the following EXCEPT that _____.
    A. it saves patients the time and effort of calling the office
    B. a Web site can be quickly updated
    C. it can provide answer to FAQs (frequently asked questions)
    D. patients may not have access to the Internet

13. Faxes *are* or *are not* considered forms of original and legal documents.
    A. are
    B. are not

14. A disadvantage of e-mail messages is that _____.
    A. e-mail is available 24 hours a day
    B. messages are sent and received rapidly
    C. messages once sent are often not retrievable
    D. verification can be made that a message was sent and received

15. A _____ sentence expresses only one thought.
    A. subject
    B. simple
    C. complex
    D. compound

16. Numbers that begin a sentence should be spelled out even if they are greater than _____.
    A. 3
    B. 5
    C. 7
    D. 9

17. Which one of the following is correctly spelled?
    A. abcess
    B. abscess
    C. absces
    D. abbscess

18. Which one of the following is correctly spelled?
    A. negligence
    B. nagligance
    C. negligance
    D. neglligence

19. Which one of the following is correctly spelled?
    A. theif
    B. percieve
    C. concieve
    D. believe

20. Always use a _____ when sending a fax.
    A. typewriter
    B. letter of introduction
    C. cover sheet
    D. reference page

Sentence Completion

Complete each sentence or statement.

1. Do not send _____ information via e-mail.

2. The acronym _____ outlines the six steps to becoming a better listener.

3. I (always/all ways) go to the park after school.

4. In (awhile/a while) we will go to the beach.

5. (Its/It's) not likely the order will arrive today.

Short Answers

1. State the goal of the communication process.

_____

_____

_____

2. List and describe the three components of the communication process.

_____

_____

_____

3. List the three components of effective listening.

_____

_____

_____

4. Explain the importance of choosing the correct words.

_____

_____

_____

Critical Thinking

Cassandra brought her mother, Elizabeth Seneca, to her doctor's appointment this morning. Mrs. Seneca has been feeling poorly for the past 4 days. Cassandra does not know what exactly is wrong. Kym, the medical assistant, takes Cassandra and her mother into the examination room and notices bruises on Mrs. Seneca's arm. Mrs. Seneca glances quickly around the room and sits with a sigh in the chair. She straightens her skirt and brushes at an invisible speck repeatedly. Kym asks Mrs. Seneca how she is feeling today. Cassandra answers immediately, "She is not eating, she barely sleeps, and she won't even go outside for some fresh air." Mrs. Seneca twists an almost shredded tissue in her hands. Kym looks directly at Mrs. Seneca and asks again how she is feeling. Mrs. Seneca looks up briefly. Kym notices that her pupils are large and that her mouth is set in a firm, thin line. Mrs. Seneca mumbles a response almost under her breath. Kym moves closer to Mrs. Seneca to hear her better, and Mrs. Seneca moves back farther on her chair. Kym steps away. "Are you in pain?" Kym asks. There still is no response. Kym washes her hands and gathers the equipment together to take Mrs. Seneca's pulse, respiration, and blood pressure. When she reaches out to take Mrs. Seneca's arm to help her roll up her sleeve, Mrs. Seneca quickly looks at her daughter and then back at the floor and at the same time bats away Kym's hand.

A. In your opinion, what do you think is going on with Mrs. Seneca?

B. What verbal communication leads you to your opinion?

C. What nonverbal communication leads you to your opinion?

D. What should be Kym's next step? Why?

Internet Research

Keyword: Interpreting body language

Research three websites. Create a list of 10 body language indicators. Describe what they indicate and how you can use this knowledge as a medical assistant. Cite the source(s) of your information.

What Would You Do?

If you have accomplished the objectives in this chapter, you will be able to make better choices as a medical assistant. Take a look at this situation and decide what you would do.

Panina is a former resident of the Middle East who moved to the United States with her husband, Abed, 6 months ago. Naturally, she brings with her the cultural and ethnic contexts of her homeland. Panina awakens one morning with a pain in her breast. She becomes concerned and calls a physician's office for an appointment. Because she has difficulty understanding the English language, she misunderstands the appointment time, and Panina and Abed arrive at the office an hour late. Abed demands to accompany his wife to the examination room. Therese, the medical assistant, tells Abed that they are late for the appointment and that he must stay in the waiting room while Panina is being examined. Panina, refusing eye contact with Therese, begins to cry. Abed becomes upset and tells Therese that the only way Panina will be examined is if he accompanies her to the room to explain to the male doctor what is wrong with her. Therese refuses, and Panina and Abed leave the office, threatening to tell all their friends how this office "just does not care about patients at all."

Effective communication helps eliminate misunderstandings. If you were the medical assistant in this situation, how could you have used your understanding of effective communication skills to help?

1. What role did Panina and Abed's cultural and ethnic background play in the misunderstandings in the physician's office? What role did communication skills play in the misunderstandings?

_____

_____

_____

2. What distracters may have caused the lack of communication between Panina and Therese?

_____

_____

_____

3. What nonverbal communication between Panina and Therese could have been recognized and used to diffuse the negative situation that occurred in the physician's office?

_____

_____

_____

4. Why is an understanding of ethnicity and cultural differences so important in the medical field?

_____

_____

_____

5. What body parts are involved in the communication of body language?

_____

_____

_____

Application of Skills

1. Underline the SUBJECT in each of the following sentences.
   A. We will open the office at 8:00 a.m.
   B. The physician is in a meeting at the hospital.
   C. Sharon stayed late to inventory the supplies.
   D. The committee will adjourn and reconvene tomorrow.

2. Underline the VERB in each of the following sentences.
    A. Sam ran quickly down the hall to grab the crash cart.
    B. Tomorrow, we will begin the new research project.
    C. Chelsea booked the reservations for the medical conference.
    D. Mrs. Jones seems to be unconscious.

3. Underline the PRONOUN(s) in each of the following sentences.
    A. She looked nauseated.
    B. Please pass me the stapler.
    C. Will they be done in the examination room soon?
    D. I would like to go over the end-of-month reports this afternoon.

4. Underline the ADJECTIVE(s) in each of the following sentences.
    A. This new brand of antibacterial soap smells like fresh lemons.
    B. The physician ordered two new oak computer desks for his office and two black leather chairs.
    C. The medical assistant just hired has exceptional skills.
    D. The casting room was left in a huge mess.

5. Underline the ADVERB(s) in each of the following sentences.
    A. Mrs. Thompson carefully removed the bandages from Lincoln's infected toe.
    B. We nearly didn't make the 1:00 o'clock flight.
    C. Angela lazily thumbed through an old magazine in the waiting room.
    D. Next year we are certainly going to need a larger office.

6. Underline the PREPOSITION(s) in each of the following sentences.
    A. The new clinic is just around the corner.
    B. Henry will have to go over to the hospital before he can file the insurance forms.
    C. Mickey reached across the minor surgery tray and contaminated the sterile field.
    D. Tressa, please go behind the curtain and change into the patient gown I left for you.

7. Underline the CONJUNCTION(s) in each of the following sentences.
    A. I ordered three pairs of turquoise scrubs and two of the raspberry ones as well.
    B. He could change Mr. Crinshaw's medication, but he is concerned that it will not be as effective.
    C. Since Sara stopped eating fast food, she has lost 15 pounds, but she is still 50 pounds overweight.
    D. The biopsy was delayed because the patient was not fasting.

8. Underline the INTERJECTION(s) in each of the following sentences.
    A. Stop! That really hurts.
    B. Perfect! Just a few more stitches and we will be all done.
    C. Oh, we will need a second opinion before we operate.
    D. Wonderful, Diane, you did a great job today; thank you.

9. Using Table 9-4 as a guideline, punctuate the following sentences.
    A. Where are my new scrubs I wanted to wear them today and if I cant find them were going to be late
    B. Have you seen their lab equipment theyre going to be hiring next week I would really like to work there
    C. Dr Xaxon the world renowned physician performed the procedure impeccably
    D. Katherine has given up smoking about five times but she cannot seem to break the habit

Chapter Quiz

Multiple Choice

Identify the letter of the choice that best completes the statement or answers the question.

1. _____ is NOT a component of the communication process.
   A. Organization
   B. Message
   C. Sender
   D. Receiver

2. Based on statistics, _____ percent of all communication is nonverbal.
   A. 10
   B. 25
   C. 75
   D. 90

3. The way a message is delivered is NOT as important as the message itself.
   A. True
   B. False

4. A _____ is anything that causes the sender or receiver of a message to not give full attention to the message.
   A. detractor
   B. distracter
   C. distortion
   D. deformation

5. Assessing _____ from the receiver allows you to determine if the message was understood the way it was intended.
   A. opinions
   B. responses
   C. feedback
   D. all of the above

6. _____ involves hearing what the speaker is saying but not listening with enough effort to become personally involved in what is being said.
   A. Passive listening
   B. Active listening
   C. Aggressive listening
   D. Unconscious listening

7. Acceptable personal space is used for those times of closeness and is typically _____ feet apart.
   A. 12 to 25
   B. 10 to 15
   C. $1\frac{1}{2}$ to $2\frac{1}{2}$
   D. 1 to $1\frac{1}{2}$

8. _____ help(s) separate, emphasize, and clarify the different ideas within sentences and between groups of sentences.
   A. Capitalization
   B. Punctuation marks
   C. Proofreading marks
   D. Adjectives

9. A word that shows action in a sentence is a(n) _____.
   A. subject
   B. noun
   C. adverb
   D. verb

10. A(n) _____ converts written material or pictures into electronic impulses that are transmitted by telephone lines and recorded magnetically and can be printed as a hard copy.
    A. voice mail
    B. e-mail
    C. facsimile
    D. telephone call

11. "The hemostats fell to the floor with a clang." Select the VERB.
    A. fell
    B. to the
    C. hemostats
    D. with

12. "The three medical assistants all went to lunch together yesterday." Select the SUBJECT.
    A. yesterday
    B. three
    C. medical assistants
    D. lunch

13. "Dr. Xaxon, the world-renowned physician, performed the procedure impeccably." Select the ADJECTIVE.
    A. Dr. Xaxon
    B. world-renowned
    C. performed
    D. procedure

14. "Good grief! What now?" Select the INTERJECTION.
    A. Good grief
    B. What
    C. now
    D. All of the above

15. "Quickly! We are very nearly there, Thom." Select the ADVERB.
    A. Quickly
    B. are
    C. very nearly
    D. Thom

16. Which one of the following sentences is punctuated correctly?
    A. In 3 weeks' time we'll have to begin school again.
    B. After surviving this ordeal the patient felt relieved.
    C. He replied "I have no idea what you mean."
    D. Its such a beautiful day that Ive decided to take the day off.

17. Which one of the following sentences is punctuated correctly?
    A. The problems involved in this operation are I think numerous.
    B. Yes Helen did mention that all three of you were coming to the medical conference.
    C. The patient used to live at 1721 Gretchen Avenue Kansas City MO but has since moved to 3rd Street West Holland Way Dubuque Iowa.
    D. Chris did not see how he could organize, write, and proofread the paper in only 2 hours.

18. Which one of the following sentences is punctuated incorrectly?
    A. Having cut the roses she decided to bring them to her friend in the hospital.
    B. Jillian, who had worked in the dress shop all summer, hoped to work there again during the Christmas holidays.
    C. "Oh no" Max exclaimed, "I think that Dr. Holmes wanted Mrs. Jenson's file immediately."
    D. I hope that someday, we can redecorate the reception area.

19. Which statement is correctly written?
    A. Wear are my new scrubs? I wanted to where them today, and if I can't find them wear going to be late.
    B. Were are my new scrubs? I wanted to wear them today, and if I can't find them where going to be late.
    C. Where are my new scrubs? I wanted to wear them today, and if I can't find them we're going to be late.
    D. Where are my new scrubs? I wanted to we're them today, and if I can't find them we're going to be late.

20. Which statement is correctly written?
    A. Have you seen their lab equipment? They're going to be hiring next week. I would really like to work there.
    B. Have you seen there lab equipment? Their going to be hiring next week. I would really like to work their.
    C. Have you seen they're lab equipment? Their going to be hiring next week. I would really like to work there.
    D. Have you seen their lab equipment? Their going to be hiring next week. I would really like to work they're.

10

OBJECTIVES

You will be able to do the following after completing this chapter:

Key Terms
1. Define, appropriately use, and spell all the Key Terms for this chapter.

Role of the Medical Assistant
2. Understand the role of the medical assistant in patient communication.
3. Explain the concept of *holistic* care.
4. List five ways you can improve communication with patients, and explain how better communication improves patient care and results in good service.
5. Explain the importance of handling patient complaints effectively.

Different Cultures
6. List three ways to establish trust with patients of different cultures.

Patients with Special Needs
7. List five considerations for communicating with a patient who is visually impaired.
8. List seven ways to communicate effectively with a patient who has hearing impairment.
9. List three considerations for accommodating patients with other physical disabilities.
10. List six considerations for communicating effectively with elderly patients.
11. List six considerations for communicating effectively with children.
12. Explain the considerations for communicating with patients with a below-normal ability to reason or think, with mental impairments, or with developmental delays.
13. Explain the importance of communicating effectively with the caregivers and families of mentally impaired and developmentally delayed patients.

Patient-Centered Professionalism
14. Analyze a realistic medical office situation and apply your understanding of effective communication with patients to determine the best course of action.
15. Describe the impact on patient care when medical assistants consistently apply the principles of effective communication when interacting with patients.

COMMUNICATING WITH PATIENTS

KEY TERMS

holistic Involving all health needs of the patient, including physical, emotional, social, economic, and spiritual needs (e.g., holistic patient care).

litigation A lawsuit.

maturation Growth and developmental process involving a person's physical, social, and emotional functioning.

rapport Harmonious relationship that considers both the physical and the emotional needs of those involved.

What Would You Do?

Read the following scenario and keep it in mind as you learn about communicating with patients in this chapter.

Mr. Joplin is a spry 82-year-old and still lives in his own home. His wife died about a year ago, but Mr. Joplin has no severe medical problems and is able to care for himself. He does have visual problems caused by cataracts in his left eye, as well as joint stiffness related to his age. John, the medical assistant, approaches Mr. Joplin to escort him to the examining room. John shouts at Mr. Joplin as if he has a hearing difficulty, then walks away without assisting Mr. Joplin from the chair. When John reaches the door, he looks over his shoulder, rolls his eyes, and shouts, "Do you need some help?" Mr. Joplin looks away and refuses any assistance. Dr. Smith examines Mr. Joplin and asks John to explain the treatment so Mr. Joplin will comply. John hurriedly tells Mr. Joplin one time what is expected, then returns him to the waiting room. Several days later, Mr. Joplin calls the office to tell the receptionist to cancel his next appointment because he is going to find a new physician.

John's poor communication skills caused Dr. Smith to lose Mr. Joplin as a patient. If you were the medical assistant in this situation, what would you have done to communicate more effectively with Mr. Joplin?

Communicating effectively with patients should be the primary goal of the medical office staff. As a medical assistant you will be expected to listen to, understand, and even anticipate patient needs. Each patient must be treated as an individual, and the staff's actions must convey to patients that each individual is important.

This chapter helps you learn to apply the principles of effective communication with patients in a medical setting.

≋ ROLE OF THE MEDICAL ASSISTANT

As an employee, the medical assistant has a responsibility to the physician and the patient to provide quality care. Communicating effectively with patients is a key factor in providing quality care. The medical assistant's role in promoting effective communication is to focus on the "customers" (patients) and their needs, strive for continuous improvement, and effectively handle patient complaints.

Focusing on the Patient

Patients and their families feel respected and well taken care of when their needs are met and their concerns are addressed immediately. When patients perceive that they are important to the health care team, they tend to follow the physician's plan of care. The medical assistant is the communication link between the patient and the physician, and thus the medical assistant–patient relationship could be key to the success of a patient's treatment. By using positive communication techniques, medical assistants can help ensure that patient needs are met and that their experience is positive (Fig. 10-1).

Keep in mind that patients' needs are not limited to their illness alone. **Holistic** health care deals with all the needs of the patient, including physical, emotional, social, economic, and spiritual needs. All of a patient's needs influence his or her behavior and compliance with treatment. This is why medical assistants must address all patient needs. A patient may not comply with treatment when he or she is nervous, angry, frightened, or confused about the illness or has financial problems. You must use what

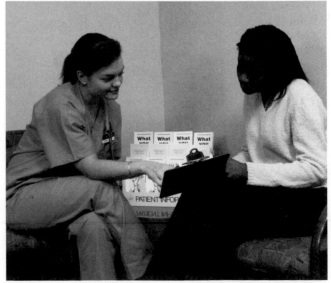

Fig. 10-1 Through positive communication techniques, the medical assistant can meet the needs of the patient.

you have learned about human relations and behavior to develop a working **rapport** with patients.

A patient undergoing treatment for muscle spasms definitely has physical needs, but you must also consider the patient's emotional needs and feelings about treatment. Consider where this patient is on Maslow's Hierarchy of Needs. If the muscle spasms result in missed work, the patient may be worried about money for treatment, food, rent, and other necessities.

Box 10-1 lists ways you can apply the principles of communication to address patient needs and concerns.

Striving for Improvement

Finding better ways to communicate with patients results in quality service and patient care. Identifying the patient's understanding of the disease process, treatments involved, and tests to be performed is necessary to meet the needs of the patient. You can assess patient understanding and improve communication in the following ways:

- Communicate in simple, everyday language.
- Ask patients to write down questions so the issues can be explained, reinforced, and discussed to clear up misunderstandings.
- Match your approach to the patient's level of readiness and ability to learn (Fig. 10-2).
- Identify any barriers to communication that may be evident, such as a history of noncompliance, a language barrier, reading ability, or physical or emotional state.
- Do not be afraid to say, "I don't know the answer." Remember that medical assistants do not know everything, but they do know how to find the answers.

Box 10-2 provides suggestions for improving communication during patient teaching.

Fig. 10-2 The medical assistant needs to individualize teaching techniques to match the patient's level of readiness.

BOX 10-1 **Ten Principles of Communication in the Medical Assistant—Patient Relationship**

1. Greet every patient and family member with a smile and a kind word.
2. Introduce yourself.
3. Explain all procedures before beginning the procedure and provide updates, no matter how minor.
4. Leave sufficient time for questions and answers.
5. Be available to listen when the patient has a need to complain or talk.
6. Try to resolve an issue without delay, or find someone who can resolve it.
7. Maintain a pleasant demeanor throughout the day even when stressed.
8. Dismiss the patient with a smile and a kind word.
9. Provide clear written instructions so that the patient is aware of follow-up plans.
10. Keep the patient informed with prompt phone calls (when appropriate) regarding test results. Remember that the patient is anxious and waiting.

Modified from "The Ten Commandments of Communication," courtesy Valentina M. Ramos, RN, Novi, Michigan.

BOX 10-2 **Effective Communication for Patient Teaching**

1. Assess the patient's readiness to learn.
2. Include the patient's family or support group in the treatment plan, if the patient agrees.
3. Allow adequate time for demonstration and return demonstration by the patient. Use positive reinforcement such as, "Yes, that is correct."
4. Provide time for questions and concerns to be expressed by the patient. Provide honest answers only within the scope of medical assisting training.
5. Assist patients in fitting the new behavior or procedure into their normal activities (e.g., a patient required to exercise may need suggestions for starting a routine).
6. Use age-appropriate wording and learning materials for better understanding.
7. Chart patient's reactions and comments concerning their level of understanding.

Use Table 10-1 to review positive communication techniques and Table 10-2 for barriers to communication.

Handling Patient Complaints

A patient may complain if he or she perceives the quality of the service to be unsatisfactory. Patient complaints generally fall into one of the following two categories:

1. *Administrative complaints* occur when the patient is unhappy with the performance of the support staff. Dissatisfaction may come from miscommunication or misunderstandings related to billing issues, telephone response time, waiting time, or office reception.

2. *Medical complaints* involve dissatisfaction with appointment access, poor referral follow-up, quality of service by the physician or clinical personnel, and limitation or denial of benefits.

Handling patient complaints requires the cooperation of all members of the health care team. Working together reduces the risk of a complaint not being handled promptly and can help relieve patient anxiety and hostility. Often, patients are angry and upset as well as hostile when voicing complaints. First, move the patient to a quiet area where he or she can express frustration out of view of the rest of the patients. Remain calm and matter-of-fact, and never return anger with anger. Handling patient complaints effectively can reduce

TABLE 10-1   Positive Communication Techniques

Technique and Meaning	Example	Value
Clarifying—seeks additional input from the patient to make clear that which is vague and to better understand the message received	**Patient:** "When I walk, I have this terrible pain in my leg." **MA:** "Tell me what you mean by terrible" or "Describe this pain."	Ensures no miscommunication and demonstrates to the patient a true interest in what the patient is saying
Focusing—expands or develops a single idea or point of view	**Patient:** "I have so many things I'm responsible for: my kids, my husband, my parents, my job." **MA:** "Of all the responsibilities you've mentioned, which is causing you the most worry?"	Directs the patient's energies to one topic
Reflecting—directs the patient's ideas, actions, thoughts, and feelings back to the patient	**Patient:** "I am so upset. I thought I would be well by now!" **MA:** "You sound upset that you're not fully recovered from your stroke?"	Allows the patient to hear and think about what he or she said and indicates that the patient's point of view has value
Restating—paraphrasing or repeating the main thought or idea expressed by the patient	**Patient:** "I can't sleep. I stay awake all night." **MA:** "You are having a problem sleeping?"	Lets the patient know that he or she has communicated his or her thoughts effectively
Silence—periods of no verbal communication	**Patient:** "I don't know how to explain it." **MA:** Needs to be aware of patient's nonverbal behavior. Says nothing but continues to maintain eye contact and show interest.	Can convey acceptance, support, and concern and allows the patient to organize his or her thoughts
Summarizing—organizes and sums up that which has gone on before and is a statement of main ideas expressed during an interaction	**Patient:** Interaction has taken place between the patient and the medical assistant. **MA:** "We have discussed . . ."	Important process because it serves as a review of information exchanged and allows both the patient and the medical assistant to come to an agreement about what has been discussed

MA, Medical assistant.

TABLE 10-2	Barriers To Effective Communication	
Technique and Meaning	**Example**	**Threat**
Defending—attempt to protect someone or something from negative verbal attack	**Patient:** "I don't like the way my doctor is handling my care." **MA:** "I'm sure your doctor has your best interests in mind."	Does not allow a patient to express an opinion; blocks further communication
Changing topics—introducing unrelated subjects	**Patient:** "I'm feeling depressed." **MA:** "Nice weather we're having."	Redirects patient's concerns and implies that his or her concerns are of no value
Making stereotyped comments—using trite or meaningless responses	**Patient:** "I'm too scared to have surgery." **MA:** "It's for your own good."	Implies patient's thoughts are unimportant
Rejecting—refusing to discuss ideas or topics with the patient	**Patient:** "I might as well just die and get it over with." **MA:** "That's silly! I don't want to hear that."	Closes off topic from further discussion and may cause patient to feel rejected

MA, Medical assistant.

the risk of **litigation** (a lawsuit). The following guidelines are useful for handling patient complaints:

- Take all complaints *seriously*. Write out all the facts of the complaint, no matter how trivial. Some complaints cannot be resolved, but they can be addressed.
- Use *tactful* (nonoffensive) language when responding to a complaint, and reassure the patient that the complaint will be investigated. Give the patient a time frame for resolution, and follow through with this plan.
- *Always* alert the physician or office manager about an unhappy patient so that he or she can defuse the situation immediately.
- *Always* inform the physician or office manager of any statements made by the patient that reflect a negative attitude. The patient's statements may reflect noncompliance with the prescribed treatment and could compromise the patient's ability to heal properly.

A large number of lawsuits result from careless actions or comments made by physicians and office staff when patients complain. A medical practice is less likely to be sued if the staff shows genuine concern for the patient's well-being by taking steps to correct problems promptly. Patients may not always remember what you did or what you said, but they will always remember *how* you made them feel. Another reason to take patient complaints seriously is that they may affect how managed care companies and state and federal agencies view the practice. Medicare has strict guidelines for handling patient complaints, and failure to follow them can lead to loss of service privileges.

PATIENT-CENTERED PROFESSIONALISM

- How does understanding the many aspects of a patient's illness (including effects on the patient's lifestyle, work, and family) allow medical assistants to provide better patient care?
- What can medical assistants do to improve their communication skills with the patient? How can a medical assistant with good communication skills affect the patient's experience?
- Why do you think patients are less likely to sue when their complaints have been taken seriously?

DIFFERENT CULTURES

You have learned how culture and belief systems affect patient behavior. In the same way, culture and belief systems also affect the way patients perceive what the health care team says and does. It is important to understand how to communicate effectively with patients of different cultures. Providing high-quality patient care means meeting patient needs in a manner that invokes trust, shows respect for cultural beliefs, and allows patients to maintain their dignity. This can only be accomplished by understanding patients' cultural systems and standard health procedures, family interactions, and value systems. Using your understanding of patients' cultural systems in your communication approach and eliminating negative personal beliefs will help you provide quality care to patients of all cultures.

Approach

As you have learned, your actions (nonverbal communication) and words (verbal communication) should take into consideration the patient's beliefs and level of understanding. All treatment plans must allow patients to maintain their self-esteem and help establish trust in the health care team. Ways to accomplish this are as follows:

- Involve the patient and patient's family in the decision-making process when possible. Encourage them to include their cultural beliefs if appropriate.
- Ask the patient's opinion, and encourage the patient to discuss issues and potential problems.
- Do not embarrass or anger the patient by arguing about his or her beliefs.
- Be sensitive to patients' needs as individuals to help avoid cultural conflicts.
- Demonstrate active listening, or patients may feel that they are not important to you.
- Provide honest feedback to patients continuously to demonstrate respect for their feelings.

As a medical assistant, you must strive to accommodate every patient's needs. When given individualized care and shown respect, a patient is more likely to follow a treatment plan.

Personal Beliefs

All patients need to be treated with dignity and respect. You will encounter patients whose cultural beliefs differ from your own. Stereotyping and any form of discrimination are not acceptable and cannot be tolerated. You must get rid of any negative beliefs so they do not affect your communication with or care for patients.

Not listening to or refusing to understand a particular culture's point of view limits the effectiveness of the health care process. If you show resistance in accepting a patient's cultural heritage or religious beliefs, this may weaken or destroy the trust that is necessary for effective treatment. The following guidelines can help you eliminate personal beliefs that are barriers to effective communication with patients:

- Do a perception check. Discuss your interpretation of the situation with the patient to see if it is correct; be specific.
- Listen to the patient's explanation and be empathetic to his or her situation.
- Answer questions within your scope of training. With the physician's guidance, explain the reasons for the needed changes and the importance of compliance.

- After the physician has explained the possible consequences of not following a treatment plan, be supportive.
- Respect the patient's decision and avoid a judgmental attitude.

Remember that the physician guides the patient care process. The medical assistant's role is an extension of the quality care process. You represent your physician, so "mirror your physician's image" to show acceptance of cultural differences.

PATIENT-CENTERED PROFESSIONALISM

- How can the medical assistant know if patients of other cultures understand what is expected of them?
- What nonverbal communication do you currently use that could be misinterpreted by a patient of a different culture?

PATIENTS WITH SPECIAL NEEDS

In previous chapters you learned how important it is to place yourself in the patient's situation. Empathy allows you to consider how a patient might feel and helps you anticipate the patient's needs. When working with patients who have special needs, this tactic is especially important. Patients with special needs may have increased anxiety because of their current illness and unfamiliar surroundings. You have a responsibility to recognize this and strive to reduce their anxiety. Do not rush these patients. Be helpful, but do not take away their dignity by automatically assuming they are not able to do something. Always ask if you can help first. If one method of communication is not working, combine it with another approach (e.g., visual aids, help from family members). Patients with special needs include those with disabilities, children and elderly persons, those with lower levels of understanding, and those with mental impairment.

Disabilities

There are many types of disabilities. In the medical office you will work with patients who have impaired vision, impaired hearing, diminished mental capacity, and other physical disabilities. It is important to understand how to apply effective communication skills with patients having all types of disabilities.

Visual Impairment

Vision problems, such as *total blindness, presbyopia, macular degeneration, cataracts,* and *glaucoma,* all affect the ability to see. Patients may have varying degrees of sight. Unless totally blind, a patient may benefit from having written materials enlarged. A totally blind patient can benefit from instructions given on an audiocassette. Always encourage questions and obtain feedback. Guidelines for communicating with patients who have visual difficulties include the following:

- Make the patient comfortable in the unfamiliar surroundings.
- Always explain what you are going to do and alert patients before touching them (e.g., "Mr. Samuel, I am going to give you an injection in your right upper arm").
- Prevent patients from falling into or over objects by providing verbal directions (e.g., "Mrs. Jones, I will need for you to move forward four steps to the chair").
- Do not increase voice volume (these patients are not hearing-impaired).

Hearing Impairment

Hearing loss is suspected when a patient speaks or responds inappropriately to a situation. Sometimes families will comment on the patient's social withdrawal and the increased volume of the television or the radio. When you are aware of a patient's hearing loss, it is best to communicate by restating directions. Also, provide the patient with written directions. Several ways to communicate effectively with a hearing-impaired patient are as follows:

- Directly face the patient when speaking.
- When the patient is not facing you, touch the patient's arm or shoulder before speaking.
- Speak clearly in a natural tone and at a normal rate of speech; do not yell or shout.
- Use hand gestures and facial expressions as cues.
- Use visual examples and reading materials.
- Involve family or close friends and provide them with all information given to the patient.
- Minimize distractions from the environment.

Other Physical Disabilities

There are many other types of physical disabilities. Physically disabled patients require attention directly associated with their impairments. When helping physically disabled patients set goals, the medical assistant encourages realistic goals using their existing abilities to help them achieve the highest possible satisfaction and enrichment in life. Because of advances in biomedical engineering, many devices now allow disabled people to become more functional and less dependent on others.

Patients with disabilities do not expect sympathy or special considerations. They do expect that you care about them as individual patients with unique needs. Your tone of voice should reflect this caring attitude.

Age

As people age, they experience a decline in vision and hearing. This makes it difficult for the elderly patient to collect information from the surroundings. In addition, changes occur in the senses of smell, taste, and touch. Box 10-3 offers suggestions for communicating with elderly patients effectively.

At the other end of the spectrum are pediatric patients. When communicating with children, use wording and methods that are appropriate to their age, ethnicity, and level of understanding. Be familiar with the growth and developmental stages of children so that you can communicate more effectively with them and their parents. Box 10-4 provides tips for communicating with children.

Intelligence

Some patients with special needs may have difficulty understanding or a below-normal ability to think and reason. You must determine the patient's level of understanding and adjust your communica-

---

BOX 10-3 Communicating with Elderly Patients

- Be an empathetic listener. This shows recognition of the aging person's hearing and visual changes, fatigue, and pain (Fig. 10-3).
- If the patient wears a hearing aid, allow time for the person to adjust the volume if necessary.
- Do not shout at a hearing-impaired patient. Shouting is often associated with anger or displeasure. Speak in a low tone of voice close to the patient's good ear or directly in front of the person.
- Be careful of body language. If an elderly patient perceives you as "too busy," the patient may not report serious concerns.
- Speak clearly and slowly, using short sentences with slight pauses. Do not give lengthy explanations.
- Be patient, and wait for the elderly patient to respond. The aging process may delay the speed at which elderly patients can organize their thoughts and speech.

BOX 10-4   Communicating with Children

- Use dolls, pictures, and other models to enhance communication.
- Let children speak at their own speed. Do not rush or supply words for them; let them complete their own thoughts and sentences.
- Encourage children to talk about themselves.
- Talk to children with words they can easily understand.
- Recognize situations that might be upsetting to children and try to reassure them.
- Allow children to handle safe medical equipment (e.g., stethoscope) (Fig. 10-4).

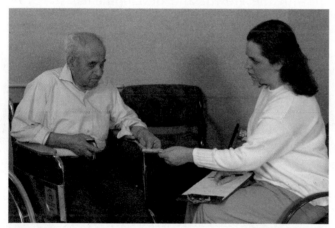

Fig. 10-3 The medical assistant must recognize that the aging process puts limitations on the elderly patient.

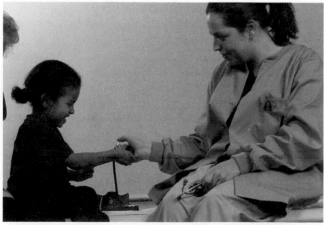

Fig. 10-4 Children understand procedures better if they handle the equipment.

tion accordingly. You can adjust communication in these situations in the following ways:

- Use both verbal and nonverbal clues to assess both the patient's ability to read and the patient's educational and emotional background.
- Allow more time for recall because people process information at different speeds. The aging process can also delay recall.
- Do not overload the patient with information. Instead, provide small portions and evaluate feedback before moving forward with new information.

Finally, determine how well the information has been received by asking questions or by having the patient do a return demonstration.

Mental Impairment

The ability to process new information and apply it appropriately in a given setting reflects a patient's mental functioning. A person is diagnosed as mentally challenged when the person functions at a lower-than-normal intellectual level. People who are mentally challenged cannot think abstractly. They learn through repetition and habit (e.g., using the same routine daily). When communicating with mentally challenged patients, the atmosphere must be relaxed, and only one direction should be given at a time.

To communicate effectively with mentally impaired patients, you must obtain information from the caregiver about the patient's habits, routines, and personal terminology (e.g., nicknames). Rushing these individuals causes stress and may reduce their cooperation. Mentally challenged patients need to be treated with the same respect that all patients deserve.

Developmentally delayed patients are those who lag behind in **maturation.** They should not be confused with mentally impaired patients. Areas of concern with these patients include not only their mental ability but also their physical, social, and emotional functioning. To communicate effectively with developmentally delayed patients, the medical assistant needs to address their level of maturation, not their chronological age. For example, an infant who is deprived of physical contact or nutrition will not progress at the same rate as an infant who receives these basic needs. The way you interact with this infant may be quite different from the way you interact with the infant who has received the basic needs.

Providing caregivers with a list of available community resources is a valuable service. Many communities have support groups and special day care centers equipped to handle mentally handicapped or developmentally delayed individuals.

PATIENT-CENTERED PROFESSIONALISM

- How does understanding the emotional and physical needs of a patient with special needs improve the quality of care?
- Why is it important to understand a patient's limitations? Give an example of how understanding a patient's limitations can result in a positive patient experience.

CONCLUSION

Communication may be the best tool that medical assistants have to establish a trusting relationship with patients and encourage compliance with their treatment plan. Every patient is a unique individual. A patient's culture, beliefs, background, age, intelligence, and abilities (seeing, hearing, sensing, thinking, comprehending) all need to be analyzed to establish a communication process that best fits the patient's communication and learning style. The ability to apply the principles of effective communication to your daily interaction with patients takes much effort and practice. However, your efforts will be reflected in the positive relationships you establish with patients and the high-quality, professional care you provide.

SUMMARY

Reinforce your understanding of the material in this chapter by reviewing the curriculum objectives and key content points below.

1. Define, appropriately use, and spell all the Key Terms for this chapter.
   - Review the Key Terms if necessary.
2. Understand the role of the medical assistant in patient communication.
   - A medical assistant is expected to be an active listener and to understand and anticipate the patient's needs. A medical assistant also needs to communicate to patients their treatment plan, instructions for medication, and follow-up appointments.
3. Explain the concept of *holistic* care.
   - The holistic approach to health care is concerned with all the patient's needs: physical, emotional, social, economic, and spiritual.

4. List five ways you can improve communication with patients, and explain how better communication improves patient care and results in good service.
   - Communication with patients can be improved by listening actively, involving the patient and family with decision making, being sensitive to the patient's needs, encouraging the patient to discuss issues and problems, and providing feedback to the patient.
   - Better communication improves patient care because the treatment plan (the message) has been delivered correctly by the medical assistant and has been accepted by the patient.
   - Focusing on the patient's needs and striving for improvement achieves quality care and service.
5. Explain the importance of handling patient complaints effectively.
   - Patients must believe that their complaints have been addressed effectively by the practice. Unhappy patients are more likely to sue or to report their dissatisfaction with the practice to others (other family members, patients, or health care workers).
   - Handling patient complaints is a skill that requires practice and the cooperation of all staff members.
   - Reducing lawsuits in the medical office starts with the patient-staff relationship.
6. List three ways to establish trust with patients of different cultures.
   - When dealing with cultural beliefs you do not understand, it is important to show respect.
   - You need good communication skills when interacting with patients who have cultural beliefs that are different from your own.
   - Allow the patient to maintain self-esteem at all times.
7. List five considerations for communicating with a patient who is visually impaired.
   Keep in mind that patients with visual impairments can have varying degrees of sight.
   - Use written materials with large print.
   - Consider using audiocassettes for patient instruction.
   - Orient the patient to unfamiliar surroundings ("There is a chair on your left in this room").
   - Give verbal visual cues when necessary ("Step down and turn around").
   - Alert the patient before touching the patient ("I'm going to wash your eye out now").

8. List seven ways to communicate effectively with a patient who has hearing impairment. Nonverbal communication is especially important to patients with hearing impairments.
   - Provide written instructions whenever possible.
   - Restate directions and instructions frequently.
   - Face patients when you are speaking to them.
   - Speak clearly and at a normal rate; do not yell or shout.
   - Involve family and caregivers.
   - Use hand gestures and facial expressions if appropriate.
   - Minimize distractions (e.g., close the door, turn down the radio).

9. List three considerations for accommodating patients with other physical disabilities.
   - Patients with special needs (e.g., those with walkers, crutches, wheelchairs, or oxygen tanks) require multiple approaches depending on their individual circumstances. Do not rush these patients.
   - Be careful ushering these patients through doorways.
   - These patients may need assistance in the bathroom.

10. List six considerations for communicating effectively with elderly patients.
    - The aging process causes many changes in the ability to process sensory information.
    - Refer to Box 10-3.

11. List six considerations for communicating effectively with children.
    - Adjust your communication to the level of the child.
    - Refer to Box 10-4.

12. Explain the considerations for communicating with patients with a below-normal ability to reason or think, with mental impairments, or with developmental delays.
    - When assessing a patient's ability to learn, acknowledge the patient's life experiences as well as formal education.
    - Review the patient's understanding of the information provided by asking questions or by having the patient perform a return demonstration of the procedure.
    - Mental impairment is diagnosed when the intellectual level is lower than the accepted range.
    - A developmentally delayed patient requires a level of communication based on maturational level, not chronological age.

13. Explain the importance of communicating effectively with the caregivers and families of mentally impaired and developmentally delayed patients.
    - Family members can provide information on the patient's life and experiences. This information can be used to communicate effectively with the patient.
    - Family members can assist the patient in complying with the treatment plan.

14. Analyze a realistic medical office situation and apply your understanding of effective communication with patients to determine the best course of action.
    - Age, intelligence, special needs, and culture all affect the way medical assistants communicate with patients.
    - Communication approaches should be varied according to the needs of each patient.

15. Describe the impact on patient care when medical assistants consistently apply the principles of effective communication when interacting with patients.
    - When patients see the medical office staff as diligent, responsive, and caring, they are more understanding when misunderstandings occur.
    - Effectively communicating with patients of all types requires empathy, patience, effective listening, and understanding of the needs of the individual patient.

FOR FURTHER EXPLORATION

Research holistic health. It is important for the medical assistant to understand how holistic treatments can be used together with conventional medicine. Learn more about holistic treatments to enhance your own understanding.

Keywords: Use the following keywords in your search: holistic, holistic medicine, holistic treatment.

Chapter Review

Vocabulary Review

Matching

Match each term with the correct definition.

A. litigation

B. holistic

C. maturation

D. rapport

_____ 1. A growth-and-development process involving a patient's physical, social, and emotional functioning

_____ 2. Lawsuit

_____ 3. Effective relationship that considers both the physical and emotional needs

_____ 4. Involving all health needs of the patient, including physical, emotional, social, economic, and spiritual needs

Theory Recall

True/False

Indicate whether the sentence or statement is true or false.

_____ 1. Communicating effectively with patients is a key factor in providing quality care.

_____ 2. Patient complaints should be handled directly by the physician.

_____ 3. Patients with disabilities expect sympathy and special considerations.

_____ 4. When communicating with children, use wording and methods that are appropriate to their age.

_____ 5. Use both verbal and nonverbal clues to assess a patient's ability to read and comprehend information.

Multiple Choice

Identify the letter of the choice that best completes the statement or answers the question.

1. _____ does NOT apply when expecting a patient to comply with treatment plans.
   A. Patient's physical state
   B. Patient's emotional state
   C. Patient's educational background
   D. None of the above, because all do apply

2. Which one of the following is NOT important in effective communication for patient teaching?
   A. Assessing patient's readiness to learn
   B. Including patient's family or support group in treatment plans
   C. Patient's dietary habits
   D. Providing time for questions

3. Developmentally delayed patients are those who are behind in _____.
   A. maturation
   B. intelligence
   C. education
   D. physical abilities

4. When communicating with children, do all of the following EXCEPT _____.
   A. use technical terms to explain all procedures
   B. use dolls and pictures to enhance communication
   C. allow children to handle "safe" medical equipment.
   D. encourage them to talk about themselves

5. The ability to process new information and to apply it appropriately in a given setting reflects a patient's _____ functioning.
   A. verbal
   B. nonverbal
   C. mental
   D. emotional

6. Which one of the following is NOT an effective means of communicating with a patient who is hearing impaired?
   A. Directly face the patient when speaking.
   B. Speak louder and more quickly.
   C. Use visual examples.
   D. Both A and B

7. All of the following are appropriate ways to communicate effectively with patients EXCEPT to _____.
   A. involve the patient's family in decision making
   B. argue with the patient about his or her beliefs that conflict with their medical treatment
   C. provide honest feedback
   D. both B and C

8. _____ health care deals with all of the health needs of the patient.
   A. Allopathic
   B. Holistic
   C. Generic
   D. Western

9. Three of the following statements pertain to considerations that should be made when accommodating patients with physical disabilities. Which one does NOT pertain?
   A. Restate directions and instructions frequently.
   B. Do not rush special needs patients.
   C. Special needs patients may require assistance in the bathroom.
   D. Be careful ushering a special needs patient through doorways.

10. Which one of the following does NOT apply when working with patients who are visually impaired?
    A. Use written material with large print.
    B. Face the patient directly when speaking.
    C. Give verbal clues when necessary.
    D. Alert patients before touching them.

Sentence Completion

Complete each sentence or statement.

1. The medical assistant must use the skills he or she has learned about human relations and behavior to develop a working _____ with patients.

2. Finding better ways to _____ with patients results in quality service and patient care.

3. A patient may _____ if he or she perceives the quality of the service to be unsatisfactory.

4. _____ occurs when the patient is unhappy with the performance of the support staff in a medical facility.

5. Use _____ language when responding to a complaint, and reassure the patient that the complaint will be investigated.

Short Answers

1. Explain the concept of holistic care.

_____

_____

2. Explain the importance of handling patient complaints effectively.

_____

_____

3. List seven ways to effectively communicate with a patient who has a hearing impairment.

_____

_____

_____

4. List six considerations for communicating effectively with elderly patients.

_____

_____

_____

_____

5. What questions should a medical assistant ask himself or herself when doing an inventory of the patient's readiness to follow a new health treatment plan?

_____

_____

_____

_____

Application of Skills

1. Select a partner in class for this activity. Partner A should be blindfolded, while Partner B navigates Partner A through a 10-minute period. Then they switch places for an additional 10 minutes. Pay particular attention to effectively communicating with the blindfolded partner. Write one paragraph journaling the experience from both perspectives, first being the caregiver and then being the visually impaired person.

2. Using cotton balls or earplugs, perform the above activity but this time as a hearing impaired person.

Critical Thinking

Using the paragraphs written in the Application of Skills section, exchange papers with your partner.

A. How did your partner feel about you as the caregiver and your ability to effectively communicate?

_____

_____

_____

_____

B. What did you learn from performing this activity that will help you to become a better medical assistant?

_____

_____

_____

_____

C. Have you ever assisted a physically challenged individual in the past? If so, what have you learned from that experience? If not, look for an opportunity to do so within the next 2 days and then answer the above question.

_____

_____

_____

_____

_____

_____

Internet Research

Keyword: Americans With Disabilities Act

Locate the answer to following question: "Who is a 'qualified individual with a disability'?" Cite the source(s) of your information.

What Would You Do?

If you have accomplished the objectives in this chapter, you will be able to make better choices as a medical assistant. Take a look at this situation and decide what you would do.

Mr. Joplin is a spry 82-year-old and still lives in his own home. His wife died about a year ago, but Mr. Joplin has no severe medical problems and is able to care for himself. He does have visual problems caused by cataracts in his left eye, as well as joint stiffness related to his age. John, the medical assistant, approaches Mr. Joplin to escort him to the examining room. John shouts at Mr. Joplin as if he has a hearing difficulty, then walks away without assisting Mr. Joplin from the chair. When John reaches the door, he looks over his shoulder, rolls his eyes, and shouts, "Do you need some help?" Mr. Joplin looks away and refuses any assistance. Dr. Smith examines Mr. Joplin and asks John to explain the treatment so Mr. Joplin will comply. John hurriedly tells Mr. Joplin one time what is expected, then returns him to the waiting room. Several days later, Mr. Joplin calls the office to tell the receptionist to cancel his next appointment because he is going to find a new physician.

John's poor communication skills caused Dr. Smith to lose Mr. Joplin as a patient. If you were the medical assistant in this situation, what would you have done to communicate more effectively with Mr. Joplin?

1. Did John need to speak in a loud voice to Mr. Joplin, or did he stereotype Mr. Joplin because of his age and visual impairments?

_____

_____

_____

2. Did John show professionalism? List three ways that John could have improved his interaction with Mr. Joplin.

_____

_____

_____

_____

3. What body language did John display that exhibited negative thoughts about Mr. Joplin?

_____

_____

_____

_____

4. What role did Mr. Joplin's age play in this interaction?

_____

_____

_____

_____

5. What steps could John have taken to show that he really wanted Mr. Joplin to comply with the physician's treatment plan?

_____

_____

_____

_____

6. What role did the receptionist play in this scenario? What should she have done when Mr. Joplin canceled his appointment?

_____

_____

_____

_____

Chapter Quiz

Multiple Choice

Identify the letter of the choice that best completes the statement or answers the question.

1. The growth and development process involving patient's physical, social, and emotional functioning is called _____.
   A. holistic health care
   B. litigation
   C. Americans With Disabilities Act
   D. maturation

2. Communicating ineffectively with patients is a key factor in providing quality care.
   A. True
   B. False

3. All of a patient's needs influence his or her behavior and compliance with treatment.
   A. True
   B. False

4. Which one of the following is NOT a means of assessing a patient's understanding or a method to improve communication?
   A. Communicating in technical/medical terms
   B. Asking patients to write down questions
   C. Identifying any communication barriers
   D. Not being afraid to say, "I don't know"

5. Which one of the following is NOT a category of reasons for which patients complain?
   A. Administrative complaints
   B. Medical complaints
   C. Laboratory complaints
   D. All of the above are complaint categories

6. Take all complaints seriously, but write down only the facts that feel important to you.
   A. True
   B. False

7. Always inform the physician and/or office manager of any statements made by the patient that reflect a negative attitude.
   A. True
   B. False

8. A large number of _____ result from careless actions or comments made by physicians and office staff when patients complain.
   A. warnings
   B. threats
   C. lawsuits
   D. thank-you cards

9. All treatment plans must allow patients to maintain their _____ and help establish trust in the health care team.
   A. self-esteem
   B. modesty
   C. confidence
   D. All of the above

10. You must get rid of all positive beliefs so they do not affect your communication with or care for patients.
    A. True
    B. False

11. A medical assistant must answer only questions within his or her scope of training. With the physician's guidance, he or she may explain the reasons for the needed changes and the importance of compliance.
    A. True
    B. False

12. A medical assistant must never accept the patient's decisions regarding medical care if it is not in alignment with his or her personal beliefs.
    A. True
    B. False

13. When working with patients with special needs, it is extremely important to ask if they would like assistance before assuming they are incapable of performing a task.
    A. True
    B. False

14. In working with visually impaired patients, you must NEVER _____.
    A. provide verbal directions
    B. yell so they will hear you more clearly
    C. alert the patient before touching them
    D. all of the above

15. Patients with disabilities do NOT expect sympathy or special considerations.
    A. True
    B. False

16. A person is diagnosed as mentally challenged when he or she functions at a higher-than-normal intellectual level.
    A. True
    B. False

17. Developmentally delayed patients are those behind in maturation.
    A. True
    B. False

18. Very few communities actually have support groups or special day care centers equipped to handle mentally handicapped or developmentally delayed individuals.
    A. True
    B. False

19. A medical assistant is expected to be an active listener and to understand and anticipate the patient's needs.
    A. True
    B. False

20. An unhappy patient is more likely to sue.
    A. True
    B. False

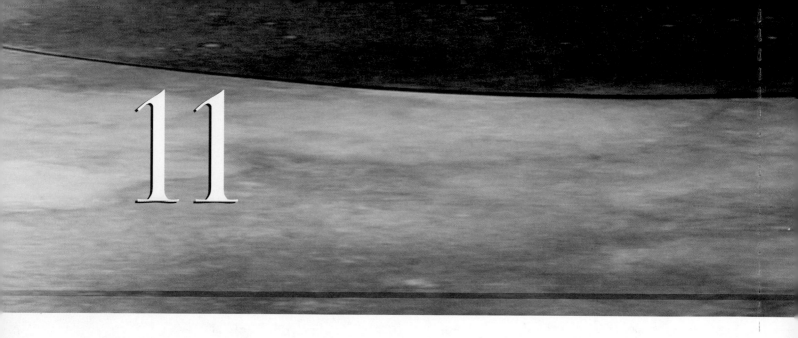

CURRICULUM OBJECTIVES

You will be able to do the following after completing this chapter:

Key Terms
1. Define, appropriately use, and spell all the Key Terms for this chapter.

Purpose and Contents of Medical Records
2. Explain the purpose of a medical record.
3. List three uses of the medical record.
4. Explain how the medical record protects the legal interests of the patient, the health care provider, and the medical practice.
5. Demonstrate the correct procedure for pulling patient records.
6. Demonstrate the correct procedure for registering a patient.
7. List and describe seven basic forms used to start a new patient's medical record.
8. Demonstrate the correct procedure for creating a medical record for a new patient using alphabetical, color-coded tabs.
9. List five examples of forms that could be added to an established patient's medical record as care is provided.
10. Demonstrate the correct procedure for adding documents to an existing patient record.
11. Demonstrate the correct procedure for protecting the confidentiality of patients and their medical records.
12. Differentiate between *source-oriented* and *problem-oriented* records.
13. Describe where progress notes fit into the POMR format of organizing a patient's record, and explain the acronym SOAP.

Charting in the Patient's Record
14. Explain the importance of documenting all services provided to the patient.
15. Identify specific actions as "Do"s or "Don't"s of charting in patients' medical records.
16. List the three steps for correcting an entry error in the patient's medical record.

Selecting a Filing System
17. State the three considerations for selecting a filing system.
18. State the three components of a filing system plan that should be recorded in detail in the office procedure manual.
19. Differentiate among vertical drawer, lateral open-shelf, lateral drawer, and movable lateral file cabinets.
20. List six supplies typically used with a filing system.

MEDICAL RECORDS AND CHART DOCUMENTATION

Filing Methods

21. List four methods of filing and briefly explain each.
22. Discuss the advantages and disadvantages of alphabetical filing.
23. List the areas addressed in the 10 rules for alphabetical filing.
24. Discuss the advantages and disadvantages of numerical filing.
25. Differentiate between *straight-number* filing and *terminal-digit* filing.

Basic Filing Procedures

26. List in order the five steps of preparing and filing medical records and briefly describe each.
27. Demonstrate the correct procedure for filing medical records using the alphabetical system.
28. Demonstrate the correct procedure for filing medical records using the numerical system.
29. Differentiate between *active* and *inactive* files.
30. Explain the need to purge files regularly in a medical practice.

Patient-Centered Professionalism

31. Analyze a realistic medical office situation and apply your understanding of charting and filing medical records to determine the best course of action.
32. Describe the impact on patient care when medical assistants understand the importance of accurate documentation and efficient filing of medical records.

KEY TERMS

acronym Word formed from the first letter of several words (e.g., SOAP).

active files Current patient files.

aging labels (year labels) Labels on a chart that identify the year.

alphabetical filing Filing method that uses the alphabet to determine how files are arranged.

caption Words that describe the contents, name, or subject matter on a label.

charting Process of documenting events and services concerning a patient's care.

coding Process of underlining a keyword to indicate how a document should be filed.

conditioning Process of removing staples and paper clips and mending a document before filing.

continuity of care Care of the patient rendered by health care providers, with the medical record documenting all treatment by providers.

cross-reference Notification system showing a file stored in more than one place.

database Information source and storage.

direct filing Filing system that requires knowing only the patient's name to initiate or locate the file.

electronic medical record (EMR) Patient medical records kept in a computer file; also called "paperless chart."

entry Written description of care provided to the patient.

filing Process of putting documents in a folder.

guides Dividers used to separate file folders.

inactive files Files of patients who have not been seen within a certain time span set by the medical practice (e.g., 3 years).

KEY TERMS—*cont'd*

indexing Process of determining how a record will be filed.

indirect filing Numerical filing system that requires a list containing cross-references of numbers and names to locate a file.

key unit First unit to be filed.

labels Stickers or other items that identify contents in a folder.

medical record Patient record that contains information about the patient's treatment history.

numerical filing Method of arranging files using numbers.

objective Concrete and factual; can be seen or measured.

out guides Separators that replace a file folder when it is removed from the file cabinet; contains a notation of the date and the name of who signed out the file.

plan Action created to solve a problem, as in a patient treatment plan.

problem list List of a patient's medical complaints.

problem-oriented medical record (POMR) Chart format that is arranged according to a patient's health complaint.

progress notes Data concerning a patient's medical care and its results.

provider Health care facility (e.g., medical office) or the personnel (e.g., physician, medical assistant) rendering medical treatment to a patient.

purge To clean out, as with excessive data in patient files.

releasing Marking or placing initials on a document to indicate it can be filed.

SOAP Type of chart format that divides each patient problem into *s*ubjective data, *o*bjective data, *a*ssessment, and *p*lan for treatment.

sorting Arranging documents in a particular order for filing ease.

source-oriented format Chart format that has dividers that separate the different types of patient information.

subjective Information supplied by the patient that cannot be proven.

terminal-digit filing Method of filing that organizes records by their final digits.

tickler file Reminder aid that organizes events by date.

work-related injury Injury that has occurred to an employee when performing the duties of his or her job.

What Would You Do?

Read the following scenario and keep it in mind as you learn about medical records and chart documentation in this chapter.

Deanna is a new administrative medical-assisting extern at Dr. Juanea's office. Shirley, the office manager, asks Deanna to prepare a file for a new patient who will be seen tomorrow in the office. Shirley tells Deanna to be sure that she has color-coded the file folder and that the necessary forms have been included inside. In this office the medical records are problem-oriented, and all records are SOAP format; both are new concepts to Deanna, who was taught to prepare source-oriented records. After Deanna has prepared the new patient's file, Shirley asks her to pull the necessary records for tomorrow's appointments from the lateral open-shelf file cabinet containing patient records filed in alphabetical order. As she pulls the records, Deanna is to annotate the patient list for tomorrow's schedule. With the assistance of Shirley, Deanna will also purge the inactive patient records.

Would you be able to perform these tasks?

When health care professionals care for a patient, they must document what they observed and what medical services were provided. This information goes into a patient's chart, which contains the patient's medical record. The medical record includes not only examination and test results, procedures, diagnoses, and treatment plans but also information provided by the patient about his or her health and family history, current symptoms, and recent life changes. Medical records are confidential documents that must be filed carefully so the patient's information can be retrieved when needed. Handling medical records is an important part of a medical assistant's duties.

PURPOSE AND CONTENTS OF MEDICAL RECORDS

Medical records are important to the functioning of a practice in many ways. It is important to understand their purpose, as well as what types of information, forms, and documentation are contained in a patient's medical record.

Purpose

Medical records provide evidence of patient assessments, interventions, and communications. Because the medical record is a permanent and legal document, care must be taken to preserve its contents. File management begins when the patient is seen in the medical office and medical information is collected (e.g., family history, past history, known allergies) and ends when the file is destroyed. The patient's record can be used in the following ways:

- Continuity of care among health care providers

- Filing insurance claims
- Resolving legal matters such as lawsuits

To serve its purpose, the patient's medical record must contain all the details about the patient's illness and care provided to the patient. In addition, remember that all information contained within the medical record is confidential. Only those involved in the care of the patient may discuss the patient's care. Financial information should never be placed in the patient's record because it is not information that is needed by health care **providers** for continuing care.

FOR YOUR INFORMATION

Documentation
Keep this in mind: **If it is not documented, it was not done.**

The medical assistant must make certain all care provided, including any treatments and communications, is documented to protect the legal interests of the patient, medical practice, and the physician.

Contents

Within each patient's medical record are several forms. The forms required for a specialty practice will vary according to the type of documentation required. The importance of these forms cannot be stressed enough because they provide the information needed to support the course of treatment (e.g., test results, consultation reports). Medical assistants need to be familiar with the type of information in a medical record as well as the various forms a medical record may take.

Data Records

Before a patient comes to the office, the patient's file is "pulled" (Procedure 11-1). If the patient is

Procedure 11-1 Pull Patient Records

TASK: Before the start of the business day, pull patient records for the daily appointment schedule.

EQUIPMENT AND SUPPLIES
- Appointment book, appointment list
- Pen
- Tape
- Stapler
- Two-hole punch
- Patient records

SKILLS/RATIONALE

1. **Procedural Step. Locate and review the day's appointment schedule in the appointment book.**
2. **Procedural Step. Generate the daily appointment list (type, photocopy, or print from the computer).**
   Rationale. This provides all office personnel with a list of the appointments for the day, allowing each person to prepare for their part in providing for patients.
3. **Procedural Step. Identify the full name of each scheduled patient and the reason for the visit.**
   Rationale. The full name will be used in locating the patient's record from the office filing system.
4. **Procedural Step. Pull the patients' records from the filing system; place a checkmark next to each patient's name on the appointment book as each record is pulled.**
   Rationale. This determines that the correct records have been pulled and that none has been omitted.
5. **Procedural Step. Review each record for completeness.**
   Rationale. It is important that each record is thoroughly reviewed to ensure that all information has been entered correctly, that any previously ordered tests have been performed, and that the results have been returned and documented in the patient's record.
6. **Procedural Step. Annotate the appointment list with any special considerations.**

Rationale. This alerts the physician or staff that special concerns must be addressed with the patient, such as needing to discuss scheduling a surgery or needing a copy of the patient's insurance card.

7. **Procedural Step. Arrange all records sequentially by appointment time.**
   NOTE: Some offices will arrange the schedule's patient records alphabetically. This is helpful when the patient cancels or arrives late or if another patient must be seen ahead of the scheduled time. Records are easier to access because you do not need to know the appointment time to find the record. How to organize records depends on the preference of the facility.
   Rationale. This provides an efficient and time-saving method of organizing the patient's record and ensures that everything is available for the physician before seeing the patient.
8. **Procedural Step. Place the records in a specified location that is out of view from unauthorized persons.**
   Rationale. Confidentiality of patient information must be ensured at all times, yet the records need to be in a convenient place.

---

new, the patient is "registered," and a medical record is started with some basic forms (Procedure 11-2). The following are examples of information and forms included in standard file assembly:

- *Patient registration (or patient information) form.* This form contains demographic and billing information (e.g., Social Security number, address, phone number, marital status, insurance carrier). This information is used for administrative office functions such as

scheduling, insurance, filing, and billing statements (Fig. 11-1).
- *Health history.* This form contains a collection of **subjective** information about the patient (e.g., description of current complaint in the patient's words, symptoms, physical signs). This information can be obtained by the medical assistant during an interview or by having the patient fill out the form before the first appointment. It contains the chief complaint, details of the present illness, current illnesses,

Procedure 11-2 Register a New Patient

TASK: Complete a registration form for a new patient, obtaining all required information for credit and insurance claims.

EQUIPMENT AND SUPPLIES
- Registration form (patient information form)
- Pen
- Clipboard
- Private conference area

SKILLS/RATIONALE

1. **Procedural Step. Establish new patient status.**
2. **Procedural Step. Obtain and document the required information.**
   a. Full name, birth date, name of spouse (if married)
   b. Home address, telephone number (include zip code and area code)
   c. Occupation, name of employer, business address, telephone number
   d. Social Security number and driver's license number, if any
   e. Name of referring physician, if any
   f. Name and address of person responsible for payment
   g. Method of payment
   h. Health insurance information
   i. Name of primary carrier (and secondary carrier, if applicable)
   j. Type of coverage
   k. Group policy number
   l. Subscriber number
   m. Assignment of benefits, if required

   Rationale. This information is necessary for credit and insurance claims.

3. **Procedural Step. Review the entire form.**
   Rationale. This helps to ensure that information is complete and legible.

---

and social, occupational, and family history (Fig. 11-2).

- *Consent to treat form.* This is a legal form that protects all health care personnel when caring for the patient by signifying that the patient has been informed of treatment risks and alternatives.
- *Consent to use and disclose health information form.* This is a form that must be signed before any patient information can be released (e.g., to the insurance company for payment).
- *History and physical form.* This form is used by the physician to assess the patient's past problems and current state of health.
- *Progress notes.* Notes entered into the patient's record are used to update the status of the patient's health. Included with each **entry** (a written description of what care was provided for the patient) is the date, time, signature, and credentials of the person charting. This is done each time the patient is seen by a health care provider. Progress notes include the patient's current symptoms (chief complaint) as documented by the medical assistant, vital signs, diagnosis if known, treatment plan, and

evaluation of plan to date. These are all documented by the health care provider.

- *Medication log (list).* This is a list of the current medications taken by the patient. A notation should also be made to include over-the-counter (OTC) medication and herbal and natural preparations.

Forms added to an established patient's medical record as services are provided could include radiographic reports, laboratory reports, diagnostic procedures, consultation reports, and hospital reports, such as discharge summaries (Fig. 11-3).

Procedure 11-3 outlines the creation of a patient file.

Procedure 11-4 shows how to add items to an established medical record. As each document is added to the patient's record, the latest information is always placed on top in chronological order because it indicates the patient's current status.

NOTE: If an established patient sees the physician for a **work-related injury,** a new file must be made because all health information before the injury is *not* to be made available to the employer.

REGISTRATION
(PLEASE PRINT)

Home Phone: _____   Today's Date: _____

PATIENT INFORMATION

Name_____   Soc. Sec.#_____
　　　　Last Name　　　　　　　　First Name　　　　　Initial

Address_____   Phone _____

City _____ State _____ Zip _____

Single ___ Married ___ Widowed ___ Separated ___ Divorced ___   Sex M___ F___   Age ___   Birthdate _____

Patient Employed by_____   Occupation _____

Business Address _____   Business Phone _____

By whom were you referred? _____

In case of emergency who should be notified? _____   Phone _____
　　　　　　　　　　　　　　　　　　　　Last Name　　　　　　Relationship to Patient

PRIMARY INSURANCE

Person Responsible for Account _____
　　　　　　　　　　　　　　Last Name　　　　　　　　　First Name　　　　　Initial

Relation to Patient _____ Birthdate _____ Soc. Sec.#_____

Address (if different from patient's) _____   Phone _____

City _____ State _____ Zip _____

Person Responsible Employed by_____   Occupation _____

Business Address _____   Business Phone _____

Insurance Company_____

Contract # _____ Group # _____ Subscriber # _____

Name of other dependents covered under this plan _____

ADDITIONAL INSURANCE

Is patient covered by additional insurance?　____Yes ____ No

Subscriber Name _____ Relationship to Patient _____ Birthdate _____

Address (if different from patient's) _____   Phone _____

City _____ State _____ Zip _____

Subscriber Employed by_____   Business Phone _____

Insurance Company_____

Contract #_____ Group # _____ Subscriber # _____

Name of other dependents covered under this plan _____

ASSIGNMENT AND RELEASE

I, the undersigned, certify that I (or my dependent) have insurance coverage with _____
　　　　　　　　　　　　　　　　　　　　　　　　　　　　　　　　Name of Insurance Company(ies)
and assign directly to Dr. _____ insurance benefits, if any, otherwise payable to me for services rendered. I understand that I am financially responsible for all charges whether or not paid by insurance. I hereby authorize the doctor to release all information necessary to secure the payment of benefits. I authorize the use of this signature on all insurance submissions.

_____   _____   _____
　Responsible Party Signature　　　　　　　　　Relationship　　　　　　　　　　　Date

© 1996 BIBBERO SYSTEMS, INC.　PETALUMA, CALIFORNIA

Fig. 11-1　Example of information sheet for a new patient. *(Courtesy Bibbero Systems, Inc., Petaluma, Calif; phone [800] 242-2376; fax [800] 242-9330; www.bibbero.com.)*

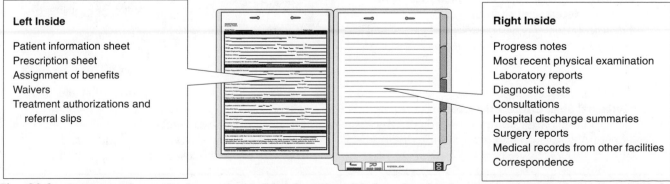

PART A — PRESENT HEALTH HISTORY (continued)

IV. GENERAL HEALTH, ATTITUDE AND HABITS (continued)

Have you recently had any changes in your: If yes, please explain:
- Marital status?   No ___ Yes ___
- Job or work?   No ___ Yes ___
- Residence?   No ___ Yes ___
- Financial status?   No ___ Yes ___
- Are you having any legal problems or trouble with the law?   No ___ Yes ___

PART B — PAST HISTORY

I. FAMILY HEALTH

Please give the following information about your immediate family:

Relationship	Age, If Living	Age At Death	State of Health Or Cause of Death
Father			
Mother			
Brothers and Sisters			
Spouse			
Children			

Have any blood relatives had any of the following illnesses? If so, indicate relationship (mother, brother, etc.)

Illness	Family Members
Asthma	
Diabetes	
Cancer	
Blood Disease	
Glaucoma	
Epilepsy	
Rheumatoid Arthritis	
Tuberculosis	
Gout	
High Blood Pressure	
Heart Disease	
Mental Problems	
Suicide	

II. HOSPITALIZATIONS, SURGERIES

Please list all times you have been hospitalized.

Year	Operation

III. ILLNESS AND MEDICAL PROBLEMS

Please mark with an (X) any of the following. If you are not certain when an illness started,

Illness	(X)
Eye or eye lid infection	
Glaucoma	
Other eye problems	
Ear trouble	
Deafness or decreased hearing	
Thyroid trouble	
Strep throat	
Bronchitis	
Emphysema	
Pneumonia	
Allergies, asthma or hay fever	
Tuberculosis	
Other lung problems	
High blood pressure	
Heart attack	
High cholesterol	
Arteriosclerosis (hardening of arteries)	
Heart murmur	
Other heart condition	
Stomach/duodenal ulcer	
Diverticulosis	
Colitis	
Other bowel problem	
Hepatitis	
Liver trouble	
Gallbladder trouble	

Page 2 © 1979, 1983 Bibbero Systems Inte... (REV. 6/92)

PART C — BODY SYSTEMS REVIEW

MEN: Please answer questions 1 through 12, then skip to question 18.
WOMEN: Please start on question 6.

ONLY
- Have you had or do you have prostate trouble? .... No ___ Yes ___
- Do you have any sexual problems or with impotency? .... No ___ Yes ___
- Have you ever had sores or lesions on your penis? .... No ___ Yes ___
- Have you ever had any discharge from your penis? .... No ___ Yes ___
- Do you ever have pain, lumps or swelling in your testicles? .... No ___ Yes ___
- Check here if you wish to discuss any special problems with the doctor.

Is it sometimes hard to start your urine flow? .... Rarely/Never ___ Occasionally ___ Frequently ___
Is urination ever painful? ....

19-711-4   5/83   Page 3

ANDRUS/CLINI-REC® HEALTH HISTORY QUESTIONNAIRE

Chart No. _____
Identification Information   Today's Date _____
Name _____   Date of Birth _____
Occupation _____   Marital Status _____

PART A — PRESENT HEALTH HISTORY

I. CURRENT MEDICAL PROBLEMS

Please list the medical problems for which you came to see the doctor. About when did they begin?

Problems	Date Began

What concerns you most about these problems?

If you are being treated for any other illnesses or medical problems by another physician, please describe the problems and write the name of the physician or medical facility treating you.

Illness or Medical Problem	Physician or Medical Facility	City

II. MEDICATIONS

Please list all medications you are now taking, including those you buy without a doctor's prescription (such as aspirin, cold tablets or vitamin supplements)

III. ALLERGIES AND SENSITIVITIES

List anything that you are allergic to such as certain foods, medications, dust, chemicals, or soaps, household items, pollens, bee stings, etc., and indicate how each affects you.

Allergic To:	Effect	Allergic To:	Effect

IV. GENERAL HEALTH, ATTITUDE AND HABITS

- How is your overall health now? .... Health now: Poor ___ Fair ___ Good ___ Excellent ___
- How has it been most of your life? .... Health has been: Poor ___ Fair ___ Good ___ Excellent ___

In the past year:
- Has your appetite changed? .... Appetite: Decreased ___ Increased ___ Stayed same ___
- Has your weight changed? .... Weight: Lost ___ lbs. Gained ___ lbs. No change ___
- Are you thirsty much of the time? .... Thirsty: No ___ Yes ___
- Has your overall 'pep' changed? .... Pep: Decreased ___ Increased ___ Stayed same ___
- Do you usually have trouble sleeping? .... Trouble sleeping: No ___ Yes ___
- How much do you exercise? .... Exercise: Little or none ___ Less than I need ___ All I need ___
- Do you smoke? .... Smokes: No ___ Yes ___ If yes, how many years? ___
- How many each day? .... ___ Cigarettes ___ Cigars ___ Pipesfull
- Have you ever smoked? .... Smoked: No ___ Yes ___ If yes, how many years? ___
- How many each day? .... ___ Cigarettes ___ Cigars ___ Pipesfull
- Do you drink alcoholic beverages? .... Alcohol: No ___ Yes ___ I drink ___ Beers ___ Glasses of Wine ___ Drinks of hard liquor - per day
- Have you ever had a problem with alcohol? .... Prior problem: No ___ Yes ___
- How much coffee or tea do you usually drink? .... Coffee/Tea: ___ cups of coffee or tea a day.
- Do you regularly wear seatbelts? .... Seatbelts: No ___ Yes ___

DO YOU:	Rarely/Never	Occasionally	Frequently
Feel nervous?			
Feel depressed?			
Find it hard to make decisions?			
Lose your temper?			
Worry a lot?			
Tire easily?			
Have trouble relaxing?			
Have any sexual problems?			

DO YOU:	Rarely/Never	Occasionally	Frequently
Ever feel like committing suicide?			
Feel bored with your life?			
Use marijuana?			
Use "hard drugs"?			
Do you want to talk to the doctor about a personal matter? No ___ Yes ___			

Created and Developed by "Medical Economics" Professional Systems
Copyright © 1979, 1983 Bibbero Systems International, Inc.
STOCK NO. 19-711-4   5/83   Page 1

CONFIDENTIAL

Fig. 11-2 General health history questionnaire. *(Courtesy Bibbero Systems, Inc., Petaluma, Calif; phone [800] 242-2376; fax [800] 242-9330; www.bibbero.com.)*

Left Inside

Patient information sheet
Prescription sheet
Assignment of benefits
Waivers
Treatment authorizations and referral slips

Right Inside

Progress notes
Most recent physical examination
Laboratory reports
Diagnostic tests
Consultations
Hospital discharge summaries
Surgery reports
Medical records from other facilities
Correspondence

Fig. 11-3 Contents of a medical record. *(Modified from Hunt SA: Saunders fundamentals of medical assisting, Philadelphia, 2002, Saunders.)*

Procedure 11-3 Initiate a Patient File for a New Patient Using Color-Coded Tabs

TASK: Set up and organize a file that contains the personal data necessary for a complete record and any other information required by the medical office for a new patient. This should be done using an alphabetical, color-coded filing system.

EQUIPMENT AND SUPPLIES
- End-cut file folder
- A-Z color-coded tabs (self-adhesive)
- Blank file label (self-adhesive)
- Color-coded year label (annual age dating label)
- Medical alert, or other label types as appropriate
- Forms:

Patient information	Prescription flow sheet
Assignment of benefits	Laboratory reports
Waiver	Diagnostic reports
Treatment authorizations	Consultation reports
Referral slips	Hospital discharge summaries
Health history	Surgery reports
Progress notes	Miscellaneous correspondence
Visit log	

SKILLS/RATIONALE

1. **Procedural Step. Obtain and review a completed patient information form.**
   Rationale. This document provides basic demographic and billing and insurance information. Reviewing the form verifies completeness of personal data and insurance information.

2. **Procedural Step. Place the completed and reviewed form on the left inside cover of the file, using the method preferred by the medical facility (see Fig. 11-1).**
   Rationale. Placing the patient information on the left inside cover of the medical file helps medical assistants and others using the file to find and verify information quickly and keeps demographic information separate from the medical record.

3. **Procedural Step. Place a progress note form and prescription flow sheet on the inside right cover of the file with the progress note form on top. File additional forms in reverse chronological order, meaning the *most recent* on top, followed by the next most recent, and so forth.**
   Rationale. Documents typically included on the right inside cover of a file pertain directly to patient care. Filing these forms in reverse chronological order allows for the most current event or treatment to be on top and most easily accessible.

4. **Procedural Step. Create a file label.**
   Indent three spaces from the left edge of the label on the second line from the top of the label, then type the patient's last name and first name, followed by the middle initial and any title on the file label. This is referred to as *indexing order*. Some offices will include the date of birth (DOB).
   Rationale. By typing the file folder labels the same way for each patient, using correct indexing order, filing is neater, more consistent, and more efficient, and retrieving files is simpler.

5. **Procedural Step. Attach the file label in the center of the file tab.**

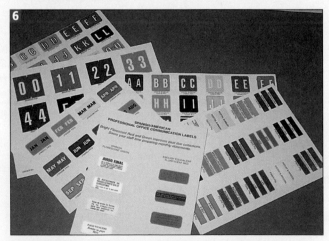

6. **Procedural Step. Attach alphabetical, color-coded labels.**
   Identify the first two letters of the patient's last name (e.g., "Jones" would be J and O) and apply on either the lower or upper portion of

Procedure 11-3 Initiate a Patient File for a New Patient Using Color-Coded Tabs—cont'd

the end tab (depending on office policy), below the file label.

> NOTE: Some offices will also use the patient's DOB.

> Identify the first initial of the patient's first name and place this letter tab ¼ inch above the file label.

> NOTE: Some offices will not use the first initial.

> NOTE: Label placement can differ from office to office.

> *Rationale. Using the first initial will assist in locating files, especially for patients with the same last name.*

7. **Procedural Step. Attach the current year "aging" label above the first-name initial tab.**
    Rationale. The year label identifies the year in which the patient was last seen.

8. **Procedural Step. Compile the file. Place the patient information, health history, and other forms in the patient's file.**

9. **Procedural Step. Attach a "Medical Alert" label on the front of the file.**
    Rationale. If the patient has identified a medical condition (e.g., allergy, diabetes, pacemaker, etc.) on the patient information form, a medical alert label must be placed on the front of the file to alert all medical personnel.

10. **Procedural Step. Prepare a ledger card or enter the patient information into a computerized management program.**
    Rationale. A ledger card is basically a place to keep a record of all services and fees, insurance payments, patient payments, insurance adjustments, and to maintain the patient's current balance. A computer software program, such as Lytec or Medisoft, can automate this process.

11. **Procedural Step. Attach an encounter form (superbill) to the outside of the patient's file.**
    Rationale. This form is attached before the patient sees the physician and provides a place for the physician to indicate the charges for the visit.

FOR YOUR INFORMATION

Ownership

The *physician* owns the medical record, but the *patient* owns the information. The Health Insurance Portability and Accountability Act (HIPAA) Privacy Rule gives the patient the right to examine and obtain a copy of his or her health information and request corrections. This rule requires health care providers to notify patients about their privacy rights, implement privacy policies and procedures, and secure patient records and information so they are not available to unauthorized personnel. See Box 11-1 for more information.

Procedure 11-5 explains the legal implications associated with confidentiality issues regarding patients and their medical records.

Format Guidelines

Most medical offices use a paper medical record. As technologies advance, computerized medical records will become more prominent. Computerized methods are already becoming the norm in large facilities. The paper medical record has two main formats: the source-oriented format and the problem-oriented format.

Source-Oriented Record

When a medical office uses the **source-oriented format** to organize a medical record, the record

BOX 11-1   Documentation and HIPAA Regulations

1. If patient care is not documented, it is as though it did not happen.
2. Health Insurance Portability and Accountability Act (HIPAA) regulations protect the privacy of personal health records by limiting access to a patient's medical records.
3. HIPAA regulations require providers to issue a written statement to each patient informing them about how the patient's health information may be used.
4. Patients have a right to review their medical records, seek corrections, and/or receive a copy of their medical record.
5. The patient's "Protected Health Information" (PHI) cannot be revealed without the patient's consent, and only on a need-to-know basis. This includes written, verbal, and electronic communications of PHI.
6. Patient files must not be out in the open where a patient's name could be seen. Files must be held in a secure area away from view (e.g., in file holder facing backward).
7. When employees are away from their desk, patient information cannot be left on a computer screen or displayed by an open file left on the desk or a message book left open for viewing.
8. All patient appointment schedules must be in a secure location. Schedules cannot be taped to the wall in the examination room, hallway, or any place where another person can view a patient's name.

Procedure 11-4 Add Supplementary Items to an Established Patient File

TASK: Add supplemental documents and progress notes to patient files, observing standard steps in filing while creating an orderly file that facilitates ready reference to any item of information.

EQUIPMENT AND SUPPLIES
- Patient file
- Assorted documents
- Stapler
- Clear tape
- Two-hole punch
- Alphanumerical sorter

SKILLS/RATIONALE

1. **Procedural Step. Retrieve the appropriate patient file from the file storage area.**
   Rationale. This ensures that supplemental forms are filed in the correct patient's file.

2. **Procedural Step. Condition the document.**
   Remove all extraneous materials such as paper clips or pins, mend any tears with tape, staple related pages together, and punch holes if needed.
   Rationale. Conditioning a document ensures that it is in good condition and is processed and ready to be filed. Leaving paper clips on documents causes the document to become attached to other nonrelated materials.

3. **Procedural Step. Release the document.**
   Be sure that the document has been marked, that it has been reviewed by the appropriate person, and that it is ready for filing. This mark may be a person's initials, a checkmark, or a "FILE" stamp.
   Rationale. Most medical offices have a policy that physicians need to review all reports and then initial them before they are filed. This helps ensure that the physician has seen the report and that it was not accidentally overlooked prior to filing.

4. **Procedural Step. Index and code the document.**
   Indexing refers to deciding where it needs to be filed, such as in a medical record or elsewhere (e.g., office accounting file). *Coding* refers to writing on or marking a document to indicate how it should be filed (e.g., by patient last name) once you have determined where it should be filed (indexing).
   Rationale. This ensures that the document is correctly filed for easy retrieval for future reference.

5. **Procedural Step. Sort for filing.**
   Arrange documents and papers in proper filing sequence before taking them to the filing storage area where they will be filed. Some offices will use a "desktop sorter" to facilitate this process. (A desktop sorter has a series of dividers between which papers are placed in filing sequence.) Sorters typically have different means of classification to allow you to sort in multiple ways (e.g., alphabetically, numerically, days of the week).
   Rationale. The use of a sorter makes the filing process much more efficient because it saves the medical assistant time, and the sorting can be accomplished while sitting at a desk in between answering phones and greeting patients.

6. **Procedural Step. File each document according to categories into the established patient's file, with the most recent document on top.**

7. **Procedural Step. Return the file to the storage cabinet.**

has dividers to separate the medical information. Each divider has a color tab with the heading of the section on it. When a document is added to a section, the most recently dated document is placed on top. Typical dividers include the following:

- History and physical examination
- Progress notes
- Medications
- Ancillary reports (e.g., laboratory, pathology, radiology)
- Operative reports
- Correspondence

When a physician wants to review a specific report, the appropriate tab is located, and the report can easily be reviewed. The source-oriented format is used most frequently in medical offices and hospitals.

Procedure 11-5 Maintain Confidentiality of Patients and Their Medical Records

TASK: Explain through role playing how confidentiality of patient issues and their medical records is maintained.

EQUIPMENT AND SUPPLIES
- Authorization form for "Release of Medical Records"

SKILLS/RATIONALE

1. **Procedural Step. Select a partner to be a patient as you assume the role of the administrative medical assistant.**
   Rationale. This provides you with the opportunity to interact one-on-one when explaining the procedures involved in maintaining patient confidentiality.

2. **Procedural Step. Explain to the "patient" through role playing how the integrity of confidences shared in the office is maintained regarding the following medical office topics:**
   a. Attorneys calling the office to gain information about a patient.
   b. Release of information about a minor.
   c. Advertising and media.
   d. Computerized medical records.
   Rationale. The partner should assume the above roles and ask questions pertaining to each of the topics, providing you, the medical assistant, with the opportunity to explain each situation.

3. **Procedural Step. Explain to the "patient" through role playing how confidences shared in the office are maintained regarding the following specialty topics:**
   a. Child abuse
   b. Sexually transmitted diseases (STDs)
   c. Sexual assault
   d. Mental health
   e. AIDS and HIV
   f. Substance abuse

   Rationale. The "patient" should assume roles and ask questions regarding the above topics, providing you, the medical assistant, with the opportunity to explain each situation.

4. **Procedural Step. Explain to the "patient" through role playing how the following situations regarding confidentiality issues are handled in the medical office:**
   a. Subpoenaed medical records.
   b. HIPAA guidelines.
   c. Areas of mandated disclosure by state and federal regulations.
   Rationale. This provides you with the opportunity to practice explaining sensitive information with a patient and answering patient questions.

5. **Procedural Step. Explain to the "patient" through role playing the "Patient's Bill of Rights."**
   Rationale. This provides you with the opportunity to learn and comprehend patients' rights so that you are confident in presenting this information to a patient.

6. **Procedural Step. Explain to the "patient" through role playing and complete an authorization form for release of medical records.**
   Rationale. This provides you with the opportunity to understand how medical records are released so that you are confident in presenting this information to a patient.

Problem-Oriented Record

The **problem-oriented medical record (POMR)** is arranged according to the patient's health complaint. Each complaint is seen as a problem or condition that needs further action (e.g., treatment, patient education). The following four stages are used to resolve a problem when using the POMR format of organizing a patient's health record:

1. A **database** (information source) is established. This is composed of subjective information (thoughts, feelings, ideas) and **objective** information (concrete facts) identified in the patient interview and obtained during the health history, chief complaint, present illness, physical examination, laboratory procedures, and diagnostic tests. This information will be stored in paper files or, in larger facilities where electronic charting is done, in a computer database.

2. Using the information provided by the database identifies a **problem list** (Fig. 11-4). Each problem is given a specific number and is used when referring to all treatments performed and diagnostic testing conducted for the problem.

3. A **plan** of action is created for each problem. This may include laboratory and diagnostic tests, patient education, and treatment (e.g., starting medication regimen).

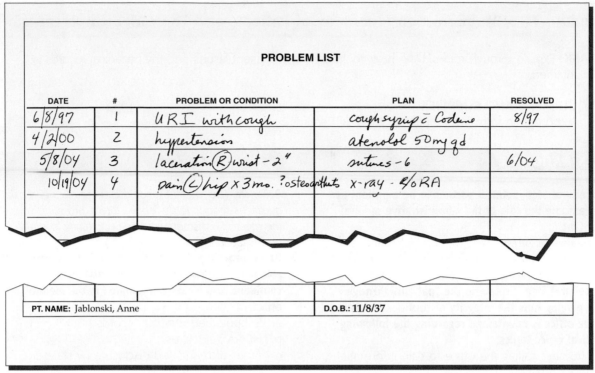

Fig. 11-4 Example of a problem list. *(From Hunt SA: Saunders fundamentals of medical assisting, Philadelphia, 2002, Saunders.)*

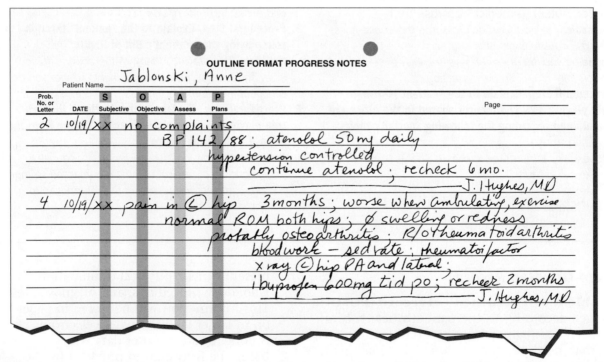

Fig. 11-5 Example of SOAP charting related to a problem list. *(From Hunt SA: Saunders fundamentals of medical assisting, Philadelphia, 2002, Saunders.)*

4. **Progress notes** follow each identified problem in a **SOAP** format (Fig. 11-5). Progress notes start with each problem numbered and include the following four categories:

- *Subjective data.* Information received from the subject, or the information provided by the patient as a chief complaint (e.g., "I'm dizzy," "my stomach hurts").
- *Objective data.* The objective information obtained through the physical examination

and the review of symptoms, or the information that is observed (e.g., rash, fever).

- *Assessment.* The assessment of the clinical diagnosis, or final diagnosis based on the information found from the chief complaint and the physical examination (e.g., physician's conclusion of reported problem based on data presented).
- *Plan.* The plan of action, or the treatment action to be taken (e.g., antibiotics for 7 days).

POMR formatting is extremely advantageous when more than one physician is (or will be) treating the patient because all information pertaining to a specific 'problem' can be located in a concise format.

PATIENT-CENTERED PROFESSIONALISM

- What is the possible outcome if the legal, ethical, and moral standards of records management are not followed?
- What purpose do the various data forms serve?
- What formats are used for documentation in a patient's medical record?

CHARTING IN THE PATIENT'S RECORD

Charting is the process of documenting events in written form. It is an important part of the patient's care because it communicates the patient's condition and the care received. Because the patient's record is a legal document, it is the medical practice's best defense against lawsuits and provides documentation for third-party payers. For these reasons, charting must be legible and accurate. Corrections to the record must be made according to established guidelines.

Guidelines

Charting must communicate that the patient has received quality care and medically necessary services. All services provided must be documented, even if the service is not billable; for example, phone calls made and diagnostic procedures scheduled are not billable, but they must be documented to show continuity of patient care.

The medical assistant frequently is responsible for recording results of procedures performed. When all members of the health care team document all relevant information in the medical record, this helps the team to improve patient care, gain full reimbursement for care provided, and protect the provider legally. See Box 11-2 for charting "do"s and "don't"s.

BOX 11-2 Charting "Do"s and "Don't"s

Do:
- Verify the name on the file before charting.
- Check to be certain the patient's name appears on each document page. The name should be in place before filing.
- Begin all entries with the date and time. Conclude with your signature and credentials.
- Use black ink because it is easier to photocopy.
- Use military time to avoid confusion (Box 11-3) if this is office policy.
- Chart all pertinent observations. Use patient quotes when possible.
- Write neatly and legibly, using proper grammar and approved abbreviations. (Wording must be accurate, clear, and concise.)
- Chart the plan of care and the physician's orders that were done, with the results and the patient's responses immediately after the procedure.
- Chart all patient teaching, precautions, and assessments of the patient's understanding.
- Chart patient's noncompliance or failure to follow treatment.

- Fill in all blank spaces and lines on a preprinted form, even if you only add "N/A" (not applicable) or draw a line through the space.
- Chart as soon as care is given; never wait and chart later.

Don't:
- Rely on memory to chart important information.
- Criticize treatment in the notes.
- Draw conclusions or make assumptions.
- Add procedures done previously to the chart.
- Erase or alter chart notes in any way.
- Chart anything you did not see or do.
- Change the patient's wording.
- Use abbreviations that are not standard and approved by the office.
- Leave empty spaces at the end of a line.
- Skip lines between entries.
- Leave space before your signature.
- Guess at spelling.

BOX 11-3 · Samples of Standard and Military Time

Standard	Military	Standard	Military
1:00 a.m.	0100	1:30 PM	1330
9:20 a.m.	0920	2:00 PM	1400
10:10 a.m.	1010	3:45 PM	1545
11:00 a.m.	1100	4:15 PM	1615
Noon	1200	Midnight	2400

A method used to convert military time into standard time is to subtract 2 from any given time after noon. Remove the first digit from the military time and subtract 2. For example:

1300 = 300 − 2 = 1 p.m. or   After 12 noon, add
1700 = 700 − 2 = 5 p.m.   1200 to the hour and
                             convert minutes
                             1:30 = 130 + 1200
                                      or 1330

(Illustration from Gerdin J: Health careers today, *ed 3, St Louis, 2003, Mosby.)*

The ultimate goal is to provide accurate, legible, consistent, and concise entries. If an entry is illegible, the fact that the service was provided cannot be established; it is as though it were never provided or documented at all. If an entry is illegible, a misinterpretation of the procedure could result. Chart all entries in black ink because black ink photocopies the best. (Different offices may have different procedures; many facilities allow *only* black ink, whereas some institutions require blue ink because it also photocopies well and makes it easier to identify the "original" entry.)

All entries in a patient's record should begin with the date of the encounter. A line should be drawn at the end of the entry to the space for the signature to prevent information from being inserted at a later date.

Box 11-4 lists the charting information needed for complete documentation in a patient record.

BOX 11-4 · Charting Information Needed for Complete Documentation in the Patient Record

Chief Complaint
Date
Time
Symptoms as told by the patient (in patient's own words, if possible)
Proper signature

Procedure
Date
Time
Type (e.g., vital signs)
Results
Patient reaction
Proper signature

Medications
Date
Time
Name of medication
Dosage given
Route
Site (if injection)
Patient reaction
Proper signature

Specimen Collection
Date
Time
Type/site (e.g., urine, blood)
Results
Proper signature

To Outside
Test requested
Date sent
Place sent
Proper signature

Diagnostic Tests and Lab Tests
Date
Time
Type of test ordered
Schedule date (if known)
Place being performed
Proper signature

Laboratory Test Results
Date
Time
Name of test
Results

From Outside (Telephone)
Record results on appropriate form
Laboratory report to physician for review, then filed with chart
Proper signature

Patient Education
Date
Time
Type of instructions
Signed form stating patient understood instructions and medical assistant to witness
Proper signature

Missed Appointments, Telephone Requests, Prescription Refills
Date
Time
Situation (e.g., refill request, missed appointment)
Proper signature

Correction Procedures

When charting, the medical assistant may find it necessary to make corrections on the patient's medical record. *Never* use correction fluid (e.g., Wite-Out) or erase in the medical record. The proper way to correct an entry follows (Fig. 11-6):

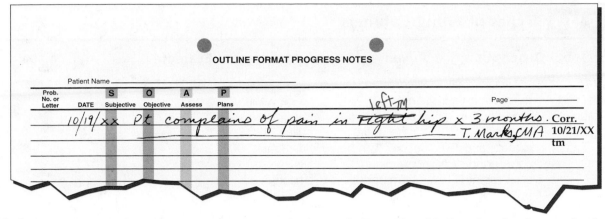

Fig. 11-6 Example of appropriate way to correct a medical record. *(From Hunt SA:* Saunders fundamentals of medical assisting, *Philadelphia, 2002, Saunders.)*

1. Draw a line through the errors.
2. Insert the correction above the error.
3. In the margin, write "correction" or "corr" ("err" or "error" is also used), your initials (or your name in full), and the date.

NOTE: The appropriate correction procedure may be subject to the medical practice's policy; some practices may require you to write your name in full when making a correction, not just your initials.

PATIENT-CENTERED PROFESSIONALISM

• Why is it important that the patient's medical record follow established guidelines?

SELECTING A FILING SYSTEM

When choosing a filing system, a medical office must determine what types and volume of documents will be filed. In most cases, more than one type of filing system will be used. For example, a *numerical* (numeric) system may be used for patient records, whereas an *alphabetical* (alphabetic) system may be used for business records; subject and geographic filing might be used for research or correspondence. Each method, with the exception of the numerical system, uses alphabetical concepts.

When choosing a filing system, the practice needs to consider the following:

• Available space
• Available budget
• Potential volume of patient records
• Selection of supplies
• Types of storage equipment

• Type of filing system best suited to the medical practice's needs

Once selected, a plan must be made for the filing system, and details must be entered into the practice's policy and procedures manual. The plan should contain the following components:

• Maintenance of the system and records
• Retrieval of the records
• Security of all records held in the office

Equipment

Several styles of file cabinets are used in the medical office. The selection of a file cabinet depends on what types of records are to be stored. Table 11-1 compares four different types of filing cabinets. Files may also be stored with automated or computerized systems.

Automated Files

Automated files can be used only in large facilities (e.g., hospitals) because of their cost and space requirements. The operator indicates the shelf needed, and the shelf is automatically moved into position by a motor, thereby eliminating the need for any pushing and pulling of cabinets and shelves.

Computerized Files

As computerization becomes more sophisticated in medical offices, the use of the **electronic medical record (EMR)** is growing in popularity and will soon become an industry standard. The data (information) can be entered from a computer station or laptop in any facility where a patient is receiving treatment. This information includes nursing notes, radiology reports, and laboratory results. The EMR is advantageous for the following reasons:

TABLE 11-1	**Types of Filing Cabinets**			
Type	**Description**	**Advantages**	**Disadvantages**	**Example**
Vertical (or drawer) file cabinet	Each drawer pulls out toward user. Often used for business records and correspondence. Typical cabinet holds about 700 files	Records are more protected in case of fire. Records can be examined from above. Usually locks	Requires more space when the drawer is pulled out. Holds about 700 files, so use limited in a medical setting. Danger of tipping if more than one drawer is open at once	
Lateral open-shelf file cabinet	Has stationary shelves and door cover that slides up and back into cabinet. Files are removed by pulling them out laterally. Usually holds about 1000 records	Patient records stored horizontally for quick retrieval. Misfiling easily seen and corrected if color-coded system used; helps keep records in proper order. Can be locked	Lateral open-shelf files require more room than vertical files	

TABLE 11-1	Types of Filing Cabinets—cont'd			
Type	**Description**	**Advantages**	**Disadvantages**	**Example**
Lateral drawer (or horizontal drawer) file cabinet	Has movable shelves that roll out sideways Patient records are filed from right to left Entire record label is visible Holds more records but requires more wall space than vertical file	Holds more records than vertical file cabinet Can be locked	More space is required for lateral or horizontal drawer file cabinets than for vertical cabinets	
Rotary (or movable lateral) file cabinet	Electronically or manually powered to rotate or move files in position to be accessed Maximizes use of space and holds large volume of records	Use of space is maximized Large volumes of records can be held	Provides less privacy and protection than file cabinets that can be closed completely and locked Normally kept in locked room	

(Vertical cabinet from Chester GA: *Modern medical assisting*, Philadelphia, Saunders, 1998. Lateral drawer cabinet courtesy Bibbero Systems, Inc., Petaluma, Calif; phone [800] 242-2376; fax [800] 242-9330; www.bibbero.com. Rotary cabinet courtesy Mayline Group, Sheboygan, Wis.)

- All entries are legible.
- The record can be accessed by multiple practitioners at the same time.
- Missing records do not become a problem.
- Once the information is entered into the computer, the record is instantaneously complete.
- Release of patient information to other providers and insurance companies is much easier.

- Printouts are easily retrieved.
- The maintenance and storage of paper records are eliminated.

Along with these benefits come responsibilities. Records must be "password" protected to allow entry only on a "need to know" basis, and computer screens must be situated so that they are not in view of the general public.

Filing Supplies

In addition to the physical filing cabinet or system itself, supplies are needed to hold, organize, and label documents, records, and forms.

Color-Coding/A-Z File Guides

Guides, or dividers, are used to separate file folders into sections and indicate a letter, number, or range of letters. Guides are larger than file folders and made of a material heavier than a file folder (e.g., fiberboard, pressboard). Their purpose is to facilitate record filing and retrieval by separating file space into recognizable and easily handled groupings.

Out Guides

Out guides are dividers of a different size and color than a file folder. Out guides should always be used when a file is removed from file storage. The out guide is placed in the space where the patient's record was filed. Its purpose is to allow the medical office to identify the precise location of a file and who has the file. Out guides should have a place to write the date, time, and name of the person removing the file. When used properly, out guides significantly reduce the time lost in locating missing files. Think of an out guide as a bookmark you place in a book that you are reading to save your place (Fig. 11-7).

File Folders

File folders are used to contain patient documents. They can be purchased in several color and size selections. Tabs (full cut, half cut, third cut, fifth cut) extend along the top edge or side edge and are used to indicate what is in the file with the addition of a label. The top-cut (tab) folder is stored in a vertical file cabinet, and the folder with the tab on the side is stored in a lateral cabinet.

File folders may be purchased with inside dividers and fasteners attached to the inside covers to hold documents.

File Labels

Labels are used to identify the contents of the file. Labels can indicate a patient's name or provide other information about the patient (e.g., allergy, advance directives) (Fig. 11-8). The label has space for a **caption** (words that describe the contents, name of a person, or subject). Most labels are self-adhesive and should always be typed or computer-printed for clarity.

Aging Labels

Aging labels (year labels) are adhesive, color-coded labels used to indicate the last year a patient was seen in the medical office. When pulling files for office appointments, always make sure the file has a current year label on it if appropriate. Current year labels are placed over the top of the outdated year label, so there is always only one year's date (label) visible on the file. The last two digits of the year are used. Aging labels help when purging files for inactive status.

Color-Coded Labels

A color-coding system consists of labels that indicate a number, a letter, or an *alphanumerical* (letters, numbers) character. An alphabetical or numerical color-coded system assigns each letter, number, or preprinted numbering sequence a different color. Subject files can also be color coded, with each subject area being assigned a different color. The advantage of using a color-coding system is that files can be retrieved faster and misfiled records are easy to see (Fig. 11-9).

Fig. 11-7 Out guides. *(Courtesy Bibbero Systems, Inc., Petaluma, Calif; phone [800] 242-2376; fax [800] 242-9330; www.bibbero.com.)*

PATIENT-CENTERED PROFESSIONALISM

- What information is necessary when choosing a file storage system?
- What supplies are needed for a filing system?
- How can a well-organized filing system benefit the patients in the medical practice?

FILING METHODS

A medical office will select a filing method for patient and office records that meets the needs of the practice. Common filing systems are alphabeti-

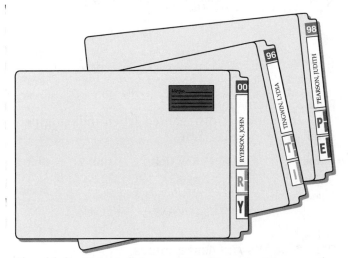

Fig. 11-8 File labels allow the physician and medical staff to quickly see important information about the patient. *(Courtesy Bibbero Systems, Inc., Petaluma, Calif; phone [800] 242-2376; fax [800] 242-9330; www.bibbero.com.)*

Fig. 11-9 Color labels used for filing. In this case, the alphabetical system is used: the first label indicates the first letter of the last name, and the second label indicates the second letter of the last name. Labels for the year of the patient's last visit are also color-coded. *(From Hunt SA: Saunders fundamentals of medical assisting, Philadelphia, 2002, Saunders.)*

cal, numerical, alphanumerical, and subject filing. Each has distinctive qualities that accommodate different record needs. Patient records are filed either by the patient's name or by a numerical method. Business records and correspondence can be filed alphabetically or by subject.

Alphabetical Filing

The **alphabetical filing** method uses letters of the alphabet to determine how files are arranged. Using the same sequence as the letters of the alphabet, files are organized by last names of people or names of businesses. This is the most common method of filing.

The **indexing** process is the determination of how a record will be filed. Each name is broken into units. All personnel responsible for filing activities must be consistent in their filing procedures. The office must determine how each piece of information is to be filed, and not allow any deviation. This should be established in the medical practice's policy and procedures manual.

Advantages and Disadvantages

Alphabetical filing is the most common system used in small to medium-sized medical practices. It is considered a **direct filing** system because finding a patient file or business folder only requires knowing the correct name. As with any system, alphabetical filing has advantages and disadvantages.

ADVANTAGES
- Alphabetical filing is the easiest system to learn
- Alphabetical filing allows for easy training of new staff members
- Only one sorting is required

DISADVANTAGES
- The correct spelling of the name must be known to find a folder
- As the medical practice grows and the volume of patients increases, each alphabetical section will expand, requiring periodic shifting of file sections in the file drawers or cabinets
- Unauthorized personnel could have easier access to files

Rules for Efficient Alphabetical Filing

The key objective to effective filing is to be able to retrieve the appropriate record or information quickly when it is needed. The Association of Records Managers and Administrators (ARMA) has established rules to assist in efficient alphabetical filing. Without specific rules, the filing process becomes inefficient. The purpose of indexing rules is to provide consistency among the office staff when filing information, whether it is business or patient related.

Read each rule and study the examples provided. Understanding how names are divided into the indexing units is the first step to alphabetical filing. If the **key unit,** or first unit (e.g., the first letter or character), is similar, move on to the second and succeeding units until a difference is apparent. For example, "Sanders" would be filed before "Santos" because "d" comes before "t" in the alphabet (*d* and *t* are the first letters in each name that are different). Before moving on to the next rule, fully understand the current rule.

RULE 1: SEQUENCING ORDER
Personal Names. Personal names are indexed accordingly:
- The last name is the *key unit*, or first unit
- The first name or initial is the second unit
- The middle name or initial is the third unit. In some medical offices, the preference is to spell out the middle name

NOTE: If an initial represents a unit, this initial will precede a unit consisting of a complete name beginning with the same letter (e.g., T. Jones would be filed before Tamara Jones). Keep in mind the rule that *nothing comes before something*—because no additional letter is immediately after the letter T. in T. Jones, this name would come before Tamara Jones, which has the letter *a* immediately after the *T.*

Name	Key Unit	Unit 2	Unit 3
Douglas A. Telle	Telle	Douglas	A
Amanda B. Telley	Telley	Amanda	B
John J. Telly	Telly	John	J

When a person's last name could be mistaken for the first name, a **cross-reference** folder should be made (e.g., Lee Wong).

Key Unit	Unit 2	
Wong	Lee	
Lee	Wong	See Wong, Lee

Business Names. Business names are indexed as written, using newspapers, letterhead, and trademarks as a guide. Each word in the business name has its own unit. If a person's name appears in the business name, it remains as written.

Name	Key Unit	Unit 2	Unit 3
Johnny Appleseed Farm	Johnny	Appleseed	Farm
Jumpin' Box Toys	Jumpin	Box	Toys

RULE 2: MISCELLANEOUS WORDS AND SYMBOLS
Prepositions, articles, conjunctions, and symbols are considered separate indexing units.
- Prepositions: in, out, at, on, by, to, of, with.
- Articles: a, an, the (when appearing as the first word of a business name, articles are indexed last or discarded; articles have no significance in filing).
- Conjunctions: and, but, or, nor
- Symbols: &, $, ¢, #, % (symbols are spelled in full—e.g., and, dollar, cent, number, percent).

Name	Key Unit	Unit 2	Unit 3	Unit 4
A Big Top Company	Big	Top	Company	(A)
Big & Small Clothing	Big	and	Small	Clothing
$ and ¢ Store	Dollar	and	Cent	Store
The Mom & Pop	Mom	and	Pop	(The)

RULE 3: PUNCTUATION
All punctuation is disregarded when indexing personal and business names.

Name	Key Unit	Unit 2	Unit 3
Barney's Tea Room	Barneys	Tea	Room
Elaine C. Jones-Smith	JonesSmith	Elaine	C
Hide-Away Motel	HideAway	Motel	

RULE 4: INITIALS AND ABBREVIATIONS
Personal. Initials, abbreviations of personal names, and nicknames are indexed as they are written.

Name	Key Unit	Unit 2	Unit 3
J. John Smith	Smith	J	John
Bill James Smith	Smith	Bill	James
Wm. James Smith	Smith	Wm	James

Business. Single letters representing a business or organization are indexed as written. If a single letter is separated by a space, each letter is indexed separately. An **acronym** (word formed from the first few letters of several words) is indexed as one unit. Television and radio station call letters are considered one unit.

Name	Key Unit	Unit 2	Unit 3	Unit 4
CNN	CNN			
S A C Furniture	S	A	C	Furniture
T & A Clinic	T	and	A	Clinic
IBM	IBM			

RULE 5: TITLES.

Personal and Professional Titles. Professional titles (Dr., Prof.), general titles (Mr., Ms., Mrs.), and professional, numeric, and seniority suffixes are always indexed last.

Name	Key Unit	Unit 2	Unit 3	Unit 4
James J. Jameston, M.D.	Jameston	James	J	MD
Ms. Joan Summers, CMA	Summers	Joan	Ms	CMA
Joseph K. Suthe, II	Suthe	Joseph	K	II
Senator Mary Toth	Toth	Mary	Senator	

Religious Titles. Religious titles not followed by a last name are indexed as written.

Name	Key Unit	Unit 2	Unit 3
Brother John	Brother	John	
Father John Jones	Jones	John	Father

Titles in Business Names. Titles used in the name of a business are indexed as written.

Name	Key Unit	Unit 2	Unit 3
Mr. Jay's Coffee	Mr	Jays	Coffee
Uncle Ben's China	Uncle	Bens	China

RULE 6: PREFIXES

A foreign name that has a prefix or an article included is combined with the last name to become the key unit, without the use of spaces. However, using uppercase and lowercase letters is allowed for the articles.

Name	Key Unit	Unit 2
Robert de la Guard	delaGuard	Robert
Tom De Marce	DeMarce	Tom
Jerry Los Angel	LosAngel	Jerry
Saint John's Church	SaintJohns	Church
St. John's Rectory	SaintJohns	Rectory
Van der Mills' Clothing	VanderMills	Clothing

NOTE: "St." is indexed as if it were spelled out (as with "Saint" John's Rectory).

RULE 7: NUMBERS IN BUSINESSES

Numbers spelled out are indexed in the file alphabetically (e.g., "Five-Spot Shop" would come before "Two Brothers Restaurant"). Numbers expressed in digit form are indexed before alphabetical letters or words (as in "7 Eleven"). Arabic numerals (1, 2, 3) are filed *before* Roman numerals (I, II, III); thus in the file, the chart for "7 Eleven" would come before "II Club."

Name	Key Unit	Unit 2
7 Eleven	7	Eleven
II Club	II	Club
One Towing	One	Towing

RULE 8: ORGANIZATIONS AND INSTITUTIONS

Banks, colleges, hotels, schools, and so forth are indexed as written. The letterhead of the organization or institution provides the correct reference.

Name	Key Unit	Unit 2	Unit 3	Unit 4
1st Union Bank	1	Union	Bank	
First Atlantic Credit Union	First	Atlantic	Credit	Union
M.L.K. High School	MLK	High	School	
R.F.K. Institute of Art	RFK	Institute	of	Art

RULE 9: IDENTICAL NAMES

When names (whether they are personal or business names) are identical, the filing order is determined by *address*. The following guidelines prevail:
- City name
- State name (if cities are identical)
- Street name (if city and state names are identical)
- House or building numbers (if the above are identical)
- If street address and building names are included in the address, disregard the building name
- Zip codes are never indexed

Name	Key Unit	Unit 2	Unit 3	Unit 4	Unit 5	Unit 6	Unit 7
Mrs. Sally Fieds 67 Atkins Ave Albany, NY 32141	Fieds	Sally	Mrs	Albany	NY	Atkins	Ave
Mrs. Sally Fieds 63 Atkins Blvd Albany, NY 32147	Fieds	Sally	Mrs	Albany	NY	Atkins	Blvd

Because addresses may change frequently, most medical offices use the date of birth or Social Security number rather than addresses when names are identical, using year, month, and date. For example, the file of Mrs. Sally Fieds with a birthdate of 7/12/74 would come before the file of Mrs. Sally Fieds with a birth date of 2/9/78. When using Social Security numbers, Mrs. Sally Fieds 190-xx-0106 would come before Mrs. Sally Fieds 206-xx-1789 in the file.

Name	Key Unit	Unit 2	Unit 3	Unit 4	Unit 5
James Smith Birth date: January 2, 1999	Smith	James	1999	January	2
James Smith Birth date: April 2, 2001	Smith	James	2001	April	2

Rule 10: Government Names

All government agencies are first indexed by United States Government, using "United" as the key unit, "States" as unit 2, and "Government" as unit 3, then the agency. The fourth and succeeding units are the main words in the name of the department.

Name	Key Unit	Unit 2	Unit 3	Unit 4	Unit 5
U.S. Government Department of the Treasury	United	States	Government	Treasury	Department

NOTE: The phone book can be a good resource for help in finding the correct alphabetical filing.

Numerical Filing

In the **numerical filing** method, patient files are given numbers and arranged in numerical sequence. Medical assistants must consider the following two factors when using a numerical filing system:

1. How to assign the number.
2. How to file the records once the number is assigned.

Medical offices that have a large number of patient files may choose to keep medical records according to an assigned number. For example, the number may be assigned on the basis of the patient's Social Security number or the patient's order of registration as a new patient. The numerical system is an **indirect filing** method because a listing of patient names must be used to locate the correct number.

Advantages and Disadvantages

As with the alphabetical filing method, there are advantages and disadvantages to the numerical method.

Advantages

- Numerical filing is the most confidential system.
- Expansion is unlimited.
- Misfiled folders are easy to locate.
- It is easy to remove inactive files when numbers are assigned according to patient order of registration (because the age of the file will be apparent by its number).

Disadvantages

- To find a folder, the correct number must be known. This is accomplished by either using a password to access the patient's computerized file or having access to a master list of patient's names that provides the patient's number. This makes locating every file a two-step process.
- A file list must be constantly updated and maintained.
- Numbers could be transposed without being detected.
- It is easy to misfile.

Methods

The two most common methods by which filing can be done numerically are straight-number filing and terminal-digit filing.

Straight-Number Filing

Straight-number filing is the most common form of numerical filing. File folders are filed in numerical sequence. Thus files in straight-number filing would appear as #3456, #3457, #3458, and so on. When using straight-number filing, as the numbers increase, so do the files. The longer the number, the harder it may become to file, because that area of numbers will be the highest concentration of newer patient files.

Terminal-Digit Filing

Terminal-digit filing organizes a number by the final digits of the number. The digits are usually separated into groups of two or three. For example, the file number 107654 can be separated into groups of twos. The last two digits (terminal digits) (54) identify the file drawer number; the second two digits (76) identify the number of the file guide; and the first two digits (10) provide the number of the file folder behind the file guide (Fig. 11-10).

Subject Filing

Subject filing is most frequently used with correspondence or research. If the physician is starting a research project about hypertension, all correspondence on this subject will be labeled "hypertension." This allows all materials on a particular subject to be kept in one folder.

Color Coding

A color-coding system can be used with alphabetical or numerical filing and in combined alphanumerical files. Several companies offer color-coded tabs; the medical assistant must follow the manufacturer's directions. Color coding makes filing easier and draws attention to misfiled folders.

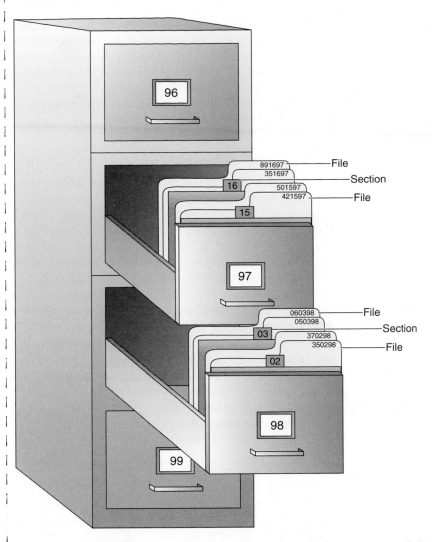

Fig. 11-10   Vertical file cabinet, showing use of terminal-digit filing method.

Tickler File

If the medical office does not use a computerized "reminder" system, an effective reminder aid is the **tickler file**. This type of file "tickles the memory" about upcoming events (e.g., license renewal, payments, call-back appointments). A tickler file can be organized by putting the event to be remembered on a 3 × 5 card and placing it behind a numbered date guide. This system allows you to file reminders for any month of the year ahead, on a year-round basis.

≋ REVIEW OF BASIC FILING PROCEDURES

Medical assistants need to be familiar with the basic steps for preparing and filing, as well as for purging and retaining files for maintenance.

Steps for Preparing and Filing

Preparing documents for filing involves the following steps:

Step 1: **Conditioning.** The files must be in good condition before they are filed. This requires removing all staples and paper clips, mending any torn edges on the document, and verifying that the patient's name appears on each page of a multiple-page document.

Step 2: **Releasing.** A file is "released" when a mark (e.g., checkmark, initials) is placed on the document indicating it should be filed. For example, releasing would occur after a physician has read a patient's lab report and checks it off for filing in the patient's record. The physician or other authorized staff member, depending on the information classification, performs this step.

Some offices use a rubber stamp to mark when a document is ready for filing. It has a place for the date and the provider's initials.

Step 3: **Indexing** and **coding.** Indexing indicates where the document is to be filed, and coding provides a mark (underlining or highlighting) with the keyword (often the patient's last name). This action also separates business documents from patient information.

Step 4: **Sorting.** The documents must be arranged (sorted) for filing. An alpha sorter has tabs labeled A-Z and can be used to sort all papers by patient last name. Or, a document sorter with captions on the tabs indicating subject areas (e.g., lab reports, consultation reports) can be used to initially sort documents of a similar nature.

Step 5: **Filing.** Once this stage is reached, filing can occur. Filing is the process of putting all documents in the folder. It is important to remember that when a document is added to an established file, the most recently dated document should be placed on top.

After documents have been prepared for filing, they can either be filed immediately or placed in an alphabetical sorter for filing later.

Procedure 11-6 outlines the process for alphabetical filing.

Procedure 11-7 shows the process for numerical filing.

Purging and Retention

Active files are kept in a file cabinet where they are easy to retrieve. These medical files are for patients who are routinely scheduled for care. **Inactive files** are the files of patients who have not visited the practice within a certain time span (set by the practice). Some larger practices with a high volume of patients will **purge** (clean out) records every 1 or 2 years. Purging is the preparation of a file to go from active status to inactive status. Smaller practices may purge less frequently.

Purging depends on the amount of storage available and the turnover and volume of patients in the practice. These files are usually stored "off site," but they can also be placed on *microfiche* (a small sheet of film containing reduced images) or can be microfilmed to reduce storage space. New computer software programs are also available for scanning

---

Procedure 11-6   File Medical Records Using the Alphabetical System

TASK: Correctly file a set of patient records using an established alphabetical filing system.

NOTE: Filing medical records by an alphabetical system is an activity related to the competency of organizing a patient's medical record.

EQUIPMENT AND SUPPLIES
- Patient files
- Alphanumerical sorter

SKILLS/RATIONALE

1. **Procedural Step. Retrieve the appropriate patient files from the file storage area.**
2. **Procedural Step. Complete any documentation needed.**
3. **Procedural Step. Add any supplemental forms or records generated according to office procedure.**
4. **Procedural Step. Sort the files alphabetically, using a "desktop sorter" if possible.**
   Rationale. The use of a sorter makes the filing process much more efficient because it saves the medical assistant significant time.

5. **Procedural Step. Remove the files from the sorter and return the files to the storage cabinet, correctly filing them alphabetically into the appropriate sequence.**
   Rationale. Specific indexing rules must be followed when filing, whether alphabetical or numerical. This ensures that the document is easy to retrieve for future reference.

Procedure 11-7 File Medical Records Using the Numerical System

TASK: Correctly file a set of patient records, using an established numerical filing system.

EQUIPMENT AND SUPPLIES
- Patient files
- Numerical sorter

TASK/RATIONALE

1. **Procedural Step. Retrieve the appropriate patient files from the file storage area.**
2. **Procedural Step. Complete any documentation necessary.**
3. **Procedural Step. Add any supplemental forms or records generated according to office procedure.**
4. **Procedural Step. Sort the files numerically, using a "desktop sorter" if possible. The office filing system may be straight number or terminal digit.**

Rationale. The use of a sorter makes the filing process much more efficient because it saves the medical assistant significant time.

5. **Procedural Step. Remove the files from the sorter, and return the files to the storage cabinet, correctly filing them into the appropriate numerical sequence.**

---

inactive patient records onto a computer (compact) disk (CD) for storage. This method is compact and cost-efficient, and office staff can be easily trained to do this.

Depending on office file space, files are usually purged every year, or even monthly in large practices. Purging of medical records can also mean removing unnecessary old materials from the medical record, such as paid insurance claims and unneeded notes (e.g., phoned-in lab results). Each office should have a policy indicating when files are to be removed from main file storage.

Most state statutes require that medical records be kept (retained) at least 7 years from the last information entry date. The American Medical Association (AMA) recommends keeping adult records for 10 years and keeping records for 3 years after a minor reaches the age of majority (which varies from state to state, usually age 18 or 21). If a file is to be discarded, the documents should be shredded or burned. This protects the confidentiality of its contents. Some medical offices contract with a business that provides this service. The outside service must follow the same guidelines for confidentiality of patient records as the medical office. Both the office and the outside service are bound by HIPAA guidelines.

PATIENT-CENTERED PROFESSIONALISM

- What function does preparing documents serve?
- What does purging documents accomplish?

CONCLUSION

Medical records are the confidential, legal documents used to record the health care services provided to an individual at a medical facility. Medical records are used in planning, coordinating, and evaluating a patient's care, as well as for protecting the interests of the patient, practice, and health care provider in case of lawsuit.

To handle the essential information and documentation in the medical record effectively and efficiently, medical assistants need to know how to generate, update, file, store, and maintain these records. Accuracy is necessary; if a service is not documented on the medical record, it is considered to have never happened. In order for patients to receive the best care possible, their medical records must be handled with as much diligence and competence as the services provided to them for care and treatment.

SUMMARY

Reinforce your understanding of the material in this chapter by reviewing the curriculum objectives and key content points below.

1. Define, appropriately use, and spell all the Key Terms for this chapter.
   - Review the Key Terms if necessary.
2. Explain the purpose of a medical record.
   - A patient's medical record provides legal evidence of assessment, interventions, and communication between health care providers and the patient.
   - If a patient's care is not documented, it is considered not done.
3. List three uses of the medical record.
   - Laboratory reports, consultation letters, and other documentation provide information to support the course of treatment.
   - Medical records are used to track progress, file insurance claims, and resolve legal matters such as lawsuits.
4. Explain how the medical record protects the legal interests of the patient, the health care provider, and the medical practice.
   - The medical record is a legal document and is a record of the services provided, the communications, and the other interactions between the patient and the provider, either the physician or the medical facility.
   - The medical record can be used as evidence in a lawsuit.
5. Demonstrate the correct procedure for pulling patient records.
   - Review Procedure 11-1.
6. Demonstrate the correct procedure for registering a patient.
   - Review Procedure 11-2.
7. List and describe seven basic forms used to start a new patient's medical record.
   - The forms required for different types of practices may vary.
   - Typical forms included in the medical record are the patient information form, health history, consent to treat form, consent to use and disclose health information form, history and physical, progress notes, and medication log (list).
8. Demonstrate the correct procedure for creating a medical file for a new patient using alphabetical, color-coded tabs.
   - Review Procedure 11-3.
9. List five examples of forms that could be added to an established patient's medical record as care is provided.

- Various radiographic reports, laboratory reports, diagnostic procedure reports, consultation reports from other physicians, and hospital reports (operative, pathology) could be added to an existing patient's medical record.

10. Demonstrate the correct procedure for adding documents to an existing patient record.
    - Review Procedure 11-4.
11. Demonstrate the correct procedure for protecting the confidentiality of patients and their medical records.
    - Review Procedure 11-5.
12. Differentiate between *source-oriented* and *problem-oriented* records.
    - A source-oriented format organizes a patient's file into sections according to the source of the documents (e.g., x-ray reports, consultations).
    - A problem-oriented medical record is organized according to the patient's health problem.
13. Describe where progress notes fit into the POMR format of organizing a patient's record, and explain the acronym SOAP.
    - The POMR (problem-oriented medical record) is arranged according to the patient's health complaint. There are four components of the POMR: database, problem list, plan, and progress notes.
    - The progress notes are written in a SOAP format, which consists of subjective data, objective data, assessment, and plan.
14. Explain the importance of documenting all services provided to the patient.
    - All services provided to a patient must be clearly documented in order to receive reimbursement for care provided (prove medical necessity), establish a legal record of all treatment, and provide for continuity of care should the patient be transferred to other health care providers.
15. Identify specific actions as "Do"s or "Don't"s of charting in patients' medical records.
    Do:
    - Use direct quotations from the patient when possible.
    - Chart the plan of care, results, physician's orders, and patient's responses immediately after performing the procedure.
    - Chart all patient teaching, precautions, and assessment of patient understanding.
    - Make sure all charting entries are accurate and legible.
    - Use black ink.
    Don't:
    - Chart anything you have not personally witnessed or performed.

- Chart from memory.
- Chart your personal opinions about the patient or treatment rendered.
- Write carelessly or illegibly.
- Use correction fluid or erase any entries.

16. List the three steps for correcting an entry error in the patient's medical record.
    - Draw a line through the incorrect entry.
    - Insert the correction above the error, indicating a correction is being made.
    - Include the name or initials of the person making the correction with the date.

17. State the three considerations for selecting a filing system.
    - Volume of patient files.
    - Budget allocated for equipment purchase.
    - Space available for the equipment.

18. State the three components of a filing system plan that should be recorded in detail in the office procedure manual.
    - A plan must be made for the maintenance, retrieval, and security of all records held in the office. This plan should be indicated by office policy and procedure.

19. Differentiate among vertical drawer, lateral open-shelf, lateral drawer, and movable lateral file cabinets.
    - *Vertical drawer:* Each drawer pulls out toward you. Folders are filed front to back in the drawer and removed by lifting them up and out of the drawer.
    - *Lateral open shelf:* Stationary shelves with a door cover that flips up and back. Folders are filed side to side and removed by pulling them out laterally.
    - *Lateral drawer:* Movable shelves that roll out sideways. Folders are filed from right to left and removed by pulling them out laterally.
    - *Movable lateral file:* Cabinets rotate manually or automatically for file selection.

20. List six supplies typically used with a filing system.
    - Cabinets
    - A-Z guides or numerical guides
    - Appropriate-size file folders
    - Out guides
    - Various types of alphanumerical labels
    - Special-alert labels (e.g., allergies, collection)

21. List four methods of filing and briefly explain each.
    - *Alphabetical filing* is by a patient's last name.
    - *Straight-number filing* is based on the entire number as the key unit.
    - *Terminal-digit filing* uses the last two digits of the patient's identifying number as the key unit for determining file placement.

- *Subject filing* is used in research studies and is organized by subject matter.

22. Discuss the advantages and disadvantages of alphabetical filing.
    - Alphabetical filing is the easiest method to learn and only requires one sorting.
    - A disadvantage is that unauthorized personnel could have easier access to files.

23. List the areas addressed in the 10 rules for alphabetical filing.
    - Filing rules relate to sequencing order, miscellaneous words and symbols, punctuation, initials and abbreviations, titles, prefixes, numbers in businesses, organizations and institutions, identical names, and government names.
    - In general, if the key unit of more than one file is alike, move on to the second and succeeding units until a difference is apparent.

24. Discuss the advantages and disadvantages of numerical filing.
    - Numerical filing is the most confidential method, and expansion is unlimited.
    - A disadvantage is that the correct number must be known to find a folder, making locating a file a two-step process.

25. Differentiate between *straight-number* filing and *terminal-digit* filing.
    - Straight-number filing is the most common method, and files follow in whole-number sequence.
    - Terminal-digit filing organizes a number by its final digits.

26. List in order the five steps of preparing and filing medical records and briefly describe each.
    - *Conditioning.* Documents must be prepared by removing staples and paper clips.
    - *Releasing.* Documents must have a release mark, meaning they are ready to be filed.
    - *Indexing and coding.* Documents must be indexed according to their source (e.g., all lab reports) and coded according to how they will be filed (e.g., patient's last name).
    - *Sorting.* Documents must be sorted for filing.
    - *Filing.* Documents must be filed according to established procedure (e.g., alphabetical or numerical).

27. Demonstrate the correct procedure for filing medical records using the alphabetical system.
    - Review Procedure 11-6.

28. Demonstrate the correct procedure for filing medical records using the numerical system.
    - Review Procedure 11-7.

29. Differentiate between *active* and *inactive* files.

- Active files are those currently in use.
- Inactive files are those of patients not seen within a specified time span set by the medical practice.

30. Explain the need to purge files regularly in a medical practice.
    - Files are purged, or moved from active status to inactive status, to keep the main file storage area as up-to-date as possible and to allow for expansion of active files.

31. Analyze a realistic medical office situation and apply your understanding of charting and filing medical records to determine the best course of action.
    - Each medical office should have its own policies on how medical records should be charted, filed, stored, and purged.
    - Understanding how to create and maintain medical records helps the practice to run more efficiently and provides protection in legal matters. It also improves continuity of patient care by providing accurate documentation and accessibility to a patient's record.

32. Describe the impact on patient care when medical assistants understand the importance of accurate documentation and efficient filing of medical records.

- Physicians use medical records to monitor patient treatment and progress; also, when patients are referred to other physicians, continuity of care transfers easily.
- Medical records provide information needed to support the course of treatment and establish medical necessity; if they are inaccurate or incomplete, patient care is negatively affected.
- Accurate medical records protect both the patient and the practice; they also help ensure that payment of insurance claims is timely.

FOR FURTHER EXPLORATION

Research the topic of medical records to learn more about how private medical information has become. The tradition of physician-patient privilege was the only protection of patient privacy for many years. HIPAA set a national standard for privacy for health information, but is it enough?

Keywords: Use the following keywords in your search: HIPAA, AHIMA, medical records, medical information, privacy rights.

Chapter Review

Vocabulary Review

Matching

Match each term with the correct definition.

A. acronym

B. active file

C. aging labels

D. caption

E. coding

F. conditioning

G. cross-reference

H. database

I. electronic medical record

J. filing

K. indexing

L. key unit

M. numerical filing

N. out guides

O. problem-oriented medical record

P. progress notes

Q. purge

R. SOAP

S. sorting

T. terminal-digit filing

_____ 1. Patient medical records kept in a computer file; also called "paperless chart"

_____ 2. Data concerning a patient's medical care and its results

_____ 3. Method of filing that organizes records by their final digits

_____ 4. Words that describe the contents, name, or subject matter on a label

_____ 5. Method of arranging files using numbers

_____ 6. To clean out, as with excessive data in patient files

_____ 7. Type of chart format that divides each patient problem into subjective data, objective data, assessment, and plan for treatment

_____ 8. Process of removing staples and paper clips and mending a document before filing

_____ 9. Information source and storage

_____ 10. Separators that replace a file folder when it is removed from the file cabinet; contains a notation of the date and the name of the person who signed out the file

_____ 11. Arranging documents in a particular order for filing ease

_____ 12. Process of underlining a keyword to indicate how a document should be filed

_____ 13. Word formed from the first letter of several words

_____ 14. Chart format that is arranged according to a patient's health complaint

_____ 15. First unit to be filed

_____ 16. Notification system showing a file stored in more than one place

_____ 17. Records of current patient

_____ 18. Process of determining how a record will be filed

_____ 19. Labels on a chart that identify the year

_____ 20. Process of putting documents in a folder

Theory Recall

True/False

Indicate whether the sentence or statement is true or false.

_____ 1. Medical records provide evidence of patient assessments, interventions, and communications.

_____ 2. Progress notes are a list of the current medications taken by the patient.

_____ 3. SOAP formatting is extremely advantageous when more than one physician is treating the patient because all information pertaining to a specific problem can be located in a concise format.

_____ 4. The proper method of correcting errors in a medical record is to use correction fluid and re-enter the correct information.

_____ 5. The caption on a file label is used to identify the contents of the file.

Multiple Choice

Identify the letter of the choice that best completes the statement or answers the question.

1. The _____ process is the determination of how a record will be filed.
   A. indexing
   B. sorting
   C. annotating
   D. none of the above

2. In alphabetical filing, a _____ name is used as the key indexing unit.
   A. first
   B. middle
   C. last
   D. any of the above

3. Which of the following names would be filed before Mary Lynn Sommers?
   A. Mary Anne Winters
   B. M. Sorenson
   C. Mary Samuels
   D. Miriam Sommers

4. Which of the following names would be filed first?
   A. John Johnston
   B. Johnny Johnsten
   C. J. Jackson
   D. Jeremiah Jacobson

5. Which one of the following would be filed first?
   A. Professor Elijah Carlson
   B. President Eldon Anderson
   C. Congressman Elliason
   D. General George Franklin

6. _____ filing organizes a number by the final digits of the number.
   A. End-numerical
   B. Alpha-numerical
   C. First-digit
   D. None of the above

7. A file is "_____" when a checkmark is placed on the document indicating it should be filed.
   A. conditioned
   B. indexed
   C. sorted
   D. released

8. Inactive files are the files of a patient who has not visited the practice in _____.
   A. a time span set by the practice
   B. 1 year
   C. 3 years
   D. 7 years

9. A _____ is a reminder aid that organizes events by date.
   A. database file
   B. tickler file
   C. giggle file
   D. reminder file

10. Which one of the following files is NOT a standard form included in a patient record?
    A. Health history
    B. Consent to treatment
    C. Birth certificate
    D. Consent to disclose health information

11. If an established patient sees the physician for a _____, a new file must be made because the patient's complete health information would not be made available to an employer.
    A. pregnancy
    B. home-related injury
    C. work-related injury
    D. natural disaster

12. _____ regulations require providers to issue a written statement to each patient telling them about how the patient's health information may be used.
    A. HIPAA
    B. OSHA
    C. CLIA
    D. State

13. When a file for a new patient is being created, the first step in the procedure is to _____.
    A. create a file label
    B. attach alphabetical, color-coded labels
    C. attach an encounter form
    D. obtain and review a patient information form

14. If two patients have the exact same name, which of the following would determine which patient's file is filed first?
    A. Address
    B. Date of birth
    C. Social Security number
    D. The patient who has seen the physician more frequently

15. A _____ medical record is arranged according to the patient's health complaint.
    A. CCPH
    B. POMR
    C. SOAP
    D. none of the above

16. "My ankle hurts" is which one of the following types of information?
    A. Subjective
    B. Objective
    C. Assessment
    D. Plan

17. Which one of the following is "objective information"?
    A. There is swelling and bruising of the ankle and foot.
    B. The foot is hot to the touch.
    C. When the patient is walking to the examination room, you notice it is painful for the patient to put weight on the foot.
    D. All of the above is objective information.

18. All entries in a patient's record should begin with the _____.
    A. patient's name
    B. date of the encounter
    C. physician's signature
    D. none of the above

19. When choosing a filing system, the practice needs to consider all of the following EXCEPT _____.
    A. available space
    B. potential volume of patients
    C. available budget
    D. what is esthetically pleasing

20. _____ has established rules to assist in efficient alphabetical filing.
    A. ARMA
    B. AAMA
    C. AHIMA
    D. None of the above

21. Which one of the following is a disadvantage to numerical filing?
    A. Expansion is unlimited.
    B. It is more confidential.
    C. It is easy to misfile.
    D. It is easy to remove inactive files.

22. The filing system that has stationary shelves and a door cover that slides up and back into a cabinet and can hold approximately 1000 records is a _____ file cabinet.
    A. vertical
    B. drawer
    C. lateral, open-shelf
    D. lateral, drawer

23. As computerization becomes increasingly sophisticated in medical offices, the use of electronic medical records is growing in popularity and will soon become the industry standard. Which one of the following is NOT an advantage of this type of system?
    A. All entries are legible.
    B. The record can be accessed by multiple practitioners at the same time.
    C. There is an inability to secure all records and maintain confidentiality.
    D. Printouts are easily retrieved.

24. _____ are dividers of a different size and color than a file folder. They should always be used when a file is removed from the storage system.
    A. Manila envelopes
    B. Out guides
    C. Book markers
    D. File labels

25. The _____ filing method uses letters of the alphabet to determine how files are arranged.
    A. Mendoza
    B. Alphabetical
    C. Numerical
    D. Indexing

Sentence Completion

Complete each sentence or statement.

1. _____ is the acronym for the Association of Records Mangers and Administrators.

2. Professional titles, general titles, and professional numeric and seniority suffixes are always indexed _____.

3. _____, articles, conjunctions, and symbols are considered separate indexing units.

4. In the _____ filing method, patient files are given numbers and arranged in numerical sequence.

5. Because patient addresses may change frequently, most medical offices use the patient's date of birth or _____ rather than the address when two patient names are identical.

6. Numbers expressed in digit form are indexed before alphabetical letters or words and _____ are filed before Roman numerals.

7. The files filed using the _____ filing method are more likely to be misfiled, and they must be constantly updated and maintained.

8. _____ filing is the most common form of numerical filing.

9. _____ a file before being filed ensures the file is in good condition because all staples and paper clips are removed and any torn edges are mended.

10. If the medical office does not have a computerized reminder system, it is an excellent idea for the medical assistant to create a(n) _____ about upcoming events such as license renewal, payments, and call-backs.

Short Answers

1. List the three steps for correcting an entry error in the patient's medical record.

_____

_____

_____

2. State the three considerations for selecting a filing system.

_____

_____

_____

3. Discuss the advantages and disadvantages of numerical filing.

_____

_____

_____

4. Discuss the advantages and disadvantages of alphabetical filing.

_____

_____

_____

5. List six supplies typically used with a filing system.

_____

_____

_____

6. Explain the need to purge files regularly in a medical practice.

_____

_____

_____

Critical Thinking

Mr. Meredith called the office this morning inquiring about the status of lab results for his wife, Sharon. Sharon was seen last Friday in the office, and the lab results came in this morning. The lab reports have been filed in her patient file and are in a stack of files on Dr. Henry's desk for review. Describe how you would handle this call.

Internet Research

Keyword: Alphanumerical filing systems, terminal digit filing systems

Choose one of the following topics to research: alphanumerical filing systems or terminal digit filing systems. Write a two-paragraph report supporting your topic. Cite your source. Be prepared to give a 2-minute oral presentation should your instructor assign you to do so.

What Would You Do?

If you have accomplished the objectives in this chapter, you will be able to make better choices as a medical assistant. Take a look at this situation and decide what you would do.

Deanna is a new administrative medical-assisting extern at Dr. Juanea's office. Shirley, the office manager, asks Deanna to prepare a file for a new patient who will be seen tomorrow in the office. Shirley tells Deanna to be sure that she has color-coded the file folder and that the necessary forms have been included inside. In this office, the medical records are problem oriented, and all records are SOAP format; both are new concepts to Deanna, who was taught to prepare source-oriented records. After Deanna has prepared the new patient's file, Shirley asks her to pull the necessary records for tomorrow's appointments from the lateral open-shelf file cabinet containing patient records filed in alphabetical order. As she pulls the records, Deanna is to annotate the patient list for tomorrow's schedule. With the assistance of Shirley, Deanna will also purge the inactive patient records.

Would you be able to perform these tasks?

1. Why is the medical record necessary? What are its uses?

   _____

   _____

   _____

2. What is meant by "color-coding" a patient file?

   _____

   _____

   _____

3. What forms should Deanna be sure are in the new record?

   _____

   _____

   _____

4. What is meant by "problem-oriented" medical records?

   _____

   _____

   _____

5. What does SOAP mean?

_____

_____

_____

6. What is a "source-oriented" patient record?

_____

_____

_____

7. What are the advantages of open-shelf filing? What are the disadvantages?

_____

_____

_____

8. Why is alphabetical filing advantageous? What are the disadvantages?

_____

_____

_____

9. What will Deanna do to "annotate" a patient list?

_____

_____

_____

10. What is "purging" a file or a record? Why should patient records be purged on a regular basis?

_____

_____

_____

Chapter Quiz

Multiple Choice

Identify the letter of the choice that best completes the statement or answers the question.

1. _____ is a method of arranging files using straight numbers.
   A. Alphabetical filing
   B. Numerical filing
   C. Terminal digit filing
   D. Problem-oriented filing

2. _____ is the process of determining how a record will be filed.
   A. Conditioning
   B. Indexing
   C. Coding
   D. Purging

3. Word(s) that describe the content's name or subject matter on a label is (are) _____.
   A. acronym
   B. key unit
   C. cross-reference
   D. caption

4. _____ is a chart format that uses dividers to separate the different types of patient information.
   A. Problem-oriented medical record format
   B. Electronic medical record format
   C. Source-oriented format
   D. None of the above

5. A type of chart format that divides each patient problem into subjective data, objective data, assessment, and plan for treatment is _____.
   A. SOAP
   B. POMR
   C. SOBP
   D. WRI

6. A _____ is entered into the patient's record and is used to update the status of the patient's health. These are added to the patient's chart each time the patient visits the office.
   A. problem list
   B. tickler file
   C. progress note
   D. caption

7. The physician owns the medical record, but the patient owns the information.
   A. True
   B. False

8. When might a medical assistant use a patient's date of birth as an indexing unit for filing?
   A. Never
   B. When two patients have the same name and same address
   C. When two patients have the same name but different addresses
   D. When a patient does not have a permanent address

9. Which one of the following names would be filed first?
   A. Lolita Gonzales
   B. Edward Green III
   C. Cleo Gonzales Esq.
   D. Juanita Esperanza

10. Which one of the following names would be filed second?
    A. Lolita Gonzales
    B. Edward Green III
    C. Cleo Gonzales Esq.
    D. Juanita Esperanza

11. Which one of the following names would be filed first?
    A. Aurelia Hunter
    B. Laura Hinkleman
    C. Sister Mary Catherine
    D. Kimberly Edades

12. Which one of the following names would be filed first?
    A. Timothy O'Shea
    B. Simon Samuelson
    C. Kelly Sherwin
    D. Belinda deLarue

13. Professional titles and professional, numerical, and seniority suffixes are always indexed _____.
    A. first
    B. second
    C. last
    D. does not matter

14. Which one of the following is a charting "DON'T"?
    A. Chart anything you did not see or do.
    B. Use black ink because it is easier to photocopy.
    C. Verify the name on the file before charting.
    D. All of the above are Don'ts.

15. Which one of the following is NOT part of the decision when selecting a filing system?
    A. Selection of supplies
    B. Types of storage equipment
    C. Available space
    D. All of the above would be considered when selecting a filing system.

16. In which filing system are records more protected in case of fire?
    A. Lateral-open shelf
    B. Vertical-drawer
    C. Rotary
    D. Lateral-drawer

17. _____ filing is most commonly used in small to medium-sized offices.
    A. Alphabetical
    B. Numerical
    C. Terminal-digit
    D. Geographical

18. Which one of the following is a disadvantage of direct filing?
    A. The correct spelling of the name must be known to find a folder.
    B. Alphabetical filing is the easiest system to learn.
    C. Only one sorting is required.
    D. None of the above

19. All punctuation is disregarded when indexing personal and business names.
    A. True
    B. False

20. When filing, the first name of the patient is considered the key unit.
    A. True
    B. False

12

"Many ambitious people spend the first half of their life ruining their health to earn money and the second half spending that money to regain their health."
—**Bashir Quereshi**

OBJECTIVES

1. Recognize and use terms related to the anatomy and physiology of the nervous system.
2. Recognize and use terms related to the pathology of the nervous system.
3. Recognize and use terms related to the diagnostic procedures for the nervous system.
4. Recognize and use terms related to the therapeutic interventions for the nervous system.

MEDICAL TERMINOLOGY OF THE NERVOUS SYSTEM

CHAPTER AT A GLANCE

ANATOMY AND PHYSIOLOGY

ANS	cranial nerves	neuralgia	spinal nerves
axon	dendrite	neuron	sympathetic nervous system
brain stem	diencephalon	neurotransmitter	synapse
cerebellum	gray matter	parasympathetic nervous	white matter
cerebrospinal fluid	meninges	system	
cerebrum	myelin sheath	somatic	
CNS	nerve root	spinal cord	

WORD PARTS

PREFIXES	SUFFIXES	COMBINING FORMS	
hemi-	-graphy	cerebell/o	meningi/o, mening/o
mono-	-lepsy	cerebr/o	myel/o
para-	-paresis	cord/o	neur/o
quadri-	-plegia	crani/o	osm/o
	-rrhaphy	dur/o	radicul/o
		encephal/o	rhiz/o
		esthesi/o	somn/o
		gangli/o	vag/o
		gli/o	

KEY TERMS

anosmia	hemiplegia	paraparesis	subdural hematoma
cerebral palsy (CP)	hydrocephalus	paresthesia	syncope
cerebrovascular accident (CVA)	lumbar puncture (LP)	Parkinson disease (PD)	transcutaneous electrical nerve
coma	meningitis	polysomnography (PSG)	stimulation (TENS)
craniotomy	migraine	quadriplegia	transient ischemic attack (TIA)
encephalitis	multiple sclerosis (MS)	sciatica	vertigo
epilepsy	neurorrhaphy	shingles	

FUNCTIONS OF THE NERVOUS SYSTEM

Possibly the most complex and poorly understood system, the nervous system plays a major role in **homeostasis** (hoh mee oh STAY sis), keeping the other body systems coordinated and regulated to achieve optimal performance. It accomplishes this goal by helping the individual respond to his or her internal and external environments.

The nervous and endocrine systems are responsible for communication and control throughout the body. There are three main **neural** functions, which are as follows:

1. Collecting information about the external and internal environment *(sensing)*.
2. Processing this information and making decisions about action *(interpreting)*.
3. Directing the body to put into play the decisions made *(acting)*.

For example, the sensory function begins with a stimulus (e.g., the uncomfortable pinch of tight shoes). That information travels to the brain, where it is interpreted. The return message is sent to react to the stimulus (e.g., remove the shoes).

◆ Exercise 12-1: FUNCTIONS OF THE NERVOUS SYSTEM

Circle the correct answer.

1. The action of the nervous system can be divided into three functions: sensing → *(interpreting, controlling)* → acting.
2. The nervous system has the responsibility of communication and control throughout the body, along with the *(gastrointestinal, endocrine)* system.
3. The function of maintaining a steady state is called *(homeostasis, stimulation)*.

ANATOMY AND PHYSIOLOGY

Organization of the Nervous System

To carry out its functions, the nervous system is divided into two main subsystems. (Fig. 12-1 provides a schematic of the divisions.) The **central nervous system (CNS)** is composed of the brain and the spinal cord. It is the only site of nerve cells called **interneurons** (in tur NOOR ons), which connect sensory and motor neurons. The **peripheral nervous system (PNS)** is composed of the nerves that extend from the brain and spinal cord to the tissues of the body. These are organized into 12 pairs of cranial nerves and 31 pairs of spinal nerves. The PNS is further divided into voluntary and involuntary neurons, which may be **afferent** (or **sensory**), carrying impulses to the brain and spinal cord, or **efferent** (or **motor**), carrying impulses from the brain and spinal cord to either voluntary or involuntary muscles.

PNS nerves are further categorized into two subsystems:

Somatic (soh MAT ick) **system:** This system is *voluntary* in nature. These nerves collect information from and return instructions to the skin, muscles, and joints.

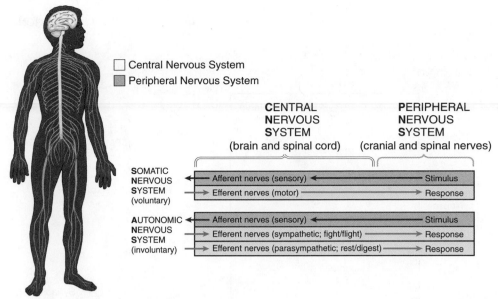

Fig. 12-1 The nervous system. Afferent nerves carry nervous impulses from a stimulus toward the central nervous system (CNS). Efferent nerves carry the impulse away from the CNS to effect a response to the stimulus.

Autonomic (ah toh NAH mick) **system:** Mostly *involuntary* functions are controlled by this system as sensory information from the internal environment is sent to the CNS, and, in return, motor impulses from the CNS are sent to involuntary muscles: the heart, glands, and organs.

⬥ Exercise 12-2: Organization of the Nervous System

Fill in the blanks.

1. The two main divisions of the nervous system are the ___CNS___ and the ___PNS___.

Circle the correct answer.

2. Sensory neurons (*transmit*, *receive*) information (*to*, *from*) the CNS.
3. Motor neurons, also called (*efferent*, *afferent*) neurons, transmit information (*to*, *from*) the CNS.
4. The (*somatic*, *autonomic*) nervous system is voluntary in nature, whereas the (*somatic*, *autonomic*) nervous system is largely involuntary.

Cells of the Nervous System

The nervous system is made up of the following two types of cells:

1. Parenchymal cells, or **neurons,** the cells that carry out the work of the system
2. Stromal cells, or **glia** (GLEE uh), the cells that provide a supportive function

Neurons

The basic unit of the nervous system is the nerve cell, or neuron (Fig. 12-2). Not all neurons are the same, but all have the following features in common. **Den-**

DID YOU KNOW?

Small collections of nerve cell bodies outside the brain and spinal cord (i.e., in the PNS) are called **ganglia** (GANG glee uh) (*sing.* ganglion).

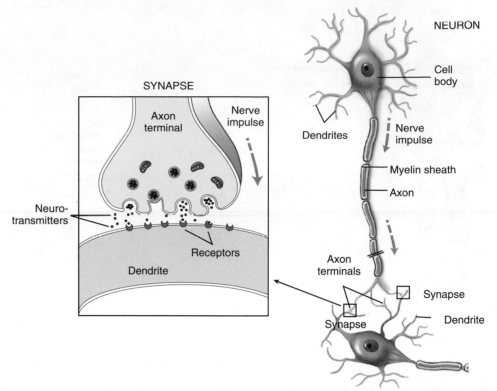

Fig. 12-2   The nerve cell (neuron) with an inset of a synapse. *(From Seidel HM, Ball JW, Dains JI, et al:* Mosby's guide to physical examination, *ed 5, St Louis, 2003, Mosby.)*

drites (DEN drytes), projections from the cell body, receive **neural impulses,** also called **action potentials,** from a **stimulus** of some kind. This impulse travels along the dendrite and into the cell body, which is the control center of the cell. This cell body contains the nucleus and surrounding cytoplasm.

From the cell body, the impulse moves out along the **axon** (AX on), a slender, elongated projection that carries the nervous impulse toward the next neuron. The **terminal fibers** are the final branching of the axon and the site of the **axon terminals** that store the chemical **neurotransmitters.** In neurons *outside* the CNS, the axon is covered by a material called **myelin** (MY uh lin), which is a substance produced by **Schwann** (shvahn) **cells** that coat the axons.

From the axon's terminal fibers, the neurotransmitter is released from the cell to travel across the space between these terminal fibers and the dendrites of the next cell. This space is called the **synapse** (SIN aps) (see Fig. 12-2). The impulse continues in this manner until its destination is reached.

Glia

These supportive, or stromal, cells are also called **neuroglia** (noo RAH glee ah). They accomplish their supportive function by physically holding the neurons together and also protecting them. One type of neuroglia, the **astrocytes** (AS troh sites), connect neurons and blood vessels and form a structure called the **blood-brain barrier (BBB)** that prevents or slows the passage of some drugs and disease-causing organisms to the CNS.

COMBINING FORMS FOR CELLS OF THE NERVOUS SYSTEM

MEANING	COMBINING FORM	MEANING	COMBINING FORM
body	somat/o	nerve	neur/o, neur/i
ganglion	gangli/o, ganglion/o	star	astr/o
glue	gli/o	tree	dendr/o

◆ Exercise 12-3: CELLS OF THE NERVOUS SYSTEM

1. List words connected by arrows to show the path of the action potential from initial stimulus to synapse.

_____

Matching.

_____ 2. star

_____ 3. body

_____ 4. nerve

_____ 5. ganglion

_____ 6. glue

_____ 7. tree

A. ganglio/o
B. gli/o
C. somat/o
D. dendr/o
E. astr/o
F. neur/o

The Central Nervous System

As stated previously, the CNS is composed of the **brain** and the **spinal cord**.

The Brain

The brain is one of the most complex organs of the body. It is divided into four parts: the **cerebrum** (suh REE brum), the **cerebellum** (sair ih BELL um), the **diencephalon** (dye en SEF fuh lon), and the **brain stem** (Fig. 12-3).

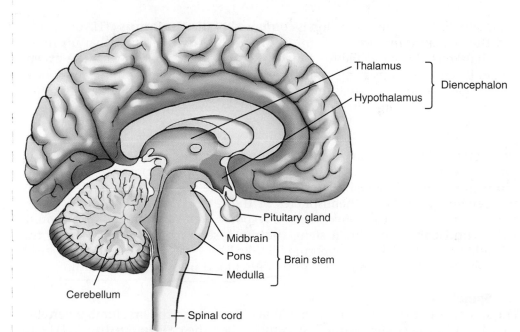

Fig. 12-3 The brain.

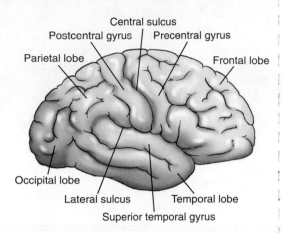

Fig. 12-4   The cerebrum.

CEREBRUM.   The largest portion of the brain, the cerebrum is divided into two halves, or hemispheres (Fig. 12-4). It is responsible for thinking, reasoning, and memory. The surfaces of the hemispheres are covered with **gray matter** and are called the **cerebral cortex.** Arranged into folds, the valleys are referred to as **sulci** (SULL sye) (*sing.* sulcus), and the ridges are **gyri** (JYE rye) (*sing.* gyrus). The cerebrum is further divided into sections called **lobes,** which each have their own functions:

1. The **frontal lobe** contains the functions of speech and the motor area that controls voluntary movement on the contralateral side of the body.
2. The **temporal** (TEM pur rul) **lobe** contains the auditory and olfactory areas.
3. The **parietal** (puh RYE uh tul) **lobe** controls the sensations of touch and taste.
4. The **occipital** (ock SIP ih tul) **lobe** is responsible for vision.

CEREBELLUM.   Located inferior to the occipital lobe of the cerebrum, the **cerebellum** coordinates voluntary movement but is involuntary in its function. For example, walking is a voluntary movement. The coordination needed for the muscles and other body parts to walk smoothly is involuntary and controlled by the cerebellum.

DIENCEPHALON.   The diencephalon is composed of the **thalamus** (THAL uh mus) and the structure inferior to it, the **hypothalamus** (HYE poh thal uh mus). The thalamus is responsible for relaying sensory information (with the exception of smell) and translating it into sensations of pain, temperature, and touch. The hypothalamus activates, integrates, and controls the peripheral autonomic nervous system, along with many functions, such as body temperature, sleep, and appetite.

BRAIN STEM.   The brain stem connects the cerebral hemispheres to the spinal cord. It is composed of three main parts: **midbrain, pons** (ponz), and **medulla oblongata** (muh DOO lah ob lon GAH tah). The midbrain connects the pons and cerebellum with the hemispheres of the cerebrum. It is the site of reflex centers for eye and head movements in response to visual and auditory stimuli. The second part of the brain stem, the pons, serves as a bridge between the medulla oblongata and the cerebrum. Finally, the lowest part of the brain stem, the medulla oblongata, regulates heart rate, blood pressure, and breathing.

The Spinal Cord
The spinal cord extends from the medulla oblongata to the first lumbar vertebra (Fig. 12-5). It then extends into a structure called the **cauda equina** (KAH dah

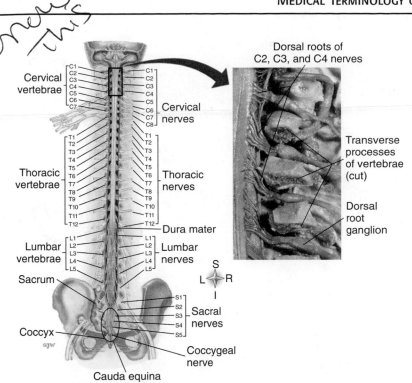

Fig. 12-5   The spinal cord with an inset of a cervical segment showing emerging cervical nerves. *(From Thibodeau GA, Patton KT: The human body in health and disease, ed 4, St Louis, 2005, Mosby.)*

eh KWY nah). The spinal cord is protected by the bony vertebrae surrounding it and the coverings unique to the CNS called **meninges** (meh NIN jeez). The spinal cord is composed of **gray matter,** the cell bodies of motor neurons, and **white matter,** the myelin-covered axons or nerve fibers that extend from the nerve cell bodies. The 31 pairs of spinal nerves emerge from the spinal cord at the **nerve roots**.

MENINGES.   Meninges act as protective coverings for the CNS and are composed of three layers separated by spaces (Fig. 12-6). The **dura mater** (DUR ah MAY tur) is the tough, fibrous, outer covering of the meninges; its literal meaning is *hard mother.* The space between the dura mater and arachnoid membrane is called the **subdural space.** Next comes the **arachnoid** (uh RACK noyd) **membrane,** a thin, delicate membrane that takes its name from its spidery appearance. The **subarachnoid space** is the space between the arachnoid membrane and the pia mater, containing **cerebrospinal fluid (CSF).** CSF is also present in cavities in the brain called **ventricles.** Finally, the **pia mater** (PEE uh MAY tur) is the thin, vascular membrane that is the innermost of the three meninges; its literal meaning is *soft mother.*

The Peripheral Nervous System

The **peripheral nervous system** is divided into 12 pairs of **cranial nerves** that conduct impulses between the brain and the head, neck, thoracic, and abdominal areas, and 31 pairs of **spinal nerves** that closely mimic the organization of the vertebrae and provide innervation to the rest of the body. If the nerve fibers from several spinal nerves form a network, it is termed a **plexus** (PLECK sus). Spinal nerves are named by their location (cervical, thoracic, lumbar, sacral, and coccygeal) and by number. Cranial nerves are named by their number and also their function or distribution.

DID YOU KNOW?

Cauda equina is a Latin term meaning horse tail.

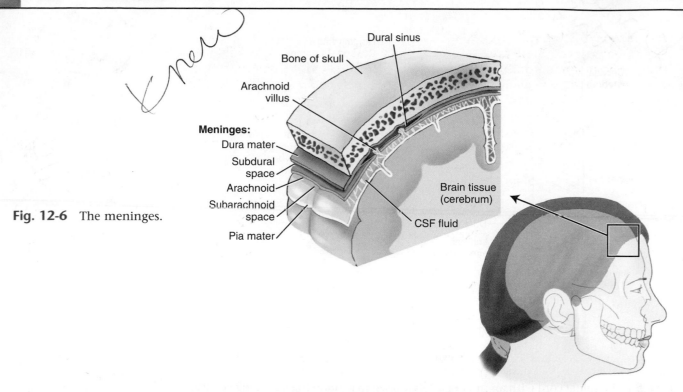

Fig. 12-6   The meninges.

The Cranial Nerves

NUMBER	NAME	ORIGIN OF SENSORY FIBERS	EFFECTOR INNERVATED BY MOTOR FIBERS
I	Olfactory	Olfactory epithelium of nose (smell)	None
II	Optic	Retina of eye (vision)	None
III	Oculomotor	Proprioceptors* of eyeball muscles	Muscles that move eyeball; muscles that change shape of lens; muscles that constrict pupil
IV	Trochlear	Proprioceptors* of eyeball muscles	Muscles that move eyeball
V	Trigeminal	Teeth and skin of face	Some muscles used in chewing
VI	Abducens	Proprioceptors* of eyeball muscles	Muscles that move eyeball
VII	Facial	Taste buds of anterior part of tongue	Muscles used for facial expression; submaxillary and sublingual salivary glands
VIII	Vestibulocochlear (Auditory)		None
	Vestibular branch	Semicircular canals of inner ear (senses of movement, balance, and rotation)	
	Cochlear branch	Cochlea of inner ear (hearing)	
IX	Glossopharyngeal	Taste buds of posterior third of tongue and lining of pharynx	Parotid salivary gland; muscles of pharynx used in swallowing
X	Vagus	Nerve endings in many of the internal organs (e.g., lungs, stomach, aorta, larynx)	Parasympathetic fibers to heart, stomach, small intestine, larynx, esophagus, and other organs
XI	Spinal accessory	Muscles of shoulder	Muscles of neck and shoulder
XII	Hypoglossal	Muscles of tongue	Muscles of tongue

*Proprioceptors are receptors located in muscles, tendons, or joints that provide information about body position and movement.

Dermatomes (DUR mah tomes) are skin surface areas supplied by a single afferent spinal nerve. These areas are so specific that it is actually possible to map the body by dermatomes (Fig. 12-7). This specificity can be demonstrated in patients with shingles, who show similar patterns as specific peripheral nerves are affected (see Fig. 12-12).

The **autonomic nervous system (ANS)** consists of nerves that regulate involuntary function. Examples include cardiac muscle and smooth muscle. The motor portion of this system is further divided into the sympathetic nervous system and the parasympathetic nervous system, two opposing systems that provide balance in the rest of the body systems:

- The **sympathetic nervous system** is capable of producing a "fight-or-flight" response. This is the one part of the nervous system that helps the individual respond to perceived stress. The heart rate and blood pressure increase, digestive processes slow, and sweat and adrenal glands increase their secretions.

- The **parasympathetic nervous system** tends to do the opposite of the sympathetic nervous system—slowing the heart rate, lowering blood pressure, increasing digestive functions, and decreasing adrenal and sweat gland activity. This is sometimes called the "rest and digest" system.

An example of a sensory response follows:

"Eight-year-old Joey is hungry. He decides to sneak some cookies before dinner. Afraid his mother will see him, he surreptitiously takes a handful into the hall closet and shuts the door. As he begins to eat, the closet door flies open. Joey's heart begins to race as he whips the cookies out of sight. When he sees it's only his sister, he relaxes and offers her a cookie as a bribe not to tell on him."

Joey's afferent (sensory) somatic neurons carried the message to his brain that he was hungry. This message was interpreted by his brain as a concern, and the response was to sneak cookies from the jar and hide himself as he ate them. When the closet door flew open, his sensory neurons perceived a danger and triggered a sympathetic "fight-or-flight" response, which raised his heart rate and blood pressure and stimulated his sweat glands. When the intruder was perceived to be harmless, his parasympathetic nervous system took over and reduced his heart rate, bringing it back to normal. The same afferent fibers perceived the intruder in two different ways, with two different sets of autonomic motor responses (sympathetic and parasympathetic).

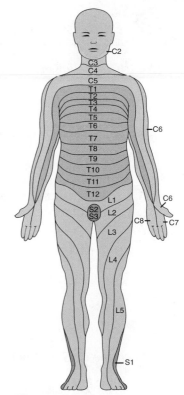

Fig. 12-7 Dermatomes. Each dermatome is named for the spinal nerve that serves it.

☒ BE CAREFUL!

The term *dermatome* can be used to describe an instrument that cuts thin slices of skin for grafting, and the term also signifies a mesodermal layer in early development, which becomes the dermal layers of the skin.

COMBINING FORMS FOR THE NERVOUS SYSTEM

MEANING	COMBINING FORM	MEANING	COMBINING FORM
brain	encephal/o	nerve root	radicul/o, rhiz/o
cerebellum	cerebell/o	skin	dermat/o
cerebrum	cerebr/o	spinal cord	cord/o, myel/o
dura mater	dur/o	spine	spin/o
meninges	mening/o, meningi/o	vertebra	spondyl/o, vertebr/o

◈ **Exercise 12-4: CENTRAL AND PERIPHERAL NERVOUS SYSTEM**

know this

Match the following parts of the brain with their functions.

_H_ 1. pons

_B_ 2. parietal cerebral lobe

_F_ 3. hypothalamus

_A_ 4. temporal cerebral lobe

_C_ 5. midbrain

_I_ 6. cerebellum

_D_ 7. occipital cerebral lobe

_B_ 8. thalamus

_G_ 9. frontal cerebral lobe

_E_ 10. medulla oblongata

A. auditory and olfactory activity
B. relays sensory information
C. reflex center for eye and head movements
D. sensation of vision
E. regulates heart rate, blood pressure, and breathing
F. regulates temperature, sleep, and appetite
G. speech and motor activity
H. connects medulla oblongata and cerebrum
I. coordinates voluntary movement
J. sensation of touch and taste

Match the CNS part with its combining form.

_____ 11. cerebellum

_____ 12. spinal cord

_____ 13. meninges

_____ 14. nerve root

_____ 15. dura mater

_____ 16. cerebrum

_____ 17. brain

_____ 18. skin

_____ 19. spine

A. meningi/o
B. myel/o
C. dur/o
D. rhiz/o
E. dermat/o
F. cerebr/o
G. spin/o
H. cerebell/o
I. encephal/o

20. Name the three layers of the meninges and the spaces between in order, from innermost to outermost.

_____

Circle the correct answer.

21. The peripheral nervous system has *(12, 31)* pairs of cranial nerves and *(12, 31)* pairs of spinal nerves.
22. *(Afferent, Efferent)* nerves carry nerve impulses toward the CNS.
23. The *(sympathetic, parasympathetic)* nervous system is capable of producing a "rest and digest" response.

⊠ BE CAREFUL!

Don't confuse *dysarthria* (difficulty with speech) and *dysarthrosis* (any disorder of a joint).

≋ **PATHOLOGY**

The signs and symptoms for this system encompass many systems because of the nature of the neural function: communicating, or failing to communicate, with other parts of the body.

Terms Related to Signs and Symptoms

TERM	WORD ORIGIN	DEFINITION
Amnesia am NEE zsa		Loss of memory caused by brain damage or severe emotional trauma.
Aphasia ah FAY zsa	*a-* without *phas/o* speech *-ia* condition	Lack or impairment of the ability to form or understand speech. Less severe forms include **dysphasia** (dis FAY zsa) and **dysarthria** (dis AR three ah).
Asthenia as THEE nee ah	*a-* without *-sthenia* condition of strength	Muscle weakness.
Athetosis ath uh TOH sis		Continuous, involuntary, slow, writhing movement of the extremities.
Aura OR uh		Sensation that may precede an epileptic seizure or the onset of some types of headache. May be a sensation of light or warmth.
Dysphagia dis FAY zsa	*dys-* difficult *phag/o* eat *-ia* condition	Condition of difficulty with swallowing.
Fasciculation fah sick yoo LAY shun		Involuntary contraction of small, local muscles.
Gait, abnormal		Disorder in the manner of walking. An example is **ataxia** (uh TACK see uh), a lack of muscular coordination, as in cerebral palsy.
Hypokinesia hye poh kih NEE sza	*hypo-* deficient *kinesi/o* movement *-ia* condition	Decrease in normal movement; may be due to paralysis.
Parasomnia pair uh SOM nee ah	*para-* abnormal *somn/o* sleep *-ia* condition	Disorder of sleep. **Hypersomnia** is excessive depth or length of sleep; **insomnia** is the inability to sleep or stay asleep; and **somnambulism** (som NAM byoo lih zum) is walking in one's sleep.
Paresthesia pair uhs THEE zsa	*para-* abnormal *esthesi/o* feeling *-ia* condition	Feeling of prickling, burning, or numbness.
Seizure SEE zhur		Neuromuscular reaction to abnormal electrical activity within the brain (see Fig. 12-19). Causes include fever or epilepsy, a recurring seizure disorder; also called **convulsions**. Types of seizures include **tonic clonic (grand mal),** accompanied by temporary loss of consciousness and severe muscle spasms; **absence seizures (petit mal)** accompanied by loss of consciousness exhibited by unresponsiveness for short periods without muscle involvement. **Status epilepticus** (STA tis eh pih LEP tih kus) is a condition of intense, unrelenting, life-threatening seizures.
Spasm SPAZ um		Involuntary muscle contraction of sudden onset. Examples are hiccups, tics, and stuttering.
Syncope SINK oh pee		Fainting. A **vasovagal** (VAS soh VAY gul) **attack** is a form of syncope that results from abrupt emotional stress involving the vagus nerve's effect on blood vessels.
Tremors TREH murs		Rhythmic, quivering, purposeless skeletal muscle movements seen in some elderly individuals and in patients with various neurodegenerative disorders.
Vertigo	See **Did You Know?** box.	Dizziness. Abnormal sensation of movement when there is none, either of one's self moving or of objects moving around oneself.

DID YOU KNOW?

Vertigo is derived from a Latin term meaning *to turn*.

DID YOU KNOW?

The term *acalculia* comes from the Greek word for stone. Shepherds once used stones to keep track of (calculate) the number of sheep in the fields, using one stone for each sheep that went out in the morning and the same number of stones when the sheep returned that evening.

Terms Related to Learning and Perceptual Differences

TERM	WORD ORIGIN	DEFINITION
Acalculia ay kal KYOO lee ah	*a-* without *calcul/o* stone *-ia* condition See **Did You Know?** box.	Inability to perform mathematical calculations.
Ageusia ah GOO zsa	*a-* without *geus/o* taste *-ia* condition	Absence of the ability to taste. **Parageusia** (pair ah GOO zsa) is an abnormal sense of taste or a bad taste in the mouth.
Agnosia ag NOH zsa	*a-* without *gnos/o* knowledge *-ia* condition	Inability to recognize objects visually, auditorily, or with other senses.
Agraphia ah GRAFF ee ah	*a-* without *graph/o* record *-ia* condition	Inability to write.
Anosmia an NOS mee ah	*an-* without *osm/o* sense of smell *-ia* condition	Lack of sense of smell.
Apraxia ah PRACK see ah	*a-* without *prax/o* purposeful movement *-ia* condition	Inability to perform purposeful movements or to use objects appropriately.
Dyslexia dis LECK see ah	*dys-* bad *lex/o* word *-ia* condition	Inability or difficulty with reading and/or writing.
Romberg sign		Indication of loss of the sense of position, in which the patient loses balance when standing erect, with feet together and eyes closed.

◆ Exercise 12-5: NEUROLOGICAL SIGNS, SYMPTOMS, AND PERCEPTUAL DIFFERENCES

Match the neurological signs, symptoms, and perceptual differences with their combining forms.

_____ 1. sthen/o   _____ 6. gnos/o   A. taste
                                                    B. words
_____ 2. phas/o   _____ 7. graph/o   C. knowledge
                                                    D. strength
_____ 3. somn/o   _____ 8. lex/o   E. stone
                                                    F. sense of smell
_____ 4. calcul/o   _____ 9. osm/o   G. record
                                                    H. speech
_____ 5. geus/o   I. sleep

Match the sign/symptom with its meaning.

_____ 10. syncope   _____ 13. aura   A. dizziness
                                                    B. involuntary contraction of
_____ 11. vertigo   _____ 14. fasciculation   small muscles
                                                    C. loss of memory
_____ 12. amnesia   D. fainting
                                                    E. premonition

Terms Related to Congenital Disorders

TERM	WORD ORIGIN	DEFINITION
Cerebral palsy (CP) SAIR uh brul PALL zee	*cerebr/o* cerebrum *-al* pertaining to	Motor function disorder as a result of permanent, nonprogressive brain defect or lesion caused perinatally. Neural deficits may include paralysis, ataxia, **athetosis** (a thih TOE sis) (slow, writhing movements of the extremities), seizures, and/or impairment of sensory functions.
Huntington chorea koh REE ah		Inherited disorder that manifests itself in adulthood as a progressive loss of neural control, uncontrollable jerking movements, and dementia.
Hydrocephalus hye droh SEFF uh lus	*hydr/o* water *-cephalus* head	Condition of abnormal accumulation of fluid in the ventricles of the brain; may or may not result in mental retardation.
Spina bifida SPY nah BIFF uh dah	*bi-* two *-fida* split	Condition in which the spinal column has an abnormal opening that allows the protrusion of the meninges and/or the spinal cord. This is termed a **meningocele** (meh NIN goh seel) or **meningomyelocele** (meh nin go MY eh loh seel) (Fig. 12-8).
Tay-Sachs tay sacks		Inherited disease that occurs mainly in people of Eastern European Jewish origin; characterized by an enzyme deficiency that results in CNS deterioration.

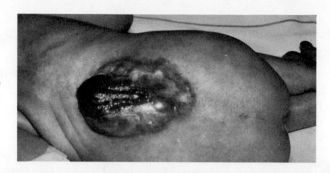

Fig. 12-8 Meningomyelocele. *(From Zitelli BJ, Davis HW: Atlas of pediatric physical diagnosis, ed 4, St Louis, 2002, Mosby.)*

Terms Related to Traumatic Conditions

TERM	WORD ORIGIN	DEFINITION
Coma KOH mah		Deep, prolonged unconsciousness from which the patient cannot be aroused; usually the result of a head injury, neurological disease, acute hydrocephalus, intoxication, or metabolic abnormalities.
Concussion kun KUH shun		Serious head injury characterized by one or more of the following: loss of consciousness, amnesia, seizures, or a change in mental status.
Contusion, cerebral kun TOO zhun		Head injury of sufficient force to bruise the brain. Bruising of the brain often involves the brain surface and causes extravasation of blood without rupture of the pia-arachnoid; often associated with a concussion.
Hematoma Hee muh TOH mah	*hemat/o* blood *-oma* tumor, mass	Localized collection of blood, usually clotted, in an organ, tissue, or space, due to a break in the wall of a blood vessel (Fig. 12-9).

⊠ BE CAREFUL!

Although the word origin of the term *hematoma* means a blood tumor, this is a misnomer. A hematoma is a mass of blood that has leaked out of a vessel and pooled.

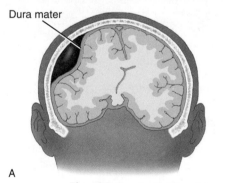

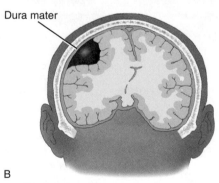

Dura mater　　　　　　　　　　　　Dura mater

A　　　　　　　　　　　　　　　　B

Fig. 12-9 **A,** Epidural hematoma. **B,** Subdural hematoma.

◈ Exercise 12-6: CONGENITAL AND TRAUMATIC CONDITIONS

Fill in the blanks with the correct congenital disorder term listed below.

Tay-Sachs, hydrocephalus, cerebral palsy, spina bifida, Huntington chorea

1. A condition characterized by an abnormal opening of the spine, allowing the protrusion of the

   meninges and possibly the spinal cord. _____

2. An inherited disorder resulting in dementia and a progressive loss of neural control beginning in

   adulthood. _____

3. A condition characterized by an accumulation of fluid in the ventricles of the brain. _____

4. An inherited disease of people of Eastern European descent that results in a deterioration of the brain and spinal cord as a result of an enzyme deficiency. _____

5. Permanent motor function disorder as a result of brain damage during the perinatal period. _____

Fill in the blanks with the correct trauma term listed below.

cerebral contusion, concussion, coma, epidural hematoma, subdural hematoma

6. Prolonged unconsciousness from which the patient cannot be aroused is termed _____.

7. Head injury accompanied by amnesia, loss of consciousness, seizures, and/or change in mental status is called a/an _____.

8. Bruising of the brain with hemorrhage and swelling is a/an _____.

9. Collection of blood, if above the dura mater, is described as a/an _____, or if below it, a/an _____.

Terms Related to Degenerative Disorders

TERM	WORD ORIGIN	DEFINITION
Alzheimer disease (AD) ALLTZ hye mur		Progressive, neurodegenerative disease in which patients exhibit an impairment of cognitive functioning. The cause of the disease is unknown. Alzheimer is the most common cause of dementia (Fig. 12-10).
Amyotrophic lateral sclerosis (ALS) ay mye oh TROH fick LAT ur ul sklih ROH sis	*a-* no *my/o* muscle *troph/o* development *-ic* pertaining to *later/o* side *-al* pertaining to	Degenerative, fatal disease of the motor neurons, in which patients exhibit progressive asthenia and muscle atrophy; also called **Lou Gehrig disease.**
Dementia deh MEN sha	*de-* lack of *ment/o* mind *-ia* condition	Chronic, progressive, organic mental disorder characterized by chronic personality disintegration; symptoms include confusion, disorientation, stupor, deterioration of intellectual capacity and function, and impairment of memory, judgment, and impulse control.
Guillain-Barré syndrome GEE on bar AY		Autoimmune disorder of acute polyneuritis producing profound myasthenia that may lead to paralysis.
Multiple sclerosis (MS)	*sclerosis* condition of hardening	Neurodegenerative disease characterized by destruction of the myelin sheaths on the CNS neurons (demyelination) and their abnormal replacement by the gradual accumulation of hardened plaques. The disease may be progressive or characterized by remissions and relapses. Cause is unknown (Fig. 12-11).
Parkinson disease (PD)		Progressive neurodegenerative disease characterized by tremors, fasciculations, slow shuffling gait, hypokinesia, dysphasia, and dysphagia.

⊠ BE CAREFUL!

MS stands for both musculoskeletal system and multiple sclerosis.

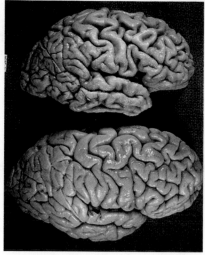

Fig. 12-10 Alzheimer disease. The affected brain *(top)* is smaller and shows narrow gyri and widened sulci compared with the normal, age-matched brain *(bottom)*. *(From Damjanov I, Linder J: Pathology: a color atlas, St Louis, 2000, Mosby.)*

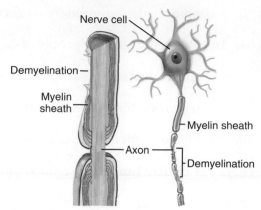

Fig. 12-11 Nerve sheath demyelination seen in multiple sclerosis.

Terms Related to Nondegenerative Disorders

TERM	WORD ORIGIN	DEFINITION
Bell palsy PALL zee		Paralysis of the facial nerve. Unknown in cause, the condition usually resolves on its own within 6 months (Fig. 12-12).
Epilepsy EP ih lep see	*epi-* above *-lepsy* seizure	Group of disorders characterized by some or all of the following: recurrent seizures, sensory disturbances, abnormal behavior, and/or loss of consciousness. The two main types of seizures are **tonic clonic seizures,** characterized by involuntary muscle contractions and loss of bowel and bladder control, and **absence seizures,** characterized by sudden short-term loss of consciousness. Causes may be trauma, tumor, intoxication, chemical imbalance, or vascular disturbances.
Narcolepsy NAR koh lep see	*narc/o* sleep *-lepsy* seizure	Disorder characterized by sudden attacks of sleep.
Tourette syndrome tur ETTS		Abnormal condition characterized by facial grimaces, tics, involuntary arm and shoulder movements, and involuntary vocalizations, including **coprolalia** (kop pro LAYL yah) (the use of vulgar, obscene, or sacrilegious language).

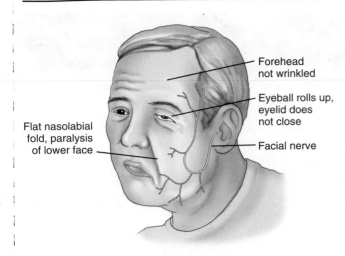

Fig. 12-12 The facial characteristics of Bell palsy.

Labels in figure: Forehead not wrinkled; Eyeball rolls up, eyelid does not close; Facial nerve; Flat nasolabial fold, paralysis of lower face

◆ **Exercise 12-7: DEGENERATIVE AND NONDEGENERATIVE DISORDERS**

Fill in the blank with the correct disorder listed below.

Alzheimer disease, Guillain-Barré syndrome, Bell palsy, amyotrophic lateral sclerosis, Parkinson disease, Tourette syndrome

1. A paralysis of a facial nerve. _____

2. A disease characterized by tics, facial grimaces, and involuntary vocalizations. _____

3. A progressive disease characterized by a shuffling gait, tremors, and dysphasia. _____

4. A degenerative fatal disorder of motor neurons. _____

5. A progressive, degenerative disorder of impairment of cognitive functioning. _____

6. An autoimmune disorder causing severe muscle weakness, often leading to paralysis.

_____

Matching.

_____ 7. later/o

_____ 8. narc/o

_____ 9. my/o

_____ 10. troph/o

_____ 11. myel/o

A. development
B. muscle
C. sleep
D. spinal cord
E. side

Terms Related to Infectious Diseases

TERM	WORD ORIGIN	DEFINITION
Encephalitis en seff uh LYE tis	*encephal/o* brain *-itis* inflammation	Inflammation of the brain, most frequently caused by a virus transmitted by the bite of an infected mosquito.
Meningitis men in JYE tis	*mening/o* meninges *-itis* inflammation	Any infection or inflammation of the membranes covering the brain and spinal cord, most commonly due to bacterial infection, although more severe strains are viral or fungal in nature.
Neuritis noo RYE tis	*neur/o* nerve *-itis* inflammation	Inflammation of the nerves.
Polyneuritis pall ee noo RYE tis	*poly-* many *neur/o* nerve *-itis* inflammation	Inflammation of many nerves.
Radiculitis rad ick kyoo LYE tis	*radicul/o* nerve root *-itis* inflammation	Inflammation of the root of a spinal nerve.
Sciatica sye AT ick kah		Inflammation of the sciatic nerve. Symptoms include pain and tenderness along the path of the nerve through the thigh and leg.
Shingles SHIN guls		Acute infection caused by the latent varicella zoster virus (chicken pox), characterized by the development of vesicular skin eruption underlying the route of cranial or spinal nerves; also called **herpes zoster** (HER pees ZAH ster) (Fig. 12-13).

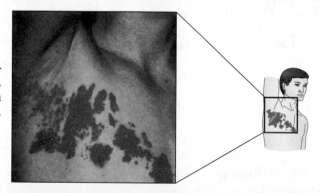

Fig. 12-13 Shingles on dermatome T4. *(From Thibodeau GA, Patton KT:* The human body in health and disease, *ed 4, St Louis, 2005, Mosby.)*

Terms Related to Vascular Disorders

TERM	WORD ORIGIN	MEANING
Cerebrovascular accident (CVA) seh ree broh VAS kyoo lur	*cerebr/o* cerebrum *vascul/o* vessel *-ar* pertaining to	Ischemia of cerebral tissue due to an occlusion (blockage) from a thrombus (*pl.* thrombi) or embolus (*pl.* emboli), or as a result of a cerebral hemorrhage. Results of a stroke depend on the duration and location of the ischemia. These sequelae may include paralysis, weakness, speech defects, sensory changes that last more than 24 hours, or death. Also called **stroke, brain attack, cerebral infarction,** and **apoplexy** (A poh pleck see) (Fig. 12-14).
Migraine		Headache of vascular origin. May be classified as *migraine with aura* or *migraine without aura.*
Transient ischemic attack (TIA) TRANS ee ent is KEE mick	*ischem/o* hold back *-ia* condition	TIA has the same mechanisms as a CVA, but the sequelae resolve and disappear within 24 hours; also known as a **ministroke.**

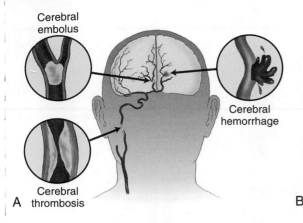

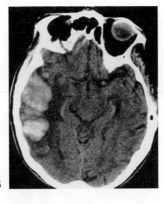

A

B

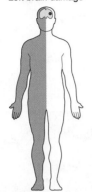

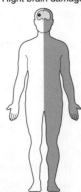

Left brain damage

Right brain damage

C

Right side paralysis
Speech and memory deficits
Cautious and slow behavior

Left side paralysis
Perceptual and memory deficits
Quick and impulsive behavior

Fig. 12-14 Cerebrovascular accident (CVA). **A,** Events causing stroke. **B,** Magnetic resonance imaging (MRI) showing hemorrhagic stroke in right cerebrum. **C,** Areas of the body affected by CVA. (*B from Black JM, Hawks JH, Keene A:* Medical-surgical nursing: clinical management for positive outcomes, *ed 7, Philadelphia, 2005, Saunders.*)

Terms Related to Paralytic Conditions

TERM	WORD ORIGIN	MEANING
Diplegia dye PLEE jee ah	*di-* two *-plegia* paralysis	Paralysis of the same body part on both sides of the body.
Hemiparesis hem mee pah REE sis	*hemi-* half *-paresis* slight paralysis	Muscular weakness or slight paralysis on the left or right side of the body.
Hemiplegia hem mee PLEE jee ah	*hemi-* half *-plegia* paralysis	Paralysis on the left or right side of the body.
Monoparesis mah noh pah REE sis	*mono-* one *-paresis* slight paralysis	Weakness or slight paralysis of one limb on the left or right side of the body.
Monoplegia mah noh PLEE jee ah	*mono-* one *-plegia* paralysis	Paralysis of one limb on the left or right side of the body.
Paralysis puh RAL ih sis	*para-* abnormal *-lysis* destruction	Loss of muscle function, sensation, or both; may be described according to which side is affected and whether it is the dominant or nondominant side (Fig. 12-15).
Paraparesis pair uh pah REE sis	*para-* abnormal *-paresis* slight paralysis	Slight paralysis of the lower limbs and trunk.
Paraplegia pair uh PLEE jee ah	*para-* abnormal *-plegia* paralysis	Paralysis of the lower limbs and trunk.
Quadriparesis kwah drih pah REE sis	*quadri-* four *-paresis* slight paralysis	Weakness or slight paralysis of the arms, legs, and trunk.
Quadriplegia kwah drih PLEE jee ah	*quadri-* four *-plegia* paralysis	Paralysis of arms, legs, and trunk.

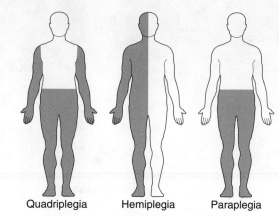

Fig. 12-15 Types of paralysis.

Quadriplegia   Hemiplegia   Paraplegia

 Exercise 12-8: INFECTIOUS, VASCULAR, AND PARALYTIC DISORDERS

Circle the correct answer.

1. An inflammation of the root of a spinal nerve is called *(polyneuritis, radiculitis)*.
2. An inflammation of the covering of the CNS is called *(meningitis, encephalitis)*.
3. An inflammation of a nerve in the thigh and leg is called *(shingles, sciatica)*.
4. Paralysis on the left or right half of the body is called *(hemiparesis, hemiplegia)*.
5. A ministroke is a *(transient ischemic attack, cerebrovascular accident)*.
6. A slight paralysis from the waist down is called *(para, mono)* paresis.

Match the suffixes and prefixes with their correct meanings.

_____ 7. hemi-   _____ 11. para-   A. one
                                                     B. slight paralysis
_____ 8. -plegia   _____ 12. -paresis   C. half
                                                     D. abnormal
_____ 9. mono-   _____ 13. di-   E. paralysis
                                                     F. four
_____ 10. quadri-   G. two

14. Three causes of occlusion that lead to a CVA are:

_____

15. The difference between a CVA and a TIA is that:

_____

Terms Related to Benign Neoplasms		
TERM	**WORD ORIGIN**	**MEANING**
Meningioma men inj ee OH mah	*meningi/o* meninges *-oma*	Slow growing, usually benign tumor of the meninges. Although benign, may cause problems because of their size and location (Fig. 12-16).
Neurofibroma new roh fye BROH mah	*neur/o* nerve *fibr/o* fiber *-oma* tumor	Benign fibrous tumors composed of nervous tissue.
Neuroma new ROH mah	*neur/o* nerve *-oma*	Benign tumor of the nerves.

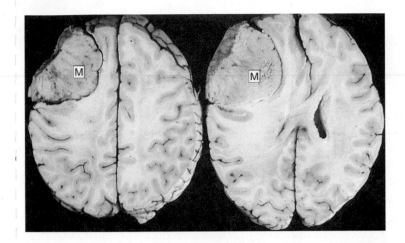

Fig. 12-16   Meningioma of the meninges of the brain. *(From Stevens A, Lowe J:* Pathology: illustrated review in color, *ed 2, St Louis, 2000, Mosby.)*

Terms Related to Malignant Neoplasms

TERM	WORD ORIGIN	DEFINITION
Astrocytoma astroh sye TOH mah	*astr/o* star *cyt/o* cell *-oma* tumor	Malignant tumor arising from star-shaped glial cells. Most common in the cerebrum in adults, but in children these rise from the brain stem, cerebrum, or cerebellum. Usually termed a *glioblastoma multiforme*.
Medulloblastoma med yoo loh blass TOH mah	*medull/o* medulla *blast/o* embryonic *-oma* tumor	Tumor arises from embryonic tissue in the cerebellum. Most commonly seen in children.
Neuroblastoma new roh blass TOH mah	*neur/o* nerve *blast/o* embryonic *-oma* tumor, mass	Highly malignant tumor arising from either the autonomic nervous system or the adrenal medulla. Usually affects children under the age of 10.

◈ Exercise 12-9: NEOPLASMS

Fill in the blank.

1. What is a benign tumor of the meninges? _____

2. What is a benign tumor of the nerves? _____

3. What is a malignant tumor of star-shaped glial cells? _____

4. What is a malignant tumor of embryonic nervous tissue that arises from the autonomic nervous

   system or the adrenal medulla in children? _____

South Shore Hospital
2243 Seaspray Dr.
Seacrest Beach, FL 32405

EMERGENCY ROOM NOTE

Physician's Report: 19-year-old female comes in today brought by ambulance with tonic clonic seizure times four. She has been seizing every 1-2 minutes for 30 seconds. Had upper extremity jerking. Gave her some Valium to start an IV and switched to IV Ativan. Seizures do not appear normal. Jerks to the upper extremities in an oddlike fashion with forward flexion and extension of her arms. Talked to her mom out in the hall and questioned whether the seizures were real. Does have some psychological issues. Psych just took her off antidepressants because of drug interactions. Vital signs are stable. Cranial nerves II through XII intact. TMs clear. Pharynx is clear.

IMPRESSION: Pseudoseizures
Diagnosis: Pseudoseizures
               Physician Sign/Date:

Nancy Connelly, MD
8/3/XX

 Exercise 12-10: EMERGENCY ROOM NOTE

Using the emergency room note above, fill in the blanks.

1. This physician is using the term "tonic-clonic seizure." What is another term for that?

   _____

2. What is a pseudoseizure? _____

3. What action is described by flexion and extension of her arms? _____

4. How do you know that she has no problems with her throat? _____

5. Which cranial nerves are functioning normally? _____

Age Matters

Pediatrics

Most children's neurological disorders are congenital ones. Cerebral palsy is usually the result of birth trauma, whereas Tay-Sachs is an inherited condition. Hydrocephalus may be detected before delivery on an ultrasound, and intrauterine prenatal procedures can be done to lessen the effects of the disorder. It should be noted that this disorder may, although infrequently, occur in adults after trauma or disease. Spina bifida is yet another congenital disorder that may be detected before birth through prenatal testing. Two pathological conditions that are not congenital but that are a concern to parents are viral and bacterial meningitis. Although viral meningitis is less severe and usually resolves without treatment, bacterial meningitis can be fatal. The vaccine that is now available and recommended is the Hib, which stands for the bacteria it protects against, *Haemophilus influenzae,* type b.

Geriatrics

The two major neurological disorders of concern as we age are cerebrovascular disease and Alzheimer disease. The first disorder manifests itself in two forms: ministrokes (transient ischemic attacks) and strokes (cerebrovascular accidents). The other disorder is Alzheimer disease, a progressive cognitive mental deterioration. It is estimated that by the age of 65, one in 10 individuals will be diagnosed with the disease. By age 85, more than half of the population will carry the diagnosis.

DIAGNOSTIC PROCEDURES

Terms Related to Imaging

TERM	WORD ORIGIN	DEFINITION
Brain scan		Nuclear medicine procedure involving intravenous injection of radioisotopes to localize and identify intracranial masses, lesions, tumors, or infarcts. Photography is done by a scintillator or scanner.
Cerebral angiography seh REE bruhl an gee OG rah fee	*cerebr/o* cerebrum *-al* pertaining to *angi/o* vessel *-graphy* process of recording	X-ray of the cerebral arteries, including the internal carotids, taken after the injection of a contrast medium (Fig. 12-17); also called **cerebral arteriography**.
Computed tomography (CT) scan	*tom/o* slice *-graphy* process of recording	Transverse sections of the CNS are imaged, sometimes after the injection of a contrast medium (unless there is suspected bleeding). Used to diagnose strokes, edema, tumors, and hemorrhage resulting from trauma.
Echoencephalography eh koh en seh fah LAH gruh fee	*echo-* sound *encephal/o* brain *-graphy* process of recording	Ultrasound examination of the brain, usually done only on newborns, because sound waves do not readily penetrate bone.
Magnetic resonance imaging (MRI)		Medical imaging that uses radiofrequency pulses in a powerful magnetic field. **Magnetic resonance angiography (MRA)** is imaging of the carotid arteries using injected contrast agents.

Continued

Terms Related to Imaging—cont'd

TERM	WORD ORIGIN	DEFINITION
Myelography mye eh LAH gruh fee	*myel/o* spinal cord *-graphy* process of recording	X-ray of the spinal canal after the introduction of a radiopaque substance.
Positron emission tomography (PET)		Use of radionuclides to visualize brain function. Measurements can be taken of blood flow, volume, and oxygen and glucose uptake, enabling radiologists to determine the functional characteristics of specific parts of the brain (Fig. 12-18). PET scans are used to assist in the diagnosis of Alzheimer disease and stroke.
Radiography		Process of making an x-ray image (with or without contrast media).
Single-photon emission computed tomography (SPECT)		An injection of a radioactive sugar substance that is metabolized by the brain, which is then scanned for abnormalities.
Ultrasonography	*ultra-* beyond *son/o* sound *-graphy* process of recording	Noninvasive imaging using high-frequency sound waves.

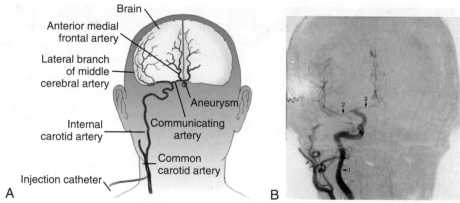

Fig. 12-17 Cerebral angiography. **A,** Insertion of dye through a catheter in the common carotid artery outlines the vessels of the brain. **B,** Angiogram showing vessels. *1,* internal carotid artery; *2,* middle cerebral artery; *3,* middle meningeal artery. (**B** *from Black JM, Hawks JH, Keene A:* Medical-surgical nursing: clinical management for positive outcomes, *ed 7, Philadelphia, 2005, Saunders.)*

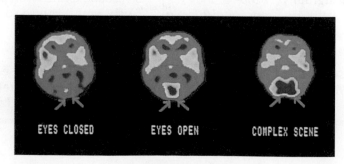

Fig. 12-18 Colorized positron emission tomography (PET) scan. (*From Thibodeau GA, Patton KT:* The human body in health and disease, *ed 4, St Louis, 2005, Mosby.)*

Terms Related to Electrodiagnostic Procedures

TERM	WORD ORIGIN	DEFINITION
Electroencephalography (EEG) ee leck troh en seff fah LAH gruh fee	*electr/o* electricity *encephal/o* brain *-graphy* process of recording	Record of the electrical activity of the brain. May be used in the diagnosis of epilepsy, infection, and coma (Fig. 12-19).
Evoked potential (EP)		Electrical response from the brain stem or cerebral cortex that is produced in response to specific stimuli. This results in a distinctive pattern on an EEG.
Multiple sleep latency test (MSLT)		Test that consists of a series of short, daytime naps in the sleep lab to measure daytime sleepiness and how fast the patient falls asleep; used to diagnose or rule out narcolepsy.
Nerve conduction test		Test of the functioning of peripheral nerves. Conduction time (impulse travel) through a nerve is measured after a stimulus is applied; used to diagnose polyneuropathies.
Polysomnography pah lee som NAH gruh fee	*poly-* many *somn/o* sleep *-graphy* process of recording	Measurement and record of a number of functions while the patient is asleep (e.g., cardiac, muscular, brain, ocular, and respiratory functions). Most often used to diagnose sleep apnea.

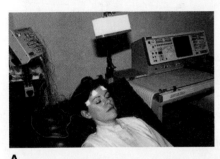

A

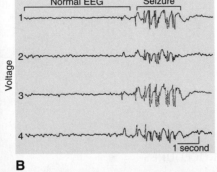

B

Fig. 12-19   EEG. **A,** Photograph of person with electrodes attached. **B,** EEG tracing showing activity in four different places in the brain. Compare the normal activity with the explosive activity that occurs during a seizure. *(From Thibodeau GA, Patton KT: The human body in health and disease, ed 4, St Louis, 2005, Mosby.)*

Terms Related to Other Diagnostic Tests

TERM	WORD ORIGIN	DEFINITION
Babinski reflex bah BIN skeez		In normal conditions, the dorsiflexion of the great toe when the plantar surface of the sole is stimulated. **Babinski sign** is the loss or diminution of the Achilles tendon reflex seen in sciatica.
Cerebrospinal fluid (CSF) analysis		Examination of fluid from the CNS to detect pathogens and abnormalities. Useful in diagnosing hemorrhages, tumors, and various diseases.
Deep tendon reflexes (DTR)		Assessment of an automatic motor response by striking a tendon. Useful in the diagnosis of stroke.
Gait assessment rating scale (GARS)		Inventory of 16 aspects of gait (how one walks) to determine abnormalities. May be used as one method to evaluate cerebellar function.
Lumbar puncture (LP)		Procedure to aspirate CSF from the lumbar subarachnoid space. A needle is inserted between two lumbar vertebrae to withdraw the fluid for diagnostic purposes. Also called a **spinal tap** (Fig. 12-20).

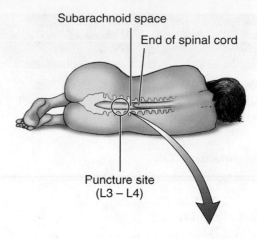

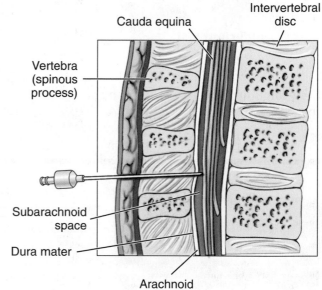

Fig. 12-20 Lumbar puncture. *(From Herlihy B, Maebius NK: The human body in health and illness, ed 2, Philadelphia, 2003, Saunders.)*

◆ Exercise 12-11: Diagnostic Procedures

Match the word part with its meaning. Some letters may be used more than once.

_____ 1. electr/o	_____ 10. arteri/o	A. sleep
		B. sound
_____ 2. cerebr/o	_____ 11. radi/o	C. artery
		D. inside
_____ 3. extra-	_____ 12. tom/o	E. spinal cord
		F. slice
_____ 4. somn/o	_____ 13. spin/o	G. outside
		H. spine
_____ 5. myel/o	_____ 14. son/o	I. brain
		J. skull
_____ 6. crani/o	_____ 15. ultra-	K. record
		L. cerebrum
_____ 7. angi/o	_____ 16. poly-	M. electricity
		N. beyond
_____ 8. intra-	_____ 17. encephal/o	O. rays
		P. many
_____ 9. -gram		Q. vessel

Circle the correct answer.

18. Walking abnormalities are measured by a *(gait assessment rating scale, deep tendon reflex)*.
19. Examination of fluid from the CNS is a/an *(evoked potential, cerebrospinal fluid analysis)*.
20. Aspiration of CSF for diagnostic purposes is a *(CT scan, spinal tap)*.
21. A record of electrical activity of the brain is an *(electroencephalogram, electrocardiogram)*.
22. A finding that indicates loss of Achilles tendon reflex is *(Babinski reflex, Babinski sign)*.
23. *(Multiple sleep latency test, Polysomnography)* is used to diagnose sleep apnea.
24. An x-ray study of cerebral arteries is called *(cerebral angiography, magnetic resonance angiography)*.
25. *(Nerve conduction test, echoencephalography)* is an ultrasound study of the brain.
26. *(Myelography, Myography)* is an x-ray of the spinal cord.

Godfrey Regional Hospital

EMERGENCY ROOM RECORD

REASON FOR VISIT:

Difficulty with speech

This 72-year-old female with past history of CVA comes in for symptoms that started on Friday. Apparently, she had an episode, which lasted approximately 15 minutes, of not being able to express her words. She says her thoughts were clear, but she was unable to say the words she wanted to say. In conjunction with that, she had some pain along the left temporal and parietal region. No visual symptoms. No obvious facial drooping according to witnesses. No weakness or paresthesias in her arms or legs. Since then has felt excessively tired and has a very mild dull headache across the frontal area.

Allergies to codeine

CURRENT MEDS:

Coumadin 4.5 mg po qd

PAST MEDICAL HISTORY:

Significant for CVA involving her right hand. She was involved in PT for approximately 1 month. Back to about 90% to 95% function. Work-up at that time included an echocardiogram and carotid Dopplers, which she says are normal. No symptoms since that time.

REVIEW OF SYSTEMS:

Otherwise unremarkable. No upper respiratory problems. Did have an eye infection and was treated with antibiotics a couple of weeks ago. No chest pain, palpitations, shortness of breath. No abdominal complaints. No dysuria or joint pain.

On exam, patient is alert and oriented. Memory is intact to conversation. HEENT exam reveals pupils equal, round, and reactive to light. Extraocular eye movements are intact. No obvious facial asymmetry is noted. Oropharynx is pink and moist. Uvula and tongue midline. Neck supple, no carotid bruits appreciated. Carotid upstrokes are of good quality and equal bilaterally. Lungs are clear to auscultation bilaterally. Heart sounds are regular, no murmurs, rubs, or gallops.

Continued

Neurological exam: cranial nerves II through XII grossly intact. Motor exam reveals good strength in both upper and lower extremities. NO gross sensory deficits. Deep tendon reflexes are of good quality and equal bilaterally. Romberg's sign is negative. Patient able to do tandem finger to nose and moving her heel up and down without difficulty. Rapid alternating movements were not tested. Able to ambulate without difficulty. No ataxia or limp.

ASSESSMENT: Expressive aphasia most likely caused by TIA or small stroke. Symptoms have resolved at this time. Remains fatigued but no neurological symptoms.

PLAN: Already on Coumadin, discussed adding a baby aspirin. She would like to discuss these options with her private doctor. Feel this is reasonable because she is stable at this time. She does have a residual headache; however, if neurological symptoms reemerge or worsen, she should have a CT scan done emergently.

Continue Coumadin 4.5 mg po q day.

Robert Rais, MD

◈ Exercise 12-12: EMERGENCY ROOM RECORD

Using the emergency room record above, answer the following questions.

1. This patient has a history of what disorder? _____

2. What term tells you that she has had no prickling, burning, or numbness in her legs? _____

3. What term tells you that she had no lack of muscular coordination? _____

4. How did her aphasia manifest itself? _____

5. Why would a CT be done emergently if her neurological symptoms worsen or reemerge? _____

≋ THERAPEUTIC INTERVENTIONS

Terms Related to Brain and Skull Interventions

TERM	WORD ORIGIN	DEFINITIONS
Craniectomy kray nee ECK tuh mee	*crani/o* skull, cranium *-ectomy* removal	Removal of part of the skull.
Craniotomy kray nee AH tuh mee	*crani/o* skull, cranium *-tomy* incision	Incision into the skull as a surgical approach or to relieve intracranial pressure; also called **trephination** (treff fin NAY shun).
CSF shunt		Tube implanted in the brain to relieve the pressure of cerebrospinal fluid as a result of hydrocephalus.
Stereotaxic radiosurgery stair ee oh TACK sick	*stere/o* 3-D *tax/o* order, arrangement *-ic* pertaining to	Surgery using radiowaves to localize structures within 3-D space.

Terms Related to Peripheral Nervous System Interventions

TERM	WORD ORIGIN	DEFINITION
Ganglionectomy gan glee oh NECK tuh mee	*gangli/o* ganglion *-ectomy* removal	Removal of a ganglion (*pl.* ganglions or ganglia).
Vagotomy vay GAH tuh mee	*vag/o* vagus nerve *-tomy* incision	Cutting of a branch of the vagus nerve to reduce the secretion of gastric acid.

Terms Related to General Interventions

TERM	WORD ORIGIN	DEFINITION
Carotid endarterectomy kuh RAH tid en dar tur ECK tuh mee	*end-* within *arter/o* artery *-ectomy* removal	Removal of the atheromatous plaque lining the carotid artery to increase blood flow and leave a smooth surface. Done to prevent thrombotic occlusions (Fig. 12-21).
Microsurgery	*micro-* small, tiny	Surgery in which magnification is used to repair delicate tissues.
Nerve block		Use of anesthesia to prevent sensory nerve impulses from reaching the CNS.
Neurectomy noo RECK tuh mee	*neur/o* nerve *-ectomy* removal	Excision of part or all of a nerve.
Neurolysis noo RAH lih sis	*neur/o* nerve *-lysis* destruction	Destruction of a nerve.
Neuroplasty noo roh PLAS tee	*neur/o* nerve *-plasty* surgical repair	Surgical repair of a nerve.
Neurorrhaphy noo ROAR ah fee	*neur/o* nerve *-rrhaphy* suture	Suture of a severed nerve.
Neurotomy noo RAH toh mee	*neur/o* nerve *-tomy* incision	Incision of a nerve.

Terms Related to Pain Management

TERM	WORD ORIGIN	DEFINITION
Cordotomy kore DAH tuh mee	*cord/o* spinal cord *-tomy* incision	Incision of the spinal cord to relieve pain.
Rhizotomy rye ZAH tuh mee	*rhiz/o* spinal nerve root *-tomy* incision	Resection of the dorsal root of a spinal nerve to relieve pain.
Sympathectomy sim puh THECK tuh mee	*sympath/o* to feel with *-ectomy* removal	Surgical interruption of part of the sympathetic pathways for the relief of chronic pain or to promote vasodilation.
Transcutaneous electrical nerve stimulation (TENS)	*trans-* through *cutane/o* skin *-ous* pertaining to	Method of pain control effected by the application of electrical impulses to the skin (Fig. 12-22).

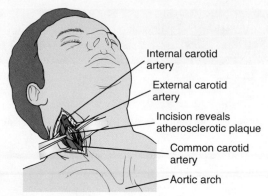

Fig. 12-21 Carotid endarterectomy. *(From Lewis SM: Medical-surgical nursing: assessment and management of clinical problems, ed 6, St Louis, 2005, Mosby.)*

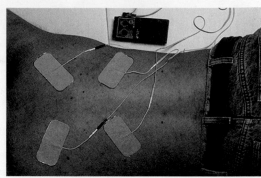

Fig. 12-22 Transcutaneous electrical nerve stimulation (TENS) treatment. *(From Lewis SM: Medical-surgical nursing: assessment and management of clinical problems, ed 6, St Louis, 2005, Mosby.)*

◈ Exercise 12-13: THERAPEUTIC INTERVENTIONS

Match the word part with its meaning.

_____ 1. stere/o

_____ 2. disk/o

_____ 3. tax/o

_____ 4. syn-

_____ 5. cutane/o

_____ 6. sympath/o

_____ 7. -desis

_____ 8. lamin/o

_____ 9. radi/o

_____ 10. rhiz/o

_____ 11. trans-

_____ 12. spondyl/o

_____ 13. -tomy

_____ 14. lob/o

_____ 15. -plasty

_____ 16. arter/o

_____ 17. gangli/o

_____ 18. crani/o

_____ 19. -ectomy

_____ 20. cord/o

_____ 21. -rrhaphy

_____ 22. neur/o

_____ 23. vag/o

_____ 24. end-

_____ 25. -lysis

A. stabilization
B. artery
C. suture
D. incision
E. within
F. intervertebral disc
G. nerve root
H. order, arrangement
I. vagus nerve
J. together
K. nerve
L. rays
M. vertebra
N. destruction
O. spinal cord
P. 3-D
Q. to feel with
R. through
S. removal
T. section
U. surgical repair
V. ganglion
W. skull
X. lamina
Y. skin

Circle the correct answer.

26. A method of pain control using electrical impulses is called *(TENS, ADL)*.
27. A method of relieving pressure of CSF from hydrocephalus is through the use of *(stereotaxic radiosurgery, CSF shunt)*.
28. Use of a local anesthetic to prevent sensory nerve impulses from reaching the CNS is called a *(nerve block, rhizotomy)*.
29. A *(cordotomy, vagotomy)* reduces the secretion of gastric acid.

PHARMACOLOGY

Analgesics: Drugs that reduce pain. Examples include morphine (MS Contin), hydrocodone (Vicodin or Lortab, in combination with acetaminophen), sumatriptan (Imitrex), acetaminophen (Tylenol), and naproxen (Anaprox). Some analgesics may be considered narcotics.

Anesthetics: Drugs that cause a loss of feeling or sensation. They can act either locally (local anesthetic) or systemically (general anesthetic), and a general anesthetic can induce unconsciousness. Examples include propofol (Diprivan) and lidocaine (Xylocaine, Lidoderm).

Anticonvulsants: Drugs that reduce the frequency and severity of epileptic or other convulsive seizures. Examples include clonazepam (Klonopin), carbamazepine (Tegretol), and phenytoin (Dilantin).

Antiparkinsonian drugs: Drugs that are effective against Parkinson disease. Examples include levodopa and carbidopa (Sinemet) and tolcapone (Tasmar).

Antipyretics: Drugs that reduce fever. Examples include aspirin (Bayer), acetaminophen (Tylenol), and ibuprofen (Advil, Motrin).

Hypnotics: Drugs that promote sleep. They may also be referred to as soporifics or somnifacients. Examples include temazepam (Restoril), zolpidem (Ambien), and flurazepam (Dalmane).

Neuromuscular blockers: Drugs that block the action of acetylcholine at the motor nerve end plate to cause paralysis. May be used in surgery to minimize patient movement. Examples include pancuronium (Pavulon), vecuronium (Norcuron), and succinylcholine (Anectine).

Sedatives: Drugs that inhibit neuronal activity to calm and relax. Examples include alprazolam (Xanax), lorazepam (Ativan), and chloral hydrate.

Stimulants: Drugs that increase synaptic activity of targeted neurons in the CNS to treat narcolepsy, attention-deficit disorder with hyperactivity, and fatigue, and to suppress the appetite. Examples include dextroamphetamine (Dexedrine), methylphenidate (Ritalin), caffeine, and phentermine (Adipex-P).

Exercise 12-14: PHARMACOLOGY

Match the drug with its effect.

_____ 1. treats PD

_____ 2. relieves pain

_____ 3. calms and relaxes

_____ 4. induces sleep

_____ 5. reduces fever

_____ 6. reduces severity of seizures

_____ 7. causes paralysis

_____ 8. causes loss of sensation

A.   anesthetic
B.   antipyretic
C.   soporific
D.   anticonvulsant
E.   sedative
F.   neuromuscular blocker
G.   analgesic
H.   antiparkinsonian drug

Abbreviations

Abbreviation	Definition	Abbreviation	Definition
AD	Alzheimer disease	MRI	Magnetic resonance imaging
ADL	Activities of daily living	MS	Multiple sclerosis
ALS	Amyotrophic lateral sclerosis	PD	Parkinson disease
ANS	Autonomic nervous system	PET scan	Positron emission tomography scan
BBB	Blood-brain barrier	PNS	Peripheral nervous system
C1-C8	Cervical nerves	PSG	Polysomnography
CNS	Central nervous system	S1-S5	Sacral nerves
CP	Cerebral palsy	SAH	Subarachnoid hemorrhage
CSF	Cerebrospinal fluid	SNS	Somatic nervous system
CT scan	Computerized tomography scan	SPECT	Single-photon emission computed tomography
CVA	Cerebrovascular accident	T1-T12	Thoracic nerves
DTR	Deep tendon reflex	TENS	Transcutaneous electrical nerve stimulation
EEG	Electroencephalogram	TIA	Transient ischemic attack
ICP	Intracranial pressure		
L1-L5	Lumbar nerves		
LP	Lumbar puncture		

◆ Exercise 12-15: ABBREVIATIONS

Spell out the following abbreviations.

1. Barry had an LP to analyze his CSF for meningitis.

   _____

2. Maria became a quadriplegic when she sustained a C2 fracture diving into the shallow end of a swimming pool.

   _____

3. Ms. Damjanov had an MRI to aid in the diagnosis of her MS.

   _____

4. The patient underwent PSG to detect abnormalities related to hypersomnia.

   _____

5. Walter needed help with his ADL after a CVA that left him with right hemiparesis.

   _____

Careers

Occupational Therapists

Occupational therapists (OTs) assist patients who have become mentally, physically, developmentally, or emotionally disabled to live independent, productive, and satisfying lives. OTs help these patients regain and build skills that are important for health and well-being, including activities of daily living (ADL): the activities usually performed in the course of a normal day in the person's life, such as eating, toileting, dressing, bathing, or brushing teeth. Aside from hospitals, work sites may include outpatient and community settings and schools. The Bureau of Labor Statistics reports that currently more than one third of OTs work part time.

All 50 states require at least a bachelor's degree; this also holds true in both Puerto Rico and Washington, D.C. To become a licensed, registered occupational therapist (OTR), an applicant must graduate from an accredited program and pass a national certification examination.

Employment is expected to increase faster than the average for all occupations through 2010. Over the long run, the demand should continue to increase as a result of growth in the number of individuals with disabilities—the baby boom generation's movement into retirement, with the concomitant incidence of heart attack and stroke. For further information, visit the American Occupation Therapy Association website at http://www.aorta.org.

Careers Related to the Nervous System

Electroneurodiagnostic Technologist

Electroneurodiagnostic technologists specialize in techniques to perform diagnostic techniques that record the electrical activity of the brain and nervous system. They perform electroencephalography (EEG), evoked potential (EP) tests, and polysomnography (PSG). Growth in this area is expected to be greater than average because of the increased use of EEG and EP tests in surgeries and the increase in sleep studies. Students may enroll in programs that range from 12 to 24 months. More information is available at the website for the American Society of Electroneurodiagnostic Technologists, Inc.: http://www.aset.org.

Polysomnography Technologist/Sleep Technologist

A relatively new specialized career is in sleep studies. These specialists are referred to as polysomnography (PSG) technologists or sleep technologists. PSG technologists use a variety of techniques to diagnose sleep disorders in patients of all ages by measuring physiological changes during the sleeping state. The disorders studied may include insomnia, hypersomnia, and somnambulism. The growth in this area is expected to be much greater than average. Some sleep technologists have a degree in respiratory therapy or nursing and earn a certificate, whereas others may apply to many of the new degree programs being offered. A good way to check on programs that are accredited is to visit the website for the Commission on Accreditation of Allied Health Education Programs (CAAHEP) at http://www.caahep.org. For more information from the Association of Polysomnographic Technologists, visit their website at http://www.aptweb.org.

Neurologist

Medical doctors who choose to specialize in the study, diagnosis, and treatment of neurological disorders are neurologists. The career path for these individuals usually includes a bachelor's degree heavy in basic science courses, a medical degree, and a residency in neurology. Neurologists may choose to further specialize in the areas of pediatric neurology, geriatric neurology, or specific disorders, such as multiple sclerosis. For more information on becoming a physician, visit the AMA website at http://www.ama.org.

Chapter Review

A. Functions of the Nervous System

1. In your own words, explain the functions of the nervous system and give an example of how one disorder illustrates a dysfunction of this system.

_____

_____

_____

B. Anatomy and Physiology

2. Explain the two main divisions of the nervous system and how they are organized.

_____

_____

3. Label the following diagrams of the brain. Include the terms and their respective combining forms where appropriate.

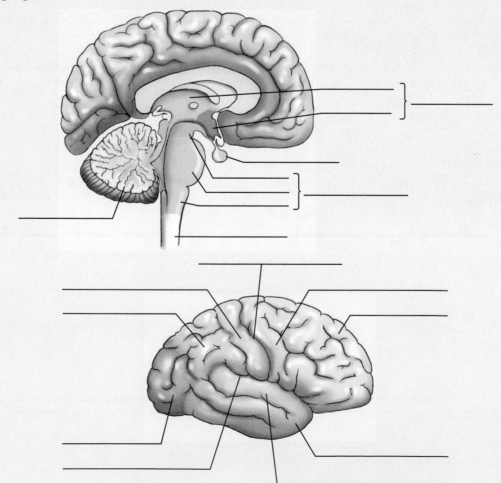

4. What are the names of the nerves that carry impulses toward the brain?

_____

5. What is the covering of the CNS? List the layers and spaces from outermost to innermost.

_____

6. The spinal nerves emerge from the spinal cord at the nerve _____.

7. A network of spinal nerves is called a/an _____.

8. What type of chemical moves across the space between two nerve cells? _____

9. What is the name of the supportive or stromal cells of the nervous system? _____

10. What part of the brain is responsible for thinking, reasoning, and memory? _____

11. Which part of the brain is responsible for the coordination of movement? _____

C. Pathology

12. A patient reports having difficulty remembering; this symptom is termed _____.

13. Ms. Roberts reports that she has problems falling asleep at night. She has _____.

14. What form of syncope is associated with abrupt emotional stress? _____

15. Cara experiences a "warning" before an epileptic seizure. What is this called? _____

16. Ms. Murphy's speech is slurred after her brain attack. She is exhibiting _____.

17. A patient who walks very slowly in an incoordinated manner, or shuffles, has an abnormal

_____.

18. Samantha has lost her sense of taste. She is exhibiting _____.

19. Zack was born with an abnormal accumulation of CSF in the ventricles of the brain. He has

_____.

20. A patient who faints is described as having _____.

21. Patients with infections of the covering of the CNS have _____.

22. Currently, the most common cause of dementia is _____.

23. What is the eponym for ALS? _____

24. A patient with a paralysis of the body from the neck down has _____.

25. In what disorder is there an abnormal opening of the spine from which the meninges and/or the

   spinal cord protrude? _____

26. A patient who has a blockage or a hemorrhage in the brain with neural deficits that last more than a

   day has had a(n) _____.

Choose the appropriate word roots, combining vowels, prefixes, and suffixes to build terms that take the place of the phrase in bold. First, write the appropriate word parts in the space provided next to their type, then assemble the term on the line after the parentheses.

Ex: Frances suffered a condition of paralysis on half of her body.

(*hemi-* prefix/ *-plegia* suffix)

hemiplegia

27. Olivia was being treated by her neurologist for an **inflammation of many nerves**.

   (_____ prefix/ _____ word root/ _____ suffix)

   _____

28. Mad cow disease is termed bovine (for cows) **inflammation of the brain**.

   (_____ word root/ _____ suffix)

   _____

29. As a result of a stroke, Michael's grandfather had a **condition of a lack of a sense of smell**.

   (_____ prefix/ _____ word root/ _____ suffix)

   _____

Decode the medical term by writing the meaning of the word part in the space provided, then using the parts to form a definition.

Ex: Monoparesis

(mono- *one* + -paresis *slight paralysis*)

slight paralysis of one (limb)

30. hypersomnia

   (hyper- _____ + somn/o _____ + -ia _____)

   _____

31. narcolepsy

   (narc/o _____ + -lepsy _____)

   _____

32. radiculitis

   (radicul/o _____ + -itis _____)

   _____

D. Diagnostic Procedures

33. What is the term for an examination of the CSF? _____

34. What is SPECT? _____

35. What imaging technique is used to diagnose strokes, edema, and tumors? _____

36. MSLT stands for _____ and is used to diagnose _____.

37. DTR is used to assist in the diagnosis of _____.

Decode the medical term by writing the meaning of the word part in the space provided, then using the parts to form a definition.

38. myelography

   (myel/o _____ + -graphy _____)

   _____

39. cerebral angiography

   (cerebr/o _____ + -al _____ angi/o _____ + -graphy _____)

   _____

40. polysomnography

   (poly- _____ + somn/o _____ + -graphy)

   _____

E. Therapeutic Interventions

41. Patients are assisted with ADL to cope with the sequelae of a stroke. What are ADL?

   _____

42. What type of surgery uses radiowaves to localize structures within 3-D spaces?

   _____

43. A tube implanted in the brain to relieve the pressure of cerebrospinal fluid is called a(n)

    _____.

44. TENS is done for the purpose of _____.

Choose the appropriate word roots, combining vowels, prefixes, and suffixes to build terms that take the place of the phrase in bold. First, write the appropriate word parts in the space provided next to their type, then assemble the term on the line after the parentheses.

45. The surgeon performed an **excision of a nerve**.

    (_____ word root/ _____ suffix)

    _____

46. Another term for a trephination is an **incision of a skull**.

    (_____ word root/ _____ combining vowel/ _____ suffix)

    _____

47. One of the repairs done after a car accident was a **surgical repair of a nerve**.

    (_____ word root/ _____ combining vowel/ _____ suffix)

    _____

Decode the medical term by writing the meaning of the word part in the space provided, then using the parts to form a definition.

48. neurolysis

    (neur/o _____ + -lysis _____)

    _____

49. rhizotomy

    (rhiz/o _____ + -tomy _____)

    _____

50. spondylosyndesis

    (spondyl/o _____ + syn- _____ + -desis _____)

    _____

F. Pharmacology

51. Epilepsy is treated by what class of drug? _____

52. Blood thinners are what class of drug? _____

53. Drugs that promote sleep are called _____

54. Drugs that relieve pain, such as aspirin, acetaminophen, and Anaprox, are called _____.

55. Roslyn took a drug to relieve her fever. That type of drug is called a(n) _____.

G. Abbreviations

Spell out the abbreviated terms.

56. Susan woke up with a loss of the use of the right side of her body. She was diagnosed with a CVA.

    _____

57. Rose had an EEG, which was used to diagnose her epilepsy. _____

58. A PET scan is especially useful in the diagnosis of AD. _____

59. When the LP was done on the patient, the needle was inserted between L3 and L4.

    _____

60. A patient with PD has dysphagia, dysphasia, and a shuffling gait. _____

H. Singulars and Plurals

Change the following terms from singular to plural.

61. gyrus _____

62. stimulus _____

63. sulcus _____

64. ganglion _____

65. thrombus _____

I. Translations

Rewrite the following sentences in your own words.

66. Mr. O'Connor had a right-sided <u>brain attack</u> that affected the <u>contralateral</u> side of his body. His symptoms included <u>hemiparesis</u> and <u>dysphasia</u>.

    _____

    _____

67. As a result of a blow to the head, the patient sustained an <u>epidural hematoma</u>.

_____

_____

68. The patient reported <u>vertigo</u> and <u>syncope</u> before her arrival at the emergency department.

_____

_____

69. The baby's <u>spina bifida</u> resulted in a <u>meningomyelocele</u>.

_____

_____

70. The neonate's <u>hydrocephalus</u> was treated with a <u>CSF shunt</u>.

_____

_____

J. Be Careful

71. What are the different definitions for dermatome?

_____

_____

72. Myel/o means spinal cord or bone marrow. In the following examples, define each term accurately, using a dictionary if necessary.

   A. myelogram _____

   B. myeloma _____

   C. osteomyelitis _____

   D. meningomyelocele _____

   E. myelitis _____

   F. myelocyte _____

   G. myelodysplasia _____

73. What is the difference between dysarthria and dysarthrosis?

_____

74. What are the two meanings for the following abbreviations?

A. BBB _____

B. MS _____

Case Study With Accompanying Medical Report

Retirement was not going quite the way Max Janovski had planned. The 75-year-old former stockbroker had been visiting his son's family when he became dizzy and fainted. He quickly regained consciousness, only to find that he had difficulty using the right side of his body, and his speech was slurred. The symptoms were of brief duration, and Max insisted that he was fine. However, his son insisted he go to the emergency department (ED). Max was admitted to the hospital and subsequently suffered a stroke while there. The stroke's sequelae required the services of a physical therapist and an occupational therapist (OT), Eduardo Menendez, to help him regain his ability to perform daily living skills.

It is likely that one of the arteries in Max's brain was initially temporarily deprived of its blood flow and hence its oxygen. This is termed a *transient ischemic attack* (TIA). The first blood clot either dislodged or disintegrated, only to be replaced by another while Max was in the hospital. This blood clot did not dissolve and subsequently caused his stroke, or cerebrovascular accident (CVA). Depending on the area affected, a neural deficit will develop when a clot lodges in the brain area. In Max's case, the clot on the left side of his brain caused weakness on his right side and slurred speech. Max was glad that his stroke had occurred in the hospital. He knew that if he hadn't been lucky enough to get help so soon, he could have suffered severe disability or died. As it was, Max had right hemiparesis and was having trouble doing things that he had always taken for granted, such as buttoning his shirt and using a spoon. Eduardo reassures Max that he will work with him on ways to feed, dress, and toilet himself.

Intravenous thrombolytic (clot buster) therapy was begun soon after Max's stroke to prevent more serious damage. Max is grateful that medicine is available, but he realizes that his physical and occupational therapy were valuable treatment options too. Eduardo helped him improve his motor skills, strength, and coordination. Eduardo acted as coach, teacher, and cheerleader and helped Max recover physically and mentally from his stroke.

South Shore Hospital
2243 Seaspray Dr.
Seacrest Beach, FL 32405

DISCHARGE SUMMARY

Patient Name: Max Janovski
MR#: 349812
Date of Admission: 07/04/05
Date of Discharge: 07/08/05
Admission Diagnosis: Rule out cerebrovascular accident
Discharge Diagnoses: (1) Cerebrovascular accident; (2) emphysema; (3) CAD.

History

This patient is a 75-year-old white male with a history of emphysema, coronary artery disease, and benign prostatic hyperplasia. His BPH was treated with a TURP in 1998. He had a triple CABG in 2000. Patient reports smoking two packs per day until 2 years ago. Denies any recent tobacco or alcohol use. He has benefited from oxygen therapy for the last 2 months.

He was admitted for an episode of vertigo and several episodes of syncope that occurred as he was visiting his son's family over the fourth of July holiday. His son brought him to the ED when he reported a loss of feeling on his right side, and his speech became slurred. These symptoms resolved before he arrived at the hospital. He has no history of headaches but has admitted to continued dizziness. Patient was admitted and experienced a right-sided CVA the following morning. Intravenous thrombolytic therapy was administered immediately, but patient remains with a right hemiparesis.

Physical Examination on Admission

Physical examination was largely negative. The patient is quiet, mildly anxious, yet cooperative. Pupils are equal and reactive. Neck is negative. There is a normal sinus rhythm with no significant murmurs. Abdomen is negative. There is no peripheral edema. Patient exhibits a minimal amount of ataxia on walking, but there are no other neurological findings.

The neurologist ordered and reviewed CT scans of head, MRIs, intracranial and extracranial MRAs, and Holter monitor readings. Cerebral hemorrhage was ruled out.

Laboratory findings included mild hypercholesterolemia and a hemoglobin of 12.1. Chest x-ray demonstrated hyperinflation, with vascular markings diminished at the apices. EEG was normal.

Patient appears to be stable at the present time and is discharged to his son's home while continuing his physical and occupational therapy. He has demonstrated a good understanding of his condition and of the need for full cooperation with his therapists to work toward regaining his independence.

An appointment has been scheduled for follow-up in 2 weeks.

_____ *J. M. Smythe, MD*

L. Health Care Report

75. Patient was admitted for vertigo and syncope. Define each.

_____

76. What is hypercholesterolemia? _____

77. What is BPH treated with TURP? _____

78. Ataxia refers to _____.

Reference

Quereshi B: Review of Jones L, Sidell M: The challenge of promoting health: exploration and action, *J R Soc Med* 90:705, 1997. Available online: ACP-ASIM Medicine in Quotations, http:www.acponline.org/cgibin/medquotes.pl.

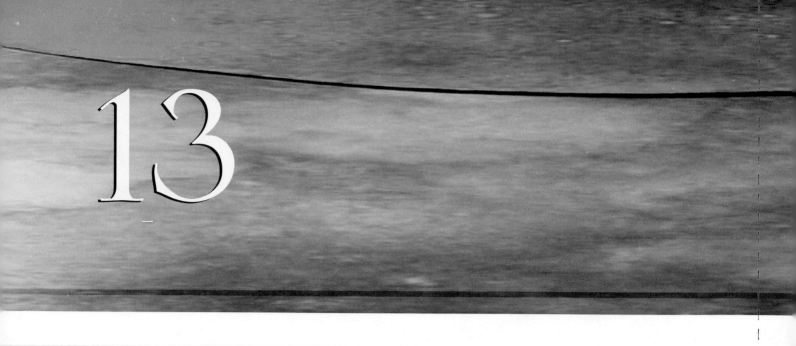

13

OBJECTIVES

You will be able to do the following after completing this chapter:

Key Terms
1. Define, appropriately use, and spell all the Key Terms for this chapter.

Structure and Function of the Nervous System
2. Describe the organization of the nervous system and identify its two main divisions.
3. Explain the role of neurons and neuroglia in a nerve impulse.
4. Describe a synapse and explain its function.

Central Nervous System
5. List the main divisions of the central nervous system (CNS).
6. Identify the parts of the brain and briefly describe the function of each.
7. Explain the purpose of cerebrospinal fluid (CSF).
8. List the cranial nerves and describe their function.
9. List the spinal nerves and describe their function.

Peripheral Nervous System
10. List the main divisions of the peripheral nervous system.
11. Describe the functions of the sympathetic and parasympathetic nervous systems.
12. List and briefly describe six types of reflex actions.

Diseases and Disorders of the Nervous System
13. List and describe nine types of signs and symptoms of neurological disease.
14. List six types of diagnostic tests and procedures for neurological disease and describe the use of each.
15. List 11 diseases and disorders of the nervous system and briefly describe the etiology, signs and symptoms, diagnosis, therapy, and interventions for each.

Mental Health
16. Describe the two-fold testing process used to determine mental health disorders.
17. List and describe seven common signs and symptoms of mental disorders.
18. List four types of tests and procedures used to diagnose mental disorders and briefly describe each.
19. List and briefly describe 20 mental health disorders.

ANATOMY AND PHYSIOLOGY OF THE NERVOUS SYSTEM

Patient-Centered Professionalism

20. Analyze a realistic medical office situation and apply your understanding of the nervous system to determine the best course of action.
21. Describe the impact on patient care when medical assistants have a solid understanding of the structure and function of the nervous system.

KEY TERMS

The Key Terms for this chapter have been organized into sections so that you can easily see the terminology associated with each aspect of the nervous system.

Structure and Function of the Nervous System

Nerve Cells and Nerve Impulses

glial cells Neuroglia that support, protect, insulate, and nourish neurons.

nerve Bundle of fibers containing neurons and blood vessels (macroscopic).

neuroglia Supporting structure of nerve tissue, located in the CNS, including phagocytic cells; do not transmit impulses.

neuron Functional unit of a nerve that sends and receives nerve impulses (microscopic).

Neurons

axon Part of the neuron attached to a cell body that carries impulses to other neurons and body tissue; conduction portion of nerve.

cell body Main part of the nerve cell.

dendrite Part of the neuron resembling tree branches that receives nerve impulses toward the cell body.

ganglion Group of neuron cell bodies along the path of a nerve outside the CNS.

integrative neurons (interneurons) Neurons in the brain and spinal cord that conduct nerve impulses between afferent (sensory) and efferent (motor) neurons.

motor (efferent) neurons Neurons that transmit nerve impulses from the CNS to muscles and glands.

myelin sheath Covering of an axon that has a whitish appearance.

myelinated Covered with myelin sheath, as over nerve fibers, and appearing as white matter.

nerve fibers Bundle of axons.

neurilemma Continuous plasma membrane around myelin sheath.

nodes of Ranvier Spaces where myelin sheath does not touch itself externally.

sensory (afferent) neurons Neurons that transmit nerve impulses to the CNS from within and outside the body.

sheath Covering.

Neuroglia

astrocytes Star-shaped nerve cells that hold blood vessels closer to nerve cells and serve as a barrier to transport water and salts between nerve cells and capillaries.

ependymal cells Nerve cells that line the brain and central cavity of the spinal cord to serve as a barrier between CSF and tissue fluid.

microglia cells Nerve cells that engulf cellular waste and destroy microorganisms in nerve tissue; special macrophages to protect CNS.

oligodendroglia cells Nerve cells that produce and maintain myelin sheath.

Nerve Impulses

dermatome Surface area of the body (skin) where afferent fibers travel from a spinal root.

nerve impulse Electrical signal that begins when a stimulus is received.

neurotransmitters Chemical substances (e.g., adrenaline or acetylcholine) that cause a nerve impulse to cross synapses.

receptor Sensory nerve ending.

KEY TERMS—cont'd

stimulus Change in the environment of a nerve cell; causes action.

synapse Space between the end of one neuron and the beginning of the next neuron.

Divisions of the Nervous System

brain Main functioning unit of the CNS, located in the skull and containing many neurons.

central nervous system (CNS) System of nerves that includes the brain and spinal cord.

peripheral nervous system (PNS) System of nerves that connect the CNS to body tissue; nervous system outside the brain and spinal cord.

Central Nervous System

arachnoid Middle layer of meninges; resembles a spiderweb.

dura mater Covering of the brain located closest to the skull and vertebral column.

pia mater Covering of the brain closest to the brain and spinal column that is delicate tissue rich with small blood vessels.

Brain

antidiuretic hormone (ADH) Hormone stored in posterior pituitary gland and needed to maintain fluid balance by reabsorption of fluids.

brain stem Stalklike portion of the brain that connects cerebral hemispheres to the spinal cord; contains the midbrain, pons, and medulla oblongata.

cerebellum "Little brain" connected to the brain stem that controls skeletal muscles for fine motor skills and coordination of voluntary muscle groups.

cerebrospinal fluid (CSF) Sterile, watery fluid formed within ventricles of the brain to cushion and protect CNS organs.

cerebrum Largest portion of the brain divided into two hemispheres responsible for thinking, sensation, and voluntary actions.

cortex Outer portion of the brain responsible for perception and initiation of voluntary movements.

cranial nerves Twelve pairs of central nerves originating within the brain.

diencephalon "Interbrain" located under the cerebrum that includes the thalamus and hypothalamus.

epidural space Space outside and between the dura mater and walls of the vertebral canal (vertebrae, skull).

equilibrium Balance.

fissures Grooves or deep folds within the cortex.

frontal lobe Part of the brain that controls voluntary muscle action, speech, and judgment.

gyri Folds in the cortex; either fissures or sulci.

hypothalamus Gland that controls activities of the pituitary gland; secretes oxytocin and ADH; regulates the autonomic nervous system, body temperatures, release of hormones, water balance.

linear Referring to a thought process that allows connections between thoughts; in a line.

medulla oblongata Lowest part of the brain stem; connects to the spinal cord and is responsible for involuntary movements.

meninges Protective covering of the brain and spinal cord.

midbrain Part of the brain connecting lower portion of the cerebellum to the pons; responsible for reflexes.

occipital lobe Lobe at the base of the posterior brain that controls vision.

oxytocin Hormone stored in the posterior pituitary gland and needed for uterine contractions during and after childbirth.

parietal lobe Lobe of the brain in the mid-cerebrum that controls sensory functions (touch, pain, temperature interpretation).

pituitary gland Master gland; under control of the hypothalamus.

pons Middle section of the brain stem that acts as a bridge between the brain and spinal cord, controlling the face, hearing, balance, blood pressure, heart rate, and respiratory patterns.

spatial Referring to the feeling of space; sense of where one "is."

subarachnoid space Space between the pia mater and arachnoid membrane; contains CSF.

subdural space Space between the dura mater and arachnoid membrane.

sulcus Shallow groove in the brain.

temporal lobe Lobe at the side of the brain over the ear that controls hearing, smell, and taste.

thalamus Area of the brain responsible for relaying messages from parts of the body; monitors sensory stimuli.

ventricles Small cavities within the brain responsible for production of CSF.

viscera Internal organs.

Spinal Cord

spinal column Bone structure (vertebrae) that surrounds and protects the spinal cord.

spinal cord Long bundle of nerves that conducts impulses to and from the brain.

spinal nerves Nerve fibers extending from the spinal cord; 31 pairs carry motor impulses from the spinal cord toward muscles or glands and organs.

Peripheral Nervous System

autonomic nervous system (ANS) System controlled by the CNS, mainly the cortex, hypothalamus, and medulla; responsible for involuntary actions of muscles and glands.

somatic nervous system System of nerves that transmits impulses to skeletal muscles and is responsible for reflex action.

Autonomic Nervous System

"fight-or-flight" response Reaction by the sympathetic nervous system to respond quickly to stressful situations.

homeostasis State of the body in balance.

parasympathetic nervous system System that returns the body back to balance after responding to a reactive state.

KEY TERMS—cont'd

sympathetic nervous system System responsible for the body's response to stress or any perceived emergency situations; "fight or flight."

Somatic Nervous System

abdominal reflex Abdominal wall draws inward on stimulation of abdominal skin.

Achilles reflex Foot extends when the Achilles tendon is tapped.

Babinski reflex Reflex when bottom of the foot is stroked; great toe extends outward and remaining toes curl.

corneal reflex Eye blinks when the cornea is touched.

patellar reflex Knee-jerk response when the patellar tendon is tapped.

plantar reflex Bottom of foot is stroked and toes flex.

reflex Involuntary reaction that results from a stimulus.

Diseases and Disorders of the Nervous System

Alzheimer disease A chronic progressive brain degeneration and dementia focusing on intellectual areas of the brain, causing loss of memory.

amyotrophic lateral sclerosis (ALS, Lou Gehrig disease) Motor neuron disease in which muscles of extremities atrophy and weaken with spasticity of the extremities.

cerebrovascular accident (CVA, stroke) Blood vessel ruptures or blood clot occludes a blood vessel in the brain, decreasing blood flow to the area of the brain.

encephalitis Infection of tissues of the brain and spinal cord.

epilepsy Disorder caused by abnormal electrical activity in the brain causing seizures.

meningitis Inflammation of the brain and spinal cord coverings.

multiple sclerosis (MS) Chronic progressive autoimmune disease caused by irritation and degeneration of the myelin sheath, which is then replaced by scar tissue.

neurologist Specialist in the medical treatment of nervous system disease.

Parkinson disease Slowly progressive degenerative disorder characterized by resting tremor, pill rolling of the fingers, and shuffling gait caused by muscle weakness and rigidity.

shingles (herpes zoster) Acute viral inflammation of the dorsal root ganglia.

tic douloureux (trigeminal neuralgia) Neuralgia of the fifth cranial nerve producing excruciating pain of the face.

transient ischemic attack (TIA) Temporary stoppage of blood to the brain; "ministroke."

Signs and Symptoms

amoebae Microscopic, single-celled parasitic organisms.

aphasia Inability to communicate through oral speech; often occurs after stroke.

gait Manner of walking.

hemiparesis Muscle weakness of the face or limb on one side of the body.

hemiplegia Paralysis of only one side of the body, often caused by stroke on the opposite side of the brain.

insidious Gradual, versus sudden, as in manifestation of disease.

Kernig sign Diagnostic sign for meningitis; patient seated or in supine position is unable to extend the knee from a flexed thigh position.

predisposing factors Factors that affect a person's susceptibility to a certain disease.

vertigo Dizziness.

Mental Health

antisocial Referring to a personality exhibiting behavior that shows a disregard for the rights of others.

attention deficit hyperactivity disorder (ADHD) Inability to focus attention for short periods or to engage in quiet activities, or both; uncontrolled compulsive behavior.

autism Disorder characterized by a preoccupation with inner thoughts and marked unresponsiveness to social contact.

bipolar disorder Disorder marked by severe mood swings from hyperactivity (mania) to sadness (depression).

conversion Resolution of a psychological conflict through the loss of body function (e.g., paralysis, blindness).

delusional disorder Condition characterized by false beliefs, including grandiose and persecutory thoughts.

dementia Irreversible impairment of intellectual capabilities.

depression Feeling of persistent sadness accompanied by insomnia, loss of appetite, and inability to experience pleasure.

general anxiety disorder (GAD) General feeling of apprehension brought on by episodes of internal self-doubt.

histrionic Showing excessive attention-seeking tendencies.

Munchausen syndrome Disorder characterized by the intentional presentation of false symptoms and self-mutilation.

narcissistic Exhibiting behavior that lacks empathy and sensitivity to the needs of others; concerned with self.

obsessive-compulsive disorder (OCD) Disorder that interferes with ability to function on a daily basis and characterized by obsessive thoughts and compulsive actions.

paranoid Feeling of exploitation or of being harmed without a credible basis.

post-traumatic stress disorder (PTSD) Severe anxiety resulting from past trauma; mental impairment that affects daily living.

psychiatry Medical science that deals with the origin, diagnosis, prevention, and treatment of developmental and emotional components of mental disorders.

psychosis Impaired perception of reality.

schizoid Showing indifference to social relationships.

schizophrenia Condition characterized by disturbances in thought content, perception, sense of self, and both personal and interpersonal relationships.

Diagnostic Procedures for the Nervous System

angiography Series of x-rays of blood vessels and lymphatics requiring a radiopaque contrast medium.

KEY TERMS—cont'd

computed tomography (CT scan) Series of x-rays taken in a transverse plane to better visualize the ventricles, subarachnoid space, and abnormalities of the brain.

electroencephalography (EEG) Measurement of electrical activity of the brain.

electromyography (EMG) Record of muscle activity that aids in diagnosing neuromuscular problems.

electroneuromyography Tests and records neuromuscular activity by electrical stimulation.

lumbar puncture (spinal tap) Withdrawal of spinal fluid for diagnostic purposes or for relief of pressure on the brain.

magnetic resonance imaging (MRI) Technique used to view soft tissues.

myelography X-rays used to view structures of the spinal cord and surrounding areas using a dye.

nerve conduction studies Measurement of peripheral nerve stimulation using electrical impulses.

positron emission tomography (PET scan) Imaging technique that evaluates physiological and biochemical processes using a glucose molecule with a radioactive material attached.

What Would You Do?

Read the following scenario and keep it in mind as you learn about the nervous system in this chapter.

Sally Jones, age 72, complained of dizziness with a loss of sensation on the left side that lasted only for a few minutes over the past few weeks. She also had a headache that lasted only during the paresthesia. She has a long history of moderately controlled hypertension for which she has taken antihypertensives "when I thought about them." Dr. Smith was concerned that she might be having TIAs. He prescribed a vasodilator and a mild analgesic for the headache when he saw her last week. Today she was brought to the emergency room with sudden left-sided hemiplegia and a headache but no aphasia. Except for the hypertension, Ms. Jones has been in relatively good health for her age. On admission, her blood pressure was 210/120 and she was semi-alert. Dr. Smith ordered a CT scan, which showed an infarct to the right frontotemporal lobes. Ms. Jones was admitted to the hospital for observation and possible treatment.

Do you understand what an infarct is and how Ms. Jones' earlier symptoms relate to it?

The nervous system is the body's communication and control system. This complex system organizes and controls voluntary and involuntary activities of the body and enables all our body systems to work together. The brain is the control center of the nervous system. It sends and receives messages through a system of nerves that functions similar to a highway system. The spinal cord can be thought of as the interstate highway. It branches off into smaller and smaller bunches of nerves (highways, main streets, side streets). In this way, our brains can send messages to and receive messages from any part of the body.

The brain sends and receives messages based on what we hear, see, taste, smell, and touch, and it allows us to react to what we sense. For example, if we see a ball coming at us, our brain helps us react by catching it or moving out of the way. This communication allows homeostasis to be maintained in the body.

To best understand the functioning of the nervous system, you need to know about its structure, the diseases and disorders that affect it, and how the sensory system communicates with it.

NERVOUS SYSTEM STRUCTURE AND FUNCTION

The nervous system is the main communication and control system of the body, allowing the other body systems to function. The nervous system organizes and controls both the voluntary and the involuntary activities of the body by means of electrical impulses. Medical assistants need to understand the structure and function of the nervous system, including its cells and nerve impulses and two major divisions (central nervous system and peripheral nervous system). This understanding will help you recognize how the nervous system is able to control the body's activities and maintain homeostasis.

Nerve Cells and Nerve Impulses

The nervous system is made up of nerves. A **nerve** is a bundle containing the fibers of many neurons and microscopic blood vessels. Nerves are protected by connective tissue and run to and from various organs and tissues in the body. As with every other body system, the smallest structural piece of the nervous system is the cell. These cells enable the whole system to function through electrical impulses that allow them to respond to stimuli.

Nerve Cells

There are two distinctive types of cells in the nervous system: neurons and neuroglia.

NEURONS

The functional unit of the nervous system is the **neuron.** A neuron is a specialized unit that receives and transmits messages in the form of nerve impulses. Neurons carry these impulses throughout the central nervous system (CNS).

Neurons are classified into three areas according to their function.

Type of Neuron	Function
Sensory (afferent) neurons	Transmit nerve impulses to the CNS from both within and outside the CNS.
Motor (efferent) neurons	Transmit impulses from the CNS to the muscles and glands of the body.
Integrative neurons (interneurons)	Conduct impulses between the afferent to the efferent neurons. Located within the brain and spinal cord.

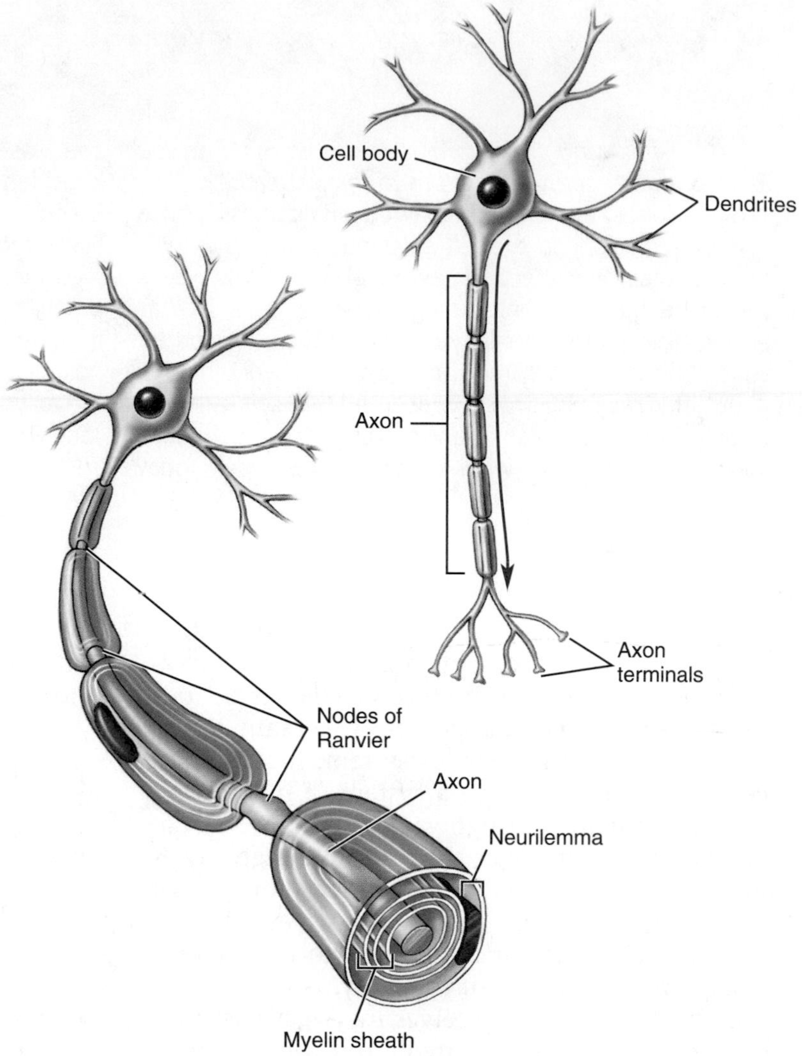

Fig. 13-1 Structure of a neuron: dendrites, cell body, axon, and axon terminals. Structure surrounding the axon is the myelin sheath. Nodes of Ranvier are the spaces between the myelin. Neurilemma surrounds the myelin sheath. The *arrow* indicates the direction in which the information moves along the axon. *(From Herlihy B, Maebius NK: The human body in health and illness, ed 2, Philadelphia, 2003, Saunders.)*

Neurons respond to stimuli by conducting impulses. Each neuron has the following parts:

- A **cell body** (main part of the cell) contains a nucleus and projections called axons and dendrites (Fig. 13-1). A group of cell bodies along the path of a nerve is a **ganglion.**
- The **axon** is attached to the cell body and carries impulses to other neurons and body tissues. A neuron has one axon with several branches. The larger the diameter of an axon, the faster the nerve impulses travel. An axon can be enclosed in a covering, or **myelin sheath,** which is not continuous. The separate parts are called the **nodes of Ranvier,** and the spaces consist of a layer of fats and proteins. Bundles of axons are **nerve fibers** and appear as white matter if **myelinated.** Not all axons are myelinated; unmyelinated axons appear as gray matter. **Neurilemma** is a continuous **sheath** around the myelin sheath.
- **Dendrites** function to receive nerve impulses. Dendrites pick up stimuli and carry the stimuli

to the cell body. Each neuron has one or more dendrites that resemble tree branches. The tips of the dendrites are referred to as "receptors" because they receive stimuli.

NEUROGLIA

The **neuroglia,** or **glial cells,** are the most numerous of the nerve cells and are mainly located within the CNS. The neuroglia are responsible for the support, protection, insulation, and nourishment of the neurons. They do not carry nerve impulses. The different types of neuroglia are classified by their function.

Type of Glial Cell	Function
Astrocytes	The most abundant type of the nerve cells; "star shaped." Astrocytes filter harmful substances from the blood circulating through the brain, forming the protective blood-brain barrier. They also transport water and salts between capillaries and neurons.

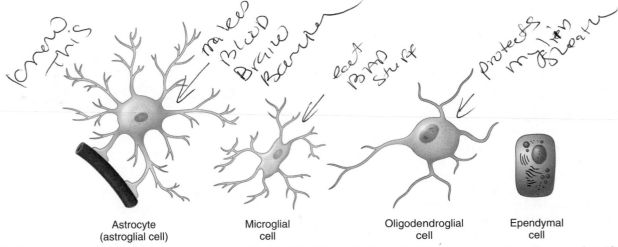

(handwritten annotations: "Know this", "Makes Blood Brain Barrier", "eat Bad Stuff", "protects myelin sheath", "neurons Glia")

Fig. 13-2 Neuroglial cells and an ependymal cell. *(Modified from Chabner DE:* The language of medicine, *ed 6, Philadelphia, 2001, Saunders.)*

Ependymal cells	Line the cavities of the brain and assist in the formation of cerebrospinal fluid.
Microglia cells	Responsible for engulfing and destroying microorganisms and cellular waste in nervous tissue.
Oligodendroglia cells	Responsible for producing the myelin sheath for neurons in the CNS.

Fig. 13-2 illustrates the various types of neuroglial cells.

Nerve Impulses

A **nerve impulse** starts when a **stimulus** (change in environment) acts on **receptors** (located on distal ends of dendrites). The stimulus must be strong enough to be sensed and appropriate for a particular neuron. For example, heat stimulates temperature receptors on the skin, and sound waves stimulate the auditory nerve; neither receptor would respond to the other stimulus.

The nerve impulse occurs as follows (Fig. 13-3).

1. The nerve is at rest.
2. An adequate stimulus occurs, and the impulse (a tiny electrical pulse) is generated.
3. The impulse travels along a myelinated axon and jumps from node to node.
4. The impulse reaches the end of the axon and moves to the muscle or gland.

When the impulse arrives at the end of the axon, there is a gap between it and the next neuron (or muscle or gland cell, depending on where the impulse is going). This gap is called a *synapse.*

SYNAPSE

A **synapse** is a microscopic space (1/100,000 of an inch wide) between the end of one neuron and the start of the next neuron. When a nerve impulse

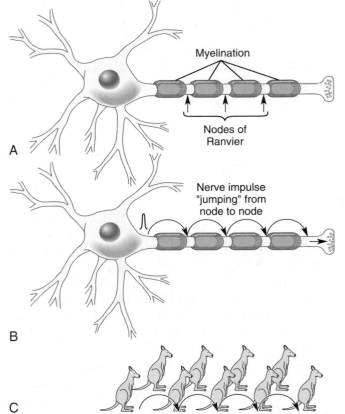

Fig. 13-3 How nerve impulses work. **A,** Myelinated axon, showing exposed axonal membrane at the nodes of Ranvier. **B,** Nerve impulse jumps from node to node toward the axon terminal. Jumping allows the nerve impulse to travel the length of the axon very fast. **C,** Jumping of nerve impulse resembles the jumping or hopping of a kangaroo. Think of how much faster a kangaroo can move by jumping rather than walking. *(From Herlihy B, Maebius NK:* The human body in health and illness, *ed 2, Philadelphia, 2003, Saunders.)*

Fig. 13-4 A, Synapse is located in the space between neuron *A* and neuron *B*. **B,** Parts of the synapse include the neurotransmitters, inactivators, and receptors. *1,* The nerve impulse travels along neuron A to its axon terminal where it causes the vesicles to merge, or fuse, with the membrane of the axon terminal *(2)*. The vesicles open and release neurotransmitter into the synaptic cleft. *3,* The neurotransmitter diffuses across the synaptic cleft and binds to the receptor sites of neuron B, causing a new nerve impulse in the dendrite of neuron B, which travels toward the cell body and axon of neuron B *(4)*. *(From Herlihy B, Maebius NK: The human body in health and illness, ed 2, Philadelphia, 2003, Saunders.)*

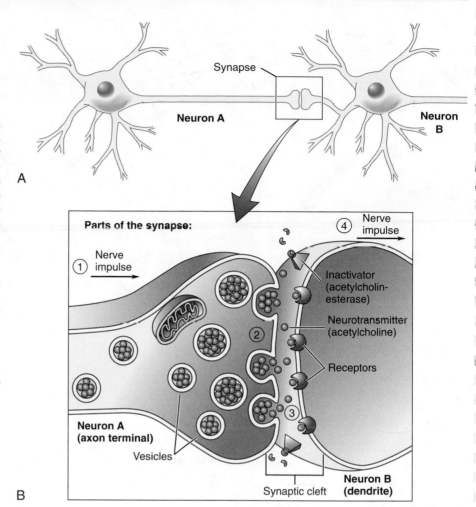

reaches the end of a neuron, the synapse helps information transmit from one neuron to another. The electrical impulse in the neuron triggers the release of chemicals **(neurotransmitters)** that carry the impulse across the junction to the next neuron (Fig. 13-4). After the impulse is transmitted across the synapse, another chemical is released so the neuron can reset itself allowing it to fire an impulse again if necessary.

Divisions of the Nervous System

As mentioned, the two main divisions of the nervous system are the **central nervous system (CNS),** which includes the brain and spinal cord, and the peripheral nervous system (PNS), which consists of a series of nerves that connect the CNS with the various tissues of the body (Fig. 13-5).

Central Nervous System

The brain and the spinal cord are protected by a membrane **(meninges)** with the following three layers (Fig. 13-6):

1. The **dura mater** is a thick covering located closest to the skull and vertebral column and contains veins that drain blood from the brain.
2. The **arachnoid** ("spiderweb") membrane, the middle layer, provides weblike space for the fluid between the second and third layers.
3. The **pia mater,** the thin membrane closest to the brain and **spinal column,** contains blood vessels to supply blood to the brain.

Box 13-1 lists protective layers and coverings for CNS structures.

BRAIN

The **brain** is a complex organ that fits inside the skull. It contains billions of neurons and has millions of synaptic connections. The brain is protected by the skull, which is made of several cranial bones, including the following:

1. Frontal
2. Parietal
3. Temporal
4. Sphenoid
5. Ethmoid

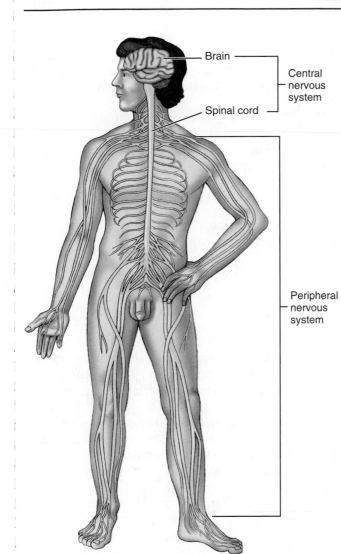

Brain

Central nervous system

Spinal cord

Peripheral nervous system

Fig. 13-5 Divisions of nervous system: central nervous system, consisting of the brain and spinal cord, and peripheral nervous system. *(From Herlihy B, Maebius NK: The human body in health and illness, ed 2, Philadelphia, 2003, Saunders.)*

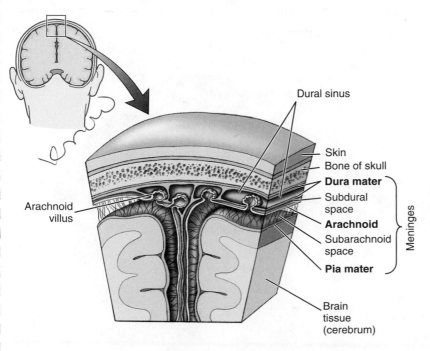

Dural sinus

Skin
Bone of skull
Dura mater
Subdural space
Arachnoid
Subarachnoid space
Pia mater

Meninges

Arachnoid villus

Brain tissue (cerebrum)

Fig. 13-6 Protective layers of central nervous system (CNS). The three layers of meninges are the dura mater, arachnoid membrane, and pia mater. Cerebrospinal fluid (CSF) circulates within the subarachnoid space. Note the arachnoid villi projecting into dural sinus for drainage of CSF. *(Modified from Herlihy B, Maebius NK: The human body in health and illness, ed 2, Philadelphia, 2003, Saunders.)*

BOX 13-1   Protection of Central Nervous System Structures

Brain	Covered by cranial bones in skull; further protection by meninges and cerebrospinal fluid
Cranial bones, vertebrae	Lined with meninges
Nerve tissue	Protected by fluid, meninges, and bones
Spinal cord	Surrounded by vertebrae and cerebrospinal fluid

As noted earlier, three-layered membranous coverings called *meninges* protect the brain. These tissues are continuous and also cover the spinal cord. The spaces between each layer are as follows:

- The **epidural space** is located outside the dura mater between the dura mater and vertebrae and skull and contains fat that acts as a cushion to absorb trauma.
- The **subdural space** is located between the dura mater and arachnoid membrane and contains a serous fluid for lubrication.
- The **subarachnoid space** is located between the pia mater and arachnoid membrane and contains **cerebrospinal fluid (CSF),** which serves as a cushion to protect the brain and spinal cord.

Cerebrospinal fluid is a sterile, watery fluid that is a combination of lymphocytes, protein, sugar, chlorides, and interstitial fluid. CSF is formed by separation of fluid from blood in the choroid plexuses (capillaries) into the ventricles of the brain.

It circulates through the ventricles and into the subarachnoid spaces of the brain and spinal cord, then is absorbed back into the blood. The amount of circulating CSF in the average adult is about 140 ml.

The 12 pairs of cranial nerves originate on the undersurface of the brain, mostly from the brain stem. The brain is divided into four main sections: cerebrum, diencephalon, brain stem, and cerebellum (Fig. 13-7).

Cranial Nerves. There are 12 pairs of **cranial nerves** attached to the brain (Fig. 13-8). The cranial nerves are numbered by Roman numerals in sequence of their origin (Table 13-1). The three types of nerve fibers represented are (1) motor (efferent—from CNS to body), (2) sensory (afferent—from body to CNS), and (3) mixed (sensory and motor).

Cerebrum. The **cerebrum** is the largest portion of the brain. It controls functions associated with thinking and voluntary activity. The outer portion of the cerebrum is the **cortex,** white soft matter covered in gray matter and arranged in folds or convolutions called **gyri.** The deeper folds, or grooves, are **fissures.** The cortex contains the areas that allow humans to learn. The higher brain functions of learning, such as reasoning, memory, and abstract thought, also occur in the cortex.

The cerebrum is divided into right and left hemispheres that are separated by a longitudinal fissure, or **sulcus.** The right hemisphere controls the left side of the body. It is responsible for auditory and tactile perception, creative functions, and **spatial** feelings. The left hemisphere controls the right side of the body. It controls language, hand movements, and **linear** thought. Each hemisphere has four lobes (Fig. 13-9), as follows:

Fig. 13-7 Four major areas of the brain: *1,* cerebrum, *2,* diencephalon, *3,* brain stem, and *4,* cerebellum. *(From Herlihy B, Maebius NK: The human body in health and illness, ed 2, Philadelphia, 2003, Saunders.)*

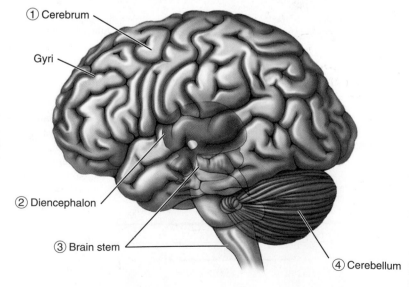

① Cerebrum
Gyri
② Diencephalon
③ Brain stem
④ Cerebellum

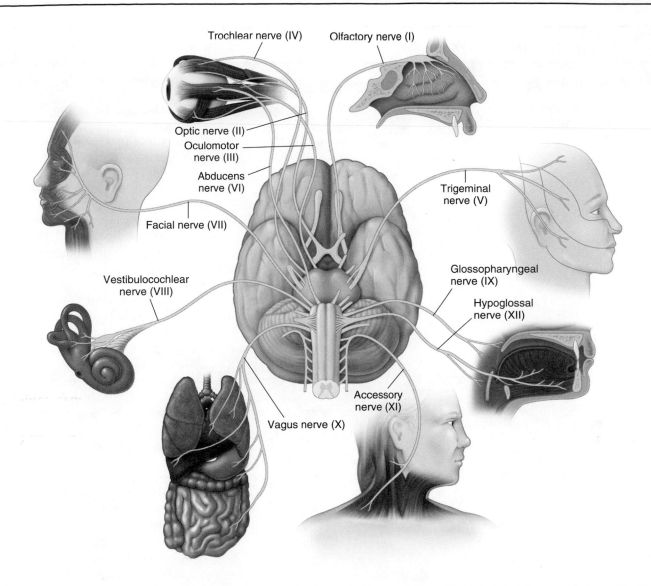

Fig. 13-8   Undersurface of the brain showing attachments of the cranial nerves. *(Modified from Thibodeau GA, Patton KT: The human body in health and disease, ed 3, St Louis, 2002, Mosby.)*

1. The **frontal lobe** controls voluntary muscles, speech, and judgment.
2. The **parietal lobe** controls sensory function, such as pain, touch, and temperature interpretation.
3. The **temporal lobe** controls hearing, smell, and taste.
4. The **occipital lobe** controls vision.

There are four **ventricles** in the brain. The ventricles contain the choroid plexus, and are small cavities responsible for the continual production of CSF, which cushions the nerve tissue of the brain and spinal cord. The ventricles align with the subarachnoid spaces and central lining of the spinal cord (Fig. 13-10).

Diencephalon. The **diencephalon** is located under the cerebrum. It encases the third ventricle of the brain and includes the thalamus and hypothalamus.

Thalamus. The **thalamus** is composed of gray matter (unmyelinated nerve tissue) and is located between the cerebrum and midbrain. Its function is to relay messages from the eyes, ears, and skin by monitoring sensory stimuli, including touch and pressure sensations, to the brain. The messages are sent to the appropriate area in the cerebrum. The thalamus has also been associated with the emotional states of pleasant and unpleasant sensations, and it is the brain's center for the perception of pain.

Hypothalamus. The **hypothalamus** is below the thalamus and connects to the CNS by controlling the activities of the "master gland," or **pituitary gland**, thus forming a link between the nervous and endocrine systems. The hypothalamus

TABLE 13-1   Cranial Nerves

Number	Name	Type	Conduct Impulses	Function
I	Olfactory	Sensory	From nose to brain	Olfaction (sense of smell)
II	Optic	Sensory	From eye to brain	Vision
III	Oculomotor	Motor	From brain to eye muscle	Controls upper eyelid muscles, eye movements, regulation of pupil size, and accommodation for close vision
IV	Trochlear	Motor	From brain to external eye muscle	Controls movement of external eye muscles
V	Trigeminal	Mixed	From brain to skin and mucous membrane of head	Controls chewing movements
				Sensation around the eye
			From teeth to brain	Sensation from eye to upper jaw and throat
			From brain to chewing muscle	Sensation in mandibular region
VI	Abducens	Motor	From brain to external eye muscles	Controls eye movement
VII	Facial	Mixed	From taste buds of tongue to brain	Controls taste, facial muscles; controls secretion of tears and saliva
			From brain to face muscle	
VIII	Vestibulocochlear	Sensory	From ear to brain	Senses of equilibrium (balance)
				Hearing
IX	Glossopharyngeal	Mixed	From throat and taste buds to brain	Controls taste (posterior third of tongue); salivation; controls swallowing muscles; blood pressure sensation
		From brain to throat muscles and salivary glands		
X	Vagus	Mixed	From throat, larynx, and organs in thoracic and abdominal cavities to brain	Controls swallowing muscles
			From brain to muscles of throat and to organs in thoracic and abdominal cavities	
XI	Accessory	Motor	From brain to shoulder and neck muscles	Controls some shoulder movements
				Controls some head movements
XII	Hypoglossal	Motor	From brain to muscles of tongue	Controls tongue muscles (swallowing and speech)

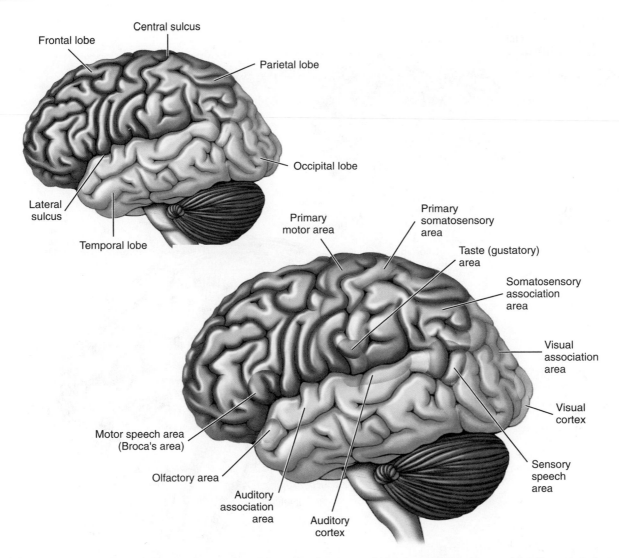

Fig. 13-9 *Upper left,* Lobes of the cerebrum: frontal, parietal, temporal, and occipital. *Lower right,* Functional areas of the cerebrum. *(From Herlihy B, Maebius NK: The human body in health and illness, ed 2, Philadelphia, 2003, Saunders.)*

produces hormones that signal the anterior pituitary gland to release its hormones into the blood for circulation. The hypothalamus also produces the hormone **oxytocin** for uterine contractions during and after childbirth and **antidiuretic hormone (ADH)** for fluid balance in the body. These two hormones are stored in the posterior pituitary gland, and their release is controlled by nerve stimulation when needed.

The hypothalamus further regulates the autonomic nervous system. This system is responsible for the involuntary activities of the internal organs **(viscera),** such as those associated with digestion and blood circulation. Body temperature, sleep cycles, appetite, thirst, and some emotions (e.g., fear, anger, pain, pleasure) are also controlled by the hypothalamus.

Brain Stem. The **brain stem** has three parts: the midbrain, pons, and medulla oblongata (Fig, 13-11).

The **midbrain** is made up of nerve tissue that connects the lower portion of the cerebrum to the pons. CSF passes from the third ventricle to the fourth ventricle in the back portion of the brain stem. Cranial nerves III and IV originate in the midbrain, which serves as a center for visual and auditory reflexes. Visual reflexes include dilation and constriction of the pupil in response to light. The auditory reflex involves movement of the head in response to sound.

The **pons,** the middle section of the brain stem, acts as a bridge between the brain and spinal cord. Cranial nerves VI, VII, VIII, and X originate in the pons, which controls areas of the face, hearing,

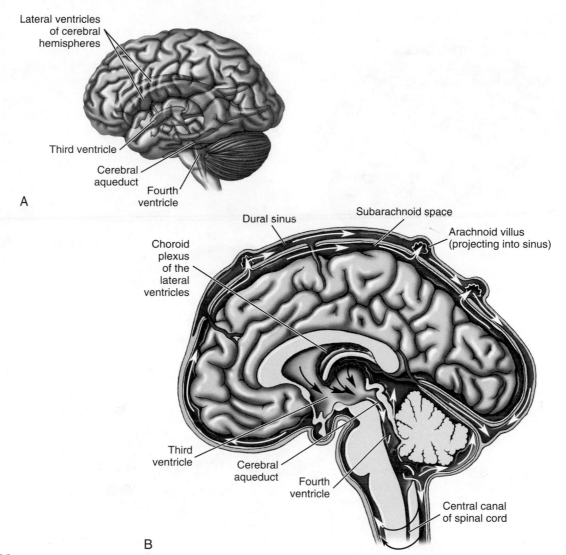

Fig. 13-10 Cerebrospinal fluid (CSF): formation, circulation, and drainage. **A,** CSF forms within lateral, third, and fourth ventricles of the brain. **B,** CSF flows down through the central canal of the spinal cord to the base. CSF also flows from fourth ventricle into subarachnoid space surrounding the brain. CSF flows into arachnoid villus, which protrudes into the dural sinuses. CSF diffuses across membrane of the villus into dural sinuses, where it mixes with venous blood. Blood in the sinuses drains CSF away from brain and into the veins. *(From Herlihy B, Maebius NK: The human body in health and illness, ed 2, Philadelphia, 2003, Saunders.)*

Fig. 13-11 Diencephalon and brain stem. Diencephalon consists of the thalamus and hypothalamus. Note relationship between hypothalamus and pituitary gland. Brain stem is composed of the midbrain, pons, and medulla. *(From Herlihy B, Maebius NK: The human body in health and illness, ed 2, Philadelphia, 2003, Saunders.)*

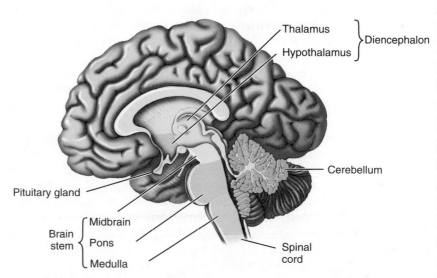

balance, blood pressure, and heart rate. Besides relaying information (sensory and motor) the pons plays a role in the breathing (rate and rhythm).

The **medulla oblongata** is the lowest portion of the brain stem. It continues into the spinal cord. The white matter forms tracts that cross from one side of the body to the other. The gray matter contains cranial nerves IX to XII and some reflex areas. The medulla is responsible for involuntary movements such as heart and respiratory rate, vasoconstriction, swallowing, coughing, sneezing, hiccupping, and vomiting.

Cerebellum. The **cerebellum** is situated below the cerebrum and is often referred to as the "little brain." The cerebellum is composed of both gray and white matter and, like the cerebrum, has two hemispheres. Connected to the brain stem by white fibers, the cerebellum controls the skeletal muscles for fine motor skills and coordination of voluntary muscle groups. The cerebellum is also responsible for maintenance of **equilibrium** (balance) and posture.

SPINAL CORD

The **spinal cord** is a long bundle of nerves that conducts impulses to and from the brain. It also serves as a reflex center to receive and transmit messages through nerve fibers. It extends from the medulla to the end of the lumbar vertebrae. The center area is composed of gray matter and the exterior portion is white matter (myelinated nerve fibers covered with fatty membrane) (Fig. 13-12). The white matter contains the ascending (sensory—afferent) and descending (motor—efferent) tracts (fiber bundles) that carry impulses to and from the brain.

Spinal Nerves. There are 31 pairs of **spinal nerves** grouped according to spinal areas: eight cervical (C1 to C8), 12 thoracic (T1 to T12), five lumbar (L1 to L5), five sacral (S1 to S5), and one coccygeal (one pair) (Fig. 13-13). Each pair joins the spinal cord by the anterior (ventral) root, which carries motor impulses away from the spinal cord toward muscles or glands. The posterior (dorsal) root carries sensory impulses into the spinal cord (Fig. 13-14).

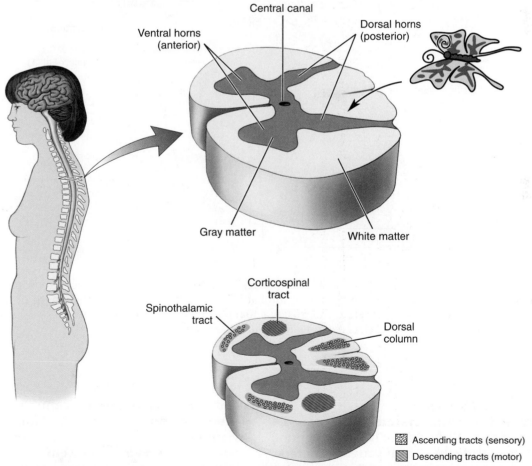

Fig. 13-12 Cross sections of spinal cord showing inner gray matter ("butterfly") and outer white matter. The butterfly wings (gray matter) are called the dorsal horns and ventral horns. The central canal is a hole in the middle of the spinal cord. The white matter shows the location of several tracts. *(From Herlihy B, Maebius NK: The human body in health and illness, ed 2, Philadelphia, 2003, Saunders.)*

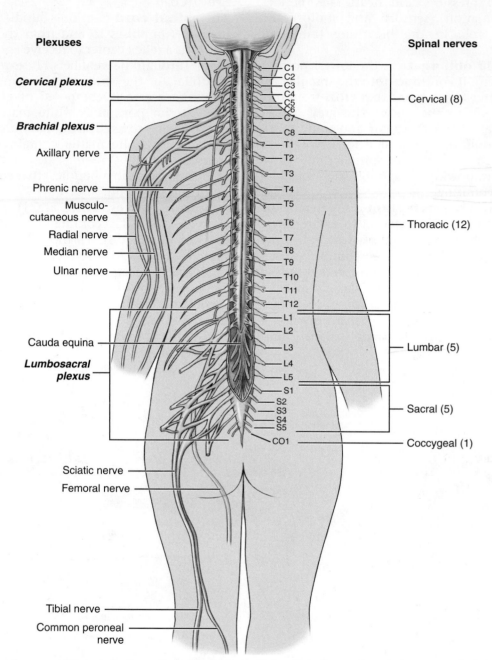

Plexuses

Cervical plexus

Brachial plexus

Axillary nerve

Phrenic nerve

Musculo-
cutaneous nerve

Radial nerve

Median nerve

Ulnar nerve

Cauda equina

*Lumbosacral
plexus*

Sciatic nerve

Femoral nerve

Tibial nerve

Common peroneal
nerve

Spinal nerves

C1
C2
C3
C4
C5
C6
C7
C8

Cervical (8)

T1
T2
T3
T4
T5
T6
T7
T8
T9
T10
T11
T12

Thoracic (12)

L1
L2
L3
L4
L5

Lumbar (5)

S1
S2
S3
S4
S5

Sacral (5)

CO1

Coccygeal (1)

Fig. 13-13 Spinal nerves (31 pairs): 8 cervical, 12 thoracic, 5 lumbar, 5 sacral, and 1 coccygeal. Spinal cord ends at first lumbar vertebra *(L1)*; cauda equina (extension of lumbar and sacral nerves) extends the length of the spinal cavity. Three major nerve plexuses (networks): cervical plexus, brachial plexus, and lumbosacral plexus. *(From Herlihy B, Maebius NK: The human body in health and illness, ed 2, Philadelphia, 2003, Saunders.)*

Peripheral Nervous System

The **peripheral nervous system (PNS)** provides information to the CNS by way of both sensory and motor activity outside the CNS. If you stub your toe, the message that your toe hurts travels from the toe up the leg to the spinal cord and informs the brain. The cranial nerves and the spinal nerves are the PNS and are classified according to their origin. The autonomic nervous system controls the involuntary actions of smooth muscles, cardiac muscles, and glands (Fig. 13-15). Another part of the PNS is the **somatic nervous system,** which transmits impulses to the skeletal muscles and is responsible for voluntary response to external stimuli by reflex action.

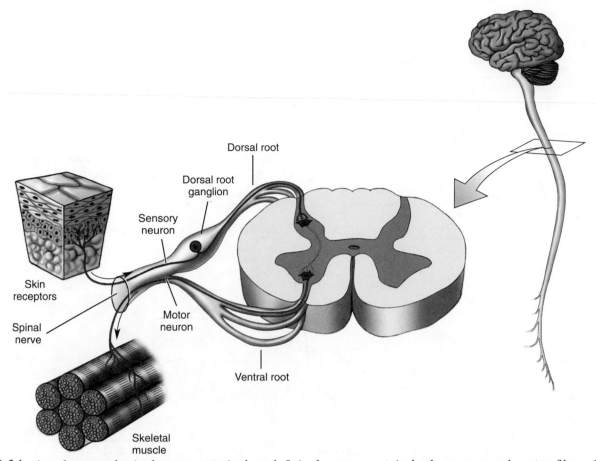

Fig. 13-14 Attachment of spinal nerves to spinal cord. Spinal nerves contain both sensory and motor fibers. Sensory neurons attach to spinal cord at the dorsal root; motor neurons attach to spinal cord at the ventral root. *(From Herlihy B, Maebius NK: The human body in health and illness, ed 2, Philadelphia, 2003, Saunders.)*

TABLE 13-2	Comparison of Sympathetic and Parasympathetic Actions	
Organ	**Sympathetic**	**Parasympathetic**
Blood vessels	Dilate to increase blood flow to brain, heart, lungs, and skeletal muscles	No effect
Bronchial tubes	Dilate to increase breathing	Constrict to decrease breathing
Heart	Strength and rate increase	Rate decreases
Intestines	Activity decreases	Activity increases
Iris of eye	Pupil dilates	Pupil constricts
Liver	Activates conversion of glycogen to glucose	No effect
Sweat glands	Increased sweating	Normal secretions

AUTONOMIC NERVOUS SYSTEM

The **autonomic nervous system (ANS)** is controlled by the CNS, mainly the cerebral cortex, hypothalamus, and medulla. The CNS also oversees the involuntary activity of the heart, glandular secretions, and involuntary muscle actions. There are two divisions to the ANS: the sympathetic nervous system and the parasympathetic nervous system (Table 13-2).

- The **sympathetic nervous system** is responsible for the body's response to stress or any perceived emergency situations. The **"fight-or-flight" response** requires the body to respond quickly, thus allowing the use of maximal exertion.

- The **parasympathetic nervous system** returns the body to a state of balance, or **homeostasis,** and is responsible for

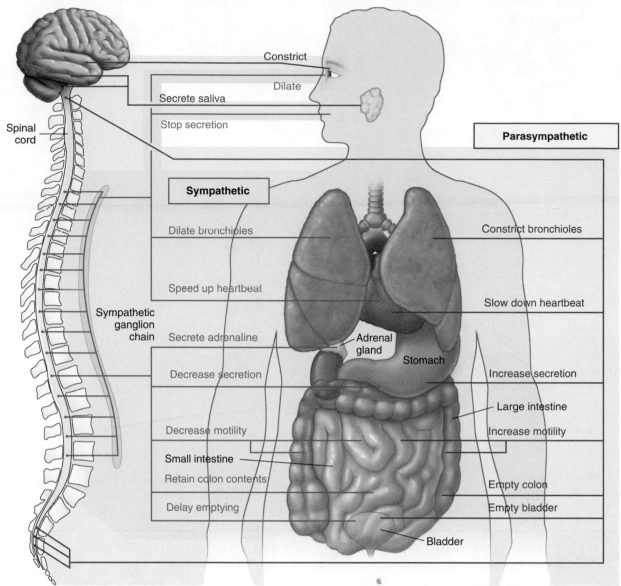

Fig. 13-15 Innervation of major target organs by the autonomic nervous system. *(Modified from Thibodeau GA, Patton KT: The human body in health and disease, ed 3, St Louis, 2002, Mosby.)*

maintaining normal activities of the body (e.g., digestion).

SOMATIC NERVOUS SYSTEM

The somatic nervous system is the voluntary movement of skeletal muscles caused by the stimuli of sensory neurons. When a stimulus is transmitted through a sensory neuron to the CNS, it crosses a synapse to a motor neuron, and an appropriate message is sent to the skeletal muscle to respond or act. This process may be a **reflex.** A reflex is an involuntary response of an individual to a given type of stimulation to a given area. Several somatic reflexes cause the skeletal muscles to contract or a glandular secretion to react. Physicians test reflexes during a physical examination.

- **Abdominal reflex** occurs when the abdominal wall draws inward in response to stroking the lateral side of the abdomen.
- **Achilles reflex** (ankle jerk) occurs when the Achilles tendon is tapped and the foot extends.
- **Babinski reflex** occurs when the bottom of the foot is stroked upward. The great toe extends outward, and the rest of the toes curl. This is normal in infants but disappears at age 1½ years and is considered abnormal after this age.
- **Corneal reflex** occurs when the cornea is touched; the eye blinks or shuts in response.
- **Patellar reflex** (knee-jerk response) occurs when the patellar tendon is tapped and the lower leg extends outward (Fig. 13-16).

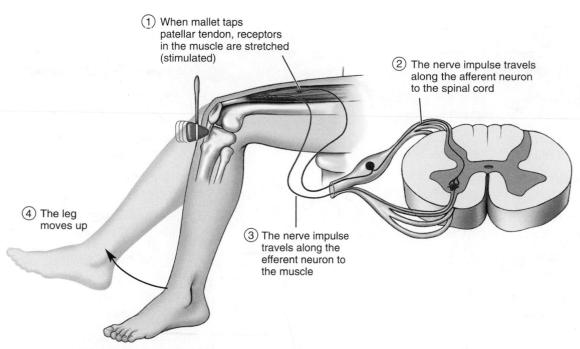

① When mallet taps patellar tendon, receptors in the muscle are stretched (stimulated)

② The nerve impulse travels along the afferent neuron to the spinal cord

④ The leg moves up

③ The nerve impulse travels along the efferent neuron to the muscle

Fig. 13-16   Knee-jerk reflex, illustrating four components of the reflex arc: *1,* stimulation of receptor; *2,* transmission of signal (sensory) toward spinal cord along afferent neuron; *3,* transmission of signal away from cord (motor) along efferent neuron; *4,* motor response of effector organ (e.g., contraction of skeletal muscle, which jerks leg upward). *(From Herlihy B, Maebius NK:* The human body in health and illness, *ed 2, Philadelphia, 2003, Saunders.)*

- **Plantar reflex** occurs when the bottom of the foot is stroked and toes flex.

PATIENT-CENTERED PROFESSIONALISM

- Why is it important for the medical assistant to understand the structure and function of the nervous system?
- Why is it important to know the difference between the CNS and the PNS and how each division depends on the other to function properly?

≋ DISEASES AND DISORDERS OF THE NERVOUS SYSTEM

As in other disease processes, listening to the patient's chief complaint, evaluating their present and past medical history, and performing a physical examination will help diagnose a neurological disease. A **neurologist** medically treats diseases of the nervous system. Drugs may be prescribed to treat neurological diseases (Table 13-3).

Medical assistants need to be able to recognize the common signs and symptoms of and diagnostic tests for the different types of neurological diseases.

- Study Box 13-2 to familiarize yourself with the common signs and symptoms.
- Study Box 13-3 to learn about common diagnostic tests.
- Study Table 13-4 to understand the diseases that affect the nervous system.

Maintaining Nervous System Health

Maintaining the health of the nervous system is important. Many ways are available to enhance the health of this system, as follows:

- Adequate diet with special attention to vitamins A, C, and B-complex, as well as protein and carbohydrates for energy
- Avoidance of substances that have an adverse affect on the nervous system (e.g., alcohol, drugs, carbon monoxide, nicotine)
- Immediate treatment of infections and injuries to minimize loss of nerve function
- Genetic counseling for parents of children with inherited disorders of the nervous system
- Screening of newborns for phenylketonuria (PKU)

Medical assistants need to be aware that some changes in the nervous system are related to age, including the following:

Text continued on p. 466

TABLE 13-3 Nervous System Drug Classifications

Drug Classification	Common Generic (Brand) Names
Analgesics Relieve pain by blocking pain impulses	meperidine (Demerol) propoxyphene (Darvon)
Anticonvulsants Prevent or reduce the severity of seizures	clonazepam (Klonopin) carbamazepine (Tegretol)
Antimigraine agents Relieve symptoms of migraine headaches	sumatriptan (Imitrex) zolmitriptan (Zomig)
Anti-infectives Reduce central nervous system infections	ceftazidime (Fortaz) ceftriaxone (Rocephin)
Antiparkinsonian agents Relieve or reduce tremors	benztropine (Cogentin) amantadine (Symmetrel)
Anti-Alzheimer agents Slow progression of disease	donepezil (Aricept) tacrine (Cognex)
Hypnotics Produce sleep	zolpidem (Ambien) secobarbital (Seconal)
Sedatives Decrease activity or excitability without causing sleep	phenobarbital (Solfoton) butabarbital (Butisol)
Anesthetics Cause loss of responsiveness to sensory stimulation	midazolam (Versed) sufentanil (Sufenta)
Vasodilators Produce relaxation of blood vessels	isosorbide dinitrate (Isordil) nitroglycerin (Nitrostat)

BOX 13-2 Signs and Symptoms of Neurological Disease

Aphasia	Inability to communicate through oral or written speech because of damage to the speech center (left hemisphere, left side of brain); an aphasic patient may be able to understand oral and written communication but is unable to formulate words to respond
Ataxia	Inability to control voluntary muscle movements because of damage to cerebellum or motor area of cerebral cortex
Diplopia	Double vision, blurred vision; vision is hampered by images not being in focus or images appearing as double
Headache	Pain or aching of or around the head (Fig. 13-17) • *Tension headaches* result from long-term contraction of skeletal muscles around face, neck, scalp, and upper back; occur bilaterally; and feel "like a tightening shower cap" • *Cluster headaches* occur unilaterally; involve an eye, temple, cheek, and forehead; start during sleep; and can last for several weeks • *Migraine headaches* are a sudden throbbing, unilateral pain with photophobia, nausea, and vomiting
Numbness, tingling	Loss of sensation, or feeling of needles piercing the skin
Pain	Localized discomfort
Paralysis	Temporary or permanent loss of function, sensation, and voluntary movement • **Hemiplegia** is paralysis of only one side of the body, often caused by stroke • *Paraplegia* is paralysis of lower trunk and extremities resulting from spinal cord injury • *Quadriplegia* is paralysis involving both upper and lower extremities
Seizures (convulsions)	Disturbances of electrical activity of the brain • Box 13-4 lists the various types of seizures
Vertigo	Dizziness

Muscle contraction headache   Cluster headache   Migraine headache

Fig. 13-17   Types of headache. *Shaded areas,* Regions of most intense pain. *(Modified from Leonard PC:* Building a medical vocabulary, *ed 5, Philadelphia, 2001, Saunders.)*

BOX 13-3   Diagnostic Tests for Central Nervous System (CNS)

Lumbar puncture (spinal tap) (Fig. 13-18)	Removal of cerebrospinal fluid (CSF) through needle inserted between third and fourth lumbar vertebrae; measures pressure in CNS, examines contaminants (e.g., blood, bacterial) in CSF
Electroencephalography (EEG) (Fig. 13-19)	Electrical impulses from brain recorded as tracings through electrodes attached to patient's scalp; measures the brain's electrical activity
Computed tomography (CT scan) (Fig. 13-20)	Better visualization of ventricles, subarachnoid space, and brain abnormalities (e.g., blood clot, tumors, cysts) than with standard radiography
Magnetic resonance imaging (MRI)	Used to view the soft tissue; therefore tumors in the gray or white matter of the CNS are easier to capture
Angiography	Requires injection of radiopaque contrast medium (dye) into a blood vessel; series of x-rays shows abnormalities of the blood vessels of the brain
Myelography	Used to view structures around spinal cord; dye injected into subarachnoid space at third and fourth lumbar vertebrae; x-rays taken of patient in multiple positions
Electroneuromyography	Used to test and record neuromuscular activity by electrical stimulation
Electromyography (EMG)	Record of muscle activity; aids in diagnosing neuromuscular problems
Nerve conduction studies	Electrical impulses stimulate peripheral nerves; measure velocity of the impulse generated

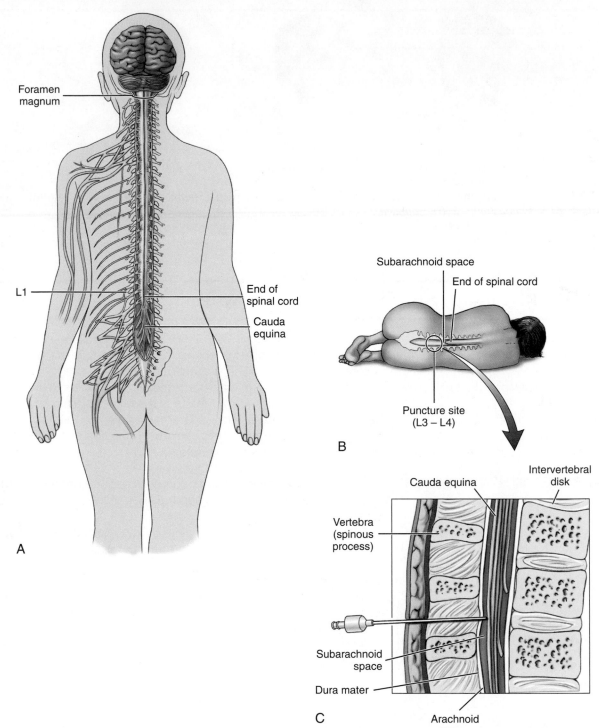

Fig. 13-18   A, Location of spinal cord, which extends from foramen magnum of occipital bone to first lumbar vertebra *(L1).* The cauda equina descends from base of the spinal cord *(L1)* to bottom of the spinal cavity. **B,** Note that spinal cord is shorter than spinal cavity. **C,** Telescoped area shows lumbar puncture (spinal tap). Needle is inserted into subarachnoid space between L3 and L4 vertebrae. Note that patient is lying so that the vertebral column is flexed; this position separates vertebrae and eases needle insertion. *(From Herlihy B, Maebius NK: The human body in health and illness, ed 2, Philadelphia, 2003, Saunders.)*

BOX 13-4 Types of Seizures

Partial Seizures
- Occur in defined areas of the brain and cause specific symptoms
- Involve involuntary muscle contractions of one body part (e.g., face, hand, arm)

Simple partial motor seizure
- Localized motor seizure (e.g., starts at thumb, spreads to hand, then to arms)
- Activities spread to adjacent areas of the brain
- Patient does not lose consciousness

Simple partial sensory seizure
- Patient experiences distorted sense of being, including hallucinations, tingling, flashing lights, and dizziness

Complex partial seizure
- Partial motor seizure that progresses to purposeless behavior (e.g., smacking lips, patting body parts)
- An *aura* (a sense of something about to happen) may precede onset of the seizure
- Mental confusion may follow the seizure

Generalized Seizures
- Affect the electrical activity of the brain in a general manner

Petit mal seizure (absence seizure)
- Change in patient's level of consciousness
- Characterized by rolling or flickering of the eyes or lids, blank stare, and slight facial movements
- Usually occurs in children and lasts 1 to 10 seconds
- Person is unaware of the seizure activity

Myoclonic seizure
- Marked (identified) by brief, involuntary muscle jerks that can occur in rhythmic patterns
- Loss of consciousness is brief

Grand mal seizure (tonic-clonic seizure)
- Begins with an outcry as air leaves the lungs and passes over vocal cords
- Patient falls to ground and loses consciousness
- Movements are first *tonic* (stiffening of muscles), then *clonic* (relaxing of muscles)
- Incontinence, labored breathing, and angina may follow
- After seizure, which lasts 2 to 5 minutes, patient may experience confusion and muscle soreness and may fall into a deep sleep

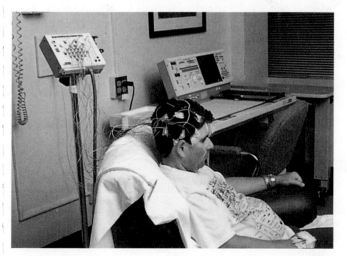

Fig. 13-19 Electroencephalography. Electrodes are attached to patient's head; patient usually remains quiet with closed eyes during EEG procedure. In certain tests, prescribed activities may be requested. *(From Chipps EM, Clanin NJ, Campbell VG: Neurologic disorders, St Louis, 1992, Mosby.)*

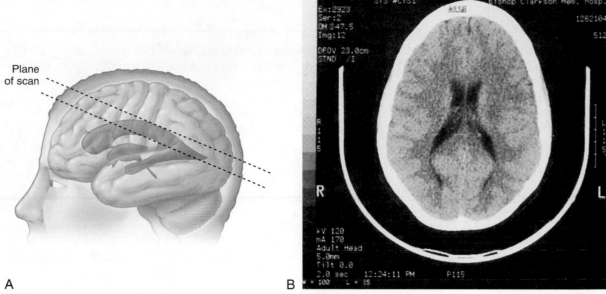

A   B

Fig. 13-20 Computed tomography (CT) of brain. **A,** CT scans are taken at various cross sections of brain. **B,** Tomogram of plane in *A* shows a normal brain. *(From Polaski AL, Tatro SE:* Luckmann's core principles and practice of medical-surgical nursing, *Philadelphia, 1996, Saunders.)*

TABLE 13-4	Diseases and Disorders of the Nervous System				
Disease and Description	**Etiology**	**Signs and Symptoms**	**Diagnosis**	**Therapy**	**Interventions**
Alzheimer disease Presenile dementia of chronic brain degeneration focusing on intellectual areas of brain; atrophy of both frontal and occipital lobes	Unknown; theories relate to gene disorders, aluminum poisoning, autoimmune disease, and viral infection	Confusion, disorientation, short-term memory failure, inability to carry out purposeful activities	Evaluation to rule out other dementia disorders; mental status exam, CT scan, MRI, EEG	Treat symptoms; administer medications to improve memory and behavioral disorders	Encourage family to provide a structured and supportive environment that ensures safety; family needs support and counseling
Amyotrophic lateral sclerosis (ALS); Lou Gehrig disease Motor neuron disease in which muscles of extremities atrophy and weaken	Unknown; theories include genetics, metabolic problems, and environmental agents	Weakness in hands and forearms that spreads to rest of body Eventual paralyses of chest muscles and vocal cords	Evidence of motor neuron involvement without sensory involvement Abnormal EMG results Blood test may show elevated protein levels Elevated protein in spinal fluid	Symptomatic Physical therapy to maintain muscle tone; speech therapy to assist with communication Ambulatory aids (cane, walkers, leg braces) Medications: muscle relaxants	Provide supportive help for family

TABLE 13-4   Diseases and Disorders of the Nervous System—cont'd

Disease and Description	Etiology	Signs and Symptoms	Diagnosis	Therapy	Interventions
Cerebrovascular accident (CVA, stroke) Blood vessel ruptures, or clot occludes blood vessel, decreasing blood flow to brain (Fig. 13-21)	Deposits of cholesterol in arteries causing occlusion, or weakness in a blood vessel wall that ruptures and causes hemorrhage	Numbness or muscle weakness of face or limb, inability to move a limb or side of body **(hemiparesis)**; inability to speak, sudden severe headache, blurred or double vision, confusion, memory loss	Diagnosed by symptoms and neurological examination, CT scan, and EEG	Depends on severity of damage; treatment of symptoms and rehabilitation to restore skills	Lifestyle changes: diet, exercise, weight management, and decrease in smoking and alcohol consumption to guard against future strokes; awareness of at-risk factors: race, age, gender, and family history
Encephalitis Infection of tissues of brain and spinal cord	Viral invasion from bite of mosquito, ticks, or **amoebae** infestation from water Some forms spread by nasal secretions or open lesions	Fever, headache, low energy, drowsiness, irritability, restlessness	History of exposure, positive **Kernig sign,*** muscle weakness CSF pressure elevated with WBCs and proteins present	Antibiotic drugs for secondary infection; sedatives for restlessness; corticosteroids to reduce swelling Maintenance of fluids, nutritional needs, and rest	Onset within 24 hours of exposure, so immediate medical attention is critical, and prophylactic treatment for family is necessary
Epilepsy Disorder caused by abnormal electrical activity in brain resulting in seizures (see Box 13-4)	Idiopathic in some cases; in other cases, caused by trauma at birth, lesions and tumors, some metabolic disorders, and toxic substance exposure	Seizure activity	Clinical history, physical exam; CT, MRI, PET, cranial x-rays, and EEG to observe brain activity	Anticonvulsant drug therapy; surgery when underlying problem is organic	During a seizure, move potentially harmful objects away from patient; do not attempt to restrain patient; educate about disease, myths, misconceptions, and importance of following prescribed drug therapy

Continued

TABLE 13-4   Diseases and Disorders of the Nervous System—cont'd

Disease and Description	Etiology	Signs and Symptoms	Diagnosis	Therapy	Interventions
Meningitis Inflammation of brain and spinal cord coverings	Usually of bacterial origin Spread through droplet contact	Fever, severe headache, stiff neck, vomiting	Results of CSF examination and cultures of respiratory tract and blood	Antibiotic agents for causative agent; analgesics for headaches and muscle aches; maintain fluid, electrolyte, and nutritional balance	Identify source; institute appropriate precautions for infective materials Vaccine for college-age students
Multiple sclerosis (MS) Chronic progressive disease caused by degeneration of myelin sheath, which is replaced with scar tissue	Unknown, but autoimmune response suspected	Onset **insidious** (gradual) with paresthesias of extremities or muscle weakness, ataxia, dizziness (vertigo), double or blurred vision (diplopia)	Elevated CSF pressure Studies indicate slowed nerve conduction; lesions may be apparent on CT and MRI	Medication therapy for muscle spasms; corticosteroids to minimize acute attacks Rest and therapy to adjust to progressive loss of function in activities of daily living (ADLs)	Provide psychological support for family and patient
Parkinson disease Slowly progressive degenerative disorder characterized by resting tremor, pill rolling of fingers, and shuffling gait	Idiopathic	Fine, slowly spreading resting tremor; shuffling of feet when walking; muscle rigidity and weakness	Clinical manifestations include impaired postural reflexes, resting tremors, and **gait** (way of walking) involvement	Symptomatic approach: medications to reduce tremors and muscle rigidity; physical therapy to maintain muscle tone; and occupational therapy to maintain ADL skills	Encourage supportive environment
Shingles (herpes zoster) Acute inflammation of dorsal root ganglia	Dormant virus from chickenpox attacks dorsal root; activated by stress, trauma, and immune disorders	Pain and rash along a **dermatome,** especially in intercostal area (Fig. 13-22)	Clinical evidence includes fever, malaise, and vesicles above affected dermatome, with pain, burning, and itching	Medications for pain and itching; antiviral agents for immuno-compromised patients	Rest and nutritional status need to be maintained

TABLE 13-4 Diseases and Disorders of the Nervous System—cont'd

Disease and Description	Etiology	Signs and Symptoms	Diagnosis	Therapy	Interventions
Tic douloureux (trigeminal neuralgia) Neuralgia of fifth cranial nerve	Unknown	Severe facial pain, especially when chewing and when exposed to cold temperatures	Tests to rule out sinus or tooth infections; symptoms include burning facial pain that occurs quickly and lasts 1 to 15 minutes	Medications to relieve discomfort; microsurgery to decompress nerve; radiosurgery to deaden nerve root	Nutritional needs must be maintained; encourage food high in calories and nutrients that require less chewing; small, frequent meals are preferred
Transient ischemic attack (TIA)† Temporary stoppage of blood to brain; "mini-stroke"	Stems from plaque emboli that block arteries in neck or vascular spasm in neck region	Temporary confusion, slurred speech, muscle weakness on one side of the body, blurred vision or diplopia that gradually subsides	Clinical history with confirming results from ultrasound of carotid or vertebral arteries	Medications to prevent plaque buildup and clot formation; surgery in patients with 70% blockage	TIAs could be warning sign of stroke

*Kernig sign occurs when a patient is in a supine position, with leg flexed at the knee and hip, and is unable to straighten the leg fully.

†**Predisposing factors** include heart disease, diabetes mellitus, and hypertension.

CSF, Cerebrospinal fluid; *CT*, computed tomography; *EEG*, electroencephalography; *EMG*, electromyography; *MRI*, magnetic resonance imaging; *PET*, positron emission tomography; *WBCs*, white blood cells.

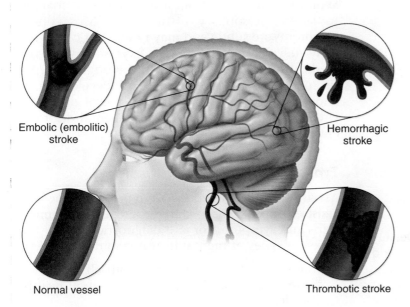

Embolic (embolitic) stroke

Hemorrhagic stroke

Normal vessel

Thrombotic stroke

Fig. 13-21 Types of stroke. Cerebrovascular accident (CVA), commonly referred to as a *stroke*, is a disruption in the normal blood supply to the brain. *Embolic* strokes are caused by emboli that break off from one area of the body and travel to the cerebral arteries. *Thrombotic* strokes are caused by plaque deposits that have built up on the interior of a cerebral artery, gradually blocking it. *Hemorrhagic* strokes are caused by a cerebral arterial wall rupture. *(Modified from Leonard PC:* Building a medical vocabulary, *ed 5, Philadelphia, 2001, Saunders.)*

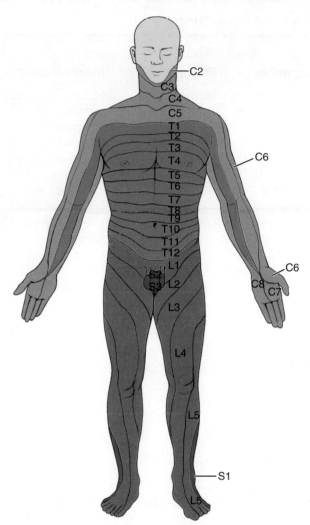

Fig. 13-22 Major nerves of the body: dermatomes. Each dermatome (segment) is named for the spinal nerve that serves it. Shingles pain follows the nerve pathways. *(From Herlihy B, Maebius NK: The human body in health and illness, ed 2, Philadelphia, 2003, Saunders.)*

- A general slowing of nerve conduction occurs with the aging process; reflexes are slower.
- A decrease in ankle-jerk reflex may affect balance.
- A decrease in nerve activity to eyes affects accommodation to changes in light.
- The senses of taste and smell decline.

Dysfunctions of the nervous system adversely affect the patient's ability to think, reason, and carry out the activities of daily living (ADLs). The nervous system allows individuals to act on input from their senses; without proper functioning of the system, ADLs can become difficult or even impossible.

MENTAL HEALTH

Because the brain is the main control center of the body, when something is wrong with its structure or functioning, the patient's mental health can be affected with neurological symptoms. Mental illnesses are psychological and behavioral and involve a wide range of problems in thought and function. Some mental illnesses are directly linked to structural or chemical problems in the brain. Others are inherited, and for some mental disorders the cause is unknown.

Mental health evaluation begins with observation. Before diagnosis of a mental health disorder, the patient is evaluated for signs of organic illness. When a physiological reason is not evident, possible psychological impairment becomes the focus.

Detecting Mental Health Disorders

Disorders of mental health are sometimes difficult to understand and diagnose. In fact, mental disorders are often misdiagnosed and go untreated. Symptoms may vary from mild behavioral changes to severe personality disturbances. Most often, symptoms are subtle and may not be noticed in the early developmental stages. **Psychiatry** is the medical science that deals with the origin, diagnosis, prevention, and treatment of developmental and emotional components of physical disorders. Drugs may be prescribed to treat mental disorders (Table 13-5).

Types of Mental Health Disorders

As with the other nervous system problems, medical assistants need to be able to recognize the common signs and symptoms of and diagnostic tests for the different types of mental health disorders.

- Study Box 13-5 to familiarize yourself with the common signs and symptoms of mental health disorders.
- Study Box 13-6 to learn about common diagnostic tests and procedures. Note that tests

TABLE 13-5 Mental Health Drug Classifications

Drug Classification	Common Generic (Brand) Drugs
Alcohol deterrents Discourage use of alcohol	disulfiram (Antabuse)
Antidepressants Relieve symptoms of depressed mood	fluoxetine (Prozac) paroxetine (Paxil)
Antimanics Control mental disorders characterized by euphoria	lithium (Lithobid) chlorpromazine (Thorazine)
Antipsychotics Control psychotic symptoms	fluphenazine (Prolixin) risperidone (Risperdal)
Anxiolytics Relieve symptoms of anxiety	alprazolam (Xanax) lorazepam (Ativan)

BOX 13-5 Common Signs and Symptoms of Mental Health Disorders

Akathisia	Inability to remain calm
Amnesia	Inability to remember
Catatonia	Immobility from emotional rather than physical cause
Delirium	Confused, unfocused, and agitated behavior
Delusion	Persistent belief in an untruth
Hallucination	Unreal sensory perception
Psychosis	Impaired perception of reality

to determine the disorders are two-fold: (1) physiological testing to identify if the origin is organic, including laboratory tests, ECG, brain scan, and MRI, and (2) psychological testing, including personality testing and other tests as appropriate for the presenting symptoms.

- Box 13-7 lists information concerning different types of mental health disorders.

CONCLUSION

The nervous system affects every other system of the body. The brain and spinal cord play a vital role in generating and transmitting information and impulses throughout the rest of the body.

Understanding the nervous system is crucial to providing effective care for and communicating clearly with patients of all ages. The growth and development of individuals affect the nervous system. The effects of aging on the nervous system vary; after age 50, people lose an estimated 1% of their neurons. When interacting with elderly patients, keep in mind that normal changes in the nervous system with aging are not the same as Alzheimer disease or dementia. Many individuals reach old age with no signs or symptoms of mental impairment.

Assessment of a patient's mental function is important because it may show changes that are

BOX 13-6 Diagnostic Tests and Procedures for Mental Health Status

Mental status examination	Assessment of patient's appearance, affect, thought processes, cognitive function, insight, and judgment
Laboratory tests	Complete blood count (CBC) with differential, blood chemistry profile, thyroid function panel, sexually transmitted disease (STD) screening
Imaging	CT scan, MRI, **positron emission tomography (PET scan)**

Psychological testing
- *Bender-Gestalt test* measures visuomotor and spatial abilities
- *Rorschach (inkblot) test* measures ability to integrate intellectual and emotional factors
- *Minnesota Multiphasic Personality Inventory (MMPI)* measures personality characteristics through forced-choice questions
- *Wechsler Adult Intelligence Scale (WAIS)* measures verbal and performance intelligence quotient (IQ)

BOX 13-7 Information Concerning Mental Health Disorders

Developmental Disorders

Autism: Disorder characterized by preoccupation with inner thoughts; marked (noticeable) unresponsiveness to social contact.

Attention deficit hyperactivity disorder (ADHD): Characterized by inability to focus attention for short periods or to engage in quiet activities, or both.

Substance-Related Disorders

Alcoholism: Physical and mental dependence on regular intake of alcohol.

Drug abuse: Use of legal or illegal drugs that cause physical, mental, or emotional harm and dependence.

Organic Mental Disorders

Dementia: Irreversible impairment of intellectual activities.

Alzheimer disease: Progressive degeneration of frontal lobe of brain.

Psychoses

Schizophrenia: Characterized by disturbances in thought content, perception, sense of self, and both personal and interpersonal relationships.

Delusional disorder: Characterized by false beliefs that include grandiose and persecutory delusions.

Mood Disorders

Depression: Feeling of persistent sadness accompanied by insomnia, loss of appetite, and inability to experience pleasure.

Bipolar disorder: Disorder marked by severe mood swings from hyperactivity *(mania)* to sadness *(depression)*.

Anxiety Disorders

General anxiety disorder (GAD): General feeling of apprehension brought on by episodes of internal self-doubt.

Obsessive-compulsive disorder (OCD): Disorder that interferes with daily functioning and is characterized by obsessive thoughts and compulsive actions (e.g., fear of germs leading to repeated cleaning).

Post-traumatic stress disorder (PTSD): Impairment that affects activities of daily living and is expressed as severe anxiety following a trauma.

Somatoform Disorders

Conversion: Resolution of psychological conflict through loss of body function (e.g., paralysis, blindness).

Munchausen syndrome: Disorder characterized by intentional presentation of false symptoms that may include self-mutilation to obtain medical care.

Personality Disorders

Paranoid: Feeling a sense of being exploited or harmed without a credible basis.

Schizoid: Showing indifference to social relationships.

Antisocial: Exhibiting behavior that shows a disregard for the rights of others.

Narcissistic: Exhibiting behavior that lacks empathy and sensitivity to the needs of others.

Histrionic: Showing excessive attention-seeking tendencies.

---

consistent with organic brain disease. Assessment also allows the medical assistant to decide if the patient has the capacity to understand treatment guidelines. Your knowledge of the nervous system will likely be used every day. Whether you are asking patients questions, assisting with medical procedures, or performing other clinical or administrative functions, your understanding of this important and complex body system will affect the care that your patients receive.

SUMMARY

Reinforce your understanding of the material in this chapter by reviewing the curriculum objectives and key content points below.

1. Define, appropriately use, and spell all the Key Terms for this chapter.
   - Review the Key Terms if necessary.
2. Describe the organization of the nervous system and identify its two main divisions.
   - The nervous system organizes and controls both the voluntary and the involuntary activities of the body by means of electrical impulses.
   - The central nervous system and peripheral nervous system work together to send information throughout the body.
3. Explain the role of neurons and neuroglia in a nerve impulse.
   - Neurons carry impulses throughout the central nervous system.
   - The neuroglial cells are responsible for the support, protection, insulation, and nourish-

ment of the neurons but do not carry nerve impulses.

4. Describe a synapse and explain its function.
   - A synapse is a microscopic space between the end of one neuron and start of the next neuron.
   - Synapses help transmit information from one neuron to another.
   - Neurotransmitters are released to send the impulse across the synapse. They prevent continuous stimulation of nerve transmission, allowing nerves to rest.

5. List the main divisions of the central nervous system (CNS).
   - The CNS is made up of the brain and spinal cord.

6. Identify the parts of the brain and briefly describe the function of each.
   - Membranous coverings called *meninges* protect the brain.
   - The cerebrum controls functions associated with thinking and voluntary activities.
   - The diencephalon includes the thalamus, which relays messages from several parts of the body and monitors sensory stimuli, and the hypothalamus, which controls the activities of the pituitary gland and produces hormones to control the release or limit the production of the hormones.

7. Explain the purpose of cerebrospinal fluid (CSF).
   - CSF cushions and protects the nervous tissue of the brain and spinal cord.

8. List the cranial nerves and describe their function.
   - There are 12 pairs of cranial nerves attached to the brain. Refer to Table 13-1.
   - Cranial nerves consist of motor (efferent), sensory (afferent), and mixed (sensory and motor) fibers.

9. List the spinal nerves and describe their function.
   - There are 31 pairs of spinal nerves.
   - Spinal nerves are grouped by location: cervical, thoracic, lumbar, sacral, and coccygeal.
   - Each pair of nerves transmits impulses to or from the spinal cord. Each forms a dermatome.

10. List the main divisions of the peripheral nervous system.
    - The autonomic nervous system and the somatic nervous systems are parts of the peripheral nervous system.

11. Describe the functions of the sympathetic and parasympathetic nervous systems.
    - The sympathetic and parasympathetic nervous systems are parts of the autonomic nervous system.

- The sympathetic nervous system is responsible for the body's response to stress ("fight or flight").
- The parasympathetic nervous system returns the body back to a state of balance.

12. List and briefly describe six types of reflex actions.
    - A reflex is an involuntary response to a given type of stimulation to a specific area.
    - Types of reflexes include abdominal (wall draws inward), Achilles (ankle jerk), Babinski (toe curl), corneal (eye blink), patellar (knee jerk), and plantar (toe flex).

13. List and describe nine types of signs and symptoms of neurological disease.
    - Refer to the Key Terms.
    - Diet, avoidance of dangerous substances, immediate treatment of infections and injuries, genetic counseling, and screening of newborns for phenylketonuria (PKU) are all ways to prevent neurological disease.

14. List six types of diagnostic tests and procedures for neurological disease and describe the use of each.
    - Refer to Box 13-3.

15. List 11 diseases and disorders of the nervous system and briefly describe the etiology, signs and symptoms, diagnosis, therapy, and interventions for each.
    - Refer to Table 13-4.

16. Describe the twofold testing process used to determine mental health disorders.
    - Tests for mental health disorders include physiological tests for body impairment and psychological tests for mental dysfunction.

17. List and describe seven common signs and symptoms of mental disorders.
    - Refer to Box 13-5.

18. List four types of tests and procedures used to diagnose mental disorders and briefly describe each.
    - Refer to Box 13-6.

19. List and briefly describe 20 mental health disorders.
    - Refer to Box 13-7.

20. Analyze a realistic medical office situation and apply your understanding of the nervous system to determine the best course of action.
    - By understanding the nervous system, you are more prepared to understand patients' perceptions and tailor education to their ability to comprehend.

21. Describe the impact on patient care when medical assistants have a solid understanding of the structure and function of the nervous system.
    - With effective communication and a good understanding of nervous system physiology,

the medical assistant can successfully encourage patients to follow their prescribed treatment plan.

FOR FURTHER EXPLORATION

Research stroke. Stroke is the third leading cause of death in the United States. To understand stroke better, a medical assistant needs to be aware of the various factors that contribute to stroke and to understand the treatment.
Keywords: Use the following keywords in your search: stroke, CVA, aphasia, brain attack, American Stroke Association.

WORD PARTS: NERVOUS SYSTEM

Structure and Function
Suffixes

-esthesia	sensation
-kinesia	movement
-lepsy	seizure
-lexia	reading
-paresis	partial paralysis
-phasia	speech
-plegia	paralysis

Combining Forms

dendr/o	tree
gangli/i, ganglion/o	ganglion
gli/o	neuroglia
neur/o, neur/i	nerve

Central Nervous System
Combining Forms

alges/o	sensitivity to pain
arachn/o	spider; arachnoid membrane
caud/o	tail
cerebell/o	cerebellum
cerebr/o	cerebrum
cortic/o	cortex
dur/o	dura mater
encephal/o	brain

WORD PARTS: NERVOUS SYSTEM—cont'd

esthesi/o	feeling
kinesi/o	movement
medull/o	medulla oblongata
mening/o, meninge/o	meninges
myel/o	spinal cord; bone marrow
narc/o	stupor; sleep
pyr/o	fire; temperature increase; fever
radicul/o	root of a spinal nerve
rhiz/o	root, nerve root
somn/o, somn/i	sleep
thalam/o	thalamus
ventricul/o	cavity

Prefixes

hemi-	half
quadri-	four
semi-	half

Mental Health
Combining Forms

ment/o	mind
phren/o	mind; diaphragm
psych/o	mind
schiz/o	split

Suffixes

-phobia	irrational fear
-mania	excited state; excessive preoccupation

Abbreviations: Nervous System

ALS	amyotrophic lateral sclerosis
ANS	autonomic nervous system
CNS	central nervous system
CSF	cerebrospinal fluid
CVA	cerebrovascular accident
EEG	electroencephalogram
LP	lumbar puncture
MS	multiple sclerosis
PNS	peripheral nervous system
REM	rapid eye movement
TIA	transient ischemic attack

Chapter Review

Vocabulary Review

Matching

Match each term with the correct definition.

A. nerve

B. neurons

C. dendrites

D. myelin sheath

E. dermatome

F. synapse

G. brain

H. hypothalamus

I.

J.

K.

L.

M.

N.

O.

_____ 1. Manner of walking

_____ 2. Functional unit of a nerve that transmits impulses; located within the CNS

_____ 3. Bone structure that surrounds and protects the spinal cord

_____ 4. Medical science that deals with the origin, diagnosis, prevention, and treatment of developmental and emotional components of physical disorders

_____ 5. Protective covering of the brain and spinal cord

_____ 6. Surface area of the body where the afferent fibers travel from a spinal root

_____ 7. Covering of an axon

_____ 8. Involuntary reaction that occurs because of a stimulus

_____ 9. Located in the skull; main functioning unit of the CNS that contains many neurons

_____ 10. Bundle of fibers containing neurons and blood vessels

_____ 11. Space from the end of one neuron to the beginning of the next neuron

_____ 12. Hormone that is stored in the posterior pituitary gland and needed for uterine contractions

_____ 13. Responsible for relaying messages from parts of the body; monitors sensory stimuli

_____ 14. Receive nerve impulses

_____ 15. Controls activities of the pituitary gland; secretes oxytocin and ADH; regulates the autonomic nervous system

Theory Recall

True/False

Indicate whether the sentence or statement is true or false.

_____ 1. The endocrine system is the main communication and control system of the body.

_____ 2. There are 16 pairs of cranial nerves.

_____ 3. A general increase in nerve conduction occurs with age.

Multiple Choice

Identify the letter of the choice that best completes the statement or answers the question.

1. Phagocytic cells that do not transmit impulses and are located within the CNS are called _____.
   A. glial cells
   B. astrocytes
   C. ganglia
   D. None of the above

2. _____ are nerve cells that engulf cellular waste and destroy microorganisms in nerve tissue.
   A. Astrocytes
   B. Ependymal cells
   C. Microglial cells
   D. Oligodendroglial cells

3. The _____ is known as the little brain.
   A. brain stem
   B. cerebellum
   C. diencephalon
   D. cerebrum

4. The middle layer of the meninges is called the _____.
   A. dura mater
   B. pia mater
   C. arachnoid
   D. none of the above

5. _____ are (is) (a) chemical substance(s) that cause(s) a nerve impulse.
   A. Neurotransmitters
   B. Aqueous humor
   C. Oxytocin
   D. Cerebrospinal fluid

6. The combining form for "brain" is _____.
   A. neur/o
   B. dur/o
   C. rhiz/o
   D. encephal/o

7. _____ are used to produce sleep.
   A. Analgesics
   B. Hypnotics
   C. Sedatives
   D. Anesthetics

8. Paxil is an example of an _____.
   A. antimanic
   B. antipsychotic
   C. anxiolytic
   D. antidepressant

9. What roman numeral is the trigeminal nerve?
   A. III
   B. IV
   C. V
   D. X

10. A _____ headache occurs unilaterally and involves an eye, temple, cheek, and forehead. These headaches start during sleep and can last for several weeks.
    A. tension
    B. cluster
    C. migraine
    D. none of the above

11. A(n) _____ is the surgical puncture performed to remove CSF for examination.
    A. spinal tap
    B. angiography
    C. myelography
    D. electroneuromyography

12. A test that measures muscle activity and aids in diagnosing neuromuscular problems is called a(n) _____.
    A. electroencephalogram
    B. angiogram
    C. electromyogram
    D. nerve conduction study

13. A _____ seizure begins with an outcry and movements that are first tonic and then clonic.
    A. petit mal
    B. myoclonic
    C. partial
    D. grand mal

14. _____ occurs when a blood vessel ruptures or a blood clot occludes a blood vessel, which decreases blood flow to the brain.
    A. ALS
    B. CVA
    C. MS
    D. TIA

15. _____ is inflammation of the brain and spinal cord coverings.
    A. Meningitis
    B. Parkinson disease
    C. Multiple sclerosis
    D. Alzheimer disease

16. Neuralgia of the fifth cranial nerve is called _____.
    A. Alzheimer disease
    B. Tic douloureux
    C. transient ischemic attack
    D. shingles

Sentence Completion

Complete each sentence or statement.

1. The functional unit of the nervous system is the _____.

2. _____ is an impaired perception of reality.

3. A(n) _____ test measures patient's ability to integrate intellectual and emotional fears.

4. _____ is an irreversible impairment of intellectual activities.

5. _____ is a disorder marked by severe mood swings from hyperactivity to sadness.

6. _____ behavior demonstrates a lack of empathy and sensitivity to the needs of others.

7. _____ is a severe anxiety following trauma. Impairment affects daily living.

8. _____ is a continuous sheath around the myelin.

Short Answers

1. Describe the organization of the nervous system and identify its two main divisions.

   _____

   _____

   _____

   _____

2. List the main divisions of the central nervous system.

   _____

   _____

   _____

3. Describe the functions of the sympathetic and parasympathetic nervous system.

_____

_____

_____

_____

_____

Application of Skills

Label the diagrams.

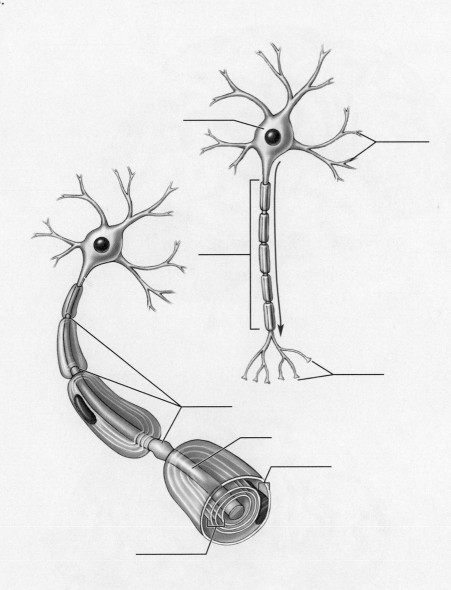

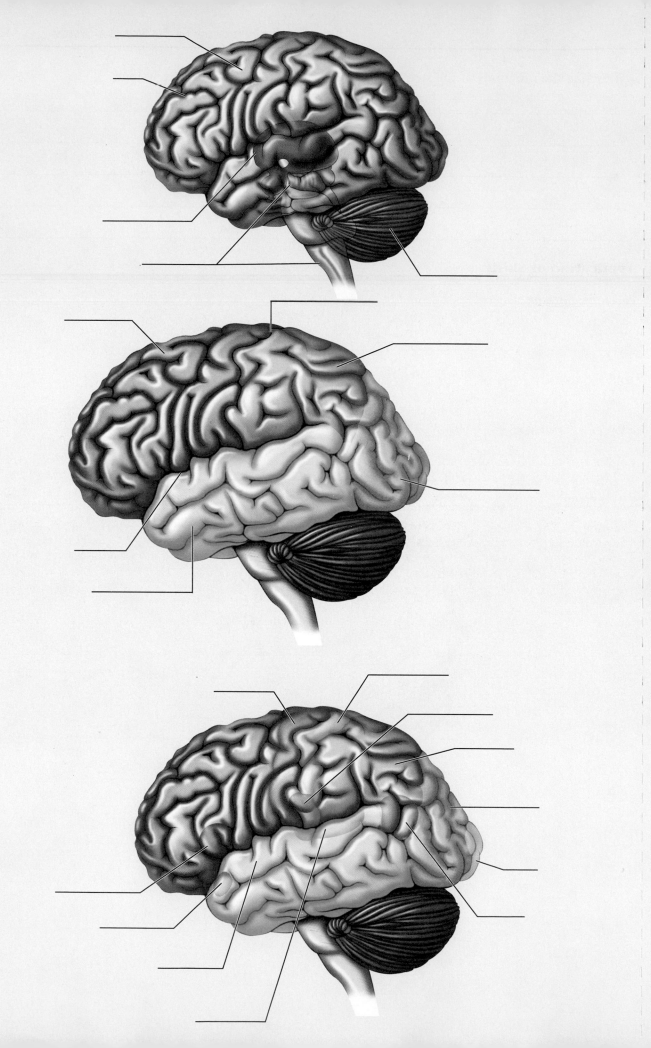

Critical Thinking

1. Describe a past event that caused your sympathetic and parasympathetic nervous systems to respond.

2. Clara Evanston is an 83-year-old patient who has been gradually exhibiting signs of Alzheimer disease. Her husband is her primary caregiver and is finding it increasingly difficult to manage her care. On Clara's recent office visit, Mr. Evanston asked you to explain the progression of Clara's symptoms and what suggestions you have for her care. Explain to Mr. Evanston the progression of symptoms and what suggestions you would give him. Research Alzheimer disease as needed.

Internet Research

Keyword: (Use the name of the condition or disease you select to write about)

Select one condition or disease from Table 13-4. Write a two-paragraph report regarding the condition or disease you selected, listing the etiology, signs and symptoms, diagnosis, therapy, and interventions. Cite your source. (You may not use the information on the tables exclusively for your report.) Be prepared to give a 2-minute oral presentation should your instructor assign you to do so.

What Would You Do?

If you have accomplished the objectives in this chapter, you will be able to make better choices as a medical assistant. Take a look at this situation and decide what you would do.

Sally Jones, age 72, complained of dizziness with a loss of sensation on the left side that lasted only for a few minutes over the past few weeks. She also had a headache that lasted only during the paresthesia. She has a long history of moderately controlled hypertension for which she has taken antihypertensives "when I thought about them." Dr. Smith was concerned that she might be having TIAs. He prescribed a vasodilator and a mild analgesic for the headache when he saw her last week. Today she was brought to the emergency room with sudden left-side hemiplegia and a headache but no aphasia. Except for the hypertension, Ms. Jones has been in relatively good health for her age. On admission, her blood pressure was 210/120 and she was semi-alert. Dr. Smith ordered a CT scan, and it showed an infarct to the right frontotemporal lobes. Ms. Jones was admitted to the hospital for observation and possible treatment.

1. What is a TIA? Why was that a precursor to the condition for which Ms. Jones was admitted to the hospital?

_____

_____

_____

2. Why were the dizziness, loss of sensation, and the headache over the past few weeks important in making a diagnosis of TIA?

_____

_____

_____

3. Why did Dr. Smith give Ms. Jones vasodilators?

_____

_____

_____

4. What is paresthesia? What is aphasia? What is hemiplegia?

_____

_____

_____

_____

5. Why was the control of blood pressure important in the prevention of illness?

_____

_____

6. Why is the paralysis on the left side of the body when the right side of the brain is involved? Why does Ms. Jones not have aphasia?

_____

_____

_____

_____

7. Why did Dr. Smith order a CT scan rather than an MRI?

_____

_____

_____

8. What is a common name for the disease process for which Dr. Smith is treating Ms. Jones?

_____

_____

9. What type of problems would you expect Ms. Jones to have given that the infarct is in the frontal and temporal lobes?

_____

_____

_____

_____

Chapter Quiz

Multiple Choice

Identify the letter of the choice that best completes the statement or answers the question.

1. The _____ of a nerve cell carry (carries) impulses to other neurons and body tissue.
   A. nodes of Ranvier
   B. dendrites
   C. synapse
   D. axon

2. _____ neurons transmit nerve impulses from the CNS to muscles and glands.
   A. Efferent
   B. Integrative
   C. Afferent
   D. None of the above

3. Star-shaped nerve cells that hold blood vessels, closer to nerve cells, and transport water and slats between nerve cells are called _____.
   A. microglial cells
   B. oligodendroglial cells
   C. astrocytes
   D. ependymal cells

4. A sterile watery fluid formed within the ventricles of the brain is _____.
   A. CNS
   B. CSF
   C. PNS
   D. PSF

5. A(n) _____ reflex extends the foot when the tendon at the heel is tapped.
   A. abdominal
   B. Achilles
   C. Babinski
   D. plantar

6. _____ is the inability to focus one's attention for short periods or for engaging in quiet activities, or both.
   A. ADHD
   B. COPD
   C. Colic
   D. Kernig's sign

7. _____ occurs when a blood vessel ruptures or a blood clot occludes a blood vessel that decreases blood flow to the brain.
   A. TIA
   B. ALS
   C. CVA
   D. OCD

8. _____ is an acute inflammation of the dorsal root ganglia of a dermatome.
   A. Meningitis
   B. Shingles
   C. Tic douloureux
   D. Encephalitis

9. _____ is a feeling of persistent sadness.
   A. Depression
   B. Anxiety
   C. Narcissism
   D. Paranoia

10. A(n) _____ is a test that records neuromuscular activity by electrical stimulation.
    A. CT scan
    B. MRI
    C. EEG
    D. EMG

11. _____ is a disorder characterized by a preoccupation with inner thoughts and marked unresponsiveness to social contact.
    A. Delusional disorder
    B. Autism
    C. Obsessive-compulsive disorder
    D. Munchausen syndrome

12. There are _____ pairs of spinal nerves.
    A. 12
    B. 31
    C. 36
    D. 42

14

OBJECTIVES

After reading this chapter and working the exercises, you should be able to:

1. Appraise the value of an attractive letter to a business.
2. Assess how the business letter reflects the public image of a medical practice.
3. Describe the specific qualities that make a letter mailable.
4. Demonstrate the three basic mechanical formats of letter preparation.
5. Demonstrate the ability to paragraph properly and to place a letter attractively on a page.
6. Use a specific letter format in preparation of a letter from draft copy typed as a single paragraph.
7. Prepare a two-page letter by following the rules for multiple-page letters.
8. Identify the unique format for "To Whom It May Concern" documents.

LETTER TRANSCRIPTION

KEY TERMS

continuation sheets The sheets of paper used to type a second and subsequent pages of a letter. These are often called *second sheets.*

full block The name of a particular letter format (see Fig. 14-1, *A*).

letter format The mechanical setup of a letter, which dictates placement of the various letter parts (Fig. 14-2).

mixed punctuation Style of letter punctuation in which a colon or a comma (only when a first name is dictated) is used after the salutation and a comma is used after the complimentary close (Fig. 14-1, *A*).

modified block The name of a particular letter format (see Fig. 14-1, *B*).

open punctuation Style of letter punctuation in which no punctuation mark is used after the salutation or complimentary close (Fig. 14-1, *B*).

Note from the Author

Correspondence was my first experience with medical transcription, and I was not as good at it as I thought I would be. I knew the proper letter mechanics and had good English grammar skills, so I thought it was going to be easy. It was not. The fact that I could not spell medical words (or understand them either, for that matter), in addition to the fact that some English words that I thought I could spell I did not spell correctly, prompted me to go to night school. No, I did not receive any training in medical transcription—it was another 10 years or so before books and classes became available. I worked on spelling, homonyms, and obscure grammar rules.

I acquired this initial job because I could take shorthand, but it was no time at all before I "talked" my employers into purchasing dictation/transcription equipment. I thought that this step surely would make a good "medical secretary"* out of the proverbial sow's ear. Alas, there was just too much more to it than that: learning to paragraph, putting punctuation marks exactly where they belonged, using numbers and symbols correctly, making sure that the finished document was perfect. (Not a word to be taken lightly, inasmuch as the overall appearance was very important, too.) However, I became proficient at doing chart notes and began to enjoy my new skills. When one of the physicians started training me to prepare operative reports, diagnostic studies, history and physical examinations, and discharge summaries, I finally found out where the "easy stuff was to be mined." Letters are hard! Good luck!

Medical transcriptionist was not a term anyone used in those days. It was many years later, in fact, before the term came into use. No one would have referred to me as a "medical language specialist," either, unless they were part of a stand-up comedy routine.

Letter preparation is unique in many ways and has several special attributes that may make it difficult to plan. These include the following:

- The overall appearance, which is challenging; unlike documents that are meant only for the medical record, the letter must be attractive. It is the personal representative of the writer and expresses his or her professional standing through both its contents and its appearance. You control its appearance, and you may in part control how it reads; thus it also represents you. The placement of the letter on the page must be considered, with top and bottom white areas taken into account and with even and equal margins maintained.
- Formats are important; traditionally, they are followed exactly.
- Paragraphing is also important, but it is not easy for the beginner to recognize when shifts to new subject matter occur.
- Correct punctuation, although important in all documents, can be a particular challenge in letters.
- Shifts of emphasis and format often are confusing. For example, the dictator may decide to place an abbreviated version of the patient's physical examination within the body of the letter. In this situation, the transcriptionist cannot expect to provide a strictly traditional document and must know how to handle variations in paragraphing.
- Lengthy lists of enclosures and/or courtesy copies can make it difficult to maintain an attractive overall appearance.
- Confusing opening and closing remarks often bewilder the novice. For example, the dictator may give both a street address and a post office box address, dictate a lengthy reference line that is not in the proper sequence, address the recipient of the document by a name other than the one previously dictated (this may be a mistake or a nickname), close the letter with unusual or nontraditional greetings or salutations (e.g., "Shalom!" "Happy New Year!" "Kindest personal regards") that were not covered in the "placement rules," or he or she may sign off with just a first name instead of the usual full name.

In this chapter, all of the standard letter transcription practices are discussed, and some variations are introduced, so you can be confident that you are setting up the document in the best possible order. It should be obvious to you by now that you are the key factor in turning out a product: the letter.

It is important that the letter be perfect in every way, beginning with "eye appeal" and with great attention paid to details. Your success depends on your ability to produce a mailable letter. In learning to identify the specific qualities that make a letter mailable, you therefore should also be able to recognize errors in form, grammar, punctuation, typing, and spelling.

QUALITIES OF A MAILABLE LETTER

1. *Placement.* The following are important aspects:
   - The content should be attractively placed on the page with the right margin fairly even. Because the right margin is not justified on medical documents, ragged right margins often occur. A maximum of five characters in variation is ideal, but sometimes this is not possible.
   - The letter should have "eye appeal," with the letterhead taken into consideration when format is chosen.
   - The letter should have picture-frame symmetry if possible.
2. *Form.* The following should be taken into consideration:
   - Correct format (such as full block or modified block).
   - Double spacing between paragraphs.
   - Consistent punctuation (open or mixed).
   - Correct use of enclosure and copy notations.
3. *Typing techniques.* There should be no keyboarding, formatting, or printout errors, such as improper word wrapping to the next line, incorrect spacing, transposition of words, typographic errors, material omitted, or words divided incorrectly at the end of a line.
4. *Proper mechanics.* You should show proper knowledge of technical writing techniques (e.g., abbreviations, numbers, and symbols).
5. *Grammar use.* The words in the letter should be used correctly in accordance with their meaning (e.g., *all ready/already*).
   - Homonyms should be used correctly (e.g., *their/there, site/sight/cite*).
   - Contractions should be avoided whenever possible.
6. *Spelling.* There must be no doubt about the correct spelling of a word, and references must be consulted without hesitation.
7. *Overall appearance.* Be sure to check the following:
   - The printout is clear and sharp, with no smudges.
   - Page startup and page breaks are correct.
   - Letterhead is not in conflict with printout.
8. *Content.* Be sure of the following:
   - The material is accurate as dictated.
   - No material is omitted.
   - No material is changed to alter the meaning of the letter.

LETTER FORMATS

Secretarial manuals illustrate and name many different formats in which letters may be prepared. The names given to these arrangements vary, but the formats are standard.

The following formats have been named to match closely the names you might already have learned and, at the same time, to describe as nearly as possible the appearance of the letter:

Full block (see Fig. 14-1, *A*). The full-block format is the most frequently used format. Notice that the date line, address, salutation, reference line, all lines of the body of the letter, complimentary close, and typed signature line are flush with the left margin. This is a popular format because no tab stops are needed. As long as it is compatible with the letterhead and the wishes of the dictator, you may use it.

Modified block (see Fig. 14-1, *B*). In the modified block format, the date line, reference line, complimentary close, and typed signature line are typed to begin just to the right of the middle of the page. This format has a little more "personality" and is compatible with most letterheads. Most dictators are comfortable with the signature area.

Notice that placement of the date line sets your format. If you place the date at the left margin, you must continue with full-block format. If you place your date at the center point, you must follow through with this format, making sure that the complimentary close and typed signature line are lined up with it.

Modified block with indented paragraphs (see Fig. 14-1, *C*). The third and final format is not as popular as the first two because of the tab stop necessary for beginning each paragraph. It is a traditional format and might be preferred by the dictator. Additional formats you may have learned in business typing classes are not used for medical letters because the formats are too informal.

Many general business offices have one letter format that is used by all the transcriptionists in the company, but you may find that there are few formal rules about letter styles for medical dictation.

Each of the following items refers to the corresponding number in Fig. 14-2; refer to this figure as I examine a business letter and discuss its components. Refer to Fig. 14-1, *D*, to see the spacing between sections. Note the placement of the reference line in particular, because it was typed in accordance with the "break-the-rule" placement.

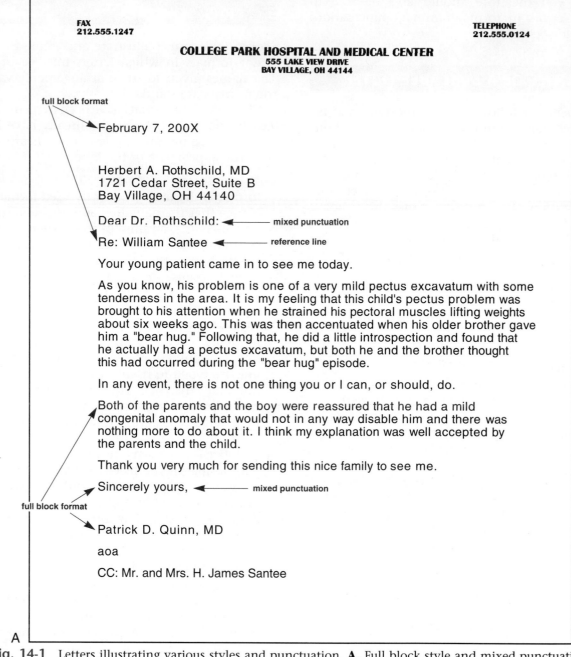

Fig. 14-1 Letters illustrating various styles and punctuation. **A,** Full block style and mixed punctuation.

Item 1: Paper

Standard $8\frac{1}{2} \times 11$ inch, 25% cotton content bond paper is most often used. The paper is usually white, although off-white or eggshell color may be preferred. Be sure that the paper is compatible with the printer and is inserted properly.

Item 2: Letterhead

The letterhead must be appropriate and current. The physician, clinic, or hospital will use stationery with his or her name (or the corporate name or institution name) and address printed on it. Other information, such as the telephone number, fax number, medical specialty, or board membership, is often included. The letterhead should be confined to the top 2 inches of the page. Refrain from using a letterhead that is continued to the bottom of the page because it makes placement difficult, and the style is unnecessary. Printed borders on the paper are equally distracting.

Many physicians choose to have steel die–engraved letterheads. Engraving establishes the finest quality letterhead; it looks professional and further enhances the appearance of the correspondence.

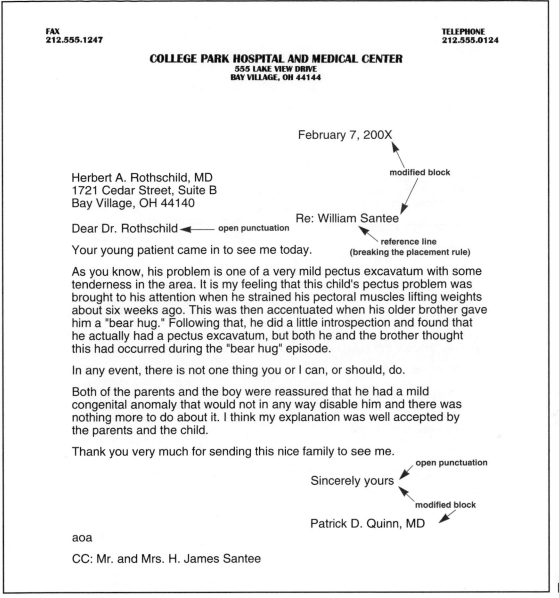

FAX
212.555.1247

TELEPHONE
212.555.0124

COLLEGE PARK HOSPITAL AND MEDICAL CENTER
555 LAKE VIEW DRIVE
BAY VILLAGE, OH 44144

February 7, 200X

modified block

Herbert A. Rothschild, MD
1721 Cedar Street, Suite B
Bay Village, OH 44140

Re: William Santee

Dear Dr. Rothschild ◄——— *open punctuation*

reference line (breaking the placement rule)

Your young patient came in to see me today.

As you know, his problem is one of a very mild pectus excavatum with some tenderness in the area. It is my feeling that this child's pectus problem was brought to his attention when he strained his pectoral muscles lifting weights about six weeks ago. This was then accentuated when his older brother gave him a "bear hug." Following that, he did a little introspection and found that he actually had a pectus excavatum, but both he and the brother thought this had occurred during the "bear hug" episode.

In any event, there is not one thing you or I can, or should, do.

Both of the parents and the boy were reassured that he had a mild congenital anomaly that would not in any way disable him and there was nothing more to do about it. I think my explanation was well accepted by the parents and the child.

Thank you very much for sending this nice family to see me.

open punctuation

Sincerely yours

modified block

Patrick D. Quinn, MD

aoa

CC: Mr. and Mrs. H. James Santee

B

Fig. 14-1, cont'd   B, Modified block style and open punctuation. Illustrates reference line that breaks the placement rule.
Continued

Embossing and color art, which are very popular on business letters, were seldom seen on physicians' letterheads until recently. However, these are gaining in popularity. Be sure to obtain the approval of your employer before you change the letterhead, the type of printing, or the quality of the paper you have been using.

Continuation sheets do not have a letterhead but are of the same color and quality as the first sheet. When using continuation sheets, be careful to print out on the face (front) of the paper. You can tell the face from the back by holding the paper to the light. The watermark (a faint symbol that is part of the paper) is visible and can be read from the face. If you print out on the back, the paper may appear to be of a different color and texture and will not match your letterhead paper. Be sure to insert the proper number of continuation sheets into the printer (and remove any spare sheets later). It is incorrect to print the second and subsequent pages on paper that happens to be in the paper tray.

Number 10 ($4\frac{1}{8} \times 9\frac{1}{2}$ inch) envelopes should match the paper in color and quality. The return address is engraved or printed to match the letterhead. Because the envelope makes the first impression on a correspondent, deliberate care must be taken in its preparation.

A variety of typefaces and setup styles are available (Fig. 14-3). You may be asked to create an appropriate letterhead when a change is made in what is currently being used. A reputable printer will provide

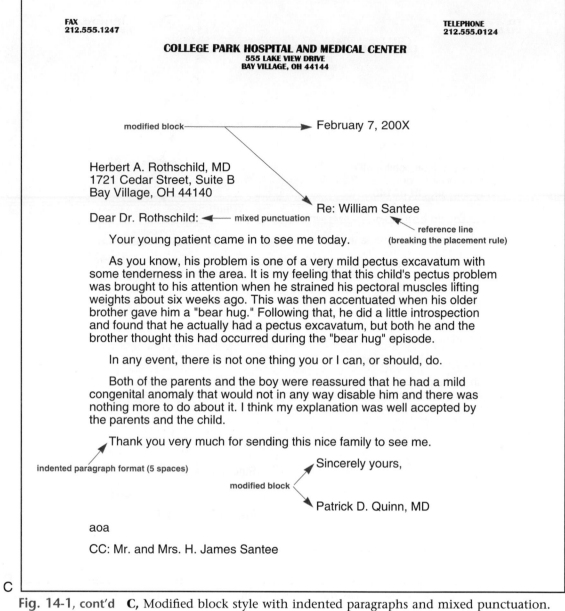

Fig. 14-1, cont'd **C,** Modified block style with indented paragraphs and mixed punctuation.

you with a list of available typefaces and will help design an attractive letterhead.

Item 3: Date

The date is in keeping with the format of the letter and is placed in line with the complimentary close and typed signature line. It is typed approximately three or four lines below the letterhead (no closer, but you may drop it farther down for a brief letter). The date used is the day on which the material was dictated and *not* the day on which it was transcribed. This point is very important because comments made in the document could reflect this date. Spell out the date in full in either the traditional or the military style. Note the use of the comma in the following example of the traditional style.

EXAMPLES:

December 22, 200X (traditional style)

22 December 200X (British and military style)

NOT: 12-22-0X or 12/11/0X

Item 4: Inside Address

The inside address is typed flush with the left margin and is begun on approximately the fifth line below the date (it may be moved up or down a line or two, depending on the length of the letter). The name of the person or firm is copied exactly as printed on the person's or firm's letterhead or as printed in the medical society directory or the telephone book. A

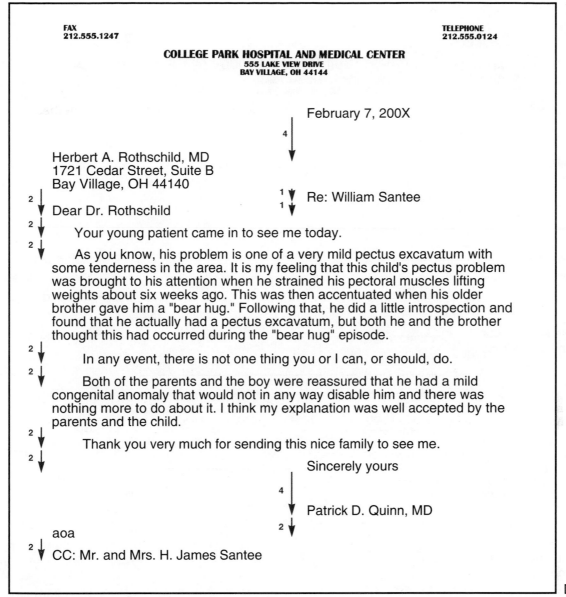

FAX
212.555.1247

TELEPHONE
212.555.0124

COLLEGE PARK HOSPITAL AND MEDICAL CENTER
555 LAKE VIEW DRIVE
BAY VILLAGE, OH 44144

February 7, 200X

Herbert A. Rothschild, MD
1721 Cedar Street, Suite B
Bay Village, OH 44140

Re: William Santee

Dear Dr. Rothschild

Your young patient came in to see me today.

As you know, his problem is one of a very mild pectus excavatum with some tenderness in the area. It is my feeling that this child's pectus problem was brought to his attention when he strained his pectoral muscles lifting weights about six weeks ago. This was then accentuated when his older brother gave him a "bear hug." Following that, he did a little introspection and found that he actually had a pectus excavatum, but both he and the brother thought this had occurred during the "bear hug" episode.

In any event, there is not one thing you or I can, or should, do.

Both of the parents and the boy were reassured that he had a mild congenital anomaly that would not in any way disable him and there was nothing more to do about it. I think my explanation was well accepted by the parents and the child.

Thank you very much for sending this nice family to see me.

Sincerely yours

Patrick D. Quinn, MD

aoa
CC: Mr. and Mrs. H. James Santee

D

Fig. 14-1, cont'd   D, Modified block style and open punctuation. Illustrates proper spacing and margin width.

courtesy title is added to a name whenever possible. If you do not know whether the person is a man or woman, omit the courtesy title. The title "Ms." is used when you do not have a title for a woman; it is also used as a substitute for "Miss" or "Mrs." because many women prefer this usage. The degree is preferred over a title in the case of a physician, and in no case should a title and a degree be used together. Use the middle initial when it is known.

EXAMPLES:

Ms. Mary T. Jordan
Professor Otis R. Laban
Drs. Reilly, Lombardo, and Hamstead

Dora F. Hodge, MD
Captain Denis K. Night, Jr.
Glenn M. Stempien, DDS
Franklyn Battencourt, Esq.
Neal J. Kaufman, MD, FACCP
Rabbi Bernice Gold
Paul Kip Barton, MD, MAJ, USN

NOT: Dr. Clifford F. Adolph, MD

Dr. Bertrum L. Storey, PhD

Ms. Janet Holloway, DO

When "doctor" is dictated and you have no way of finding out if the person being addressed is a medical doctor, an osteopath, a podiatrist, a dentist,

Item 1 — Paper

KARL ROBRECHT, MD
INTERNAL MEDICINE

Gulf Medical Group
A PROFESSIONAL CORPORATION
800 GULF SHORE BOULEVARD
NAPLES, FLORIDA 33940
TELEPHONE 262-9976

ROBERT T. SACHS, MD
PHYSICIAN AND SURGEON

2 — Letterhead

Approximately 3
blank lines
below letterhead

_____ 3 — Date

Fifth line below
date line

_____ 4 — Inside address
_____ 5 — Street address
_____ 6 — City and state
_____ Reference

Double space after
last line of address

_____ : 7 — Salutation

_____
_____
_____
_____ . 8 — Body

Single spaced with
double space
between paragraphs

_____
_____
_____
_____ .

Double space after
last line typed

_____ , 9 — Complimentary
close

Signature area

3 blank lines

_____ 10 — Typed
signature line

_____ Title

Double space   ——   11 — Reference
initials

Double space   ——   12 — Enclosure
notation

Double space   ——   13 — Distribution
notation

Fig. 14-2 Business letter setup mechanics, showing modified block format and mixed punctuation. (See text for a description of each item illustrated.)

GULF MEDICAL GROUP

A PROFESSIONAL MEDICAL CORPORATION
800 GULF SHORE BOULEVARD
NAPLES, FLORIDA 33940
865-262-9976
FAX 865-893-4353

KARL ROBRECHT, MD
INTERNAL MEDICINE

CELESTYN SACHS, MD
PHYSICIAN AND SURGEON

FAX
212.555.1247

TELEPHONE
212.555.0124

COLLEGE PARK HOSPITAL AND MEDICAL CENTER
555 LAKE VIEW DRIVE
BAY VILLAGE, OH 44140

212.555.1247

212.555.2345

COLLEGE PARK HOSPITAL AND MEDICAL CENTER
555 LAKE VIEW DRIVE
BAY VILLAGE, OH 44140

THORACIC SURGERY MEDICAL GROUP, INC.
ROBERT B. STEINWAY, MD
STEPHEN R. CLAWSON, MD
CHRISTIAN M. LOW, MD
MARY SUE LOW, MD

504 WARFORD DRIVE
SYRACUSE, NY 13223
TELEPHONE 555.567.2342

19098 CHATHAM ROAD
SYRACUSE, NY 13203
TELEPHONE 555.562.4290

Kwei-Hay Wong, MD
1654 Piikea Street
Honolulu, Hawaii 96818
Telephone 555-534-0922
Fax 555-534-9512

Diplomate, American Board
Of Otolaryngology

Ear, Nose, Throat
Head and Neck Surgery

Fig. 14-3 Letterhead styles and typefaces.

or another professional with a doctoral degree, use the title format.

EXAMPLES:

Dr. Phillip R. Wood

Dr. Suzanne P. Markson

If a business title accompanies the name, it may follow the name on the same line, or, if lengthy, it may appear on the next line. (Note the punctuation in the examples.)

EXAMPLES:

F.E. Stru, MD, Medical Director

Ms. Sheila O. Wendall
Purchasing Agent

William Peter Sloan-Wilson, MD
Captain, USN, USCG

Adrian N. Abott, MD
Chief-of-Surgery
Sinai-Lebanon Hospital

Item 5: Street Address

After the name of the person or firm is the street or post office box address. (If both are given, use the post office box address. The street address has been provided for persons visiting the firm and provides a site for express-mail deliveries. The firm may not even have the facilities for receiving regular mail on site. If the post office box is given, the person or firm has indicated that delivery to the post office box is preferred.) Abbreviations are permitted *after* the street name only; they include NW, NE, SW, and so on. Avoid abbreviating North, South, East, West, Road, Street, Avenue, or Boulevard. "Apartment" is abbreviated only if the line is unusually long. The apartment, suite, or space number is typed on the same line with the street address, separated by a comma.

EXAMPLES:

321 Madison Avenue

1731 North Branch Road, Suite B

845 Medford Circle, Apartment 54

8895 Business Park NW

PO Box 966

If all of the delivery address line information cannot be typed in a single line above the city, state, and ZIP code, then place the secondary address information (e.g., suite, apartment, building, room, space numbers) on the line immediately *above* the delivery address line. This placement may seem awkward, but it is correct. The envelope address is a copy of the inside address, and post office personnel and scanning equipment read only the last two lines of the address, so these lines must contain the street address, city, state, and ZIP codes. The mail carrier is the only one interested in the suite, apartment, or space number. When you do not know whether a suite or apartment is indicated, use the pound sign (#) and the number.

EXAMPLES: *Entire address*

Mrs. Lila Hadley
Apartment 21
1951 52nd Street
Tucson, AZ 85718

Mrs. Marijane Simmons
8840 Marshall Place, #5
Jamestown, NY 14701

James Woo
Wildflower Estates
325 Park Drive
Lakewood, CO 80215

Item 6: City and State

The name of the city is spelled out and separated from the state name with a comma. The state name may be spelled out or abbreviated and is separated from the ZIP code by one letter space and no punctuation. The United States Postal Service state abbreviations are not used without the ZIP code. (See Appendix B for these state abbreviations.)

EXAMPLE:

Honolulu, Hawaii 96918 or Honolulu, HI 96918

NOT: Honolulu, HI

Item 7: Salutation

The salutation is typed two line spaces below the last line of the address, as follows:

- Open punctuation format: no mark of punctuation used.
- Mixed punctuation format (formal): followed by a colon.
- Mixed punctuation format (informal—first name used): followed by a comma or a colon.

EXAMPLES:

Open: Dear Mr. Walsh

Mixed (formal): Dear Mr. Walsh:

Mixed (informal): Dear Don: or Dear Don,

See Fig. 14-1, *A* and *C*, for examples of mixed punctuation and Fig. 14-1, *B* and *D*, for examples of open punctuation.

EXAMPLES: *Salutations used for men, showing mixed punctuation*

Gentlemen:

Dear Mr. Sutherland:

Dear Dr. Hon:

Dear Drs. Blake and Fortuna:

Dear Dr. Blake and Dr. Fortuna:

Dear Mr. Tony Lamb and Mr. Peter Lamb:

Dear Rabbi Ruderman: (likewise, Father, Bishop, Reverend, Monsignor, Cardinal, Brother, Deacon, Chaplain, Dean, and so on)

EXAMPLES: *Salutations used for women, showing mixed punctuation*

Ladies:

Mesdames:

Dear Dr. Martin:
Dear Mrs. Clayborne:
Dear Ms. Robinson:
Dear Judge Peterson: (likewise Reverend, Rabbi, Chaplain, Dean, Deacon, Bishop, Captain, Professor, and so on)
Dear Sister Rose Anthony:
Dear Miss Thomas and Mrs. Farintino:

EXAMPLES: *Salutations used for addressing men and women together*

Dear Sir or Madam:
Ladies and Gentlemen:
Dear Doctors:
Dear Mr. and Mrs. Knight:
Dear Dr. and Mrs. Wong:
Dear Professor Holloway and Mr. Blake:
Dear Drs. Candelaria or Dear Dr. Lois Candelaria and Dr. Fred Candelaria:
Dear Mr. Clayborne and Mrs. Steen-Clayborne:
Dear Dr. Petroski and Mr. Petroski:
Dear Captain and Mrs. Philips:
Dear Dr. Mitchelson et al.: (used for addressing large groups of men and/or women)

Item 8: Body

The body of the letter is begun two line spaces after the salutation or the reference line (when used here) and is single-spaced. (Even very brief letters are single-spaced.) The first and subsequent lines are flush with the left margin unless indented paragraphs are used; in that case, the first line of each paragraph is indented one tab stop. There are always two line spaces between paragraphs.

Make use of displayed extract text when it is appropriate. This practice adds emphasis to the material, makes the letter easier to read, and supplies visual interest. This part of the letter is indented at least five letter spaces (one tab stop on left margin) from *both* left and right margins. Figs. 14-4 and 14-5 illustrate two examples of appropriate use of displayed extract text. Be sure to double-space before and after this feature.

When the speaker decides to include an outline for the proposed plan for the care of the patient, an abbreviated version of the patient's history or current status, or a brief physical examination, prepare it in the form as illustrated. Be sure you carry the block indentation to continuing pages when necessary, and remember to return to the established margin when this material is complete.

Item 9: Complimentary Close

The complimentary close is lined up with the date and is typed two line spaces below the last typed

Kwei-Hay Wong, MD
1654 Piikea Street
Honolulu, Hawaii 96818
Telephone 555-534-0922
Fax 555-534-9512

Diplomate, American Board Of Otolaryngology

Ear, Nose, Throat Head and Neck Surgery

March 27, 200X

Roy V. Zimmer, MD
6280 Jackson Drive
San Antonio, TX 78288

Re: Mrs. Florida Sanchez

Dear Roy:

Thank you for referring this pleasant young lady to my office. She was first seen on February 17, 200X.

Her past history is of no great significance and will not be reiterated at this time.

Physical examination revealed the following:

Thyroid:	Normal to palpation, with no cervical adenopathy.
Breasts:	No masses, tenderness or axillary adenopathy.
Abdomen:	Flat. Liver, kidneys, and spleen not felt. There is a well-healed McBurney scar present. No masses, tenderness, or...

Fig. 14-4 Part of a letter illustrating the use of displayed extract text set off from the rest of the letter for emphasis.

GULF MEDICAL GROUP

A PROFESSIONAL MEDICAL CORPORATION
800 GULF SHORE BOULEVARD
NAPLES, FLORIDA 33940
865-262-9976
FAX 865-893-4353

KARL ROBRECHT, MD
INTERNAL MEDICINE

CELESTYN SACHS, MD
PHYSICIAN AND SURGEON

March 27, 200X

PERSONAL

Mrs. Lila Hadley
Apartment 21
1951 52nd Street
Naples, FL 33941

Dear Mrs. Hadley:

This is in reply to your letter concerning the results of your tests that were done here
and by Dr. Galloway.

1. Intestinal symptoms, secondary to a lactase deficiency.

2. Generalized arteriosclerosis.

3. Mitral stenosis and insufficiency.

4. History of venous aneurysm.

You were seen on February 2, at which time you were having some stiffness at the shoulders, which I
felt was likely to be due to a periarthritis. (This is a stiffness of the shoulder capsule.)

Fig. 14-5 Part of a letter illustrating the use of displayed extract text set off from the rest of the letter for emphasis.

line. Only the first word is capitalized. A comma is used after the close if a colon appears with the salutation (mixed punctuation). No punctuation mark is used with the "open" format. If the author of the document dictates some other greeting at the end of the letter, such as "Kindest personal regards," "Merry Christmas to Janet and the children," "Regards in the holiday season," "Happy New Year!" and so on, type it as a final paragraph, and use the complimentary close as usual.

EXAMPLES: *Mixed punctuation*

Sincerely,

Yours very truly,

EXAMPLES: *Open punctuation*

Sincerely

Yours very truly

See Fig. 14-1, *A* to *D*, for examples of mixed and open punctuation.

Item 10: Typed Signature Line

The dictator's or writer's name is typed exactly as it appears in the letterhead, with three blank lines

inserted after the complimentary close. Press the return/enter key four times after you type the complimentary close. Then type the name, lined up with the complimentary close. If an official title accompanies the name, it may appear on the same line, preceded by a comma, or be typed on the line directly below the signature line without a comma. If the dictator signs off with just a first name, type his or her complete name (and title, if there is one).

EXAMPLE:

Sincerely,

Samuel R. Wong, MD

Chief-of-Surgery

EXAMPLE:

Yours very truly,

Kathryn B. Black, MD, Medical Director
Note the punctuation.

NOTE: An office employee using the letterhead stationery always identifies his or her position in the firm and provides a courtesy title. The title enables the correspondent to have a title to use in writing or telephoning. The title is enclosed in parentheses, or the title may accompany the name when it is signed.

EXAMPLES:

(Ms.) Lynmarie Myhre, CMT

(Mrs.) Mai Chang
Receptionist

(Miss) Paula de la Vera, CMA-A
Office Manager

Item 11: Reference Initials

The transcriptionist's initials are typed using lower-case letters two line spaces below the typed signature, flush with the left margin. Only two or three of the transcriptionist's initials are used, and humorous or confusing combinations are avoided. Do not type your initials when you type a letter for your own signature.

EXAMPLES:

crc (rather than *cc*)
db (rather than *dmb*)
dg (rather than *dog*)

NOTE: If the speaker wants his or her initials used, they precede the initials of the transcriptionist, or if the speaker differs from the person who signs the document, the speaker's, the signer's, and the transcriptionist's initials are used.

EXAMPLES:

lrc/wpd or lrc : wpd
RF : BJT : wpd

Item 12: Enclosure Notation

If the speaker is enclosing one or more items with the letter, attention is called to the item or items with a notation. The notation is typed flush with the left margin, and the number of enclosures should be noted if there is more than one. A wide variety of styles is acceptable. The underlined example is the one most commonly used.

EXAMPLES:

Enc.	<u>Enclosure</u>	Check enclosed
Enc. 2	2 Enc.	2 enclosures
Enclosures		
Enclosures: 2		

Enclosed:	1. Operative report
	2. Pathology report
	3. History and physical

NOTE: This last notation can help you ensure that all items are enclosed before the letter is sealed. The recipient's secretary should also check the enclosure line when the letter is opened to ensure that he or she has all of the mentioned items before the envelope is discarded.

Item 13: Distribution Notation

It is understood that a file copy is made of every item prepared by the transcriptionist. If a copy of the correspondence is sent *to someone else*, this fact is noted on the original version. The notation is typed flush with the left margin and is two line spaces below the reference initials or last notation made. In other words, it is the last entry on the page, unless there is a postscript. Various styles are used, and all are followed by the complete name of the recipient. A colon is used with the notation. Copies mailed out are photocopies of the original document, or the document may be printed out again and mailed. Use the abbreviation *cc* or simply *C* in capital or lowercase letters and identify the recipient of a copy of the document. The abbreviation *cc* remains correct and popular. It used to mean "carbon copy" and now means "courtesy copy."

EXAMPLES:

cc: Frank L. Naruse, MD
c: Ruth Chriswell, Business Manager
C: Hodge W. Lloyd
Copy: Carla P. Ralph, Buyer
Copies: Kristen A. Temple
Anthony R. McClintock

NOTE: *Never* type a copy notation without a name following it.

Second and subsequent copy notations are lined up under the first notation. In general, the names are ranked in alphabetical order. If you have a very lengthy list of copy notations, consider making a two- or three-column list rather than a long string that could affect another page.

EXAMPLES:

CC:	Claire Duennes, MD	Norman Szold, MD
	Sharon Kirkwood, MD	James Tanaka, MD
	Amrum Lambert, MD	Robert Wozniak, MD
	Clifford Storey, MD	Vell Yaldua, MD

≋ OTHER LETTER MECHANICS

Blind Copy

If the sender wishes a copy of the correspondence to be sent to a third party and does not wish the recipient of the original version to know that this was done, he or she will direct that a "blind copy" be mailed. Do *not* make a copy notation on the original but do make a notation on the file copy with the name of the recipient after the notation. Print out the original, and then add the *bcc* notation with the recipient's name to the master and print two copies: one to mail and one to file.

> **EXAMPLE:** *Typed on file copy and Taylor's copy*
>
> bcc: Ms. Penelope R. Taylor

Postscript

The postscript is typed two line spaces below the last reference notation and is flush with the left margin. The abbreviation *PS* followed by a colon usually introduces the item. It is no longer punctuated.

> **NOTE:** The postscript can be an afterthought or a statement deliberately withheld from the body of the letter for emphasis or a restatement of an important thought (e.g., a telephone number in a letter of application). A handwritten afterthought, added by the dictator, does not need to be introduced with "PS."

> **EXAMPLE:** *An afterthought*
>
> PS: Thanks for your offer to borrow your mountain cabin. I'll telephone you when I see I have a weekend off.

> **EXAMPLE:** *Emphasis*
>
> PS: Please do not hesitate to call on me if I can help you in any way.

If the postscript is longer than one line, indent any subsequent lines to align with the first word of the message.

If the postscript is simply something forgotten from the body of the letter such as "By the way, I will return the x-rays to your office after I see Mrs. Theobald next week," you may insert the statement in the body of the letter where the x-rays were last mentioned and then eliminate the postscript. This maneuver is easy to accomplish with the "cut and paste" feature of word processing software.

Attention Line

The attention line is no longer used in business correspondence because of the software feature that enables you to copy the inside address to the envelope. Type the recipient's name and title, if necessary, above the name of the business. The word *Attention* is no longer used unless you wish or unless you are using a title for an unknown recipient.

> **EXAMPLES:**
>
> Josephine Simmons, PhD, Administrator
> Altamont Springs Community Hospital
> 321 Fifth Avenue
> Altamont Springs, FL 32716
>
> Attention: Administrator
> Altamont Springs Community Hospital
> 321 Fifth Avenue
> Altamont Springs, FL 32716

To Whom It May Concern

The phrase *To Whom It May Concern* is used when you have no person or place to send a document. It is typed in full capitals, or the first letter of each word is capitalized. It may be typed flush with the left margin or centered on the page. Open or mixed punctuation is used with it. In general, the complimentary close is not used with this format.

When a reference line is used with this document, it is typed two line spaces below the "To Whom It May Concern" line.

> **EXAMPLE:**
>
> TO WHOM IT MAY CONCERN:
>
> RE: Rudy Carpenter, SS #576-39-9654

Reference Line

Reference lines are commonly used in medical correspondence and medicolegal reports.

A patient's name is always placed in a reference line. Using recent guidelines, some dictators avoid using the name elsewhere in the document so that the patient is identified only in this initial entry. Exact placement is determined by the letter style chosen. In some documents, a reference line may also include file numbers, name of employer, name of insurance carrier, or date of accident or injury. Examine the examples closely.

THORACIC SURGERY MEDICAL GROUP, INC.
ROBERT B. STEINWAY, MD
STEPHEN R. CLAWSON, MD
CHRISTIAN M. LOW, MD
MARY SUE LOW, MD

504 WARFORD DRIVE
SYRACUSE, NY 13223
TELEPHONE 555.567.2342

19098 CHATHAM ROAD
SYRACUSE, NY 13203
TELEPHONE 555.562.4290

August 18, 200X

TO WHOM IT MAY CONCERN

RE: Capt. R. J. Reynolds, USMC

The above-named individual has been under my care for chronic obstructive pulmonary disease since March 1999. He has seen some improvement of his symptomology . . .

Full-Block Placement (see Fig. 14-1, *A*)
- Flush with the left margin
- Two line spaces after the salutation
- Use *RE:* or *Re:* to introduce the patient's full name

EXAMPLE:

Matthew R. Bates, MD

7832 Johnson Avenue

Denver, CO 80241

Dear Dr. Bates

RE: Leah Hamlyn

Modified Block Placement
- Use when the reference line is long or contains more than one entry
- Flush with the left margin
- Two line spaces after the salutation
- Use *RE:* or *Re:* to introduce the patient's full name

EXAMPLE:

Matthew R. Bates, MD

7832 Johnson Avenue

Denver, CO 80241

Dear Dr. Bates

Re: Leah Hamlyn, Accident report E 14-78-9865

EXAMPLE:

Matthew R. Bates, MD

7832 Johnson Avenue

Denver, CO 80241

Dear Dr. Bates

RE: Leah Hamlyn
　　　Colorado Workers' Compensation Company
　　　Date of Injury: October 1, 200X

Modified Block Placement (see Fig. 14-1, *B*)
- Breaking the placement rule
- Lined up with the date
- A single line space after the last line of the address
- Use *RE:* or *Re:* to introduce the patient's full name
- A single line space between *Re:* and salutation

EXAMPLE:

October 14, 200X

Matthew R. Bates, MD

7832 Johnson Avenue

Denver, CO 80241

RE: Leah Hamlyn

Dear Dr. Bates

However, the reference line is *misplaced* so often that transcriptionists who place it correctly not only are in the minority but also begin to think that they are in error. There is no arbitrary rule about this line.

It is considered a part of the body of the letter. The problem with misplacement began when custom dictated that the "rule could be broken" when modified block format was used and the reference line was very brief. The second part of the problem occurred when dictators, unconcerned with style or format, gave information for the reference line before pronouncing the salutation. Finally, instead of inserting a single line space and then inserting the reference followed by another single line space, some transcriptionists inserted two line spaces both before and after the reference in the breaking-the-placement-rule format. Take care to place this line correctly, and begin by looking closely at and studying the following examples, which show incorrect placements. The correct versions are given in the preceding examples.

EXAMPLE: *Incorrect placement of reference line (out of place)*

Matthew R. Bates, MD

7832 Johnson Avenue

Denver, CO 80241

RE: Leah Hamlyn

Dear Dr. Bates:

EXAMPLE: *Another incorrect placement of reference line (too much space)*

Matthew R. Bates, MD

7832 Johnson Avenue

Denver, CO 80241

                                    RE: Leah Hamlyn

Dear Dr. Bates:

PERSONAL OR CONFIDENTIAL NOTATION

Personal or confidential notations are typed on the second line below the date, starting at the same point as the date. Type the notation in bold capital letters. Follow with the inside address on the fourth line down, depending on the length of the letter (see Fig. 14-5).

EXAMPLE: *Full-block format*

October 23, 200X
PERSONAL

TWO-PAGE LETTERS

If a letter is too long for one page, it must be appropriately continued on a second page or subsequent pages. The following rules apply:

1. Continue to the second page at the end of a paragraph whenever possible.
2. If a paragraph must be divided between pages, carry at least two lines of the paragraph to the second page.
3. Leave at least two lines of a paragraph on the first page.
4. Type no closer than 1 inch from the bottom of the page.
5. Do not divide the last word on the page.
6. Place headings 1 inch from the top of the page.
7. Leave two blank lines between the last line of the heading and the first line of the continuation of the letter. To do this, press the return or enter key three times at the end of the typed data in the heading.
8. To prevent the first line of a new paragraph from appearing as the last line on the page or to prevent the final line of a paragraph from printing on a new page, use the widow/orphan control feature of your word processing software. (An "orphan" is a single short line or the last few words of a paragraph left on the bottom of a page. A "widow" is a short line ending a paragraph that is positioned at the top of a page.)

The second sheet or continuation sheets are plain paper the same color, size, and quality as the letterhead paper. Headings are placed on the second sheet to identify it as belonging to the first sheet. There are two styles for page headings.

EXAMPLE: *Horizontal form*

RE: Leah Hamlyn   2   October 3, 200X
(patient's name) (page number)   (date)

EXAMPLE: *Vertical form*

RE: Leah Hamlyn
Page 2
October 3, 200X

NOTE: The page number is centered in the horizontal form. In a nonmedical letter, the name of the correspondent is listed in place of the patient's name.

Always check your printout to be sure that the page markings appear where they were intended, and take care to number each sheet in the series properly. It is an insult to ask the document author to sign a letter in which new page markings are on the bottom of the page or a few lines into a paragraph on page 2. If documents are printed off site and you do not have the opportunity to review the final printed document, be sure that someone on site checks them and the printer setup for you.

COPIES

The transcriptionist makes a copy of every item transcribed. Great care must be taken to ensure that a copy is made of every corrected original before the original is mailed. A document may need to be rushed to the mail after it is signed; therefore make it a habit to photocopy the letter *before* the signature is added. If corrections or additions are needed, make another copy and carefully discard the first photocopy. Be sure that good-quality paper is used for copies that are mailed out of the office. You might consider printing a duplicate of your original for the copy to be mailed out. The office copy becomes part of the patient's permanent record and is filed in his or her medical chart.

FILE NOTATION

You already have experience in naming your individual files. You may also need to code the document itself with your unique file name. This way transcribed documents may be retrieved easily and quickly when needed. You may be able to use your own file name; however, the dictator or organization may prefer that you use specified codes. If you can use your own codes, here are some hints for making it simple:

- Use minimum data: ID number for the dictator, patient name, and date.
- Use letters and numbers: for dates, use just the last digit of the year and then use 1 to 9 for the first nine months and o, n, and d (for October, November, and December) for the last three.
- Use a period for a separation mark.
- Place the file name as the last entry on the page.

- Decrease the font size to 8 or 9 point.
- Use the identical code as your saved file name.

EXAMPLES: *D.P.D: doctor.patient.date*

(using Fig. 14-1)
(Your ID number for Dr. Quinn is Q1)
Q1.Santee.277

Uncoded: Dr. Quinn dictated a letter about patient Santee on February 7, 2007.

(using Fig. 14-4)
(Your ID number for Dr. Wong is W3)
W3.Sanchez.327X

Uncoded: Dr. Wong dictated a letter about patient Sanchez on March 27, 200X.

PLACEMENT

Placement should have picture-frame symmetry and balance of the three blank margins and the letterhead. A good rule to follow for margins is to use 2-inch margins with short letters (fewer than 100 words), $1\frac{1}{2}$-inch margins with medium-length letters (100 to 200 words), and 1-inch margins with long letters (200 words).

To achieve symmetry and to squeeze a letter onto one page, you may adjust the spacing at the end of the letter (beginning with the typed signature line). Leave two, rather than three, line spaces for the signature and a single line space between the typed signature line, the reference initials, and other notations. If you are using the modified block format, you may type the reference initials on the same line as the typed signature line to save more space. If you still find that you cannot fit the letter on one page, reformat, widen the margins, and type the final paragraph on a second page.

The visual appeal of the letter is very important. Try to keep the right margin as even as possible, and try not to vary the line length by more than five characters.

To make a very short letter appear attractive on the page, widen the margins and increase the space between the date line and the letterhead; increase the space between the date line and the inside address.

Exercise 14-1: TYPING ASSIGNMENT

Directions:

- Retype the following material into letter form. Paragraph beginnings are indicated by the symbol ¶.
- Make a letterhead by using a computer macro to match the name of the speaker and inventing an appropriate address, or use any prepared letterhead paper as your instructor directs.
- Use full-block format, open punctuation, a reference line, and the current date. Refer to the vocabulary list at the beginning of the chapter if necessary. Pay close attention to placement and mechanics.
- Remember to use the proper state abbreviations.
- Prepare a file maintenance notation and insert it on the bottom of your document.

Save this letter after your instructor has checked it because you will need it for Self-Study 14-3.

The letter is from Laurel R. Denison, MD, and is to Gregory O. Theopolis, MD, 4509 Roessler Road, Detroit, Michigan 48224, and is in reference to Bobby West.

Dear Dr. Theopolis ¶ This 1-month-old baby was seen in my office yesterday for evaluation of difficulty with the right foot. ¶ The mother reports that this is the third sibling in the family. The older two siblings have no difficulty with the feet. When this baby was born, there was obvious deformity of the right foot, which has not corrected itself. ¶ Physical examination reveals that the hips are normal. There is internal tibial torsion. There is pes equinus; there is hindfoot supination and forefoot adduction. It is obvious that this baby has a congenital talipes equinovarus in the right foot. ¶ He was casted in the office yesterday. ¶ We do not know the prognosis yet since this is the first experience with the child. Prognosis depends on the congenital factors that caused the deformity, in the first place, and the elasticity of the tissues, in the second place. We will follow the child at weekly intervals. ¶ Thank you for the opportunity to see this baby. Sincerely

 Exercise 14-2: TYPING ASSIGNMENT

Directions:

- Retype the following material into letter form. Paragraph beginnings are indicated by the symbol ¶.
- Make a letterhead by using a computer macro to match the name of the speaker and inventing an appropriate address, or use any prepared letterhead paper as your instructor directs.
- Use modified block format, mixed punctuation, a reference line that breaks the placement rule, and the current date. Pay close attention to placement and mechanics.
- Remember to use the proper state abbreviations.
- Prepare a file maintenance notation and insert it on the bottom of your document.

This letter is from Emery R. Stuart, MD, to Walter W. von der Meyer, MD, 6754 Sunrise Circle, Ft. Lauderdale, Florida 33312. Copies should be sent to Dr. Barney P. Haber and Dr. Herbert W. Delft. (It is not necessary to make these copies; make just the notation.) The patient is Mrs. Nora George.

Dear Walter. ¶ This is a final follow-up letter on your patient, who, you will recall, was admitted to Sunrise View Hospital in February 200X for aortic valve replacement with a diagnosis of aortic stenosis. ¶ Nora has done well; she is in normal sinus rhythm, and she is well controlled on her Coumadin. She, at times, has some swelling of her hands and feet and has gained considerable weight since surgery. She needs continued close medical observation of her prothrombin level, which should be maintained at about 20% of normal, indefinitely. She should also be maintained on Lanoxin and may possibly require diuretics intermittently. ¶ We will not follow Nora any further for her heart disease. She has had an uneventful postoperative course and can continue her medical follow-up through your office or that of Dr. Herbert Delft, whichever you decide. ¶ Thank you very much for letting us see this patient with you and perform her surgery. We will be glad to see her at any time if there are any questions regarding her valve function or clinical course. Sincerely yours.

Save this letter after your instructor has checked it.

PARAGRAPHING

Paragraphs give the letter shape. The subject is divided into topics, and these topics constitute paragraphs. Paragraphs aid the reader by signaling a *new* idea with each division.

The paragraphing will contribute to the visual appeal of the letter and should be well balanced. Therefore the first and last paragraphs are usually brief, and the middle paragraphs are longer. Nevertheless, a paragraph may be of any length, and you should not hesitate to make one sentence a paragraph when it is appropriate. A series of brief paragraphs in a row, however, can be distracting to the reader. On the other hand, in a brief letter, a long paragraph may appear uninviting, and you may have to break the paragraph up to provide visual appeal.

Most speakers do not directly indicate the beginning (or end) of a paragraph, but they may give indirect clues with voice inflections or other subtle voice changes. Each new paragraph is begun with a sentence that suggests the topic or further explains it in a different way.

Correct paragraphing is not difficult with most medical letters because the letters generally follow a well-established pattern. The knowledge of this pattern will help you determine the paragraph breaks with or without vocal hints.

Physicians' letters dealing with patient care are usually narrative reports to workers' compensation carriers, consultation reports, letters of referral, follow-up notes, or discharge summaries.

The first paragraph is normally a brief introduction or explanation for the letter. In patient-related letters, the patient and his or her chief complaint are introduced in the initial brief paragraph. The next paragraph may contain the history of the complaint, along with a general description of any contributing problems in the patient's history. This material is followed in the third or fourth paragraph with the findings on examination of the patient. (At times, these remarks may be so brief that they constitute only one sentence.)

The next-to-last paragraph is confined to a medical opinion, prognosis, diagnosis, recommendation, report of tests, results of surgical procedures, detailed outlines for proposed care or treatment, evaluation of return-to-normal status, or summary. The subject is then closed in the final paragraph. At this point, the speaker may thank a referring physician, indicate what will take place next with the patient, or request some action on the patient's behalf.

◆ Exercise 14-3: SELF-STUDY

Directions: *Obtain your copy of Typing Assignment 14-1. Notice the paragraph breaks. Answer the following questions here or on a separate sheet of paper as your instructor directs.*

1. Notice that paragraph 1 is only one sentence long. What does the dictator do with this sentence?

   _____

2. Notice that paragraph 2 is three sentences long. Could the first of these sentences have been placed in

   the first paragraph? _____ Why or why not? _____

3. What is the speaker *doing* in paragraph 2? _____

4. Could any part of paragraph 3 logically be part of the second or fourth paragraph? _____

   Why or why not? _____

5. What is the speaker *doing* in paragraph 3? _____

6. Again, we have one sentence in paragraph 4. Could the transcriptionist have joined this sentence to

   paragraph 3? _____ What did the speaker *do* in this paragraph? _____

7. What is the subject of paragraph 5? _____ Could this paragraph be joined to paragraph 4?

   _____ Why or why not? _____

8. Notice the last line of paragraph 5. Could this have been a paragraph on its own? _____

   Why or why not? _____ Could you make it a part of the last paragraph? _____

   Why or why not? _____

9. What is the dictator doing in the final paragraph, number 6? _____ Do you think it is

   appropriate to have this single sentence standing as an entire paragraph? _____ Why or

   why not? _____

◆ Exercise 14-4: SELF-STUDY

Directions: *Obtain your copy of Typing Assignment 14-2. Notice the paragraph breaks. Answer the following questions here or on a separate sheet of paper as your instructor directs.*

1. Paragraph 1 tells us the type of document this is. What is it?

   _____

2. Paragraph 1: What is the subject(s) of this paragraph? _____

3. Paragraph 2: What is the speaker *doing* in this paragraph? _____ Could the last two

   sentences of this paragraph be used to form a new paragraph? _____

   Why or why not? _____

4. Paragraph 3: What is the dictator saying in this paragraph? _____ Could this paragraph

have been combined with the last two sentences of paragraph two? _____ Why or why

not? _____

5. Paragraph 4: What is the subject of this paragraph? _____ Should this be arranged as two

short paragraphs? _____

◇ Exercise 14-5: Typing Assignment

Directions:

- Retype the following material into letter form.
- Use full-block format, mixed punctuation, and the current date.
- Watch for proper paragraphing, placement, and mechanics.
- Use letterhead paper.
- Carefully mark your book where you think the paragraph breaks should be. Ask yourself whether they follow the pattern you have just learned. If they do not, consider some different breaks. Remember that there is sometimes more than one choice for a new paragraph break.
- On your final draft, write a number by each paragraph break.
- On a separate sheet of paper, type an explanation for that paragraph break, and turn it in with your letter.

The letter is from Steven A. Flores, MD, and is to another physician, Willard R. Beets, at 7895 West Sherman Street, San Diego, California 92111.

Dear Dr. Beets. I saw Mr. Tim Molton, your patient, in my office yesterday afternoon. As you will recall, Mr. Molton is a 49-year-old professional gardener who came to see you with a chronic cough and a history of expectoration of a whitish material. He brought the x-rays from your office with him, and I noted a fossa on the superficial surface of his lung. He was afebrile today and stated that he had been so since the onset of his symptoms. He did not complain of pain but did experience some dyspnea on exertion and some shortness of breath. I did not carry out a physical examination, but I did skin test him for both tuberculosis and coccidioidomycosis. I did not give him a prescription for any medication and will wait until we get the results of his skin tests. It seems to me that your diagnosis of his problem is correct, so we will proceed with that in mind. As you probably know, valley fever is endemic to San Diego; and since Mr. Molton was born and raised in New York State, he could be very susceptible. You may tell his employer that if he does have valley fever, he will have to convalesce for 1 month to 6 weeks, after which time he should be fully able to return to his normal duties. I will keep you posted on the results of his tests. Thank you very much for letting me help you with Mr. Molton's problem. Sincerely.

NOTE: *Please notice how many times the patient's name was used in this document. There is a trend toward using the patient's name only in the reference line. That style would be difficult for this dictator. You cannot change this pattern unless asked to do so. Always transcribe what is dictated.*

 Exercise 14-6: TYPING PRACTICE TEST

Directions:

- Retype this material in letter form. Use modified block format with indented paragraphs, mixed punctuation, and a reference line.
- Use letterhead paper.
- You will have to supply proper punctuation, capitalization, paragraphing, and mechanics. Good luck!

may 1 200X ian r wing m d 2261 arizona avenue suite b milwaukee wisconsin 53207 dear dr wing i saw your patient mrs elvira martinez in consultation in my office today. she brought the x-rays from your office with her. she was afebrile today but on questioning admitted a low grade fever over the past few days i removed the fluid as seen on your film of april 30 from the right lower lung field and she felt considerably more comfortable. on thoracentesis there was 50 mL of straw colored fluid her history is well known to you so i will not repeat it. on physical examination i found a well developed well nourished white female with minimal dyspnea there was no lymphadenopathy breath sounds were diminished somewhat on the right there was dullness at the right base the left lung was clear to percussion and auscultation. the remainder of the examination was negative. because of her history of chronic asthma i suggested she might consider bronchoscopy if this fluid reaccumulates. because she is a heavy smoker i insisted she stop smoking completely. if she does not she will not enjoy continuing good health although i have no idea of the actual prognosis. your patient has been returned to you for her continuing care i will be glad to see her again at any time you think it necessary thank you for letting me see this pleasant lady with you sincerely yours jon l mikosan m d ps i am enclosing a copy of the pathology report on the fluid as you can see it is negative

☰ ENVELOPE PREPARATION

A No. 10 ($4\frac{1}{8} \times 9\frac{1}{2}$ inch) envelope, printed to match your letterhead stationery, is always used with your $8\frac{1}{2} \times 11$ inch paper. The traditional style for addressing envelopes by using both uppercase and lowercase letters can now be read by the optical character readers used by the United States Postal Service. The proper formatting style that you have learned in this chapter confirms to Postal Service regulations: Single-spaced. Blocked each line to the left. Capitalized first letter of every word in the address. City, state, and ZIP code on the last line. Street address on the line above the city, state, and ZIP code. (If the apartment, suite, space, room, building, or development name or number cannot fit on the line with the street name and address, it is placed on the line above the street address.)

To print an envelope, do the following:

1. Select the default placement specifications for your printer with the proper-sized envelope. (This step ensures that the address falls within the optical character readers' read zone.)
2. Be certain that your inside address has been prepared properly.
3. Highlight the inside address on your letter.
4. Select the envelope feature of your word processing program.
5. Insert your envelope into the printer and select print. The address will be printed on the envelope.

If notations such as "Confidential," "Personal," or "Special Delivery" need to be typed on the envelope, do not type them below or alongside the address, the so-called read zone.

EXAMPLE:

Attention: Sales Director
National Paper Company
Franklin-Pratt Building
1492 Columbus Avenue North
Syracuse, NY 13224

EXAMPLE: *Poorly arranged format*

Victory R. Langworthy, MD
Medical Director
West View Community Hospital and Inland
Medical Center, Inc.
321 Roseview Drive
St. Louis, MO 63139

EXAMPLE: *Better arrangement*

Victory R. Langworthy, MD, Medical Director
West View Community Hospital and
Inland Medical Center, Inc.
321 Roseview Drive
St. Louis, MO 63139

EXAMPLE: *Poorly arranged format*

Miss Josie M. Brooks
1879 Westchester Boulevard, Apartment 170 B
Normal Heights, SD 57701

EXAMPLE: *Better arrangement*

Miss Josie M. Brooks
Apartment 170 B
1879 Westchester Boulevard
Normal Heights, SD 57701

If you are unable to print an envelope with your computer, prepare the envelope exactly as you have done your inside address. Begin typing 2 inches down from the top of the envelope and 4 inches from the left edge, so that your address will appear in the proper read zone.

Mail addressed to a foreign country should have the name of that country as the last line of the address block. Place the name two line spaces below line that has the city, state or province, and postal code. Coding varies from country to country. Type the name of the country in full capital letters.

EXAMPLE:

Prof. Wolfgang Hinz
Art Director, Rhineland Institute
Schulstrasse 21
Siegelbach, Pfalz 6751

GERMANY

EXAMPLE:

Ms. Marijane N. Woods
Manager, Abbott Realty
1804 31st Avenue SW
Calgary, AB T2T 1S7

CANADA

NOTE: There is one letter space between the city name and the two-letter abbreviation for the province or territory, followed by two letter spaces and the six-character postal code.

Mail addressed to members of the military who have Army Post Office (APO) or Fleet Post Office (FPO) addresses is set up as follows:

EXAMPLE:

Warrant Officer John R. Meadows, USAF
Company R
5th Infantry Regiment
APO New York, NY 09801

If your mail is addressed to a private mailbox (rented from a private company), insert the private mail box number (PMB) above the delivery address.

EXAMPLE:

Mr. Steven R. Madruga
PMB 9982
115 South Olive Street
Philadelphia, PA 10101

◆ Exercise 14-7: TYPING PRACTICE TEST

Directions: *Prepare envelopes for the letters you typed in Typing Assignments 14-1 and 14-2. Do not be concerned about the names (if any) in the return address block.*

≋ SIGNING AND MAILING

When the letter is ready for signature, use a paper clip to attach the envelope (and any enclosures) to the top of the letter, with the flap over the letterhead. Until you present the letter for signature, keep it in a folder to keep it clean and out of the view of any passerby. After the letter is signed and before you place it in its envelope, make sure that there are no smudges and that all enclosures are attached.

Fold the letter by bringing the bottom of the page one third up the page and then creasing. Next, fold the upper third down to within $\frac{1}{2}$ inch of the first crease and make the second crease. Insert the letter into the envelope so that when it is removed, it will open right side up. Fig. 14-6 illustrates the proper way to fold a letter.

On occasion, the dictator is unavailable to sign the mail but requests that it be sent out rather than delayed for his or her signature. You should handle this situation as directed, by signing his or her name and then adding your initials, by typing below the signature area "Dictated but not signed" and adding your initials, or by simply signing his or her name. Be particularly careful that the letter is completely error-free in every way. Keep the copy available for the dictator's return rather than filing it immediately.

No. 10 Envelope (9-½ × 4-⅛ Inches)

Fold the letter by bringing the bottom of the page one third up the page and crease. Fold down the upper third within ½ inch of the first fold and crease. Insert the last creased edge into the envelope first.

Fig. 14-6 Proper way to fold a letter for insertion into a No. 10 envelope. *(From Diehl MO:* Medical transcription guide: do's and don'ts, *ed 3, St Louis, Elsevier, 2004.)*

≋ A FINAL NOTE

Letterhead stationery in addition to the standard $8\frac{1}{2} \times 11$ inch type is often kept for brief letters or secretarial correspondence. There are two standard sizes: Monarch ($7\frac{1}{2} \times 10\frac{1}{2}$ inches) and Baronial ($5\frac{1}{2} \times 8\frac{1}{2}$ inches). Envelopes are printed to match these two sizes, and papers and envelopes should *not* be mixed. Follow the same general guidelines in preparing the envelopes, except that you should begin the address $2\frac{1}{2}$ inches from the left edge of the envelope, rather than 4 inches.

◆ Exercise 14-8: TYPING REVIEW TEST

Instruction Sheet for Retyping the Following Material into Letter Form

1. Paper: use letterhead, size $8\frac{1}{2} \times 11$

2. Envelope: use No. 10

3. Copies: single

4. Equipment: computer

5. Format: modified block, open punctuation

6. Date: May 16 plus current year

7. Mechanical needs: proper paragraphing, placement on page, *some* internal punctuation, other mechanics as may be required

8. Placement on page: proper alignment for attractiveness and "eye appeal"

9. Patient's name: LeeAnn Jensen

10. Dictator: Dr. Randolph R. Bever

11. Addressed to: Dr. Norman C. Kisbey Jr, at Post Office Box 1734, Washington, DC 20034

Dear Dr. Kisbey. Today I have seen your patient in neurosurgical consultation at your request. As you know, she is a very pleasant 40-year-old, right-handed lady who comes in with a history of seizure-like episodes beginning in January of 200X. These seizures consist of a sense of unreality and a feeling as though she were observing herself as an actress on a stage. Prior to the onset of, or associated with, these seizure-like episodes, she has noted a smell of heavy fragrant flowers. She describes the smell of the flowers as slightly unpleasant, almost funereal. Each of these so-called seizure states lasts only a few seconds and is followed by a tremendous feeling of unreality. This is also associated with a great fear that she won't be able to move and she always gets up and walks around afterward to make sure she is not paralyzed. During the episode there is no loss of cognitive ability and she is able to converse with her husband and she has virtually total recall for the entire episode. She had episodes, as described, in January and February of 200X, four in March and five in April. There is no family history of seizures. There is a story of a mild head injury at age ten and apparently she was in a moderately severe motorcycle accident about 15 years ago which resulted in a broken mandible. The neurological examination at this time is essentially normal. The extraocular movements and fundi show no abnormalities. The visual fields and confrontation testing are intact. There is no Babinski sign. The only abnormality that I could detect in the entire examination was a stiffened right shoulder which she tells me came on after a lengthy game of tennis. I could palpate no masses over the head and there were no audible bruits over the head or over either carotid bifurcation. She has been on a dose of 30 mg of phenobarbital b.i.d. and did not care to add any Dilantin. The phenobarbital keeps her in a drowsy state consequently she is not able to think creatively or participate in sports activities. She brought with her the skull x-rays and brain scan taken at University Hospital and I have reviewed them. In my opinion, they are within normal limits. In addition, she brought with her several EEG records which I have gone over. The neurologist's summary is enclosed. I thought there was a slight abnormality present in the right temporal area. At this time, I do not believe there is evidence of intracranial mass lesion or of focal neurological deficit. A number of features argue against interpreting her spells as true psychomotor seizures: Firstly, the fact that the aura is unusual, and secondly the fact that she has total recall for the entire episode. Thirdly, there is the fact that she has no postictal abnormality. My tendency at this time would be to gradually switch her over to Dilantin 30 mg t.i.d. and, in addition, place her on Diamox 125 mg each morning. I suggest the Diamox because she tells me that the "seizure" episodes tend to come on within a few days of her menstrual periods. We have agreed that if she is not markedly improved within a period of one month on this regimen she would come into the hospital for 4-vessel angiography. Thank you for the privilege of seeing this interesting patient and for thinking of me in connection with her problems. Yours sincerely. Randolph R. Bever, MD Professor of Neurosurgery, Weeks Medical School.

BLOTCHETT TOURS

8888 Malarky Drive
Fun Valley, UT 99999

1	4/1/0X

2 Ms. Glendora Kirsch
3 211 Elm Ave. Apt a
4 Losangeles, Cal. 99999

5 Dear Miss Kirsch,

6 It seems that each year about this time we sent you a
7 letter inquiring about your plans for this sumer. Each
8 year for the passed three years now we have had no answer.

9   According to our records, you wrote Blotchett Tours inquiring
10 about some information concerning different tours. We sent you our price lists,
11 departure date list, special off season excursions, etc. Wouldn't it be nice if you
12 could plan to travel this summer. Why not reserve
13 a place for yourself in one of our package deals..

14   Enclosed herewith please find an application blank for
15 you to fill out. Just return it in the business reply
16 envelope with your small check for only $35 and your Place will be assured.
17 Naturally your deposit will aply toward the full purchase of your tour. We are
18 guaranteed and bonded.

19 We will will be looking for your response soon.

20 Very Truly Yours,

21 Hank Behn, Sales rep.

≋ FOOD FOR THOUGHT

Imagine for a few minutes that you have just received the letter above in the mail. Try to read it with the assumption that it is to you personally. What is your reaction to the letter? How many errors can you find? Briefly express your opinion on a separate sheet of paper or as your instructor directs.

If nothing else, you have formed a definite opinion about this company that is based entirely on the written representation of them. It is doubtful that you would consider asking them for any information about their tours. Nor would you give them further thought other than to wonder how they stay in business. Certainly, you would not feel they could be trusted to handle a tour because they are unable to handle their correspondence.

The recipients of your office correspondence will be equally affected by the preparation and thought that go into the letters they receive from your office. It is inconsistent to ignore the fact that careless preparation could affect their opinion of *your* employer.

Student Name (print)	Instructor's Name (print)	Date

DOCUMENT EACH PATIENT IN PROPER CHARTING FORMAT.

VITAL SIGNS

	Date/Time	Patient	T	P	R	B/P	MA Signature
1.							
2.							
3.							
4.							
5.							

INJECTIONS

	Date/Time	Patient	Location	Reactions	MA Signature
INTRADERMAL					
1.					
2.					
SUBCUTANEOUS					
1.					
2.					
INTRAMUSCULAR (DELTOID)					
1.					
2.					
INTRAMUSCULAR (GLUTEAL-8th or 9th module students use Z-track technique)					
1.					
2.					

VENIPUNCTURE

	Date/Time	Patient	Location	Reactions	MA Signature
EVACUATED-TUBE METHOD					
1.					
2.					
3.					
SYRINGE METHOD [8th or 9th module students only]					
1.					
BUTTERFLY METHOD [8th or 9th module students only]					
1.					

Student Name _____ Date _____

CHECKLIST: PERFORM PROPER HANDWASHING FOR MEDICAL ␣PSIS

TASK: Prevent the spread of pathogens by aseptically washing hands, following S␣␣d Precautions.

CONDITIONS: Given the proper equipment and supplies, the student will be r␣␣ ␣ to demonstrate the proper method of performing handwashing for medical asepsis.

EQUIPMENT AND SUPPLIES
- Liquid antibacterial soap
- Nailbrush or orange stick
- Paper towels
- Warm running water
- Regular waste container

STANDARDS: Complete the procedure within _____ minutes and ␣␣e a minimum score of _____%.

Time began _____ Time ended _____

Steps	Possible Points	First Attempt	Second Attempt
1. Assemble all supplies and equipment.	5		
2. Remove rings and watch or push the watch up ␣␣␣␣earm.	5		
3. Stand close to the sink, without allowing clot␣␣␣␣␣th the sink.	5		
4. Turn on the faucets, using a paper to␣	5		
5. Adjust the water temperature to ␣␣␣␣␣ ␣␣cold. Explain why proper water temperatu␣	10		
6. Discard the paper towel ␣␣␣␣␣␣ ␣ontainer.	5		
7. Wet hands and wrist␣ ␣␣␣␣␣ ␣␣er, and apply liquid antibacterial soap. ␣␣␣␣␣ ␣ower than the elbows at all times. Hands ␣␣␣␣␣ ␣nside of the sink.	10		
8. Work soap into ␣␣␣␣␣␣ ␣ the palms together using a circular motion.	10		
9. Clean the finge␣ ␣␣␣ ␣ailbrush or an orange stick.	5		
10. Rinse hands th␣␣ ␣␣␣der running water, holding them in a downward p␣␣ ␣ allowing soap and water to run off the fingertips.	10		
11. Repeat the ␣␣␣␣ ␣ if hands are grossly contaminated.	10		
12. Dry the ha␣␣ ␣tly and thoroughly using a clean paper towel. Discard th␣ ␣␣vel in proper waste container.	10		
13. Using a d␣␣␣␣ ␣turn the faucets off, clean the area around th␣␣ ␣␣rd the towel in regular waste container.	10		
Total Point␣ *Instru␣	100		

Comments: ␣␣␣␣␣␣␣␣␣␣␣␣␣␣␣ Instructor's Signature _____

Student Name _____   Date _____

CHECKLIST: APPLY AND REMOVE CLEAN, DISPOSABLE (NONSTERILE) GLOVES

TASK: Apply and remove disposable (nonsterile) gloves properly.

CONDITIONS: Given the proper equipment and supplies, the student will be required to apply and remove nonsterile disposable gloves.

EQUIPMENT AND SUPPLIES
- Alcohol-based hand rub
- Nonsterile disposable gloves
- Biohazardous waste container

STANDARDS: Complete the procedure within _____ minutes and achieve a minimum score of _____%.

Time began _____   Time ended _____

Steps	Possible Points	First Attempt	Second Attempt
Applying Gloves			
1. Assemble all supplies and equipment.	5		
2. Select the correct size and style of gloves according to office policy.	5		
3. Sanitize hands.	10		
4. Apply gloves and adjust them to ensure a proper fit.	5		
5. Inspect the gloves carefully for tears, holes, or punctures before and after application.	5		
Removing Gloves			
1. Grasp the outside of one glove with the first three fingers of the other hand, approximately 1 to 2 inches below the cuff.	10		
2. Stretch the soiled glove by pulling it away from the hand, and slowly pull the glove downward off the hand. Usually the dominant hand is ungloved first.	10		
3. After the glove is pulled free from the hand, ball it in the palm of the gloved hand.	10		
4. Remove the other glove by placing the index and middle fingers of the ungloved hand inside the glove of the gloved hand; turn the cuff downward. Be careful not to touch the outside of the soiled glove.	10		
5. Stretch the glove away from the hand and pull the cuff downward over the hand and over the balled-up glove, turning it inside out with the balled glove inside.	10		
6. Carefully dispose of the gloves in a marked biohazardous waste container.	10		
7. Sanitize hands.	10		
Total Points Possible	100		

Comments: Total Points Earned _____   Instructor's Signature _____

Student Name _____ Date _____

CHECKLIST: MEASURE ORAL BODY TEMPERATURE USING A MERCURY-FREE GLASS THERMOMETER

TASK: Accurately measure and record a patient's oral temperature.

CONDITIONS: Given the proper equipment and supplies, the student will be required to role-play with another student or an instructor the proper method for measuring an oral body temperature using a mercury-free glass thermometer.

EQUIPMENT AND SUPPLIES
- Mercury-free glass oral thermometer
- Thermometer sheath
- Disposable gloves
- Biohazardous waste container
- Pen
- Patient's medical record

STANDARDS: Complete the procedure within _____ minutes and achieve a minimum score of _____%.

Time began _____   Time ended _____

Steps	Possible Points	First Attempt	Second Attempt
1. Assemble all supplies and equipment.	5		
2. Sanitize hands.	5		
3. Greet and identify the patient.	5		
4. Explain the procedure to the patient.	5		
5. Determine if the patient has recently had a hot or cold beverage to drink or has smoked.	5		
6. Put on gloves and remove the thermometer from its holder, without touching the bulb end with your fingers.	5		
7. Inspect the thermometer for chips or cracks.	5		
8. Read the thermometer to ensure that the temperature is well below 96.0° F. Shake down thermometer as necessary.	5		
9. Cover the thermometer with a protective thermometer sheath.	5		
10. Ask the patient to open his or her mouth and place the probe tip under the tongue.	5		
11. Ask the patient to hold, not clasp, the thermometer between the teeth and to close the lips snugly around it to form an airtight seal.	5		
12. Leave the thermometer in place for a minimum of 3 minutes.	5		
13. Remove the thermometer and read the results.	10		

Steps	Possible Points	First Attempt	Second Attempt
14. Holding the thermometer by the stem, remove the protective sheath and discard in a biohazardous waste container.	5		
15. Sanitize the thermometer following the manufacturer's recommendations.	5		
16. Remove gloves and discard in biohazardous waste container.	5		
17. Return the thermometer to its storage container.	5		
18. Sanitize hands.	5		
19. Document the results in the patient's medical record.	5		
Total Points Possible	100		

Comments: Total Points Earned _____   Instructor's Signature _____

Student Name _____   Date _____

CHECKLIST: MEASURE BODY TEMPERATURE USING A DISPOSABLE ORAL THERMOMETER

TASK: Accurately measure and record a patient's oral temperature using a disposable thermometer.

CONDITIONS: Given the proper equipment and supplies, the student will be required to perform the proper method for measuring an oral temperature using a disposable oral thermometer.

EQUIPMENT AND SUPPLIES
- Disposable thermometer
- Disposable gloves
- Biohazardous waste container
- Pen
- Patient's medical record

STANDARDS: Complete the procedure within _____ minutes and achieve a minimum score of _____%.

Time began _____   Time ended _____

Steps	Possible Points	First Attempt	Second Attempt
1. Assemble all supplies and equipment.	5		
2. Sanitize hands.	5		
3. Greet and identify the patient.	5		
4. Explain the procedure to the patient.	5		
5. Determine if the patient has recently had a hot or cold beverage to drink or has smoked.	5		
6. Put on disposable gloves.	5		
7. Open the thermometer packaging.	5		
8. Place the thermometer under the patient's tongue and wait 60 seconds.	5		
9. Remove the thermometer and read the results by looking at the colored dots.	5		
10. Discard the thermometer and gloves in a biohazardous waste container.	5		
11. Sanitize hands.	5		
12. Document results in the patient's medical record.	10		
Total Points Possible	65		

Comments: Total Points Earned _____   Instructor's Signature _____

Student Name _____   Date _____

CHECKLIST: MEASURE BODY TEMPERATURE USING A TYMPANIC THERMOMETER

TASK: Accurately measure and record a patient's temperature using a tympanic thermometer.

CONDITIONS: Given the proper equipment and supplies, the student will be required to role-play with another student the proper method for measuring the tympanic temperature using a tympanic thermometer.

EQUIPMENT AND SUPPLIES
- Tympanic thermometer
- Disposable probe cover
- Pen
- Patient's medical record
- Biohazardous waste container

STANDARDS: Complete the procedure within _____ minutes and achieve a minimum score of _____%.

Time began _____   Time ended _____

Steps	Possible Points	First Attempt	Second Attempt
1. Assemble all supplies and equipment.	5		
2. Sanitize hands.	5		
3. Greet and identify the patient.	5		
4. Explain the procedure to the patient.	5		
5. Remove the thermometer from the charger.	5		
6. Check to be sure the mode for interpretation of temperature is set to "oral" mode.	10		
7. Check the lens probe to be sure it is clean and not scratched.	5		
8. Turn on the thermometer.	5		
9. Insert the probe firmly into a disposable plastic probe cover.	5		
10. Wait for a digital "READY" display.	5		
11. With the hand that is not holding the probe, pull adult patient's ear up and back to straighten the ear canal. For a small child, pull the patient's ear down and back to straighten the ear canal.	10		
12. Insert the probe into the patient's ear and tightly seal the ear canal opening.	10		
13. Position the probe.	5		
14. Depress the activation button.	5		
15. Release the activation button and wait 2 seconds.	5		
16. Remove the probe from the ear and read the temperature.	5		

Steps	Possible Points	First Attempt	Second Attempt
17. Note the reading, making sure that the screen displays "oral" as the mode of interpretation.	5		
18. Discard the probe cover in a biohazardous waste container.	5		
19. Replace the thermometer on the charger base.	5		
20. Sanitize hands.	5		
21. Document results in the patient's medical record using Ⓣ to indicate a tympanic temperature was obtained.	10		
Total Points Possible	125		

Comments: Total Points Earned _____   Instructor's Signature _____

Student Name _____   Date _____

CHECKLIST: MEASURE RADIAL PULSE

TASK: Accurately measure and record the rate, rhythm, and quality of a patient's pulse.

CONDITIONS: Given the proper equipment and supplies, the student will be required to role-play with another student or an instructor the proper method for measuring a patient's radial pulse.

EQUIPMENT AND SUPPLIES
- Watch with a second hand
- Patient's medical record
- Pen

STANDARDS: Complete the procedure within _____ minutes and achieve a minimum score of _____%.

Time began _____   Time ended _____

Steps	Possible Points	First Attempt	Second Attempt
1. Assemble all supplies and equipment.	5		
2. Sanitize hands.	5		
3. Greet and identify the patient.	5		
4. Explain the procedure to the patient.	5		
5. Observe the patient for any signs that may indicate an increase or a decrease in the pulse rate due to external conditions.	5		
6. Position the patient.	5		
7. Place the index and middle fingertips over the radial artery while resting the thumb on the back of the patient's wrist.	10		
8. Apply moderate, gentle pressure directly over the site until the pulse can be felt.	10		
9. Count the pulse for 60 seconds.	10		
10. Sanitize hands.	5		
11. Document the results in the patient's chart; include the pulse rate, rhythm, and volume.	10		
Total Points Possible	75		

Comments: Total Points Earned _____   Instructor's Signature _____

Student Name _____   Date _____

CHECKLIST: MEASURE RESPIRATORY RATE

TASK: Accurately measure and record a patient's respiratory rate.

CONDITIONS: Given the proper equipment and supplies, the student will be required to role-play with another student the proper method for measuring a patient's respiratory rate.

EQUIPMENT AND SUPPLIES
- Watch with a second hand
- Patient's medical record
- Pen

STANDARDS: Complete the procedure within _____ minutes and achieve a minimum score of _____%.

Time began _____   Time ended _____

Steps	Possible Points	First Attempt	Second Attempt
1. Assemble all supplies and equipment.	5		
2. Sanitize hands.	5		
3. Greet and identify the patient.	5		
4. Explain the procedure to the patient.	5		
5. Count each respiration for 30 seconds and multiply by 2. (If breathing pattern is irregular, count for 1 full minute.)	15		
6. Sanitize hands.	5		
7. Document the results in the patient's chart; include the respiratory rate, rhythm, and depth. Document any irregularities found.	10		
Total Points Possible	50		

Comments: Total Points Earned _____   Instructor's Signature _____

Student Name _____   Date _____

CHECKLIST: PREPARE A PARENTERAL MEDICATION FROM A VIAL

TASK: From a vial, measure the ordered medication dosage into a 3-mL hypodermic syringe for injection.

CONDITIONS: Given the proper equipment and supplies, the student will prepare a parenteral medication from a vial in a 3-mL syringe.

EQUIPMENT AND SUPPLIES
- Vial of medication as ordered by physician
- 70% isopropyl alcohol wipes
- 3-mL syringe for ordered dose
- Needle with safety device appropriate for site of injection
- 2 × 2-inch gauze squares
- Biohazardous waste container
- Patient's medical record

STANDARDS: Complete the procedure within _____ minutes and achieve a minimum score of _____%.

Time began _____   Time ended _____

Steps	Possible Points	First Attempt	Second Attempt
1. Sanitize hands.	5		
2. Verify the order, and assemble equipment and supplies.	5		
3. Check expiration date of the medication.	10		
4. Follow the "seven rights" of medication administration.	10		
5. Check the medication against the physician's order three times before administration.	10		
6. Check the patient's medical record for drug allergies or conditions that may contraindicate the injection.	10		
7. Calculate the correct dose to be given, as necessary.	10		
8. Prepare the vial, needle, and syringe.	5		
9. Draw the amount of air into the syringe for the amount of medication to be administered.	5		
10. Remove the cover from the needle and insert the needle into the vial.	10		
11. Inject the air into vial and fill the syringe with the medication.	10		
12. Remove any air bubbles and recap the needle as necessary.	10		
13. Compare the medication to the vial label, and return the medication to its proper storage.	5		
14. Sanitize hands.	10		
Total Points Possible	115		

Comments: Total Points Earned _____   Instructor's Signature _____

Student Name _____   Date _____

CHECKLIST: ADMINISTER AN INTRADERMAL INJECTION

TASK
- Identify the correct syringe, needle gauge, and length for an intradermal injection.
- Select and prepare an appropriate site for an intradermal injection.
- Demonstrate the correct technique to administer an intradermal injection.
- Document an intradermal injection correctly in the medical record.

CONDITIONS: Given the proper equipment and supplies, the student will prepare and administer an intradermal injection.

EQUIPMENT AND SUPPLIES
- Nonsterile disposable gloves
- Medication as ordered by physician
- Tuberculin syringe for ordered dose
- Needle with safety device (26 or 27 gauge, $3/8$ inch to $1/2$ inch)
- 2 × 2-inch sterile gauze
- 70% isopropyl alcohol wipes
- Written patient instructions for post testing as appropriate
- Sharps container
- Biohazardous waste container
- Patient's medical record

STANDARDS: Complete the procedure within _____ minutes and achieve a minimum score of _____%.

Time began _____   Time ended _____

Steps	Possible Points	First Attempt	Second Attempt
1. Sanitize hands.	5		
2. Verify the order, and assemble equipment and supplies.	5		
3. Check expiration date of the medication.	10		
4. Follow the "seven rights" of medication administration.	10		
5. Check the medication against the physician's order three times before administration.	10		
6. Check the patient's medical record for drug allergies or conditions that may contraindicate the injection.	10		
7. Calculate the dose to be given, if necessary.	15		
8. Follow the correct procedure for drawing the medication into syringe.	10		
9. Greet and identify the patient, and explain the procedure to the patient.	10		
10. Select an appropriate injection site and properly position the patient as necessary to expose the site adequately.	10		
11. Apply gloves.	5		

Steps	Possible Points	First Attempt	Second Attempt
12. Prepare the injection site.	10		
13. While the prepared site is drying, remove the cover from the needle.	10		
14. Pull the skin taut at the injection site.	10		
15. Inject the medication between the dermis and epidermis. Create a wheal.	10		
16. Withdraw the needle from the injection site at the same angle as it was inserted, and activate the safety device immediately.	10		
17. Dab the area with the gauze. Do not rub.	5		
18. Discard in the syringe sharps container. Remove gloves and discard in a biohazardous container.	5		
19. Sanitize the hands.	5		
20. Check the patient.	5		
21. Read or discuss with the patient the test results.	10		
22. Sanitize hands.	5		
23. Document the procedure.	10		
Mantoux Test			
24. Check to be sure test was given 48 to 72 hours earlier.	10		
25. After sanitizing the hands and applying nonsterile gloves, gently rub the test site with a finger and lightly palpate for induration.	10		
26. Using the tape that comes with the medication, measure the diameter of the area of induration from edge to edge.	10		
27. Record the area of induration and notify the health care provider of the measurement if not within the negative range.	10		
28. Record the reading in the medical record.	10		
Total Points Possible	245		

Comments: Total Points Earned _____   Instructor's Signature _____

Student Name _____   Date _____

CHECKLIST: ADMINISTER A SUBCUTANEOUS INJECTION

TASK
- Identify the correct syringe, needle gauge, and length for a subcutaneous injection.
- Select and prepare an appropriate site for a subcutaneous injection.
- Demonstrate the correct technique to administer a subcutaneous injection.
- Document a subcutaneous injection correctly in the medical record.

CONDITIONS: Given the proper equipment and supplies, the student will prepare and administer a subcutaneous injection.

EQUIPMENT AND SUPPLIES
- Nonsterile disposable gloves
- Medication as ordered by physician
- Appropriate syringe for ordered dose of medication
- Appropriate needle with safety device
- 2 × 2-inch sterile gauze
- 70% Isopropyl alcohol wipes
- Sharps container
- Biohazardous waste container
- Patient's medical record

STANDARDS: Complete the procedure within _____ minutes and achieve a minimum score of _____%.

Time began _____   Time ended _____

Steps	Possible Points	First Attempt	Second Attempt
1. Sanitize hands.	5		
2. Verify the order, and assemble equipment and supplies.	5		
3. Check expiration date of the medication.	10		
4. Follow the "seven rights" of medication administration.	10		
5. Check the medication against the physician's order three times before administration.	10		
6. Check the patient's medical record for drug allergies or conditions that may contraindicate the injection.	10		
7. Calculate the correct dose to be given, if necessary.	15		
8. Follow the procedure for drawing the medication into the syringe.	5		
9. Greet and identify the patient, and explain the procedure.	10		
10. Select an appropriate injection site and properly position the patient as necessary to expose the site.	10		
11. Apply gloves.	5		
12. Prepare the injection site.	10		

Steps	Possible Points	First Attempt	Second Attempt
13. While the prepared site is drying, remove the cover from the needle.	5		
14. Pinch the skin at the injection site and puncture the skin quickly and smoothly, making sure the needle is kept at a 45-degree angle.	10		
15. Aspirate the syringe to check for blood. If no blood is present, inject the medication.	10		
16. Place a gauze pad over the injection site and quickly withdraw the needle from the injection site at the same angle at which it was inserted.	10		
17. Massage the injection site, if appropriate.	5		
18. Discard the syringe and needle into a rigid biohazardous container.	5		
19. Remove gloves and discard in a biohazardous waste container.	5		
20. Sanitize the hands.	5		
21. Check on the patient.	5		
22. Document procedure.	10		
Total Points Possible	175		

Comments: Total Points Earned _____   Instructor's Signature _____

Student Name _____   Date _____

CHECKLIST: ADMINISTER AN INTRAMUSCULAR INJECTION TO AN ADULT

TASK
- Identify the correct syringe, needle gauge, and length for an adult intramuscular injection.
- Select and prepare an appropriate site for a pediatric intramuscular injection.
- Demonstrate the correct technique to administer an intramuscular injection.
- Document an intramuscular injection correctly in the medical record.

CONDITIONS: Given the proper equipment and supplies, the student will prepare and administer an intramuscular injection to an adult patient.

EQUIPMENT AND SUPPLIES
- Nonsterile disposable gloves
- Medication as ordered by physician
- Appropriate syringe for ordered medication dose
- Appropriate needle with safety device (21 or 25 gauge, 1 inch to 1½ inch)
- 2 × 2-inch sterile gauze
- 70% isopropyl alcohol wipes
- Sharps container
- Biohazardous waste container
- Patient's medical record

STANDARDS: Complete the procedure within _____ minutes and achieve a minimum score of _____%.

Time began _____   Time ended _____

Steps	Possible Points	First Attempt	Second Attempt
1. Sanitize hands.	5		
2. Verify the order, and assemble equipment and supplies.	5		
3. Follow the "seven rights" of medication administration.	10		
4. Check the medication against the physician's order three times before administration.	10		
5. Check the patient's medical record for drug allergies or conditions that may contraindicate the injection.	10		
6. Check expiration date of the medication.	10		
7. Calculate the correct dose to be given.	20		
8. Greet and identify the patient, and explain the procedure.	10		
9. Select an appropriate injection site by amount and density of medication. Properly position the patient as necessary to expose the site adequately.	10		
10. Apply gloves.	5		
11. Prepare the injection site.	10		
12. While the prepared site is drying, remove the cover from the needle.	10		

Steps	Possible Points	First Attempt	Second Attempt
13. Secure the skin at the injection site.	10		
14. Puncture the skin quickly and smoothly, making sure the needle is kept at a 90-degree angle.	10		
15. Aspirate the syringe.	10		
16. Inject medication using proper technique for density of medication.	10		
17. Place a gauze pad over the injection site and quickly withdraw the needle from the injection site at the same angle at which it was inserted. Activate the safety shield over the needle.	10		
18. Massage the injection site if appropriate for medication.	10		
19. Discard the syringe and needle into a sharps container.	5		
20. Remove gloves and discard in a biohazardous waste container.	5		
21. Sanitize the hands.	5		
22. Check on the patient.	10		
23. Document procedure.	10		
Total Points Possible	210		

Comments: Total Points Earned _____   Instructor's Signature _____

Student Name _____   Date _____

CHECKLIST: ADMINISTER AN INTRAMUSCULAR INJECTION USING THE Z-TRACK TECHNIQUE

TASK: Demonstrate the correct technique to administer an intramuscular injection using the Z-track technique.

CONDITIONS: Given the proper equipment and supplies, the student will prepare and administer an intramuscular injection using the Z-track technique.

EQUIPMENT AND SUPPLIES
- Nonsterile disposable gloves
- Medication order by physician
- Appropriate syringe for ordered dose
- Appropriate needle with safety device
- 2 × 2-inch sterile gauze
- 70% isopropyl alcohol wipes
- Biohazardous waste container
- Patient's medical record

STANDARDS: Complete the procedure within _____ minutes and achieve a minimum score of _____%.

Time began _____   Time ended _____

Steps	Possible Points	First Attempt	Second Attempt
1. Sanitize hands.	5		
2. Verify the order, and assemble equipment and supplies.	5		
3. Follow the "seven rights" of medication administration.	10		
4. Check the medication against the physician's order three times before administration.	10		
5. Check the patient's medical record for drug allergies or conditions that may contraindicate the injection.	10		
6. Check expiration date of the medication.	10		
7. Calculate the correct dose to be given.	20		
8. Follow the correct procedure for drawing the medication into syringe.	10		
9. Greet and identify the patient, and explain the procedure to the patient.	15		
10. Select an appropriate injection site and properly position the patient.	5		
11. Apply disposable gloves.	5		
12. Prepare the injection site.	5		
13. While the prepared site is drying, remove the cover from the needle.	5		

Steps	Possible Points	First Attempt	Second Attempt
14. Secure the skin at the injection site by pushing the skin away from the injection site.	10		
15. Puncture the skin quickly and smoothly, making sure the needle is kept at a 90-degree angle.	10		
16. Continue to hold the tissue in place while aspirating and injecting the medication.	15		
17. Inject the medication.	10		
18. Withdraw the needle.	10		
19. Release the traction on the skin to seal the track as the needle is being removed. Activate safety shield over needle.	10		
20. Discard the syringe and needle into a rigid biohazardous container.	5		
21. Remove gloves and discard in a biohazardous waste container.	5		
22. Sanitize the hands.	5		
23. Check on the patient.	5		
24. Document the procedure.	5		
25. Clean the equipment and examination room.	10		
Total Points Possible	215		

Comments: Total Points Earned _____   Instructor's Signature _____

Student Name _____   Date _____

CHECKLIST: PERFORM VENIPUNCTURE USING THE EVACUATED-TUBE METHOD (COLLECTION OF MULTIPLE TUBES)

TASK: Obtain a venous blood specimen acceptable for testing using the evacuated-tube system.

CONDITIONS: Given the proper equipment and supplies, the student will be required to perform a venipuncture using the evacuated-tube system method of collection.

EQUIPMENT AND SUPPLIES
- Nonsterile disposable gloves
- Personal protective equipment (PPE) as required
- Tourniquet (latex-free)
- Evacuated tube holder
- Evacuated tube multidraw needle (21 or 22 gauge, 1 or 1½ inch) with safety guards
- Evacuated blood tubes for requested tests with labels (correct nonadditive or additive required for ordered test)
- Alcohol wipe
- Sterile 2 × 2-inch gauze pads
- Bandage (latex-free) or nonallergenic tape
- Sharps container
- Biohazardous waste container
- Laboratory requisition form
- Patient's medical record

STANDARDS: Complete the procedure within _____ minutes and achieve a minimum score of _____%.

Time began _____   Time ended _____

Steps	Possible Points	First Attempt	Second Attempt
1. Sanitize hands.	5		
2. Verify the order, and assemble equipment and supplies.	5		
3. Greet the patient, identify yourself, and confirm the patient's identity. Escort the patient to the proper room. Ask the patient to sit in phlebotomy chair.	5		
4. Confirm that the patient has followed the needed preparation (e.g., fasting).	10		
5. Explain the procedure to the patient.	5		
6. Prepare the evacuated tube system.	5		
7. Open the sterile gauze packet and place the gauze pad on the inside of its wrapper, or obtain sterile gauze pads from a bulk package.	10		
8. Position the remaining needed supplies for ease of reaching with nondominant hand. Place tube loosely in holder with label facing downward.	10		
9. Position and examine the arm to be used in the venipuncture.	10		
10. Apply the tourniquet.	10		
11. Apply gloves and PPE.	5		

Steps	Possible Points	First Attempt	Second Attempt
12. Thoroughly palpate the selected vein.	5		
13. Release the tourniquet.	5		
14. Prepare the puncture site using alcohol swabs.	10		
15. Reapply the tourniquet.	10		
16. Position the holder while keeping the needle covered, being certain to have control of holder. Uncover the needle.	10		
17. Position the needle so that it follows the line of the vein.	5		
18. Perform the venipuncture.	5		
19. Secure the holder. Push the bottom of the tube with the thumb of your nondominant hand so that the needle inside the holder pierces the rubber stopper of the tube. Follow the direction of the vein.	10		
20. Change tubes (minimum of two tubes) as required by test orders.	10		
21. Gently invert tubes that contain additives to be mixed with the specimen.	10		
22. While the blood is filling the last tube, release the tourniquet and withdraw the needle. Cover the needle with the safety shield.	10		
23. Apply direct pressure on the venipuncture site, and instruct the patient to raise the arm straight above the head and maintain pressure on the site for 1 to 2 minutes.	10		
24. Discard the contaminated needle and holder into the sharps container.	10		
25. Label the tubes as appropriate for lab.	10		
26. Place the tube into the biohazard transport bag.	5		
27. Check for bleeding at puncture site and apply a pressure dressing.	5		
28. Remove and discard the alcohol wipe and gloves.	5		
29. Sanitize the hands.	5		
30. Record the collection date and time on the laboratory requisition form, and place the requisition in the proper place in the biohazard transport bag.	10		
31. Ask and observe how the patient feels.	5		
32. Clean the work area using Standard Precautions.	5		
33. Document the procedure, indicating tests for which blood was drawn and the labs to which blood will be sent.	10		
Total Points Possible	250		

Comments: Total Points Earned _____   Instructor's Signature _____

Steps	Possible Points	First Attemp
31. Ask and observe how the patient feels.	5	
32. Clean the work area using Standard Precautions.	5	
33. Document the procedure.	10	
Total Points Possible NOTE: Awards points for Steps 13-14-15 OR 16-17-18, not both	255	

Comments: Total Points Earned _____ Instructor's Signature _____

Student Name _____   Date _____

CHECKLIST: PERFORM VENIPUNCTURE USING THE SYRINGE METHOD

TASK: Obtain a venous blood specimen acceptable for testing using the syringe method.

CONDITIONS: Given the proper equipment and supplies, the student will be required to perform a venipuncture using the syringe method of collection.

EQUIPMENT AND SUPPLIES
- Nonsterile disposable gloves
- Personal protective equipment (PPE) as required
- Tourniquet (latex-free)
- Test tube rack
- 10-cc (10-mL) syringe with 21- or 22-gauge needle and safety guards
- Proper evacuated blood tubes for tests ordered
- Alcohol wipe
- Sterile 2 × 2-inch gauze pads
- Bandage (latex-free) or nonallergenic tape
- Sharps container
- Biohazardous waste container
- Laboratory requisition form
- Patient's medical record

STANDARDS: Complete the procedure within _____ minutes and achieve a minimum score of _____%.

Time began _____   Time ended _____

Steps	Possible Points	First Attempt	Second Attempt
1. Sanitize hands.	5		
2. Verify the order. Assemble equipment and supplies.	5		
3. Greet the patient, identify yourself, and confirm the patient's identity. Escort the patient to the room for the blood draw. Position the patient in phlebotomy chair or on examination table.	5		
4. Confirm any necessary preparation has been accomplished (e.g., fasting). Explain the procedure to the patient.	5		
5. Prepare the needle and syringe, maintaining syringe sterility. Break the seal on the syringe by moving the plunger back and forth several times. Loosen the cap on the needle and check to make sure that the hub is screwed tightly onto the syringe.	15		
6. Place the evacuated tubes to be filled in a test tube rack on a work surface in order of fill.	15		
7. Open the sterile gauze packet and place the gauze pad on the inside of its wrapper, or obtain sterile gauze pads from a bulk package.	5		
8. Position and examine the arm to be used in the venipuncture.	10		
9. Apply gloves and PPE.	5		

Steps	Possible Points	Fi At
10. Thoroughly palpate the selected vein.	10	
11. Release the tourniquet.	10	
12. Prepare the puncture site and reapply tourniquet.	10	
13. If drawing from the hand, ask the patient to make a fist or bend the fingers downward. Pull the skin taut with your thumb over the top of the patient's knuckles.	15	
14. Position the syringe and grasp the syringe firmly between the thumb and the underlying fingers.	10	
15. Follow the direction of the vein and insert the needle in one quick motion at about a 45-degree angle.	10	
16. If drawing from AC vein, with your nondominant hand pull the skin taut beneath the intended puncture site to anchor the vein. Thumb should be 1 to 2 inches below and to the side of the vein.	15	
17. Position the syringe and grasp the syringe firmly between the thumb and the underlying fingers.	10	
18. Follow the direction of the vein and insert the needle in one quick motion at about a 15-degree angle.	10	
19. Perform the venipuncture. If flash does not occur, gently pull back on the plunger. Do not move the needle. If blood still does not enter the syringe, slowly withdraw the needle, secure new supplies, and retry the draw.	10	
20. Anchor the syringe, and gently continue pulling back on the plunger until the required amount of blood is in the syringe.	10	
21. Release the tourniquet.	5	
22. Remove the needle and cover the needle with safety shield without locking.	10	
23. Apply direct pressure on the venipuncture site, and instruct the patient to raise the arm straight above the head. Instruct the patient to maintain pressure on the site for 1 to 2 minutes.	5	
24. Transfer the blood to the evacuated tubes as soon as possible.	10	
25. Properly dispose of the syringe and needle.	10	
26. Label the tubes and place into biohazard transport bag.	10	
27. Check for bleeding at venipuncture site and place a pressure dressing.	10	
28. Remove and discard the alcohol wipe and gloves.	5	
29. Sanitize the hands.	5	
30. Record the collection date and time on the laboratory requisition form, and place the requisition in the biohazard transport bag.	10	

Student Name _____   Date _____

CHECKLIST: PERFORM VENIPUNCTURE USING THE BUTTERFLY METHOD (COLLECTION OF MULTIPLE EVACUATED TUBES)

TASK: Obtain a venous blood specimen acceptable for testing using the butterfly method.

CONDITIONS: Given the proper equipment and supplies, the student will perform a venipuncture using the butterfly method of collection.

EQUIPMENT AND SUPPLIES
- Nonsterile disposable gloves
- Personal protective equipment (PPE) as required
- Tourniquet (latex-free)
- Test tube rack
- Winged-infusion set with Luer adapter and safety guard
- Multidraw needle (22 to 25 gauge) and tube holder, or 10-cc (10-mL) syringe
- Evacuated blood tubes for requested tests with labels (correct nonadditive or additive required for ordered tests)
- Alcohol wipe
- Sterile 2 × 2-inch gauze pads
- Bandage (latex-free) or nonallergenic tape
- Sharps container
- Biohazardous waste container
- Laboratory requisition form
- Patient's medical record

STANDARDS: Complete the procedure within _____ minutes and achieve a minimum score of _____%.

Time began _____   Time ended _____

Steps	Possible Points	First Attempt	Second Attempt
1. Sanitize hands.	5		
2. Verify the order. Assemble equipment and supplies.	5		
3. Greet the patient, identify yourself, and confirm the patient's identity. Escort the patient to the proper room for venipuncture.	5		
4. Ask the patient to have a seat in the phlebotomy chair or on the examination table.	5		
5. Confirm any necessary preparation has been followed (e.g., fasting). Explain the procedure to the patient.	10		
6. Prepare the winged infusion set. Attach the winged infusion set to either a syringe or an evacuated tube holder.	15		
7. Open the sterile gauze packet and place the gauze pad on the inside of its wrapper, or obtain sterile gauze pads from a bulk package.	5		
8. Position and examine the arm to be used in the venipuncture.	10		
9. Apply the tourniquet.	10		
10. Apply gloves and PPE.	5		
11. Thoroughly palpate the selected vein.	10		

Steps	Possible Points	First Attempt	Second Attempt
12. Release the tourniquet.	10		
13. Prepare the puncture site and reapply the tourniquet.	5		
14. If drawing from the hand, ask the patient to make a fist or bend the fingers downward. Pull the skin taut with your thumb over the top of the patient's knuckles.	10		
15. Remove the protective shield from the needle of the infusion set, being sure the bevel is facing up. Position needle over vein to be punctured.	10		
16. Perform the venipuncture. With your nondominant hand, pull the skin taut beneath the intended puncture site to anchor the vein. Thumb should be 1 to 2 inches below and to the side of the vein. Follow the direction of the vein and insert the needle in one quick motion at about a 15-degree angle.	20		
17. After penetrating the vein, decrease the angle of the needle to 5 degrees until a "flash" of blood appears in the tubing.	5		
18. Secure the needle for blood collection.	10		
19. Insert the evacuated tube into the tube holder or gently pull back on the plunger of the syringe. Change tubes as required by the test ordered.	10		
20. Release the tourniquet and remove the needle.	10		
21. Apply direct pressure on the venipuncture site, and instruct the patient to raise the arm straight above the head. Maintain pressure on the site for 1 to 2 minutes, with the arm raised straight above the head.	10		
22. If a syringe was used, transfer the blood to the evacuated tubes as soon as possible.	10		
23. Dispose of the winged infusion set.	5		
24. Label the tubes and place the tube into the biohazard transport bag.	5		
25. Check for bleeding and place a bandage over the gauze to create a pressure dressing.	5		
26. Remove and discard the alcohol wipe and gloves.	5		
27. Sanitize the hands.	5		
28. Record the collection date and time on the laboratory requisition form, and place the requisition in the biohazard transport bag.	10		
29. Ask and observe how the patient feels.	5		
30. Clean the work area using Standard Precautions.	5		
31. Document the procedure.	10		
Total Points Possible	250		

Comments: Total Points Earned _____   Instructor's Signature _____

Student Name _____ Date _____

CHECKLIST: CHARTING

TASK: Create new medical records, organize contents, interview patients, and document subjective and objective data.

CONDITIONS: Given the proper equipment and supplies, the students will be required to create new medical records by labeling them correctly and organizing sample forms and/or reports within each appropriately. The student will then role-play with another student or an instructor to demonstrate how to interview a patient. Finally, using the list of common charting abbreviations (as directed) from the student handbook, the student will record the "patient's" chief complaint (subjective data) as well as every procedure in this module using the sample documentation provided on the procedure competency checklists (objective data).

EQUIPMENT AND SUPPLIES
- File folders
- Blank file labels
- Color-coded year labels
- Alphabetical labels
- Medical alert labels
- Other labels as appropriate
- Sample forms and/or reports
- Sample documentation (on procedure competency checklists)

STANDARDS: Complete the procedure within _____ minutes and achieve a minimum score of _____%.

Time began _____   Time ended _____

Steps	Possible Points	First Attempt	Second Attempt
1. Assemble all equipment and supplies.	5		
2. Create a file label (patient name).	5		
3. Attach other labels as appropriate (year, initials, medical alert).	5		
4. Organize preprinted forms appropriately within the folder.	10		
5. Review medical history form with the patient (subjective data).	10		
6. Record chief complaint (in patient's own words/subjective data).	10		
7. Document all procedures on appropriate forms using correct terminology and abbreviations (objective data).	10		
8. Record all information legibly.	10		
9. Maintain HIPAA privacy guidelines.	10		
10. Maintain professional qualities as defined.	10		
11. Clean area when finished.	5		
Total Points Possible	90		

Comments: Total Points Earned _____   Instructor's Signature _____

Student Name _____ Date _____

CHECKLIST: DIAGNOSTIC CODING

TASK: Assign the proper *International Classification of Diseases (ICD-9-CM)* code based on medical documentation to the highest degree of specificity.

CONDITIONS: Given the proper equipment and supplies, the student will assign the proper *ICD-9-CM* code based on medical documentation to the highest degree of specificity.

EQUIPMENT AND SUPPLIES
- Current *ICD-9-CM* codebook
- Medical dictionary
- Patient's medical records
- Pen or pencil
- Work product (see next pages)

STANDARDS: Complete the procedure within _____ minutes and achieve a minimum score of _____%.

Time began _____ Time ended _____

Steps	Possible Points	First Attempt	Second Attempt
1. Assemble all supplies and equipment.	5		
2. Identify the key term in the diagnostic statement.	10		
3. Locate the diagnosis in the Alphabetic Index (Volume 2, Section 1) of the *ICD-9-CM* codebook.	20		
4. Read and use footnotes, symbols, or instructions.	15		
5. Locate the diagnosis in the Tabular List (Volume 1).	10		
6. Read and use the inclusions and exclusions noted in the Tabular List.	10		
7. Assign the code to the highest degree of specificity appropriate.	20		
8. Document in the medical record.	10		
9. Ask yourself these final questions (NO points awarded for this section).	0		
a. Have you coded to the highest degree of specificity?			
b. Are there any secondary diagnoses or conditions addressed during the encounter that need to be coded?			
Total Points Possible	100		

Comments: Total Points Earned _____ Instructor's Signature _____

Student Name _____   Date _____

CHECKLIST: PROCEDURAL CODING

TASK: Assign the proper *Current Procedural Terminology* (CPT) code to the highest degree of specificity based on medical documentation for auditing and billing purposes.

CONDITIONS: Given the proper equipment and supplies, the student will assign the proper (CPT) code to the highest degree of specificity based on medical documentation for auditing and billing purposes.

EQUIPMENT AND SUPPLIES
- Current *CPT* codebook
- Medical dictionary
- Patient's medical records
- Pen or pencil
- Work product (see next pages)

STANDARDS: Complete the procedure within _____ minutes and achieve a minimum score of _____%.

Time began _____   Time ended _____

Steps	Possible Points	First Attempt	Second Attempt
1. Assemble all supplies and equipment.	5		
2. Read the introduction, guidelines, and notes of a current *CPT* codebook.	10		
3. Review all service and procedures performed on the day of the encounter; include all medications administered and trays and equipment used.	20		
4. Identify the main term in the procedure.	15		
5. Locate the main term in the alphabetical index. Review any subterms listed alphabetically under the main term.	10		
6. Verify the code sets in the tabular (numerical) list. Select the code with the greatest specificity.	10		
7. Determine if a modifier is required.	20		
8. Assign the code using all necessary steps for proper code determination.	10		
9. Ask yourself these final questions (NO points awarded for this section).	0		
a. Have you coded to the highest degree of specificity?			
b. Are there any secondary diagnoses or conditions addressed during the encounter that need to be coded?			
Total Points Possible	100		

Comments: Total Points Earned _____   Instructor's Signature _____

Student Name _____   Date _____

CHECKLIST: USE *PHYSICIAN'S DESK REFERENCE*

TASK: Demonstrate understanding of *Physician's Desk Reference's* organization by creating a fact sheet for each listed on a prepared document.

CONDITIONS: Given proper equipment and supplies, the student will be required to identify the trade and gener names for each listed drug, its classification, one indication for its use, one contraindication for its use, its usual do and administration, and any possible side effects.

EQUIPMENT AND SUPPLIES
- *Physician's Desk Reference*
- List of drugs (on following pages)
- Pen or pencil

STANDARDS: Complete the procedure within _____ minutes and achieve a minimum score of _____%.

Time began _____   Time ended _____

Steps	Possible Points	First Attempt	Second Attempt
1. Assemble all equipment and supplies.	5		
2. Create a fact sheet for each medication listed on the prepared drug list (see next page) to include the following:			
• Trade name, generic name, and drug classification	10		
• Identify indications for assigned medications	10		
• Identify contraindications for assigned medications	10		
• Identify dosage and administration of assigned medications	10		
• Identify side effects of assigned medications	10		
3. Display professional abilities through penmanship.	10		
4. Clean area.	5		
5. Proofread and correct your work and submit to your instructor. Demonstrate professionalism throughout procedure and accept constructive feedback with a problem-solving attitude.	10		
Total Points Possible	80		

Comments: Total Points Earned _____   Instructor's Signature _____

Student Name _____   Date _____

CHECKLIST: PREPARE AND MAINTAIN AN APPOINTMENT BOOK

TASK: Establish the matrix of an appointment book page and schedule a patient appointment.

CONDITIONS: Given the proper equipment and supplies, the student will be required to matrix an appointment book and schedule appointments.

EQUIPMENT AND SUPPLIES

* Appointment book assignment
* Office policy for office hours and list of physician's availability
* Pencil
* Work product (see next pages)

STANDARDS: Complete the procedure within _____ minutes and achieve a minimum score of _____ %.

Time began _____   Time ended _____

Steps	Possible Points	First Attempt	Second Attempt
1. Identify and mark the matrix according to office policy.	25		
2. Allow appointment times for emergency visits and unexpected needs.	10		
3. Schedule appointment(s) providing the needed information for appropriate patient care, for canceling appointments, and for efficient time management.	15		
Total Points Possible	50		

Comments: Total Points Earned _____   Instructor's Signature _____

WORK PRODUCT FOR
PREPARE AND MAINTAIN AN APPOINTMENT BOOK

Part I: Advance Preparation and Establishing a Matrix

Prepare Appointment Page #1 according to the following directions.

1. The date is Monday, October 13, 20XX.
2. Drs. Lawler and Hughes have hospital rounds from 8 to 9 a.m.
3. Dr. Lupez sees patients from 8 a.m. to noon, then has a medical conference.
4. Lunch is from noon until 2 p.m.
5. Dr. Lawler has a 4 p.m. meeting at the hospital.
6. Dr. Hughes and Dr. Lawler both prefer a break from 3:15 to 3:30 p.m. to catch up on telephone calls and other duties.

Part II: Scheduling Appointments

Prepare Appointment Page #2 according to the following directions. Appointments can be scheduled for subsequent days in these exercises.

7. The date is Tuesday, October 14, 20XX.
8. Lunch is from noon until 2 p.m.
9. Dr. Lawler will be out Tuesday afternoon.
10. Dr. Hughes is out of town speaking at a conference.
11. Tracey and Keith Jones would like an appointment with Dr. Lawler right before lunch. Both require new patient physical examinations, and they would like to come to the office at the same time so that they can also discuss family planning.
12. John Edgar, Lydia Perry, and June Trayner are established patients who need follow-up appointments with Dr. Lupez.
13. Wayne Harris needs a new patient appointment with Dr. Lawler as early as possible.
14. Lucy Fraser needs an appointment with Dr. Lawler or Dr. Hughes and has to make the appointment after 3:30 p.m. because she picks up her children from school.
15. Asa Nordholm, Carrie Jones, and Seicho Ando need follow-up appointments with Dr. Lawler.
16. Talia Perez called and is having trouble with her new blood pressure medication. The soonest she can get off work and come to the clinic is 2:15 p.m.
17. Paula Nolen needs an allergy shot in the morning.
18. Amy Wainwright needs a well-woman examination and can come to the clinic any time before 3 p.m.
19. Pam Billingsley wants to come to the clinic in the later afternoon for a return check about her migraine headaches.
20. Adam Angsley needs an appointment with Dr. Lawler in the afternoon.

Prepare Appointment Page #3 according to the following directions. Appointments can be scheduled for subsequent days in these exercises.

21. The date is Wednesday, October 15, 20XX.
22. All of the physicians are in the office today.
23. Lunch is from noon until 2 p.m.
24. Dr. Lawler has three rechecks today, with Ella Jones, Fred Linstra, and Mary Higgins.

25. Winston Hill is an established patient coming in for an annual physical with Dr. Lawler. His neighbor can drive him to the clinic for a 2 p.m. appointment.
26. Elnar Rosen, an established patient, needs a physical with Dr. Hughes at around 10:15 a.m.
27. A staff meeting is scheduled for 9 a.m.
28. A representative from Allied Medical Supply is demonstrating a self-scheduling computer program at 4:30 p.m. for all staff members.
29. Bob Jones needs a morning appointment with Dr. Lupez.
30. Talia Perez is extremely nauseated and needs to return to the clinic today.
31. Robin Tower is a new patient who wishes to see Dr. Lawler or Dr. Hughes.
32. Audrey Rhodes is a new patient who wishes to see Dr. Lawler.
33. Victor Garner is a follow-up patient whom Dr. Lupez saw last week in the hospital. He is new to the clinic.
34. Charlie Robinson missed his appointment today at 11 a.m. with Dr. Hughes.
35. Peter Blake calls to see if he can be seen by one of the physicians at 11:15 a.m.

Prepare Appointment Page #4 according to the following directions. Appointments can be scheduled for subsequent days in these exercises.

36. The date is Thursday, October 16, 20XX.
37. Dr. Hughes is not in the office because his daughter is having a baby.
38. Lunch is from noon until 2 p.m.
39. All patients must be seen in the morning because the clinic is closed on Thursday afternoons.
40. Cassie LeGrand is coming to the clinic as a new patient to see Dr. Lupez.
41. Cassandra LeBrock is coming to the clinic as an established patient to see Dr. Lupez.
42. Raymond Smith wants to make an appointment at 1:45 p.m. with Dr. Lawler.
43. Benjamin Charles requests an appointment with Dr. Lupez at 3:45 p.m.

Prepare Appointment Page #5 according to the following directions.

44. The date is Friday, October 17, 20XX.
45. Dr. Lupez is the only provider in the office today.
46. Lunch is from noon until 2 p.m.
47. Cassie LeGrand returns today for laboratory work and to consult with Dr. Lupez for surgery.
48. Bruce Wells is scheduled for a follow-up appointment at 10:15 a.m.
49. Ronald Trayhan calls to make an appointment with Dr. Lupez for 2:30 p.m.
50. Dr. Hughes calls to ask Dr. Lupez to see one of his young patients, Barbara Scott, at 3 p.m. for a high fever.
51. Stanley Allred calls for an appointment to see Dr. Lupez at 3 p.m.

Student Name _____   Date _____

APPOINTMENT PAGE #1

ADVANCE PREPARATION AND ESTABLISHING A MATRIX
Complete Appointment Page #1 using the information in Part I, Items 1-6.

			DAY
			DATE

			8	00 10 20 30 40 50	
			9	00 10 20 30 40 50	
			10	00 10 20 30 40 50	
			11	00 10 20 30 40 50	
			12	00 10 20 30 40 50	
			1	00 10 20 30 40 50	
			2	00 10 20 30 40 50	
			3	00 10 20 30 40 50	
			4	00 10 20 30 40 50	
			5	00 10 20 30 40 50	

Bibbero Systems Form 56-7310

APPOINTMENT PAGE #2

SCHEDULING APPOINTMENTS
Complete Appointment Page #2 using the information in Part II, Items 7-20.

			DAY							
			DATE							

Hour	Min
8	00 / 10 / 20 / 30 / 40 / 50
9	00 / 10 / 20 / 30 / 40 / 50
10	00 / 10 / 20 / 30 / 40 / 50
11	00 / 10 / 20 / 30 / 40 / 50
12	00 / 10 / 20 / 30 / 40 / 50
1	00 / 10 / 20 / 30 / 40 / 50
2	00 / 10 / 20 / 30 / 40 / 50
3	00 / 10 / 20 / 30 / 40 / 50
4	00 / 10 / 20 / 30 / 40 / 50
5	00 / 10 / 20 / 30 / 40 / 50

Bibbero Systems Form 56-7310

APPOINTMENT PAGE #3

SCHEDULING APPOINTMENTS
Complete Appointment Page #3 using the information in Part II, Items 21-35.

			DAY			
			DATE			

			8	00 10 20 30 40 50
			9	00 10 20 30 40 50
			10	00 10 20 30 40 50
			11	00 10 20 30 40 50
			12	00 10 20 30 40 50
			1	00 10 20 30 40 50
			2	00 10 20 30 40 50
			3	00 10 20 30 40 50
			4	00 10 20 30 40 50
			5	00 10 20 30 40 50

Bibbero Systems Form 56-7310

APPOINTMENT PAGE #4

SCHEDULING APPOINTMENTS

Complete Appointment Page #4 using the information in Part II, Items 36-43.

			DAY								
			DATE								

Time slots (hourly with 00–50 minute increments):
8, 9, 10, 11, 12, 1, 2, 3, 4, 5

APPOINTMENT PAGE #5

SCHEDULING APPOINTMENTS
Complete Appointment Page #5 using the information in Part II, Items 44-51.

			DAY							
			DATE							
			8	00						
				10						
				20						
				30						
				40						
				50						
			9	00						
				10						
				20						
				30						
				40						
				50						
			10	00						
				10						
				20						
				30						
				40						
				50						
			11	00						
				10						
				20						
				30						
				40						
				50						
			12	00						
				10						
				20						
				30						
				40						
				50						
			1	00						
				10						
				20						
				30						
				40						
				50						
			2	00						
				10						
				20						
				30						
				40						
				50						
			3	00						
				10						
				20						
				30						
				40						
				50						
			4	00						
				10						
				20						
				30						
				40						
				50						
			5	00						
				10						
				20						
				30						
				40						
				50						

Bibbero Systems Form 56-7310

Student Name _____   Date _____

CHECKLIST: SCHEDULE OUTPATIENT AND INPATIENT APPOINTMENTS

TASK: Schedule a patient for a physician-ordered test or procedure and admission, in both an outpatient and an inpatient setting or inpatient admission, with the time frame requested by the physician, confirm the appointment with the patient, and issue all required instructions.

CONDITIONS: Given the proper equipment and supplies, the student will be required to schedule outpatient and inpatient appointments.

EQUIPMENT AND SUPPLIES
- Physician's order for either an outpatient or an inpatient diagnostic test procedure or inpatient admission
- Patient chart
- Test preparation or preadmission instructions
- Telephone
- Work product (see next pages)

STANDARDS: Complete the procedure within _____ minutes and achieve a minimum score of _____ %.

Time began _____   Time ended _____

Steps	Possible Points	First Attempt	Second Attempt
Outpatient			
1. Schedule appointment using an order for an outpatient diagnostic test(s) or procedure(s) and the expected time frame for results.	15		
2. Precertify the procedure(s) and/or test(s) with the patient's insurance company.	10		
3. Determine patient availability.	10		
4. Contact the facility and schedule the procedure(s) and/or test(s).	10		
5. Notify the patient of the arrangements.	10		
6. Conduct follow-up.	10		
Inpatient			
1. Schedule appointment using an order for an inpatient diagnostic test or procedure and the expected time frame for results.	15		
2. Precertify the procedure(s) and/or test(s) with the patient's insurance company.	10		
3. Determine patient availability.	10		
4. Contact the facility and schedule the procedure(s) and/or test(s).	10		
5. Notify the patient of the arrangements.	10		
6. Conduct follow-up.	10		

Steps	Possible Points	First Attempt	Second Attempt
Inpatient			
1. Schedule hospital admission.	15		
2. Precertify the admission with the patient's insurance company.	10		
3. Determine patient availability.	10		
4. Contact the facility and schedule the procedure(s) and/or test(s).	10		
5. Notify the patient of the arrangements.	10		
6. Conduct follow-up.	10		
Total Points Possible	195		

Comments: Total Points Earned _____   Instructor's Signature _____

WORK PRODUCT FOR
SCHEDULE OUTPATIENT AND INPATIENT APPOINTMENTS

Complete the four referral forms on the subsequent pages for the following patients. Create fictional demographic information.

1. Cassie LeGrand is to report to Mercy Hospital for excision of a nasal polyp on Tuesday, October 24, 20XX. Dr. Lupez is her attending physician. Surgery is scheduled for Tuesday at 2 p.m. She will need blood work that morning. The procedure is considered outpatient, and Cassie will go home later that day if she does well. ICD code: 471.0.
2. Bob Jones arrives at Presbyterian Hospital to have an MRI on his right knee on Friday, November 2, 20XX. He needs an early morning appointment. ICD code: 715.8.
3. Lucille Saxton is to be admitted to the hospital for surgery because of a bowel obstruction. Her surgery date is June 14, 20XX, and she must be admitted a day in advance for laboratory work and a chest x-ray examination. ICD code: 560.9.
4. Pam Burton needs to be admitted for several tests because of her recurrent irritable bowel syndrome. She will be in the hospital for at least 3 days and should check in on July 23, 20XX in the afternoon, so that she will have taken nothing by mouth (NPO) before the blood tests are performed and x-ray films are taken the following morning. ICD Code: 564.1.

Student Name _____   Date _____

REFERRAL FORM #1

SCHEDULING INPATIENT AND OUTPATIENT ADMISSIONS AND PROCEDURES
Complete the referral from using the information for patient #1.

BLACKBURN PRIMARY CARE ASSOCIATES, P.C.
1990 Turquoise Drive • Blackburn, WI 54937
Phone 608-459-8857 • Fax 608-459-8860
Referral Form Effective Jan. 1, 20XX

Patient Name _____ **Phone #** _____
SS # _____ **DOB** _____
Diagnosis (ICD-9 Required) _____
Insurance Type _____
Referring Physician _____ **Phone** _____
Office Contact _____ **Fax** _____

REFERRAL FOR:
❑ Consult Only
❑ Evaluation and Treatment
❑ Inpatient Surgery
❑ Inpatient Admission
❑ Outpatient Surgery
❑ Outpatient Lab
❑ Outpatient X-ray
❑ Procedure Only
❑ Chiropractic
❑ Physical Therapy
❑ Back in Action Rehabilitation Program
❑ Psychophysiologic Evaluation
❑ Biofeedback
❑ Other _____

Comments
_____
_____
_____
_____
_____
_____
_____

REFERRAL TIMEFRAME:
❑ First Available Appt (within 5 business days)
❑ Stat (within 24 hr)

PROVIDER:
❑ Ron Lupez, M.D.
❑ Donald Lawler, M.D.
❑ Robert Hughes, D.O.
❑ Neil Stern, D.C.
❑ Joel Lively, P.T.

PLEASE INCLUDE THE FOLLOWING:
❑ Copy of Insurance Card
❑ Demographic Information
❑ Treatment Notes
❑ Diagnostic Reports

HOSPITAL/FACILITY
❑ Mercy Hospital
❑ Presbyterian Hospital
❑ Outpatient Surgical Complex
❑ Health and Wellness Center

Scheduled By _____

Appt Date/Time _____ Physician _____

Student Name _____   Date _____

REFERRAL FORM #2

Complete the referral form using the information for patient #2.

BLACKBURN PRIMARY CARE ASSOCIATES, P.C.
1990 Turquoise Drive • Blackburn, WI 54937
Phone 608-459-8857 • Fax 608-459-8860
Referral Form Effective Jan. 1, 20XX

Patient Name _____ **Phone #** _____
SS # _____ **DOB**_____
Diagnosis (ICD-9 Required) _____
Insurance Type _____
Referring Physician _____ **Phone** _____
Office Contact _____ **Fax** _____

REFERRAL FOR:
❑ Consult Only
❑ Evaluation and Treatment
❑ Inpatient Surgery
❑ Inpatient Admission
❑ Outpatient Surgery
❑ Outpatient Lab
❑ Outpatient X-ray
❑ Procedure Only
❑ Chiropractic
❑ Physical Therapy
❑ Back in Action Rehabilitation Program
❑ Psychophysiologic Evaluation
❑ Biofeedback
❑ Other _____

Comments

_____
_____
_____
_____
_____
_____
_____

REFERRAL TIMEFRAME:
❑ First Available Appt (within 5 business days)
❑ Stat (within 24 hr)

PROVIDER:
❑ Ron Lupez, M.D.
❑ Donald Lawler, M.D.
❑ Robert Hughes, D.O.
❑ Neil Stern, D.C.
❑ Joel Lively, P.T.

PLEASE INCLUDE THE FOLLOWING:
❑ Copy of Insurance Card
❑ Demographic Information
❑ Treatment Notes
❑ Diagnostic Reports

HOSPITAL/FACILITY
❑ Mercy Hospital
❑ Presbyterian Hospital
❑ Outpatient Surgical Complex
❑ Health and Wellness Center

Scheduled By _____

Appt Date/Time _____   Physician _____

Student Name _____   Date _____

REFERRAL FORM #3

Complete the referral form using the information for patient #3.

BLACKBURN PRIMARY CARE ASSOCIATES, P.C.
1990 Turquoise Drive • Blackburn, WI 54937
Phone 608-459-8857 • Fax 608-459-8860
Referral Form Effective Jan. 1, 20XX

Patient Name _____ **Phone #** _____
SS # _____ **DOB** _____
Diagnosis (ICD-9 Required) _____
Insurance Type _____
Referring Physician _____ **Phone** _____
Office Contact _____ **Fax** _____

REFERRAL FOR:
❑ Consult Only
❑ Evaluation and Treatment
❑ Inpatient Surgery
❑ Inpatient Admission
❑ Outpatient Surgery
❑ Outpatient Lab
❑ Outpatient X-ray
❑ Procedure Only
❑ Chiropractic
❑ Physical Therapy
❑ Back in Action Rehabilitation Program
❑ Psychophysiologic Evaluation
❑ Biofeedback
❑ Other _____

Comments
_____
_____
_____
_____
_____
_____
_____

REFERRAL TIMEFRAME:
❑ First Available Appt (within 5 business days)
❑ Stat (within 24 hr)

PROVIDER:
❑ Ron Lupez, M.D.
❑ Donald Lawler, M.D.
❑ Robert Hughes, D.O.
❑ Neil Stern, D.C.
❑ Joel Lively, P.T.

PLEASE INCLUDE THE FOLLOWING:
❑ Copy of Insurance Card
❑ Demographic Information
❑ Treatment Notes
❑ Diagnostic Reports

HOSPITAL/FACILITY
❑ Mercy Hospital
❑ Presbyterian Hospital
❑ Outpatient Surgical Complex
❑ Health and Wellness Center

Scheduled By _____

Appt Date/Time _____   Physician _____

Student Name _____   Date _____

REFERRAL FORM #4

Complete the referral form using the information for patient #4.

BLACKBURN PRIMARY CARE ASSOCIATES, P.C.
1990 Turquoise Drive • Blackburn, WI 54937
Phone 608-459-8857 • Fax 608-459-8860
Referral Form Effective Jan. 1, 20XX

Patient Name _____   **Phone #** _____
SS # _____   **DOB** _____
Diagnosis (ICD-9 Required) _____
Insurance Type _____
Referring Physician _____   **Phone** _____
Office Contact _____   **Fax** _____

REFERRAL FOR:
❏ Consult Only
❏ Evaluation and Treatment
❏ Inpatient Surgery
❏ Inpatient Admission
❏ Outpatient Surgery
❏ Outpatient Lab
❏ Outpatient X-ray
❏ Procedure Only
❏ Chiropractic
❏ Physical Therapy
❏ Back in Action Rehabilitation Program
❏ Psychophysiologic Evaluation
❏ Biofeedback
❏ Other _____

Comments
_____
_____
_____
_____
_____
_____

REFERRAL TIMEFRAME:
❏ First Available Appt (within 5 business days)
❏ Stat (within 24 hr)

PROVIDER:
❏ Ron Lupez, M.D.
❏ Donald Lawler, M.D.
❏ Robert Hughes, D.O.
❏ Neil Stern, D.C.
❏ Joel Lively, P.T.

PLEASE INCLUDE THE FOLLOWING:
❏ Copy of Insurance Card
❏ Demographic Information
❏ Treatment Notes
❏ Diagnostic Reports

HOSPITAL/FACILITY
❏ Mercy Hospital
❏ Presbyterian Hospital
❏ Outpatient Surgical Complex
❏ Health and Wellness Center

Scheduled By _____

Appt Date/Time _____   Physician _____

Student Name _____   Date _____

CHECKLIST: CREATE A MEDICAL PRACTICE INFORMATION BROCHURE

TASK: Create a patient information booklet for a "mock" medical practice.

CONDITIONS: Given the proper equipment and supplies, the student will be required to create an informational brochure for his or her "mock" practice.

EQUIPMENT AND SUPPLIES

- Computer
- Software program that allows for brochure layouts
- Examples of local medical practice brochures and local medical office policies
- Pen or pencil

STANDARDS: Complete the procedure within _____ minutes and achieve a minimum score of _____ %.

Time began _____   Time ended _____

Steps	Possible Points	First Attempt	Second Attempt
1. Write and key a short paragraph describing each of the following topics and other information as needed.			
a. Description of the practice	10		
b. Physical location of facility	10		
c. Parking options	10		
d. Telephone numbers, e-mail addresses, and Web page	10		
e. Office hours	10		
f. Names and credentials of staff members	10		
g. Types of services	10		
h. Appointment scheduling and cancellation policies	10		
i. Payment options	10		
j. Prescription refill policy	10		
k. Types of accepted insurance	10		
l. Referral policy	10		
m. Release of records policy	10		
n. Emergency protocols	10		
o. Name of a contact person in the event that the physician is unavailable	10		
p. Frequently asked questions	10		
q. Any special considerations	10		

Steps	Possible Points	First Attempt	Second Attempt
2. Proofread the keyed paragraphs.	15		
3. Determine the layout of the brochure to provide ready access of information to patient. Include the following considerations:			
a. Visually pleasing	5		
b. Placement of logo	5		
c. Name, address, and telephone number of the practice prominently placed	5		
4. Print the final version of the brochure. Submit to instructor.			
Total Points Possible	100		

Comments: Total Points Earned _____   Instructor's Signature _____

Student Name _____   Date _____

CHECKLIST: COMPLETE A MEDICAL HISTORY FORM

TASK: Obtain and record a patient's medical history using verbal and nonverbal communication skills and applying the principles of accurate documentation in the patient's medical record.

CONDITIONS: Given the proper equipment and supplies, the student will be required to role-play with another student or an instructor the proper method for obtaining and recording a patient's medical history.

EQUIPMENT AND SUPPLIES

- Medical history form (See Fig. 7-2)
- Patient's medical record
- Pen (red and black ink)
- Clipboard
- Quiet private area

STANDARDS: Complete the procedure within _____ minutes and achieve a minimum score of _____ %.

Time began _____   Time ended _____

Steps	Possible Points	First Attempt	Second Attempt
1. Assemble all supplies and equipment.	5		
2. Greet and identify the patient.	5		
3. Escort the patient to a quiet, comfortable room that is well lit and affords privacy.	5		
4. Explain why information is needed and reassure the patient that the information will be kept confidential.	10		
5. Seat the patient, and then sit near the patient at eye level.	5		
6. Review the completed portion of the medical history form, looking for omissions or incomplete answers. Verify information as needed.	15		
7. Speak clearly and distinctly; maintain eye contact as appropriate with the patient.	10		
8. Remember to record all information legibly in black ink.	5		
9. Ask the patient to state the reason for today's visit.	10		
10. Record the information briefly and concisely, using the patient's own words as much as possible.	20		
11. Ask the patient about prescription, over-the-counter, and herbal medications or treatments; record all medications the patient is taking.	10		

Steps	Possible Points	First Attempt	Second Attempt
12. Inquire about allergies to medications, food, and other substances; record any allergies in red ink on every page of the history form. Record no allergies as appropriate.	10		
13. Review and record information in all sections of the family history form.	10		
14. Thank the patient for providing the information.	10		
15. Review the record for errors before giving it to the physician.	10		
16. Use the information to complete the patient's record as directed.	10		
Total Points Possible	150		

Comments: Total Points Earned _____   Instructor's Signature _____

Student Name _____   Date _____

CHECKLIST: RECOGNIZE AND RESPOND TO VERBAL AND NONVERBAL COMMUNICATION

TASK: Recognize and respond to basic verbal and nonverbal communication.

CONDITIONS: Given the proper equipment and supplies, the student will be required to role-play with another student the proper method for recognizing and responding to basic verbal and nonverbal communication.

EQUIPMENT AND SUPPLIES

• No equipment or supplies required

STANDARDS: Complete the procedure within _____ minutes and achieve a minimum score of _____ %.

Time began _____   Time ended _____

Steps	Possible Points	First Attempt	Second Attempt
1. Greet the patient, smile to welcome the patient, and introduce yourself.	5		
2. Verify the patient's name and use it with a courtesy title, unless instructed otherwise by the patient.	5		
3. Establish a comfortable physical environment while respecting individual ethnic and cultural differences.	5		
4. Verify that the patient feels comfortable.	5		
5. Establish the topic of discussion as directed.	5		
6. Observe the patient for nonverbal communication cues.	10		
7. Ask open-ended questions. Verify that the patient understands the questions.	10		
8. Practice active listening; provide feedback.	10		
9. Near the end of the discussion, give the patient the opportunity to ask questions or provide further clarifications.	10		
10. Thank the patient for his or her comments and signal the end of the discussion.	10		
Total Points Possible	75		

Comments: Total Points Earned _____   Instructor's Signature _____

Student Name _____   Date _____

CHECKLIST: ASSIST WITH THE PHYSICAL EXAMINATION

TASK: Prepare a patient and assist the physician or health care practitioner with a general physical examination.

CONDITIONS: Given the proper equipment and supplies, the student will be required to role-play with another student or an instructor the proper method for assisting with a general physical examination.

EQUIPMENT AND SUPPLIES

- Examination table
- Table paper
- Patient gown
- Drape
- Urine specimen container
- Snellen chart
- Patient's medical record
- Balance scale
- Tongue depressor
- Plastic-backed paper towel
- Stethoscope
- Sphygmomanometer
- Otoscope
- Ophthalmoscope
- Pen (red and black ink)

STANDARDS: Complete the procedure within _____ minutes and achieve a minimum score of _____ %.

Time began _____   Time ended _____

Steps	Possible Points	First Attempt	Second Attempt
1. Sanitize hands.	5		
2. Assemble equipment and supplies.	5		
3. Obtain the patient's medical record.	5		
4. Greet and identify the patient.	5		
5. Explain the procedure to the patient.	5		
6. Measure weight and height, and document the results.	10		
7. Measure visual acuity and document the results.	10		
8. Have the patient obtain a urine sample (if office policy).	5		
9. Escort the patient to the examination room.	5		
10. Measure the patient's vital signs, and document the results.	10		

Steps	Possible Points	First Attempt	Second Attempt
11. Provide a gown and drape to the patient, and allow the patient to change into the gown. Inform the physician when the patient is ready, and make the patient's medical record available to the physician.	10		
12. Assist physician with eye examination.	10		
13. Assist physician with ear examination.	10		
14. Assist physician with nasal examination.	10		
15. Assist physician with throat examination.	10		
16. Assist physician with heart and lung examination.	10		
17. Assist physician with testing and examination of the upper extremity reflexes.	10		
18. Position the patient in each of the following positions.			
• Sitting	2		
• Recumbent	2		
• Sims'	2		
• Prone	2		
• Knee-Chest	2		
• Fowler's	2		
19. Assist the patient from the examination table as appropriate.	10		
20. Allow the patient time to change from gown to street clothes.	10		
21. Allow time for further discussion between the physician and patient regarding prescriptions, medications, and a return visit. Ask the patient if he or she has any questions.	10		
22. Document any instructions given to the patient in the medical record.	10		
23. Clean the examination room according to Standard Precautions and take used equipment to appropriate place for sanitization.	10		
24. Sanitize hands.	5		
Total Points Possible	202		

Comments: Total Points Earned _____   Instructor's Signature _____

Student Name _____ Date _____

CHECKLIST: ASSESS DISTANCE VISUAL ACUITY USING A SNELLEN CHART

TASK: Accurately measure visual acuity using a Snellen eye chart, and document the procedure in the patient's medical record.

CONDITIONS: Given the proper equipment and supplies, the student will be required to measure visual acuity using a Snellen chart.

EQUIPMENT AND SUPPLIES

- Snellen eye chart
- Eye occluder
- Well-lit examination room
- Floor mark (20 feet from chart)
- Patient's medical record
- Pen

STANDARDS: Complete the procedure within _____ minutes and achieve a minimum score of _____ %.

Time began _____   Time ended _____

Steps	Possible Points	First Attempt	Second Attempt
1. Sanitize hands.	5		
2. Assemble equipment and supplies.	5		
3. Greet and identify the patient.	5		
4. Explain the procedure to the patient.	5		
5. Ask the patient if he or she is wearing contact lenses, and observe for eyeglasses.	10		
6. Place the patient in a comfortable position 20 feet from the chart.	10		
7. Select the appropriate Snellen chart for the patient and position the center of the chart at the patient's eye level. Stand next to the chart during the test to indicate to the patient the line to be identified.	10		
8. Ask the patient to cover the left eye with the eye occluder, keeping the eye open.	10		
9. Measure the visual acuity of the right eye by asking the patient to identify verbally each letter (or picture or rotating "E" direction) in the row on the Snellen chart, starting with the 20/70 line.	10		
10. Proceed up or down the chart as necessary.	10		
11. Observe the patient for any unusual symptoms while he or she is reading the letters, such as squinting, tilting the head, or watering eyes.	10		

Steps	Possible Points	First Attempt	Second Attempt
12. Repeat the procedure to test the left eye by covering the right eye.	10		
13. Record the results appropriately, indicating the errors for each eye.	10		
14. Repeat the procedure without covering either eye.	10		
15. If appropriate, repeat the procedure without corrective lenses.	10		
16. Chart the procedure.	10		
17. Sanitize or discard the occluder as appropriate.	5		
18. Sanitize hands.	5		
Total Points Possible	150		

Comments: Total Points Earned _____   Instructor's Signature _____

Student Name _____   Date _____

CHECKLIST: ASSESS COLOR VISION USING THE ISHIHARA TEST

TASK: Measure color visual acuity accurately using the Ishihara color-blindness test.

CONDITIONS: Given the proper equipment and supplies, the student will be required to role-play with another student or an instructor the proper method for measuring color visual acuity using the Ishihara color-blindness test.

EQUIPMENT AND SUPPLIES

- Ishihara color plate book
- Cotton swab
- Well-lit examination room (natural light preferred)
- Watch with second hand
- Patient's medical record
- Pen or pencil

STANDARDS: Complete the procedure within _____ minutes and achieve a minimum score of _____ %.

Time began _____   Time ended _____

Steps	Possible Points	First Attempt	Second Attempt
1. Sanitize hands.	5		
2. Assemble equipment and supplies.	5		
3. Greet and identify the patient.	5		
4. Explain the procedure to the patient.	5		
5. In a well-lit room, use the first plate in the book as an example, and instruct the patient on how the examination will be conducted using the plate.	10		
6. Hold the color plates 30 inches from the patient.	10		
7. Ask the patient to identify the number on the plate or, using a cotton-tipped swab, to trace the winding path.	10		
8. Record the results for each plate, and continue until the patient has viewed and responded to all 11 plates.	10		
9. Appropriately record the results in the patient's medical record.	10		
10. Return the Ishihara book to its proper place.	10		
11. Discard cotton-tipped swab as appropriate.	5		
12. Sanitize hands.	5		
Total Points Possible	90		

Comments: Total Points Earned _____   Instructor's Signature _____

Student Name _____   Date _____

CHECKLIST: ASSESS NEAR VISION USING THE JAEGER CARD

TASK: Measure near visual acuity accurately using the Jaeger near-vision acuity card, and document the procedure in the patient's medical record.

CONDITIONS: Given the proper equipment and supplies, the student will be required to role-play with another student or an instructor the proper method for assessing near vision using the Jaeger card.

EQUIPMENT AND SUPPLIES

- Jaeger card
- Occluder
- Well-lit examination room
- Patient's medical record
- Pen

STANDARDS: Complete the procedure within _____ minutes and achieve a minimum score of _____ %.

Time began _____   Time ended _____

Steps	Possible Points	First Attempt	Second Attempt
1. Sanitize hands.	5		
2. Assemble equipment and supplies.	5		
3. Greet and identify the patient.	5		
4. Explain the procedure to the patient.	5		
5. In a well-lit room, seat the patient in a comfortable position.	10		
6. Provide the patient with the Jaeger card and instruct the patient to hold the card 14 to 16 inches away from the eyes. Measure the distance for accuracy.	15		
7. Ask the patient to read out loud the paragraphs on the card; cover the left eye and then the right eye with the occluder.	15		
8. Document the number at which the patient stopped reading for each eye.	10		
9. Return the Jaeger card to its proper storage place.	10		
10. Sanitize or discard the occluder as appropriate.	10		
11. Sanitize hands.	10		
Total Points Possible	100		

Comments: Total Points Earned _____   Instructor's Signature _____

Student Name _____   Date _____

CHECKLIST: PERFORM AN EYE IRRIGATION

TASK: Simulate irrigation of the patient's eye(s) to remove foreign particles and to soothe irritated tissue.

CONDITIONS: Given the proper equipment and supplies, the student will be required to demonstrate the proper method for irrigating the patient's eye(s).

EQUIPMENT AND SUPPLIES

- Sterile irrigating solution (as ordered)
- Sterile container for solution
- Sterile bottled solution with syringe tip, eye wash cup, or appropriate equipment for eye irrigation
- Disposable gloves (powder free)
- Basin for the returned solution
- Sterile gauze squares
- Disposable moisture-resistant towel
- Biohazardous waste container
- Patient's medical record
- Tissues

STANDARDS: Complete the procedure within _____ minutes and achieve a minimum score of _____ %.

Time began _____   Time ended _____

Steps	Possible Points	First Attempt	Second Attempt
1. Sanitize hands.	5		
2. Assemble equipment and supplies, and verify order.	5		
3. Obtain the patient's medical record.	5		
4. Obtain correct solution ordered by physician.	5		
5. Escort the patient to the examination room, greet and identify the patient, and ask the patient to have a seat on the end of the examination table.	5		
6. Explain procedure to patient.	5		
7. Warm the irrigating solution to body temperature by running the container under warm running tap water (98.6° to 100° F).	5		
8. Put on disposable gloves.	5		
9. Remove any debris or discharge from the patient's eyelid using moisturized gauze squares. Wipe from inner to outer canthus.	10		
10. Position the patient and apply moisture-resistant barrier to shoulder of affected side.	5		
11. Prepare the irrigating solution.	10		

Steps	Possible Points	First Attempt	Second Attempt
12. Expose the lower conjunctiva by separating the eyelids with the gloved index finger and thumb, and ask the patient to stare at a fixed spot.	10		
13. Irrigate the affected eye(s) from inner to outer canthus.	15		
14. Continue with the irrigation until the correct amount of solution has been used or as ordered by the physician.	10		
15. Dry the eyelids from the inner to the outer canthus using dry gauze squares.	10		
16. Wipe the face and neck as needed.	5		
17. Remove gloves and sanitize the hands.	5		
18. Provide any further follow-up instructions. (Inform the patient that the eyes[s] may be red and irritated. If this lasts 2 days or longer, the patient should report it to the office.) Allow for questions.	10		
19. Escort the patient to the reception area.	5		
20. Document the procedure.	10		
21. Clean the equipment and examination room.	5		
Total Points Possible	150		

Comments: Total Points Earned _____   Instructor's Signature _____

Student Name _____   Date _____

CHECKLIST: PERFORM AN EYE INSTILLATION

TASK: Simulate proper instillation of prescribed medication in the affected eye(s).

CONDITIONS: Given the proper equipment and supplies, the student will be required to perform a proper instillation of eye medication.

EQUIPMENT AND SUPPLIES

- Ophthalmic drops with sterile eyedropper, or ophthalmic ointment as ordered by physician
- Sterile gauze squares
- Tissues
- Disposable gloves (powder-free)
- Patient's medical record

STANDARDS: Complete the procedure within _____ minutes and achieve a minimum score of _____ %.

Time began _____   Time ended _____

Steps	Possible Points	First Attempt	Second Attempt
1. Sanitize hands.	5		
2. Assemble equipment and supplies.	5		
3. Obtain the patient's medical record and verify order.	5		
4. Obtain correct "ophthalmic" medication.	5		
5. Escort the patient to the examination room, greet and identify the patient, and ask the patient to have a seat on the end of the examination table.	10		
6. Explain the procedure to the patient.	10		
7. Place the patient in a sitting or supine position.	5		
8. Put on disposable powder-free gloves and prepare the medication.	5		
9. Prepare the eye for instillation. (Ask the patient to stare at a fixed spot during the instillation).	10		
10. Expose the lower conjunctival sac of the eye to be treated.	5		
11. Instill the medication according to physician's order. Instill drops in the center of the lower conjunctival sac of the affected eye, or place a thin ribbon of ointment along the length of the lower conjunctival sac from inner to outer canthus, holding the tip of the dropper or ointment tube approximately $1/2$ inch above the eye sac, never allowing the applicator to touch the eye.	15		
12. Discard any unused solution from the eye dropper, and replace the dropper into the bottle.	10		

Steps	Possible Points	First Attempt	Second Attempt
13. Ask the patient to close the eyes gently and rotate the eye. Ask patient not to squeeze the eyelids.	15		
14. Blot-dry the eyelids from the inner to the outer canthus with a dry gauze square to remove any excess medication. Use a separate tissue for each eye.	10		
15. Remove gloves and sanitize the hands.	5		
16. Provide verbal and written follow-up instructions.	5		
17. Document the procedure.	15		
18. Clean the equipment and examination room.	10		
Total Points Possible	150		

Comments: Total Points Earned _____   Instructor's Signature _____

Student Name _____   Date _____

CHECKLIST: PERFORM AN EAR IRRIGATION

TASK: Simulate irrigation of the external ear canal to remove cerumen.

CONDITIONS: Given the proper equipment and supplies, the student will be required to perform proper irrigation of an external ear to remove cerumen.

EQUIPMENT AND SUPPLIES

- Irrigating solution (may use warm tap water)
- Container to hold irrigating solution (sterile)
- Disposable gloves
- Irrigating syringe or Reiner's ear syringe
- Ear basin for drainage
- Disposable barrier drape
- Otoscope with probe cover
- Biohazardous waste container
- Gauze squares
- Towel
- Patient's medical record

STANDARDS: Complete the procedure within _____ minutes and achieve a minimum score of _____ %.

Time began _____   Time ended _____

Steps	Possible Points	First Attempt	Second Attempt
1. Sanitize hands.	5		
2. Assemble equipment and supplies.	5		
3. Obtain the patient's medical record. Verify the physician order and obtain correct solution.	5		
4. Escort the patient to the examination room, greet and identify the patient, and ask the patient to have a seat on the end of the examination table.	5		
5. Explain the procedure to the patient.	10		
6. Warm the irrigating solution to body temperature by running the container under warm tap water.	5		
7. Put on disposable gloves.	5		
8. Examine the ear.	15		
9. Position the patient by tilting the head slightly forward and toward the affected ear.	15		
10. Place a water-resistant disposable barrier on the patient's shoulder on the affected side. Provide an ear basin, and ask the patient to hold the basin snugly against the head underneath the affected ear.	10		

Steps	Possible Points	First Attempt	Second Attempt
11. Using the solution ordered to perform the irrigation, moisten cotton balls or 2 × 2-inch gauze squares and clean the outer ear.	10		
12. Pour the warmed solution into the sterile basin.	5		
13. Fill the ear-irrigating syringe with the ordered solution, being sure to expel air bubbles from the syringe.	10		
14. Straighten the ear canal as appropriate for age.	10		
15. Irrigate the ear by inserting the tip of the irrigating syringe into the ear and injecting the irrigating solution toward the roof of the canal.	20		
16. Irrigate until the solution has been used or until the desired results have been achieved. Save solution for physician to observe if appropriate.	10		
17. Examine the ear canal with the otoscope at the end of the procedure. Gently dry the outside of the ear with a cotton ball or 2 × 2-inch gauze squares.	10		
18. Explain to the patient that the ear may feel sensitive for a few hours. Have the patient lie on the examination table with the affected ear down for approximately 15 minutes.	10		
19. Remove gloves and sanitize the hands.	5		
20. Inform the physician that procedure is complete. Provide otoscope for inspection as appropriate.	5		
21. Provide clarification of questions as appropriate.	5		
22. Escort the patient to the reception area.	5		
23. Document the procedure.	10		
24. Clean the equipment and examination room.	5		
Total Points Possible	200		

Comments: Total Points Earned _____   Instructor's Signature _____

Student Name _____   Date _____

CHECKLIST: PERFORM AN EAR INSTILLATION

TASK: Simulate proper instillation of prescribed medication in the affected ear(s).

CONDITIONS: Given the proper equipment and supplies, the student will be required to demonstrate the proper method for instilling prescribed medication into an affected ear.

EQUIPMENT AND SUPPLIES

- Otic drops with sterile dropper
- Cotton balls
- Disposable gloves
- Patient's medical record

STANDARDS: Complete the procedure within _____ minutes and achieve a minimum score of _____ %.

Time began _____   Time ended _____

Steps	Possible Points	First Attempt	Second Attempt
1. Sanitize hands.	5		
2. Assemble equipment and supplies.	5		
3. Verify the physician's order.	5		
4. Obtain the patient's medical record.	5		
5. Escort the patient to the examination room, greet and identify the patient, and ask the patient to have a seat on the end of the examination table.	5		
6. Explain the procedure to the patient.	5		
7. Put on disposable gloves.	5		
8. Warm the medication, if necessary, and draw the medication into a dropper.	10		
9. Position the ear.	5		
10. Instill the medication in the ear as ordered by physician.	10		
11. Discard unused medication in dropper.			
12. Instruct the patient to rest on the unaffected side for approximately 5 minutes.	5		
13. If appropriate, place cotton ball in ear canal.	5		
14. Remove gloves and sanitize the hands.	5		
15. Provide the patient with verbal and written follow-up instructions. Allow for questions.	5		

Steps	Possible Points	First Attempt	Second Attempt
16. Escort the patient to the reception area.	5		
17. Document the procedure.	10		
18. Clean the equipment and examination room.	5		
Total Points Possible	105		

Comments: Total Points Earned _____   Instructor's Signature _____

Student Name _____   Date _____

CHECKLIST: PULL PATIENT RECORDS

TASK: Before the start of the business day, pull patient charts for daily appointment schedule.

CONDITIONS: Given the proper equipment and supplies, the student will be required to role-play with another student or an instructor the proper method for pulling patient records based on a full day's appointment schedule (10 to 12 patient files requested of 30 to 50 files).

EQUIPMENT AND SUPPLIES

- Computer
- Appointment book, appointment list
- Pen/pencil
- Tape
- Stapler
- Two-hole punch
- Patient files

STANDARDS: Complete the procedure within _____ minutes and achieve a minimum score of _____ %.

Time began _____   Time ended _____

Steps	Possible Points	First Attempt	Second Attempt
1. Assemble all equipment and supplies.	5		
2. Locate and review the day's schedule.	5		
3. Generate the daily appointment list (type, photocopy, or print from the computer).	5		
4. Identify the full name of each scheduled patient.	5		
5. Obtain the patient's records from the filing system; place a checkmark next to each patient's name on the appointment book as each record is obtained.	10		
6. Review each record for completeness.	5		
7. Annotate the appointment list with any special considerations.	5		
8. Arrange all records sequentially by appointment time.	5		
9. Place the records in a specified location that is out of view from unauthorized persons.	5		
Total Points Possible	50		

Comments: Total Points Earned _____   Instructor's Signature _____

Student Name _____ Date _____

CHECKLIST: REGISTER A NEW PATIENT

TASK: Complete a registration form for a new patient, obtaining all required information for credit and insurance claims.

CONDITIONS: Given the proper equipment and supplies, the student will be required to complete a new patient registration form by role-playing with another student or an instructor.

EQUIPMENT AND SUPPLIES

- Computer
- Registration form
- Pen
- Clipboard
- Private conference area

STANDARDS: Complete the procedure within _____ minutes and achieve a minimum score of _____ %.

Time began _____   Time ended _____

Steps	Possible Points	First Attempt	Second Attempt
1. Assemble all equipment and supplies.	5		
2. Establish a new patient status.	5		
3. Obtain and document the required information. (When role-playing this procedure, information obtained can be fictitious.)	25		
4. Review the entire form for completeness and make corrections as required.	15		
Total Points Possible	50		

Comments: Total Points Earned _____   Instructor's Signature _____

Student Name _____   Date _____

CHECKLIST: ADD SUPPLEMENTARY ITEMS TO AN ESTABLISHED PATIENT FILE

TASK: Add supplemental documents and progress notes to patient files, observing standard steps in filing while creating an orderly file that facilitates ready reference to any information.

CONDITIONS: Given the proper equipment and supplies, the student will be required to add supplementary items to an established patient file.

EQUIPMENT AND SUPPLIES

- Patient file
- Assorted documents (provided by instructor)
- Stapler
- Clear tape
- Two-hole punch
- Alphanumerical sorter

STANDARDS: Complete the procedure within _____ minutes and achieve a minimum score of _____ %.

Time began _____   Time ended _____

Steps	Possible Points	First Attempt	Second Attempt
1. Assemble all equipment and supplies.	5		
2. Retrieve the appropriate file from the file storage area.	5		
3. Condition the document.	5		
4. Release the document.	5		
5. Index and code the document.	10		
6. Sort for filing.	5		
7. File each document according to categories into the established patient's file, with the most recent document on top.	10		
8. Return file to the storage area.	5		
Total Points Possible	50		

Comments: Total Points Earned _____   Instructor's Signature _____

Student Name _____   Date _____

CHECKLIST: MAINTAIN CONFIDENTIALITY OF PATIENT INFORMATION AND MEDICAL RECORDS

TASK: Explain through role-playing how to maintain confidentiality of patient information and medical records.

CONDITIONS: Given the proper equipment and supplies, the student will be required to explain how to maintain confidentiality of patient information and medical records.

EQUIPMENT AND SUPPLIES

- Authorization form for "Release of Medical Records"
- HIPAA release form

STANDARDS: Complete the procedure within _____ minutes and achieve a minimum score of _____ %.

Time began _____   Time ended _____

Steps	Possible Points	First Attempt	Second Attempt
1. Assemble all supplies and equipment.	5		
2. Select a partner to be a patient as you assume the role of the administrative medical assistant.	5		
3. Explain to the "patient" through role-playing how the integrity of confidences shared in the office is maintained regarding the following medical office types:	15		
a. Attorney calling the office to gain information about a patient	5		
b. Release of information about a minor	5		
c. Advertising and media	5		
d. Computerized medical records	5		
4. Explain to the "patient" through role-playing how confidences shared in the office are maintained regarding the following specialty topics:	15		
a. Child abuse	5		
b. Sexually transmitted diseases	5		
c. Sexual assault	5		
d. Mental health	5		
e. AIDS and HIV	5		
f. Substance abuse	5		

Steps	Possible Points	First Attempt	Second Attempt
5. Explain to the "patient" through role-playing how the following situations regarding confidentiality issues are handled in the medical office:	15		
a. Subpoenaed medical records	5		
b. HIPAA guidelines	5		
c. Areas of mandated disclosure by state and federal regulations	5		
6. Explain to the "patient" through role-playing the "Patient's Bill of Rights."	15		
7. Explain to the "patient" through role-playing how to complete an authorization form for release of medical records.	15		
Total Points Possible	150		

Comments: Total Points Earned _____   Instructor's Signature _____

Student Name _____   Date _____

CHECKLIST: FILE MEDICAL RECORDS USING THE ALPHABETICAL SYSTEM

TASK: Correctly file a set of patient records using an established alphabetical filing system.

CONDITIONS: Given the proper equipment and supplies, the student will be required to file medical charts using the alphabetical system.

EQUIPMENT AND SUPPLIES

- Patient files
- Alphanumerical sorter
- Work product (see next pages)

STANDARDS: Complete the procedure within _____ minutes and achieve a minimum score of _____ %.

Time began _____   Time ended _____

Steps	Possible Points	First Attempt	Second Attempt
1. Assemble all supplies and equipment.	5		
2. Retrieve the appropriate patient files from the file storage area.	15		
3. Use an out guide.	10		
4. Complete documentation as appropriate.	15		
5. Add any supplemental forms or records generated according to office procedures.	15		
6. Sort the files alphabetically, using a "desktop sorter" if possible.	15		
7. Remove the files from the sorter and return the files to the storage area, correctly filing them alphabetically into the appropriate sequence.	15		
8. Remove out guide.	10		
Total Points Possible	100		

Comments: Total Points Earned _____   Instructor's Signature _____

Student Name _____   Date _____

≋ WORK PRODUCT FOR
FILE MEDICAL RECORDS USING THE ALPHABETICAL SYSTEM

DIRECTIONS
Using a blue or black pen, write the names in descending alphabetical order on the lines provided. Use the last name as the primary sequence indicator and the first name/middle initial when appropriate. Write neatly so your instructor can read it.

Filing Exercise #1

Clair Hanover	1.	_____
Ann C. White	2.	_____
Corey Melton	3.	_____
Alice Abelene	4.	_____
P. E. Simpson	5.	_____
Austin Beaumont	6.	_____
Amber Shelton	7.	_____
Elizabeth Jackson	8.	_____
A. C. White	9.	_____
Margaret Appleton	10.	_____
Gail Racine	11.	_____
Wayne Somerset	12.	_____
Nina Kenosha	13.	_____
T. C. Whitehead	14.	_____
Geraldine Temple	15.	_____
Hamilton Townsend	16.	_____
Frederick Columbia	17.	_____
Irving Edgoten	18.	_____
Jasper Springer	19.	_____
Marshall Washington	20.	_____
Charlotte Swathmore	21.	_____

Benjamin Albany   22. _____

Mary Simpson   23. _____

George Baldwin   24. _____

Aaron Evans   25. _____

Warren Lenoir   26. _____

Wesley Hudson   27. _____

Monroe Windom   28. _____

Vernon Tiffin   29. _____

Ada Manhasset   30. _____

Student Name _____   Date _____

Filing Exercise #2

Stuart Sonoma	1. _____
Gary Modesto	2. _____
Venetia Urbano	3. _____
Toshi Akabad	4. _____
Patricaia Peoria	5. _____
Richard Ruston	6. _____
Jerry Wilkerson	7. _____
Lawrence Sycamore	8. _____
Eloise Springfield	9. _____
Parket Arlington	10. _____
Tami Wilkens	11. _____
Clinton Claxton	12. _____
Rosalina Sausalito	13. _____
Olivia Osceola	14. _____
Rashid Mamoud	15. _____
Marion Pontiac	16. _____
Dexter Belvidere	17. _____
Urbans Rantoul	18. _____
Tamara Wilkins	19. _____
Portia Crane	20. _____
Vincent Purcell	21. _____
Camille Stigler	22. _____
Milton Norris	23. _____
Dale Findlay	24. _____
Roslyn Asheboro	25. _____
Ann Arbor	26. _____

Sylvia Charleroi   27. _____

Bethany Woodward   28. _____

Lorraine Wheaton   29. _____

Clark Benton   30. _____

Student Name _____   Date _____

Filing Exercise #3

Bill Evanston	1.	_____
Marion Dayton	2.	_____
Samantha La Rue	3.	_____
Betty Sloan	4.	_____
Louis Gonzalez	5.	_____
Raleigh Kroger	6.	_____
Jeannette Hammond	7.	_____
Arthur O'Leary	8.	_____
Ashley Conroy	9.	_____
Vivian Kroger	10.	_____
Parker St. Tropez	11.	_____
John Newton	12.	_____
Crystal Salem	13.	_____
Bernice Shelton	14.	_____
Dennis Dayton	15.	_____
Rosa St. Jean	16.	_____
Ruth Newton	17.	_____
Lowell Kroger	18.	_____
Winnefred Atherton	19.	_____
Damian Vincennes	20.	_____
Wendy Sloan	21.	_____
Maria del Castillo	22.	_____
Myra Savannah	23.	_____
Harvey Rosenbury	24.	_____
Julian Blythe	25.	_____
Megan O'Riley	26.	_____

Micheal Dayton   27. _____

Clinton Slidell   28. _____

Wheaton Sloan   29. _____

Colleen Kruger   30. _____

Student Name _____   Date _____

Filing Exercise #4

Allen Hobart	1.	_____
Norman Paoli	2.	_____
A & A Accounting	3.	_____
Elizabeth Parma	4.	_____
Daniel N. Jefferson	5.	_____
Camilla Beacon	6.	_____
Lasting Impressions Florist	7.	_____
James Sloan	8.	_____
Maureen O'Neill	9.	_____
Mikal Detoro Garage	10.	_____
J. T. Sloan	11.	_____
Dr. David N. Jefferson	12.	_____
Tiffany Lamps & Lighting	13.	_____
Maxine O'Neill	14.	_____
Darla Dorchester	15.	_____
Geigi Pharmaceutical	16.	_____
Dr. John Sloan	17.	_____
Wendy Wynnewood	18.	_____
Richard Lodi	19.	_____
Robin Warner	20.	_____
Penguin Cool Air Conditioning	21.	_____
Prefer Pharmacy	22.	_____
Sally Salinas	23.	_____
M. J. O'Neill	24.	_____
Edward Whiting	25.	_____
Jeff Sloan	26.	_____

David M. Jefferson   27. _____

Tony Ahilene   28. _____

Luke Mansfield   29. _____

Peggy Purcell   30. _____

Student Name _____   Date _____

CHECKLIST: FILE MEDICAL RECORDS USING THE NUMERICAL SYSTEM

TASK: Correctly file a set of patient charts, using an established numerical filing system.

CONDITIONS: Given the proper equipment and supplies, the student will be required to file medical charts using a numerical system.

EQUIPMENT AND SUPPLIES

- Patient files
- Numerical sorter

STANDARDS: Complete the procedure within _____ minutes and achieve a minimum score of _____ %.

Time began _____   Time ended _____

Steps	Possible Points	First Attempt	Second Attempt
1. Assemble all supplies and equipment.	5		
2. Retrieve the proper numerical code from the appropriate system file.	15		
3. Use an out guide.	10		
4. Complete documentation as appropriate.	15		
5. Add any supplemental forms or records generated according to office procedures.	15		
6. Sort the files numerically, using a "desktop sorter" if possible.	15		
7. Remove the files from the sorter and return the files to the storage area, correctly filing them into the appropriate numerical sequence.	15		
8. Remove out guide.	10		
Total Points Possible	100		

Comments: Total Points Earned _____   Instructor's Signature _____

Student Name _____   Date _____

WORK PRODUCT FOR
FILE MEDICAL RECORDS USING THE NUMERICAL SYSTEM

DIRECTIONS
Using a pen or pencil, identify which number in each group would be first when using straight number filing.

Filing Exercise #1

1. a. 126342
   b. 145632
   c. 126432
   d. 123642

2. a. 531200
   b. 621000
   c. 181200
   d. 882200

3. a. 432588
   b. 342588
   c. 345288
   d. 435288

4. a. 123642
   b. 123600
   c. 145632
   d. 142364

5. a. 73355
   b. 183245
   c. 93165
   d. 263054

6. a. 40801
   b. 10804
   c. 80201
   d. 10208

7. a. 81562
   b. 631795
   c. 65870
   d. 76142

8. a. 145177
   b. 415177
   c. 251770
   d. 235177

9. a. 183245
   b. 181200
   c. 185620
   d. 185632

10. Write the numbers in descending order:

201010   _____

009901   _____

000065   _____

027800   _____

001201   _____

010065   _____

136431   _____

023402   _____

136531   _____

Student Name _____   Date _____

DIRECTIONS

Using a pen or pencil, identify which number in each group would be first when using terminal digit number filing.

Filing Exercise #2

1. a. 126342
   b. 145632
   c. 126432
   d. 123642

2. a. 531200
   b. 621000
   c. 181200
   d. 882200

3. a. 432588
   b. 342588
   c. 345288
   d. 435288

4. a. 123642
   b. 123600
   c. 145632
   d. 142364

5. a. 733550
   b. 183245
   c. 931650
   d. 263054

6. a. 408010
   b. 108040
   c. 802010
   d. 102080

7. a. 815620
   b. 631795
   c. 658700
   d. 761420

8. a. 145177
   b. 415177
   c. 251770
   d. 235177

9. a. 183245
   b. 181200
   c. 185620
   d. 185632

10. Write the numbers in descending order:

    201010   _____

    009901   _____

    000065   _____

    027800   _____

    001201   _____

    010065   _____

    136431   _____

    023402   _____

    136531   _____

Page numbers followed by f indicate figures; t, tables; b, boxes.